THROUGH THE PRIESTLY MINISTRY
THE GIFT OF SALVATION

Through the Priestly Ministry the Gift of Salvation

VOLUME 1

Messages of John Paul II
to Bishops, Priests and Deacons

Compiled and indexed by
the Daughters of St. Paul

ST. PAUL EDITIONS

Addresses reprinted with permission from *L'Osservatore Romano*, English Edition.

Library of Congress Cataloging in Publication Data

John Paul II, Pope, 1920-
Through the Priestly Ministry, the Gift of Salvation

Includes index.
1. Catholic Church—Doctrinal works—Catholic authors—Addresses, essays, lectures.
I. Daughters of St. Paul. II. Title.
BX1755.J648   282   82-19528
                          AACR2

ISBN 0-8198-7322-5 cloth
      0-8198-7323-3 paper

Copyright © 1982, by the Daughters of St. Paul

Printed in the U.S.A. by the Daughters of St. Paul
50 St. Paul's Ave., Boston, MA 02130

The Daughters of St. Paul are an international congregation of religious women serving the Church with the communications media.

*To the Bishops,
successors of the Apostles,*

*to the Priests,
who share the Bishops' authority
of building up, sanctifying and ruling
the Mystical Body of Christ,*

*and to the Deacons,
consecrated for a ministry of service,
the Daughters of St. Paul
respectfully dedicate
this priceless work.*

CONTENTS

A Pledge of Fidelity to Vatican Council II 23
To the College of Cardinals in the Sistine Chapel, and to the world, October 17, 1978.

A Sign of the Universality of the Church 33
To the members of the Sacred College, in the Consistorial Hall, October 18, 1978.

In the Footsteps of St. Charles 36
To the Sacred College of Cardinals, November 4, 1978.

Doctrine and Discipline in the Priestly Life 38
To the bishops of the seventh pastoral region of the U.S.A., and to the archbishops and bishops of the fifth pastoral region of the U.S.A., November 9, 1978.

The World Today Needs Your Priestly Witness 42
To the clergy of the diocese of Rome, November 9, 1978.

Development in Freedom 49
To the participants of the plenary assembly of the Pontifical Commission Justitia et Pax, *November 11, 1978.*

Evangelization in Line with Vatican II 53
To Cardinal Reginald Delargey, together with a group of bishops from New Zealand, November 13, 1978.

Deep Pastoral Concern for the Church's Discipline 56
To a group of Canadian bishops on their ad limina *visit, November 17, 1978.*

Apostolate of Migrants and the Universality
of the Church 61
Message sent to Cardinal Baggio for the celebration of Migrant's Day.

Full Ecclesial Communion in a Spirit
of True Charity 64
To a group of bishops of Honduras on their ad limina visit, November 23, 1978.

Universality of the Church Amid
a Variety of Rites 67
To a group of bishops of the Ruthenian Byzantine Province in the U.S.A., together with the bishop of St. Maron of Brooklyn for the Maronites, November 23, 1978.

Letter to the Bishops of Hungary 69
Letter to Cardinal Lekai, dated December 2, 1978.

Role of the Family in Today's World 72
Address to the members of the General Council of the Synod of Bishops together with the officials and the "periti," December 16, 1978.

Episcopal Collegiality and Regional Autonomies 75
To the members of the Council of Episcopal Conferences of Europe gathered in Rome, December 19, 1978.

Announcement of Papal Visit to Mexico 78
To the College of Cardinals, December 22, 1978.

Man's Answer to God's Call to Service 87
Excerpts from the homily delivered at the Roman parish of St. Mary Liberator at Monte Testaccio, January 14, 1979.

To the Church in the Dominican Republic 90
To the bishops, clergy, men and women religious, and representatives of all members of the Church in the Dominican Republic, January 25, 1979.

You Are Servants of the People of God 91
Address to the priests and men religious of Mexico, in the Basilica of Our Lady of Guadalupe, January 27, 1979.

Preserve, Defend, and Communicate the Truth 95
Discourse before the representatives of all the bishops of Latin America, in the Major Seminary, Palafoxiano of Puebla de Los Angeles, January 28, 1979.

Farewell Message to Bishops of Central America
and the Antilles 118
To the episcopate of Central America and the Antilles.

The Meeting in Mexico with Its Human
and Christian Reality 119
To the Cardinals present in Rome, gathered in the Consistory Hall.

Uganda Celebrates Centenary 122
*Letter appointing Cardinal James Knox as the special
representative for the National Eucharistic Congress
which occurred between the tenth and the twentieth of
February, 1979.*

In the Service of Equity and Charity 126
*To the Court of the Sacred Roman Rota,
February 17, 1979.*

The Parish: The Presence of Christ Among Us 133
*Excerpts from homily delivered in the parish of Saint
Gregory the Great at Magliana, Rome, February 18, 1979.*

To Participants of the Liturgico-Pastoral Meeting 136
*Address to the participants in the Twenty-first Liturgico-
Pastoral Congress, February 23, 1979.*

Catechesis, Liturgy, Charity in the
Lenten Apostolate 137
*Address to the parish priest prefects of the diocese of Rome
gathered in the Roman Major Seminary, February 24, 1979.*

The Priest in the Mystery of Christ 140
*To Cardinal Poletti, and the auxiliary bishops of Rome,
the parish priests and clergy, in the Sistine Chapel,
March 2, 1979.*

First Priority: Announce the Word of God
in Its Purity and Integrity 147
*To the rectors of several major seminaries of England,
Scotland and Malta, March 3, 1979.*

A Special Time of God's Grace 150
*Address concluding the Spiritual Exercises in Matilda Chapel,
March 10, 1979.*

In the Service of Christ Throughout
His Whole Life 152
*Homily delivered during the funeral rites of the late
Cardinal Giovanni Villot, March 13, 1979.*

Like Jesus Who Came To Serve 155
*To a group of deacons from the archdiocese of Milan,
March 15, 1979.*

Colleges and Seminaries as Real Upper Rooms 157
*To numerous rectors of ecclesiastical colleges in
Rome, March 16, 1979.*

"Stewards of the Mysteries of God" 160
*To the superiors and pupils of the Pontifical Ecclesiastical
Academy, March 17, 1979.*

Hope for a Luminous Future of Evangelization 162
Letter to the Council of Presidency of CELAM, March 23, 1979.

The Gift of the Priestly Vocation 163
Homily John Paul II delivered to his old fellow-students of the Belgian College, March 31, 1979.

Real Scientific Formation in Priestly Formation 165
Address to professors, rectors and pupils, and members of the Sacred Congregation for Catholic Education, April 3, 1979.

Courage and Consistency in Apostolic Work 174
To a group of Hungarian bishops, priests, and faithful gathered in Rome, April 6, 1979.

Letter to All the Bishops of the Church 180
On the Occasion of Holy Thursday, 1979.

Letter to All the Priests of the Church 184
On the Occasion of Holy Thursday, 1979.

Perseverance and Fidelity in the Priestly Vocation 206
Homily delivered at Chrism Mass in St. Peter's Basilica, April 12, 1979.

Authenticity and Service Charisms 209
To a group of forty priests led by Cardinal Antonio Poma from the archdiocese of Bologna, April 19, 1979

Essential Elements of the Priesthood 211
To a group of priests returning to the archdiocese of Milan from a pilgrimage to Our Lady of Czestochowa, April 21, 1979.

The Gift of the Priesthood 215
To a group of deacons from the diocese of Regensburg led by Mons. Rudolf Graber, April 21, 1979.

Obedience and Joy in the Spirit of the Diaconate 216
Homily delivered at a concelebrated Mass in the Pauline Chapel, attended by eighteen new deacons of the Pontifical Irish, Scots and Rosminian College in Rome, April 21, 1979.

Apostolate in the World of Manual Labor 220
Address to a large group of diocesan priest delegates engaged in the apostolate of the world of manual labor, assembled in Rome, April 25, 1979.

Formation of Catechists 221
Address to those who had been taking part in the International Council for Catechesis, April 25, 1979.

The Joyful Commitment of Service to Humanity
Is Sustained by the Eucharist 223
Discourse delivered to a group of thirteen bishops from India on their ad limina visit, April 26, 1979.

To Do More, To Serve More, To Love More 227
To a group of bishops from Sri Lanka on their ad limina *visit, April 28, 1979.*

The Luminous Example of Mary 231
April 28, 1979.

Church's Unity Manifested in Our Communion
of Love 233
Address to the bishops of the Antilles, May 4, 1979.

"Make Every Effort to Ensure Pastoral Care
for the Family" 238
Special address to the participants in the Meeting on the Family Apostolate during the audience of May 5, 1979.

Authentic Doctrine and Holiness of Life 240
Address to a group of Indian bishops on their ad limina *visit, May 5, 1979.*

Three Passwords: Pray, Call, Respond 244
An excerpt from the message of John Paul II for the Sixteenth World Day of Prayer for Vocations, May 6, 1979.

Following the Example of Jesus,
Let Everyone Be a "Good Shepherd" 247
Excerpts from the homily of Pope John Paul II to the parish of St. Anthony of Padua at Via Tuscolana, Rome, May 6, 1979.

The Paschal Significance of the Good Shepherd 251
Excerpt from the address given at the general audience in St. Peter's Square, May 9, 1979.

Missionary Dynamism Lies in Persons Animated
by the Spirit 253
To the National Directors of the Pontifical Mission Aid Societies, May 11, 1979.

Pastoral Care and Prayer To Achieve
Revival of Vocations 256
Homily during the concelebration of Mass with all the Italian bishops in the Sistine Chapel, May 15, 1979.

Profile of the Good Shepherd 264
Excerpts from the address during the general audience in St. Peter's Square, May 9, 1979.

From the Word of the Gospel
an Invitation to Courage........................... 266
Address to the Italian bishops gathered to take part in the final session of the Sixteenth General Assembly of the C.E.I., May 18, 1979.

Keep Intact and Proclaim the Sacred Deposit
of Christian Doctrine 271
*To the staff and students of the Venerable English
College and of the Pontifical Beda College,
May 24, 1979.*

Pastoral Care for Religious Vocations 274
*To a group of bishops from Uruguay on their ad limina visit,
May 26, 1979.*

Abide in the Love of Christ 277
*Homily delivered during the ordination of twenty-six
new bishops, in the Vatican Basilica, May 27, 1979.*

To Sustain and To Guide the Community of Faith 281
*To eleven bishops of India on their ad limina visit,
May 31, 1979.*

Unity of Polish Bishops—a Recognized Source
of Spiritual Strength 285
*Address to the Polish episcopal conference which was held
in the Monastery of Jasna Gora, June 5, 1979.*

Gospel Witness in the Priestly Ministry 300
*Address to diocesan and religious clergy in the Cathedral of
Czestochowa, June 6, 1979.*

Seven Years of Community Work To Update
the Church of Krakow 304
*Homily given during the Mass in Wawel Cathedral,
June 8, 1979.*

The Work of the Local Churches for the
Strengthening of Unity 307
Address to a group of bishops from Pakistan, June 19, 1979.

Evangelization in Terms of the Future 310
*Address during a concelebrated Mass with members of the
Council of Bishops of Europe, June 20, 1979.*

Task of the Whole Community: To Transmit
the Word of God 316
*To thirteen bishops from the Tamil Nadu region of India,
June 23, 1979.*

Build the Church with Your Priesthood 321
*Homily during the ordination of eighty-eight new priests
in the Vatican Basilica, June 24, 1979.*

Value of the Evangelizing Mission 324
*Address to the participants in the national Study Meeting,
June 28, 1979.*

Consistory for the Creation of Fourteen
   New Cardinals 326
   *To those participating in the Consistory for the creation
   of Cardinals, for the provision of Churches and for the
   postulation of the sacred Pallia, June 30, 1979.*

The Church as a Sign of God's Salvific Will 337
   *Homily delivered during the solemn concelebration of
   Mass in the Vatican Basilica with fourteen new Cardinals,
   July 1, 1979.*

The Baptism of Blood of the Church of Rome 341
   *Address at the general audience in St. Peter's Square,
   July 4, 1979.*

Irreplaceable Presence of the Priest in the
   Evangelizing Work of the Church 345
   *To a group of bishops of Colombia on their ad limina visit,
   July 6, 1979.*

Apostolic Work of the Roman Curia 348
   *Address to the large crowd assembled in St. Peter's Square,
   July 11, 1979.*

Exemplary Fidelity in Ecclesial Service 353
   *Homily during the concelebrated solemn funeral rite for
   Cardinal Alfredo Ottaviani in the Vatican Basilica,
   August 6, 1979.*

A Long Life at the Service of the Lord
   and His Church 356
   *Homily delivered at the funeral Mass for Cardinal Alberto
   di Jorio, September 6, 1979.*

Let Us Go to Christ: He Will Cure Us 359
   *Homily delivered during a Mass celebrated on
   September 9, 1979, at the Monastery of Grottaferrata
   in the Alban Hills.*

Dialogue with Christ in His Church 364
   *Homily delivered for the episcopal ordination of His
   Excellency, Most Rev. Jozef Tomko, in the Sistine Chapel,
   September 15, 1979.*

The Lovable Figure of Cardinal Wright 368
   *Homily delivered during the Mass celebrated for the soul of
   Cardinal John Joseph Wright on September 22, 1979.*

The Family and the Young in the Church's Future 371
   *Address on September 25, 1979, to a group of bishops from
   Paraguay on their ad limina visit.*

Gather All Men in Christ 373
Address of September 25, 1979, to the bishops from Colombia on their ad limina visit.

Unfading Crown of Glory 377
To priests, seminarians and students from Scotland, September 26, 1979.

The Unfathomable Mystery of Life and Death 377
To the Cardinals and faithful gathered to participate in the Mass celebrated on the first anniversary of the death of John Paul I, September 28, 1979.

The Church of Europe Owes a Debt of Gratitude
to the Church in Ireland 381
To the Catholic bishops gathered in Ireland for the Holy Father's visit, September 29, 1979.

Support of the Pope and Church in the Ministry
of Bishops.. 383
To the Irish bishops on September 30, 1979.

Homage to the Tradition of Faith and of Christian Life
in Ireland 393
Address delivered to those gathered to meet the Holy Father in Clonmacnois, Ireland, September 30, 1979.

What the People Expect of You Is Fidelity
to the Priesthood 394
To priests, religious, missionaries and seminarians in St. Patrick's College, Maynooth, Ireland, October 1, 1979.

"I Am Happy To Be in Your Midst" 400
To the priests, religious, seminarians and faithful gathered in the Cathedral of Holy Cross, Boston, October 1, 1979.

Who Will Separate Us from Christ? 401
Address to numerous bishops, priests, religious, seminarians and faithful at St. Patrick's Cathedral in New York, October 3, 1979.

Sacramental Priesthood Is Truly a Gift from God 403
To priests and religious gathered in the Civic Center of Philadelphia, October 4, 1979.

Fidelity to the Truth in Love 412
To the bishops of the episcopal conference of the United States at Quigley South Seminary, Chicago, October 5, 1979.

Mary Is the Model of the Church 427
Homily delivered to the priests, deacons, and members of the archdiocesan council gathered in St. Matthew's Cathedral, Washington, D.C., October 6, 1979.

Evangelization and Apostolate of Priestly Vocations 428
To the bishops of Chile on their ad limina visit, October 13, 1979.

Consistent Testimony of Faith
in a Brilliant Catechesis 435
*Homily delivered during the beatification of the Spanish
priest, Henry de Ossó y Cevelló, October 14, 1979.*

Be Teachers of Religious and Social Truth 441
To the bishops of Peru on their ad limina *visit,
October 20, 1979.*

I Follow Your Labor as a Father 446
To heads of the Apostolic Union of the Clergy.

Theological Research Must Help the Church
to Ever Deeper Knowledge of the Mystery
of Jesus Christ 447
*To the International Theological Commission on their tenth
anniversary, October 26, 1979.*

The Apostolate of the Family, a Priority
in the Task of Bishops 453
To the bishops from Argentina on their ad limina *visit,
October 28, 1979.*

Let the Church Be Faithful to the Task
of Evangelizing 458
To the bishops of Colombia on their ad limina *visit,
October 29, 1979.*

The Religious Spirit of Your People Augurs Well
for the Spread of the Gospel 462
To the bishops from Mexico on their ad limina *visit,
October 30, 1979.*

We Celebrate with Our Dead the Hope
of an Eternal Life 466
*Homily given at a Mass celebrated at the cemetery of Verano
in Rome, All Saints' Day, 1979.*

United in Truth and Charity 470
*To 120 Cardinals present at the opening of the plenary meeting
of the Sacred College, November 5, 1979.*

An Important Stage on the Way to Collegiality 482
*Address to the Sacred College of Cardinals, in the Synod Hall
in the Vatican, November 9, 1979.*

To Lighten the Trials of Those Who Suffer
for Their Fidelity 486
*Homily preached in a solemn concelebration in the
Byzantine-Ukrainian Rite, in which episcopal ordination
was conferred on Archbishop Myroslav Lubachivsky,
November 12, 1979.*

Communion of Grace and Mission 490
> *To a group of bishops from Venezuela on their* ad limina *visit, November 15, 1979.*

Intense Work for Native Vocations 495
> *To a group of bishops and of prelates from Colombia on their* ad limina *visit, November 20, 1979.*

Genuine Renewal 499
> *Excerpt from the general audience of December 9, 1979.*

Evangelization: Fundamental Mission of the Church 499
> *To a group of bishops of Ecuador on their* ad limina *visit, December 11, 1979.*

Be Priests and Pastors of True Justice 504
> *To about seventy participants in the seventh course for judges and officials of tribunals at the Pontifical Gregorian University, gathered in the Sala Clementina, December 13, 1979.*

Live Your Vocation with Authenticity, Intensity 508
> *To a group of ecclesiastical assistants of International Catholic Organization, at Villa Cavalletti, Grottaferrata, December 13, 1979.*

Conform Always to the Image of Christ the Priest 511
> *To those visited by the Pope in the Pontifical Mexican College in Rome, December 13, 1979.*

The Church Today in Defense of the Dignity
of Every Person 513
> *To the Sacred College of Cardinals, the Pontifical Household, the Curia and the Roman Prelature, December 22, 1979.*

The Episcopate: the Sacrament of the Way 533
> *Homily during the episcopal ordination of three bishops, in St. Peter's Basilica, on January 6, 1980, the Feast of the Epiphany.*

May the Teaching of the Council
Guide Our Thoughts and Actions 538
> *Homily during the Eucharistic concelebration starting the Synod of the Dutch Bishops, January 14, 1980.*

Unity Is Conversion to Christ 542
> *Homily preached during the Eucharistic concelebration in the Pauline Chapel with the Fathers taking part in the Synod of Dutch Bishops, January 25, 1980.*

Let No One Feel Neglected by the Pope 544
> *Message to the bishops, priests and people of Mexico, on the first anniversary of the Pope's pilgrimage there.*

Our Task—To Proclaim the Sacredness of Life 546
Message sent to the 150 bishops of the United States and Canada who met in Dallas, Texas, from January 28 to 31, 1980.

We All Sincerely Desire a Church Which Corresponds to Christ's Will 548
Homily preached during the Eucharistic concelebration in the Sistine Chapel, which concluded the Synod of Dutch Bishops, January 31, 1980.

The Pursuit of Truth Is the Supreme Norm of Justice 558
To the Court of the Sacred Roman Rota, February 4, 1980.

A Great Common Commitment 566
To the Roman clergy in the Hall of the Lateran University, February 21, 1980.

Renewed Commitment and True Solidarity 577
To the directors of the National Federation of the Italian Clergy, February 22, 1980.

Permanent Significance of the Christian Family 578
Delivered to the Council of the General Secretariat of the Synod of Bishops, February 23, 1980.

On the Mystery and Worship of the Eucharist 585
Letter to all the bishops of the Church, February 24, 1980.

Be Open to the Gifts of the Holy Spirit 618
Address delivered at the end of the spiritual exercises held in the Matilda Chapel, March 1, 1980.

In the Service of the Renewal and Pastoral Progress of Rome 622
To those the Holy Father visited in the offices of the Vicariate of Rome, at St. John Lateran, March 4, 1980.

Priests for the Church and for the Men of Today 625
To the clergy of the dioceses of Spoleto and Norcia, and priests from other parts of Umbria, March 23, 1980.

To Strengthen the Experience of Unity and Cooperation 630
Homily delivered to Cardinal Josyf Slipyj and fourteen other Ukrainian bishops, March 24, 1980.

New Vigor of Religious Life in Ukrainian Catholic Church 637
Address of the Holy Father at the meeting of the Extraordinary Synod of the Ukrainian Bishops, March 24, 1980.

Persevere in Love! 642
To fourteen newly-ordained priests from St. Peter's Philosophical and Theological Institute, March 24, 1980.

Continuation of Your Church Assured 644
   *To Cardinal Josyf Slipyj, and the other Ukrainian bishops at
   the end of their Extraordinary Synod, March 27, 1980.*

We Are Priests of Christ's Priesthood 646
   *Homily given at the Mass for the blessing of the chrism in the
   Vatican Basilica, April 3, 1980.*

You Are Called to a Ministry of Charity 649
   *To numerous newly-ordained deacons, their relatives and the
   superiors of the various colleges, April 11, 1980.*

Joyful Awareness of Your Own Identity 651
   To concelebrants outside the Turin Cathedral, April 13, 1980.

The Church Wishes To Collaborate in the Progress
of Nicaragua 655
   To the seven bishops of Nicaragua, April 17, 1980.

Need To Evangelize, Reflect and Pray 659
   *Address for the Seventeenth World Day of Prayer for
   Vocations, April 27, 1980.*

A Pledge of Fidelity to Vatican Council II

On October 17, 1978, the day after his election as Supreme Pontiff, Pope John Paul II celebrated Mass together with the College of Cardinals in the Sistine Chapel. At the end of the Mass, His Holiness spoke as follows to the Cardinals and to the world.

Our venerable brothers, beloved children of Holy Church, and all men of good will who listen to us: One expression only, among so many others, comes immediately to our lips at this moment, as after our election to the See of the blessed Peter, we present ourself to you. The expression, which, in evident contrast with our obvious limitations as a human person, highlights the immense burden and office committed to us, is this: "O the depth... of the wisdom and knowledge of God! How unsearchable are his judgments and how inscrutable his ways!" (Rom. 11:33) In fact, who could have foreseen, after the death of Pope Paul VI whom we always remember, the premature decease of his most amiable Successor, John Paul I? How could we have been able to foresee that this formidable heritage would have been placed on our shoulders? For this reason, it is necessary for us to meditate upon the mysterious design of the provident and good God, not indeed in order to understand, but, rather, that we may worship and pray. Truly we feel the need to repeat the words of the psalmist who, raising his eyes aloft, exclaimed: "From whence does my help come? My help comes from the Lord" (Ps. 120:1-2).

These totally unforeseen events, happening in so brief a time, and the inadequacy with which we can respond to that invitation impel us to turn to the Lord and to trust completely in Him. But they also prevent us from outlining a program for our pontificate which would be the fruit of long reflection and of precise elaboration. But to make up for this, there is at hand a certain compensation, as it were, which is itself a sign of the strengthening presence of God.

It is less than a month since all of us, both inside and outside these historic walls of the Sistine Chapel, heard Pope John Paul I speaking at the very beginning of his ministry, from which one might have hoped much. Both on account of the memory that is yet fresh in the mind of each one of us and on account of the wise reminders and exhortations contained in the allocution, we consider that we cannot overlook it. That same address, as in the circumstances in which it was given, is truly apposite and clearly maintains its validity here and now at the start of this new pontifical ministry to which we are bound and which, before God and the Church, we cannot avoid.

We wish, therefore, to clarify some basic points which we consider to be of special importance. Hence—as we propose and as, with the help of God, we confidently trust—we shall continue these not merely with earnestness and attention, but we shall also further them with constant pressure, so that ecclesial life, truly lived, may correspond to them. First of all, we wish to point out the unceasing importance of the Second Vatican Ecumenical Council, and we accept the definite duty of assiduously bringing it into effect. Indeed, is not that universal Council a kind of milestone as it were, an event of the utmost importance in the almost two thousand year history of the Church, and consequently in the religious and cultural history of the world?

However, as the Council is not limited to the documents alone, neither is it completed by the ways of applying it which were devised in these post-conciliar years. Therefore, we rightly consider that we are bound by the primary duty of most diligently furthering the implementation of the decrees and directive norms of that same Universal Synod. This indeed we shall do in a way that is at once prudent and stimulating. We shall strive, in particular, that first of all an appropriate mentality may flourish. Namely, it is necessary that, above all, outlooks must be at one with the Council so that in practice those things may be done that were ordered by it, and that those things which lie hidden in it or—as is usually said—are "implicit" may become explicit in the light of the experiments made since then and the demands of changing circumstances. Briefly, it is necessary that the fertile seeds which the Fathers of the Ecumenical Synod, nourished by the Word of God, sowed in good ground (cf. Mt. 13:8, 23) —that is, the important teachings and pastoral deliberations—should be brought to maturity in that way which is characteristic of movement and life.

This general purpose of fidelity to the Second Vatican Council and express will, insofar as we are concerned, of bringing it into effect, can cover various sections: missionary and ecumenical affairs, discipline, and suitable administration. But there is one section to which greater attention will have to be given, and that is the ecclesiological section. Venerable brethren and beloved sons of the Catholic world, it is necessary for us to take once again into our hands the "Magna Charta" of the Council, that is, the Dogmatic Constitution *Lumen gentium*, so that with renewed and invigorating zeal we may meditate on the nature and function of the Church, its way of being and acting. This should be done not merely in order that the vital communion in Christ of all who believe and hope in Him should be accomplished, but also in order to contribute to bringing about a fuller and closer unity of the whole human family. John XXIII was accustomed to repeat the following words: "The Church of Christ is the light of the nations." For the Church—his words were repeated by the Council—is the universal sacrament of salvation and unity for the human race (cf. LG 1, 48; AG 1).

The mystery of salvation which finds its center in the Church and is actualized through the Church; the dynamism which on account of that same mystery animates the People of God; the special bond, that is, collegiality, which "with Peter and under Peter" binds together the sacred pastors; all these are major elements on which we have not yet sufficiently reflected. We must do so in order to decide in face of human needs, whether these be permanent or passing, what the Church should adopt as its mode of presence and its course of action. Wherefore, the assent to be given to this document of the Council, seen in the light of Tradition and embodying the dogmatic formulae issued over a century ago by the First Vatican Council, will be to us pastors and to the faithful a decisive indication and a rousing stimulus, so that—we say it again—we may walk in the paths of life and of history.

In order that we may become better informed and more vigilant in undertaking our duty, we particularly urge a deeper reflection on the implications of the collegial bond. By collegiality the bishops are closely linked with the Successor of the blessed Peter, and all collaborate in order to fulfill the high offices committed to them: offices of enlightening the whole People of God with the light of the Gospel, of sanctifying them with the means of grace, of guiding them with pastoral skill. Undoubtedly, this collegiality extends to the appropriate development of institutes—some new, some updated—by which is procured the greatest unity in outlook, intent, and activity in the work of building up the Body of Christ, which is the Church (cf. Eph. 4:12; Col. 1:24). In this regard, we make special mention of the Synod of Bishops, set up before the end of the Council by that very talented man, Paul VI (cf. Apostolic Letter, given "motu proprio," *Apostolica Sollicitudo; AAS* LVII, 1965, pp. 775-780).

But besides these things, which remind us of the Council, there is the duty in general of being faithful to the task we have accepted and to which we ourself are bound before all others. We, who are called to hold the Supreme Office in the Church, must manifest this fidelity with all our might and for this reason we must be a shining example both in our thinking and in our actions. This indeed must be done because we preserve intact the deposit of faith, because we make entirely our own the commands of Christ, who, after Peter was made the rock on which the Church was built, gave him the keys of the kingdom of heaven (cf. Mt. 16:18-19), who bade him strengthen his brethren (cf. Lk. 22:32), and to feed the sheep and the lambs of His flock as a proof of his love (cf. Jn. 21:15-17). We are entirely convinced that in no inquiry, which may take place today into the "ministry of Peter" as it is called —so that what is proper and peculiar to it may be studied in greater depth every day—can these three important passages of the holy Gospel be omitted. For it is a question of the various parts of the office, which are bound up with the very nature of the Church so that its internal unity may be preserved and its spiritual mission placed in safe hands. These parts were not only committed to St. Peter but also to his lawful Successors. We are also convinced that this high office must always be related to love as the source from which it is nourished and as it were the climate in which it can be expanded. This love is as it were a necessary reply to the question of Jesus, "Do you love me?" So we are pleased to repeat these words of St. Paul, "The love of Christ constrains us" (2 Cor. 5:14), because we want our ministry to be from the outset a ministry of love, and we want to show and declare this in every possible way.

In this matter we will strive to follow the meritorious examples of our immediate Predecessors. Who does not remember the words of Paul VI, who preached "the civilization of love" and almost a month before his death declared in a prophetic way: "I have kept the faith" (cf. Homily on Feast of Sts. Peter and Paul: *AAS* LXX,

1978, p. 395), not indeed to praise himself but after fifteen years full of apostolic ministry to examine his conscience more strictly?

But what can we say of John Paul I? It seems to us that only yesterday he emerged from this assembly of ours to put on the papal robes—not a light weight. But what warmth of charity, nay, what "an abundant outpouring of love"—which came forth from him in the few days of his ministry and which in his last Sunday address before the Angelus he desired should come upon the world. This is also confirmed by his wise instructions to the faithful who were present at his public audiences on faith, hope and love.

Beloved brothers in the episcopate and dear children, fidelity, as is clear, implies not a wavering obedience to the Magisterium of Peter, especially in what pertains to doctrine. The "objective" importance of this Magisterium must always be kept in mind and even safeguarded because of the attacks which in our time are being leveled here and there against certain truths of the Catholic Faith. Fidelity too implies the observance of the liturgical norms laid down by ecclesiastical authority and, therefore, has nothing to do with the practice either of introducing innovations of one's own accord and without approval, or of obstinately refusing to carry out what has been lawfully laid down and introduced into the sacred rites. Fidelity also concerns the great discipline of the Church of which our immediate Predecessor spoke. This discipline is not of such a kind that it depresses or, as they say, degrades. It seeks to safeguard the right ordering of the Mystical Body of Christ with the result that all the members of which it is composed, united together, perform their duties in a normal and natural way. Moreover, fidelity signifies the fulfillment of the demands of the priestly and religious vocation in such a way that what has freely been promised to God will always be carried out insofar as the life is understood in a stable, supernatural way.

Finally, insofar as the faithful are concerned—as the word itself signifies—fidelity of its very nature must be a duty in keeping with their condition as Christians. They show it with ready and sincere hearts and give proof of it either by obeying the sacred pastors whom the Holy Spirit has placed to rule the Church of God (cf. Acts 20:28), or by collaborating in those plans and works for which they have been called.

Nor at this point must we forget the brethren of other Churches and Christian confessions. For the cause of ecumenism is so lofty and such a sensitive issue that we may not keep silent about it. How often do we meditate together on the last wish of Christ, who asked the Father for the gift of unity for the disciples? (cf. Jn. 17:21-23) Who does not remember how much St. Paul stressed "the unity of the spirit" from which the followers of Christ might have the same love, being of one accord, of one mind? (cf. Phil. 2:2, 5-8) Therefore, one can hardly credit that a deplorable division still exists among Christians. This is a cause of embarrassment and perhaps of scandal to others. And so we wish to proceed along the road which has happily been opened and to encourage whatever can serve to remove the obstacles, desirous as we are that through common effort full communion may eventually be achieved.

We turn also to all men, who as children of almighty God are our brothers whom we must love and serve, to make known to them without any sense of boasting but with sincere humility our intention to really devote ourself to the continual and special cause of peace, of development and justice among nations. In this matter we have no desire to interfere in politics or to take part in the management of temporal affairs. For just as the Church cannot be confined to a certain earthly pattern, so we in our approach to the urgent questions of men and peoples are led solely by religious and moral motives. Following Him who gave that perfect way to His followers, so that they might be the "salt of the earth" and the "light of the world" (Mt. 5:13-16), we wish to strive to strengthen the spiritual foundations on which human society must be based. We feel that this duty is all the more urgent the longer that discords and dissensions last, which in not a few parts of the world provide material for struggles and conflicts and even give rise to the more serious danger of frightful calamities.

Therefore, it will be our constant care to direct our attention to questions of this kind and to deal with them by timely action, forgetful of our own interests and motivated by the spirit of the Gospel. One may at this point at least share the grave concern which the College of Cardinals, during the interregnum, expressed concerning the dear land of Lebanon and its people. For it we all greatly desire peace with freedom. At the same time we wish to extend our hand to all peoples and all men at this moment and to open our heart to all who are oppressed, as they say, by any injustice or discrimination with regard to either economic or social affairs, or even to political matters, or even to freedom of conscience and the freedom to practice their religion, which is their due. We must aim at this: that all forms of injustice which exist today should be given consideration by all in common and should be really eradicated from the world, so that all men may be able to live a life worthy of man. This also belongs to the mission of the Church which has been explained in the Second Vatican Council, not only in the Dogmatic Constitution *Lumen gentium* but also in the Pastoral Constitution *Gaudium et spes*.

Brothers, dear sons and daughters, the recent happenings of the Church and of the world are for us all a healthy warning: how will our pontificate be? What is the destiny the Lord has assigned to His Church in the next years? What road will mankind take in this period of time as it approaches the year 2000? To these bold questions the only answer is: "God knows" (cf. 2 Cor. 12:2-3).

The course of our life which has brought us unexpectedly to the supreme responsibility and office of apostolic service is of little interest. Our person—we ought to say—should disappear when confronted with the weighty office we must fill. And so a speech must be changed into an appeal. After praying to the Lord, we feel the need of your prayers to gain that indispensable, heavenly strength that will make it possible for us to take up the work of our Predecessors from the point where they left off.

After acknowledging their cherished memory, we offer to each one of you, our venerable brothers whom we remember with gratitude, our greeting. We extend a greeting which is both trusting and encouraging to all our brothers in the episcopate, who in different parts of the world have the care of individual Churches, the chosen sections of the People of God (cf. CD 11) and who are co-workers with us in the work of universal salvation. Behind them, we behold the order of priesthood, the band of missionaries, the companies of religious men and women.

At the same time we earnestly hope that their numbers will grow, echoing in our mind those words of the Savior, "The harvest is great, the laborers are few" (Mt. 9:37-38; Lk. 10:2). We behold also the Christian families and communities, the many associations dedicated to the apostolate, the faithful who even if they are not known to us individually are not anonymous, not strangers, nor even in a lower place, for they are included in the glorious company of the Church of Christ. Among them we look with particular affection on the weak, the poor, the sick, and those afflicted with sorrow.

Now, at the beginning of our universal pastoral ministry, we wish to open to them our heart. Do not you, brothers and sisters, share by your sufferings in the passion of our Redeemer, and in a certain way complete it? (cf. Col. 1:24) The unworthy Successor of St. Peter, who proposes to explore "the unsearchable riches of Christ" (Eph. 3:8), has the greatest need of your help, your prayers, your devotedness or "sacrifice," and this he most humbly asks of you.

We also wish, most beloved brothers and sons who hear us, because of our undying love for the land of our birth, to greet in a very special way all the citizens of Poland, "ever faithful," and the bishops, priests, and people of the Church of Krakow. United in this greeting by an indissoluble bond are memories, affections, the sweet love of the fatherland, and hope.

In this grave hour which gives rise to trepidation, we cannot do other than turn our mind with filial devotion to the Virgin Mary, who always lives and acts as a Mother in the mystery of Christ, and repeat the words *"Totus tuus"* (all thine) which we inscribed in our heart and on our coat of arms twenty years ago on the day of our episcopal ordination. We cannot but invoke Sts. Peter and Paul and all the saints and blessed of the universal Church.

In this same hour we greet everyone, the old, those in the prime of life, adolescents, children, babes newly born, with that ardent sentiment of fatherhood which is already welling up from our heart. We express the sincere wish that all "may grow in the grace and knowledge of our Lord and Savior Jesus Christ," as the Prince of the Apostles desired (2 Pt. 3:18). And to all we impart our first apostolic blessing, that it may procure not only for them but for the whole human family an abundance of the gifts of the Father who is in heaven. Amen.

A Sign of the Universality of the Church

The Holy Father's first audience was for the members of the Sacred College whom he received in the Consistorial Hall on October 18, 1978. After the address of homage by Cardinal Confalonieri, the Dean of the College, His Holiness spoke to them as follows.

Revered brothers!

What can I say, what do I wish to say to you at this meeting, while all of us are certainly still moved by the ecclesial events of these days?

In the first place I thank the Cardinal Dean for the noble words which, interpreting your sentiments, he has addressed to me. And in particular I express gratitude for the act of extraordinary confidence which you have shown with regard to my humble person, electing me as Peter's Successor in the See of Rome. Only in the light of faith is it possible to accept with interior tranquillity and with confidence the fact that by virtue of your choice it has fallen to me to become the Vicar of Christ on earth and visible Head of the Church.

AN ACT OF COURAGE

Venerable brothers, it was an act of confidence and at the same time of great courage to have wished to call a "non-Italian" as Bishop of Rome. One cannot say any more, but can only bow one's head before this decision of the Sacred College.

Never, perhaps, as in these recent events which have involved the Church, depriving her twice in two months of her universal Pastor, have the Christian people felt and experienced the importance, the delicacy, the responsibility of the tasks that the Sacred College of Cardinals had to perform. And never as in this period—we must recognize with real satisfaction—have the faithful shown such affectionate esteem and such benevolent understanding for their Eminences. The intense and prolonged applause addressed to you at the end of the Mass *Pro eligendo Papa* and at the announcement of the election of the new Pontiff, was the most expressive, exalting and moving proof.

The faithful have really understood, revered brothers, that the purple you wear is the sign of that faithfulness "unto the shedding of your blood," which you promised the Pope with a solemn oath. Yours is a garment of blood, which recalls and presents the blood that the apostles, the bishops, the Cardinals have shed for Christ in the course of the centuries. I remember, at this moment, the figure of a great bishop, St. John Fisher, created Cardinal—as is known—when he was imprisoned for his faithfulness to the Pope of Rome. On the morning of June 22, 1535, while he was preparing to offer his head to the executioner's axe, he exclaimed facing the crowd: "Christian people, I am about to die for faith in the holy Catholic Church of Christ." I would also venture to add that also in our times there are persons who have not been spared, who are still not spared, the experience of prison, sufferings, humiliation for Christ.

May this unshakeable faithfulness to the Bride of Jesus be always the badge of honor and the preeminent boast of the College of Cardinals.

SENSE OF BROTHERHOOD

I would like to stress another element in this short meeting of ours: the sense of brotherhood, which in this recent period has been manifested and strengthened more and more within the Sacred College: "Behold, how good and pleasant it is when brothers dwell in unity!" (Ps. 132[133]:1) The Sacred College has had to deal twice, and in a very short space of time, with one of the most delicate problems of the Church: that of the election of the Roman Pontiff. And on this occasion the true universality of the

Church has shone forth. It was really possible to see what St. Augustine affirms: "The Church itself speaks the languages of all peoples.... Spread among the peoples, the Church speaks all languages" *(In Ioannis Evang. Tractat.,* XXXII, 7; *PL* 35, 1645).

CONCORDANT IN ONE FAITH

Ecclesial experiences, needs and problems are complex, varied, and sometimes even different. But this variety has been—and certainly will be—always *concordant in one faith,* as the same Bishop of Hippo reminds us when he emphasizes the beauty and variety of the clothes of the queen-Church: "These languages constitute the variety of the vesture of the queen. Just as every variety of dress is harmonized in unity, so too, all languages in regard to the one faith" *(Enarrat. in psal.* XLIV, 23: *PL* 36, 509).

It is difficult for me not to express deep gratitude to the Holy Father, Paul VI, for the fact that he decided to give the Sacred College such a wide, international, intercontinental dimension. Its members, in fact, come from the farthest ends of the earth. That makes it possible not only to accentuate the universality of the Church, but also the universal aspect of Rome.

In a few days you will all return to your posts of responsibility: most of you to your dioceses; others to the Departments of the Holy See; all to continue with ever-increasing commitment the pastoral ministry, which is weighed down with responsibilities, worries and sacrifices, but also comforted by the grace of the Lord and by the spiritual joy He gives His faithful servants. But, though at the head of the particular Churches, always participate in concern for the whole Church, living and putting into practice with all your might what the Second Vatican Council recommends: "As lawful successors of the Apostles and as members of the episcopal college, bishops should always realize that they are linked one to the other, and should show concern for all the Churches. For by divine institution and the requirement of their apostolic office, each one in concert with his fellow bishops is responsible for the Church" (CD 6; cf. *ibidem* 3; LG 23).

LET THE CHURCH BE BLESSED

Invoking on you all, on the faithful entrusted to your pastoral zeal and on all dear to you, the grace of Christ and the watchful protection of Mary, "Mother of the Church," I would like to impart my apostolic blessing with great affection. I would like to do so first for you, and afterwards with you all: in this way let the Church be blessed everywhere by the new Bishop of Rome and by the whole College of Cardinals, whose members come from all over the world and are close to him.

In the Footsteps of St. Charles

On November 4, 1978, the feast of St. Charles Borromeo, the Holy Father received the Sacred College of Cardinals, who presented to him their fervent and cordial good wishes for his name day. His Holiness, John Paul II, delivered the following address.

I wish to thank you heartily for the expressions of benevolence with regard to my person. Name days always draw the attention and the benevolence of those closest to us—of members of the family—upon the person who bears a given name. This name reminds us of the love of our parents, who, on giving it, wished to determine somehow the place of their child in that community of love which the family is. They were the first to address him with this name, and together with them, his brothers and sisters, relatives, friends and companions. And so the name marks out the man's path among men, among the men closest to him and fondest of him.

But the mystery of the name goes further. The parents, who gave their child his name in Baptism, wished to define his place in the great gathering of love which the family of God is. The Church on earth strives continually towards the dimensions of this family in the mystery of the communion of saints. By naming their child, the parents wish to bring him into the continuity of this mystery.

My beloved parents gave me the name Karol (Charles), which was also my father's name. Certainly, they could never have foreseen (they both died young) that this name would open up for their child the way among the great events of the Church of today.

St. Charles! How often I have knelt before his relics in Milan Cathedral; how often I have thought about his life, contemplating in my mind the gigantic figure of this man of God and servant of the Church, Charles Borromeo, Cardinal, Bishop of Milan, and a man of the Council. He is one of the great protagonists of the deep reform of the sixteenth-century Church, carried out by the Council of Trent, which will always remain linked with his name. He is also one of the creators of the institution of ecclesiastical seminaries, which has been reconfirmed in all its substance by the Second Vatican Council. Moreover, he was a servant of souls, who never let himself be intimidated; a servant of the suffering, of the sick, of those condemned to death.

My patron saint!

In his name my parents, my parish, my country intended to prepare me right from the beginning for an extraordinary service of the Church, in the context of today's Council, with the many tasks united with its implementation, and also in all the experiences and sufferings of modern man.

May God reward you, revered brothers, Cardinals of the holy Roman Church, for having, on this day, together with me, wished to venerate St. Charles in my unworthy person. May God reward all those who do so together with you.

If only I could imitate him, at least partly!

I hope that your prayers, the prayers of all good, noble, benevolent men, my brothers and sisters, will help me in this.

And now, before I conclude this talk, allow me to address you particularly, revered and dear Dean of the Sacred College, who bear the same name, Charles.

We have a common patron saint and we celebrate our name day on the same day.

I reciprocate your good wishes. And I do so from the bottom of my heart, with deep gratitude.

The Dean of the Sacred College has shown me great benevolence on these first days of my pontificate. Whenever he speaks, his words are full of love and dedication; and I welcome the expressions he has addressed to me today as a sign of extraordinary support for my first steps at the beginning of my new mission. I thank him heartily.

And I pray that St. Charles, our common patron saint, will bless his person for his whole life, for all the days full of love for the Church and marked by the spirit of dedication and service which edified us all.

With my special apostolic blessing.

Doctrine and Discipline in the Priestly Life

On November 9, 1978, the Holy Father, John Paul II, received the bishops of the seventh pastoral region of the U.S.A., as also the archbishops and bishops of the fifth pastoral region of the U.S.A. Both groups of prelates were in Rome for their canonical ad limina *visit. In reply to a speech of homage by His Eminence, Cardinal Cody, His Holiness gave the following address.*

Dear brothers in our Lord Jesus Christ,

One of the greatest consolations of the new Pope is to know that he has the love and support of all the People of God. Like the Apostle Peter in the Acts of the Apostles, the Pope is powerfully sustained by the fervent prayers of the faithful. And so it is a special joy for me today to be with you, my brothers in the episcopate, the pastors of the local Churches in the United States of America. I know that you bring with you the deep faith of your people, their profound respect for the mystery of Peter's role in God's design for the universal Church, and their love for Christ and His brethren. In the Providence of God I have been able to visit your land and to know some of your people personally. Thus our being together is itself a celebration of the unity of the Church. It is also an attestation of our acceptance of Jesus Christ in the totality of His mystery of salvation.

I UNDERSTAND YOUR NEEDS

As Servant and Pastor and Father of the universal Church, I wish at this moment to express my love for all those who are specially called to work for the Gospel, all those who actively collaborate with you in your dioceses to build up the kingdom of God. Like yourselves, I learned as a bishop to understand at firsthand the ministry of priests, the problems affecting their lives, the splendid efforts they are making, the sacrifices that are an integral part of their service to God's people. Like yourselves, I am fully aware of how much Christ depends on His priests in order to fulfill in time His mission of redemption. And like yourselves I have worked with the religious, endeavoring to give witness to the esteem that the Church has for them in their vocation of consecrated love, and urging them always to full, generous collaboration in the corporate life of the ecclesial community. All of us have seen abundant examples of authentic *evangelica testificatio*. Now I ask you all to take my greetings to the clergy and religious, to assure them all of my understanding, my solidarity, my love in Christ Jesus and in the Church.

I am aware also that my pastoral obligations extend to the whole community of the faithful. During this audience I would like to offer a few basic reflections that I am firmly convinced are relevant for each local Church in its entirety. In establishing priorities, my Predecessors Paul VI and

John Paul I chose topics of extreme importance, and all of their exhortations and directives to the American bishops I ratify with full knowledge and personal conviction. In the last *ad limina* address to the bishops of the U.S.A. my immediate Predecessor spoke on the Christian family. Already during the first weeks of my pontificate I too have had occasion to speak on this theme, and to extol its importance. Yes, may all the wonderful Christian families in God's Church know that the Pope is with them, united in prayer, in hope, in confidence. The Pope confirms them in their mission given them by Christ Himself, proclaims their dignity, and blesses all their efforts.

I am thoroughly convinced that families everywhere and the great family of the Catholic Church will be greatly served—a real pastoral service will be rendered to them—if a renewed emphasis is placed on the role of doctrine in the life of the Church. In God's plan a new pontificate is always a new beginning, evoking fresh hopes and giving new opportunities for reflection, for conversion, for prayer and for resolves.

PURITY OF DOCTRINE AND SOUND DISCIPLINE

Under the care of Mary, Mother of God and Mother of the Church, I wish to commit my pontificate to the continued genuine application of the Second Vatican Council, under the action of the Holy Spirit. And in this regard, nothing is more enlightening than to recall the exact words with which, on the opening day, John XXIII wished to spell out the orientation of this great ecclesial event: "The greatest concern of the Ecumenical Council is this: that the sacred deposit of Christian doctrine should be more effectively guarded and taught." This far-seeing vision of Pope John is valid today. It was the only sound basis for an Ecumenical Council aimed at pastoral renewal; it is the only sound basis for all our pastoral endeavors as bishops of the Church of God. This, then, is my own deepest hope today for the pastors of the Church in America, as well as for all the pastors of the universal Church: "that the sacred deposit of Christian doctrine should be more effectively guarded and taught." The sacred deposit of God's word, handed on by the Church, is the joy and strength of our people's lives. It is the only pastoral solution to the many problems of our day. To present this sacred deposit of Christian doctrine in all its purity and integrity, with all its exigencies and in all its power, is a holy, pastoral responsibility; it is, moreover, the most sublime service we can render.

And the second hope that I would express today is a hope for the preservation of the great discipline of the Church—a hope eloquently formulated by John Paul I on the day after his election: "We wish to maintain intact the great discipline of the Church in the life of priests and of the faithful, as the history of the Church, enriched by experience, has presented it throughout the centuries with examples of holiness and heroic perfection, both in the exercise of the evangelical virtues and in service to the poor, the humble, the defenseless."

These two hopes do not exhaust our aspirations or our prayers, but they are worthy of intense pastoral efforts and apostolic diligence. These efforts and diligence on our part are in turn an expression of real love and concern for the flock entrusted to our care by Jesus Christ, the chief Shepherd—a pastoral charge to be exercised within the unity of the universal Church and in the context of the collegiality of the episcopate.

These hopes for the life of the Church—purity of doctrine and sound discipline—intimately depend on every new generation of priests who, with the generosity of love, continue the Church's commitment to the Gospel. For this reason, Paul VI showed great wisdom in asking the American bishops "to fulfill with loving personal attention your great pastoral responsibility to your seminarians: know the content of their courses, encourage them to love the Word of God and never to be ashamed of the seeming folly of the cross" (Address of June 20, 1977). And this is my ardent desire today: that a new emphasis on the importance of doctrine and discipline will be the postconciliar contribution of your seminaries, so that "the word of the Lord may speed on and triumph" (2 Thes. 3:1).

And in all your pastoral labors you can be sure that the Pope is united with you and close to you in the love of Jesus Christ. All of us have a single goal: to prove faithful to the pastoral trust committed to us, to lead the People of God "in right paths for his name's sake" (Ps. 23:3), so that, with pastoral accountability, we can say with Jesus to the Father: "As long as I was with them, I guarded them with your name which you gave me. I kept careful watch, and not one of them was lost..." (Jn. 17:12).

In the name of Jesus, peace to you and to all your people. With my apostolic blessing.

The World Today Needs Your Priestly Witness

The first meeting of Pope John Paul II with the clergy of the diocese of Rome took place on November 9, 1978. After the address of homage by the Cardinal Vicar Ugo Poletti, the Pope delivered the following speech.

Lord Cardinal,

1. I wish to thank you heartily for the words addressed to me at the beginning of this meeting of ours today. Together with the Cardinal Vicar, Mons. the Vicegerent and the auxiliary bishops, the clergy of the diocese of Rome are present here to meet the new Bishop of Rome, whom Christ designated by means of the Cardinals' vote in the conclave on October 16, after the sudden death of beloved Pope John Paul I. I must confess to you, dear confreres, that I greatly desired and looked forward to this meeting. However, taking over the succession to my venerable Predecessors—barely three months, in fact, have

passed since the death also of the great Pope Paul VI—I thought it should be done gradually. All the more so in that the circumstances are so unusual.

The succession of the Bishops of Rome, after 455 years, includes a Pope who comes from beyond the frontiers of Italy. Therefore, I considered it necessary that the taking possession of the diocese of Rome, together with the solemn entrance into the Basilica of St. John Lateran, should be preceded by a period of preparation. In the meantime, I wished to take my place in that magnificent movement of Christian tradition in Italy expressed by the figures of its patron saints: St. Francis of Assisi and Saint Catherine of Siena. After this preparation, I wish to carry out the fundamental duty of my pontificate, that is, to take possession of Rome as a diocese, as the Church of this city, and officially assume responsibility for this community, this tradition, which has its origins in St. Peter the Apostle. I am deeply aware of having become Pope of the universal Church because of being Bishop of Rome. The ministry (*munus*) of the Bishop of Rome, as Peter's Successor, is the root of universality.

ESSENTIAL PROBLEMS ARE NOT NEW

Our meeting today, on the feast of the Dedication of the Lateran Basilica, is, as it were, an inauguration of the solemn act which will take place next Sunday. I greet the Cardinal Vicar, the Vicegerent, the bishops and all the priests gathered here, both diocesan and religious. I extend the most cordial welcome to all on behalf of Christ the Savior.

2. I listened with great attention to the Cardinal Vicar's address. I add that, even before our meeting today, he has been so kind as to inform me about various questions concerning the diocese of Rome, and in particular about the pastoral activity which weighs on your shoulders, dear brother priests, in it, the first in dignity among the dioceses of the Church.

As I was listening to the address, I realized with joy that the most essential problems are not new to me. They are part of all my preceding experience. As a result of twenty years of episcopal service and nearly fifteen of pastoral guidance in one of the most ancient dioceses of Poland, the Archdiocese of Krakow, these problems relive in my memories, forcing me to compare them with one another, though remaining aware—as is obvious—of the difference in the situations. I am perfectly aware of what evangelization and pastoral activity mean in a city whose historic center is rich in churches that are becoming empty, while at the same time new districts and suburbs are springing up for which it is necessary to provide; often even struggling to obtain new churches, new parishes, and the other fundamental conditions for evangelization. I remember the admirable, zealous and often heroic priests, with whom I was able to share the concern and the struggles. Along this way, faith, nourished by tradition, acquires new strength. Secularization, planned or springing from habits and tendencies among the inhabitants of a large city, stops when it meets a living testimony of faith, which also clearly shows the social dimension of the Gospel.

I know too, dear brothers, the significance of the individual institutions and structures which the Cardinal Vicar of Rome has been good enough to mention. That is, the Curia, in our case the Vicariate of Rome, the Prefectures and the respective Council of Parish Priest Prefects and the Priests' Council. I have learned to give their rightful value to all these forms of group work. They are not only administrative structures, but centers by means of which our priestly communion is expressed and realized, as well as the union of the pastoral service and of evangelization. In my preceding episcopal work the Priests' Council rendered me great service, both as a community, and as a meeting place to share, together with the bishop, common solicitude for the whole life of the "presbyterate" and for the effectiveness of its pastoral activity.

Among the institutions that the Cardinal Vicar enumerated in his address, the following three were always very near and dear to me in my preceding service as bishop: the diocesan seminary, the University of Theological Sciences, and the parish.

How I wish I could contribute to their development! The seminary is, in fact, "the apple" not only of the bishop's eye, but of that of the whole local and universal Church. The University of Theological Sciences—in this case the Lateran University—will be as dear to me as the Theology Faculty in Krakow, with the attached institutes, was and remains dear to me. With regard to the parish, how profoundly true I find the affirmation that the bishop feels more at ease "in the parish"! How I loved the visits to the parishes—the fundamental organizational cells of the Church and at the same time of the community of the People of God! I hope that I will be able to continue them here too, in order to get to know your problems and those of the parishes. In this connection, we have already had preliminary talks with His Eminence and his bishops.

3. Everything I say refers to you and concerns you directly, dear brother priests of Rome. As I meet you here for the first time and greet you with sincere affection, I have still before my eyes and in my heart the "presbyterate" of the church of Krakow—all our meetings on various occasions, the numerous talks that had their beginning right from the years in the seminary, the meetings of priests, ordination groups of each of the seminary classes to which I was invited and in which I took part with joy and benefit!

THE FUNDAMENTAL CONDITION OF UNION

It will certainly not be possible to transfer all that here, in the new conditions of work, but we must do our utmost to be close, to form the *unum*, priestly communion, composed of all the diocesan and religious clergy, and of all the priests from various parts of the world who work in the Roman Curia and who also dedicate themselves solicitously to the pastoral ministry. This communion of priests among themselves and with the bishop is the fundamental condition of union among the whole People of God. It constructs its unity in pluralism and in Christian solidarity. The union of priests with the bishop must become the source of the mutual union of priests among themselves and of groups of priests. This union, at the basis of which we find awareness of our own great mission, is expressed by means of the exchange of services and experiences, availability for collaboration, commitment in all pastoral activities—both in the parish and in catechesis—or in guiding the apostolic action of the laity.

Dear brothers, we must love our priesthood from the bottom of our heart, as a great "social sacrament." We must love it as the essence of our life and of our vocation, as the basis of our Christian and human identity. None of us can be divided in himself. The sacramental priesthood, the ministerial priesthood, calls for particular faith, for particular commitment of all the forces of body and soul, for special awareness of one's vocation as an exceptional vocation. Each of us must thank Christ on his knees for the gift of this vocation: "What shall I render to the Lord for all his bounty to me? I will lift up the cup of salvation and call on the name of the Lord" (Ps. 116).

We must take, dear brothers, "the cup of salvation." We are necessary for men, we are immensely necessary, and not part-time, not half-time like "employees"! We are necessary as those who bear witness and reawaken in others the need to testify. And if it may sometimes seem that we are not necessary, it means that we must begin to bear witness more clearly, and then we will see how much the modern world needs our priestly testimony, our service, our priesthood.

We must give and offer the men of our time, our faithful, the people of Rome, this testimony of ours with our whole human existence, with our whole being. Priestly testimony, yours, beloved priest confreres, and mine, involves the whole of our person. Yes, the Lord seems, in fact, to speak to us:

"I need your hands to continue to bless, / I need your lips to continue to speak, / I need your body to continue to suffer. / I need your heart to continue to love, / I need you to continue to save" (Michel Quoist, "Preghiere").

Let us not deceive ourselves that we are serving the Gospel if we try to "water down" our priestly charism through exaggerated interest in the vast field of temporal problems, if we wish to "secularize" our way of living and acting, if we cancel even the external signs of our priestly vocation. We must keep the sense of our singular vocation, and this "singularity" must be expressed also in our exterior garb. Let us not be ashamed of it! Yes, we are in the world! But we are not of the world!

PRIESTLY VOCATIONS FOR ROME

The Second Vatican Council recalled to us this splendid truth regarding the "universal priesthood" of the whole People of God, which is derived from participation in the one priesthood of Jesus Christ. Our "ministerial" priesthood, rooted in the sacrament of Holy Orders, differs essentially from the universal priesthood of the faithful. And it was constituted in order to enlighten more effectively our brothers and sisters who live in the world—that is, the laity—about the fact that in Jesus Christ we are all a "kingdom of priests" for the Father. The priest reaches this purpose through the ministry of the word and of the sacraments, which is specifically his, and above all, through the Eucharistic Sacrifice, for which he alone is authorized; the priest realizes all this also through a suitable lifestyle. Therefore, our priesthood must be clear and expressive. And if, in the tradition of our Church, it is closely linked with celibacy, this is due precisely to the clarity and "evangelical" expressiveness referred to in our Lord's words on celibacy "for the kingdom of heaven" (cf. Mt. 19:12).

The Second Vatican Council and one of the first Synods of Bishops, that of 1971, gave great attention to the above-mentioned questions. We recall, moreover, that during this Synod, Pope Paul VI raised to the altars Blessed Maximilian Kolbe, a priest. Today I wish to refer to all that was stated then, as well as to this priestly testimony of my fellow countryman.

I would like to entrust to you yet another problem which I have particularly at heart: priestly vocations for this dear city of ours and beloved diocese of Rome! Share this concern and solicitude of mine, dear priests! Go back to your most personal memories. At the beginning of your vocation is there not, perhaps, an exemplary priest who guided you in your first steps towards the priesthood? Is not your first thought, your first desire to follow the Lord linked, perhaps, with the concrete person of a priest-confessor, a priest-friend? Let your grateful thought, your heart overbrimming with thankfulness go back to this priest. Yes, the Lord needs intermediaries, instruments, to make His voice, His call, heard. Dear priests, offer yourselves to the Lord to be His instruments in calling new workers to His vineyard. There is no lack of generous youths.

With great humility and love I ask Christ, the one eternal Priest, through the intercession of His Mother and ours, so venerated in the image known all over the world as *Salus Populi Romani*, that our common priestly and pastoral service in this diocese, the most venerable one in the universal Church, may be blessed and bear abundant fruit. Referring then to Jesus Christ's priestly prayer, I end with these words: "Holy Father, keep them in your name which you have given me, that they may be one...and none of them lost...that they may be consecrated in truth" (Jn. 17:11, 12, 19).

Development in Freedom

On November 11, 1978, Pope John Paul II received in audience participants in the plenary assembly of the Pontifical Commission Justitia et Pax, *to whom he delivered the following address.*

Dear friends,

I am counting on you, I am counting on the Pontifical Commission *Iustitia et Pax*, to help me and to help the whole Church to repeat to the men of this time, with pressing insistence, the appeal which I addressed to them on beginning my Roman and universal ministry, on Sunday, October 22:

"Do not be afraid! Open, yes, fling the doors wide open to Christ! Open to His power of salvation the frontiers of states, economic and political regimes, the immense fields of culture, civilization and development. Do not be afraid! Christ knows what there is in man! And He is the only one who knows it."

BREAK DOWN PARTITIONS

We are living in times in which everything should urge us to break down partitions: the keener perception of the universal solidarity of men and peoples; the necessity of safeguarding the common environment and inheritance of mankind; the necessity of reducing the weight and the deadly threat of armaments; the duty of rescuing from want millions of men who would find again, with the means of leading a decent life, the possibility of bringing new energies to the common effort. Now, before the amplitude and the difficulties of the task, we can see nearly everywhere a reflex of hardening. At the source, there is fear: fear above all of man and his responsible freedom, fear which is often increased by the concatenation of violence and repression. And, finally, fear of Jesus Christ, either because people do not know Him, or because, among Christians themselves, the experience—demanding, but life-bringing—of an existence inspired by His Gospel is no longer sufficiently lived.

OPEN UP TO CHRIST

The first service that the Church must render to the cause of justice and peace is to call upon men to open up to Jesus Christ. In Him they will learn again their essential dignity as children of God, made in God's image, endowed with unsuspected possibilities which make them capable of facing up to the tasks of the hour, bound to one another by a brotherhood which has its roots in God's fatherhood. In Him they will become free for a responsible service. Let them not be afraid! Jesus Christ is not an alien or a competitor. He does not offend anything that is authentically human, either in persons, or in their different scientific and social achievements. Nor is the Church an alien or a competitor. "The Church," says the Constitution *Gaudium et spes*, "by reason of her role and competence, is not identified with any political community nor bound by ties to any political system. It is at once the sign and the safeguard of the transcendental dimension of the human person" (76). Opening man up to God, the Church prevents him from shutting himself up in any ideological system whatsoever; it opens him up to himself and to others and makes him available to create something new in the dimensions of the present requirements of the evolution of mankind.

With the central gift of Jesus Christ, the Church brings to the common work, not a prefabricated model, but a dynamic inheritance—doctrinal and practical—which developed in contact with the changing situations of this world, under the impulse of the Gospel as the source of renewal, with a disinterested will for service and attention for the poorest (cf. OA 42). The whole Christian community takes part in this service. But the Council opportunely desired, and Paul VI effected with the Pontifical Commission *Iustitia et Pax*, the creation of an "organization of the universal Church whose task it would be to arouse the Catholic community to promote the progress of areas which are in want and foster social justice between nations" (no. 90).

It is to this universal service that you are called, beside the Pope and under his guidance. You exercise it in a spirit of service and in a dialogue—which it will be necessary to develop—with the episcopal conferences and different organisms which, in communion with them, are pursuing the same task. You exercise it in an ecumenical spirit by tirelessly seeking and adapting the forms of cooperation calculated to further the unity of Christians in thought and in action.

Without prejudice to the numerous questions to which the Commission gives its attention, you have dedicated this general assembly to the subject of the development of peoples. The Church has been present from the outset at this immense effort, and she has followed its hopes, difficulties and disappointments. A serene appreciation of the positive results, even when insufficient, must help to overcome the present hesitations. You have made a point of studying the whole range of problems which the necessary pursuit of the work begun raises—at the level of the international community, in the internal life of each people, at the level also of elementary communities—in the way of conceiving and realizing new ways of life. In order that the Church may be able to say the word of hope which is expected of her and to strengthen the spiritual and moral values, without which there cannot be any development, she must listen, patiently and with sympathy, to the men and institutions that are working hard at the task at all levels, and measure the obstacles to be overcome. There can be no trickery with the reality which it is desired to change.

ATTENTION TO THOSE WHO SUFFER

Priority attention for those who are suffering from radical poverty, for those who are suffering from injustice, certainly coincides with a fundamental concern of the Church; similarly the concern to conceive models of development which, in order to ask for sacrifices, are careful not to sacrifice essential personal and social freedoms and rights, without which, moreover, they would soon condemn themselves to a dead-end. And Christians will want to be in the vanguard in order to bring forth convictions and ways of life which will break decisively with a frenzy for consumption, so exhausting and joyless.

Thank you, Lord Cardinal, for the words through which you expressed to me the filial and devoted sentiments of the whole commission. Your presence at the head of this organism is a pledge that peoples that are poor, but rich in humanity, will be at the heart of its concerns. Thank you, brother bishops, thank you all, dear friends, who bring to the Commission and to myself your human and apostolic competence and experience. Thank you, all members of the Curia present here: Due to you, the dimension of human and social advancement can better penetrate the activity of the other congregations and departments; in return, the activity of the Commission *Iustitia et Pax* will be able to be integrated better and better in the Church's overall mission.

IN FAVOR OF JUSTICE

You know, in fact, to what extent the Council and my Predecessors took it to heart to set the action of the Church in favor of justice, peace, development, and liberation, in the frame of reference of its evangelizing mission. Against confusion which is always springing up again, it is important not to reduce evangelization to its fruits for the earthly city: The Church owes it to men to give them access to the source, to Jesus Christ. So the Dogmatic Constitution *Lumen gentium* remains the "magna charta" of the Council: in its light all the other texts take on their full dimension. The Pastoral Constitution *Gaudium et spes* and everything it inspires are not minimized, but strengthened, by it.

In Christ's name, I bless you, yourself and your collaborators, those who are dear to you, and your beloved countries, and especially those who are sorely tried. Turning again to the subject of the audience last Wednesday, may the Lord help us, may He help all our brothers, to set out along the ways of justice and peace!

Evangelization in Line with Vatican II

The Holy Father received in audience on the morning of November 13, 1978, Cardinal Reginald Delargey, Archbishop of Wellington, together with a group of bishops of New Zealand, and spoke to them as follows.

Dear brothers in our Lord Jesus Christ,

I shall always be grateful to God for having given me the opportunity to visit New Zealand. Even though my stay among you in 1973 was a brief one, it gave me great joy. Be assured that my memories of these days are still vivid, and that they constitute one more reason for me to do everything in my power to be of service to your beloved people in the Gospel of Christ. And today it is my hope, with God's grace, to fulfill my papal ministry towards you, my brother bishops: as successor of Peter I desire to confirm you in the Apostle's profession of faith, so that you in turn may continue with fresh vigor and new strength to preach Jesus Christ, the Son of the living God, and to assist your people to realize to the full their Christian dignity and to attain their final destiny.

The Second Vatican Council wanted to avoid every semblance of triumphalism in the Church. In this regard it pointed out that Christ calls His Church "to that continual reformation of which she always has need, insofar as she is an institution of people here on earth" (UR 6). The Council never had any intention of claiming that the Church always has at hand facile solutions to individual problems (cf. GS 33); it did, however, positively wish to emphasize the teaching role of the Church: the fact that she is endowed with light from God, in order to offer solutions to problems that affect humanity (cf. GS 12). The Council desired that through the preaching of the Gospel all people would be illumined by the light of Christ that shines on the face of the Church (cf. LG 1).

The Church truly reflects the light of Christ, and from Christ she has received a message that answers the fundamental aspirations of the human heart. In the Pastoral Constitution on the Church in the Modern World we are reminded that "bishops, who are assigned the task of ruling the Church of God, should, together with their priests, so preach the message of Christ that all the earthly activities of the faithful will be bathed in the light of the Gospel" (GS 43). As bishops, you are constantly trying to fulfill this role of pastoral service, to bring the treasure of God's Word to bear relevantly on the life of each member of the flock, to bring the light of Christ into the lives of individuals and communities.

I wish to assure you today that I am deeply aware of the bonds that unite us in the Church and in her hierarchical communion. You have my prayers and support for all your apostolic labors. In particular, I am at one with you in your mission of defending human life in all its stages. In all your catechetical endeavors, in all your work for Catholic education, you can count on the solidarity of the universal Church. What an important work it is to provide children with Catholic schools, in which they can "grow up in every way into him who is the head, into Christ!" (Eph. 4:15) What a great challenge it is for a bishop to guard the deposit of Christian doctrine, so that each new generation can receive the fullness of the apostolic faith! And to what deep paternal sensitivity and spiritual leadership the bishop is called, in order effectively to associate the whole diocese with himself in exercising the collective vigilance that is needed for maintaining true Catholic education! Through word and example and prayer, the bishop must inspire each member of the Christian family to do his or her part, so that the light of Christ will touch all people in each vital aspect of modern living.

Despite difficulties and obstacles, we must never falter in our commitment to work for the re-establishment of Christian unity, according to the ardent desire of the heart of Christ. The orientation of the Ecumenical Council is decisive, and its call for conversion and holiness of life is even more imperative today than it was fourteen years ago when this appeal was made: "Let all Christ's faithful remember that the more purely they strive to live according to the Gospel, the more they are fostering and even practicing Christian unity" (UR 7). The great ecumenical heritage of the Council was succinctly summarized by Paul VI in the closing lines of his testament, which I propose once again to your prayerful meditation and to that of the whole Church: "Let the work of drawing closer to our separated brethren be carried on, with much understanding, with much patience, with great love; but without deviation from the true Catholic doctrine." This delicate work is beyond human power; only the Holy Spirit can bring it to completion. With the intensity of love we must pray to the Father: "Thy kingdom come, Thy will be done."

With these reflections I reiterate my affection in Christ Jesus for all the Catholic people and for all your fellow citizens in New Zealand. My special love is with the poor, the sick, the suffering. I send a particular greeting to the Maori people, encouraging them to remain strong in faith and fervent in love.

My apostolic blessing "to all of you that are in Christ" (1 Pt. 5:14).

Deep Pastoral Concern for the Church's Discipline

On November 17, 1978, the Holy Father, John Paul II, received a group of Canadian bishops who had been in Rome for their ad limina *visit. During the audience, the Pope addressed the bishops as follows.*

Dear brothers in our Lord Jesus Christ,

It is a rich source of pastoral strength to assemble together in the name of Jesus and in the unity of His Church. For me personally, it is a real joy to welcome you as brothers in the episcopate, partners in the Gospel, pastors of a great section of the People of God in Canada. Your dioceses are immensely important for the universal Church, and for me, whom the inscrutable design of God has now placed in the See of Peter to be the servant of all.

According to the Second Vatican Council, the very notion of a diocese is "a portion of God's people entrusted to a bishop to be guided by him with the assistance of his clergy, so that, loyal to its pastor and formed by him into one community in the Holy Spirit through the Gospel and the Eucharist, it constitutes one particular Church in which the one, holy, Catholic and apostolic Church of Christ is truly present and active" (CD 11). This is the mystery of God's love that we are reflecting on today: the bishop as pastor of a particular Church in which Catholic unity abides.

This unity is effected and ensured by the Gospel and the Eucharist. Indeed the Council reminds us: "Among the principal duties of bishops, the preaching of the Gospel occupies an eminent place" (LG 25). The bishop finds his identity in evangelizing, in being a herald of that Gospel which St. Paul assures us is "the power of God for salvation to every one who has faith" (Rom. 1:16). At the highest level of our ministry of evangelization is the Eucharist, which we faithfully acknowledge with the Council as "the source and summit of all evangelization" (PO 5).

From God's Word and its supreme enactment in the Eucharist we draw gladness and strength in order to be father and brother and friend to our priests, who have the vital task of collaborating with us in communicating the mystery of Christ. May the joy that the Gospel generates in our own lives be contagious for the ministry of our priests, and help them to realize how much Christ needs them in His mission of salvation.

At the tomb of Peter we are also humbly seeking grace to fulfill our responsibility to our entire flock with renewed fortitude and even greater pastoral love. It is with the power of the Gospel of Christ that we confront all the pastoral situations and problems linked to our ministry. Only on this basis can we build the Church, which is the germ and beginning of God's kingdom on earth and the leaven of all society. Through the power of God's Word we find energy to promote justice, witness to love, uphold the sacredness of life and proclaim the dignity of the human person and his transcendent destiny. In short, with the power of the Gospel we go forth serenely and confidently to proclaim "the unsearchable riches of Christ" (Eph. 3:8).

Because of the centrality of God's Word, we are called to give absolute pastoral priority to the ever more effective guarding and teaching of the deposit of faith. In this regard St. Paul challenges us constantly to apostolic vigilance: "Before God and before Jesus Christ, who is to be judge of the living and the dead, I put this duty to you, in the name of His appearing and of His kingdom: proclaim the message and, welcome or unwelcome, insist on it. Refute falsehood, correct error, call to obedience—but do all with patience and with the intention of teaching" (2 Tm. 4:1-3).

At the same time, as bishops we are urged to a deep pastoral concern for the sacred discipline common to the whole Church (cf. LG 23). This brings with it a need for a sensitivity to the delicate and sovereign action of the Holy Spirit in the life of our people, and a humble realization that this action is accomplished in a special way through the ministry of the bishops who, united with the entire

Episcopal College and with Peter its head, are promised the assistance of the Holy Spirit, so that they may effectively lead the faithful to salvation.

At this moment in the life of the Church there are two particular aspects of sacramental discipline that are worthy of the special attention of the universal Church, and I wish to mention them, in order to assist bishops everywhere. These matters form part of that general discipline of which the Apostolic See has prime responsibility, and in which the Pope wishes to sustain his brethren in the episcopate and to offer a word of encouragement and pastoral orientation for the spiritual well-being of the faithful. These two matters are the practice of first Confession before first Communion and the question of general absolution.

After some initial experimentation had been conducted, Paul VI in 1973 reiterated the discipline of the Latin Church in regard to first Confession. In a spirit of exemplary fidelity, numerous bishops, priests, deacons, religious, teachers and catechists set out to explain the importance of a discipline which the supreme authority of the Church had confirmed, and to apply it for the benefit of the faithful. Ecclesial communities were comforted to know that the universal Church gave renewed assurance for a pastoral matter in which, previously, honest divergence of opinion existed. I am grateful to you for your own vigilance in this regard and ask you to continue to explain the Church's solicitude in maintaining this universal discipline, so rich in doctrinal background and confirmed by the experience of so many local Churches. With regard to the children who have reached the age of reason, the Church is happy to guarantee the pastoral value of having them experience the sacramental expression of conversion before being initiated into the eucharistic sharing of the Paschal Mystery.

As Supreme Pastor, Paul VI manifested similar deep solicitude for the great question of conversion in its sacramental aspect of individual confession. In an *ad limina* visit earlier this year he referred at some length to the pastoral norms governing the use of general absolution (Address of April 20, 1978, to bishops from the United States), showing that these norms are in fact linked to the solemn teaching of the Council of Trent concerning the *divine precept* of individual confession. Once again he indicated the altogether *exceptional* character of general absolution. At the same time he asked the bishops to help their priests "to have an ever greater appreciation of the splendid ministry of theirs as confessors.... Other works, for lack of time, may have to be postponed or even abandoned, but not the confessional." I thank you for what you have done and will do to show the importance of the Church's wise discipline in an area that is so intimately linked with the work of reconciliation. In the name of the Lord Jesus, let us give assurance, in union with the whole Church, to all our priests of the great supernatural effectiveness of a persevering ministry exercised through auricular confession, in fidelity to the command of the Lord and the teaching of His Church. And once again let us assure all our people of the great benefits derived from frequent confession. I am indeed convinced of the words of my Predecessor, Pius XII: "Not without the inspiration of the Holy Spirit was this practice introduced into the Church" (*AAS* 35, 1943, p. 235).

Our Lord Jesus Christ Himself insisted on the essential indissolubility of marriage. His Church must not allow His teaching on this matter to be obscured. She would be untrue to her Master if she did not insist, as He did, that whoever divorces his or her marriage partner and marries another commits adultery (Mk. 10:11-12). The unbreakable union between husband and wife is a great mystery or sacramental sign in reference to Christ and the Church. It is by preserving the clarity of this sign that we will best manifest the love that it signifies: the supernatural love that unites Christ and the Church, that binds together the Savior and those whom He saves.

And in all your apostolic activities be assured of my fraternal love. I am at one with you and your clergy—for whom I pray daily—in thanking God for the many graces bestowed on the people of your dioceses: for their renewed sense of collective solidarity in the mission of the Church, for fresh signs of spiritual awakening, for increased devotion to God's Word, for deeper understanding of social responsibility, and for the fortitude of the young in responding to the call of Christ. May the renewal that we all desire also include a preservation and strengthening of the great Canadian heritage of evangelical service, especially in furnishing missionaries in large numbers throughout the Church, in order to preach the Gospel of Christ. May the joy and peace of Christ Jesus be powerfully communicated through your pastoral ministry and through that of your beloved priests. And may all of us find encouragement and perseverance in realizing fully that "our fellowship is with the Father and with his Son Jesus Christ" (1 Jn. 1:3).

Following joyfully in the footsteps of your predecessors, you have come, dear brothers, to kneel on the tomb of the Apostle Peter, as I did so often myself, coming from Krakow.

This personal and community step, always a moving one, implies a very deep meaning, an extremely demanding commitment. We all know that, in dependence on Christ, who is the only cornerstone, the humble fisherman of Galilee was called the Rock of the Church by Jesus Himself. It is this Rock which enables the People of God to grow through time and space on solid foundations, that is, on the essential faith, to be linked deeply and permanently with Christ, the Source of life, to maintain and reconstruct unity among the disciples, to resist the wear and tear of time and of external—and sometimes internal—movements of dissolution and disintegration. Oh! certainly, the Holy Spirit is always at work, and I rejoice with you at the unexpected renewals, the real deepening of faith that you find in your communities. They are the fruits of the Spirit. But the pastors that we are must remain vigilant and clearsighted, in hope and humility. The forces of dissolution and disintegration are also at work. The parable of the wheat and the tāre is still relevant today. It is for that reason that we, we the pastors first of all, must profess loudly and clearly the faith, the doctrine of the Church, the whole doctrine of the Church. It is for that reason that we must adhere, and boldly draw along the adherence of the faithful to the sacramental discipline of the Church, guarantee of the continuity and the authenticity of Christ's saving action, guarantee of the dignity and the unity of Christian worship, and finally guarantee of the real vitality of the People of God. That is what the service of the salvation of souls—which we have in common—demands. That is what the visit *ad limina Apostolorum* implies above all.

May the Lord Jesus Himself help you to become, with Peter, the rock on which your communities are built. My service is to help to strengthen you. I will accompany you in prayer in your ministry. Pray for me, too. And let us bless together all your dear diocesan communities.

Apostolate of Migrants and the Universality of the Church

From the beginning of Advent, Migrant's Day is celebrated in the local churches at successive moments of the liturgical year. For these celebrations, the Holy Father, John Paul II, continuing the happy practice established by Paul VI, had the following message sent to Cardinal Baggio, President of the Pontifical Commission for the Apostolate of Migrations and Tourism.

Lord Cardinal,

As his late Predecessor, Paul VI, was accustomed to do, Pope John Paul II is happy to give his support to the celebrations for Migrant's Day, fixed by the episcopates at different moments of the liturgical year. And the Holy Father carries out this act also in memory of Pope John Paul I, the son of migrants and particularly sensitive to the needs of all migrants, to whom he showed his deep affection even if the shortness of his pontifical ministry did not enable him to testify to it with official acts.

The situation of all those who are obliged to look for a living, and work outside their own country is well known to His Holiness. Throughout his episcopate, he often visited communities of emigrant Poles, very flourishing Catholic communities in spite of the frequent difficulties they meet with. Whole generations, who keep an admirable attachment to their original ethnical roots, are the evident proof of this.

Referring to the appreciable number of interventions of the Roman Pontiffs and of the Apostolic See in this field of migration, one cannot but note the clear-sightedness of the Church, concerned to promote good understanding among peoples and groups of different original cultures, in conformity with the fundamental concept of unity in plurality and plurality in unity.

This basic principle always inspires the action of the Church in all its extent and must guide all those who are called to exercise an apostolate among emigrants: priests and laity, religious men and women. In a world moving towards its unification and which feels more and more the need to overthrow barriers of race, culture and nationality, the evangelizing action of the Church, in all the realities of the phenomenon of migration, takes on ever greater value. But this aspect, which is certainly very important, contributes to highlight the deep nature of the mission of the Church, and to make her advance towards increasing transparentness and authenticity.

The apostolate of emigrants has brought forth recently a set of valuable experiences which have found expression, so to speak, in the Instruction *De pastorali migratorum cura* issued by the Congregation for Bishops *(AAS* 61, 1969, pp. 614-643) and in the recent Letter to the episcopal conferences, "Church and Human Mobility," published by the Pontifical Commission for the Apostolate of Migrations and Tourism *(AAS* 70, 1978, pp. 357-378).

This apostolate is an apostolate of the Church and of the whole Church. The particular elements, which the concrete situations require, not only do not exempt any of the ecclesial communities from their duties, but emphasize their common responsibility.

This year, it seems useful to stress the necessity of qualitative and quantitative progress in the priestly ministry among emigrants.

The world congress which was to have taken place at the beginning of the month of October, if the sudden death of Pope John Paul I had not made it necessary to postpone it, had very opportunely been entrusted with the task of studying the responsibilities of bishops and priests in the present situation of emigration.

Preceding, therefore, the joyful meeting of the future participants in the congress, which will take place in the Vatican, the Holy Father proposes already to the reflection of the People of God some very simple ideas on the subject of the congress.

"The harvest is abundant, and the workers few": if the number of diocesan priests and religious, dedicated to the service of emigrants, has providentially increased, it does not yet meet the pastoral needs. It is necessary to make more fertile the ground of the apostolate of migrants. The Christian communities affected by their exodus must, therefore, develop their sensitiveness with regard to those who have had to depart. It is important that the Christian communities in the host country should look for missionaries and open wide their arms to them. The conviction must become deeper in everyone that emigrants cannot be deprived of those whose mission it is to break the bread of God's Word, taking into account the habits and language corresponding to their mentalities.

Missionaries of migrants must become more and more aware of their specific priestly mission. They are sent by Christ, through the call of the Church. Their task is a very difficult one. It calls for deep and continual concern with their priestly identity and the specific character of their pastoral work. The instructions of St. Gregory the Great, recalled by John Paul I to the clergy of Rome, suit them perfectly: the pastor of souls must continually be in dialogue with God without ever forgetting men, and he must dialogue with men without ever forgetting God.

That is the secret which also makes it possible to share, deeply and effectively, all the concerns and all the aspirations of our brother migrants, in order to be their support, their comfort, their sure guide, and thus contribute to their social advancement.

The Holy Father assures all those who have emigrated all over the world, especially children and the aged, of his feelings of deep affection. He prays for them, hoping that they, too, will pray for him and for his ministry as supreme Pastor of the Church. He is glad to impart his fatherly blessing to all.

Happy to transmit this message to you, I beg you to accept, Lord Cardinal, my cordial devoted regards in our Lord.

Giovanni Cardinal Villot

Full Ecclesial Communion in a Spirit of True Charity

On November 23, 1978, Pope John Paul II received a group of bishops of Honduras for their visit ad limina Apostolorum. *His Holiness delivered the following address.*

Venerated brothers in the episcopate,

After the individual meeting with each of you, today I have the pleasure of receiving collectively all the members of the episcopate of Honduras, in the framework of the visit *ad limina Apostolorum* which you are carrying out in these days.

If during our preceding contact we spoke of particular aspects of each of your dioceses, now I would like to deal with some subjects that affect the life of the Church in Honduras as a whole.

Through your words and the reports presented, I saw to my joy that evangelization work in Honduras has been intensified in the last few years and that religious practice has increased with it, while at the same time the religious formation of the people, particularly in certain sectors, has improved. These are reasons for hope, which at the same time make us think of the main difficulty that the Church meets with in your country, due to the scarcity of priests.

I am well aware that the Catholic laity of Honduras, God be thanked, has been becoming more and more aware of its responsibility within the Church, and is contributing positively to the ecclesial task of spreading the Gospel message. This contribution, which denotes a new maturity of Christian awareness in the laity, is very praiseworthy, and must continue and be intensified as far as possible.

But it must not make us forget the irreplaceable and specific place that priests have in the sanctification of the People of God, appointed as they are by the Lord "to hold in the community of the faithful the sacred power of Order, that of offering sacrifice and forgiving sins, and to exercise the priestly office publicly on behalf of men in the name of Christ" (PO 2).

It is a question of vital importance for the Church. From it is derived the precise duty of giving absolute priority to the fostering of vocations to the priesthood, and likewise to the consecrated life. It is a great task which must be undertaken with all diligence, with the subsequent training of those who have been called, to a strong sense of faith and service for the world today.

To create an environment propitious to the flourishing of vocations, the ecclesial community will have to offer a testimony of life in conformity with the essential values of the Gospel. In this way they will be able to arouse generous souls, directed towards complete commitment to Christ and others, with confidence in the Lord and in the reward promised to those who serve Him faithfully.

Thinking of your priests, I wish to urge you with special interest to dedicate particular pastoral care to your collaborators, so that they may always keep alive their own priestly identity and the ecclesial donation they have made. Help them with your example and words to be well aware of the greatness of their task as continuers of Christ's mission of salvation, and of the necessity of adapting themselves better and better to it.

That will require a constant effort not to conform to this world (cf. Rom. 12:2), in order to revive every day the grace they possess by means of the imposition of hands (cf. 2 Tm. 1:6), and to live for Christ, who lives in them (cf. Gal. 2:20). Only in this spirit of faith will priests be fully conscious of the sublime value of their state and mission.

In the exercise of the sacred ministry, to give full efficacy to the work of evangelization, it is essential to maintain close communion between bishops and priests. The former, in a spirit of true charity and exercising their authority in an attitude of service (cf. Mt. 20:28); the latter, in faithfulness to the guidelines received from their Ordinary, aware that they form "one family of which the bishop is the father" (CD 28). For that reason I call on your priests to realize that nothing stable or constructive can be obtained in their ministry, if they claim to exercise it outside communion with their own bishop; far less, if against him. Not to mention the harm and confusion that such attitudes create among the faithful.

Beloved brothers: I would like to be able to deal here with so many other questions. Let my word of encouragement in your pastoral action suffice for the present. On returning to your country, transmit this word of the Pope's encouragement to priests and seminarians, to religious priests and brothers—such an important part of your collaborators—to sisters and to the laity. Take to them the affectionate greeting of the Pope, who remembers them in his prayers, encourages them in their respective ecclesial commitments, and willingly blesses them.

Universality of the Church Amid a Variety of Rites

On November 23, 1978, Pope John Paul II received a group of bishops of the Ruthenian Byzantine Province in the U.S.A., together with the bishop of St. Maron of Brooklyn for the Maronites.

Dear brothers, sharers in the episcopal ministry to the Church of Christ,

We greet you with deep respect and affection. The Christian faithful whom you serve are citizens of a nation that is still young, yet they are heirs of two of the ancient traditions that enrich the one Catholic Church. In welcoming you we therefore embrace also the Churches in your charge, expressing our heartfelt veneration and our love for them.

The Church is indeed enriched by such venerable traditions and would be much poorer without them. Their variety contributes in no small measure to her splendor. They enshrine many great artistic and cultural values, the loss of which would be sorely felt. Each of them is in itself worthy of great admiration and wonder.

Yet these traditions are no mere adornment of the Church. United in brotherhood, they are important means at the disposal of the Church for displaying to the world the universality of Christ's salvation and fulfilling her mission of making disciples of all nations.

The variety within brotherhood that is seen in the Catholic Church, far from being detrimental to the Church's unity, rather manifests it, showing how all peoples and cultures are called to be organically united in the Holy Spirit through the same faith, the same sacraments, and the same government.

Each tradition must value and cherish the others. The eye cannot say to the hand: "I have no need of you"; for, if all were a single organ, where would the body be? (cf. 1 Cor. 12:19, 21) The Church is Christ's Body and the various parts of the body are intended to serve the good of the whole and to collaborate with each other for that end.

Each individual tradition has its own contribution to make to the good of the whole. Each one's understanding of the faith is deepened by the doctrine contained in the works of the Fathers and spiritual writers of the others, by the theological riches stored in the others' liturgies as they have developed over the centuries under the guidance of the Holy Spirit and of legitimate ecclesiastical authority, and by the others' ways of living the faith that they have received from the Apostles. Each one can find support in the examples of zeal, fidelity and holiness that are provided by the others' history.

The Second Vatican Council declared that "all should realize that it is of supreme importance to understand, venerate, preserve and foster the exceedingly rich liturgical and spiritual heritage of the Eastern Churches, in order faithfully to preserve the fullness of Christian tradition" (UR 15). The Council also declared that the Eastern Churches' "entire heritage of spirituality and liturgy, of discipline and theology, in their various traditions, belongs to the full catholic and apostolic character of the Church" (*ibidem*, 17).

My brother bishops, I do most heartily respect and appreciate the venerable traditions to which you belong, and I desire to see them flourish.

I would wish every member of the Catholic Church to cherish his or her own tradition. "It is the mind of the Catholic Church that each individual Church or rite retain its traditions whole and entire, while adjusting its way of life to the various needs of time and place" (OE 2). You and the Churches over which you preside should accordingly treasure your heritage and take care to hand it on in its integrity to future generations.

I would also wish each member of the Catholic Church to recognize the equal dignity of the other rites within her unity. Each rite is called to assist the others, working together in harmony and good order for the good of the whole and not for its own particular welfare.

I give assurance of my prayers for all the members of your Churches in the United States of America. I pray also for your fellow citizens and for your brethren in the countries from which your ancestors came. For most of you those countries are close to my own native land. For one of you it means one of the most sorely tried areas in the world today, namely Lebanon, an area that deserves from all of us special prayers for the ending of enmity and oppression within it, in order that its inhabitants may be able to dwell there in peace and understanding.

Let us join in invoking on all your people the blessing of almighty God.

Letter to the Bishops of Hungary

Monsignor Luigi Poggi, representative of the Holy See in Hungary for talks with the civil authorities of the country, brought the following letter of John Paul II, dated December 2, 1978, to Cardinal Lekai, Archbishop of Esztergom, President of the Episcopal Conference of Hungary.

To our esteemed brother Cardinal Ladislaus Lekai, Archbishop of Esztergom and to the other bishops of Hungary,

Within a few days the Most Reverend Luigi Poggi will once again go to this country of yours as the representative of the Holy See for talks with the authorities of your nation. In the past, as often as such matters had to be dealt with, he brought you the cordial greetings of our lamented Predecessor Pope Paul VI as proof of the spiritual union with him.

Therefore, observing the same custom at this time, we wish with this letter to convey to you, dear brothers, a like greeting. We think that this is highly opportune, since we have been given this occasion, which comes so soon after this new pontificate has been entered upon by us. Moreover, the same representative of the Holy See, who in the name of His Holiness Paul VI visited you quite often, comes now in the name of John Paul II, who by the will of Christ, became the Successor of blessed Peter after only thirty-three days of the pontificate of John Paul I, who will never be forgotten. We wish, then, dear brothers, that Archbishop Luigi Poggi will now be the interpreter for you of that same pastoral concern which the Supreme Pastor feels strongly for the Church of your fatherland. It was also the object of so much solicitude on the part of previous Popes. There are indeed a number of reasons for this.

And yet to all those reasons referred to above, there is now added the special consideration of our origin and country and of the See of Krakow itself from which we were called to the See of Peter in Rome. We cannot pass over all these considerations in silence. Indeed they impel us, dear brothers, to speak to you in this letter. For our Polish origin and our belonging to that nation which is closely linked with the people of Hungary by several ties, by ties of a common history, of close proximity, a royal dynasty, and of similar fortunes, clearly require that since this opportunity has presented itself, we should of necessity keep each of these considerations before our eyes. Moreover, in the cathedral in Krakow, which we had to leave to accept the Roman heritage of the Apostles, the relics of that daughter of Hungary, Queen Hedwig, whom the Church in Poland for many centuries has called "blessed," are devoutly venerated: a queen, we say, of outstanding merits whom all the people of Poland, but especially the youth, honor with a love that is lasting.

If, therefore, esteemed and dear brothers, we honor the memory of these things, we do so to add the fullest possible historical significance to this first contact of ours, as it were, established by this letter. Past ages have given your people a very high place indeed in the history of the whole of Europe, and especially with regard to the advancement of the Church and of the Christian religion.

But St. Stephen, the patron of Hungary, stands out as a proof and in some way as a sign of the same high position. We rightly consider him both the patron of your fatherland, the apostle of the Faith, and the founder of the Church in Hungary. It is just over a thousand years since these remarkable beginnings. At the same time they indicate the commencement of the entire history of the Church, of the people, and of the civil community in Hungary.

Turning our thoughts, then, to all these facts and circumstances, we wish at the same time to state that we are convinced that the Catholic Church, which has played such an important role in the history of Hungary, can also continue to shape the spiritual image, as it were, of your country by bringing to your sons and daughters the same light of the Gospel of Christ which for so many centuries illuminated the way of life for your citizens. Indeed we desire very much that through your episcopal ministry, the pastoral care of the priests, the religious, and laity, the same light may continue to exercise a great influence on the minds, consciences, and hearts of men. May it also show them the meaning of the precept of charity, a respect for the dignity of every man, a desire for a freedom that is ennobling, together with a love for vigorous activity for the common good and for all those personal, family, and social virtues which are necessary for the attainment of such good. Strive, esteemed and dear brothers, to devote yourselves with good advantage to all these aims by your apostolic witness, your zeal for the salvation of souls, your love for your national traditions, and your union with the Successor of St. Peter and the entire college of bishops in the Church of Christ. Finally, together with this fraternal greeting we send the apostolic blessing to you and to the whole ecclesial community over which Christ has placed you as pastors and teachers (cf. Eph. 4:11).

Thus through you, the interpreters of our fatherly good will, we wish our greeting to reach all the people of

Hungary. Mindful of its remarkable achievements, we pray God to give it an abundance of peace and continued greater prosperity.

From the Vatican, the second day of December in the year 1978, the first of our pontificate.

Role of the Family in Today's World

On the morning of December 16, 1978, the Holy Father, John Paul II, received in audience the members of the General Council of the Synod of Bishops together with the officials and the "periti."

At the beginning of the audience the President, Cardinal Höffner, gave a loyal address of homage to the Holy Father. Pope John Paul II replied with the following address.

Revered brothers,

I am indeed overcome with joy because it has been given to me to speak to you today. For the Council of the General Secretariat of the Synod of Bishops is a body that is both dear and familiar to me. It is really the circle in which I grew in maturity, as it were. Allow me to recall that after the last session of the Synod of Bishops held in the month of October 1977 I was re-appointed as a member of the same Council for a further period of three years.

If, as the result of another decision which the College of Cardinals took on the sixteenth of October of this year my mandate has ceased to exist, nevertheless I feel that I am closely connected with the Council. For this reason— I like to repeat something which pleases me—I am very happy to see you. What you put before me is also a part —perhaps not a very small part—of my own personal experience.

Indeed this experience actually expresses the teaching of the Second Vatican Council on the collegiality of bishops. This collegiality, however, becomes daily more urgent in the very life of the Church of our time.

There is re-echoed what John Paul I said in his first address when he uttered these words: "We greet all the bishops of the Church of God, 'each of whom represents his own Church, whereas all together with the Pope represent the entire Church in a bond of peace, love and unity' (LG 23) and whose collegiality we very much wish to strengthen" (*AAS*, LXX, 1978, pp. 696-697). This very statement was confirmed a few weeks later by his Successor in his first address and in these words: "We particularly urge a deeper reflection on the implications of the bond of collegiality. By it the bishops are closely linked with the Successor of the blessed Peter and all work together in order to fulfill the high offices entrusted to them: offices of enlightening the whole People of God with the light of the Gospel, of sanctifying them with the means of grace, and of governing them with pastoral skill. Undoubtedly, this collegiality extends also to the appropriate development of institutes—some new, some brought up-to-date—by which is procured the greatest unity in outlook, intent, and activity in the work of building up the body of Christ. In this regard, we make special mention of the Synod of Bishops" (*AAS*, LXX, 1978, p. 922).

The principle concerning collegiality laid down by the Council can without doubt be expressed and put into effect in various ways. My illustrious predecessor, Paul VI, spoke of this theme when he addressed the Fathers who had come together for the Extraordinary Synod in the year 1969. "We believe," he said, "that we have already given proof of this will to give practical increase to episcopal collegiality, both by instituting the Synod of Bishops, in recognizing the episcopal conferences, and in associating some brothers in the episcopate and pastors residing in their dioceses with the ministry that belongs to our Roman Curia; and if the grace of the Lord assists us and brotherly concord facilitates our mutual relations, the exercise of collegiality in other canonical forms will be able to have wider development.... The Synod...will be able to throw light on the existence and the growth of episcopal collegiality in suitable canonical terms and at the same time strengthen the teaching of the First and the Second Vatican Councils concerning the power of St. Peter's Successor and that of the College of Bishops with the Pope, its head" *(AAS,* LXI, 1969, pp. 717-718). All the previous sessions dealt with these matters which are very effective in realizing in the practical life that plan for the renewal of the Church which is contained in the teaching of the Second Vatican Council.

The themes which were discussed in the last two sessions of the Synod of Bishops make this clear to us. The principal question and, as it were, the crux of the matter, seems to be evangelization. This is immediately followed by catechesis, by which evangelization becomes especially effective. The fruit of the first Synod, held in the year 1974, was the Apostolic Exhortation of Paul VI, *Evangelii nuntiandi.* But the fruit of the Synod held in the year 1977 has not yet appeared. I hope that it will be published in the early part of next year. We certainly need documents of this kind, which spring from the fruitful, and at times difficult, practical life of the Church, and which, conversely, give new growth to that same life.

We are certainly convinced of the great importance of the theme "The Role of the Christian Family in the World of Today," which has been proposed for the Synod to be held in the year 1980. This theme is not unconnected with the previous ones; it moves in the same furrow, as it were. However, it must be observed that the family is not only the "object" of evangelization and catechesis, it is also and indeed above all the "fundamental subject" of evangelization. This is gathered from the whole teaching of the Second Vatican Council about the People of God and the apostolate of the laity. This is the main field, as it were, in which the same teaching is put into practice and consequently where the renewal of the Church according to the mind of the same Council is brought about.

Certainly, revered brothers, you have to take upon yourselves and to endure a heavy task! I thank you very much for your diligence, especially the Secretary General of the Synod of Bishops, Ladislaus Rubin, Titular Bishop of Serta, and each of the members of the Council of the General Secretariat. Nor do I wish to pass over the "periti" and the officials who have their own duties in the same Secretariat. I encourage you all and I urge you to continue this noble work which in this age brings not a little vitality and growth to the Church.

Finally, as a special mark of our affection for you I willingly impart to you the apostolic blessing, as a pledge of heavenly assistance.

Episcopal Collegiality and Regional Autonomies

On December 19, 1978, the Holy Father received in audience the members of the Council of Episcopal Conferences of Europe, gathered in Rome for the annual plenary assembly. The group of bishops was led by the President of the Council, Archbishop Roger Etchegaray of Marseilles, with the two Vice-Presidents, Most Rev. John Baptist Musty, titular Bishop of Botriana, and Archbishop Jerzy Stroba of Poznan. John Paul II delivered the following address.

Dear brothers,

I am very happy to receive you, for I attach great importance to these plenary meetings of your Council, in which bishops delegated by each of the episcopal conferences of the whole of the European continent take part.

1. This collaboration is carried out in conformity with the statutes which were canonically approved by the Holy See on January 10, 1977. It consists in exchanging regularly information, experiences and points of view on the main pastoral problems raised in your countries. It also leads you to undertake together duties which assume a European dimension.

It is one of the ways of incarnating collegiality, in the framework of which the teaching of the Second Vatican Council can yield all its fruit. Collegiality means the mutual opening and brotherly cooperation of bishops in the service of evangelization, of the mission of the Church. An opening and cooperation of this kind are necessary, not only at the level of the local Churches and the universal Church, but also at the level of continents, as is testified by the vitality of other regional organisms—even if the statutes are a little different—such as the Latin American Episcopal Council (CELAM), the Symposium of Episcopal Conferences of Africa and Madagascar (SECAM) or the Federation of the Asian Bishops' Conference (FABC), to mention only these great assemblies. The Pope and the Holy See make a point of promoting these organisms, at the various levels of collegial cooperation, it being understood that regional or continental bodies do not replace the authority of each bishop or of each of the episcopal conferences as regards decisions, and that their research is set in the framework of the more general orientations of the Holy See, in close liaison with Peter's Successor. And in the present case, the European dimension seems to the Pope very important and even necessary.

2. The Council of European Episcopal Conferences (CEEC), among its numerous exchanges and activities, has taken an important initiative: it organizes a symposium of European bishops every three years. The symposium scheduled to take place this year was not held owing to the death of my two Predecessors and the conclaves that followed. The preparation is continuing on the subject: youth and faith. It is a very important subject: it must be approached with great objectivity and with the hope of the apostles who know that Christ's message can and must touch the young of every generation.

I had the good fortune to take part in the 1975 symposium and to give a conference to it. I wish to recall at least some of the thoughts that Paul VI had expressed then on receiving us. They were thoughts concerning Europe, its Christian heritage and its Christian future. He called on us to "awaken the Christian soul of Europe in which its unity is rooted"; to purify and bring back to their source the evangelical values still present but, as it were, disarticulated, geared to purely earthly aims; to awaken and strengthen consciences in the light of the faith preached in season and out of season; to cause their flame to converge above all barriers... (cf. *AAS*, 67, 1975, pp. 588-589).

In line with these thoughts, Paul VI established Saint Benedict as the patron saint of Europe, and now the fifteenth centenary of the birth of this great saint is approaching.

3. Europe is not the first cradle of Christianity. Even Rome received the Gospel thanks to the ministry of the Apostles Peter and Paul, who came here from the country of Jesus Christ. But, in any case, it is true that Europe became, for two millennia, the bed, as it were, of a great river in which Christianity spread, making fertile the land of the spiritual life of the peoples and nations of this continent. And under this impetus, Europe became a mission center, the influence of which spread to the other continents.

The Council of European Episcopal Conferences constitutes a special representation of the Catholic episcopates of Europe. We must hope that all episcopates are fully represented in this organization, with the possibility of taking a real part in it. It is only under these conditions that the analysis of the essential problems of the Church and of Christianity can be complete. It is a question of the problems of the Church and of Christianity, approached also in an ecumenical perspective. For if it is true that the whole of Europe is not Catholic, it is nearly all Christian. Your Council must become a kind of breeding-ground in which there is expressed, developed and matured not only awareness of what Christianity was yesterday, but responsibility for what it must be tomorrow.

It is with these sentiments that I present to you my best wishes for Christmas and the new year, for the intention of each of you, your Council, all the episcopates that you represent and all the nations of this continent, with which Providence has linked the history of Christianity so eloquently.

Announcement of Papal Visit to Mexico

On the morning of December 22, 1978, Pope John Paul II met the College of Cardinals who had come to present their Christmas greetings. In reply to an address of homage read by Cardinal Villot on behalf of the Dean of the Sacred College, Cardinal Confalonieri, who was not well, His Holiness spoke as follows.

Dearest brothers of the Sacred College and sons of the Roman Church!

1. To that address which has just now been delivered to me, in the name of all you here present, I can only reply with the very briefest expression, but one animated by great affection: my deepest thanks. Thank you, because your visit on this vigil of the holy feast of Christmas is not a mere gesture of protocol, taking its inspiration from a traditional custom, however gracious. But it is an act so rich in warmth of sentiment that it affords me yet a further proof, if there were any need for such—and there is not—of the fact that although I have been elected Pope scarcely two months now, and have left behind my beloved land of Poland and my own diocese of Krakow, I have received in exchange another land here in Rome and a Church as vast as the world.

Christmas is the feast of home and family affections. It is a return to the side of the infant Jesus, come to be our brother, a return to our own birth and, by an interior journey, to the primordial roots of our very existence, surrounded by the dear faces of our parents, our relatives, our fellow countrymen. Christmas is an invitation, therefore, to think over our own birth, in the concrete circumstances peculiar to each one of us. Just as it is natural for me to return in thought, on a wave of colorful memories, to my home in Wadowice, so it is natural for each of you to return to the warmth of hearth and home.

But now your devoted and solicitous presence this morning comes to weave itself into my personal and private thoughts, unleashing, as it were, an irrepressible emotion, and bringing me back to another and much higher reality. I mean the new reality that has devolved upon me by the choice that precisely you, Lord Cardinals, together with your other confreres scattered throughout the world made on that fateful day for me, October 16. *Vos estis corona mea* (You are my crown) I can repeat to you with the Apostle (cf. Phil. 4:11): you have extended my family circle and have become by a very special title "my kinsmen" according to that transcendent, and yet very real communion, which creates bonds as staunch as those of any human family, that communion which is called and is ecclesial life.

So I thank you, therefore, for this choral offering of best wishes, which you do not offer me on your own but together with all those whom you represent. And I reciprocate, with all my heart, wishing for each of you, as well as for all those closest to you, an abundant outpouring of heavenly grace and of that very human kindness of our Savior, Jesus Christ (cf. Ti. 2:11).

2. I know well how my Predecessor, Paul VI, of happy memory, during the course of similar gatherings taking place in this hall during the exacting and distinguished span of his fifteen-year pontificate, always preferred to widen the horizon to include the duties of his pastoral mission. He used to recall the salient facts of the Church and the world, not only to give precise content to this talk with his most qualified collaborators, but also to bring specific focus to the situation by a careful examination of the most recent events.

Such an opportunity also presents itself to me today in a form both similar and diverse, but perhaps somewhat easier.... What happened this year? Or, more exactly: what happened after sunset on August 6, when that remarkable Pontiff closed his eyes on the scenes of this world to open them in the light of heaven, where he entered to receive the prize of the good and faithful servant (cf. Mt. 25:2)? The events are well known, and it is certainly not necessary to recall them, even less so in your presence, since you were not merely spectators, but active participants and, in great measure, protagonists. None of us—I might say with the disciple of Emmaus—is so much a stranger in Rome as to be ignorant of *quae facta sunt in illa his diebus* (what events have taken place here in these days) (cf. Lk. 24:8).

In journalistic or bureaucratic terms, there has been talk of "avvicendamento" (change), or even of a twofold "change" at the summit of the Church, so that within one year—as has been noted—we have had three Popes! This is objectively true, but it certainly does not exhaust the discussion of what happened in the succession to the Apostolic See and of what is most substantial and determinant in this: I mean the formidable heritage of the very ministry of Peter, which manifested itself in the short span of these crucial years during the pontificate of Paul VI, and which at the same time was enriched by the seed and sap, the renewing impulses, and the programmatic orientations of the Conciliar sessions.

And one ought to add, too, that the brief, but very intense, service of Pope John Paul I has marked this already complex heritage, bringing to it a more definite pastoral connotation. Thus, I myself, who have been called to take it up, feel day by day the truly enormous weight of such a great responsibility.

So, should we then be speaking of summits or power? Oh no, my brothers; the service of Peter—as I intimated in the Sistine Chapel the day after my election—is essentially a task of self-giving and love. This is how I mean my humble ministry to be.

In this I take comfort, especially, in the certitude, or even more, in the indestructible faith in the power of Jesus Christ the Lord, who has promised to His Church an indefectible assistance (cf. Mt. 28:20); and to His Vicar, even more so than to all the other pastors, He whispers persuasively: *Modicae fidei, quare dubitasti?* (You of little faith, why did you doubt?) (Mt. 14:31) But I also take comfort in the help that you offer me, of which I have had daily confirmation, even during this first period of pontifical beginnings, in many ways and with much efficiency.... So here I take up again the theme of best wishes to you, concluding with a renewed invitation to raise up your prayers for me. Let fellowship in prayer and charity take the highest priority among the forms of your precious collaboration with me.

3. After a look at the Church, one's thoughts turn quite naturally—as also Pope Paul's used to turn—to the world that surrounds it. How has human society fared during this year which has just come to an end? And how is it faring just now? We all need to look at the facts, and even more at the connections between them, in order to grasp —as far as possible—their sense and direction. Here we might ask, for example, is the cause of peace among men progressing or stagnating? And the answer comes back anxious and uncertain, when we discover, in different countries, the persistence of virulent tensions, which frequently give rise to furious outbreaks of violence.

Peace, unfortunately, remains rather precarious, while it is all too easy to catch a glimpse of the fundamental motives which are ready to threaten it. Where there is no justice—who doesn't know this—there can be no peace, because injustice is itself a disorder, and the words of the prophet remain ever true: *Opus iustitiae pax.* (The work of justice is peace.) (Is. 32:17) Likewise, where there is no respect for human rights—I mean those inalienable rights which are inherent in every man by his very nature—there can be no peace, because every violation of personal dignity favors rancor and the spirit of revenge. Moreover, where there is no moral formation to favor the growth of good, there can be no peace, because it is always necessary to keep watch and contain the destructive tendencies which nestle in the heart of man.

I do not want to linger on these thoughts, my brothers, but I want to extract from all this a certain indicative point. Studying this theme, it seems even more necessary to consolidate the spiritual bases of peace, continuing with courage and with perseverance that *pedagogy of peace* of which Paul VI was such an authoritative master. In the Message for the World Day of Peace, published just yesterday, I took up his exposition on education for peace, and I repeat to you—as to all men, who are my brothers—the invitation to deepen this theme and assimilate it.

Just how urgent the need is to pledge oneself to the cause of peace has been confirmed by the sad news coming recently from the continent of South America.

The dispute which has grown ever more aggravated in these recent days between Argentina and Chile, notwithstanding the lively appeal for peace sent to the authorities on the part of the episcopates of the two countries, vigorously supported by my Predecessor, Pope John Paul I, is a cause for deep sorrow and personal anxiety.

Moved by the paternal affection that I bear to both of these dear nations, I, myself, on the vigil of the meeting scheduled for December 12 in Buenos Aires between their Ministers of Foreign Affairs and upon which so many hopes had rested, manifested directly to the two Presidents my own fears, my prayers, and my encouragement in seeking through calm and responsible examination a way of safeguarding that peace so ardently desired by both peoples.

The answers I received are full of respect and expressions of good will. Yet, notwithstanding the acceptance in principle, on the part of both contenders, of recourse to the mediating intervention of this Holy See, in the concrete difficulties then at issue, the common proposal has not been acted upon. The Holy See would not have refused such an appeal, even in the knowledge of the delicacy and complexity of the question, considering the higher interests of peace as prevailing over the political and technical aspects of the quarrel.

Yesterday, when faced with the ever more alarming news arriving here about the aggravated circumstances and what some consider the possibly imminent precipitation of the situation, I made known to the parties concerned my disposition—indeed, my desire—to send to the two capitals my own special representative, in order to have more direct and concrete information about the respective positions, and in order to examine and search together for the possibilities of an honorable and peaceful settlement of the question.

In the evening came the news of the acceptance of such a proposal on the part of both of the governments, with expressions of gratitude and confidence which, while they comfort me, make me feel even more the responsibility that such an intervention involves, but from which the Holy See is determined not to allow herself to shrink. Thus, since both of the parties jointly emphasize the urgency of such an intervention, the Holy See will proceed with all possible solicitude.

Meanwhile, I wish to renew my sorrowful appeal to the authorities that any steps be avoided which could bear unforeseen consequences—or even all too foreseeable ones—of harm and suffering for the populations of the two brother nations. Thus, I invite all to lift up a fervent prayer to the Lord that the violence of arms may not have the advantage over peace.

4. And now I want to give you some good news as a sort of happy firstfruits of initiatives and events, different among themselves, but all demonstrative of the multiform presence and activity of Holy Church.

a) The first news is that, towards the end of next January, I hope to go—please God—to Mexico in order to participate at the *Third General Assembly of the Latin American Episcopate,* which is to take place—as you know—at Puebla de los Angeles. This is an event of the most relevant ecclesial importance, not only because in the vast continent of Latin America, called the Continent of Hope, the Catholic faithful are present as the clear majority. But it is so also by reason of that special interest, and even more, those great expectations which are focused upon that meeting, and which it will be the authentic historical credit of the bishops who govern those ancient and new Churches to transform into comforting reality. But, before going to the seat of the conference, I shall make a stop at the celebrated Sanctuary of Our Lady of Guadalupe. It is there, in fact, that I wish to draw that higher solace and necessary stimulus—the good auspices, as it were—for my mission as the Pastor of the Church, and especially for my first contact with the Church of Latin America. The essential point of a most ardently desired encounter with this Church will be precisely such a religious pilgrimage to the feet of the holy Virgin, in order to venerate her, to implore her help, and to ask her for inspiration and counsel for my brothers from the entire continent.

It is a joy for me to affirm all this on the vigil of Christmas, the moment when all—pastors and faithful—are reunited around the Mother who, as she once gave to the world the Savior Jesus in the stable at Bethlehem, still gives Him to us in the inexhaustible fruitfulness of her virginal and spiritual maternity. I pray that my presence in her beautiful sanctuary on Mexican soil may contribute to our finding Christ again through her—through her as Mother, not only for the people of that same land, but for all the nations of Latin America.

As far as the theme assigned to the meeting at Puebla is concerned, you are already familiar with it, together with the wise advice contained in the preparatory document set forth by CELAM: "Evangelization in the present and in the future of Latin America." Well then, the relevance of this theme, its theological, ecclesiological, pastoral, doctrinal, and practical implications, the very amplitude of the area in which it will be necessary to apply each concrete resolution, are so very evident that I do not need to explain the reason for my decision. As Paul VI wished to be present at the second assembly, during the International Eucharistic Congress of Bogotà, so I shall be present among the brothers convened there for the new assembly with the aim of witnessing to them and to their priests and faithful the esteem, the confidence, the hope of the universal Church, and to increase their courage in the common pastoral task. Someone has said that the future of the Church "is being played out" in Latin America. Even if, on a general plane, this future is hidden in God, according to His design that goes beyond the projects of men and socio-historical conditions (cf. Rom. 11:33; Acts 16:6-9), this sentence contains a truth of its own, because it signifies how much the fate of the Church of the Central and South American continent is in solidarity with that of the one and undivided Church of Christ.

So, for now, I send out my very best wishes to that select assembly.

b) The second announcement refers to the decision to open to scholars the *Secret Vatican Archives* to include the whole pontificate of Pope Leo XIII. Such a decision, awaited some time now by the world of culture, falls opportunely in the year 1978, which marks—as you well know—a double centenary: that of the death of the servant of God, Pius IX, and that of the successive elevation to the Chair of Peter of Gioacchino Pecci, whose ministry, which lasted fully twenty-five years, "usque ad summam senectutem" (unto exceeding old age), carried over into the first years of our own century. So it is that the Holy See, consenting to the free perusal of the letters and documents concerning this ample and hardly unimportant period, running from 1878 to 1903, which marks the entry into the twentieth century, opens into investigation a panorama of singular richness in the service of historical truth, witnessing also to the ever active presence of the Church in the world of culture.

c) Much along the same lines of thought is the plan to honor the memory of my great Predecessor, Paul VI. On the one hand, to his perpetual memory, the great Audience Hall, desired by him and entrusted to the ingenious skill of the architect, Pier Luigi Nervi, will from now on be called "Aula Paolo VI" (Hall of Paul VI). On the other hand, in order to treasure the patrimony that came about during the last year of his pontificate, the "autographs" (handwritten letters) of so many famous persons, which were offered to him during the course of his eightieth birthday, will be made available to the public. I consider, in fact, that one of my most specific duties is to continue and develop the interest that Paul VI constantly demonstrated in the cause of culture and art: this earned for him so much respect and brought such great prestige to the Church.

Thus, brothers and dear sons, I have replied to your well-wishing; I have officially anticipated here certain plans; I have recommended myself to your prayers and to the prayers of all. The contacts I have had until now with you urge me to make clear the meaning of this communion. I thank God that I have already been able to become acquainted personally with one sector of my closest collaborators, those of the Secretariat of State, and I have every intention of continuing, as soon as I possibly can, the visits to the other departments of the Roman Curia, in the conviction that reciprocal acquaintance favors the best coordination of our forces, tending—according to the respective functions of each—to the same focal center of reference: the growth of the People of God in faith and charity.

So, here we are at Christmas, and Jesus is coming. May He find us all—as the Preface of Advent augurs—vigilant in our expectation, exulting in our praise, ardent in our charity, under the gently reassuring gaze of her who, as Mother of Jesus, was and is also our Mother. May it be so, with my warmest blessing.

Man's Answer to God's Call to Service

On January 14, 1979, the Holy Father John Paul II went to visit the Roman parish of St. Mary Liberator at Monte Testaccio. In the course of the Eucharistic Liturgy the Pope delivered a homily, from which are taken the following excerpts.

Dear brothers and sisters!

1. We have listened to the Word of God in today's liturgy, which speaks to us in the text of the book of Samuel, the letter of St. Paul to the Corinthians, and the Gospel of St. John. Although these texts which we have heard are very different, the Word of God of this Sunday speaks to us above all of one question: "vocation," the "call." This is stressed in the description contained in the book of Samuel: God calls a boy by name; He calls him in a perceptible voice, speaking his name. Samuel hears the voice and wakes up from sleep three times, and for three times he fails to understand whose voice it is, who is calling him by name. Only on the fourth time, instructed by Eli, does he give a suitable answer: "Speak, Lord, for your servant hears" (1 Sm. 3:9).

CHRIST'S INVITATION

This passage from the book of Samuel enables us to understand more thoroughly the vocation of the first Apostles, of Andrew and Peter, called by Jesus Christ. They, too, accept the call, and follow Jesus; first Andrew, who announces to his brother: "We have found the Messiah"; then, in his turn, Simon, to whom Jesus, during their first meeting, announces his new name, "Cephas" ("which means Peter," Jn. 1:42).

When we then follow the thought that St. Paul expresses in the letter to the Corinthians, our subject seems to open to a further dimension. The Apostle writes to those to whom his letter is addressed: "Do you not know that your body is a temple of the Holy Spirit within you, which you have from God? You are not your own; you were bought with a price" (1 Cor. 6:19-20).

God, who calls man to His service and assigns a task to him, has a fundamental right to do so. He alone has this right, because He is the Creator and Redeemer of each of us. If He calls us, if He invites us to follow a given way, He does so in order that we will not dissipate His work; in order that we may respond with our own lives to the gift received from Him; in order that we may live in a way worthy of man, who is "a temple of God"; in order that we may be able to carry out that particular duty which He wishes to entrust to us.

A LIVING COMMUNITY

...I would like this moving and generous readiness to accept God's call to be always present in all the many faithful of this parish, to form a living Christian community, joyful and proud to be able to say "yes" to Christ and to the Church.

My affectionate thought goes in the first place to the *parish priest* and his collaborators, who unselfishly dedicate their energies to the good of the parish; it goes to the *children*, who give consolation and hope; to the *adolescents*, who are beginning their first steps, which may also be difficult ones, towards the commitments of life; to the *young*, who seek joy, the fullness of joy; to *adults*, eager to contribute with all their might to the construction of a more just and more serene society; to *fathers* and *mothers*, who wish to preserve and renew the strength of their indissoluble union; to the *sick*, who suffer in body and in spirit; to the *old*, eager for understanding, affection, and the respect they deserve.

ST. MARY LIBERATOR

This title, with which you invoke the Blessed Virgin here, is a very significant one; man appreciates freedom very much, but at the same time he often does not know how to use it; he uses it badly. Often the wrong use of freedom results in man's losing it; he ceases to be free.

Christ teaches us the good and perfect use of freedom. St. Paul was particularly aware of this, when he wrote to the Galatians: "For freedom Christ has set us free" (Gal. 5:1).

The Mother of Christ collaborates with her Son in this great work which He wishes to carry out in each of us. And she does so in a motherly way, and with such love that only a mother can express.

Dear brothers and sisters!

Let us entrust our freedom to Mary. She will help us to discover that real good which freedom contains.

She will help us to make the best use of freedom; she who "liberates," as every mother does. We know very well that often the very awareness that she is there, hearing everything that has the power to embarrass us, discourage us, humiliate us, takes great weights from our hearts.

Sometimes a word of hers, a look of hers, a smile of hers, is enough.

She "liberates" with kindness, in a motherly way.

Man, who has fallen into the depths and is "entangled" in many snares, needs this certainty that there is someone who thinks of him as of her own son; someone for whom he has not lost his value.

She is the Mother who "liberates" by means of love.

I beseech you, Mother of God, patron saint of this parish, be a liberator for all your sons and your daughters.

St. Mary Liberator, pray for us!

To the Church in the Dominican Republic

The first meeting of John Paul II with the bishops, clergy, men and women religious, and representatives of all members of the Church in the Dominican Republic, took place in the Cathedral of Santo Domingo, on January 25, 1979. Cardinal Octavio Antonio Beras Rojas, Archbishop of Santo Domingo, delivered an address of homage and welcome to the Holy Father, who replied as follows:

Lord Cardinal, brothers in the episcopate, beloved sons,

It is but a few moments since I had the happiness to arrive in your country, and now I feel a new joy on meeting you in this cathedral, dedicated to the Annunciation, where so many of you have desired to come to see the Pope: the primatial cathedral, which stands beside what was the first archiepiscopal see in America.

My thanks go in the first place to you, Lord Cardinal, for your kind words; they have filled my spirit with satisfaction, admiration and hope.

I wish to tell you that the Pope, too, desires to be with you, in order to know you and love you even more. My only regret is not to be able to meet and speak with each one of you.

But although that is not possible, rest assured that no one is excluded from the affection, from the memory, of the common father who, even though far away, thinks of you and prays for your intentions.

In order that this meeting may be more intimate, let us pray for a moment and ask the Lord, through the intercession of Our Lady of High Grace, whose image is present here, to grant that you may always be good children of the Church, that you may grow in the faith, and that yours may be a life worthy of Christians.

I very willingly impart my blessing to you, to your fellow countrymen and members of your families, and above all to the sick and to those who are suffering.

And you, too, pray for the Pope.

You Are Servants of the People of God

The Holy Father delivered the following address to the priests and men religious of Mexico, who were represented in large numbers at the meeting with the Pope which took place on January 27, 1979, in the Basilica of Our Lady of Guadalupe.

Beloved priests, diocesan and religious,

One of the meetings I was most looking forward to during my visit to Mexico is that which I have with you, here in the Sanctuary of our venerated and beloved Mother of Guadalupe.

See in it a proof of the Pope's affection and solicitude. He, as the Bishop of the whole Church, is aware of your irreplaceable role. He feels very close to those who are keystones in the ecclesial task, as the main collaborators of the bishops, participants in Christ's saving powers, witnesses, proclaimers of His Gospel, encouraging the faith and apostolic vocation of the People of God. And here I do not wish to forget so many other consecrated souls, precious collaborators, though without the priestly character, in many important sectors of the Church apostolate.

Not only do you have a special presence in the Church apostolate, but also your love for man through God is conspicuous among students at different levels, among the sick and those in need of assistance, among men of culture, among the poor who demand understanding and support, among so many persons who have recourse to you in search of advice and encouragement.

For your self-sacrificing dedication to the Lord and to the Church, for your closeness to man, receive my thanks in Christ's name.

Servants of a sublime cause, the fate of the Church largely depends on you in the sectors entrusted to your pastoral care. That makes it necessary for you to be deeply aware of the greatness of the mission you have received and of the necessity of better and better adapting yourselves to it.

It is a question, in fact, beloved brothers and sons, of the Church of Christ—what respect and love this must inspire in us!—which you have to serve joyfully in holiness of life (cf. Eph. 4:13).

This high and exacting service cannot be carried out without a clear and deep-rooted conviction of your identity as priests of Christ, depositaries and administrators of God's mysteries, instruments of salvation for men, witnesses of a kingdom which begins in this world but is completed in the next. In the light of these certainties of faith, why doubt about your own identity? Why hesitate about the value of your own life? Why waver on the path which you have chosen?

To preserve or strengthen this firm and persevering conviction, look at the model, Christ; renew the supernatural values in your existence; ask for strength from above, in the assiduous and trusting conversation of prayer. It is indispensable for you, today as yesterday. And also be faithful to frequent practice of the sacrament of reconciliation, to daily meditation, to devotion to the Virgin by means of the recitation of the rosary. In a word, cultivate union with God by means of a deep inner life. Let this be your first commitment. Do not be afraid that the time dedicated to the Lord will take anything away from your apostolate. On the contrary, it will be the source of fruitfulness in the ministry.

You are persons who have made the Gospel a profession of life. You must draw from the Gospel the essential principles of faith—not mere psychological or sociological principles—which will produce a harmonious synthesis between spirituality and ministry; without permitting a "professionalization" of the latter, without diminishing the esteem that your celibacy or consecrated chastity, accepted for love of the kingdom in an unlimited spiritual fatherhood (cf. 1 Cor. 4:15), must win for you. "To them (priests) we owe our blessed regeneration"—St. John Chrysostom affirms—"and knowledge of true freedom" *(On the Priesthood*, 4-6).

You are participants in Christ's ministerial priesthood for the service of the unity of the community. A service which is realized by virtue of the authority received to direct the People of God, to forgive sins and to offer the Eucharistic Sacrifice! (cf. LG 10; PO 2) A specific priestly service, which cannot be replaced in the Christian community by the common priesthood of the faithful, which is essentially different from the former! (LG 10)

You are members of a particular Church, whose center of unity is the bishop (CD 28), towards whom every priest must observe an attitude of communion and obedience. Religious, on their side, with regard to pastoral activities, cannot deny to the local hierarchy their loyal collaboration and obedience, on the pretext of exclusive dependence on the universal Church (cf. CD 34; *Joint Document of the Sacred Congregation for Religious and for Secular Institutes and of the Sacred Congregation for the Bishops*, May 14, 1978). Far less would it be admissible for priests or religious to practice a parallel to that of the bishops—the only authentic teachers in the faith—or of the Episcopal Conferences.

You are servants of the People of God, servants of faith, administrators and witnesses of Christ's love for men; a love that is not partisan, that excludes no one, although it is addressed preferably to the poorest. In this connection, I wish to remind you of what I said not long ago to the Superiors General of the Religious in Rome: "The soul that lives in habitual contact with God and moves within the ardent ray of His love is able to defend itself easily against the temptation of particularisms and contrasts that create the risk of painful divisions; it is able to interpret in the correct light of the Gospel the options for the poorest and for each of the victims of human selfishness, without giving way to socio-political radicalisms which are seen in the long run to be inopportune and self-defeating" (November 24, 1978).

You are spiritual guides who endeavor to direct and improve the hearts of the faithful in order that, converted, they may live love for God and their neighbor and commit themselves to the betterment of man and to increasing his dignity.

You are priests and religious; you are not social or political leaders or officials of a temporal power. For this reason I repeat to you: "Let us not be under the illusion that we are serving the Gospel if we 'dilute' our charism through an exaggerated interest in the wide field of temporal problems" (Address to the Clergy of Rome). Let us not forget that temporal leadership can easily be a source of division, while the priest must be a sign and agent of unity and brotherhood. Secular functions are the specific field of action of laymen, who have to improve temporal matters with the Christian spirit (AA 4).

Beloved priests and religious: I would say many other things to you, but I do not wish to make this meeting too long. I will say some things on another occasion, and I refer you to them.

I conclude, repeating to you my great confidence in you. I have great hopes in your love for Christ and for men. There is a great deal to be done. Let us set out with renewed enthusiasm, united with Christ, under the motherly gaze of the Virgin, Our Lady of Guadalupe, the sweet Mother of priests and religious. With the affectionate blessing of the Pope, for you and for all the priests and religious of Mexico.

Preserve, Defend, and Communicate the Truth

On Sunday, January 28, 1979, in the Major Seminary Palafoxiano of Puebla de Los Angeles, there opened the Third General Conference of the Latin American Episcopate. Before the representatives of all the bishops of Latin America John Paul II delivered the following discourse.

Beloved brothers in the episcopate,

This hour that I have the happiness to experience with you is certainly an historic one for the Church in Latin America. World opinion is aware of this, as are the faithful members of your local Churches, and especially you yourselves are aware of it, you who will be the protagonists and leaders of this hour.

It is also an hour of grace, marked by the drawing near of the Lord, by a very special presence and action of the Spirit of God. For this reason we have confidently invoked that Spirit, at the beginning of our work. For this reason also I now wish to implore you, as a brother to very beloved brothers: all the days of this Conference and in every one of its acts, let yourselves be led by the Spirit, open yourselves to His inspiration and His impulse, let it be He and no other spirit that guides and strengthens you.

Under the guidance of this Spirit, for the third time in the last twenty-five years you, the bishops of all the countries representing the episcopate of the continent of Latin America, have gathered together to study more deeply together the meaning of your mission in the face of the new demands of your peoples.

The Conference that is now opening, convoked by the revered Paul VI, confirmed by my unforgettable Predecessor John Paul I, and reconfirmed by myself as one of the first acts of my pontificate, is linked with the Conference now long past, held in Rio de Janeiro, which had as its most notable result the birth of CELAM. But it is linked even more closely with the second Conference, of Medellín, of which it marks the tenth anniversary.

In these last ten years, how much progress humanity has made, and, with humanity and at its service, how much progress the Church has made! This third Conference cannot disregard that reality. It will, therefore, have to take as its point of departure the conclusions of Medellín, with all the positive elements that they contained, but without ignoring the incorrect interpretations at times made and which call for calm discernment, opportune criticism, and clear choices of position.

You will be guided in your debates by the Working Document, prepared with such care so as to constitute the constant point of reference.

But you will also have at hand Paul VI's Apostolic Exhortation *Evangelii nuntiandi*. With what care the great Pontiff approved as the Conference's theme: "The present and the future of evangelization in Latin America!"

Those who were close to him during the months when the Assembly was being prepared can tell you this. They can also bear witness to the gratitude with which he learned that the basic material of the whole Conference would be this text, into which he put his whole pastoral soul, as his life drew to a close. Now that he has "closed his eyes to this world's scene" (Testament of Paul VI), this document becomes a spiritual testament that the Conference will have to scrutinize with love and diligence, in order to make it the other obligatory point of reference, and in order to see how to put it into practice. The whole Church is grateful to you for the example that you are giving, for what you are doing, and what other local Churches will perhaps do in their turn.

The Pope wishes to be with you at the beginning of your labors, and he is thankful to the Father of lights from whom comes down every perfect gift (cf. Jas. 1:17), for having been able to be with you at yesterday's Solemn Mass, under the maternal gaze of the Virgin of Guadalupe, as also at the Mass this morning. I would very much like to stay with you in prayer, reflection and work: be sure that I shall stay with you in spirit, while the "anxiety for all the churches" (2 Cor. 11:28) calls me elsewhere. I wish at least, before continuing my pastoral visit through Mexico and before my return to Rome, to leave you as a pledge of my spiritual presence a few words, uttered with the solicitous care of a Pastor and the affection of a Father; words which are the echo of my main preoccupations regarding the theme you have to deal with and regarding the life of the Church in these beloved countries.

I
Teachers of the Truth

It is a great consolation for the universal Father to note that you come together here not as a symposium of experts, not as a parliament of politicians, not as a congress of scientists or technologists, however important such assemblies may be, but as a fraternal encounter of pastors of the Church. And as pastors you have the vivid awareness that your principal duty is to be teachers of the truth. Not a human and rational truth, but the truth that comes from God, the truth that brings with it the authentic liberation of man: "You will know the truth, and the truth will make you free" (Jn. 8:32); that truth which is the only one that offers a solid basis for an adequate "praxis."

I.1. To be watchful for purity of doctrine, the basis in building up the Christian community, is, therefore, together with the proclamation of the Gospel, the primary and irreplaceable duty of the pastor, the teacher of faith. How often St. Paul emphasized this, convinced as he was of the seriousness of the accomplishment of this duty (cf. 1 Tm. 1:3-7; 18-20; 4:11, 16; 2 Tm. 1:4-14). Over and above unity in love, unity in truth is always urgent for us. The beloved Pope Paul VI, in the Apostolic Exhortation *Evangelii nuntiandi*, said: "The Gospel entrusted to us is also the word of truth. A truth which liberates and which alone gives peace of heart is what people are looking for when we proclaim the Good News to them. The truth about God, about man and his mysterious destiny, about the world.... The preacher of the Gospel will therefore be a person who even at the price of personal renunciation and suffering always seeks the truth that he must transmit to others. He never betrays or hides truth out of a desire to please men, in order to astonish or to shock, nor for the sake of originality or a desire to make an impression.... We are the pastors of the faithful people, and our pastoral service impels us to preserve, defend, and to communicate the truth regardless of the sacrifices that this involves" (EN 78).

TRUTH CONCERNING JESUS CHRIST

I.2. From you, pastors, the faithful of your countries expect and demand above all a careful and zealous transmission of the truth concerning Jesus Christ. This truth is at the center of evangelization and constitutes its essential content: "There is no true evangelization if the name, the teaching, the life, the promises, the kingdom and the mystery of Jesus of Nazareth, the Son of God, are not proclaimed" (cf. EN 22).

From the living knowledge of this truth will depend the vigor of the faith of millions of people. From it will also depend the strength of their support of the Church and of their active presence as Christians in the world. From this knowledge there will derive choices, values, attitudes and modes of behavior capable of orienting and defining our Christian life and of creating new people, and hence a new humanity, for the conversion of the individual and social conscience (cf. EN 18).

It is from a solid Christology that there must come light on so many doctrinal and pastoral themes and questions that you intend to study in these coming days.

I.3. And then we have to confess Christ before history and the world with a conviction that is profound, deeply felt and lived, just as Peter confessed Him: "You are the Christ, the Son of the living God" (Mt. 16:16).

This is the Good News in a certain sense unique: the Church lives by it and for it, just as she draws from it everything that she has to offer to people, without any distinction of nation, culture, race, time, age or condition. For this reason "from that confession of faith (Peter's) the sacred history of salvation and of the People of God could not fail to take on a new dimension" (Homily of Pope John Paul II at the solemn inauguration of his pontificate, October 22, 1978).

This is the one Gospel, and "even if we, or an angel from heaven, should preach to you a gospel contrary to that which we preached to you, let him be accursed," as the Apostle wrote in very clear terms (Gal. 1:8).

I.4. In fact, today there occur in many places—the phenomenon is not a new one—"re-readings" of the Gospel, the result of theoretical speculations rather than authentic meditation on the Word of God and a true commitment to the Gospel. They cause confusion by diverging from the central criteria of the faith of the Church, and some people have the temerity to pass them on, under the guise of catechesis, to the Christian communities.

In some cases either Christ's divinity is passed over in silence, or some people in fact fall into forms of interpretation at variance with the Church's faith. Christ is said to be merely a "prophet," one who proclaimed God's kingdom and love, but not the true Son of God, and therefore not the center and object of the very Gospel message.

In other cases people claim to show Jesus as politically committed, as one who fought against Roman oppression and the authorities, and also as one involved in the class struggle. This idea of Christ as a political figure, a revolutionary, as the subversive Man from Nazareth, does not tally with the Church's catechesis. By confusing the insidious pretexts of Jesus' accusers with the—very different

—attitude of Jesus Himself, some people adduce as the cause of His death the outcome of a political conflict, and nothing is said of the Lord's will to deliver Himself and of His consciousness of His redemptive mission. The Gospels clearly show that for Jesus anything that would alter His mission as the Servant of Yahweh was a temptation (cf. Mt. 4:8; Lk. 4:5). He does not accept the position of those who mixed the things of God with merely political attitudes (cf. Mt. 22:21; Mk. 12:17; Jn. 18:36). He unequivocally rejects recourse to violence. He opens His message of conversion to everybody, without excluding the very publicans. The perspective of His mission is much deeper. It consists in complete salvation through a transforming, peacemaking, pardoning and reconciling love. There is no doubt, moreover, that all this is very demanding for the attitude of the Christian who wishes truly to serve his least brethren, the poor, the needy, the emarginated; in a word, all those who in their lives reflect the sorrowing face of the Lord (cf. LG 8).

I.5. Against such "re-readings," therefore, and against the perhaps brilliant but fragile and inconsistent hypothesis flowing from them, "Evangelization in the present and future of Latin America" cannot cease to affirm the Church's faith: Jesus Christ, the Word and the Son of God, becomes man in order to come close to man and to offer him, through the power of His mystery, salvation, the great gift of God (cf. EN 19 and 27).

This is the faith that has permeated your history and has formed the best of the values of your peoples and must go on animating, with every energy, the dynamism of their future. This is the faith that reveals the vocation to harmony and unity that must drive away the dangers of war in this continent of hope, in which the Church has been such a powerful factor of integration. This is the faith, finally, which the faithful people of Latin America, through their religious practices and popular piety, express with such vitality and in such varied ways.

From this faith in Christ, from the bosom of the Church, we are able to serve men and women, our peoples, and to penetrate their culture with the Gospel, to transform hearts, and to make systems and structures more human.

Any form of silence, disregard, mutilation or inadequate emphasis of the whole of the mystery of Jesus Christ that diverges from the Church's faith cannot be the valid content of evangelization. "Today, under the pretext of a piety that is false, under the deceptive appearance of a preaching of the Gospel, some people are trying to deny the Lord Jesus," wrote a great bishop in the midst of the hard crises of the fourth century. And he added: "I speak the truth, so that the cause of the confusion that we are suffering may be known to all. I cannot keep silent" (Saint Hilary of Poitiers, *Contra auxentium*, 1-4). Nor can you, the bishops of today, keep silent when this confusion occurs.

This is what Pope Paul VI recommended in his opening discourse at the Medellín Conference: "Talk, speak out, preach, write. United in purpose and in program, defend and explain the truths of the faith by taking a position on the present validity of the Gospel, on questions dealing with the life of the faithful and the defense of Christian conduct..." (Pope Paul VI's Discourse, I).

I too will not grow weary of repeating, as my duty of evangelizing the whole of mankind obliges me to do: "Do not be afraid. Open wide the doors for Christ. To His saving power open the boundaries of states, economic and political systems, the vast fields of culture, civilization and development" (the Pope's Homily at the Inauguration of the Pontificate, October 22, 1978).

THE TRUTH CONCERNING THE CHURCH'S MISSION

I.6. You are teachers of the truth, and you are expected to proclaim unceasingly, but with special vigor at this moment, the truth concerning the mission of the Church, object of the Creed that we profess, and an indispensable and fundamental area for our fidelity. The Church was established by the Lord as a fellowship of life, love and truth (LG 9) and as the body, the *Pleroma* and the sacrament of Christ, in whom the whole fullness of deity dwells (LG 7).

The Church is born of our response in faith to Christ. In fact, it is by sincere acceptance of the Good News that we believers gather together in Jesus' name in order to seek together the kingdom, build it up and live it (cf. EN 13). The Church is "the assembly of those who in faith look to Jesus as the cause of salvation and the source of unity and peace" (LG 9).

But on the other hand we are born of the Church. She communicates to us the riches of life and grace entrusted to her. She generates us by Baptism, feeds us with the sacraments and the Word of God, prepares us for mission, leads us to God's plan, the reason for our existence as Christians. We are her children. With just pride we call her our Mother, repeating a title coming down from the centuries, from the earliest times (cf. Henri de Lubac, *Meditation sur l'Eglise*).

She must, therefore, be called upon, respected and served, for "one cannot have God for his Father, if he does not have the Church for his Mother" (St. Cyprian, *De Unitate*, 6, 8); one cannot love Christ without loving the Church which Christ loves (cf. EN 16), and "to the extent that one loves the Church of Christ, he possesses the Holy Spirit" (St. Augustine, *In Ioannem tract.*, 32, 8).

Love for the Church must be composed of fidelity and trust. Stressing, in the first discourse of my pontificate, my resolve to be faithful to the Second Vatican Council and my desire to dedicate my greatest care to the ecclesiological area, I called on people to take once again into their hands the Dogmatic Constitution *Lumen gentium* in order to "meditate with renewed and invigorating zeal on the nature and function of the Church, her way of being and acting...not merely in order that the vital communion in Christ of all who believe and hope in Him should be accomplished, but also in order to contribute to bringing about a fuller and closer unity of the whole human family" (First Message of John Paul II to the Church and the World, October 17, 1978).

Now, at this surpassing moment in the evangelization of Latin America, I repeat the call: "Assent to this document of the Council, seen in the light of Tradition and embodying the dogmatic formulae issued a century ago by the First Vatican Council, will be for us, pastors and faithful, a clear signpost and urgent incentive for walking—let us repeat—the paths of life and history" *(ibid.)*.

I.7. There is no guarantee of serious and vigorous evangelizing activity without a well-founded ecclesiology.

The first reason is that evangelization is the essential mission, the distinctive vocation and the deepest identity of the Church, which has in turn been evangelized (EN 14-15; LG 5). She has been sent by the Lord and in her turn sends evangelizers to preach "not their own selves or their personal ideas, but a Gospel of which neither she nor they are the absolute masters and owners, to dispose of it as they wish" (EN 15). A second reason is that "evangelization is for no one an individual and isolated act; it is one that is deeply ecclesial" (EN 60), which is not subject to the discretionary power of individualistic criteria and perspectives but to that of communion with the Church and her pastors (cf. *ibid.*).

How could there be authentic evangelizing, if there were no ready and sincere reverence for the sacred Magisterium, in clear awareness that by submitting to it the People of God are not accepting the word of men but the true Word of God? (cf. 1 Thes. 2:13; LG 12) "The 'objective' importance of this Magisterium must always be kept in mind and also safeguarded, because of the attacks being levelled nowadays in various quarters against some certain truths of the Catholic Faith" (First Message of John Paul II to the Church and the World, October 17, 1978).

I well know your attachment and availability to the See of Peter and the love that you have always shown it. From my heart I thank you in the Lord's name for the deeply ecclesial attitude implied in this, and I wish you yourselves the consolation of counting on the loyal attachment of your faithful.

I.8. In the abundant documentation with which you have prepared this Conference, especially in the contributions of many Churches, a certain uneasiness is at times noticed with regard to the very interpretation of the nature and mission of the Church. Allusion is made, for instance, to the separation that some set up between the Church and the kingdom of God. The kingdom of God is emptied of its full content and is understood in a rather secularist sense: It is interpreted as being reached not by faith and membership in the Church but by the mere changing of structures and social and political involvement, and as being present wherever there is a certain type of involvement and activity for justice. This is to forget that "the Church receives the mission to proclaim and to establish among all peoples the kingdom of Christ and of God. She becomes on earth the seed and beginning of that kingdom" (LG 5).

In one of his beautiful catechetical instructions, Pope John Paul I, speaking of the virtue of hope, warned that "it is wrong to state that political, economic and social liberation coincides with salvation in Jesus Christ, that the *Regnum Dei* is identified with the *Regnum hominis.*"

In some cases an attitude of mistrust is produced with regard to the "institutional" or "official" Church, which is considered as alienating, as opposed to another Church of the people, one "springing from the people" and taking concrete form in the poor. These positions could contain different, not always easily measured, degrees of familiar ideological forms of conditioning. The Council has reminded us what is the nature and mission of the Church. It has reminded us how her profound unity and permanent up-building are contributed to by those who are responsible for the ministry of the community and have to count on the collaboration of the whole People of God. In fact, "if the Gospel that we proclaim is seen to be rent by doctrinal disputes, ideological polarizations or mutual condemnations among Christians, at the mercy of the latter's differing views on Christ and the Church and even because of their different concepts of society and human institutions, how can those to whom we address our preaching fail to be disturbed, disoriented, even scandalized?" (EN 77)

THE TRUTH CONCERNING MAN

I.9. The truth that we owe to man is, first and foremost, a truth about man. As witnesses of Jesus Christ we are heralds, spokesmen and servants of this truth. We cannot reduce it to the principles of a system of philosophy or to pure political activity. We cannot forget it or betray it.

Perhaps one of the most obvious weaknesses of present-day civilization lies in an inadequate view of man. Without doubt, our age is the one in which man has been most written and spoken of, the age of the forms of humanism and the age of anthropocentrism. Nevertheless, it is paradoxically also the age of man's deepest anxiety about his identity and his destiny, the age of man's abasement to previously unsuspected levels, the age of human values trampled on as never before.

How is this paradox explained? We can say that it is the inexorable paradox of atheistic humanism. It is the drama of man being deprived of an essential dimension of his being, namely, his search for the infinite, and thus faced with having his being reduced in the worst way. The Pastoral Constitution *Gaudium et spes* plumbs the depths of the problem when it says: "Only in the mystery of the Incarnate Word does the mystery of man take on light" (GS 22).

Thanks to the Gospel, the Church has the truth about man. This truth is found in an anthropology that the Church never ceases to fathom more thoroughly and to communicate to others. The primordial affirmation of this anthropology is that man is God's image and cannot be reduced to a mere portion of nature or a nameless element in the human city (cf. GS 12 and 14). This is the meaning of what St. Irenaeus wrote: "Man's glory is God, but the recipient of God's every action, of His wisdom and of His power is man" (St. Irenaeus, *Adversus Haereses*, III, 20, 2-3).

I made particular reference to this irreplaceable foundation of the Christian concept of man in my Christmas Message: "Christmas is the feast of man.... Man is an object to be counted, something considered under the aspect of quantity.... Yet at the same time he is a single being, unique and unrepeatable...somebody thought of and chosen from eternity, someone called and identified by his own name" (Christmas Message, 1).

Faced with so many other forms of humanism that are often shut in by a strictly economic, biological or psychological view of man, the Church has the right and the duty to proclaim the truth about man that she received from her Teacher, Jesus Christ. God grant that no external compulsion may prevent her from doing so. God grant, above all, that she may not cease to do so through fear or doubt, through having let herself be contaminated by other forms of humanism, or through lack of confidence in her original message.

When a pastor of the Church proclaims clearly and unambiguously the truth about man that was revealed by Him who "knew what was in man" (Jn. 2:25), he must therefore be encouraged by the certainty of doing the best service to the human being.

This complete truth about the human being constitutes the foundation of the Church's social teaching and the basis also of true liberation. In the light of this truth, man is not a being subjected to economic or political processes; these processes are instead directed to man and are subjected to him.

Without doubt, this truth about man that the Church teaches will go out strengthened from this meeting of pastors.

II
Signs and Builders of Unity

Your pastoral service of truth is completed by a like service of unity.

II.1. *Unity among bishops*

Unity will be, first of all, unity among yourselves, the bishops. "We must guard and keep this unity," the Bishop St. Cyprian wrote in a moment of grave threats to communion between the bishops of his country, "especially we bishops who preside over the Church, in order to give witness that the episcopate is one and indivisible. Let no one mislead the faithful or alter the truth. The episcopate is one" *(De Ecclesiae Catholicae Unitate,* 6-8).

This unity of bishops comes not from human calculations and strategy but from on high: from serving one Lord, from being animated by one Spirit, and from loving one and the same Church. It is unity resulting from the mission that Christ has entrusted to us, the mission that has been evolving on the Latin-American continent for almost half a millennium, and that you are carrying forward with stout hearts in times of profound changes as we approach the close of the second millennium of redemption and of the Church's activity. It is unity around the Gospel, the body and blood of the Lamb, and Peter living in his Successors; all of which are different signs, but all of them highly important signs, of the presence of Jesus among us.

What an occasion you have, dear brothers, for living this unity of pastors in this Conference! In itself it is a sign and result of an already existing unity; but it is also an anticipation and beginning of a unity that must be more and more close and solid. Begin your work in a climate of brotherly unity: even now let this unity be a component of evangelization.

II.2. *Unity with priests, religious and faithful*

Let unity among the bishops be extended by unity with priests, religious and faithful. Priests are the immediate collaborators of the bishops in their pastoral mission, and their mission would be compromised if close unity did not reign between priests and bishops.

Men and women religious are also especially important subjects of that unity. I well know the importance of their contribution to evangelization in Latin America in the past and in the present. They came here at the dawn of the discovery and accompanied the first steps of almost all the countries. They worked continuously here together with the diocesan clergy. In some countries more than half, in other countries the great majority, of the body of priests are religious. This would be enough to show how important it is here, more than in other parts of the world, for religious not only to accept but to seek loyally an unbreakable unity of aim and action with their bishops. To the bishops the Lord entrusted the mission of feeding the flock. To religious it belongs to blaze the trails for evangelization. It cannot be, it ought not to be, that the bishops should lack the responsible and active, yet at the same time, docile and trusting collaboration of the religious, whose charism makes them ever more ready agents at the service of the Gospel. In this matter everybody in the ecclesial community has the duty of avoiding magisteria other than the Church's magisterium, for they are ecclesially unacceptable and pastorally sterile.

The laity also are subjects of that unity, whether involved individually or joined in apostolic associations for the spreading of the kingdom of God. It is they who have to consecrate the world to Christ in the midst of their daily duties and in their various family and professional tasks, in close union with and obedience to the lawful pastors.

In line with *Lumen gentium*, we must safeguard the precious gift of ecclesial unity between all those who form part of the pilgrim People of God.

III
Defenders and Promoters of Human Dignity

III.1. Those familiar with the Church's history know that in all periods there have been admirable bishops deeply involved in advancing and valiantly defending the human dignity of those entrusted to them by the Lord. They have always been impelled to do so by their episcopal mission, because they considered human dignity a Gospel value that cannot be despised without greatly offending the Creator.

This dignity is infringed on the individual level when due regard is not had for values such as freedom, the right to profess one's religion, physical and mental integrity, the right to essential goods, to life.... It is infringed on the social and political level when man cannot exercise his right of participation, or when he is subjected to unjust and unlawful coercion, or submitted to physical or mental torture, etc.

I am not unaware of how many questions are being posed in this sphere today in Latin America. As bishops, you cannot fail to concern yourselves with them. I know that you propose to carry out a serious reflection on the relationships and implications between evangelization and human advancement or liberation, taking into consideration, in such a vast and important field, what is specific about the Church's presence.

Here is where we find, brought concretely into practice, the themes we have touched upon in speaking of the truth concerning Christ, the Church and man.

III.2. If the Church makes herself present in the defense of, or in the advancement of man, she does so in line with her mission, which, although it is religious and not social or political, cannot fail to consider man in the entirety of his being. The Lord outlined in the parable of the Good Samaritan the model of attention to all human needs (cf. Lk. 10:29ff.), and He said that in the final analysis He will identify Himself with the disinherited—the sick, the imprisoned, the hungry, the lonely—who have been given a helping hand (cf. Mt. 25:31ff.). The Church has learned in these and other pages of the Gospel (cf. Mk. 6:35-44) that her evangelizing mission has, as an essential part, action for justice and the tasks of the advancement of man (cf. Final Document of the Synod of Bishops, October 1971), and that between evangelization and human advancement there are very strong links of the orders of anthropology, theology and love (cf. EN 31); so that "evangelization would not be complete if it did not take into account the unceasing interplay of the Gospel and of man's concrete life, both personal and social" (EN 29).

Let us also keep in mind that the Church's action in earthly matters such as human advancement, development, justice, the rights of the individual, is always intended to be at the service of man, and of man as she sees him in the Christian vision of the anthropology that she adopts. She therefore does not need to have recourse to ideological systems in order to love, defend and collaborate in the liberation of man: at the center of the message of which she is the depositary and herald she finds inspiration for acting in favor of brotherhood, justice, and peace; against all forms of domination, slavery, discrimination, violence, attacks on religious liberty and aggression against man, and whatever attacks life (cf. GS 26, 27 and 29).

III.3. It is therefore not through opportunism nor thirst for novelty that the Church, "the expert in humanity" (Paul VI, Address to the United Nations, October 4, 1965), defends human rights. It is through a true *evangelical commitment*, which, as happened with Christ, is a commitment to the most needy. In fidelity to this commitment, the Church wishes to stay free with regard to the competing systems, in order to opt only for man. Whatever the miseries or sufferings that afflict man, it is not through violence, the interplay of power and political systems, but through the truth concerning man, that he journeys towards a better future.

III.4. Hence the Church's constant preoccupation with the delicate question of property. A proof of this is the writings of the Fathers of the Church through the first thousand years of Christianity (cf. St. Ambrose, *De Nabuthe*, c. 12, n. 53; *PL* 14, 747). It is clearly shown by the vigorous teaching of St. Thomas Aquinas, repeated so many times. In our own times, the Church has appealed to the same principles in such far-reaching documents as the social encyclicals of the recent Popes. With special force and profundity, Pope Paul VI spoke of this subject in his encyclical *Populorum progressio* (cf. 23-24; cf. also MM 106).

This voice of the Church, echoing the voice of human conscience and which did not cease to make itself heard down the centuries in the midst of the most varied social and cultural systems and conditions, deserves and needs to be heard in our time also, when the growing wealth of a few parallels the growing poverty of the masses.

It is then that the Church's teaching, according to which all private property involves a social obligation, acquires an urgent character. With respect to this teaching, the Church has a mission to carry out: she must preach, educate individuals and collectivities, form public opinion, and offer orientations to the leaders of the peoples. In this way she will be working in favor of society, within which this Christian and evangelical principle will finally bear the fruit of a more just and equitable distribution of goods, not only within each nation but also in the world in general, ensuring that the stronger countries do not use their power to the detriment of the weaker ones.

Those who bear responsibility for the public life of the states and nations will have to understand that internal peace and international peace can only be ensured if a social and economic system based on justice flourishes.

Christ did not remain indifferent in the face of this vast and demanding imperative of social morality. Nor could the Church. In the spirit of the Church, which is the spirit of Christ, and relying upon her ample and solid doctrine, let us return to work in this field.

It must be emphasized here once more that the Church's solicitude looks to the whole man.

For this reason, for an economic system to be just, it is an indispensable condition that it should favor the development and diffusion of public education and culture. The more just the economy, the deeper will be the conscience of culture. This is very much in line with what the Council stated: that to attain a life worthy of man, it is not possible to limit oneself to *having more*, one must aspire to *being more* (cf. GS 35).

Therefore, brothers, drink at these authentic fountains. Speak with the language of the Council, of John XXIII, of Paul VI It is the language of the experience, of the suffering, of the hope of modern humanity.

When Paul VI declared that development is "the new name of peace" (PP 76), he had in mind all the links of interdependence that exist not only within the nations but also those outside of them, on the world level. He took into consideration the mechanisms that, because they happen to be imbued not with authentic humanism but with materialism, produce on the international level rich people ever more rich at the expense of poor people ever more poor.

There is no economic rule capable of changing these mechanisms by itself. It is necessary, in international life, to call upon ethical principles, the demands of justice, the primary commandment which is that of love. Primacy must be given to what is moral, to what is spiritual, to what springs from the full truth concerning man.

I have wished to manifest to you these reflections which I consider very important, although they must not distract you from the central theme of the Conference: We shall reach man, we shall reach justice, through evangelization.

III.5. In the face of what has been said hitherto, the Church sees with deep sorrow "the sometimes massive increase of human rights violations in all parts of society and of the world.... Who can deny that today individual persons and civil powers violate basic rights of the human person with impunity: rights such as the right to be born, the right to life, the right to responsible procreation, to work, to peace, to freedom and social justice, the right to participate in the decisions that affect people and nations? And what can be said when we face the various forms of collective violence like discrimination against individuals and groups, the use of physical and psychological torture perpetrated against prisoners or political dissenters? The list grows when we turn to the instances of the abduction of persons for political reasons and look at the acts of kidnapping for material gain which attack so dramatically family life and the social fabric" (Message of John Paul II to the Secretary General of the United Nations Organization on December 2, 1978: 30th Anniversary of the Declaration of Human Rights). We cry out once more: Respect man! He is the image of God! Evangelize, so that this may become a reality; so that the Lord may transform hearts and humanize the political and economic systems, with man's responsible commitment as the starting point!

III.6. Pastoral commitments in this field must be encouraged through a correct Christian idea of liberation. The Church feels the duty to proclaim the liberation of millions of human beings, the duty to help this liberation become firmly established (cf. EN 30); but she also feels the corresponding duty to proclaim liberation in its integral and profound meaning, as Jesus proclaimed and realized it (cf. EN 31). "Liberation from everything that oppresses man but which is, above all, liberation from sin and the evil one, in the joy of knowing God and being known by Him" (EN 9). Liberation made up of reconciliation and forgiveness. Liberation springing from the reality of being children of God, whom we are able to call "Abba, Father" (Rom. 8:15); a reality which makes us recognize in every man a brother of ours, capable of being transformed in his heart through God's mercy. Liberation that, with the energy of love, urges us towards fellowship, the summit and fullness of which we find in the Lord. Liberation as the overcoming of the various forms of slavery and man-made idols, and as the growth of the new man. Liberation that, in the framework of the Church's proper mission, is not reduced to the simple and narrow economic, political, social or cultural dimension, and is not sacrificed to the demands of any strategy, practice or short-term solution (cf. EN 33).

To safeguard the originality of Christian liberation and the energies that it is capable of releasing, one must at all costs avoid any form of curtailment or ambiguity, as Pope Paul VI said: "The Church would lose her fundamental meaning. Her message of liberation would no longer have any originality and would easily be open to monopolization and manipulation by ideological systems and political parties" (EN 32). There are many signs that help to distinguish when the liberation in question is Christian and when on the other hand it is based rather on ideologies that rob it of consistency with an evangelical view of man, of things and of events (cf. EN 35). They are signs drawn from the content of what the evangelizers proclaim or from the concrete attitudes that they adopt. At the level of content, one must see what their fidelity is to the Word of God, to the Church's living Tradition and to her Magisterium. As for attitudes, one must consider what sense of communion they have with the bishops, in the first place, and with the other sectors of the People of God; what contribution they make to the real building up of the community; in what form they lovingly show care for the poor, the sick, the dispossessed, the neglected and the oppressed, and in what way they find in them the image of the poor and suffering Jesus, and strive to relieve their need and serve Christ in them (cf. LG 8). Let us not deceive ourselves: the humble and simple faithful, as though by an evangelical instinct, spontaneously sense when the Gospel is served in the Church and when it is emptied of its content and is stifled with other interests.

As you see, the series of observations made by *Evangelii nuntiandi* on the theme of liberation retains all its validity.

III.7. What we have already recalled constitutes a rich and complex heritage, which *Evangelii nuntiandi* calls the social doctrine or social teaching of the Church (cf. EN 38). This teaching comes into being, in the light of the Word of God and the authentic Magisterium, from the presence of Christians in the midst of the changing situations of the world, in contact with the challenges that result from those situations. This social doctrine involves, therefore, both principles for reflection and also norms for judgment and guidelines for action (cf. OA 4).

Placing responsible confidence in this social doctrine—even though some people seek to sow doubts and lack of confidence in it—to give it serious study, to try to apply it, to teach it, to be faithful to it: all this is the guarantee, in a member of the Church, of his commitment in the delicate and demanding social tasks, and of his efforts in favor of the liberation or advancement of his brothers and sisters.

Allow me, therefore, to recommend to your special pastoral attention the urgent need to make your faithful people aware of this social doctrine of the Church.

Particular care must be given to forming a social conscience at all levels and in all sectors. When injustices grow worse and the distance between rich and poor increases distressingly, the social doctrine, in a form which is creative and open to the broad fields of the Church's presence, must be a valuable instrument for formation and action. This holds good particularly for the laity: "...it is to the laity, though not exclusively to them, that secular duties and activity properly belong" (GS 43). It is necessary to avoid supplanting the laity and to study seriously just when certain forms of supplying for them retain their reason for existence. Is it not the laity who are called, by reason of their vocation in the Church, to make their contribution in the political and economic dimensions, and to be effectively present in the safeguarding and advancement of human rights?

IV
Some Priority Tasks

You are going to consider many pastoral themes of great significance. Time prevents me from mentioning them. Some I have referred to or will do so in the meetings with the priests, religious, seminarians and lay people.

IV.1. The themes that I indicate here have, for different reasons, great importance. You will not fail to consider them, among the many others that your pastoral far-sightedness will indicate to you.

a) The Family: Make every effort to ensure that there is pastoral care for the family. Attend to this field of such primary importance in the certainty that evangelization in the future depends largely on the "domestic Church." It is the school of love, of the knowledge of God, of respect for life and for human dignity. The importance of this pastoral care is in proportion to the threats aimed at the family. Think of the campaigns in favor of divorce, of the use of contraceptive practices, and of abortion, which destroy society.

b) Priestly and religious vocations: In the majority of your countries, in spite of an encouraging awakening of vocations, the lack of vocations is a grave and chronic problem. There is a huge disproportion between the growing population and the number of agents of evangelization. This is of great importance to the Christian community. Every community has to obtain its vocations, as a sign of its vitality and maturity. Intense pastoral activity must be reactivated, starting with the Christian vocation in general and from enthusiastic pastoral care for youth, so as to give the Church the ministers she needs. Lay vocations, although they are so indispensable, cannot compensate for them. Furthermore, one of the proofs of the laity's commitment is an abundance of vocations to the consecrated life.

c) Youth: How much hope the Church places in youth! How much energy needed by the Church abounds in youth, in Latin America! How close we pastors must be to the young, so that Christ and the Church and love of the brethren may penetrate deeply into their hearts.

Conclusion

At the end of this message I cannot fail to invoke once again the protection of the Mother of God upon your persons and your work during these days. The fact that this meeting of ours is taking place in the spiritual presence of Our Lady of Guadalupe, who is venerated in Mexico and in all the other countries as the Mother of the Church in Latin America, is for me a cause for joy and a source of hope. May she, the "Star of evangelization," be your guide in your future reflections and decisions. May she obtain for you from her divine Son:

—the boldness of prophets and the evangelical prudence of pastors,

—the clearsightedness of teachers and the reliability of guides and directors,

—courage as witnesses, and the calmness, patience and gentleness of fathers.

May the Lord bless your labors. You are accompanied by select representatives: priests, deacons, men and women religious, lay people, experts and observers, whose collaboration will be very useful to you. The whole Church has its eyes on you, with confidence and hope. You intend to respond to these expectations with full fidelity to Christ, the Church, and humanity. The future is in God's hands, but in a certain way God places that future with new evangelizing momentum in your hands, too. "Go therefore and make disciples of all nations" (Mt. 28:19).

Farewell Message to Bishops of Central America and the Antilles

At the moment of leaving Mexico, the Holy Father addressed the following message to the episcopate of Central America and the Antilles.

Beloved brothers,

Before leaving the soil of Mexico, I feel the necessity of sending a fatherly greeting to you and, through you, to all the faithful entrusted to your pastoral care.

A greeting marked by the sign of sorrow at not having been able to visit these beloved sons, although so near your countries.

A sorrow that is manifested in a deeper expression of love.

Tell them that the Pope, during the days he lived in the New Continent, thought of them a great deal and prayed a great deal for them.

The material closeness, due to my visit to Mexico, has made me feel more vividly my affection and interest in the whole of Latin America; and in particular, during my brief stay in Santo Domingo, I remembered with special love the whole archipelago of the Antilles.

Now that my thought and my affection are closer to you, there comes to my mind, in a special way, the memory of the material calamities that not long ago befell some countries, particularly Guatemala and Nicaragua. We thank God that the process of reconstruction is continuing in a satisfactory way.

If you could understand how much the Pope desires that the peoples of these countries should be understood in their whole dimension as human beings, and that those who have in their hands the possibility and the power should exercise it in complete justice, which is the condition of peace and development among peoples!

The Pope returns to Rome, but his word remains with you: may it be a constant stimulus to you to continue to work every day with renewed effort, in order that the great love for your countries may be manifested through your commitment in favor of the welfare and brotherly life of this great family which is made up by one and all of the countries of the American continent.

Imparting his blessing to the bishops, and through them to all the peoples of these lands, the Pope wishes to consolidate, increase, and deepen these ties that have been established thanks to his pastoral mission.

Praise to almighty God who has permitted us, on account of the Conference of the Latin American Episcopate, to make the center of the Church in American lands for some days, days that are all-important for the present and the future of evangelization in this great and beloved continent.

The Meeting in Mexico with Its Human and Christian Reality

On his return to the Apostolic Palace, John Paul II was welcomed in the Consistory Hall by the Cardinals present in Rome. They expressed to him their cordial congratulations for the positive result in Latin America. After listening to an address of homage delivered by the Dean of the Sacred College, Cardinal Carlo Confalonieri, the Holy Father spoke as follows.

Lord Cardinals,

1. At the moment when my first missionary journey ends, I raise my deepest thanks to God for the great experience He has granted me of living in the fullness of an apostolic work which occupied, with particular intensity, every hour of the past days.

2. I considered it my duty to undertake this journey (connected with the work of the Third General Assembly of

the Latin American Episcopate in Puebla, announced some time ago), following, in this, the example of my Predecessor Paul VI of venerated memory, who wished to inaugurate this new form in carrying out the papal office in the Church.

3. It is difficult to speak fully of this unforgettable experience while the thousand voices I listened to still re-echo in my mind, and while the memories of what I was able to see, of the persons that I was able to meet, and of the subjects I had occasion to tackle, are still so immediate and alive.

4. It will be necessary to return to all that for a long time in prayer, reflection, and in my heart. But I can say right now that this journey, after the short but significant stop at Santo Domingo, was an exceptional meeting with Mexico in its human and Christian reality, a meeting with the People of God of this country, which responded with a great act of faith to the presence of the Pope. This meeting, which started in Guadalupe, the heart of the Mexican Church, extended to reach the stages of Puebla in Oaxaca, Guadalajara, and Monterrey.

5. With the riches of its contents and the multiplicity of its manifestations, this meeting offers, in a certain sense, a living context for the tasks which, together with the bishops of Latin America, we tackled within the Third General Assembly of that episcopate. The latter, which, as you know, opened on last January 27, with the solemn concelebration at the Sanctuary of the Virgin of Guadalupe, continues at Puebla, on the subject "Evangelization in the present and future of Latin America," until next February 12, when it concludes.

Introducing its work on January 28, I addressed to the South American Church, with great hope and confidence, a message which was made concretely universal by the presence of the media of social communications, and by that of the professionals of information (who gave great coverage to every stage of my short but intense journey).

It will certainly be necessary to speak more than once of the significance of the work of Puebla and of the individual problems tackled there, examining the various subjects again.

6. Now, returning to the Apostolic See after seven days, I feel the need to thank heartily all those, at every level, who helped to prepare and organize this journey; it has been a great success, although it took place in such a short time.

I would like to thank also all those who bore with me the weight of this journey: Their Excellencies Caprio, Casaroli, Martin, Marcinkus, Msgr. Noè, and all the other persons of the suite; press, radio and television; and all the lay people who followed me throughout the whole journey.

7. Finally, for the welcome you have given me, allow me to express my thanks particularly to you and to the whole College of Cardinals, whom I felt so close in prayer and in their hearts in the course of these unforgettable days; especially to the Cardinal Dean who has interpreted so well the sentiments of you all, and to the Cardinal Secretary of State for the precious work he carried out so generously in the days of my absence.

May the Virgin of Guadalupe, to whom I have prayed so much in these days, through her intercession, give strength to our commitment in order that the hopes raised by the apostolic journey that I have concluded today will not be disappointed.

Uganda Celebrates Centenary

From the tenth to the twentieth of February, 1979, many events took place in Uganda to celebrate the centenary of the evangelization of the country. The center of the celebrations was the National Eucharistic Congress. Pope John Paul II sent the following letter to Cardinal James Knox appointing him to be his special representative for these celebrations in Uganda.

To our esteemed brother, Cardinal James Robert Knox, health and apostolic blessing.

We turn our thoughts to Africa, so ready to hear the Gospel; in particular to Uganda, which for the past hundred years has eagerly accepted the truth of Christianity; it has also produced splendid fruits of sanctity. For there, as is well known, a considerable number of witnesses for the faith preferred to die rather than to dishonor it; and by the shedding of their blood they affirmed their observance of the divine law. Of their number, Pope Paul VI, our Predecessor, canonized in 1964 Charles Lwanga, Matthias Kalemba Murumba (or Mulumba) and their twenty companions. During the solemn rite he spoke as follows: "These African martyrs add a new page to that list of victorious persons which we call the martyrology, and in which we find the most magnificent as well as the most tragic of stories. We consider it a page which is worthy to be added to those wonderful accounts of ancient Africa, which we who live today, being men of little faith, thought would never be repeated. We think, for example, of those moving accounts of the Scillitan martyrs, of the martyrs of Carthage, of the martyrs of Utica, that 'Massa Candida' of whom St. Augustine and Prudentius tell us, of the Egyptian martyrs of whom St. John Chrysostom writes with such admiration, and of the martyrs of the persecution by the Vandals. Who could ever have thought that in our times new accounts would be added to these which would be no less heroic and no less glamorous?" (*AAS*, LVI, 1964, p. 905)

Indeed, we must state that this martyrdom took place just a few years after the Catholic religion had been brought to Uganda. Therefore, we rightly feel that this land was in some way already disposed to receive the Christian religion; namely, it was waiting, as it were, for the seed of the Gospel and once this was sown, in a short time an abundant harvest of fruits resulted.

Therefore, the decision of the hierarchy of Uganda to celebrate with festive ceremonies the completion of the hundred years since the first missionaries came to that land and to hold a National Eucharistic Congress, is to be praised. We know that our esteemed brother, Cardinal Emmanuel Nsubuga, Archbishop of Kampala, and his assistants have worked very hard to prepare for these solemn celebrations, and that the bishops of Uganda in a joint pastoral letter have fittingly exhorted the clergy, the religious, and the faithful to prepare for them.

Moreover, we recall that our Predecessor Paul VI in the year 1969 was the first of the supreme Pastors of the Church to go to Africa, and indeed to Uganda, to attend the episcopal conference of that continent, to honor the above-mentioned martyrs in their own country, and to attend to other matters relating to religion. We, too, desire to take part, at least through the Cardinal who will be our personal representative, in these celebrations which will soon take place there. Wherefore, by this letter we appoint and nominate you, our esteemed brother, as our extraordinary envoy, instructing you to preside in our name at the official celebrations. Since we know the qualities of mind and heart with which you are endowed, we are sure that you will carry out this duty for the greater increase of the glory of God, so that not a few and no small benefits will result to the Church in that region.

"How beautiful are the feet of those who preach good news!" (Rom. 10:15) The first men to announce Christ to the Ugandans were Simeon Lourdel, a priest, and Brother Amans Delmas, members of the Society of Missionaries of Africa or "The White Fathers," who on February 17, 1879, after crossing Lake Victoria, landed at Entebbe. Some months later, three other members of the same religious family joined them.

They settled at Nabulagala where they celebrated the Eucharistic Sacrifice for the first time in Uganda; and in the following year their first baptism was that of four aborigines. The cross of Christ then was set up in this place from which its light went forth. Although more than once serious difficulties arose, the Catholic Faith enjoyed a happy and strong increase, especially because new laborers came into that vineyard. Also, care was taken to see that sacred ministers were recruited from the Ugandans themselves. This happened in such a way that in the year 1953, by the farsightedness of Pius XII, likewise our Predecessor, the sacred hierarchy was able to be established in that region.

Thus looking back over the hundred years which have been marked by such a happy progress, we paternally exhort all our sons living there, whom we hold very dear, steadfastly to preserve the precious gift of the Faith and, encouraged by this jubilee, to strive to live by it more diligently every day; remembering that it is nourished by the word of duly appointed preachers and by the liturgical life by which "minds are raised to God, so that they may offer Him the worship which reason requires and more copiously receive His grace" (SC 33). But even more must be done. One must strive to spread the Gospel more widely, because "the obligation of spreading the Faith is imposed on every disciple of Christ according to his ability" (LG 17); namely, it is necessary that the Church in Uganda, founded by missionaries, should itself be missionary.

By a praiseworthy decision, as we have said above, a Eucharistic Congress is being held on the occasion of the solemn celebrations of the centenary. Rightly indeed is this august sacrament honored by social worship. In it, not only divine grace but the Author Himself of grace, Christ the Lord, is contained. The Eucharist is the bond of charity, indeed, "because there is one bread, we who are many are one body for we all partake of the one bread" (1 Cor. 10:17). Therefore, St. John Chrysostom aptly adds: "But if from the same bread we all become also the very same thing, why do we not show towards each other the same love and for that reason become one?" (In Epist. 1 ad Cor., Hom. 24, 2, PG 61, 200) Certainly it is to be greatly desired that in this Eucharistic Congress the flame of true brotherhood may be enkindled, by which Christians are inspired to heal others' wounds, whether of mind or body, to help those in trouble, to refresh those in need.

But to put all these noble and lofty things into practice one must also ask the help of the Blessed Virgin Mary, who is the Mother of the Church. We confidently commit to her care the present life and the future fortunes of the whole of the Catholic community in Uganda.

Motivated by pastoral love and zeal, we have decided to write these things to you on the occasion of the forthcoming solemn celebrations. Moreover, may the apostolic blessing which we willingly impart to you in the Lord, our esteemed brother, to the above-mentioned Cardinal Archbishop of Kampala, to the other bishops, to the civil authorities, to the priests, to the religious, and to all the faithful who will come together for the same jubilee, confirm the wish we make that from these solemn celebrations as much fruit as possible may be reaped.

Given at St. Peter's, Rome, on the seventeenth day of January, in the year 1979, the first of our pontificate.

In the Service of Equity and Charity

On February 17, 1979, the Holy Father received in audience the members of the Court of the Sacred Roman Rota. John Paul II delivered the following address.

I am grateful to you for this visit and, in particular, I thank your revered dean, who has interpreted your sentiments.

I greet you all warmly, and I am happy to have this opportunity of meeting, for the first time, those who incarnate *par excellence* the judicial function of the Church in the service of truth and charity for the building up of the Body of Christ, and to recognize in them, as in all the administrators of justice and in experts of canon law, professionals with a vital task in the Church; indefatigable witnesses to a higher justice in a world marked by injustice and violence; and, therefore, precious collaborators in the pastoral activity of the Church herself.

SUPPORTING THE HUMAN PERSON

1. As you well know, the commitment and the effort to interpret the thirst for justice and dignity that men and women feel deeply in modern times are also part of the vocation of the Church. And in this function of proclaiming and upholding man's fundamental rights in all stages of his existence, the Church is comforted by the international community, which has recently celebrated with special initiatives the thirtieth anniversary of the universal Declaration of Human Rights, and has proclaimed 1979 the International Year of the Child.

The twentieth century will perhaps characterize the Church as the main bulwark supporting the human person in the whole span of his earthly life, right from his conception. In the evolution of ecclesial self-consciousness, the human-Christian person meets not only with recognition but also and above all with an open, active and harmonious protection of his basic rights, in harmony with those of the ecclesial community. This, too, is an essential task of the Church, which, on the ground of person-community relations, offers a model of integration between the orderly development of society and the fulfillment of the personality of the Christian in a community of faith, hope, and charity (cf. LG 8).

EDUCATIVE FUNCTION

Canon law carries out a highly educative function on the individual and social plane, with the intention of creating an orderly and fruitful society, in which germinates and matures the complete development of the human-Christian person. The latter, in fact, can be fulfilled only to the extent to which exclusive individuality is denied, since his vocation is at once personal and communitarian. Canon law permits and fosters this characteristic improvement, since it leads to the overcoming of individualism. From negation of oneself as exclusive individuality, it leads to affirmation of oneself as genuine sociality by means of recognition and respect of the other as a "person" endowed with universal, inviolable, and inalienable rights, and invested with transcendent dignity.

But the task of the Church, and her historical merit, of proclaiming and defending man's fundamental rights at all times and places, does not exempt her but, on the contrary, obliges her to be a *speculum iustitiae* before the world. The Church has a specific responsibility of her own in this connection.

CONTINUAL CHALLENGE

This fundamental option, which represents an awareness of the whole "People of God," continually challenges and stimulates all ecclesiastics—and in particular those who, like you, have a special task in this regard—to "love righteousness and justice" (Ps. 33:5). In fact, it applies particularly to agents of the ecclesiastical courts, to those who must "judge righteously" (Ps. 7:9; 9:8; 67:5; 96:10 and 13; 98:9, etc.). As my revered Predecessor, Paul VI, affirmed, you who dedicate yourselves to service of the noble virtue of justice, can be called, according to the beautiful name already used by Ulpian, *"Sacerdotes iustitiae"*; because it is a question, in fact, of "a noble and lofty ministry, on the dignity of which there is reflected the very light of God, the primordial and absolute Justice, the pure source of all earthly justice. Your *'ministerium iustitiae,'* which must always be faithful and irreproachable, is to be considered in this light; it can then be understood how it must shun the slightest stain of injustice, in order to preserve for this ministry its character of clear purity" *(Insegnamenti di Paolo VI,* II 1965, 29-30).

TO RESPECT THE PERSON

2. The great respect due to the rights of the human person, which must be safeguarded with all care and solicitude, must induce the judge to exact observance of rules of procedure, which are precisely the guarantees of the rights of the person.

The ecclesiastical judge, furthermore, will not only have to keep in mind that "the primary exigency of justice is to respect persons" (L. Bouyer, *L'Eglise de Dieu, Corps du Christ et temple de l'Esprit,* Paris 1970, 599), but, beyond justice, he will have to aim at equity, and, beyond this, at charity (cf. Fr. Andrieu-Guitrancourt, *Introduction sommaire à l'étude du droit en géneral et du droit canonique en particulier,* Paris 1963, 22).

Along this line, confirmed by history and by experience, the Second Vatican Council had declared that "all men must be treated with justice and humanity" (DH 7), and, also with regard to civil society, it had spoken of "a system of positive law providing for a suitable division of the functions and organs of public authority and an effective and independent protection of rights" (GS 75). On these premises, on the occasion of the reform of the Curia, the Constitution *Regimini ecclesiae universae* established that a second section should be set up in the Supreme Court of the Apostolic Signatura, with the competence of settling the *"contentiones...ortas ex actu potestatis administrativae ecclesiasticae, et ad eam, ob interpositam appellationem seu recursum adversus decisionem competentis Dicasterii, delatas quoties contendatur actum ipsum legem aliquam violasse" (AAS* 59 [1967] 921-22).

To recall finally the unexcelled portrait that Pope Paul VI drew of him, "the ecclesiastical judge is, essentially, that *quaedam iustitia animata* of which St. Thomas speaks, quoting Aristotle; he must therefore feel and carry out his mission in a priestly spirit, acquiring, together with knowledge (juridical, theological, psychological, social, etc.), great and habitual self-mastery, with thoughtful concern to grow in virtue in order not to run the risk of dimming, with the screen of a defective and distorted personality, the celestial rays of justice which the Lord bestows on him for the correct exercise of his ministry. Thus he will be, even in passing judgment, a priest and pastor of souls, *solum Deum prae oculis habens" (Insegnamenti di Paolo VI,* IX [1971] 65-66).

A PROBLEM OF RELATIONSHIP

3. I wish to mention a problem with which the observer of the phenomenology of civil society and of the Church is at once confronted: that is, the problem of the relationship between protection of rights and ecclesial communion. There is no doubt that the consolidation and safeguarding of ecclesial communion is a basic task which gives substance to the whole system of canon law and guides the activities of all its members. The very juridical life of the Church, and therefore also judicial activity,

is in itself—by its very nature—pastoral: *"inter subsidia pastoralia, quibus Ecclesia utitur, ut homines ad salutem perducat, est ipsa vita iuridica"* (Insegnamenti di Paolo VI, XV [1977] 124). It must, therefore, be animated in its operation by the Holy Spirit, to whose voice minds and hearts must open.

On the other hand, protection of rights and the relative control of the acts of public administration constitute, for the public authorities themselves, a guarantee of unquestionable value. In the context of a possible rupture of ecclesial communion and of the absolute necessity of its recomposition, together with the various preliminary institutions (such as *aequitas*, *tolerantia*, arbitration, settlement, etc.), law of procedure is an ecclesial fact, as an instrument to overcome and solve conflicts. In fact, in the perspective of a Church which protects the rights of the individual faithful, but also promotes and protects the common good as an indispensable condition for the complete development of the human and Christian person, penal discipline also has a positive place. Also, the penalty inflicted by the ecclesiastical authority (but which actually is recognition of a situation in which the subject has put himself), must be seen, in fact, as an instrument of communion; that is, as a means of recuperating the lack of individual good and common good revealed in the anti-ecclesial, sinful and scandalous behavior of members of the People of God.

Pope Paul VI clarifies further: *"Sed iura fundamentalia baptizatorum non sunt efficacia neque exerceri possunt, nisi quis officia ipso baptismate cum illis connexa agnoscat, praesertim, nisi persuasum sibi habeat* eadem iura in communione Ecclesiae esse exercenda; *immo haec iura pertinere ad aedificationem Corporis Christi, quod est Ecclesia, ideoque eorum exercitium ordini et paci convenire, non autem licere, ut detrimentum afferant"* (ibid., 125).

If, moreover, the believer recognizes, under the impulse of the Spirit, the necessity of a deep ecclesiological conversion, he will transform the assertion and exercise of his rights into the assumption of duties of unity and solidarity for the implementation of the superior values of the common good. I recalled this explicitly in the message to the Secretary of the UN for the thirtieth anniversary of the Declaration of Human Rights: "While insisting—and rightly so—on the vindication of human rights, one should not lose sight of the obligations and duties that go with those rights. Every individual has the obligation to exercise his basic rights in a responsible and ethically justified manner. Every man and woman has the duty to respect in others the rights claimed for oneself. Furthermore, we must all contribute our share to the building up of a society that makes possible and feasible the enjoyment of rights and the discharge of the duties inherent in those rights" (Message to the Secretary General of the United Nations, in *L'Osservatore Romano*, December 11-12, 1978, p. 2).

RESPONSIBILITY OF MINISTERS OF JUSTICE

4. In the existential experience of the Church, the words "law," "judgment" and "justice," though in the midst of the imperfections and difficulties of every human system, recall the model of a higher justice, the justice of God, which is set as the goal and as an inescapable term of comparison. That entails a formidable commitment in all those who "exercise justice."

In the historical effort for a balanced integration of values, stress has sometimes been laid more on "social order" to the detriment of the autonomy of the person. But the Church has never ceased to proclaim the "dignity of the human person as known through the revealed Word of God and by reason itself" (DH 2). She has always delivered *miserabiles personas* from every form of oppression, denouncing situations of injustice, when man's fundamental rights and his very salvation required it, and asking —respectfully, but clearly—that such situations contrary to justice should be put right.

In conformity with its transcendent mission, the "ministry of justice" entrusted to you puts you in a position of special responsibility to make more and more transparent the face of the Church, *speculum iustitiae*, a permanent incarnation of the Prince of justice, in order to sweep the world along to a blessed age of justice and peace.

I am certain that all those who collaborate in judicial activity in the Church, especially the prelates auditors, the officials and all the personnel of the apostolic court, as well as the lawyers and prosecuting attorneys, are fully aware of the importance of the pastoral mission in which they take part, and are happy to carry it out diligently and with dedication, following the example of so many outstanding jurists and zealous priests, who, with admirable solicitude, dedicated to this tribunal their gifts of mind and heart.

I am happy to recall at this moment Cardinal Boleslao Filipiak, called to the heavenly country last year; and I also wish to pay tribute to the example of diligence and self-denial of the revered Mons. Carlo Lefebvre, from whose precious experience the Holy See continues to benefit after he left the service at the Sacred Roman Rotà a few months ago.

My gratitude also goes to the prelates auditors who, for reasons of health, have not been able to continue their service.

To all of you my deep gratitude and sincere appreciation, with the assurance of my prayer: May the Lord accompany you with His assistance, and may my encouragement and blessing sustain you.

The Parish: the Presence of Christ Among Us

During the celebration of Mass in the parish of St. Gregory the Great at Magliana, Rome, on February 18, 1979, the Pope delivered a homily, from which are taken these excerpts.

In the Gospel of today we read that at Capernaum, in the house in which Jesus stayed, *"many were gathered together"* (Mk. 2:2). There was not room for them all in the house, so great was the number of those who wished to listen to "the word that He was preaching," and to see what He did.

And lo, in the midst of this crowd, Jesus does a very significant thing when a paralytic is put in front of Him, lowered through an opening in the roof for lack of other space. Jesus first of all says to this man, "My son, your sins are forgiven" (Mk. 2:5). At these words a murmur arises among those who, with mistrust, have followed Christ's action. These are scribes who (rightly) affirm, "Who can forgive sins but God alone?" (Mk. 2:7) But it had only been aversion to Jesus that had dictated this objection to them: "Why does this man speak thus? It is blasphemy!" (Mk. 2:7) Jesus, in a certain sense, reads their thoughts and gives an answer: " 'Which is easier, to say to the paralytic, "Your sins are forgiven," or to say, "Rise, take up your pallet and walk"? That you may know that the Son of man has authority on earth to forgive sins'—he said to the paralytic—'I say to you, rise, take up your pallet and go home' " (Mk. 2:9-11).

Everything happens as Jesus has ordered.

Jesus cures an incurable man.

He works a miracle. By so doing, He gives the proof that He has the power on earth to forgive sins. And as the scribes have affirmed that only God has this power, they should now draw the conclusion of what they themselves had sustained in words.

Jesus reaffirms the presence of God among the crowd.

Jesus reaffirms the divine power, proper to Him, of forgiving sins.

Jesus proves, at the same time, that the evil of sin is more dangerous and worrying than physical illness (in this case, serious and chronic disease). He is the Savior who has come, in the first place, to remove this serious evil.

LIVING SECTION OF THE PEOPLE OF GOD

What does this passage of the Gospel say to us gathered here?

"Many were gathered together" then. And today, too, many are gathered. And I am thinking not only of the persons present in this church now, but of all the inhabitants of the Magliana area. For some time now, people who came to Rome from various parts have been gathering here. A large district has sprung up; at the same time, a new parish has come into being which now contains forty-five thousand persons. It is a very large parish.

What does "parish" mean?

Parish means: Christ's presence among men. Parish means a set of persons; it means a community in which and with which Jesus Christ reconfirms the presence of God. The parish is a living part of the People of God.

While I say these things, your thought goes instinctively to your experience here, day after day, in the concrete context of your parish. Many of you, beginning with the parish priest, Don Pietro Cecchelani, knew this parish, so to speak, in its infancy, when the community met in a small chapel which could hold at most two hundred persons. It is not necessary to go back very far in the years: The parish was constituted, in fact, on December 13, 1963.

How much distance has been covered since then! The district has grown at a bewildering pace, rising from the 4,500 inhabitants of the beginnings to the present 45,000 and more. But, at the same time, the Christian community has also grown, and not just in numbers: Around the Word of God, proclaimed by the priests, re-echoed by the catechists, borne witness to by the faithful in everyday life, there has been formed a community of persons who know one another, help one another, and love one another. An open, lively community, aware of the immense riches constituted by the Gospel of Christ, and therefore straining to proclaim it to the mass of the indifferent, the "distant."

Evangelization—rightly felt as a primary commitment—occupies the priests, the sisters of the two communities present in the parish, the youthful groups of the catechists; and it is developed not only in the ordinary forms, but also by means of new approaches, such as by reading and meditating on the Gospel in homes, in the so-called "block groups," in which several families gather together for a moment of reflection and communion.

THE CHRISTIAN COMMUNITY

For all of you, and for your pastors in particular, let Pope St. Gregory, who was a great master in the pastoral art, be an example and guide. He recalled that the pastor of souls "must be near everyone with the language of compassion and understanding"; but he pointed out, at the same time, that to do this, he "must be able, to an extraordinary extent, to rise above all others through prayer and contemplation" (cf. *Regola Past.* II, 5). In the intimacy of conversation with God and in the regenerating contact with His grace, he can find the light and wisdom necessary to "adapt his word to the audience listening to him, so that it may be grasped by the mind of everyone, without losing the power of being edifying for all" *(ibid.,* II, prol.). May this happen in your parish! Then will be realized among you that which St. Gregory, in a poetic image, indicated as the ideal of every Christian community: that is, to be like a "well-tuned lyre" which, skillfully touched by the artist, raises to God the harmonious sound of its melody (cf. *ibid.).*

Before concluding, I would like to tell you my joy in knowing that in your parish there is a chapel dedicated to the Blessed Maximilian Kolbe, the great apostle of our century. Together with him and with Pope St. Gregory, I entrust you all to the Blessed Lady who is the Mother of the Church, and who is invoked confidently by the inhabitants of this city of ours as *Salus Populi Romani*.

In the liturgy of today the prophet Isaiah says:

"Behold, I am doing a new thing...do you not perceive it? I will make a way in the wilderness and rivers in the desert.... The people whom I formed for myself [will] declare my praise" (Is. 43:19-21).

May all this take place among you.

This is what the Bishop of Rome, Pope John Paul II, on the occasion of today's visit, wishes for the parish of St. Gregory, at Magliana.

To Participants of the Liturgico-Pastoral Meeting

On February 23, 1979, the Holy Father John Paul II received in audience participants in the Twenty-first Liturgico-Pastoral Congress promoted by the Work of Kingship on the fiftieth anniversary of its foundation. The Holy Father delivered the following address.

Dear brothers and sisters,

In the first place, I thank Cardinal Fernando Antonelli for the appreciated words of homage which he addressed to me also on our behalf. And I thank all of you also, for visiting me in such large numbers at the conclusion of the Twenty-first National Liturgico-Pastoral Congress, promoted by the "Work of the Kingship of Our Lord Jesus Christ."

I know you are studying the very topical subject, "Liturgy and forms of piety, for a renewal of popular piety." I hope you will succeed in showing in its right light, and in a well-balanced way, the mutual relationship between both these important aspects of Christian religious life, so that each one may respect and promote the requirements and identity of the other.

But I also wish to recall that the fiftieth anniversary of the foundation of the above-mentioned "Work of Kingship" falls this year. I am well aware that this association was founded by the indefatigable and well-deserving Franciscan, Father Agostino Gemelli, who characterized it with the purpose of a twofold promotion, liturgical and ascetical. And it is a pleasure for me, today, cordially to acknowledge before you the great good done in so many years by this institution: both with the many publications, ancient and recent, and with the numerous initiatives of fruitful meetings of study and prayer.

I am happy, therefore, to formulate sincere wishes for the further development of the "work," in conformity with the spirit of the Founder, in harmony with other similar institutes, and in faithful collaboration with the bishops: May it always contribute to educating and bringing new Christian life to wide sectors of the holy Church of God in Italy.

It is with these wishes and with fatherly affection that I grant the special apostolic blessing to you all, as a token of the necessary heavenly graces.

Catechesis, Liturgy, Charity in the Lenten Apostolate

In the course of his visit on February 24, 1979, to the Roman Major Seminary, the Holy Father met the parish priest prefects of the diocese, to whom he delivered the following address.

Dear friends:

1. At the end of this brotherly meeting, I feel the deep need to express to you cordially my joy and satisfaction at this meeting of ours: joy, because I find myself once more with a specialized group of priests of my Roman diocese; satisfaction, because I have been able to see personally the seriousness and pastoral commitment which animate you all.

In the articulated structure of the diocese, you have the delicate task of acting as liaison between the "presbyterium" and the bishop; of ensuring and strengthening also the continual and effective concord of priests in the sphere of the respected prefectures, in order that the overall apostolate may be coordinated with the purposes of a more and more homogeneous and prompt effectiveness. The circle of this twofold union is widened and strengthened even more in the prefects' community meetings, as is that of today, in order to study together, in a wide survey, the pastoral problems of the Church in Rome, as is laid down in the Apostolic Constitution *Vicariae potestatis in urbe* (7-8).

In this perspective, the function and the mission of the prefect and of the council of prefects take on great significance for the diocesan apostolate, since they condition its necessary and desirable compactness, as well as its orderly and logical method.

On you, in particular, there falls the responsibility that the diocese of Rome may really be, like the early community of Jerusalem, "of one heart and soul" (Acts 4:32).

2. It is the first time I have officially met the prefects of the diocese of Rome, and this happy circumstance brings back to my memory the many meetings with the prefects of my diocese in Krakow. At these meetings, over which I presided, I conversed in a brotherly way with my priests and discussed our common responsibilities as pastors and guides of souls. The close collaboration which existed between bishop and prefect was a guarantee of serene availability for the solution of the various complex problems which ecclesial life presented day after day.

3. I listened with deep interest to the three reports on the "Lenten apostolate" in Rome. It intends to move in three directions, with a concrete approach: catechesis; liturgical celebrations; the commitment of charity. I hope and trust that, in such a rich and significant liturgical time as is that of Lent, now imminent, not only the priests of the

diocese but all the faithful will be made aware of these three fundamental aspects of Christian life.

I listened with particular attention to the evaluation of this pastoral year's Second Assembly of the Roman Clergy which took place on last February 15. In it you studied the subject of the clergy of Rome faced with the requirements of the diocese, stressing four points: the requirements of an authentic communion; the structures of participation and collegiality; solidarity and equalization between the clergy and the parishes; and finally, the problem of vocations.

I was positively impressed by the spirit that animated the meeting, by the high number of participants, and by the truly priestly commitment with which you tackled such delicate problems. I hope that concrete spiritual fruit will come from it.

I also think that some ideas, which I listened to at this meeting today, will certainly be a precious help for me to prepare the address which I will deliver to the Roman clergy in the audience that will take place for the beginning of Lent. In this connection, I would be sincerely grateful to you if you would add some other suggestions, either orally or in writing, because, as the book of Proverbs notes: "a wise man listens to advice" (Prv. 12:15).

To all of you my esteem and affection. May the faithful of the whole Church, looking to their brothers and priests of the diocese of Rome, subscribe to the words that St. Paul addressed to the Romans: "Your faith is proclaimed in all the world" (Rom. 1:8).

With this wish, I bless you paternally.

The Priest in the Mystery of Christ

On March 2, 1979, under the leadership of His Eminence, Cardinal Poletti, and the auxiliary bishops of Rome, the parish priests and clergy, both secular and regular, of the diocese of Rome were received in the Sistine Chapel by the Holy Father, who addressed them as follows.

1. We meet at the beginning of Lent. In this period, each of us must renew, that is, find again in some way, above all, his own "Christian being"; the identity that springs from belonging to Christ, first of all through Baptism. The whole tradition of the Lenten period is turned in this direction, and in the ancient practice of the Church its completion was precisely the Baptism of catechumens.

Let us recall that the fundamental substratum of our "priesthood" is our "Christian being"; our "priestly identity" has its roots in our "Christian identity" *(christianus—alter Christus; sacerdos—alter Christus).*

Preparing with all our brothers in the faith for the renewal of baptismal promises on the vigil of Holy Saturday, we are preparing in a special way for the renewal of priestly promises in the liturgy of Holy Thursday—the day of priests. The whole time of Lent must serve for this preparation.

ELEMENTS OF HOLINESS

2. The Second Vatican Council set forth clearly and precisely the essence of the holiness characteristic of priests (Decree on the Ministry and Life of Priests). We must seek the concrete forms of this holiness, by exercising the many tasks that belong to our vocation and our pastoral ministry.

If we ask ourselves what are the elements that characterize the holiness to which the priest is called, the elements that constitute, so to speak, its *specificum*, they can rightly be indicated in two closely complementary aspects. These I would formulate as follows: a) a man completely possessed by the mystery of Christ; b) a man who builds the community of the People of God in a quite special way.

a) The priest is placed at the very center of the mystery of Christ, who constantly embraces humanity and the world, the visible creation and the invisible one. He acts, in fact, *in persona Christi*, particularly when he celebrates the Eucharist: by means of his ministry Christ continues to carry out His work of salvation in the world. Rightly, therefore, with the Apostle Paul every priest can exclaim: "This is how one should regard us, as servants of Christ and stewards of the mysteries of God" (1 Cor. 4:1).

It is not difficult to perceive the implications that spring from this fact. I will limit myself to indicating the following:

—If the purpose of his ministry is the sanctification of others, it is obvious that the priest must feel involved in a commitment of personal holiness. He cannot "stand aside," he cannot "dispense himself," from this commitment, without condemning himself thereby to a life that is not authentic, or, to use the words of the Gospel, without changing from a "good shepherd" into a "hireling" (cf. Jn. 10:11-12).

—Then there is the implication constituted by the old theological problem of the relationship between *opus operatum* and *opus operantis*. The supernatural efficacy of the sacraments depends directly on *opus operatum*; but the Second Vatican Council stressed forcefully the importance of *opus operantis*. Do you remember the words of the Decree *Presbyterorum ordinis?* "While it is possible for God's grace to carry out the work of salvation through unworthy ministers, yet God ordinarily prefers to show His wonders through those men who are more submissive to the impulse and guidance of the Holy Spirit and who, because of their intimate union with Christ and their holiness of life, are able to say with St. Paul: 'It is no longer I who live, but Christ who lives in me' (Gal. 2:20)" (no. 12).

UNITY OF LIFE

—Finally, the problem of the "style" of the interior life of the priest in care of souls has its place here. The Council tackled it with courageous clarity: "Priests"—the Decree just quoted points out—"who are perplexed and distracted by the very many obligations of their position may be anxiously inquiring how they can reduce to unity their interior life and their program of external activity. This unity of life cannot be brought about merely by an outward arrangement of the works of the ministry nor by the practice of spiritual exercises alone, though this may help to foster such unity. Priests can, however, achieve it by following in the fulfillment of their ministry the example of Christ the Lord, whose meat was to do the will of Him who sent Him that He might perfect His work" (no. 14).

These words constitute a specific reinterpretation of the many precious reflections that have matured in the course of the centuries on the relationship between *active life* and *contemplative life*. One thing is certain: if the priest's conscience is imbued with the immense mystery of Christ, if it is completely possessed by it, then all his activities, even the most absorbing ones (active life) will find a root and nourishment in contemplation of the mysteries of God (contemplative life), whose "steward" he is.

BUILDING THE COMMUNITY

b) The second aspect of the priest's vocation to holiness I have located in his task of building the community of the People of God. It might seem an "exterior" aspect, bound up with the institutional dimension of the Church and therefore not significant from the point of view of personal holiness. Yet the whole teaching of the Second Vatican Council, which goes back, moreover, to the most genuine sources of ecclesiology, indicates also in this sector the *proprium* of priestly holiness. The priest, won over by the mystery of Christ, is called to win others over to this mystery: he lives this "social" dimension of his priesthood within the structures of the Church-institution. The priest is not only the man "for others"; he is called to help "others" to become a community, that is, to live the social significance of their faith. In this way, the commitment with which the priest "gathers" (and does not "scatter": cf. Mt. 12:30), the commitment with which he "builds" the Church, becomes the measure of his holiness.

The greeting with which he begins the Eucharistic liturgy: "The communion of the Holy Spirit be with you all," becomes his program: the priest is the spokesman and the intermediary of this communion. He must, therefore, cultivate in himself an attitude of brotherhood and solidarity, he must learn the art of collaboration, the sharing of experiences, and mutual aid. A living part of the presbyterium, which gathers closely round its bishop, he must feel continually urged to a missionary projection towards those who are far off, who are not yet part of the "one fold" (cf. Jn. 10:16).

And finally: since believers walk in time, sustained by hope of the definitive meeting with Christ in His glory, the priest builds the community of brothers by taking his place within it as a witness to eschatological hope. The faithful to whom he is sent expect from him, as the decisive seal of his mission, a clear and unmistakable testimony to eternal life and to the resurrection of the flesh. Also the commitment of celibacy must be considered in this light; it then appears as a very important contribution to the building up of the Church and, therefore, as an element characterizing the spirituality of the priest.

AN ACCEPTABLE TIME

3. Beloved sons, I have lingered over a sketch of the main features of our priestly identity, because the period of

Lent is really "the acceptable time" (2 Cor. 6:2) for an opportune revision of life before the extraordinary gift of vocation.

It is a revision that each one must carry out within the community both of the presbyterium and of the parish, so that it may be expressed in a renewed commitment of Christian life on the part of all. Lent has always marked a relaunching of pastoral activities within the parishes: once there used to be parish missions, special practices of piety, community penitential exercises. Today, in the changed environmental conditions, the commitment for the renewal of Christian life will have to be expressed in other forms.

The meetings which I have already been able to have with leaders of the diocesan presbyterium have permitted me to realize the promising flourishing of initiatives planned for this Lent, in the sectors of catechesis, liturgical celebrations, and commitment of charity. I wish to take advantage of this circumstance to express to you my sincere appreciation and cordial encouragement. Work, beloved sons, without letting yourselves be discouraged by difficulties and failures. Profit from experience to perfect new initiatives, to seek new ways on which to go to meet men, our brothers, and bring them the "Word that saves," a Word for which they are hungering, perhaps without knowing it. The priest as pastor must always imitate Christ—the Pastor who seeks.

This search, carried out together with the Good Shepherd in a disinterested and often deeply felt way, confers on his priesthood that stamp of authenticity which is so essential both from the point of view of his priestly personality and from the merely human one which impresses itself on the consideration and esteem of all those who approach him.

We must take great care not to "split" our personality as priests. We must take great care not to allow our priesthood to stop being the "most essential" thing for us, the "unifying" element of all our concerns. It must never become something "secondary" and "supplementary."

PRIESTLY FORMATION

4. This is the fundamental object of our work on ourselves, of our interior life, in a word, of permanent priestly formation in its threefold aspect: spiritual, pastoral, and intellectual.

We are formed "in order to" carry out priestly activity, and we are formed "through" priestly activity. In this field we must have a genuine healthy ambition. It must be important for us to carry out the service of the Word as effectively as possible. *(How* do I preach? *How* do I catechize?) It must be our concern to reach souls, to help men in their problems of conscience: confession, spiritual direction—particularly of the persons consecrated to God. (Sometimes complaints are heard of the lack of good directors.)

We must, certainly, be with the suffering and the needy. On their side. But we must always be with them "as priests."

GETTING ACQUAINTED

5. I have been Bishop of Rome for only a few months. I am gradually beginning to know my new diocese. I realize that my "universal" mission is based on that "particular" one, and therefore I am trying to dedicate myself to the latter as much as I can, availing myself of the great help of the Cardinal Vicar of Rome, of Monsignor the Vicegerent, and of the auxiliary bishops. In these months I have had the opportunity to visit some parishes, first contacting the pastors of each of them.

They have been very fine experiences, in which I had confirmation of the attractive spontaneity of the people, of the open and confident availability of the priests, of the generous vivacity of the laity, especially of the young. In this connection, I am happy to take the opportunity to thank the Cardinal Vicar, their Excellencies the bishops of the zones, the clergy and faithful, for the cordiality and warmth of their welcome.

I am counting on these meetings a great deal. It is my intention to make them coincide, as far as possible, with the more thorough visits carried out by the individual bishops of the pastoral areas. I consider it very useful, in these circumstances, to contact directly the groups of laity who are apostolically committed in the parish. Among the latter, I would like to stress in particular the catechetical groups, made up both of parents and of young people, whose work, especially in this time in which there is a lack of priests, is seen to be more and more necessary. Only the commitment of select and well-prepared groups, who are able to involve also the families of the children in that effort of reaching maturity in faith which catechesis must be, can cope with the serious problems raised by a secularized society.

SEEKING VOCATIONS

On the basis of collaboration with the families and in the context of a deep dialogue with the young, the apostolate of vocations must be developed. It is really unnecessary for me to dwell on its urgency here. Of course, the fact that this specific pastoral action is more difficult in a city with millions of inhabitants must not be found surprising. If, however, it is carried out methodically and with commitment, it might turn out in the long run to be even more effective in such a wide sphere. I would lay stress, in any case, particularly on the necessity that priests should ask the Lord of the harvest to help them to be effective mediators, by their own lives and by their own instructions, in this work of promotion of vocations.

6. Concluding this meeting with you, my thought flies to the forthcoming Holy Thursday, when the whole presbyterium—secular and religious priests—will again be gathered around its bishop. That is the day of our priestly unity. We must seek a concrete form of this unity, particularly here in Rome, where—as is known—the clergy is particularly differentiated. We must think of what can

serve to deepen this unity and also of what can be done to grasp that which might hinder it.

From the report that was presented to your assembly on last February 15, the subject of which was: "The clergy of Rome faced with the requirements of the diocese," I was able to realize the effort you are making to revive and increase the structures of participation and collegiality, as well as to consolidate the ties of solidarity and communion. It is a program that deserves all encouragement, because it corresponds responsibly to those requirements of brotherhood which are derived from common priestly ordination, common service, and a common mission. Cultivate, as the usual and conscious attitude of your spirit, a real *affectus collegialis,* as I would call it in analogy with the bond of collegiality which unites the bishops. This, too, is part of your specific spirituality.

Taking leave of you, I clasp you all to me in one spiritual embrace, and I bless you all willingly. When, at Easter time, you visit the families of your parishes, take to them the greeting and the blessing of the Bishop of Rome, the humble Successor of Peter, Pope John Paul II.

First Priority: Announce the Word of God in Its Purity and Integrity

On March 3, 1979, Pope John Paul II received the rectors of several major seminaries of England, Scotland, and Malta. The Holy Father addressed them as follows.

The presence here this morning of a group of rectors of seminaries, including important Pontifical Colleges in this city, brings to my mind many considerations. There are many thoughts that I, as Bishop of Rome and Pastor of the universal Church, wish to share with you, my beloved brothers and sons in the priesthood of our Lord Jesus Christ. But I also hope that my words today will be known by other seminary rectors throughout the world, and that through them the expression of my love will reach all their students.

Today, then, my first thought is for all the seminarians. I ask you to take back to them my greetings, assuring them, in my name, how much their fidelity means to the Church, how much the future of evangelization depends on their generosity, and how great a role they are called to play in that authentic renewal of the People of God that was willed by the Second Vatican Council. Yes, my message to the seminarians is one of profound interest in their welfare and of deep affection for them as future partners in the Gospel of Christ.

Precisely because of the great hope that I have in the seminarians of this generation, I am particularly pleased to reflect with you, their rectors, on the task that is yours. You have been called by your bishops to exercise a role of special spiritual leadership in the Church of Christ. And today I wish to speak to you about certain fundamental issues, in order to confirm you in your mission.

By meditating, yourselves, on these issues you will see ever more clearly the goal of your own specific ministry of service in the training of future priests. You will thus have clear criteria for knowing what the Church desires, above all else, to be at the foundation of seminary life; you will have clear guidelines for determining the priorities of your institutions, and those means that are truly apt to put these priorities into practice.

In a word, the first priority for seminaries today is the teaching of God's Word in all its purity and integrity, with all its exigencies and in all its power. The Word of God—and the Word of God alone—is the basis for all ministry, for all pastoral activity, for all priestly action. The power of God's Word constituted the dynamic basis of the Second Vatican Council, and John XXIII pointed out clearly on the day it opened: "The greatest concern of the

Ecumenical Council is this—that the sacred deposit of Christian doctrine should be more effectively guarded and taught" (Discourse of October 11, 1962). And if the seminarians of this generation are to be adequately prepared to take on the heritage and challenge of this Council, they must be trained above all in God's Word: in "the sacred deposit of Christian doctrine." We all know what love St. Paul had for the Word of God, and with what urgency his words apply to all the priests of the Church: "Guard the truth that has been entrusted to you by the Holy Spirit" (2 Tm. 1:14). In fulfilling this holy responsibility, seminaries must play a primary role and give an outstanding witness.

A second issue of great importance that deeply affects seminaries today is that of ecclesiastical discipline. With simplicity and forthrightness John Paul I spoke to his clergy about the "great discipline" (Discourse of September 7, 1978). On that occasion he stated: "The 'great discipline' requires a suitable atmosphere. And first of all, an atmosphere of recollection *(raccoglimento)."* It is my conviction that with this suitable atmosphere, and through the grace of God, the great discipline required for seminaries will be achieved and joyfully maintained. And the reason for all of this is found in the impelling love of Christ and His brethren. The sacrifice, effort and generosity entailed in the preparation for the priesthood have meaning only if they are done *propter regnum Dei.* They are possible only with prayer.

When the Word of God is seen as the basis of all seminary life and training, and when the great discipline of the Church is embraced by the seminarians as a service to charity, then the seminaries themselves become, in the words of Paul VI, "Houses of deep faith and authentic Christian asceticism, as well as joyful communities sustained by Eucharistic piety" (Discourse of April 16, 1975).

In the years ahead all of us must work for the purification of the Church, in accordance with the Gospel, and following the directives of the Second Vatican Council. In so doing, we hope to offer to the Savior His Church—holy and worthy of His love: a Church in which numerous young men are imbued with the mystery of Christ, and, basing their lives on His Word, give themselves in generous preparation for His ministry.

This preparation and training depends to a great extent on you. I repeat: You have been called to exercise a role of special spiritual leadership in the Church. Christ depends on you and is with you. And the Pope is with you and blesses you.

A Special Time of God's Grace

On March 10, 1979, concluding the practice of the Spiritual Exercises which had taken place in the Matilda Chapel in the Vatican that week, the Holy Father delivered the following address.

Dear brothers!

At this moment we want, above all, to express together our gratitude to Christ the Lord who, during the past days, has gathered us in this place, in St. Matilda's Chapel in the Vatican, where the Pope and his closest collaborators have taken part in the Spiritual Exercises of Lent. These Exercises are a special time of God's grace for us. They are the Lenten gift that our Lord and Master has prepared for us. They are so indispensable for us; our souls were looking forward to them intensely. Among the many tasks, among the important duties to which we attend, each of us appreciates particularly the days that permit us to consider exclusively the most essential problems and to apply, in a certain way, to all the other matters that compose our everyday life, *the deepest measure, which is Christ Himself.*

The Father Preacher of the Exercises has tried in the first place to make everyone see Christ. We are heartily grateful to him for this, and now I express this gratitude on behalf of all the participants. The Father Moderator raised, together with us, the fundamental questions; we could say, the eternal questions. He raised them in the old way, which is, however, always fresh and new. These questions, in fact, never lose their topicality; they never fall into decay, and we always listen to them as new and original problems. *Cur Deus homo? Cur Deus panis? Quomodo Christum predicare?* The Father Preacher of these Exercises outlined the great themes of our Faith, our life, our ministry, illustrating them with his own pastoral experiences and referring to the characteristic aspects of our times. He left space for the reflection of each one. He was sincere with his particular audience. He followed the great movement of the thought and life of the modern Church, while always remaining in this concrete place, which was our "upper room" of Spiritual Exercises, with the men gathered in it, that is, us.

Every human work is according to the measure of the man. In the work of the Spiritual Exercises the most important thing is always the following: that the man should be a faithful messenger. Just as our Father Moderator said on the first evening, referring to the Angelus: the name of this messenger is not important; what counts is the message itself.

The most important thing is that this message should reach the heart, that it should sink into the soil of the soul and act for a long time in this soil into which it has been thrown in the same way as grain is thrown.

Our desires meet on this, and it is just with these wishes that I want to thank the Reverend Father. These wishes are at the same time for us, for the participants. May Christ the Lord grant them through the intercession of His Mother, to whom the Reverend Father often directed our attention, referring to the figure of the Blessed Maximilian Kolbe. May this final blessing become for us all a token of the fulfillment of these wishes, which we formulate for one another at the end of the Spiritual Exercises.

In the Service of Christ Throughout His Whole Life

On March 13, 1979, the Holy Father presided over the solemn liturgy for the funeral rites of the late Cardinal Giovanni Villot.

Thirty-four Cardinals, including the Archbishop of Paris, Francois Marty, and the Archbishop of Lyons, Alexandre Charles Renard, concelebrated with the Holy Father.

The Holy Father delivered the following homily.

Beloved brothers and sons,

1. We are gathered here around the coffin of our brother. He passed away so unexpectedly. Just a week ago it was difficult to think that he would leave us, that his hour was so near. It was difficult to think so. He still seemed full of life and strength—in accordance with his age, of course—but he seemed full of it.... We felt deeply grieved when we learned from the doctors that, in spite of these appearances, his organism was exhausted and defenseless.

He has left us. The Lord of life has called him to Himself. *Deus, cui omnia vivunt....*

At this moment, in front of his coffin, we gather around the altar. We celebrate the Holy Sacrifice: we who lived so close to him every day. This liturgy of ours, this concelebration is, in a certain sense, a continuation of all the days spent together with him, of all the meetings, the conversations, the collaboration.

2. The Cardinals and I have still clearly in our minds what he said to us, as Camerlengo of the Holy Roman Church, on two solemn occasions, during the celebration of the votive Mass to the Holy Spirit *pro eligendo Summo Pontifice*. Twice: first, after Pope Paul VI's death and then, just a few weeks later, after the death of Pope John Paul I. He spoke here, in this very place. Let us recall what he said:

"At this moment, a serious and delicate one, Lord Cardinals, the sacred liturgy gathers us all together and causes us to pray for the election of the Pope, which, with the Lord's help, we are about to begin. We know that, in accordance with His ineffable promise, Jesus is in our midst.... The thought occurs to us spontaneously, Lord Cardinals, that Jesus is addressing us particularly, at this solemn hour of the Conclave—as He addressed the Apostles gathered in the Upper Room—that He is looking into our eyes, one by one, asking us for complete correspondence (in the limits, of course, of our human weakness) with His will, with His forestalling love, by means of a deeper union with Him, a truer brotherly charity among ourselves, and, above all, convinced faithfulness in carrying out the task that is assigned to us."

And again, on the following October 14, commenting on the words of Jesus: "Greater love has no man than this, that a man lay down his life for his friends" (Jn. 15:13), he observed: "Let us reflect, brothers, that all of us—it is certain—but in a very special way the one we will elect, must give our life for the multitude of the redeemed; *ut amici Christi efficiantur*. The whole mystical mission of the Church is contained in this concept; and, since God uses men as ordinary instruments, it can clearly be seen what is the spirit that must animate those He chooses to exercise an office as pastor, as guide, and to make the Gospel message known for the first time. We ourselves, to the extent to which we wish to consider ourselves His friends—with all our failings—are such only and exclusively by virtue of His death."

He prepared the Conclave twice, together with the whole College of Cardinals. He was the Secretary of State of Pope Paul VI and later of John Paul I. After my election, he expressed his readiness to leave this office. I asked him to remain, however, at least for a certain time; and he remained. He served the Church with his experience, his advice, his competence. I am grateful to him for this. And I cannot but express my regret that this cooperation has been interrupted so suddenly.

3. At this moment, it is difficult to consider the whole life of the deceased. Our frequent meetings go back to the

times of the Second Vatican Council in which he was very active in the capacity of Under-Secretary. Following upon the death of his predecessor, he was called to the archepiscopal see of Lyons, and also entered the College of Cardinals. After the Council, he was called to enter the direct service of the Holy See as Prefect of the Sacred Congregation for the Clergy. In May, 1969, Pope Paul VI called him to the office of his Secretary of State.

He brought to this key post his pastoral experience as a bishop and before that as a priest, matured in long years of service of the Church in France, which boasts the title of "firstborn daughter of the universal Church."

In the future, biographers will show us the life and work of Cardinal Giovanni Villot in all their fullness. Today, allow us to repeat only the words of the Gospel: "If any one serves me, he must follow me; and where I am, there shall my servant be also; if any one serves me, the Father will honor him" (Jn. 12:26). Just so. This one thing only is important; it is, in fact, the essential thing. He followed Christ. He was always there where He called him. He served. The measure of his whole life is in this service.

4. The measure of life. Yes. This life has already its measure. It is already completed, it has reached its end. We are in the presence of this completion. And in this consists the grandeur of the moment we are living now, the dignity of this meeting in which are fulfilled, in our brother, the Lord's words: "Unless a grain of wheat falls into the earth and dies, it remains alone; but if it dies, it bears much fruit" (Jn. 12:24). Only then. When it dies.... It is necessary to die in order that man's life may bear full fruit. The hour has come in which Cardinal Giovanni Villot's life can produce its full fruit in God. No life of man in his earthly dimensions can bear such fruit; and it is a fruit that goes beyond life, exclaiming: "I know that my Redeemer lives," as Job exclaimed in his ordeal (cf. Job 19:25).

5. Death is always man's last experience, and it is inescapable. A difficult experience, before which the human soul feels fear. Did not Christ Himself say: "Now is

my soul troubled. And what shall I say, 'Father, save me from this hour'? And he added at once: 'No, for this purpose I have come to this hour. Father, glorify your name' " (Jn. 12:27).

Father, glorify!

There remains that last cry of the soul, in such contrast with the experience of death, with the experience of the destruction of the body, in which "the whole creation has been groaning in travail together until now"! (Rom. 8:22) Yet, groaning and suffering the pains of death, it does not cease to wait "with eager longing for the revealing of the sons of God" (Rom. 8:19). And we know "that the sufferings of this present time are not worth comparing with the glory that is to be revealed to us" (Rom. 8:18).

Let us too, then, before this coffin, in the spirit of that special communion that united us, give expression to these desires:

Father, forgive! Father, absolve! Father, purify! Purify in the measure of the holiness of Your face.

And finally: Father, glorify!

With all humility, but at the same time with all the realism of our faith and hope, let us raise this prayer beside the coffin of our brother, Cardinal Giovanni Villot, Secretary of State.

Like Jesus Who Came To Serve

On March 15, 1979, the Holy Father received in audience a group of deacons from the Archdiocese of Milan, led by the Auxiliary Bishop and Rector of the diocesan Seminary, Monsignor Bernardo Citterio. John Paul II delivered the following address.

Beloved deacons of the Archdiocese of Milan!

I complied very willingly with your desire to have a special meeting with me, as your rector, Bishop Bernardo Citterio who accompanies you today, had communicated some time ago.

I greet you all, therefore, with particular affection, seeing in you the younger recruits, who are about to be brought in as workers to that elect portion of the Lord's vineyard which is the Church of Milan.

My word, in this circumstance, cannot but be of satisfaction and joy at this truly ecclesial event, but also of encouragement and exhortation to show that you are not only worthy of your call, but also generous in responding to divine grace.

As you well know, "deacon" means "minister," that is, "servant." And this is a fundamental and stable qualification which marks you irrevocably; you will not renounce it, on the contrary, you will stress it still more when you become priests in a few months with the laying on of hands of your archbishop. Let the "ministry" really be the definition of your life: as it was for Jesus, who "came not to be served but to serve" (Mk. 10:45), or as for Barnabas and Paul, whom the ancient Council of Jerusalem described as "men who have risked their lives for the sake of our Lord Jesus Christ" (Acts 15:26).

It is to each of you that the Lord intends to repeat: "Where I am, there shall my *diakonos* be also" (Jn. 12:26). And where is Jesus? Today as then, He is on various fronts: in the celebration of the Eucharist and consequent sacramental presence, in the proclamation of the Gospel, in the daily necessities of the poor, in the Christian community which is His body, in the Successors of His Apostles. All these functions or spheres of the life of the Church must find you, too, present, ready, completely available and joyful. May it never happen to you to be reproved by your own community, as happened to the unknown Archippus, to whom, according to Paul's testimony, the faithful had to say: "See that you fulfill the ministry which you have received in the Lord" (Col. 4:17).

Complete dedication to your pastoral duty, made in a disinterested spirit and in joy, will be the best witness you can bear: the witness that the Lord and the Church expect of you; and at the same time, it will mark the success of your life.

May my fatherly apostolic blessing, which desires to be a cordial token of these wishes, accompany you always.

Colleges and Seminaries as Real Upper Rooms

On March 16, 1979, the Holy Father received in audience numerous rectors of Ecclesiastical Colleges in Rome who have met in these days to discuss the subject: "Our young people in the context of youth today." The Holy Father delivered the following address.

Beloved brothers!

At the conclusion of your annual meeting you wished to meet the Pope, to receive from him a word of encouragement and guidance. I must tell you that I, too, have desired this meeting in order to get to know you personally, to express to you my deep gratitude for the delicate ministry you carry out as rectors of the Ecclesiastical Colleges of Rome, and to communicate some reflections to you, simply and sincerely.

SENSE OF THE CHURCH

1. In these two days of your meeting you have meditated on, and studied together, the subject: "Our young people in the context of youth today," analyzing it from various aspects.

Let the students of your colleges—seminarians or young priests—coming from all the continents, be formed first and foremost to a deep *sense of the Church*. They must love the Church intensely as "Christ loved the church and gave himself up for her" (cf. Eph. 5:25). The Second Vatican Council did not fail to inculcate this fundamental element for the priest's formation: "The students should be thoroughly penetrated with a sense of the mystery of the Church, which this holy Council has set particularly in relief. Their sense of the Church will find expression in a humble and filial attachment to the Vicar of Christ and, after ordination, in their loyal cooperation with the bishop, in harmony with their fellow priests. By this means they will bear witness to that unity which draws men to Christ" (OT 9). Love for the Church, our Mother, which is manifested concretely in responsible and effective personal action, in order that she may show herself, and always be, "in splendor, without spot or wrinkle or any such thing, that she might be holy and without blemish" (Eph. 5:27). The holier the seminarians and the priests are, the holier the Church will be.

GIFT OF PROVIDENCE

2. Your students come from all over the world to this city of Rome, the geographical center of Catholicism. They bear within them their temperament, their original culture, their diversified historical experiences, their desire to prepare themselves, in the diocese of Peter's Successor, for the future ministry. This they will carry out in their dioceses and in their nations, after having enriched themselves with the great religious and cultural values which the city has accumulated in the centuries and continues to offer to souls desirous of truth, goodness and beauty. The experience of the stay in Rome is for a seminarian or for a young priest a real gift of Providence: the prayerful visits to its splendid basilicas, to the catacombs, to the tombs of the innumerable martyrs and saints, to the monuments of its age-old history, specialized study at the pontifical universities, the stay in the ecclesiastical colleges: all this has a deep impact on the personality and development of a young man.

I hope that your students will be able, with sound discernment, to collect and treasure all these elements for their own human and priestly formation. But, on the other hand, I also hope that Rome will always be able to offer these spiritual riches and never disappoint the expectations and hopes of these young people, and not distort or destroy the image they had formed of it. May they be able to make their own, and repeat of the diocese of Rome, the words that St. Ignatius of Antioch addressed to it with fervent enthusiasm: "The Church, beloved and illuminated in the will of Him who willed all things that exist,... worthy of God, veneration and praise" *(Letter to the Romans,* Introd.).

AN INTIMATE SPIRIT

3. I would like, finally, to express the sincere hope that the community life practiced in the ecclesiastical colleges will not be reduced to a mere set of exterior relations, but that it will imitate the spirit that animated that of the Apostles and of the first disciples in the Upper Room: "All these...devoted themselves to prayer, together with... Mary the Mother of Jesus" (Acts 1:14). This is just what the seminaries, colleges, and ecclesiastical boarding schools of Rome must be: real Upper Rooms, in which a life of intense personal and community prayer is breathed; a life of reciprocal, active and hard-working charity; a life of mutual spiritual aid to be always faithful to one's vocation and to the sacred commitments assumed before God, the Church, and one's own conscience.

And let the young be able to perceive and discover in you rectors not only the superior who must concern himself with the smooth, orderly, and disciplined running of a house, but the serene guide, the father, the brother, the friend, and, above all, the priest, who, in his behavior, irradiates the presence of Christ (cf. Gal. 2:20).

With these wishes, I willingly impart a special apostolic blessing to all of you and to the young people of your colleges.

"Stewards of the Mysteries of God"

On March 17, 1979, the Holy Father received in audience the superiors and pupils of the Pontifical Ecclesiastical Academy and delivered the following address.

I wish to express my satisfaction with you, dear pupils of the Pontifical Ecclesiastical Academy, gathered here—led by your president, Most Reverend Cesare Zacchi—to manifest to the Vicar of Christ sentiments of devotion and your priestly promise of faithfulness.

I thank you for the generous gift of your youth to the Church and to her visible head, and I am happy to talk to you, dear priests, like a father among his sons, in an atmosphere of cordiality and simplicity, to you who have begun or have completed the courses of preparation for service of the Holy See in the Pontifical Representations. It is natural that the Pope should love to express to you his expectations and hopes, and want to encourage you vigorously to undertake, in a spirit of faith and trusting abandonment in the Lord, the apostolic labors that are waiting for you.

Yours, in fact, will be an eminently pastoral service, a direct *diakonia* for the good of the local Churches, with a view to making their union with the apostolic See more and more operative. The Pontifical Representative and his collaborators must be, in the different countries, the visible testimony, as it were, of the presence of him who has been chosen, in Peter's succession, to be the foundation of unity and the center of cohesion of the whole Church, and has received the charism of strengthening his brothers (Lk. 22:32).

Therefore, in the accomplishment of your work, which is not without sacrifices, nearly always hidden, and sometimes not sufficiently appreciated, keep in mind that you are "servants of Christ and stewards of the mysteries of God" (1 Cor. 4:1) in the specific and delicate task of giving a perceptible voice, in the different parts of the world, to him whom Jesus willed to be the rock of the Church.

It is easy to understand, then, how the Holy See follows with solicitude your cultural preparation, with the intention of ensuring for you easy possession of all those instruments, notions, and knowledge which will be necessary for the exercise of your apostolate. However, what is important above all, for the Pope and for this apostolic See, is your sanctification; your exemplary priestly life, animated by deep convictions of faith, by a vision of the world and of history that is always theological, because the priest, as I said recently to the parish priests and clergy of Rome, "is placed at the very center of the mystery of Christ, who constantly embraces humanity and the world, the visible and invisible creation." You will not be able to carry out your particular ministry fruitfully if your heart is not full of the dedication of Christ, in order to act, you too, *in persona Christi*, for the salvation of brothers. Human knowledge, necessary though it is, of the languages, the customs, the traditions and the history of the peoples whom you approach, would be vain and ineffective, if you did not bring in your heart the spirit of Christ who, in adherence to the Father's plan of salvation, gave Himself for us.

I wish to address a special wish to those of you who are about to leave the Academy to assume, before long, your first office in the various Pontifical Representations. May the Lord sustain your work with His grace; the Pope, be certain, accompanies you with his benevolence, his affection and his prayer.

Invoking on all the protection of the Blessed Virgin, I willingly and gratefully bless your beloved president, his collaborators, the whole teaching staff and each of you, with particular warmth, together with your families, as a token of abundant heavenly gifts and consolations.

Hope for a Luminous Future of Evangelization

The Holy Father sent the following letter of March 23, 1979, to the Council of Presidency of CELAM, expressing his satisfaction at the results reached by the Puebla Conference and hoping for a luminous future for evangelization in Latin American countries.

Beloved brothers in the episcopate,

The intense work of the Third General Conference of the Latin American Episcopate, which I had the privilege of inaugurating personally and which I followed with particular love and interest with regard to the Church of this continent in the different stages of its development, is condensed in these pages which you have laid in my hands.

I remember vividly and with great pleasure my meeting with you, united in the same love and solicitude for your peoples, in the Basilica of Our Lady of Guadalupe and then in the seminary of Puebla.

This document, the fruit of assiduous prayer, deep reflection, and intense apostolic zeal, offers—as you intended—a rich set of pastoral and doctrinal guidelines on questions of supreme importance. It must serve, with its precious criteria, as a light and permanent stimulus for evangelizing in the present and future of Latin America.

You can feel satisfied and optimistic at the results of this conference, carefully prepared by CELAM with the jointly responsible participation of all the episcopal conferences. The Church of Latin America has been strengthened in its vigorous unity, in its own identity, in the determination to meet the needs and the challenges attentively considered throughout your assembly. It really represents a great step forward in the essential mission of the Church, that of evangelizing.

Your experiences, rules, concerns and aspirations, in faithfulness to the Lord, to His Church and to Peter's See, must become life for the communities which you serve.

For this reason you will have to propose in all your episcopal conferences and particular Churches plans with concrete goals, at the corresponding levels and in harmony with CELAM in the continental sphere.

God grant that all ecclesial communities will soon be informed and penetrated by the spirit of Puebla and the directives of this historic conference.

May the Lord Jesus, the Evangelizer *par excellence*, and Himself the Good Tidings, bless you abundantly.

May the Blessed Virgin, Mother of the Church and Star of evangelization, guide your steps in a renewed evangelizing impulse of the Latin American continent.

The Gift of the Priestly Vocation

On March 31, 1979, John Paul II met again his old fellow-students of the Belgian College. The Pope concelebrated a Mass with twenty-two of them and delivered the following homily.

Dear friends,

The Eucharist we are celebrating together is the sign of particular unity with Christ, the one eternal Priest, who "entered once for all into the Holy Place, taking...his own blood" (Heb. 9:12). The same Christ is always present in the Church "to the close of the age" (Mt. 28:20). He dwells in her, gathering the People of God round the table of the Word and of the Eucharist. He dwells in her through our priestly service.

When we find ourselves around the altar in this way today, in this communion that we initiated formerly at the Belgian College in Rome, our hearts are then filled with gratitude for the gift of the priestly vocation, because He has chosen us so that we may go and bear fruit (Jn. 15:16), because, entrusting His mysteries to us, He has entrusted to us men who have "redemption through his blood" (Eph. 1:7). Looking at all that with the eyes of faith, we feel our worthlessness, and we are always ready to repeat: "We are unworthy servants." (Lk. 17:10). We always feel, too, the greatness of God, and we thank God for this gift. "O give thanks to the Lord, for he is good" (Ps. 106:1).

Today, we wish to address this gratitude to one another. The Lord wishes us to know how to be grateful to men, to look at our life from the point of view of the gifts received through men, our brothers. Thus I would like today, with you, to look back on those years which gathered us within the walls of the old Belgian College, situated at 26 Via del Quirinale, in the neighborhood of St. Andrew's Church where St. Stanislaus Kostka, the patron saint of youth, died and rests.

Some thirty years separate us from that time. One might yield to the laws of time which bring us, among other things, to forgetfulness. But the voice of the heart is stronger, which asks us to keep things in our memory and think of them again with gratitude. Today we thank Christ who bestowed on us the grace of being together, in this important period of our lives, when we were still in the first years of our priesthood or preparing for it. *"Ecce quam bonum et quam iucundum habitare fratres in unum":* "Behold, how good and pleasant it is when brothers dwell in unity!" (Ps. 133:1)

We thank God for having let us be brothers for one another, and our gratitude is also reciprocal among us. He let us live this brotherhood which unites men coming from different families, different nations, different continents, for that was how He gathered us then. We say: Thanks for what each one was for the others at that time and for what everyone was for everyone. Thanks for the way we shared with others our qualities of intelligence, character and heart. Thanks for the place that the studies then in progress had, in this mutual exchange, as well as the apostolic and pastoral experiences in which each one of us was already engaged. Thanks for what sacred Rome was for us, as we learned to know it systematically as the capital of antiquity and the capital of Christendom. Thanks for what was the experience of Europe, of the world, of each of our countries, which were then picking themselves up after the sufferings of the Second World War.

Let us think finally of what our superiors were for us: our revered rector, Cardinal de Furstenberg, who is present in our midst today; and also our bishops who came to see us, who visited us at the college, as well as other ecclesiastics, the apostles of their time, such as Father Cardijn, not to mention the learned professors, the preachers of retreats, the directors of conscience: What have they been for us?

We want to speak of all that, in the first place, to Christ Himself, beginning with this concelebration, this liturgy. And this concelebration permits us also to express ourselves to one another. We also wish to renew this spirit that we received through the "laying on of hands" (cf. 2 Tm. 1:6), and this union of hearts, the secret of which the Lord Himself knows. Amen!

Real Scientific Formation in Priestly Formation

On April 3, 1979, the Holy Father received in audience rectors, professors, and pupils of the pontifical universities, seminaries, and ecclesiastical hostels and colleges, in the presence of Cardinals, bishops and officials of the Sacred Congregation for Catholic Education, which is celebrating its plenary meeting these days.
John Paul II delivered the following address.

Beloved brothers and sons,

Allow me to address, in the first place, the Cardinal Prefect Gabriel-Marie Garrone, to whom I wish to express sincere thanks both for his presence, and for the noble words he has just pronounced. Everyone knows the commitment with which he has striven, for long years, as the principal person responsible for the guidance of the Sacred Congregation for Catholic Education. Well-known, too, is the contribution which he made, with the sensitiveness of a pastor attentive and open to the requirements of the new times, from the preparatory phase, to the Second Vatican Council. These are merits which I wish to acknowledge publicly today, while to the Cardinals who, as members of the same Congregation, have gathered for the annual plenary session, to the secretary, and to the under-secretary, I extend my deepest gratitude. I then address my cordial greeting to the professors, superiors, and students of the Roman centers of academic studies.

OF SPECIAL CONCERN

At the opening of the meeting, I would like to start with a personal reference: for several years I had the opportunity to take part in the work of the Sacred Congregation, and it was a very precious experience for me. Because not only did I draw great benefit from it, but, at the same time, I was able to compare it with experiences in my field of pastoral work in Poland.

As you well know, Catholic schools of every order and level are the object of the concern of this Congregation; but the ecclesiastical seminaries are the object of very special concern. This immediately brings up the serious and delicate problem of priestly vocations, without forgetting, of course, the problem of the superior institutes of various types: the universities, theological faculties, the other faculties of ecclesiastical studies, etc. And also in this connection, I must recall that I took part in the important work of the Congregation for the preparation of the new Apostolic Constitution, which will replace—as a legislative document—the Constitution *Deus scientiarum Dominus.* On the basis of the mandate of the Second Vatican Council, a "temporary" document had already been published in May, 1968: *Normae quaedam ad Constitutionem Apostolicam "Deus scientiarum Dominus" de studiis academicis ecclesiasticis recognoscendam.*

Subsequently, after consultation of all the sectors interested in doctrine and in Catholic teaching, abundant material has been collected to draw up the new Constitution, which will have to be promulgated shortly. Now— and this is a third premise of psychological and personal character—all the problems concerning Christian education, the particular significance of science in the historical experience of the Church, the present mission of the Church herself in this field, are subjects especially close and congenial to me. In fact, I greatly appreciate this sector of the Church's activity, because I have great esteem for human culture: *Genus humanum arte et ratione vivit.* If man—as I wrote in my first encyclical—is "the primary and fundamental way for the Church" (cf. RH, III, 14), how could the latter not take an interest in what, even at the simple natural level, is directly connected with the elevation of man? How could she remain extraneous to the needs and the ferments, the labor and the goals, the difficulties and the achievements of culture today? Would not such a lack of interest and extraneousness be almost a shirking of her own responsibilities and an act of omission owing to the *vulnus* that would result in her own evangelizing function? Interpreting the supreme command of Christ, I am of the opinion that the pregnant significance and the multiple implication of the words *docete* and *docentes* (cf. Mt. 28:18-19; in the Greek text *matheteúsate* and *didáskontes)* are never stressed enough.

You understand, therefore, how, according to such a broad and high perspective, today's meeting takes place not only with you here present, but, at least indirectly and certainly intentionally, includes teachers and students of all Catholic institutes of instruction and education, scattered all over the world. Their tasks, their mission, their "creative" contribution to the universal mission of the Church, are, as it were, the background to this solemn audience today.

ESTEEM AND CONFIDENCE

2. In a more immediate and direct environment, however, the audience gathers a select and large group of representatives of the superior institutes of Rome, and that gives me great joy. I desired this meeting deeply, and I am happy that it takes place just at the time when the Cardinals and other representatives of the episcopate are gathered for the annual session at the Sacred Congrega-

tion, which is in charge of the organization and animation of the mission of the Church in the scientific and educational field.

The initiative for our meeting came from the rectors of the Roman institutes, with whom I have already had an opportunity to discuss the preliminaries of problems so important for the life of the Church in the Eternal City. These institutes, in fact, represent a special wealth of this Church: On the one hand, they welcome a large group of professors, scientists, and scholars who, thanks to their intelligence and their preparation, do honor to doctrine and to the Faith; on the other hand, they are open to students all over the world, and constitute, therefore, a significant and inspiring "sample" of the nationalities, languages, cultural elements and ritual varieties of the Catholic world. For this reason, and not only now, they have won well-deserved international recognition.

As for me, I wish to name them separately here, as a proof of my esteem and confidence in them, and these sentiments are intended to confirm and extend in time—I would say—those of so many Predecessors of mine on Peter's Chair. Here, in the first place, is the group of universities that bear the title "Pontifical": the Gregorian, entrusted to the sons of St. Ignatius and rich in a centuries-old and well-tested teaching and scientific experience; the Lateran which, being close, and not just topographically, to St. John's Patriarchal Basilica and the Major Seminary of Rome, has a typical Roman character and a special function; then the Urbanian University, intended specifically for the primary cause of evangelization and for the formation of the clergy for the missions; and then the University of St. Thomas Aquinas, known as the *Angelicum*, at which I had the good fortune to attend an industrious two years' course, which I have always remembered; and finally the Salesian which, though recently founded, wishes to win recognition with a note of originality in the area of the pedagogical disciplines.

QUALIFIED FORCES

There follow the Anselmian and Antonian *Pontifical Athenaea*, directed by the religious of St. Benedict and St. Francis. Then, further, the Biblical and the Oriental *Institutes* and the *Institutes* for Sacred Music and Christian Archaeology. And finally the *Theological Faculties* of St. Bonaventure, *Teresianum, Marianum.* Including also the Institute of Arabic Studies and the *Auxilium* Faculty, the Academic Centers existing in Rome amount altogether to 16, with a total number of over 950 lecturers and about 7,000 matriculated students. Are they many, are they few? Beyond the quantitative datum, which is variable in itself and, in any case, not absolute, there is the grandiose and consoling panorama of a whole series of *living and highly qualified forces;* there is the *reality of wealth* which, before being cultural and doctrinal, is of a spiritual nature; *this admirable complex of didactic structures* is at the disposal not only of the Catholic Church, but also of the human society which the Church is called to serve.

To confirm the prestige and the further potentialities of these forces, it is sufficient to draw attention to two facts:

a) The first is the multiplicity of the *scientific specializations,* which exist within these same centers. It is not possible to talk of duplication or of useless schools, because, if the schema of the fundamental sacred disciplines (beginning with the queen-science, theology) is found and functions—as is obvious—in them all, there is in each one a characteristic note, as it were, such as to give it an original place in the general framework of ecclesiastical studies. I am thinking, in this connection, of the various "specialties" and "superior schools" of modern conception, which have been created, with brilliant intuition, in more recent years. This is a response to the cultural growth of the world.

b) The other fact that I wish to recall in terms of praise is that the above-mentioned "specialties" and, therefore, the specialized institutes in question, are available for a fruitful collaboration with other "specialties" and institutes. In this way, to the objective requirement, which today is emerging more and more in scientific activity and methodology—*the requirement of so-called interdisciplinarity*—and to the need of avoiding cultural particularism and fragmentation, you have likewise responded with open, intelligent, generous, and fruitful collaboration. And it is a pleasure for me to recognize the importance of this active cultural exchange, which means improving the coordination of initiatives, a timely comparison of results, and balanced assignment of the researches to be carried out. All that, while it promotes the general increase of good studies, also multiplies contacts between persons to their mutual advantage, stimulates integration among the various institutes, and bears witness to the liveliness and vitality of the pace of studies within the Church.

REAL SCIENTIFIC FORMATION

3. But at this point, I would like to emphasize above all the importance of a *real scientific formation in priestly formation as a whole,* as I recall also in the Letter that I will address to priests for the forthcoming Holy Thursday. If the Church sets such store by the promotion of higher studies and, therefore, the preparation of adequate structures, she does so "ultimately" to carry out better her mission in the world and to serve the cause of man better. But she does so "directly" to prepare those to whom, to such a large extent, this mission and this service are delegated: that is, the priests. To be complete and adapted to the requirements of the times, the formation of priests must also be scientific.

And the reason, or rather, reasons for this more demanding preparation are so evident that all explanation seems to me superfluous. Necessary, first and foremost, in the sacred ministries is a *sound general culture,* as a fruitful and receptive soil for new seeds, admitting of more luxuriant developments. Then they must be started on their way and helped to reach a *real and proper specialization at the university level*, which will make them capable of taking part in the creative processes of culture in any type of society in which the Church finds herself carrying out her mission (cf. OT 38).

Here, then, are the two elements of this formation: general culture and specialized culture. Actually, the necessity of a rich doctrinal store for the formation of a mature priestly personality, such as is suitable for one who must be a pastor and teacher and is called to carry out multiform services connected with the vocation of the priest, pastor, and teacher, can never be sufficiently stressed.

BASED ON "SCIENCE OF FAITH"

Today this is a task of unusual and great responsibility. We need men with a deep knowledge of the problems of man and of the world. But this knowledge cannot stop at the purely human and secular level: It will have to be based, above all, on the "science of faith." It will have, in fact, to spring from a precise attitude of faith, from an active exercise of faith, which means communion and conversation with the Word of God, the Teacher who teaches and dictates "ab intus": *Ille., qui consulitur, docet, qui in interiore homine habitare dictus est Christus, id est incommutabilis Dei Virtus atque sempiterna Sapientia* (St. Augustine, *De Magistro* 11, 38; P.L. 32, 1216; cf. Eph. 3:16; 1 Cor. 1:24). We need priests endowed with a sound theological sense, listening attentively to Holy Scripture, Tradition, and the Magisterium. We need priests who, teaching faith and morality, will construct and not destroy. All this presupposes doctrinal completeness, intellectual honesty, faithful adherence to the "sacred deposit," awareness of participation in the "prophetic function" of Christ: in a word, a maturity of superior quality is necessary.

"EXISTENCE OF ROME"

4. In this vast set of problems, reference to which would deserve a far longer development, I wish to point out another aspect. I consider, in fact, that special attention must be paid to the "existence of Rome," as an element of that formation which brings to every local Church a wholesome and extremely fruitful leaven of universality. Saying this, I draw on the memories of the time of my studies in Rome and also of the experiences I had during my subsequent contacts with "sacred Rome," which offers vital sap and nourishment to every Christian, and particularly to every priest. What does Rome teach? *Hic saxa ipsa loquuntur*, it can rightly be said. Oh, it is not rhetorical to lay stress on this historico-environmental fact: Rome, a unique city in the world, is the center of irradiation of Christian faith. It is necessary, therefore, to be aware of this fact, it is necessary to be worthy of it; it is necessary to respond to—and to collaborate with—the exemplary function that is incumbent on Rome with regard to the whole Catholic world. And you young people, who have the fortune to study in Rome, must "profit" by this stay and by the teaching that is imparted to you here. You must draw firmness of faith and breadth of perspectives from the memories that the witness of the Apostles Peter and Paul, the blood of the innumerable martyrs, the vestiges of a religious situation that is now bimillenary, have concentrated here.

FERVENT GOOD WISHES

5. It is in this spirit that, as Easter draws near, I address my confident good wishes to all members of the superior institutes. And it is in this spirit that I express my fervent good wishes to the Congregation for Catholic Education, to its venerated and well-deserving Prefect, to the Cardinals and Bishops. To one and all, connected by a commitment which, though having different expressions and forms, is in purpose unitarian because it is directed to

the same goal, I recommend to live this solemn hour of the Church with attentive and clear awareness (cf. RH I, 1). As mankind is approaching the year two thousand, it is not permissible for the People of God to delay, to stop, or to move back. The Church must walk in history with her eyes turned backwards *(Ecclesia retro-oculata)* and at the same time forwards *(Ecclesia ante-oculata)*, but, above all, fixed upwards towards Christ, her Lord *(Ecclesia supra-oculata): levatis ad Dominum oculis....* It is from above, in fact, it is from Him that she gets inspiration, strength, resistance, courage. And how could the members of the People of God remain inactive?

RECALL THE 1971 SYNOD

Beloved brothers and sons, the post-conciliar period brought with it a set of questions for the Church, as if continuing the fundamental questions of the Second Vatican Council: *Ecclesia Dei, quid dicis de te ipsa?* Now it would be a form of reticence not to speak of the crisis that occurred; or to deny, for example, that certain questions were sometimes raised in a "radical" form and assumed a character of "contestation"; or to ignore that the latter, among other things, concerned and almost attacked the ministerial priesthood, the priestly vocation, as well as the seminary as an institution. There is no need, moreover, to recall the heat of some debates and polemics. Yet so many discussions have brought about opportune clarifications and definitions. After study of those problems had been resumed—let it suffice to think of the 1971 Synod—after the objections or the new elements of the various questions had been thoroughly examined, things returned to their proper places, and significant confirmations have been derived. It can be said that, thanks to this critical and self-critical effort, we are already beginning to pass from the "negative" phase to a "positive" implementation of Vatican II, that is, to that authentic renewal or *aggiornamento* which was among the aims of the lovable Pontiff who courageously decided on it.

HOLY VOCATIONS

With all those present I pray to the Lord Jesus, in His Paschal Mystery, in order that such a renewal may be manifested in the vast sector of education and instruction, in particular by means of a new flourishing of holy vocations in all the local Churches. I say priestly, religious, and missionary vocations: vocations that are mature thanks to the institutions in question, that is, seminaries, studentates and university centers; vocations mature with that maturity of which witnesses to the Gospel have need in our times which are so difficult and heavy with responsibilities. *Spes non confundit!* (Rom. 5:5) Not all the difficulties are overcome, but it is now time to go on our way, with hope that is never disappointed, relying on the unfailing help of Him who, if He entrusted the Church to men, guaranteed that He would not abandon them: *Ecce ego vobiscum sum omnibus diebus* (Mt. 28:20). With an expression that was dear to my Predecessor and Father, Paul VI, I will therefore say: Onward in the Lord's name and with my affectionate blessing!

Courage and Consistency in Apostolic Work

On April 6, 1979, John Paul II received in audience a group of Hungarian bishops, priests, and faithful gathered in Rome to take part in the solemn celebrations for the fourth centenary of the foundation of the Germanic-Hungarian College and for the fiftieth anniversary of the Hungarian Ecclesiastical Institute. The group was led by the Cardinal Primate of Hungary, László Lékai. The Holy Father delivered the following address.

Revered and dear brothers,

1. I cannot but manifest to you the deep joy I feel today at my first meeting with such a large group of prelates, priests, and faithful, led by Cardinal László Lékai, gathered in Rome for the fourth centenary of the foundation of the Germanic-Hungarian College.

This date was already solemnly celebrated last Sunday in the presence of Cardinals and prelates, high Hungarian authorities, the Ambassadors of the Federal Republic of Germany and of Austria, and other personalities. The high mission carried out, for centuries, by the Germanic-Hungarian College in forming holy and learned priests, who not infrequently rose to high responsibilities in the Church, was recalled on that occasion.

As is known, in 1579 my Predecessor, Gregory XIII, founded the Hungarian College. Shortly before, in the year 1573, he had set up the new Germanic College, associating himself ideally with an intention of St. Ignatius of Loyola.

Since the Hungarian College could not be endowed with sufficient means, the Pope, in the year following its foundation, that is, in 1580, united it with the Germanic College and gave instructions to the Apostolic Nuncio Malaspina to send twelve students to Rome from Hungary. But the Pontifical Representative was able to send only one, since your nation was under foreign occupation at that time.

A great many zealous priests, and also bishops of high prestige, came out of this college: Let it suffice to mention the great personalities of Emeric Losy, George Lippay, George Szelepczenyi, who, in the seventeenth century, organized the life of the Church, then afflicted by divisions. I do not want to pass over in silence the figure of Benedict Kisdy, whose admirable hymns still ring out in your churches. But above them all towers the great thinker, theologian, and orator of last century, Otokar Prolaszka, Bishop of Szekesfehérvár.

This mission, as regards Hungary, has been interrupted for some time; but there is news that it will resume in the near future. I therefore formulate fervent wishes that the Hungarian priests who are formed in the Germanic-Hungarian College will be a glory for the Church and for their country.

I greet particularly the aforesaid Cardinal Primate, my confreres in the episcopate, and all the other former students of the Germanic-Hungarian College, present here or who have remained in Hungary.

But in these days you are also celebrating the fiftieth anniversary of the opening in Rome of the Hungarian Ecclesiastical Institute, which received the seal of the approval of the Holy See in 1940.

I am happy to recall that, also in this institute, hosts of priests have been educated and formed for the good of the Church and of their country. I have pleasure in greeting the prelates, former pupils or also rectors of the institute; and with them I intend to greet, with esteem and affection, all the priests who attended the Hungarian Ecclesiastical Institute in Rome.

The Church, Mother and Teacher, has the right and the duty to found and direct institutes, in which she can form and educate her children in full freedom. "Holy Mother Church," the Second Vatican Council affirms, "in order to fulfill the mandate she received from her divine Founder to announce the mystery of salvation to all men and to renew all things in Christ, is under an obligation to promote the welfare of the whole life of man, including his life in this world insofar as it is related to his heavenly vocation; she has, therefore, a part to play in the development and extension of education" (GE, Preface). And again: "...The sacred synod, therefore, affirms once more the right of the Church freely to establish and conduct schools of all kinds and grades, a right which has already been asserted time and again in many documents of the Magisterium. It emphasizes that the exercise of this right is of the utmost importance for the preservation of liberty of conscience, for the protection of the rights of parents, and for the advancement of culture itself" *(ibid.* 8).

The happy occasion of the fiftieth anniversary of the opening of your institute in Rome gives you and me the opportunity for a short reflection on the fundamental and primary importance, for the very life of the Church, of the formation of priests who are at the same time *holy;* that is, who live intensely in union with Christ (cf. Jn. 15:9f.), modeling their life on His (Gal. 2:20; Phil. 1:21) and carrying out day by day the demands, sometimes hard ones, of the Gospel (cf. Mt. 16:24; Mk. 8:34); and who are also *learned,* that is, with a deep knowledge of the Word of God, the Sacred Doctrine, the teaching of the Magisterium of the Church, and capable of communicating this teaching to enlighten and guide the faithful, thus proving to be true "Ministers of the Word" (cf. Lk. 1:2, Acts 6:4; 20:24; 2 Cor. 6:7; 2 Tm. 2:15).

I sincerely hope that the directors and teaching staff of the two institutes mentioned, as well as their students, are striving with all their might towards these aims, carrying out what the Second Vatican Council earnestly recommends, when it speaks of major seminaries and, therefore, also of ecclesiastical institutes: "In them the whole training of the students should have as its object to make them true shepherds of souls after the example of our Lord Jesus Christ, Teacher, Priest, and Shepherd. Hence, they should be trained for the ministry of the Word, so that they may gain an ever increasing understanding of the revealed Word of God, making it their own by meditation, and giving it expression in their speech and in their lives. They should be trained for the ministry of worship and sanctification, so that by prayer and the celebration of the sacred liturgical functions they may carry on the work of salvation through the Eucharistic Sacrifice and the sacraments. They should be trained to undertake the ministry of the shepherd, that they may know how to represent Christ to men" (cf. PT 4).

2. Faced with this qualified group of prelates, priests, and faithful of noble Hungary, there come, spontaneously, remembrance, admiration, and veneration of St. Stephen —the King who, between the tenth and the eleventh century, obtaining recognition of the kingdom from my Predecessor Sylvester II, started your glorious history and became, rightly, the father of the country, the apostle of

the Catholic Faith, and the founder of the Church in Hungary. Always be proud of this great saint, who was able to unite, in perfect harmony, consistency with the Christian faith, faithfulness to the Church, and love of his own nation!

I manifested my sentiments of good will and affection for you in my letter addressed on last December 2, to the Cardinal Primate, the prelates and, thereby, also to all my dear brothers and sons in Hungary. In this letter I wrote that I was convinced that the Catholic Church, which has had such an important part in Hungarian history, will be able, also in the future, to continue, in a certain sense, to mold the spiritual face of your country; irradiating on her sons and daughters that light of the Gospel of Christ, which has illuminated the lives of your fellow citizens for so many centuries.

At this meeting of ours, I wish to renew to you the expression of my sentiments, and urge you to continue to work, with zeal and dedication, always in harmony with one another. I have learned with deep satisfaction that you are dedicating yourselves, with special and increased commitment, to *the formation of youth.* This is a primary duty of the Church, which is aware that "young people exert a very important influence in modern society" (AA 12). They seek truth, solidarity and justice; they dream and wish to contribute to the construction of a better society, in which selfishness will be banned, but the originality and uniqueness of human persons respected; they seek a global and exhaustive answer to man's fundamental problems, such as those concerning the essential and existential meaning of life. Answer these demands, these questions of the young, with constant zeal, presenting to them Christ, His Person, His life, His message: a demanding one, it is true, but *charged with hope and love.* "Our spirit is set in one direction," I wrote recently, "the only direction for our intellect, will and heart is—towards Christ our Redeemer, towards Christ, the Redeemer of man. We wish to look towards Him—because there is salvation in no one else but

Him, the Son of God—repeating what Peter said: 'Lord, to whom shall we go? You have the words of eternal life,' (Jn. 6:68; cf. Acts 4:8-12)" (RH II, 7). Continue with these efforts of yours. The Lord will help you in every circumstance with His comfort and with His grace.

3. Concluding this meeting, I address an affectionate greeting to you present here, to your priests and faithful, and to all the other prelates, priests, and faithful of Hungary, the Kingdom of Mary. Always be firm in faith in God and in Christ (cf. 1 Cor. 16:13; Col. 1:23: 2:7; Heb. 4:14; 1 Pt. 5:9) and hand down clearly to future generations this incomparable gift of the Lord! (cf. Rom. 6:17; 1 Cor. 11:23; 15:3; 2 Tm. 2:2)

I invoke on your nation the motherly protection of the Blessed Virgin, its heavenly Queen; of holy King Stephen; of St. Elizabeth of Hungary, *pauperum consolatrix* and *famelicorum reparatrix*; of Blessed Hedwig, Queen of Poland, the splendid gift that your people bestowed on my country of origin in the fourteenth century; of all the saints, men and women, that Hungary has given, for the glory of God, to the Church and to the world.

My respectful greeting and good wishes are also addressed to the civil authorities, as to all Hungarians who do not share your faith.

To all of you, prelates, priests, men and women religious, and the faithful of Hungary, I impart an abundant apostolic blessing.

Letter to All the Bishops of the Church

ON THE OCCASION OF HOLY THURSDAY, 1979

Venerable brothers in the episcopate,

The great day is drawing near when we shall share in the liturgy of Holy Thursday together with our brothers in the priesthood and shall meditate together on the priceless gift in which we have become sharers by virtue of the call of Christ the eternal Priest. On that day, before we celebrate the liturgy *In Cena Domini*, we shall gather together in our cathedrals to renew before Him who became for us "obedient unto death"[1] in total self-giving to the Church, His spouse, our giving of ourselves to the exclusive service of Christ in His Church.

On this holy day, the liturgy takes us inside the Upper Room, where, with grateful heart, we set ourselves to listen to the words of the divine Teacher, words full of solicitude for every generation of bishops called, after the Apostles, to take upon themselves care for the Church, for the flock, for the vocation of the whole People of God, for the proclamation of God's Word, for the whole sacramental and moral order of Christian living, for priestly and religious vocations, for the fraternal spirit in the community. Christ says: "I will not leave you orphans; I will come back to you."[2] It is precisely this Sacred Triduum of the passion, death and resurrection of the Lord that re-evokes in us, in a vivid way, not only the memory of His departure, but also faith in His return, in His continuous coming. Indeed, what is the meaning of the words: "I am with you always; yes, to the end of time"?[3]

Venerable and dear brothers, in the spirit of this faith, which fills the entire Triduum, it is my desire that, in our vocation and our episcopal ministry, we should feel in a special way this year—the first of my pontificate—that unity which the Twelve shared in when together with our Lord they were assembled for the Last Supper. It was precisely there that they heard those words that were most complimentary and at the same time most binding: "I shall not call you servants any more, because a servant does not know his master's business; I call you friends, because I have made known to you everything I have learned from my Father. You did not choose me, no, I chose you; and I commissioned you to go out and to bear fruit, fruit that will last."[4]

Can anything be added to those words? Should one not rather pause in humility and gratitude before them, given the greatness of the mystery we are about to celebrate? There then takes root even deeper within us our awareness of the gift that we have received from the Lord through our vocation and our episcopal ordination. In fact the gift of the sacramental fullness of the priesthood is greater than all the toils and also all the sufferings involved in our pastoral ministry in the episcopate.

The Second Vatican Council reminded us and clearly showed us that this ministry, while being a personal duty of each one of us, is nevertheless something that we carry out in the brotherly communion of the whole of the Church's episcopal College or "body." While it is right that we should address every human being, and especially every Christian as "brother," this word takes on an altogether special meaning with regard to us bishops and our mutual relationships: in a certain sense it goes back directly to that brotherhood which gathered the Apostles about Christ; it goes back to that friendship with which Christ honored them and through which He united them to one another, as is attested by the words of John's Gospel quoted above.

Therefore, venerable and dear brothers, we must express the wish, today especially, that everything that the Second Vatican Council so wonderfully renewed in our awareness should take on an ever more mature character of collegiality, both as the principle of our collaboration *(collegialitas effectiva)* and as the character of a cordial fraternal bond *(collegialitas affectiva)*, in order to build up the Mystical Body of Christ and to deepen the unity of the whole People of God.

As you gather in your cathedrals, with the diocesan and religious priests who make up the *presbyterium* of your local Churches, your dioceses, you will receive from them—as is provided for—the renewal of the promises that they placed in the hands of you, the bishops, on the day of their priestly ordination. With this in mind, I am sending to the priests another letter that—as I hope—will enable you and them to live even more deeply this unity, this mysterious bond that joins us in the one priesthood of Jesus Christ, brought to completion with the sacrifice of the Cross, which merited for Him entrance "into the sanctuary."[5] Venerable brothers, I hope that these words of mine addressed to the priests, at the beginning of my ministry in the See of St. Peter, will also help you to strengthen ever more that communion and unity of the whole *presbyterium*[6] which have their basis in our collegial communion and unity in the Church.

And may there be a renewal of your love for the priests whom the Holy Spirit has given and entrusted to you as the closest collaborators in your pastoral office. Take care of them like beloved sons, brothers and friends. Be mindful of all their needs. Have particular solicitude for their spiritual advancement, for their perseverance in the grace of the sacrament of the priesthood. Since it is into your hands they make—and each year renew—their priestly promises, and especially the commitment to celibacy, do everything in your power to ensure that they remain faithful to these promises, as is demanded by the holy tradition of the Church, the tradition that sprang from the very spirit of the Gospel.

May this solicitude for our brothers in the priestly ministry also be extended to the seminaries, which constitute, in the Church as a whole and in each of her parts, an eloquent proof of her vitality and spiritual fruitfulness, which are expressed precisely in readiness to give oneself exclusively to the service of God and of souls. Today, every possible effort must again be made to encourage vocations, to form new generations of priests. This must be done in a genuinely evangelical spirit, and at the same time by "reading" properly the signs of the times, to which the Second Vatican Council gave such careful attention. The full reconstitution of the life of the seminaries throughout the Church will be the best proof of the achievement of the renewal to which the Council directed the Church.

Venerable and dear brothers: everything that I am writing to you, as I prepare to live Holy Thursday intensely —the "feast of priests"— I wish to link up closely with the desire that the Apostles heard expressed that day by the lips of their beloved Teacher: "Go out and bear fruit, fruit that will last."[7] We can bear this fruit only if we remain in Him: in the vine.[8] He told us this clearly in His words of farewell on the day before His Passover: "Whoever remains in me, with me in him, bears fruit in plenty; for cut off from me you can do nothing."[9] Beloved brothers, what more could I wish you, what more could we wish one another, than precisely this: to remain in Him, Jesus Christ, and to bear fruit, fruit that will last?

Accept these good wishes. Let us strive to deepen ever more our unity; let us strive to live ever more intensely the sacred Triduum of the Passover of our Lord Jesus Christ.

From the Vatican, April 8, Passion Sunday (Palm Sunday), in the year 1979, the first of the Pontificate.

Footnotes

1. Phil. 2:8.
2. Jn. 14:18.
3. Mt. 28:20.
4. Jn. 15:15-16.
5. Cf. Heb. 9:12.
6. Cf. LG 28.
7. Jn. 15:16.
8. Cf. Jn. 15:1-8.
9. Jn. 15:5.

Letter to All the Priests of the Church

ON THE OCCASION OF HOLY THURSDAY, 1979

Dear brother priests,

1. FOR YOU I AM A BISHOP, WITH YOU I AM A PRIEST

At the beginning of my new ministry in the Church, I feel the deep need to speak to you, to all of you without any exception, priests both diocesan and religious, who are my brothers by virtue of the sacrament of Orders. From the very beginning I wish to express my faith in the vocation that unites you to your bishops, in a special communion of sacrament and ministry, through which the Church, the Mystical Body of Christ, is built up. To all of you, therefore, who, by virtue of a special grace and through a singular gift of our Savior, bear "the burden of the day and the heat"[1]—in the midst of the many tasks of the priestly and pastoral ministry, I have addressed my thoughts and my heart from the moment when Christ called me to this See, where St. Peter, with his life and his death, had to respond until the end to the question: Do you love me? Do you love me more than these others do?[2]

I think of you all the time, I pray for you, with you *I seek the ways of spiritual union and collaboration*, because by virtue of the sacrament of Orders, which I also received from the hands of my bishop (the Metropolitan of Krakow, Cardinal Adam Stephen Sapieha, of unforgettable memory), you are my brothers. And so, adapting the words of St. Augustine,[3] I want to say to you today: "For you I am a bishop, with you I am a priest." Today, in fact, there is a special circumstance that impels me to confide to you some thoughts that I enclose in this Letter: It is the nearness of Holy Thursday. It is this, the annual feast of our priesthood, that unites the whole presbyterium of each diocese about its bishop in the shared celebration of the Eucharist. It is on this day that all priests are invited to renew, before their own bishop and together with him, the promises they made in their priestly ordination; and this fact enables me, together with all my brothers in the episcopate, to be joined to you in a special unity, and especially to be in the very heart of the mystery of Jesus Christ, the mystery in which we all share.

The Second Vatican Council, which so explicitly highlighted the collegiality of the episcopate in the Church, also gave a new form to the life of the priestly communities, joined together by a special bond of brotherhood, and united to the bishop of the respective local Church. The whole priestly life and ministry serve to deepen and strengthen that bond; and a particular responsibility for the various tasks involved by this life and ministry is taken on by the priests' councils, which, in conformity with the thought of the Council and the Motu Proprio *Ecclesiae sanctae*[4] of Paul VI, should be functioning in every diocese. All this is meant to ensure that each bishop, in union with his presbyterium, can serve ever more effectively the great cause of evangelization. Through this service the Church realizes her mission, indeed her very nature. The importance of the unity of the priests with their own bishop on this point is confirmed by the words of St. Ignatius of Antioch: "Strive to do all things in the harmony of God, with the bishop presiding to represent God, the presbyters representing the council of the Apostles, and the deacons, so dear to me, entrusted with the service of Jesus Christ."[5]

2. LOVE FOR CHRIST AND THE CHURCH UNITES US

It is not my intention to include in this Letter everything that makes up the richness of the priestly life and ministry. In this regard I refer to the whole tradition of the Magisterium and of the Church, and in a special way to the doctrine of the Second Vatican Council, contained in the Council's various documents, especially in the Constitution *Lumen gentium* and the Decrees *Presbyterorum ordinis* and *Ad gentes*. I also wish to recall the Encyclical of my Predecessor Paul VI, *Sacerdotalis caelibatus*. Finally, I wish to place great importance upon the Document *De sacerdotio ministeriali*, which Paul VI approved as the fruit of the labors of the 1971 Synod of Bishops, because I find in this document—although the session of the Synod that elaborated it had only a consultative form—a statement of essential importance regarding the specific aspect of the priestly life and ministry in the modern world.

Referring to all these sources, which you are familiar with, I wish in the present Letter *only to mention a number of points* which seem to me to be of extreme importance at this moment in the history of the Church and of the world. These are words that are dictated to me by my love for the Church, which will be able to carry out her mission to the world only if—in spite of all human weakness—she maintains her fidelity to Christ. I know that I am addressing those whom only the love of Christ has enabled, by means of a specific vocation, to give themselves to the service of the Church and, in the Church, to the service of man for the solution of the most important problems, and especially those regarding man's eternal salvation.

Although at the beginning of these considerations I refer to many written sources and official documents, nevertheless I wish to refer especially to that living source which is our shared love for Christ and His Church, a love that springs from the grace of the priestly vocation, the love that is the greatest gift of the Holy Spirit.[6]

3. "CHOSEN FROM AMONG MEN... APPOINTED TO ACT ON BEHALF OF MEN"[7]

The Second Vatican Council deepened the idea of the priesthood and presented it, throughout its teaching, as the expression of the inner forces, those "dynamisms," whereby the mission of the whole People of God in the Church is constituted. Here one should refer especially to the Constitution *Lumen gentium*, and re-read carefully the relevant paragraphs. The mission of the People of God is carried out through the sharing in the office and mission of Jesus Christ Himself, which, as we know, has a triple dimension: it is the mission and office of Prophet, Priest and King. If we analyze carefully the conciliar texts, it is obvious that one should speak of a triple dimension of Christ's service and mission, rather than of three different functions. In fact, these functions are closely linked to one another, explain one another, condition one another and clarify one another. Consequently, it is from this threefold unity that our sharing in Christ's mission and office takes its origin. As Christians, members of the People of God, and subsequently, as priests, sharers in the hierarchical order, we take our origin from the combination of the mission and office of our Teacher who is Prophet, Priest and King, in order to witness to Him in a special way in the Church and before the world.

The priesthood in which we share through the sacrament of Orders, which has been for ever "imprinted" on our souls through a special sign from God, that is to say the "character," *remains in explicit relationship with the common priesthood of the faithful,* that is to say the priesthood of all the baptized, but at the same time it differs from that priesthood "essentially and not only in degree."[8] In this way the words of the author of the Letter to the Hebrews about the priest, who has been "chosen from among men...appointed to act on behalf of men,"[9] take on their full meaning.

At this point, it is better to re-read once more the whole of this classical conciliar text, which expresses the basic truths on the theme of our vocation in the Church:

> "Christ the Lord, high priest taken from among men (cf. Heb. 5:1), made the new people 'a kingdom of priests to God, his Father' (Rv. 1:6, cf. 5:9-10). The baptized, by

regeneration and the anointing of the Holy Spirit, are consecrated to be a spiritual house and a holy priesthood, that through all the works of Christian men they may offer spiritual sacrifices and proclaim the perfection of him who has called them out of darkness into his marvelous light (cf. 1 Pt. 2:4-10). Therefore all the disciples of Christ, persevering in prayer and praising God together (cf. Acts 2:42-47), should present themselves as a sacrifice, living, holy and pleasing to God (cf. Rom. 12:1). They should everywhere on earth bear witness to Christ and give an answer to everyone who asks a reason for the hope of an eternal life which is theirs (cf. 1 Pt. 3:15).

Though they differ essentially and not only in degree, the common priesthood of the faithful and the ministerial or hierarchical priesthood are nonetheless ordered one to another; each in its own proper way shares in the one priesthood of Christ. The ministerial priest, by the sacred power that he has, forms and rules the priestly people; in the person of Christ he effects the Eucharistic Sacrifice and offers it to God in the name of all the people. The faithful indeed, by virtue of their royal priesthood, participate in the offering of the Eucharist. They exercise that priesthood, too, by the reception of the sacraments, prayer and thanksgiving, the witness of a holy life, abnegation and active charity."[10]

4. THE PRIEST AS A GIFT OF CHRIST FOR THE COMMUNITY

We must consider down to the smallest detail not only the theoretical meaning but also the existential meaning of the mutual "relation" that exists between the hierarchical priesthood and the common priesthood of the faithful. The fact that they differ not only in degree but also in essence is a fruit of a particular aspect of the richness of the very priesthood of Christ, which is the one center and the one source both of that participation which belongs to all the baptized and of that other participation which is reached through a distinct sacrament, which is precisely the sacrament of Orders. This sacrament, dear brothers, which is specific for us, which is the fruit of the special grace of vocation and the basis of our identity, by virtue of its very nature and of everything that it produces in our life and activity, serves to make the faithful aware of their common priesthood and to activate it[11]: the sacrament reminds them that they are the People of God and enables them "to offer spiritual sacrifices,"[12] through which Christ Himself makes us an everlasting gift to the Father.[13] This takes place, above all, when the priest "by the sacred power that he has...in the person of Christ *(in persona Christi)* effects the Eucharistic Sacrifice and offers it to God in the name of all the people,"[14] as we read in the conciliar text quoted above.

Our sacramental priesthood, therefore, is a "hierarchical" and at the same time "ministerial" priesthood. It constitutes a special *ministerium*, that is to say "service," in relation to the community of believers. It does not however take its origin from that community, as though it were the community that "called" or "delegated." The sacramental priesthood is truly a gift for this community and comes from Christ Himself, from the fullness of His priesthood. This fullness finds its expression in the fact that Christ, while making everyone capable of offering the spiritual sacrifice, calls some and enables them to be ministers of His own sacramental Sacrifice, the Eucharist—in the offering of which all the faithful share —in which are taken up all the spiritual sacrifices of the People of God.

Conscious of this reality, we understand how our priesthood is "hierarchical," that is to say connected with the power of forming and governing the priestly people[15] and *precisely for this reason "ministerial."* We carry out this office, through which Christ Himself unceasingly "serves" the Father in the work of our salvation. Our whole priestly existence is and must be deeply imbued with this service, if we wish to effect in an adequate way the Eucharistic Sacrifice *in persona Christi.*

The priesthood calls for a particular integrity of life and service, and precisely such integrity is supremely fitting for our priestly identity. In that identity there are expressed, at the same time, the greatness of our dignity and the "availability" proportionate to it: It is a question of the humble readiness to accept the gifts of the Holy Spirit and to transmit to others the fruits of love and peace, to give them that certainty of faith from which derive the profound understanding of the meaning of human existence and the capacity to introduce the moral order into the life of individuals and of the human setting.

Since the priesthood is given to us so that we can unceasingly serve others, after the example of Christ the Lord, the priesthood cannot be renounced because of the difficulties that we meet and the sacrifices asked of us. Like the Apostles, we have left everything to follow Christ[16]; therefore, we must persevere beside Him also through the cross.

5. IN THE SERVICE OF THE GOOD SHEPHERD

As I write, there pass before the eyes of my soul the vast and varied areas of human life, areas into which you are sent, dear brothers, like laborers into the Lord's vineyard.[17] But for you there holds also the parable of the flock,[18] for, thanks to the priestly character, you share in the *pastoral charism*, which is a sign of a special relationship of *likeness to Christ, the Good Shepherd*. You are precisely marked with this quality in a very special way. Although care for the salvation of others is and must be a task of every member of the great community of the People of God, that is to say also of all our brothers and sisters who make up the laity—as the Second Vatican Council so amply declared[19]—nevertheless you priests are expected to have a care and commitment which are far greater and different from those of any lay person. And this is because your sharing in the priesthood of Jesus Christ differs from their sharing, "essentially and not only in degree."[20]

In fact, the priesthood of Jesus Christ is the first source and expression of an unceasing and ever effective care for our salvation, which enables us to look to Him precisely as the Good Shepherd. Do not the words "the good shepherd is one who lays down his life for his sheep"[21] refer to the sacrifice of the cross, to the definitive act of Christ's priesthood? Do they not show all of us that Christ the Lord, through the sacrament of Orders, has made us sharers in His priesthood, the road that we too must travel? Do these words not tell us that our vocation is a singular *solicitude for the salvation of our neighbor?* that this solicitude is a special *raison d'être* of our priestly life? that it is precisely this solicitude that gives it meaning, and that only through this solicitude can we find the full significance of our own life, perfection and holiness? This theme is taken up, at various places, in the conciliar Decree *Optatam totius.*[22]

However, this matter becomes more comprehensible in the light of the words of our same Teacher, who says: "For anyone who wants to save his life will lose it; but anyone who loses his life for my sake, and for the sake of the gospel, will save it."[23] These are mysterious words, and they seem like a paradox. But they cease to be mysterious if we try to put them into practice. Then the paradox disappears, and the profound simplicity of their meaning is fully revealed. May all of us be granted this grace in our priestly life and zealous service.

6. "THE SUPREME ART IS THE DIRECTION OF SOULS"[24]

The special care for the salvation of others, for truth, for the love and holiness of the whole People of God, for the spiritual unity of the Church—this care that has been entrusted to us by Christ, together with the priestly power, is exercised in various ways. Of course there is a difference in the ways in which you, dear brothers, fulfill your priestly vocation. Some in the ordinary pastoral work of parishes; others in mission lands; still others in the field of activities connected with the teaching, training and education of youth, or working in the various spheres and organizations whereby you assist in the development of social and cultural life; yet others near the suffering, the sick, the neglected, and sometimes, you yourselves bedridden and in pain. These ways differ from one another, and it is just impossible to name them all one by one. They are necessarily numerous and different, because of the variety in the structure of human life, in social processes, and in the heritage and historical traditions of the various cultures and civilizations. Nevertheless, within all these differences, *you are always and everywhere the bearers of your particular vocation:* you are bearers of the grace of Christ, the eternal Priest, and bearers of the charism of the Good Shepherd. And this you can never forget; this you can never renounce; this you must put into practice at every moment, in every place and in every way. In this consists that "supreme art" to which Jesus Christ has called you. "The supreme art is the direction of souls," wrote St. Gregory the Great.

I say to you therefore, quoting these words of his: strive to be "artists" of pastoral work. There have been many such in the history of the Church. There speak to each of us, for example, St. Vincent de Paul, St. John of Avila, the holy Curé d'Ars, St. John Bosco, Blessed Maximilian Kolbe, and many, many others. Each of them was different from the others, was himself, was the son of his own time and was "up to date" with respect to his own time. But this "bringing up to date" of each of them was an original response to the Gospel, a response needed precisely for those times; it was the response of holiness and zeal. There is no other rule apart from this for "bringing ourselves up to date," in our priestly life and activity, with our time and with the world as it is today. Without any doubt, the various attempts and projects aimed at the "secularization" of the priestly life cannot be considered an adequate "bringing up to date."

7. STEWARD AND WITNESS

The priestly life is built upon the foundation of the sacrament of Orders, which imprints on our soul the mark of an indelible character. This mark, impressed in the depths of our being, has its "personalistic" dynamism. *The priestly personality* must be *for others* a clear and plain *sign and indication.* This is the first condition for our pastoral service. The people from among whom we have been chosen and for whom we have been appointed[25] want above all to see in us such a sign and indication, and to this they have a right. It may sometimes seem to us that they do not want this, or that they wish us to be in every way "like them"; at times it even seems that they demand this of us. And here one very much needs a profound "sense of faith" and "the gift of discernment." In fact, it is very easy to let oneself be guided by appearances and fall victim to a fundamental illusion in what is essential. Those who call for the secularization of priestly life and applaud its various manifestations will undoubtedly abandon us when we succumb to temptation. We shall then cease to be necessary and popular. Our time is characterized by different forms of "manipulation" and "exploitation" of man, but we cannot give in to any of these.[26] In practical terms, the only priest who will always prove necessary to people is the priest who is conscious of the full meaning of his priesthood: the priest who believes profoundly, who professes his faith with courage, who prays fervently, who teaches with deep conviction, who serves, who puts into practice in his own life the program of the beatitudes, who knows how to love disinterestedly, who is close to everyone, and especially to those who are most in need.

Our pastoral activity demands that we should be close to people and all their problems, whether these problems be personal, family or social ones, but it also demands that we should be close to all these problems "in a priestly way." Only then, in the sphere of all those problems, do we remain ourselves. Therefore, if we are really of assistance in those human problems, and they are sometimes very difficult ones, then we keep our identity and are really faithful to our vocation. With great perspicacity we must seek, together with all men, truth and justice, the true and definitive dimension of which we can only find in the Gospel, or rather in Christ Himself. Our task is to serve *truth and justice* in the dimensions of human "temporality," but *always in a perspective* that is the perspective *of eternal salvation*. This salvation takes into account the temporal achievements of the human spirit in the spheres of knowledge and morality, as the Second Vatican Council wonderfully recalled,[27] but it is not identical with them, and in fact it goes higher than them: "The things that no eye has seen and no ear has heard...all that God has prepared for those who love him."[28] Our brethren in the faith, and unbelievers too, expect us always to be able to show them this perspective, to become real witnesses to it, to be dispensers of grace, to be servants of the Word of God. They expect us to be men of prayer.

Among us there are also those who have united their priestly vocation in a special way with an intense life of prayer and penance in the strictly contemplative form of their religious orders. Let them remember that their priestly ministry also in this form is—in a special way—"ordered" to the great solicitude of the Good Shepherd—solicitude for the salvation of every human being.

And this we must all remember: that it is not lawful for any of us to deserve the name of "hireling," that is to say the name of one "to whom the sheep do not belong," one who, "since he is not the shepherd and the sheep do not belong to him, abandons the sheep and runs away as soon as he sees the wolf coming, and then the wolf attacks and scatters the sheep; this is because he is only a hired man and has no concern for the sheep."[29] The solicitude of every good shepherd is that all people "may have life and have it to the full,"[30] so that none of them may be lost,[31] but should have eternal life. Let us endeavor to make this solicitude penetrate deeply into our souls; let us strive to live it. May it characterize our personality, and be at the foundation of our priestly identity.

8. MEANING OF CELIBACY

Allow me at this point to touch upon the question of priestly celibacy. I shall deal with it summarily, because it has already been considered in a profound and complete way during the Council, and subsequently in the Encyclical *Sacerdotalis caelibatus,* and again at the ordinary session of the 1971 Synod of Bishops. This reflection has shown itself to be necessary both in order to present the matter in a still more mature way, and also in order to explain even more deeply the meaning of the decision that the Latin Church took so many centuries ago and to which she has sought to be faithful, and desires to maintain this fidelity also in the future. The importance of the question under consideration is so great, and its link with the language of the Gospel itself so close, that in this case we cannot reason with categories different from those used by the Council, the Synod of Bishops and the great Pope Paul VI himself. We can only seek to understand this question more deeply and to respond to it more maturely, freeing ourselves from the various objections that have always —as happens today too—been raised against priestly celibacy, and also freeing ourselves from the different interpretations that appeal to criteria alien to the Gospel, to Tradition and to the Church's Magisterium—criteria, we would add, whose "anthropological" correctness and basis in fact are seen to be very dubious and of relative value.

Nor must we be too surprised at all the objections and criticisms which have intensified during the postconciliar period, even though today in some places they seem to be growing less. Did not Jesus Christ, after He had presented the disciples with the question of the renunciation of marriage "for the sake of the kingdom of heaven," add these significant words: "Let anyone accept this who can"?[32] The Latin Church has wished, and continues to wish, referring to the example of Christ the Lord Himself, to the apostolic teaching and to the whole Tradition that is proper to her, that *all those who receive the sacrament of Orders should embrace this renunciation "for the sake of the kingdom of heaven."* This tradition, however, is linked with respect for different traditions of other Churches. In fact, this tradition constitutes a characteristic, a peculiarity and a heritage of the Latin Catholic Church, a tradition to which she owes much and in which she is resolved to persevere, in spite of all the difficulties to which such fidelity could be exposed, and also in spite of the various symptoms of weakness and crisis in individual priests. We are all aware that "we have this treasure in earthen vessels"[33]; yet we know very well that it is precisely a treasure.

Why is it a treasure? Do we wish thereby to reduce the value of marriage and the vocation to family life? Or are we succumbing to a Manichean contempt for the human body and its functions? Do we wish in some way to devalue love, which leads a man and a woman to marriage and the wedded unity of the body, thus forming "one flesh"?[34] How could we think and reason like that, if we know, believe and proclaim, following St. Paul, that marriage is a "great mystery" in reference to Christ and the Church?[35] However, none of the reasons whereby people sometimes try to "convince us" of the inopportuneness of celibacy corresponds to the truth, the truth that the Church proclaims and seeks to realize in life through the commitment to which priests oblige themselves before ordination. The essential, proper and adequate reason, in fact, is contained in the truth that Christ declared when He spoke about the renunciation of marriage for the sake of the kingdom of heaven, and which St. Paul proclaimed when he wrote that each person in the Church has his or her own particular gifts.[36] Celibacy is precisely a "gift of the Spirit." A similar though different gift is contained in the vocation to true and faithful married love, directed towards procreation according to the flesh, in the very lofty context of the sacrament of Matrimony. It is obvious that this gift is fundamental for the building up of the great community of the Church, the People of God. But if this community wishes to respond fully to its vocation in Jesus Christ, there will also have to be realized in it, in the correct proportion, that other "gift," the gift of celibacy "for the sake of the kingdom of heaven."[37]

Why does the Latin Catholic Church link this gift not only with the life of those who accept the strict program of the evangelical counsels in religious institutes but also with the vocation to the hierarchical and ministerial priesthood? She does it because celibacy "for the sake of the kingdom" is not only an eschatological sign; it also has a great social meaning, in the present life, for the service of the People of God. Through his celibacy, the priest becomes the "man for others," in a different way from the man who, by binding himself in conjugal union with a woman, also becomes, as husband and father, a man "for others," especially in the radius of his own family: for his wife, and, together with her, for the children, to whom he gives life. The priest, by renouncing this fatherhood proper to married men, seeks another fatherhood and, as it were, even another motherhood, recalling the words of the Apostle about the children whom he begets in suffering.[38] These are children of his spirit, people entrusted to his solicitude by the Good Shepherd. These people are many, more numerous than an ordinary human family can embrace. The pastoral vocation of priests is great, and the Council teaches that it is universal: it is directed towards the whole Church,[39] and therefore it is of a missionary character. Normally, it is linked to the service of a particular community of the People of God, in which each individual expects attention, care and love. The heart of the priest, in order that it may be available for this service, must be free. Celibacy is a sign of a freedom that exists for the sake of service. According to this sign, the hierarchical or "ministerial" priesthood is, according to the tradition of our Church, more strictly "ordered" to the common priesthood of the faithful.

9. TEST AND RESPONSIBILITY

The often widespread view that priestly celibacy in the Catholic Church is an institution imposed by law on those who receive the sacrament of Orders is the result of a misunderstanding, if not of downright bad faith. We all know that it is not so. Every Christian who receives the sacrament of Orders commits himself to celibacy with full awareness and freedom, after a training lasting a number of years, and after profound reflection and assiduous prayer. He decides upon a life of celibacy only after he has reached a firm conviction that Christ is giving him this "gift" for the good of the Church and the service of others. Only then does he commit himself to observe celibacy for his entire life. It is obvious that such a decision obliges not only by virtue of a law laid down by the Church but also by virtue of personal responsibility. It is a matter here of *keeping one's word to Christ and the Church.* Keeping one's word is, at one and the same time, a duty and a proof of the priest's inner maturity; it is the expression of his personal dignity. It is shown in all its clarity when this keeping one's promise to Christ, made through a conscious and free commitment to celibacy for the whole of one's life, encounters difficulties, is put to the test, or is exposed to temptation—all things that do not spare the priest, any more than they spare any other Christian. At such a moment, the individual must seek support in more fervent prayer. Through prayer, he must find within himself that attitude of humility and sincerity before God and his own conscience; prayer is indeed the source of strength for sustaining what is wavering. Then it is that there is born a confidence like the confidence expressed by St. Paul in the words: "There is nothing that I cannot master with the help of the One who gives me strength."[40] These truths are confirmed by the experience of many priests and proved by the reality of life. The acceptance of these truths constitutes the basis of fidelity to the promise made to Christ and the Church, and that promise is at the same time the proof of genuine fidelity to oneself, one's own conscience, and one's own humanity and dignity. One must think of all these things especially at moments of crisis, and not have recourse to a dispensation, understood as an "administrative intervention," as though in fact it were not, on the contrary, a matter of a profound question of conscience and a test of humanity. God has a right to test each one of us in this way, since this earthly life is a time of testing for every human being. But God also wishes us all to emerge victorious from such tests, and He gives us adequate help for this.

Perhaps, not without good reason, one should add at this point that the commitment to married fidelity, which derives from the sacrament of Matrimony, creates similar obligations in its own sphere; this married commitment sometimes becomes a source of similar trials and experiences for husbands and wives, who also have a way of proving the value of their love in these "trials by fire." Love, in fact, in all its dimensions, is not only a call but also a duty. Finally, we should add that our brothers and sisters joined by the marriage bond *have the right to expect from us*, priests and pastors, good example and *the witness of fidelity to one's vocation until death*, a fidelity to the vocation that we choose through the sacrament of Orders just as they choose it through the sacrament of Matrimony. Also in this sphere and in this sense we should understand our ministerial priesthood as "subordination" to the common priesthood of all the faithful, of the laity, especially of those who live in marriage and form a family. In this way, we serve in "building up the body of Christ" [41]; otherwise, instead of cooperating in the building up of that body we weaken its spiritual structure. Closely linked to this building up of the body of Christ is the authentic development of the human personality of each

Christian—as also of each priest—a development that takes place according to the measure of the gift of Christ. The disorganization of the spiritual structure of the Church certainly does not favor the development of the human personality and does not constitute its proper testing.

10. EVERY DAY
WE HAVE TO BE CONVERTED ANEW

"What must we do, then?"[42]: dear brothers, this seems to be your question, just as the disciples and those who listened to Christ the Lord asked Him so often. What must the Church do, when it seems that there is a lack of priests, when their absence makes itself felt especially in certain countries and regions of the world? How are we to respond to the immense needs of evangelization, and how can we satisfy the hunger for the Word and the Body of the Lord? The Church, which commits herself to maintaining priestly celibacy as a particular gift for the kingdom of God, *professes faith in and expresses hope in* her Teacher, Redeemer and Spouse, and at the same time in Him who is "Lord of the harvest" and "giver of the gift."[43] In fact, "every perfect gift is from above, coming down from the Father of lights."[44] We for our part cannot weaken this faith and confidence with our human doubting or our timidity.

In consequence, we must all be converted anew every day. We know that this is a fundamental exigency of the Gospel, addressed to everyone,[45] and all the more do we have to consider it as addressed to us. If we have the duty of helping others to be converted we have to do the same continuously in our own lives. Being converted means returning to the very grace of our vocation; it means meditating upon the infinite goodness and love of Christ, who has addressed each of us and, calling us by name, has said: "Follow me." Being converted means continually "giving an account" before the Lord of our hearts about our service, our zeal and our fidelity, for we are "Christ's servants, stewards entrusted with the mysteries of God."[46] Being converted also means "giving an account" of our negligences and sins, of our timidity, of our lack of faith and hope, of our thinking only "in a human way" and not "in a divine way." Let us recall, in this regard, the warning that Christ gave to Peter himself.[47] Being converted means, for us, seeking again the pardon and strength of God in the sacrament of Reconciliation, and thus always beginning anew, and every day progressing, overcoming ourselves, making spiritual conquests, giving cheerfully, for "God loves a cheerful giver."[48]

Being converted means "to pray continually and never lose heart."[49] *In a certain way prayer is the first and last condition for conversion,* spiritual progress and holiness. Perhaps in these recent years—at least in certain quarters—there has been too much discussion about the priesthood, the priest's "identity," the value of his presence in the modern world, etc., and on the other hand there has been too little praying. There has not been enough enthusiasm for actuating the priesthood itself through prayer, in order to make its authentic evangelical dynamism effective, in order to confirm the priestly identity. It is prayer that shows the essential style of the priest; without prayer this style becomes deformed. Prayer helps us always to find the light that has led us since the beginning of our priestly vocation, and which never ceases to lead us, even though it seems at times to disappear in the darkness. Prayer enables us to be converted continually, to remain in a state of continuous reaching out to God, which is essential if we wish to lead others to Him. Prayer helps us to believe, to hope and to love, even when our human weakness hinders us.

Prayer likewise enables us continually to rediscover the dimensions of that kingdom for whose coming we pray every day, when we repeat the words that Christ taught us. Then we realize *what our place is in the realization of the petition: "Thy kingdom come,"* and we see how necessary we are in its realization. And perhaps, when we pray, we shall see more easily those "fields...already white for harvest"[50] and we shall understand the meaning of Christ's words as He looked at them: "So ask the Lord of the harvest to send laborers to his harvest."[51]

We must link prayer with continuous work upon ourselves: this is the *formatio permanens*. As is rightly pointed out by the Document on this theme issued by the Sacred Congregation for the Clergy,[52] this formation must be both interior, that is to say, directed towards the deepening of the priest's spiritual life, and must also be pastoral and intellectual (philosophical and theological). Therefore, since our pastoral activity, the proclamation of the Word and the whole of the priestly ministry depend upon the intensity of our interior life, that activity must also find sustenance in assiduous study. It is not enough for us to stop at what we once learned in the seminary, even in cases where those studies were done at university level, which the Sacred Congregation for Catholic Education resolutely recommends. This process of intellectual formation must last all one's life, especially in modern times, which are marked—at least in many parts of the world—by the widespread development of education and culture. To the people who enjoy the benefits of this development we must be *witnesses* to Jesus Christ, and properly qualified ones. As teachers of truth and morality, we must tell them, convincingly and effectively, of the hope that gives us life.[53] And this also forms part of the process of daily conversion to love, through the truth.

Dear brothers: you who have borne "the burden of the day and the heat,"[54] who have put your hand to the plough and do not turn back,[55] and perhaps even more those of you who are doubtful of the meaning of your vocation or of the value of your service: think of the places where people anxiously await a priest, and where for many years, feeling the lack of such a priest, they do not cease to hope for his presence. And sometimes it happens that they meet in an abandoned shrine, and place on the altar a stole which they still keep, and recite all the prayers of the

Eucharistic liturgy; and then, at the moment that corresponds to the transubstantiation a deep silence comes down upon them, a silence sometimes broken by a sob...so ardently do they desire to hear the words that only the lips of a priest can efficaciously utter. So much do they desire Eucharistic Communion, in which they can share only through the ministry of a priest, just as they also so eagerly wait to hear the divine words of pardon: *Ego te absolvo a peccatis tuis!* So deeply do they feel the absence of a priest among them!... Such places are not lacking in the world. So if one of you doubts the meaning of his priesthood, if he thinks it is "socially" fruitless or useless, reflect on this!

We must be converted every day, we must rediscover every day the gift obtained from Christ Himself in the sacrament of Orders, by penetrating the importance of the salvific mission of the Church and by reflecting on the great meaning of our vocation in the light of that mission.

11. MOTHER OF PRIESTS

Dear brothers, at the beginning of my ministry I entrust all of you to the Mother of Christ, who in a special way is our Mother: the Mother of priests. In fact, the beloved disciple, who, as one of the Twelve, had heard in the Upper Room the words "Do this in memory of me,"[56] was given by Christ on the cross to His Mother, with the words: "Behold your son."[57] The man who on Holy Thursday received the power to celebrate the Eucharist was, by these words of the dying Redeemer, given to His Mother as her "son." All of us, therefore, who receive the same power through priestly ordination have in a certain sense a prior right to see her as our Mother. And so I desire that all of you, together with me, should find in Mary the Mother of the priesthood which we have received from Christ. I also desire that you should entrust your priesthood to her in a special way. Allow me to do it myself, *entrusting to the Mother of Christ* each one of you —without any exception—in a solemn and at the same time simple and humble way. And I ask each of you, dear brothers, to do it yourselves, in the way dictated to you by your own heart, especially by your love for Christ the priest, and also by your own weakness, which goes hand in hand with your desire for service and holiness. I ask you to do this.

The Church of today speaks of herself especially in the Dogmatic Constitution *Lumen gentium.* Here too, in the last chapter, she proclaims that she looks to Mary as to the Mother of Christ, because she calls herself a mother and wishes to be a mother, begetting people for God to a new life.[58] Now, dear brothers: How near you are to this cause of God! How deeply it is imprinted upon your vocation, ministry and mission. In consequence, in the midst of the People of God that looks to Mary with immense love and hope, you must look to her with exceptional hope and love. Indeed, you must proclaim Christ who is her Son; and who will better communicate to you the truth about Him than His Mother? You must nourish human hearts with Christ: And who can make you more aware of what you are doing than she who nourished Him? "Hail, true Body, born of the Virgin Mary." In our "ministerial" priesthood there is *the wonderful and penetrating dimension of nearness to the Mother of Christ.* So let us try to live in that dimension. If I may be permitted to speak here of my own experience, I will say to you that in writing to you I am referring especially to my own personal experience.

As I communicate all this to you, at the beginning of my service to the universal Church, I do not cease to ask God to fill you, priests of Jesus Christ, with every blessing and grace, and as a token of this communion in prayer I bless you with all my heart, in the name of the Father and of the Son and of the Holy Spirit.

Accept this blessing. Accept the words of the new Successor of Peter, that Peter whom the Lord commanded:

"And once you have recovered, you in your turn must strengthen your brothers."[59] Do not cease to pray for me together with the whole Church, so that I may respond to that exigency of a primacy of love that the Lord made the foundation of the mission of Peter, when He said to him: "Feed my lambs."[60] Amen.

From the Vatican, April 9, Passion Sunday (Palm Sunday), in the year 1979, the first of the Pontificate.

FOOTNOTES

1. Cf. Mt. 20:12.
2. Cf. Jn. 21:15ff.
3. *Vobis enim sum episcopus, vobiscum sum Christianus:* Serm. 340, 1: *PL* 38, 1483.
4. Cf. I art. 15.
5. *Epistula ad Magnesios*, VI, 1: *Patres apostolici* I, ed. Funk, p. 235.
6. Cf. Rm. 5:5; 1 Cor. 12:31; 13.
7. Heb. 5:1.
8. Dogmatic Constitution *Lumen gentium*, no. 10.
9. Heb. 5:1.
10. Dogmatic Constitution *Lumen gentium*, no. 10.
11. Cf. Eph. 4:11,12.
12. Cf. 1 Pt. 2:5.
13. Cf. 1 Pt. 3:18.
14. Dogmatic Constitution *Lumen gentium*, no. 10.
15. Cf. Dogmatic Constitution *Lumen gentium*, no. 10.
16. Cf. Mt. 19:27.
17. Cf. Mt. 20:1-16.
18. Cf. Jn. 10:1-16.
19. Cf. Dogmatic Constitution *Lumen gentium*, 11.
20. Dogmatic Constitution *Lumen gentium*, 10.
21. Jn. 10:11.
22. Cf. 8-11; 19-20.
23. Mk. 8:35.
24. Saint Gregory the Great, *Regula pastoralis*, I, 1: *PL* 77, 14.
25. Cf. Heb. 5:1.
26. "Let us not deceive ourselves in thinking we serve the Gospel, if we try 'to dilute' our priestly charism...": Pope John Paul II, *Discourse to the Clergy of Rome* (November 9, 1978), no. 3: "L'Osservatore Romano" (November 10, 1978), p. 2.
27. Cf. Pastoral Constitution *Gaudium et spes*, 38-39, 42.
28. 1 Cor. 2:9.
29. Jn. 10:12-13.
30. Jn. 10:10.
31. Cf. Jn. 17:12.
32. Mt. 19:12.
33. Cf. 2 Cor. 4:7.
34. Gn. 2:24; cf. Mt. 19:6.
35. Cf. Eph. 5:32.
36. Cf. 1 Cor. 7:7.
37. Mt. 19:12.

38. Cf. 1 Cor. 4:15; Gal. 4:19.
39. Cf. Decree *Presbyterorum ordinis*, 3, 6, 10, 12.
40. Phil. 4:13.
41. Eph. 4:12.
42. Lk. 3:10.
43. Mt. 9:38; cf. 1 Cor. 7:7.
44. Jas. 1:17.
45. Cf. Mt. 4:17; Mk. 1:15.
46. 1 Cor. 4:1.
47. Cf. Mt. 16:23.
48. 2 Cor. 9:7.
49. Lk. 18:1.
50. Jn. 4:35.
51. Mt. 9:38.
52. Cf. Circular Letter of November 4, 1969: *AAS* 62 (1970), pp. 123ff.
53. Cf. 1 Pt. 3:15.
54. Mt. 20:12.
55. Cf. Lk. 9:62.
56. Lk. 22:19
57. Jn. 19:26.
58. Cf. Dogmatic Constitution *Lumen gentium*, Chapter VIII.
59. Lk. 22:32.
60. Jn. 21:16.

Perseverance and Fidelity in the Priestly Vocation

On the morning of April 12, 1979, Pope John Paul II was chief celebrant at the concelebrated Chrism Mass in St. Peter's Basilica. 2,500 priests concelebrated with the Holy Father. His Holiness gave the following homily.

1. Today, on the threshold of His holy Triduum, we wish in a particular way to profess our faith in Christ, in Him whose passion we must renew in the spirit of the Church, so that all "shall look on him whom they have pierced" (Jn. 19:37), and the present generation of the earth's inhabitants will bewail and lament Him (cf. Lk. 23:27). This is the Christ, He in whom God comes to mankind as Lord of history; "I am the Alpha and the Omega... who is and who was and who is to come" (Rv. 1:8).

This is the Christ "who loved me and gave himself for me" (Gal. 2:20), Christ, who came to obtain for us "with his own blood...an eternal redemption" (Heb. 9:12);

Christ: the "Anointed," the Messiah. Once Israel, on the eve of her liberation from slavery in Egypt, marked the doors of the houses with the blood of the lamb (cf. Ex. 12:1-14). Behold, the Lamb of God is among us, He whom the Father Himself anointed with power and with the Holy Spirit, and sent into the world (cf. Jn. 1:29; Acts 10:36-38).

Christ: the *Anointed*, the Messiah. During these days, with the power of the Holy Spirit's anointing, with the power of the fullness of the sanctity which is in Him, and in Him alone, He will cry to God "with a loud voice" (Lk. 23:46), the voice of humiliation, of annihilation, of the cross: "O Lord, my strength. The Lord is my rock, and my fortress and my deliverer, my God, my rock, in whom I take refuge, my shield, and the horn of my salvation, my stronghold" (Ps. 17[18]:2).

Thus He will cry for Himself and for us.

2. Today we celebrate the liturgy of the Chrism, through which the Church, on the threshold of these holy days, *wants to renew the sign of that power of the Spirit which she has received from her Redeemer and Bridegroom.*

This power of the Spirit—grace and sanctity, which is in Him—is imparted, at the price of the passion and death, to mankind through the sacraments of the faith. Thus the People of God is continuously built up, as the Second Vatican Council teaches: "The faithful, by virtue of their royal priesthood, participate in the offering of the Eucharist. They exercise that priesthood, too, by the reception of the sacraments, prayer and thanksgiving, the witness of a holy life, abnegation and active charity" (LG 10).

With this holy oil, Oil of the Catechumens, the catechumens will be anointed during Baptism, to be able to be then anointed with the holy Chrism. They will receive this anointing a second time in the sacrament of Confirmation. They will also receive it—if called—during ordinations:

deacons, priests, and bishops. In the sacrament of the sick, all invalids will receive the anointing with the oil of the sick (cf. Jas. 5:14).

Today we wish to prepare the Church for the new year of grace, for the administration of the sacraments of the faith, which have their center in the Eucharist. All the sacraments, both those whose sign is anointing, and those administered without this sign, such as Penance and Matrimony, signify an effective participation in the power of Him whom the Father Himself anointed and sent into the world (cf. Lk. 4:18).

Today, Holy Thursday, we celebrate the *liturgy of this power*, which reached its fullness in the weaknesses of Good Friday, in the torments of Christ's passion and agony, because it was through all that suffering that He procured grace for us: "Grace to you and peace...from Jesus Christ, the faithful witness, the first-born of the dead, and the ruler of kings on earth" (Rv. 1:4-5).

3. Through His abandonment to the Father, *through His obedience until death*, He also made us a *"kingdom of priests"* (Rv. 1:6).

He proclaimed it on the solemn day on which He shared bread and wine with the Apostles, as His body and blood for the world's salvation. And it is just today that we are called to live this day: the feast of priests. Today our hearts newly respond to the mysteries of the supper table, at which Christ, with the first Eucharist, said: "Do this in remembrance of me" (Lk. 22:19), thus instituting the sacrament of the priesthood. And thus what the prophet Isaiah had said centuries before came to pass: "You shall be called the priests of the Lord, men shall speak of you as the ministers of our God" (Is. 61:6).

Today we feel the warmest desire to be present at the altar for this eucharistic concelebration and to render *thanks for the particular gift* which the Lord has conferred on us. Conscious of the greatness of this grace, we further wish to renew the vows which each one of us, on the day of his own ordination, made to Christ and to the Church, depositing them in the hands of the bishop. In renewing them, we ask for the grace of fidelity and perseverance. We also ask that the grace of the priestly vocation may fall on the ground of many young souls, and that it may take root in them as seeds which yield a hundredfold (cf. Lk. 8:8).

Today, bishops in their cathedrals throughout the world do likewise, as is required of them. Together with priests they renew the vows made on the day of their ordination. Let us join with them with yet more ardor *through brotherhood in the faith and in the vocation* that we attained at the supper table as the particular legacy bequeathed us by the Apostles.

Let us persevere in this great priestly community, as servants of the People of God, and as disciples and lovers of Him who was made obedient unto death, and who came into the world not to be served, but to serve! (cf. Mt. 20:28)

Authenticity and Service Charisms

On April 19, 1979, the Holy Father received in audience a group of about forty priests from the Archdiocese of Bologna, led by the Archbishop, Cardinal Antonio Poma. John Paul II delivered the following address.

Lord Cardinal,

The meeting this morning is gladdened by these young priests of your archdiocese, on whom you laid hands in the course of the last decade. It seems to me I can read on your face the legitimate pride of a father who sees himself surrounded by a large and strong group of sons, on whom he knows he can rely for the present and for the future. Let my cordial greeting go to you, therefore, Lord Cardinal, and to these priests of yours, with an open and sincere welcome.

It always gives me special joy to be able to talk to priests, because it seems to me I can at once find myself in agreement with them owing to the ideals, hopes, joyful and sad experiences, in a word, the vocation which, by providential divine disposition, unites us. The spontaneous desire I feel in these cases would be to listen to the problems of each one, to ask questions about apostolic initiatives, the difficulties met with, the results obtained, projects for the future. I would then like to be able to converse, in brotherly communion of spirit, about the mystery of divine election, the greatness of the mission to which we are called, and the formidable responsibilities which we bear. To talk about them in order to revive in us awareness of the irreplaceable role that the ministerial priesthood must carry out in service of the People of God.

I entrusted some thoughts on this fundamental ecclesial function of ours to the Letter which I addressed to all priests on the occasion of the recent liturgical celebration of Holy Thursday. I trust that it was received by you, beloved sons, with the same open-heartedness with which I wrote it; and I hope that your attentive, intelligent, available reflection will dwell on it, so that it may strengthen and spur each one of you to persevere joyfully in the donation of himself to Christ and to the Church.

I would like here just to note that there are two requirements particularly felt by the clergy, especially the young: the demand for authenticity and the demand for closeness to the man of our times. They are two exigencies worthy of great consideration, because they express a sincere desire for consistency with one's own mission.

Glancing through the text of the above-mentioned Letter, you will have found that I indicated in likeness to Christ, "the Good Shepherd," the most valid criterion of priestly authenticity (cf. no. 5), and in the commitment to offer others the testimony of a priestly personality that is for everyone "a clear and plain sign and indication" (cf. no. 7), the most effective way of effecting a "significant" presence among modern men. It is not, in fact, by giving in to the promptings of an easy secularization, expressed either in the abandonment of the ecclesiastical habit, or in the assimilation of worldly habits, or in the taking up of a secular trade, it is not in this way that we can approach modern man effectively.

This assimilation might perhaps give, at first sight, the impression of an immediacy of contacts; but what use would it be if it were to be "paid for" with loss of the specific evangelizing and sanctifying charge, which makes the priest the salt of the earth and the light of the world? The risk that the salt may lose its taste or the light be smothered is already clearly put forward by Jesus in the Gospel (cf. Mt. 5:13-16). What would be the use of a priest so "assimilated" to the world as to become a camouflaged part of it and no longer a transforming leaven?

These are—I am sure—your convictions also; and it is for this reason that to be able to contemplate such a fine and promising group of young priests, closely gathered round their bishop, fills my soul with joy. Thanking you again, therefore, for this visit of yours, in which I see the attestation of an intense desire for ever closer communion with Peter's Successor, I willingly assure you of a special memory at the altar of the Lord, and in His name I bestow upon you all my fatherly apostolic blessing, which can be extended to your families and to the souls entrusted to your generous ministry.

Essential Elements of the Priesthood

On April 21, 1979, the Holy Father received in audience a group of priests from the archdiocese of Milan on their way back from a pilgrimage to Our Lady of Czestochowa, made on the occasion of the 25th anniversary of their ordination. John Paul II delivered the following address.

Beloved priests of Milan!

Celebrating the twenty-fifth anniversary of your priestly ordination, you desired to solemnize it with a personal meeting with the Pope, on your return from a devout pilgrimage to Poland, my beloved native land, to the Marian sanctuary of Czestochowa.

And I thank you heartily for this filial devotion of yours, and I receive you with deep and sincere affection and extend my greeting to all. I embrace you, indeed, with all the love that must flow from our common priesthood and from my mission as universal Father. Welcome, then, you superiors who come from Milan, a city famous all over the world for its adventurous history and its intelligent industry; a diocese of great bishops, holy priests, and committed laymen; the land of the painstaking and thoughtful pastoral ministry of my venerated Predecessor Paul VI!

Welcome, you who have been pilgrims in my homeland, where the long and painful vicissitudes of history are interwoven with a Christian faith that is always sincere and real!

But welcome above all to you priests who are celebrating your priestly jubilee!

Twenty-five years of priesthood are so many! They are a mystical and precious cathedral constructed with over ten thousand holy Masses celebrated, with thousands and thousands of absolutions imparted, with innumerable baptisms, marriages, anointings of the sick, administered by means of the divine powers conferred by Jesus Himself through the Apostles and the golden chain of the laying on of hands!

What can we do if not express our thanks and repeat with the Psalmist: *"Misericordias Domini in aeternum cantabo"* (Ps. 89:2)?

Twenty-five years of priesthood also mean a period of long experience and concrete reflection on the priest's real identity. After so many years of industrious ministry in the Lord's vineyard and harvest, after having "borne the burden of the day and the scorching heat" (Mt. 20:12), it is possible to deduce more easily the essential elements of the Catholic priesthood, strengthening ourselves to persevere and as a lesson for all confreres.

1. Our interior strength lies in our vocation.

We have been called! This is the fundamental truth that must instill courage and joy in us! Jesus Himself said to the Apostles: "You did not choose me, but I chose you and appointed you that you should go and bear fruit and that your fruit should abide" (Jn. 15:16). And the author of the Letter to the Hebrews cautions: "One does not take the honor upon himself, but he is called by God!" (Heb. 5:4)

The call was at first an inner one, mysterious, caused by various reasons; but then, after the long and necessary preparation in the seminary, under the direction of prudent and responsible superiors, it became official, guaranteed, when the Church called us and consecrated us by means of the bishop.

No one, in fact, would dare to become a minister of Christ, in continual contact with the Almighty! No one would have the courage to shoulder the weight of consciences and accept in this way a sacred and mystical solitude!

The call gives us the strength to be what we are with constancy and faithfulness: In moments of serenity, but above all in moments of crisis and discouragement, we say to ourselves: "Courage! I have been called!" *"Ecce ego, mitte me"* (Is. 6:8).

2. Our joy is the Eucharist.

Let us recall the words of the Divine Master to the Apostles: "I have called you friends, for all that I have heard from my Father I have made known to you" (Jn. 15:15).

The priest is first of all for the Eucharist and lives by the Eucharist. We can "consecrate" and meet Christ personally with the divine power of transubstantiation; we can receive in Communion Jesus living, true, real; we can distribute to souls the Word, incarnate, dead and risen again for the salvation of the world! Every day we are in private audience with Jesus!

So always make holy Mass the driving force of the day, the personal meeting with Him who is our only true joy. An adequate preparation and appropriate thanksgiving are, therefore, absolutely necessary at every holy Mass, to be able to savor the joy of the priesthood.

3. Finally, our concern must be love and service of souls, in the place that Providence has assigned to us through our superiors. Wherever we may be, in the bustling parishes of metropolises as in remote mountain villages, there are always persons to love, to serve and to save. We can always meditate on those consoling words that will mark our eternal destiny: "Well done, good and faithful servant; you have been faithful over a little, I will set you over much; enter into the joy of your master!" (cf. Mt. 25:23)

May these words of mine accompany you as a memory of your twenty-fifth anniversary, while I ask you to pray for me, for all priests and that the Lord may bring forth many vocations.

May you be assisted, enlightened and strengthened by the Blessed Virgin, whom I address with the very words spoken by Paul VI at the resumption of the Second Vatican Council: "O Mary, look on us your sons, look on us, brothers and disciples and apostles and continuers of Jesus. Make us aware of our vocation and our mission; make us not unworthy of assuming, in our priesthood, in our word, in the offering of our lives for the faithful entrusted to us, the representation, the personification of Christ. You, full of grace, make the priesthood, which honors you, also be holy and immaculate!" (October 11, 1963)

And may my comforting blessing always remain with you!

The Gift of the Priesthood

On April 21, 1979, the Holy Father received in audience a group of deacons from the diocese of Regensburg led by the Bishop, Mons. Rudolf Graber. John Paul II delivered the following address.

Your Excellency,
Mr. Regens, dear deacons,

I greet you heartily in the joy of the Easter octave at this short meeting. May the peace of the risen Lord be with you all!

That you wished, during your stay in the Eternal City, to pay a visit also to the Bishop of Rome, confirms your belief in his universal mission for the whole Church at the same time. As Successor of St. Peter, the first courageous witness to the resurrection of Christ, it is his duty today to strengthen brothers in faith (cf. Lk. 22:31f.).

I would now like to carry out this task towards you with special joy by heartily congratulating you as deacons on the gift of grace of your vocation and by encouraging you on your way to the priesthood. It is something great to be chosen by God for closer participation in His Son's mission of salvation for the redemption of mankind. The grace of the vocation to the priesthood is, as I stressed recently in my Letter to the priests: "the greatest gift of the Holy Spirit" (no. 2).

It is a precious treasure, which we carry, it is true, in frail vessels, but which, precisely for this reason, must be all the more carefully preserved.

Grasp this gift with both hands, without hesitation and anxious reservations, with full availability in the service of the People of God, with courageous and self-sacrificing love of Christ and of His Church! Be convinced from the first—to draw your attention particularly to another word from the above-mentioned Letter—and prepare yourself conscientiously for it: "The only priest who will always prove necessary to people is the priest who is conscious of the full meaning of his priesthood: the priest who believes profoundly, who professes his faith with courage, who prays fervently, who teaches with deep conviction, who serves, who puts into practice in his own life the program of the beatitudes, who knows how to love disinterestedly, who is close to everyone, and especially to those who are most in need" (no. 7).

Let my special prayer for you and at the same time my sincere wish for your bishop and your diocese be that such a fulfilled priesthood may be allotted to each of you through the grace of God and your personal religious effort. The convincing example of good priests will also be the most effective means for the promotion of new priestly vocations! For this purpose I willingly impart the apostolic blessing to you all for rich graces of Christ, the risen and eternal High Priest.

Obedience and Joy in the Spirit of the Diaconate

On April 21, 1979, the Holy Father presided at a concelebrated Mass in the Pauline Chapel, attended by eighteen new deacons of the Pontifical Irish, Scots and Rosminian Colleges in Rome. With the Pope there concelebrated the three rectors, Eamonn Marron, Sean O'Kelly, Denis Cleary, and also the other superiors of the three institutes. After the Gospel, His Holiness gave the following homily.

Dearly beloved deacons,

In the long history of the Church in Rome, it is not uncommon to see deacons associated with the Pope in his ministry, to see deacons at his side. And this morning it is a special joy for me to be surrounded by deacons, as our relationship—our ecclesial communion—reaches its highest expression in the holy Sacrifice of the Mass.

Our joy is enhanced—yours and mine—to have some of your parents and loved ones here. All of us have come to celebrate the Paschal Mystery and to experience the love of Jesus. His is a sacrificial love—a love that moved Him to lay down His life for His people and to take it up again. And His sacrificial love has been manifested with great generosity in your parents' lives, and today it is very fitting that they should have an exceptional moment of serenity, satisfaction and wholesome pride.

REJOICE AND EXULT

As we commemorate the resurrection of the Lord Jesus, we reflect on His various appearances, as recorded in the reading from the Acts of the Apostles: His appearance to Mary Magdalene, to the two disciples, to the eleven Apostles. We renew our faith—our holy Catholic Faith—and *we rejoice and exult because the Lord is truly risen, alleluia!* Today more than ever before we are conscious of what it means to be an Easter people and to have the alleluia as our song.

The Easter event—the bodily resurrection of Christ—pervades the life of the whole Church. It gives to Christians everywhere strength at every turn in life. It makes us sensitive to humanity with all its limitations, sufferings and needs. The resurrection has immense power to liberate, to uplift, to bring about justice, to effect holiness, to cause joy.

But for you, deacons, there is a particular message this morning. By your sacred ordination *you have been associated in a special way with the Gospel of the risen Christ.* You have been commissioned to render a special type of service, *diaconia,* in the name of the risen Lord. During the ordination ceremony the bishop told each of you: "Receive the Gospel of Christ, whose herald you now are. Believe what you read, teach what you believe, and practice what you teach." And so you are called to take the words of the Acts of the Apostles to heart. In the rank of deacons you have come to be associated with Peter and John and all the Apostles. You support the apostolic ministry and share in its proclamation. Like the Apostles *you too must feel impelled to proclaim by word and deed the resurrection of the Lord Jesus.* You too must experience the need to do good, *to render service in the name of the crucified and risen Jesus*—to bring God's Word into the lives of His holy people.

CHRIST'S VICTORY

In today's first reading we hear the Apostles saying: "We cannot but speak of what we have seen and heard." And you are called, in the obedience of faith, to proclaim, on the basis of their testimony—on the basis of what has been handed down in the Church under the guidance of the Holy Spirit—the great mystery of the risen Lord, who in His very act of resurrection communicates eternal life to all His brethren because He communicates His victory over sin and death. Remember that the Apostles by their proclamation of resurrection were a challenge and reproof to many. And they were warned never to speak again in the name of the risen Jesus. But their response was immediate and clear: "You must judge whether in God's eyes it is right to listen to you and not to God."

And in this obedience to God they found the supreme measure of paschal joy.

It is the same for you, the new deacons of this Easter season. As the associates of the bishops and priests of the Church, *your discipleship will be marked by these two characteristics: obedience and joy.* Each, in its own way, will show the authenticity of your lives. Your ability to communicate the Gospel will depend on your adherence to the faith of the Apostles. The effectiveness of your *diaconia* will be measured by the fidelity of your obedience to the mandate of the Church. It is the risen Christ who has called you, and it is His Church that sends you forth to proclaim the message transmitted by the Apostles. And it is the Church that authenticates your ministry. Be confident that the very power of the Gospel you proclaim will fill you with the most sublime joy: sacrificial joy, yes, but the transforming joy of being intimately associated with the risen Jesus in His triumphant mission of salvation. All the disciples of Jesus, and you deacons by a special title, are called to share the immense Easter joy experienced by our Blessed Mother. At the resurrection of her Son, we see Mary as *Mater plena sanctae laetitiae*, becoming for all of us *Causa nostrae laetitiae*.

Obedience and joy are then true expressions of your discipleship. But they are also conditions for your effective ministry, and at the same time gifts of God's grace—effects of the very mystery of the resurrection that you proclaim.

SPECIAL RESOLVE

Dear deacons, I speak to you as sons and brothers and friends. This is a day of special joy. *But let it also be a day of special resolve.* In the presence of the Pope, under the gaze of the Apostles Peter and Paul, in the company of Stephen, before the witness of your parents, and in the communion of the universal Church, *renew again your ecclesial consecration to Jesus Christ,* whom you serve and whose lifegiving message you are called to transmit in all its purity and integrity, with all its exigencies and in all its power. And know that it is with immense love that I repeat to you and to your brother deacons throughout the Church the words of this morning's Gospel, the words of our Lord Jesus Christ: "Go out to the whole world, proclaim the Good News to all creation."

This is the meaning of your ministry. This will be your greatest service to humanity. This is your response to God's love. Amen.

Apostolate in the World of Manual Labor

Before his general audience address on April 25, 1979, Pope John Paul II addressed as follows the large group of diocesan priest delegates engaged in the apostolate of the world of manual labor, who had assembled in Rome for their annual congress.

A cordial greeting now goes to the large group of priests, diocesan delegates for the apostolate of manual labor, who are concluding in Rome today their annual congress, organized by the National Office of the Italian Episcopal Conference for the Apostolate in the World of Manual Labor.

Beloved priests, I express to you my deep satisfaction with the interesting program you have carried out in the last few days for a more effective "Apostolate of Manual Labor in Italian Churches."

As you well know, the Church follows with all care and anxiety the vast, varied and, sometimes, dramatic social question regarding the workers. Since she "cannot remain insensible to whatever serves man's true welfare, any more than she can remain indifferent to what threatens it" (RH 13), she constantly safeguards the Christian meaning of work and at the same time the inviolable dignity of the worker, which is all the more sacred the more it is recognized as having the first place which man occupies in the scale of values. Work, in fact, is for man, and not man for work. It must aim at serving man and not at subduing him: if that were not so, man again would become a slave and his stature would be measured—alas!—only with the yardstick of suffocating materialism.

It is necessary to reconsider the figure and the situation of the worker, so that he may be enabled to be more of a man and to regain his true greatness as collaborator in God's creative work when he imprints on matter the sign of his active mind.

It is up to you, dear priests, to make every effort in order that this wish may come true, so that the space between the Church and the factory may be lessened and the smoke of incense mingle, in its ascent to heaven, with that of industries. In your pastoral action take care, in the first place, of those who are still suffering because of the heaviness and unhealthiness of their work, uncertainty about their employment, the insufficiency of their dwellings and of their wages. But take care also and above all in order that the workers may be able to rediscover and support the inborn tendency to the highest values of the spirit: faith, hope, and justice. Succeed, in a word, in projecting the light of the Gospel upon the difficult but attractive world of manual work.

And for you priests, and those who help you in your work of human and Christian solidarity, I pray to the heavenly Father, imploring from Him, through the Blessed Virgin, Mother of the divine Workman, a special apostolic blessing.

Formation of Catechists

During the general audience on April 25, 1979, the Holy Father gave the following brief address to those who had been taking part in the International Council for Catechesis.

I now wish to address a special greeting to members of the International Council for Catechesis, composed of bishops, priests, sisters and lay experts, who have met here in Rome in these days to examine the important subject of the "Formation of Catechists," and who, together with the superiors and some officials of the Sacred Congregation for the Clergy, which organized the meeting, have come here to express to the Pope their ecclesial communion.

I thank you, dear brothers, for this significant presence of yours and, even more, for your active commitment in updating the delicate and important sector of catechesis, which is certainly the *opus princeps* of the Church's mission. The theme you have chosen is too vast and important for me to be able to refer to it here: I will limit myself, therefore, to a short and simple exhortation. I am of the opinion that in the catechist's formation, over and above all problems regarding the content and the method of teaching, uprightness of life and sincerity of Christian faith are necessary. Neither cultural preparation nor pedagogical skill are sufficient to make the revealed truths accessible to the mentality of modern man. These are necessary things, but they are not enough: The catechist must have *a soul*, which lives and brings life to everything he professes. In this connection I am glad to leave you, as an inspiring motive, some expressions of St. Bonaventure of Bagnoregio, who, in his *Itinerarium mentis in Deum*, admonished the teachers of his time, with sculptural clarity, as follows: *"Nemo credat quod sibi sufficiat lectio sine unctione, speculatio sine devotione, investigatio sine admiratione, circumspectio sine exsultatione, industria sine pietate, scientia sine charitate, intelligentia sine humilitate, studium absque divina gratia, speculum absque sapientia divinitus inspirata"* (Itinerarium mentis in Deum, Introduction, no. 4).

All that demands of the catechist, of course, great love for Jesus Christ, our Master. It demands readiness to listen to His voice and follow Him daily in order to be able to learn how He spoke, in His continual catechesis, to children, to the young, to the learned and to the ignorant.

This is, dear brothers, the brief thought I wished to express to you. May the Holy Spirit sustain you in your work, and the Blessed Virgin, *Sedis Sapientiae*, encourage you in difficulties. To all of you my fatherly blessing, which I willingly bestow also on all those who are engaged in various capacities in the delicate field of catechesis.

The Joyful Commitment of Service to Humanity Is Sustained by the Eucharist

The Holy Father received, on April 26, 1979, a group of thirteen bishops of India on their ad limina Apostolorum *visit. The bishops, coming from Bengal and the Northeast section of the country, were led by His Eminence, Cardinal Trevor Lawrence Picachy, Archbishop of Calcutta. Pope John Paul delivered the following discourse to the group.*

Dear brothers in our Lord Jesus Christ,

For all of us, this is an hour of faith. We have come together as bishops of the Church of God, united in Christ, united in a wonderful communion of faith and love, united in a mission of evangelization and service to humanity—a mission that originates from a mandate received from the Savior of the world.

This faith of ours is first of all expressed in thanksgiving to God for the marvelous works that He continues to bring about in the lives of the faithful committed to our pastoral care. You have come to reflect with me on what the Holy Spirit is accomplishing today in the local Churches of the Bengal and Northeastern regions of India, and to give praise to the glory of divine grace.

This faith is likewise expressed in fraternity—in the fraternity with which we gather together to consider the exigencies of our apostolic ministry. In this brotherhood of faith, we all experience the great joy of being apostles—successors to the original Twelve. Jesus Christ, today and always, is the center of our interest; He is the meaning of our lives. We also have the consciousness of belonging to the College of Bishops, of being in solidarity with the other members, of enjoying the support throughout the universal Church of all our brothers in the episcopate. Above all, we have the supreme consolation of knowing that the Lord Jesus is in our midst: *"Ecce ego vobiscum sum"* (Mt. 28:20).

This is then, indeed, an hour of faith—an opportunity to renew our faith at the tomb of the Apostle Peter, who confessed that Jesus is "the Christ, the Son of the living God" (Mt. 16:16), and that He alone has "the words of eternal life" (Jn. 6:68). We are here, moreover, to rededicate ourselves to our mission of faith, which is to proclaim God's word, to proclaim God's gift of salvation in Jesus Christ.

Our awareness, in faith, of the Lord's presence inspires us to pursue our mission with confidence and humble self-assurance. We know that with God's help there is no challenge that cannot be met, no obstacle that cannot be overcome for the kingdom of God. With St. John we attest: "This is the victory that overcomes the world, our faith" (1 Jn. 5:4). The message of faith that we offer freely and without constraint rests not on the wisdom of men but rather on the power of God (cf. 1 Cor. 2:5).

The power of God was strikingly manifested in the Paschal Mystery of Jesus of Nazareth; it pervaded the teaching of the Apostles, and it is active in our day. Above all, this power of God is active through the Eucharistic Sacrifice. It is here that we ourselves, together with our priests, must go to find the main source of that pastoral love (cf. PO 14) which enables us to live a life of faith, a life of selfless love modeled on that of the Good Shepherd.

In a full and active sharing in the Eucharistic Sacrifice and in the entire liturgical life of the Church, all our people find the primary and indispensable source of the true Christian spirit (cf. SC 14). Here they draw the strength to be able to give to the world the witness of faith, the witness of love. The joyful commitment of service to humanity in need can only be sustained by power derived from the Eucharistic Christ. And it is He who inspires in the hearts of the faithful an ever greater appreciation of the needs of His brethren.

The effectiveness of the laity, and in particular of Christian families, to give to the world the witness of faith and love is conditioned by their spiritual dynamism, which is nowhere more available than in the Eucharist. The youth of your local Churches can only come to full maturity in Christ through the power of the Eucharist. God's gift of priestly and religious vocations is mysteriously related to the reverent participation of God's people in the Eucharist.

Brethren, in this hour of faith that we are celebrating together, it is fitting that we should concentrate on the Eucharist, which is the very mystery of faith. The Eucharist is our source of hope for the future. The success of our ministry is linked to it; the well-being of God's people depends on it. With the Second Vatican Council we must continually point out that the Eucharist is "the source and summit of all Christian life" (LG 11). It is the heart of our ecclesial communities. To rededicate ourselves to our ministry of faith as bishops requires a clear vision of our service in the perspective of the Eucharist. The full expression of human concern and love will be effected only through the Eucharist. All the great issues of your pastoral ministry are related to the Eucharistic Christ. He, and He alone, directs, through the power of His presence and the dynamism of His salvific action, the inner life of the ecclesial communities committed to your pastoral care. This profound truth motivated the appeal which I made to the universal Church in my recent encyclical and which I repeat today: "Every member of the Church, especially bishops and priests, must be vigilant in seeing that this sacrament of love shall be at the center of the life of the People of God..." (RH 20).

In the same encyclical, I spoke also about the close link between the Eucharist and Penance, emphasizing how personal conversion must constantly be pursued with renewed endeavor so that partaking in the Eucharist may not lack its full redeeming effectiveness. In particular, I noted the need to guard the sacrament of Penance, and I stressed that the faithful observance of the centuries-old "practice of individual confession with a personal act of sorrow and the intention to amend and make satisfaction" is an expression of the Church's defense of "man's right to a more personal encounter with the crucified, forgiving Christ," and of Christ's "right to meet each one of us in that key moment...of conversion and forgiveness" *(ibid.)*. Brethren, let us never grow tired of extolling the value of individual confession. The documents that I cited in *Redemptor hominis* make reference to a point of capital importance: "the solemn teaching of the Council of Trent concerning the divine precept of individual confession" (cf. Note 179, *Ad limina* Address of Paul VI: April 20, 1978).

Seen in this perspective, the diligent observance by all the priests of the Church of the pastoral norms of *Sacramentum paenitentiae* in regard to general absolution is both a question of loving fidelity to Jesus Christ and to His redemptive plan, and the expression of ecclesial communion in what Paul VI called "a matter of special concern to the universal Church and of regulation by her supreme authority" *(ibid)*. Of particular importance for all the bishops of the world is Paul VI's great pastoral appeal: "Moreover, we ask you, the bishops, to help your priests to have an ever greater appreciation of this splendid ministry of theirs as confessors (cf. LG 30). The experience of centuries confirms the importance of this ministry. And if priests deeply understand how closely they collaborate, through the sacrament of Penance, with the Savior in the work of conversion, they will give themselves with ever greater zeal to this ministry.... Other works, for lack of time, may have to be postponed or even abandoned, but not the confessional" *(ibid.)*.

Our ministry is indeed a ministry of faith, and the supernatural means to effect our goal are commensurate with the wisdom and power of God. The Eucharist and Penance are great treasures of Christ's Church.

In all the challenges and joys of our ministry, in all our hopes and disappointments, in all the difficulties inherent in proclaiming Christ and His uplifting message for the cause of man and human dignity, let us reflect, in faith, that Christ's power, and not our own, guides our steps and supports our efforts. Today, in the fraternity of collegiality that is ours, we can hear Christ speaking to us: *Ecce ego vobiscum sum.* And when you return to your people, endeavor to communicate the same message of faith, confidence and strength to the whole community—to the priests, religious and laity who make up with you the People of God. *Ecce ego vobiscum sum.* Particularly in the Eucharist.

But before we part, before you return to the field of your apostolic labors, let us rekindle, dear brothers, the gift of God that is ours as bishops. In the words of St. Paul: "God did not give us a spirit of timidity but a spirit of power and love and self-control" (2 Tm. 1:7). In this way, then, go forth to exercise your ministry of faith.

I ask you to take my greeting to your local Churches: to convey my love for all your people, to express my special gratitude to your co-workers in the priesthood, to the religious and to all who are your partners in the Gospel. My particular encouragement goes to the teachers and the catechists. In the unity of faith, in the love of the Redeemer, I embrace you all, saying with the Apostle Peter: "Peace to all of you who are in Christ" (1 Pt. 5:14).

To Do More, To Serve More, To Love More

On April 28, 1979, Pope John Paul II received in audience a group of bishops from Sri Lanka who had come on their ad limina *visit. The Holy Father addressed them as follows.*

Dear brothers in our Lord Jesus Christ,

As we assemble in the unity of the episcopate, our thoughts turn spontaneously to Jesus Christ. We are supremely conscious of the urgency which pervaded His soul, and which He expressed in the words: "I must proclaim the Good News of the kingdom of God...because that is what I was sent to do" (Lk. 4:43).

In reflecting on this mission of Christ, we understand the evangelizing nature of His Church; at the same time we obtain new insights into our own mission as bishops communicating the Word of God. At the center of the Good News that we are called to proclaim is the great mystery of redemption and, especially, the Person of the Redeemer. All our efforts as pastors of the Church are directed to making the Redeemer better known and loved. We find our identity as bishops in preaching "the unsearchable riches of Christ" (Eph. 3:8), in transmitting His salvific message of revelation.

Absolute fidelity to the special evangelizing task inherent in our episcopal office becomes the aim of our daily lives. The following words of my recent encyclical apply above all to us bishops: "We perceive intimately that the truth revealed to us by God imposes on us an obligation. We have, in particular, a great sense of responsibility for this truth. By Christ's institution the Church is its guardian and teacher, having been endowed with a unique assistance of the Holy Spirit in order to guard and teach it in its most exact integrity" (RH 12).

For this reason, we are intent on maintaining the purity of the Catholic Faith; we are vigilant that the content of evangelization corresponds to the message preached by Christ, transmitted by the Apostles, and authenticated by the Church's Magisterium over the centuries. Day after day we speak to our people about the name, the teaching, the life, the promises, the kingdom and the mystery of Jesus of Nazareth, the Son of God. We clearly and explicitly proclaim before the entire world that salvation is a gift of God's grace and mercy, and that it is offered to all in Jesus Christ, the Son of God, who died and rose from the dead. We preach a transcendent and eschatological salvation begun in time but to be fulfilled only in eternity.

At the same time evangelization involves an explicit message about the rights and duties of every human being. The Gospel message is necessarily linked to human advancement under the aspects of both development and liberation, since it is not possible to proclaim Christ's new commandment of love without promoting in justice and peace the well-being of man.

Our efforts, moreover, to bring this universal message into the lives of each ecclesial community, and to transpose it into language that is readily understood, must be made in close harmony with the whole Church, for we know that to adulterate the content of the Gospel, under the pretext of adapting it, is to dissipate its power. Ours is a grave responsibility, but one that we face with serenity and confidence, convinced as we are, in accordance with the Lord's promise, that the Spirit of truth guides us, provided we remain faithful to the communion of Christ's Church.

It is also significant to note in Paul VI's great treatise on evangelization how forcefully he insists that effective evangelization depends on holiness of life (cf. EN 21, 26, 41, 76). The Gospel must be proclaimed by witness, the witness of a Christian life lived in fidelity to the Lord Jesus. And just as all categories of people in the Church are invited to fulfill their role in the task of evangelization, so also everyone is earnestly exhorted to true holiness of life.

In reflecting on evangelization, it is fitting to dwell also on that unity which Jesus came to effect. In transmitting to His disciples the words that His Father gave Him, Jesus prayed that they would be truly one (cf. Jn. 17:8, 11). By His Gospel, Christ overcame the divisions of sin and human weakness, reconciling us to the Father, and leaving us as a legacy His new commandment of love. He was to die in order "to gather in unity the scattered children of God" (Jn. 11:52).

This unity among ourselves and among our people is the proof of our discipleship, the gauge of our fidelity to Jesus. The unity to which we are summoned is a unity of faith and love, which supersedes alienation among brethren and overcomes human divisions. The unity enjoined by Jesus also guarantees the effectiveness of our witness to the world: "By this all men will know that you are my disciples, if you have love for one another" (Jn. 13:35).

The same evangelizing Christ who tells us that He must proclaim the Good News also tells us that "the Son of Man came not to be served but to serve" (Mt. 20:28). Christ thus invites us, His members, to share His role of kingly service; Christ calls His Church to the service of man. This element I also endeavored to emphasize in *Redemptor hominis:* "Inspired by eschatological faith, the Church considers an essential, unbreakably united element of her mission this solicitude for man, for his humanity, for the future of men on earth and, therefore, also for the course set for the whole of development and progress. She finds the principle of this solicitude in Jesus Christ Himself, as the Gospels witness" (no. 15).

As an expression then of her understanding of the Gospel, the Church mobilizes herself in renewed charity for service to the world. She freely commits herself in all her members to exercise the charity of Christ. And one of the most important services that Christians can render is to love their brethren with the love with which they have been loved: a personal love manifested in understanding, compassion, sensitivity to need, and a desire to communicate the love of Christ's heart. In speaking of the human dimension of the redemption, I wrote: "Man cannot live without love. He remains a being that is incomprehensible for himself, his life is senseless, if love is not revealed to him, if he does not participate intimately in it" (RH 10).

Understanding this, we see that there is immense room in the world for the charity of Christ. The service of our love is without limits. We are constantly called to do more, to serve more, to love more.

Dear brothers, besides these brief reflections on evangelization and service—which are not meant to be complete—there are many other things I would like to talk to you about, in order to encourage you in your pastoral mission, so that you in turn may encourage your priests, religious, seminarians and lay people. But I am sure that in our ecclesial communion itself you will find strength and inspiration to pursue your ministry, building up, through the power of the Holy Spirit, the communities of the faithful entrusted to your pastoral care.

I commend you to the intercession of Mary, the Immaculate Virgin Mother of God, asking her to sustain you in fidelity and joy. I send my apostolic blessing with you to your people, into the Churches and into the homes of Sri Lanka—"The Pearl of the Indian Ocean"—to the old and to the young, to all in suffering and in need. My love is with you all in Jesus Christ and in His Gospel.

The Luminous Example of Mary

April 28, 1979

To my venerable brother, Alberto Cosme do Amaral, Bishop of Leiria (Portugal):

On next May 13, another great pilgrimage will be made to the sanctuary of Fatima, the program of which I was glad to know. For I am complying in this simple way with the desire you thought right to express to me that the new Successor of St. Peter, in the first year of his pontificate, should be present spiritually among the many pilgrims from Portugal and from all over the world who will gather in that blessed place.

In harmony, therefore, with this prayerful assembly, I cordially desire to wish pastors, priests, men and women religious, and beloved faithful—pilgrims to Fatima—that grace and peace may be abundant in all for deep knowledge of God and of Jesus Christ our Lord (cf. 2 Pt. 1:2). They will come to venerate the Mother of the Church and, in the light of her luminous example and through her merits and intercession, they will go there to worship God, to offer Him expiation, to attract His mercy, and implore help and graces for the Church and mankind. I would like to share in some way and stimulate this aspiration that leads you to unite with Blessed Mary, the Mother of the true God and our Mother, and to trust in the motherly love she put in the mystery of redemption and in the life of the Church; the deep necessity of faith, hope and charity, in the hour in which we are living, drives us to that.

For we actually find ourselves in an hour of radiant hope, in which the Church perceives that she is very close to man, really and deeply tied to mankind and to its history (cf. GS 1). But it is also an hour full of responsibility in which the Church herself feels with greater force that a deep bond with Christ the Redeemer of man is indispensable for her.

And then, "Brethren, what shall we do?" To this question, once asked of St. Peter, his humble Successor replies with the same word: "Repent..." (Acts 2:38). And conversion—as we are well aware, it is at the center of the message of Fatima—is a continual commitment to seek and bear witness to "deep knowledge of God and of Jesus Christ our Lord," the way of eternal life (cf. Jn. 13:3), which necessarily passes through penitence (cf. Lk. 13:3) and through prayer (cf. Jn. 15:5), which is for the Church in our day more than a need, a categorical imperative.

For this reason, a "pilgrim" with the pilgrims to Fatima, I exhort you to pray to Mary, through Mary and with Mary, holy Mother of God and Mother of the Church and Our Lady Help of Christians, trusting in her fullness of grace, manifesting to her filial love and sincere devotion based on a resolution of faithfulness to Christ, faithfulness to the Church, and faithfulness to men, our brothers. And may it be our Lady, our protectress, who presents to God the supplications I call on you to make in union with Christ, "mediator between God and men" (1 Tm. 2:5):

—for harmony within our holy Catholic Church, so that we may live and bear witness to the mystery of redemption before all those whom Christ embraced and embraces with inexhaustible love;

—for the sanctification of the whole People of God—sacred ministers, consecrated persons, families, youth, children—that there may be vocations for consecration to service of the kingdom and to the evangelical witness of charity;

   —for peace, justice, and brotherhood among men and among peoples; for those who are homeless, or live without peace, without religious freedom, without love and without hope; above all, for the little ones in this "International Year of the Child";

   —for one and all of the pilgrims gathered in this sanctuary, for their loved ones, for their land and their country; that the Lord may comfort, protect and bless all.

   With these wishes and with my heart in prayer, in token of abundant grace and peace, I bless everyone in the name of the Father, and of the Son and of the Holy Spirit.

Church's Unity Manifested in Our Communion of Love

On May 4, 1979, John Paul II received in audience the bishops of the Antilles, led by Archbishop Samuel Carter of Kingston, Jamaica. His Holiness addressed them as follows.

Dear brothers in our Lord Jesus Christ,

   With deep fraternal love I welcome you today.

   As members and observers of the Antilles Episcopal Conference you have assembled at the tomb of the Apostle Peter—and together with his Successor—in order to celebrate your unity in Christ and in the Church. Since you come from a conference that serves so many different nations and peoples of the Caribbean and the mainland, I believe you are in a position to reflect with special interest on the great theme of Church unity. I also believe that the emphasis of the Second Vatican Council on the mystery of the Church as "a sign and instrument of intimate union with God and of the unity of the whole human race" (LG 1) has a particularly deep meaning for all of you. And because reflection on this theme is both a cause of immense joy and of pastoral strength, I present it to you this morning, asking the Holy Spirit, by whose power the Church is unified in her ecclesial communion and her ministry (cf. LG 4) to bestow on us the grace for which Christ prayed: that we may be *"consummati in unum"* (Jn. 17:23).

Communion and ministry are indeed two great aspects of the Church's unity, of which we are the servants and guardians. To see the Church as a communion is to gain insight into the heart of her mystery, and into the identity of our ministry as bishops, who are called to proclaim that "our fellowship is with the Father and His Son Jesus Christ" (1 Jn. 1:3).

The communion that we promote and foster is a communion of faith in God. We believe in the Father, who out of His infinite love reveals Himself, and who through the power of the Holy Spirit gives us salvation in His Incarnate Word. We believe in our Lord Jesus Christ, who by His death gathers together in the unity of His Church the scattered children of God (cf. Jn. 11:52).

For us bishops this communion of faith is the basis of our apostolic task of building up the Church by proclaiming the Gospel, each of us finding solidarity with St. Paul as he says: "For this Gospel I was appointed a preacher and apostle and teacher..." (1 Tm. 1:11). Our communion of faith also sheds light on the unity of our ministry, in which, with the universal Church, we announce the unchanging message of salvation in Christ. Our communion of faith imposes on us the great responsibility, in which we are sustained by God's power, of giving to our people the fullness of Christian doctrine. In his last talk on the very day he died, my Predecessor John Paul I spoke of this from the standpoint of the People of God, saying: "Among the rights of the faithful, one of the greatest is the right to receive God's word in all its entirety and purity, with all its exigencies and power" (Address to Bishops from the Philippines, September 28, 1978).

The unity of the Church is likewise manifested in our communion of love, a love that is greater than our own powers and that is infused into us at Baptism, a love whereby we love God with all our heart and soul and mind, and our neighbor as ourself (cf. Mt. 22:37-39). Saint Augustine presents us with a great insight of truth when he says: "Loving God comes first as a commandment, but loving our neighbor comes first as an activity" (*"Dei dilectio prior est ordine praecipiendi, proximi autem dilectio prior est ordine faciendi": In Ioann. Tract.* 17). On the basis of this understanding, our ministry takes on new vigor as we reach out to all people to bring them Christ's love, to put into practice His commandment of love. In the communion of love we find the sustaining force for serving humanity. From the Gospel message we learn to honor man and promote the inescapable exigencies of human dignity, and to help humanity pursue the task of building the civilization of love.

In the expression of the Second Vatican Council, the great unity willed by Christ for His Church is modeled on and finds its source in the unity of the Blessed Trinity and subsists in the Catholic Church (cf. LG 8; UR 2, 3). And yet we know that the task of promoting the restoration of unity among all Christians is far from complete. It is a task that we have received from the Lord. Fidelity to Jesus Christ requires that we should pursue with vigor the cause of Christian unity. In our own day the Holy Spirit has powerfully communicated to the world the urgency of this matter: *"ut omnes unum sint"* (Jn. 17:21). This goal of the Ecumenical Council is clear, and as Pope, I have stated that "since the moment of my election I have formally committed myself to promote the carrying out of its norms and guidelines, seeing this as one of my first duties" (Address to the Secretariat for Promoting Christian Unity, November 18, 1978).

At the same time we must be willing to commit ourselves to making the effort and to adopting the means which lead to Christian unity. The Council makes detailed suggestions. Of particular importance is the question of examining our own fidelity to Christ: We are constantly called to conversion or change of heart. It is useful today to repeat the Council's emphasis that "this change of heart and holiness of life, along with public and private prayers for the unity of Christians, should be regarded as the soul of the whole ecumenical movement, and can rightly be called 'spiritual ecumenism' " (UR 8).

It is inevitable, and indeed salutary, that as Christians strive towards the restoration of unity they should feel the pain of existing divisions. As I pointed out in the above-mentioned talk: "A sickness is not healed by giving painkillers but by attacking its causes." We must continue to work humbly and resolutely to remove the real divisions, to restore that full unity in faith which is the condition for sharing in the Eucharist. Of great importance is the fact that "in every Eucharistic Celebration it is the whole faith of the Church that comes into play; it is ecclesial communion in all its dimensions that is manifested and realized" *(ibid.)*. Sharing in the Eucharist, therefore, presupposes unity in faith. Intercommunion between divided Christians is not the answer to Christ's appeal for perfect unity. God has set an hour for the realization of His salvific design for Christian unity. As we yearn for this hour, in common prayer and dialogue, and endeavor to offer an ever more purified heart to the Lord, we must also wait for the Lord's action. It must be said and said again that the restoration of Christian unity is above all a gift of God's love. Meanwhile, on the basis of our common Baptism and the patrimony of faith that we already share, we must intensify our common witness to the Gospel and our common service to humanity. In this context I would repeat the words I spoke during my recent visit to Nassau: "With deep respect and fraternal love I wish also to greet all the other Christians of the Bahamas"—and today I add:

of all the Antilles—"all who confess with us that 'Jesus Christ is the Son of God' (1 Jn. 4:15). Be assured of our desire to collaborate loyally and perseveringly, in order to attain by God's grace the unity willed by Christ the Lord."

Dear brothers in the episcopate, this mystery of unity in Christ and His Church must be lived to the full by the People of God, and the basis and center of every Christian community is the celebration of the Eucharist (cf. PO 6). I ask you to remind your faithful of the real privilege that is theirs to assemble for Sunday Mass, to be united with Christ in His worship of the Father. Sunday Mass is indeed of primary value in the life of the faithful, not in the sense that their other activities lack importance and meaning in Christian living, but rather in the sense that Sunday Mass sustains, ennobles and sanctifies all that they do throughout the week.

When you return to the field of your pastoral labors, I ask you to assure all the priests once more of my love, and to make every effort to live, together with them, the unity of ecclesial communion and ministry in all its intensity. The missionaries, still necessary in your lands, have a special place in my heart and in the heart of Christ the Savior. I also commend the seminarians to your pastoral care, so that they may learn by experience how intensely personal is the love that they will be called to manifest in the name of Christ the Good Shepherd, who knows His sheep by name. And to those who collaborate with you for the cause of the Gospel, in particular the catechists, I send the expression of my gratitude. My special support goes to the Christian families striving to exemplify the covenant of God's love and the unity of Christ's Church.

Before concluding, I make an appeal for the young people of your local Churches. Within the communion of the Church they constitute a sign of the youth and dynamism of the Church herself; they are the hope of her future. Let us do everything in our power so that the young people will be trained in justice and truth and nourished by God's Word, so that rejecting all deceptive ideologies they may live in real freedom as brothers and sisters of Jesus Christ.

To all united with you in the communion of the Church I send my apostolic blessing, invoking the intercession of Mary the Queen of heaven and Mother of the risen Christ.

"Make Every Effort To Ensure Pastoral Care for the Family"

On May 5, 1979, during the audience in St. Peter's Square, the Holy Father spoke specially to participants in the Meeting on the Family Apostolate which was taking place in Rome under the auspices of the Italian Episcopal Conference.

And now I am really happy to address a special greeting to participants in the meeting on the Family Apostolate, which is taking place here in Rome these days, and especially to my dear brothers in the episcopate who are taking part in it.

I thank you for this visit, beloved, which, if it offers you the possibility of tightening your ties of faithfulness and communion with the Successor of Peter, gives me the opportunity of talking briefly on a subject of vital importance for the society and the Church of our time.

The meeting of these days on the Family Apostolate certainly concerns a focal aspect of the lives and responsibilities of the baptized. Its topical interest is confirmed doubly, both from a positive and from a negative point of view. On the one hand, in fact, you anticipate, at least partly, the subject of a specialized ecclesial event such as the future Fifth Synod of Bishops, which will deal precisely with "The functions of the Christian family in the modern world." On the other hand, serious reflection on the subject is required by the mere fact that the psychological, social and ideological climate of today has often considerable disturbing effects on marriage and family life.

NEED OF PASTORAL CARE

My duty, therefore, is to praise and stimulate every initiative aimed at safeguarding, educating and promoting first the awareness and then the practical fulfillment of the commitments belonging to the reciprocal relations between Christian families and the ecclesial community. I am glad to repeat to you, because it is universally valid, what I already said at Puebla to the bishops of Latin America: "Make every effort to ensure that there is pastoral care for the family. Attend to this field of such primary importance in the certainty that evangelization in the future depends largely on the 'domestic church.'" Likewise the recent document of the Italian Episcopal Conference on "Evangelization and the Sacrament of Marriage" expresses itself well when it affirms that "the family must be not only the object of the responsible action of the various structures of civil society, but it must become a responsible collaborator" (no. 117). For this to happen, an efficacious education to complete maturity—human and Christian—of married couples, of the children, and of both together, is necessary.

SERENITY AND GROWTH

In a world in which the supporting function of many institutions seems to be failing and especially the quality of town life is deteriorating in a dreadful way, the family can and must become a place of real serenity and harmonious growth; not, indeed, in order to isolate itself in forms of proud self-sufficiency, but to offer the world a luminous testimony that the recuperation and complete advancement of man is possible if the latter has as its starting point and frame of reference the healthy vitality of the primary cell of the civil and ecclesial fabric.

The Christian family, therefore, must change more and more into a community of love, such as to make it possible to overcome, in faithfulness and harmony, the inevitable difficulties of everyday life; into a community of life, in order to give rise to, and cultivate joyfully, precious new existences in the image of God; into a community of grace, which will constantly make the Lord Jesus Christ its own center of gravity and focal point, in such a way as to make the commitment of each one fruitful and to draw ever-new vigor in the daily progress.

A NEW DYNAMISM

My most cordial approval and encouragement go to you, who dedicate yourselves in such a specialized way to such fundamental problems, with the hope that your labor will really be advantageous, in view of a real impact of families renewed in Christ for a new dynamism of the Church and for the general well-being of human society.

The fatherly apostolic blessing, which I willingly impart to you all and to those who support your precious work, is a sincere token of these wishes.

Authentic Doctrine and Holiness of Life

On May 5, 1979, the Pope received in audience a group of Indian bishops on their ad limina *visit. He addressed them as follows.*

Dear brothers in our Lord Jesus Christ,

It is a joy for me to have this second visit, within such a short time, from a group of bishops from India. I welcome you today, as I welcomed your brother bishops last week, in the love of Christ.

As you gather in Rome for your *ad limina* visit, you seem to echo the sentiments expressed by all the bishops of the Church as they assembled for the Second Vatican Council: "Coming together in unity...we carry in our hearts the hardships, the bodily and mental distress, the sorrows, longings, and hopes of all the peoples entrusted to us" (Message to Humanity, October 20, 1962). On my part, I embrace, in you, all the beloved people whom you are called to serve.

It is my earnest hope that this visit will give you renewed vigor and strength for your pastoral labors, that you will experience gladness in knowing—in vividly realizing—that all your apostolic zeal is supported by the universal Church. It is shared by the Pope, as one who in the mystery of the Church represents "the chief Shepherd" (1 Pt. 5:4), and endeavors to fulfill in His name a ministry of universal service. In particular, it is my desire to encourage you, my brothers in the episcopate—indeed, to confirm you in faith (cf. Lk. 22:32), not merely by words or actions, but in virtue of a charism implanted in the Church by her Founder, Jesus Christ, and activated by His Spirit. This, then, is the meaning of our meeting as we gather in unity, as we assemble in the celebration of our ecclesial and hierarchical communion.

I am aware through study, and now through our personal meetings, of a number of the issues that make up your daily solicitude on behalf of the Gospel. I am spiritually united with you as you face—with courage, confidence and perseverance—the various obstacles that beset your ministry, and hinder you in your work of evangelization and service to humanity. With my prayer I follow you in your pastoral work, blessing in particular every initiative undertaken to increase the numbers of collaborators in the Gospel, every effort made to see that students for the priesthood are trained in authentic doctrine and holiness of life. I express my deep interest in your catechetical programs, in your education of the youth and in the youth apostolates, in your efforts to defend the sanctity of marriage and to consolidate the unity of God's people in faith and love, as well as to infuse a missionary consciousness into everyone. I desire to be close to you, in fraternal understanding and shared concern, as you, on your part, strive to be close to your people in all their aspirations for human well-being and for the fullness of life in Christ. Be assured of my support for what is done in your local Churches—on the part of the clergy, religious and laity—to help the needy, the poor, the sick: to show solidarity, to enkindle hope, and to diffuse the love of Christ's heart. In all of this, brethren, I am one with you in the holy name of Jesus.

With the passing of the years and in the face of the great issues of the modern world, as well as before the inscrutable designs of God's Providence for the Church, we cannot but be more and more convinced with the Psalmist of a fundamental principle—the fact that "Our help is in the name of the Lord" (Ps. 128:4). For us, as disciples of Christ, ministers of the Gospel and leaders of God's people, it is absolutely essential that this principle should become a whole attitude of mind and norm of conduct.

Our help is indeed in the name of our Lord Jesus Christ! This luminous truth, dear brothers, is of immense relevance, and it has direct bearing on all our pastoral activity, since all our activity is carried out under the sign of the holy name of Jesus, by the power of His grace, and for His glory alone.

The message that we proclaim is proclaimed in His name—in the name of Jesus, the Savior of the world. Ours is a proclamation of salvation in Him—salvation in His name. This truth is the explicit object of apostolic teaching, being proclaimed by the Apostle Peter under the inspiration of the Holy Spirit. And today the Successor of Peter wishes to proclaim it anew, to you and with you and for you, and for your people: "There is salvation in no one else, for there is no other name under heaven given by which we must be saved" (Acts 4:12).

It is in the name of Jesus that all our ministry is performed. Repentance and the forgiveness of sins are preached in His name to all nations (cf. Lk. 24:47). We ourselves have been washed and sanctified and justified in the name of our Lord Jesus Christ (cf. 1 Cor. 6:11). Through faith we have "life in his name" (Jn. 20:31). Moreover, the Holy

Spirit Himself has been sent to us by the Father in the name of Jesus (cf. Jn. 14:26). In a ceaseless proclamation of Christ's universal mediation and in a solemn and explicit confession of His divinity, the prayer of all generations of Christians is presented to the Father: *per Dominum nostrum Iesum Christum Filium tuum.* In this name there is help for the living, consolation for the dying, and joy and hope for the whole world.

We are called to invoke this name, to praise this name, and to proclaim this name to our brethren. Our whole lives and ministry must be directed to the glory of this name. This attitude corresponds to the will of God; it is in deepest conformity with the Father's plan to constitute Christ as the Head of the Church, "the first-born among many brethren" (Rom. 8:29), and the fulfillment of all creation. It is with profound conviction and deep love that the Church addresses her Redeemer with the words: *Tu solus sanctus, tu solus Dominus, tu solus Altissimus, Iesu Christe.* The effectiveness of our supernatural mission requires that we act always in the name of Jesus, precisely in order "that primacy may be his in everything" (Col. 1:18).

In this way, dear brothers, let us face obstacles, confront challenges, accept successes; let us do everything "in the name of the Lord Jesus" (Col. 3:17). And in word and deed let us exclaim: *Non nobis, Domine, non nobis, sed nomini tuo da gloriam* (Ps. 115:1).

Three Passwords: Pray, Call, Respond

The following is an excerpt from the message of John Paul II for the XVI World Day of Prayer for Vocations, on May 6, 1979.

Dear brothers in the episcopate,
Dear sons and daughters throughout the world:

This is the first time that the new Pope is speaking to you on the occasion of the World Day of Prayer for Vocations.

In the first place, let my and your affectionate and grateful remembrance go to the late Pope Paul VI. We are grateful, because during the Council he established this day of prayer for all vocations to special consecration to God and the Church. We are grateful, because every year, for fifteen years, he highlighted this day with his words as a teacher, and encouraged us with his pastor's heart.

Following his example, I now turn to you on this Sixteenth World Day, to confide to you a number of things that I have very much at heart, almost like three passwords: pray, call, respond.

PRAY FOR LABORERS

1. First of all, *pray*. The reason why we must pray is certainly a big one, if Christ Himself commanded us to do it: "Pray therefore the Lord of the harvest to send out laborers into his harvest" (Mt. 9:38). Let this day be a public witness of faith and obedience to the Lord's command. So celebrate it in your cathedrals: the bishops together with the clergy, the men and women religious, the missionaries, those aspiring to the priesthood and the consecrated life, the people, the young people, many young people. Celebrate it in the parishes, communities, shrines, colleges and the places where there are people who are suf-

fering. From every part of the world let this insistent prayer rise to heaven, to ask the Father what Christ wanted us to ask.

A DAY FULL OF HOPE

Let it be a day full of hope. May it find us gathered together, as though in a worldwide Upper Room, "in continuous prayer, together with...Mary the Mother of Jesus" (Acts 1:14), confidently awaiting the gifts of the Holy Spirit. In fact, on the altar of the Eucharistic Sacrifice round which we gather in prayer, it is the same Christ who prays with us and for us, and assures us that we shall obtain what we ask for: "If two of you agree on earth about anything they ask, it will be done for them by my Father in heaven. For where two or three are gathered in my name, there am I in the midst of them" (Mt. 18:19f.). There are many of us gathered in His name, and we ask only for what He wants. In view of His solemn promise, how can we fail to pray with minds full of hope?

Let this day be a center of spiritual radiation. Let our prayer spread out and continue in the churches, communities, families, the hearts of, the faithful, as though in an invisible monastery from which an unbroken invocation rises to the Lord.

"COME, FOLLOW ME!"

2. *Call.* I would now like to speak to you, brothers in the episcopate, and to your collaborators in the priesthood, in order to strengthen and encourage you in the ministry which you are already laudably exercising. Let us be faithful to the Council, which exhorted bishops to "foster priestly and religious vocations as much as possible, and take a special interest in missionary vocations" (CD 15).

Christ, who commanded prayer for the laborers in the harvest, has also personally called those laborers. The words of His call are preserved in the treasure of the Gospel: "Follow me, and I will make you fishers of men" (Mt. 4:19). "Come, follow me" (Mt. 19:21). "If anyone serves me, he must follow me" (Jn. 12:26). The words of His call are entrusted to our apostolic ministry, and we must make them heard, like the other words of the Gospel, "to the end of the earth" (Acts 1:8). It is Christ's will that we should make them heard. The People of God have a right to hear them from us.

The admirable pastoral programs of the individual churches, the organizations for vocations that, in accordance with the Council, have the task of promoting all pastoral activity for vocations (cf. OT 2), open the way and prepare the good ground for the Lord's grace. God is always free to call whom He wishes and when He wishes, in accordance with "the immeasurable riches of his grace in kindness towards us in Christ Jesus" (Eph. 2:7). But usually He calls by means of us and our words. So, do not be afraid to call. Go among your young people. Go and meet them personally and call them. The hearts of many young people, and not so young people, are ready to listen to you. Many of them are looking for something to live for; they are waiting to discover a worthwhile mission, to devote their lives to it. Christ has attuned them to His call and yours. We must call. The Lord will do the rest, He who offers each individual his or her special gift, according to the grace that has been given to that person (cf. 1 Cor. 7:7; Rom. 12:6).

Let us carry out this ministry wholeheartedly. Let us open our minds, as the Council wishes, "to transcend the boundaries of each diocese, nation, religious community, and rite. Responding to the needs of the whole Church, special help should be given to those places where workers for the Lord's vineyard are more urgently called for" (OT 2). What I have said to the bishops and their cooperators in the priestly order I would also like to say to religious superiors, to the heads of secular institutes, and to the leaders of missionary life, so that each one can play his or her part, according to individual responsibilities, with a view to the general good of the Church.

Following the Example of Jesus, Let Everyone Be a "Good Shepherd"

On May 6, 1979, on the occasion of the World Day of Prayer for Vocations, the Holy Father visited the parish of St. Anthony of Padua at Via Tuscolana, Rome, where he celebrated Mass. The following are excerpts from his homily.

Beloved brothers and sisters!

Today, in the whole of the Catholic Church, the day for priestly and religious vocations is being observed. I am happy to keep it with you, here in Rome, in the center of Christianity, and in your parish entrusted to the priests of the Congregation of "Rogationists," whom I greet cordially.

This Sunday has been dedicated to this supreme and essential need precisely because the liturgy presents to us the figure of Jesus, the "Good Shepherd."

The Old Testament already usually speaks of God as the Shepherd of Israel—the people of the covenant—chosen by Him to carry out the plan of salvation. Psalm 22 is a marvelous hymn to the Lord, the Shepherd of our soul:

"The Lord is my shepherd, I shall not want; / he makes me lie down in green pastures, / he leads me beside still waters, / he restores my soul. / He leads me in paths of righteousness.... / Even though I walk through the valley of the shadow of death, / I fear no evil; / for you are with me..." (Ps. 22:1-3).

The prophets Isaiah, Jeremiah, and Ezekiel often return to the subject of the people as "the Lord's flock": "Behold your God!"... "He will feed his flock like a shepherd, he will gather the lambs in his arms..." (Is. 40:11). Above all, they announce the Messiah as a Shepherd who will really feed His sheep and not let them go astray any more: "I will set up over them one shepherd, my servant David, and he shall feed them: he shall feed them and be their shepherd..." (Ez. 34:23).

This sweet and moving figure of the shepherd is a familiar one in the Gospel. Even if times have changed owing to industrialization and urbanism, it always keeps its fascination and effectiveness; and we all remember the touching and poetic parable of the Good Shepherd who goes in search of the lost sheep (Lk. 15:3-7).

In the early times of the Church, Christian iconography used a great deal and developed the subject of the Good Shepherd, whose image often appears, painted or sculpted, in the catacombs, sarcophagi and baptismal fonts. This iconography, so interesting and reverent, testifies to us that, right from the early times of the Church, Jesus "the Good Shepherd" struck and moved the hearts of believers and non-believers, and was a cause of conversion, spiritual commitment and comfort. Well, Jesus "the Good Shepherd" is still alive and true today in our midst, in the midst of the whole of mankind, and He wants to let each of us hear His voice and feel His love.

1. *What does it mean to be the Good Shepherd?*
Jesus explains it to us with convincing clearness.

—The shepherd knows his sheep and the sheep know him. How wonderful and consoling it is to know that Jesus knows us one by one; that for Him we are not anonymous persons; that our name—that name which is agreed upon by loving parents and friends—is known to Him! For Jesus we are not a "mass," a "multitude"! We are individual "persons" with an eternal value, both as creatures and as redeemed persons! He knows us! He knows me and loves me and gave Himself for me! (Gal 2:20)

—The shepherd feeds his sheep and leads them to fresh and abundant pastures. Jesus came to bring life to souls, and to give it in superabundance. And the life of souls consists essentially in three supreme realities: truth, grace, glory. Jesus is the truth, because He is the Word Incarnate. He is the "head of the corner," as St. Peter said to the rulers of the people and elders, the stone on which alone it is possible to construct the family, social, and political edifice: "There is salvation in no one else, for there is no other name under heaven given among men by which we must be saved" (Acts 4:11-12).

Jesus gives us "grace," that is, divine life, by means of Baptism and the other sacraments. Through "grace," we become participants in the very trinitarian nature of God! An immense mystery, but of inexpressible joy and consolation!

Jesus, finally, will give us the glory of paradise, complete and eternal glory, where we will be loved and will love, participants in God's own happiness which is infinite even in joy! "It does not yet appear what we shall be," St. John comments, "but we know that when he appears we shall be like him, for we shall see him as he is" (1 Jn. 3:3).

—The shepherd defends his sheep; he is not like the mercenary who flees when the wolf arrives, because he does not care about the sheep at all. Unfortunately, we know very well that there are still mercenaries in the world who sow hatred, malice, doubt, confusion of ideas and of the senses. Jesus, on the contrary, with the light of His divine word and with the strength of His sacramental and ecclesial presence, forms our minds, strengthens the will, purifies sentiments, and thus defends and saves from so many painful and dramatic experiences.

The shepherd even offers his life for his sheep. Jesus realized the project of divine love by means of His death on the cross! He offered Himself on the cross to redeem man: every individual man, created by love for the eternity of love!

—Finally, the shepherd feels the desire to increase his flock. Jesus clearly affirms His universal concern: "And I have other sheep, that are not of this fold; I must bring them also, and they will heed my voice. So there shall be one flock, one shepherd" (Jn. 10:16). Jesus wants all men to know Him, love Him and follow Him.

2. *Jesus wanted the priest in the Church as the "Good Shepherd."*

The parish is the Christian community, enlightened by the example of the Good Shepherd, around its own parish priest and priest collaborators.

In the parish the priest continues the mission and the task of Jesus; therefore, he must "feed the flock," he must teach, instruct, give grace, defend souls from error and evil, console, help, convert and, above all, love.

Therefore, with all the anxiety of my heart as Pastor of the universal Church I say to you: love your priests! Esteem them, listen to them, follow them! Pray for them every day. Do not leave them alone either at the altar or in daily life!

And never stop praying for priestly vocations and for perseverance in the commitment of consecration to the Lord and to souls. But, above all, create in your families an atmosphere suitable for the flourishing of vocations. And, you parents, be generous in responding to God's plans for your children.

3. *Finally, Jesus wants everyone to be a "good shepherd."*

Above all, let persons consecrated to God—religious, sisters, those who belong to the secular institutes—be "good shepherds" in society. Today and always we must pray for all religious vocations, male and female, in order that this testimony of religious life in the Church may be more and more numerous, alive, intense, and always efficacious. Today more than ever the world needs convinced witnesses, who are completely consecrated!

The Paschal Significance of the Good Shepherd

The following is an excerpt of the address given at the general audience in St. Peter's Square on May 9, 1979. The Holy Father spoke as follows.

The Good Shepherd, according to Christ's words, is just he who, *"seeing the wolf come," does not flee, but is ready to risk his own life,* struggling with the beast of prey so that none of the sheep will be lost. If he were not ready to do so, he would not be worthy of the name of Good Shepherd. He would be a hireling, but not a shepherd.

This is Jesus' allegorical discourse. Its essential meaning lies precisely in this, that "the Good Shepherd lays down his life for the sheep" (Jn. 10:11); and this, in the context of the events of Holy Week, means that Jesus, dying on the cross, laid down His life for every man and for all men.

SOLICITUDE FOR SALVATION OF THE WORLD

The allegory of the Good Shepherd and, in it, the image of the fold are of fundamental importance to understand what the Church is and what tasks she has to carry out in the history of man. Not only must the Church be a "fold," but she must actualize this mystery, which is always being accomplished between Christ and man: the mystery of the Good Shepherd, who lays down His life for the sheep. This is what St. Augustine says of her: "Will He, who sought you first when you despised Him instead of seeking Him, despise you, O sheep, if you seek Him? Begin, therefore, to seek Him, the one who sought you first and carried you on His shoulders. Make His words come true: *The sheep that belong to me listen to my voice and follow me*" (*Enarrationes in Psalmos*, Ps. LXIX, 6).

The Church, which is the People of God, is, at the same time, a historical and social reality, in which this mystery is continually renewed and actualized in different ways. And different men have their active part in this *solicitude for the salvation of the world, for the sanctification of one's neighbor,* which is and does not cease to be the solicitude characteristic of the crucified and risen Christ. Such is certainly, for example, the solicitude of parents with regard to their children. What is more, it is the solicitude of every Christian, without any difference, with regard to his neighbor, the brothers and sisters that God puts on his way.

This pastoral solicitude is, of course, particularly the vocation of pastors—priests and bishops. And they in particular must fix their eyes on the figure of the Good Shepherd, meditate on all the words spoken by Christ, and measure their own life by them.

Let us permit St. Augustine to speak once more: "If only good shepherds be not lacking! Far be it from us that they should be lacking, and far be it from divine mercy not to call them forth and establish them. It is certain that if there are good sheep, there are also good shepherds; in fact, it is from good sheep that good shepherds are derived" (*Sermones ad populum,* I, Sermo XLIV, XIII, 30).

ST. STANISLAUS

In accordance with the evangelical discourse on the Good Shepherd, the Church reconstructs every year in her own liturgy *the life and death of St. Stanislaus,* Bishop of Krakow. His memory in the liturgical calendar of the universal Church is celebrated on April 11—the date of his death in 1079 at the hands of King Boleslas the Bold; in Poland, on the other hand, the feast of this principal patron is traditionally celebrated on May 8.

This year it is 900 years, nine centuries, since the moment in which—following the liturgical texts—we can repeat of him that he laid down his life for his sheep (cf. Jn.

10:11). And even if this death is so distant from us in time, it keeps the eloquence of a special testimony.

In the course of history my fellow citizens united spiritually round the figure of St. Stanislaus, especially in difficult periods.

In the current year, a year of great jubilee, as the first Polish Pope, who until a short time ago was the successor of St. Stanislaus in the episcopal see of Krakow, I wish to participate in the solemnity in honor of the patron saint of Poland.

Together with all those who celebrate this solemnity we wish to approach again Christ the Good Shepherd, who "lays down his life for the sheep," in order that He may be our strength for future centuries and for the new generations.

Missionary Dynamism Lies in Persons Animated by the Spirit

On May 11, 1979, the Holy Father received in audience the National Directors of the Pontifical Mission Aid Societies, accompanied by His Excellency Mons. Simon Lourdusamy, President of the Superior Council of these Societies. John Paul II delivered the following address.

Dear brothers and sons,

I am very happy to meet the National Directors of the Pontifical Mission Aid Societies. I know that every year you meet round Mons. Simon Lourdusamy, the President of the Superior Council of these Societies, to allocate the sums you have helped to collect, which are distributed entirely to Christian communities in need. On my side, it is the first time I have had the pleasure of receiving you and encouraging you.

The work of solidarity you are carrying out is a magnificent and necessary one. It is typical of the real charity that must reign among all members of the Mystical Body of Christ. It is a concrete expression of ecclesial fellowship, about which people like to talk so much today. An example is found in the very first Christian generation, when the Apostle Paul invites the Churches to participate in the collection in favor of the "saints" of Jerusalem who were at that time in a critical material situation. It is above all a necessity in order that evangelization may be carried on with adequate means in the young Churches or in Churches which are sorely tried.

Missionary dynamism, it is true, lies in persons animated by the Spirit of Pentecost, anxious to bring the Good News to all their brothers and sisters in the world, exactly because it is a question of their salvation and of Christ's will. There may even exist a very strong religious vitality, while means are poor, because it is based on the holiness of evangelizers and the active participation of Christians. But precisely, true zeal cannot help seeking not luxury or ease, but at least a decent subsistence and fair remuneration for Gospel workers; catechetical means worthy of an education to faith that is adapted and deep; possibilities for correct formation of priests, sisters, catechists, married couples, and lay apostles; structures of pastoral coordination which permit exchange, reflection, concerted action, particular care for the young, assistance for those in want, the setting up of places of spiritual renewal, etc.

Now, all this aid must come from Christians themselves: from those of the community concerned in the first place, who must aim at providing for their own needs as far as possible, but also from communities that are better off from the material point of view. The latter, opening up boldly to missionary solidarity—whether it is a question of individuals, families, parishes, dioceses—draw benefit themselves in apostolic dynamism; they become witnesses of religious vitality to the younger members, which may be an awakening for them. It is also necessary that public opinion should understand well this necessity of helping mission Churches. That is your main task. Last century, a magnificent movement arose when the great missionary societies came into being. Today, generosity is often manifested in an admirable way, but you must take care to maintain it and broaden it, particularly by associating the young generations with it, perhaps with new methods. For you see, maybe, that certain communities which are, however, quite rich, are too much concerned with the economic difficulties of the present and with their own problems, or are less aware of missionary duty, though they are touched by the material misery of starving countries. The Pontifical Mission Aid Societies which you are directing at the national level must, therefore, carry out first of all this work of education to charity and to missionary charity. I am anxious to tell you how much the universal Church appreciates your task and, presiding over the charity of all the Churches, I thank you deeply on their behalf. Do not let yourselves be discouraged. Improve your action. Consolidate missionary cooperation continually.

Not only do you prepare in this way the atmosphere for greater generosity, for sharing and exchanges expanded to the plane of means, but you also bring forth missionary vocations. On the Fourth Sunday of Easter, we prayed for vocations. If they are necessary everywhere, how much more so in mission territories, where, for lack of courageous and systematic evangelization, the ground remains fallow, or rather, alas, it becomes the field of ideologies alien to Christian faith. Yes, your educative concern must aim also at bringing forth missionary vocations of priests, religious men and women, and laity, in old Christian communities as in young communities. The latter, moreover, whose Directors of Mission Aid Societies I have the pleasure of greeting, are experiencing here and there an exemplary reawakening of vocations.

May the Holy Spirit enlighten and strengthen your zeal! May the Blessed Virgin obtain for you His graces which will enable you to open souls to charity! Receive my affectionate apostolic blessing.

Pastoral Care and Prayer To Achieve Revival of Vocations

On May 15, 1979, all the Italian bishops, gathered in Rome for the Sixteenth General Assembly of their episcopal conference, concelebrated Mass with John Paul II in the Sistine Chapel.
The Holy Father delivered the following homily.

Revered and beloved confreres of the Italian episcopate!

1. "Let not your hearts be troubled" (Jn. 14:1).

Christ utters these words when He has to leave this world, for He says: "I go...I will come again" (cf. Jn. 14:2-3). He utters them, aware that "the ruler of this world is coming" (Jn. 14:30), while He Himself will have to face the ordeal of the cross. Far more than His disciples, He is aware of what will happen to Him, of the course events will take in the next few days, and of how the history of the Church and of the world will proceed. Yet He utters these words which contain an appeal for courage: "Let not your hearts be troubled." And almost in contrast with all of which He was deeply conscious, He precedes this appeal with a greeting of peace, with the assurance of peace: "Peace I leave with you; my peace I give to you" (Jn. 14:27).

As can be seen, we are in this magnificent paschal setting, nearly always in the Upper Room: there where the Church, on Holy Thursday, received the Eucharist, and where, at Pentecost, she was to receive the Spirit of truth. We are at the beginnings of the Church.

THROUGH TRIBULATIONS

2. At the same time, we already enter her history. As in a kaleidoscope, there pass before us the events which bear witness how the words uttered by Jesus Christ in the Upper Room are put into practice in the lives of the first generation of Christians, which is the apostolic generation.

In today's liturgy, in fact, we find ourselves in the tracks of the first missionary journey of St. Paul who, persecuted by the Jews and threatened with death, proclaims the Gospel. At Lystra, after stoning him, they dragged him out of the city and left him alone when they thought he was dead. But Paul gets up and returns to the city, later going to Iconium and Antioch. Everywhere he organizes the Church, "appointing elders for them in every church" (Acts 14:23). He considers the ordeals he has to face as a normal thing, since in no other way, but only through many tribulations we must enter the kingdom of God (cf. Acts 14:22). In these words, we hear, as it were, an echo of the words that the Lord addressed to the disciples on the way to Emmaus: "Was it not necessary that the Christ should suffer these things and enter into his glory?" (Lk. 24:26)

In this way the early Church grows from all these experiences: It grows by means of the faith that springs from the proclamation of the Gospel made by the Apostles and sustained by prayer and fasting; it grows through the power of God's own grace. And those who construct it bear witness to it.

THAT THE CHURCH MAY GROW

3. The duty of all of us, who today are celebrating the Eucharist together here in the Sistine Chapel, is to serve in order that the Church may grow in our age, grow in these difficult times of ours; that it may grow also in the midst of adversities and threats; that it will be able to assume the fruit of the new experiences of this Italian land, of this people, which, for two thousand years, has been so closely linked with the history of the Gospel and St. Peter's See—this people whose history is entirely imbued, in an exceptional way, with the spiritual influence of Christianity. It is not necessary, in fact, to explain what is the position of Rome and, therefore, of Italy in the context of the whole Catholic Church. It is a question of a privilege, not due to

attributions of human origin, far less to usurpation of power, but corresponding to a mysterious plan of the Lord, for it was He who drove His Apostles Peter and Paul towards the shores of Italy and along the way to Rome to bring the proclamation of the Gospel and to confirm it with the sacrifice of their lives.

For this reason, at the important moment of our common service, I meet you today, venerable and dear brothers of the individual Churches of Italy, in an official way, after the numerous meetings I have had here and there with many of you in the last few months. I owe you in the first place a greeting, which is inspired both by sentiments of respect and friendship for each of you and by the far higher reasons of faith and charity. And—I beg you, beloved brothers—kindly take this greeting of mine to the faithful of each of the Churches entrusted to you.

BISHOPS OF THE CHURCH TOGETHER

You are bishops of the Church of God which is in Italy: or rather—because of the well-known geographical, historical, and theological reasons which, providentially intermingled, put Rome at the center of Italy and at the same time of the Catholic world—it is necessary to say: We are the bishops of this Church; together you and I are. And in me, called to Rome, *nullis meis meritis, sed sola dignatione misericordiae Domini*, that calls for a special consciousness of being the Vicar of Christ and Pastor of the universal Church precisely because I am Peter's Successor in this blessed Roman See; and I say, further, the consequent responsibility of having to think and operate—in line, certainly, with the *"sollicitudo omnium ecclesiarum"* of which St. Paul spoke (2 Cor. 11:28)—with very special attention and care for the increase of the spiritual and religious life of this holy city.

And from here, by natural connection or expansion, this special solicitude extends to the other Churches which are near the Church of Rome: the ancient suburbicarian sees, then the Churches of the region of Latium, then those comprised in the ancient *Patrimonium S. Petri*, and gradually to all those in the whole of Italy. It is precisely pastoral duty which obliges me to promote the cause of evangelization and to stimulate ecclesial life in the whole peninsula, with the contribution of full dedication and constant and humble commitment.

PARTICULAR PROBLEMS

4. A bishop with you and like you of the Church in Italy, I cannot ignore the particular problems that arise in our days, in the concrete framework of the social, cultural, and civil circumstances in which the whole country lives. I will tell you, in this connection, that last March I was able to read the well-thought-out "introduction," which your President, Antonio Cardinal Poma, delivered to the Permanent Council of the Italian Episcopal Conference (CEI) specifically in view of this Sixteenth General Assembly. It should be kept in mind, he said, that "the ministry of evangelization is carried out and reaches maturity at a given time and in a particular area, which we must know and evaluate." I have examined, too, the draft of the pastoral document on "Seminaries and Priestly Vocations" which you will discuss in these days. I am aware that this document constitutes the program for the year 1979-80 and, pointing out that it bears the same date as my recent *Letter to Priests*, I emphasize with pleasure that it agrees with what is for me a motive for most devoted care.

Without wishing now to anticipate conclusions that should spring from the reflection of your assembly, I am anxious to express, by way, as it were, of personal adherence, my sincere satisfaction at this work. This sentiment is prompted by a series of points contained in it: for example, the consistency of the theme of sacred vocations and seminaries with the subjects dealt with in preceding years, which all hinged on evangelization, and the last of which was entitled precisely "evangelization and ministries"; furthermore, the topical interest of the theme and its correspondence with the requirements of the present time, in which the drop that has taken place in the last fifteen years or so is making more acute the problem of the service that is specifically assigned to the ministerial priesthood within the People of God.

Now, in the middle of our Eucharistic assembly, we must look at the question of vocations in its exact ecclesiological and Christological dimension, and we must, above all, make it the object of more insistent invocation to "the Lord of the harvest." Every priestly vocation, as it springs from the voice of the Lord, is assigned to service of the Church, and it is therefore within the Church that the problem of the desired revival of sacred vocations must be inserted, studied, and solved. While keeping in mind sociostatistical investigations, we must convince ourselves that this problem is connected in the closest way with the whole of ordinary pastoral care. Vocation means a relationship, in the first place, with the life of the parish, the influence of which is of fundamental importance for it from the most different points of view: those of liturgical animation, the community spirit, the validity of Christian witness, the personal example of the parish priest and the priests who assist him. But there is a quite special relationship with family life: where there is an effective and enlightened family apostolate, just as it becomes normal to accept life as a gift from God so it is easier for God's voice to resound and to find a more generous hearing. There is another special relationship with the apostolate of youth, because there is no doubt that, if the young are followed, assisted, and educated in faith by priests who live their priesthood in a worthy way, it will not be difficult to pick out and discover those among them who are called, and to help them to walk along the way indicated by the Lord. You understand, beloved brothers, how necessary a great mobilization of apostolic forces is in this connection, starting from the fundamental environments of Christian life: the parishes, families, youth associations and groups.

As for the Christological aspect, it is likewise essential, in order to discern clearly the fitness and quality of those called, to look to Christ the eternal Priest and take from Him, from His ministry, from His priesthood, the exact measure and draw the genuine lines of priestly service. And, above all, prayer remains indispensable: we must pray tirelessly, we must pray even today, even now, in such a way that, thanks to this concelebration of ours, there will grow in us not only awareness of the problem of vocations but also the certainty of unfailing divine assistance. Once more we wish to, and must, pray fervently "the Lord of the harvest to send out laborers into his harvest" (Mt. 9:38; Lk. 10:2). It will be a prayer raised in Christ's name; it will, therefore, be granted and will help you greatly in the work of deep study and reflection which you are about to dedicate to such a serious and delicate subject.

REGARDING THE CATECHISM

5. I also know of other particular subjects to which, venerable brothers, you will give your attention in these days. For them, too, I must express to you my approval and appreciation. I am thinking of the fine text of the "Catechism of the Young," regarding which I repeat publicly what I have already written to His Eminence, the President, who presented me with a copy of it in advance: it is a text which is to be recommended for its pastoral wisdom and pedagogical experience. And I know of the other volume which, with equal commitment, is being prepared for adults. But with regard to the predominant theme, I wish to point out the fundamental value of catechesis for the revival of vocations. If ordinary pastoral care finds in catechesis one of its highest forms and one of its most suitable means, it follows that catechesis, as well as meeting the general purpose of evangelization, can also be directed to the specific purpose of vocations. I must, therefore, repeat what I have already said of pastoral care: it is necessary to give great development to the catechesis

of youth, as well as to the catechesis of the family. The latter subject is directly linked with the theme already chosen for the next Synod of Bishops. I know that the C.E.I. is already looking to this assembly which will meet next year, and has started the necessary preliminary researches in order to be able to offer the work of the Synod the contribution, always precious, of the Church in Italy. This, too, gives me sincere pleasure, in the conviction that the subject of the family and its tasks in the modern world is really one of prime importance.

There is, further, the circumstance of the Twentieth National Eucharistic Congress; announcing it, I will say that it has been decided to celebrate it in 1983, to place it at a suitable interval from the International Congress of the same name, which—as you know—will be held at Lourdes in 1981. To these and other, though minor, initiatives, there go immediately my interest, my approval and solidarity.

BOND OF COLLEGIAL UNION

6. With these thoughts and with these problems, we enter, venerated and dear brothers, upon the annual assembly of the pastors of the Church which is in Italy from the Alps to Sicily. And we listen to what the Lord says to us, as He said to the Apostles gathered in the Upper Room. We recall that His were words of peace: "Let not your hearts be troubled..." (Jn. 14:1); you heard what I said to you—I am going now and later I shall return (cf. Jn. 14:2, 3).

The same affirmation will be repeated by Him before the ascension: "I am with you always, to the close of the age" (Mt. 28:20). We accept these words with great faith. Christ is really with us and calls us to peace and fortitude. The human heart can be troubled in different ways. It can be troubled by fear which paralyzes interior forces, but it can also be troubled by that fear which springs from concern for a great good, for a great cause; from creative fear, I would say, which is manifested as a deep sense of responsibility.

The Second Vatican Council, which proposed to us such a true image of the modern world, at the same time called the whole Church to a deeper sense of responsibility for the Gospel, for the history of human salvation. This pastoral responsibility for brothers, for our fellow countrymen, weighs on each of us. It weighs in a particular way on the Successor of St. Peter, to whom Christ said "strengthen your brethren" (Lk. 22:32); and I take it up with regard to the beloved "Church which is in Italy," in the bond of collegial union with you, venerable and dear brothers!

Let us recall that the Church is a community of the People of God. Our pastoral responsibility for the Church is carried out essentially through the fact that we make all those that God has entrusted to us aware of their own responsibility, and educate them to this responsibility for the Church, and take up this responsibility in fellowship with them. This is the task that confronts the Italian episcopate, as it confronts, moreover, all the episcopates in the world. It is necessary to make the whole People of God aware of their responsibility and to share it with everyone; it is necessary to drive home to each one his own rights and duties in all fields of Christian life, individual, family, social and civil; it is necessary to unearth, so to speak, all the great resources of energy that lie in the souls of modern Christians and, indirectly, in all men of good will.

The Latin word *"confirma"* (Lk. 22:32) means "strengthen," "make stronger"; but it also means the following: *help* (brethren) *to find again the sources of this energy*, which are found in the two thousand years of Christianity on this earth: the energy, I say, that the whole modern world likewise needs. And this "confirma" rests for all of us, venerable and dear brothers, on the evangelical *confide* and *confidite* (cf. Mt. 9:2; Jn. 16:33). It is necessary to have trust in Christ, it is necessary to trust

Christ who conquered by means of the cross. We must have trust! And let us pray to His holy Mother to teach us to have this trust always, without any limit. Amen.

Profile of the Good Shepherd

The following are excerpts of the address Pope John Paul II gave during the general audience in St. Peter's Square on May 16, 1979.

INTELLECTUAL CERTAINTY

"I am the Good Shepherd," Jesus says. "I know my own and my own know me, as the Father knows me and I know the Father" (Jn. 10:14-15). How marvelous this knowledge is! What knowledge! It reaches as far as eternal Truth and Love, the name of which is the "Father"! That particular knowledge, which gives rise to sheer trust, comes precisely from this source. Mutual knowledge: *"I know...and they know."*

Christ revealed Himself precisely in this way. His words: "I know my own and my own know me" find a definitive confirmation in the words that follow: "I lay down my life for the sheep" (cf. Jn. 10:11-15).

That is the interior profile of the Good Shepherd.

FOLLOWING THE SHEPHERD

During the history of the Church and Christianity there has never been a lack of men *to follow Christ the Good Shepherd.* Certainly they are not lacking today either. More than once the liturgy refers to this allegory to present to us the figures of some saints when the day of their feast arrives in the liturgical calendar. Last Wednesday we recalled St. Stanislaus, patron saint of Poland, whose ninth centenary we are celebrating this year. On the feast of this bishop-martyr we reread the Gospel of the Good Shepherd.

Today I would like to refer to another personage, since *the 250th anniversary of his canonization* falls this year, too. It is a question of the figure of St. John Nepomucene. On this occasion, at the request of Cardinal Tomasek, Archbishop of Prague, I sent personally to him a special letter for the Church in Czechoslovakia.

Here are some sentences from this letter:

EXAMPLE AND ZEAL

"The grand figure of St. John has examples and gifts for everyone. History presents him to us first as dedicated to study and to preparation for the priesthood. Aware as he was that, in the expression of St. Paul, he would be changed into another Christ, he incarnates in himself the ideal of the expert of God's mysteries, straining as he did for the perfection of virtues; that of the parish priest who sanctifies his faithful with the example of his life and with zeal for souls; and that of the vicar-general as well, carrying out his duties punctiliously in the spirit of ecclesial obedience.

"In this office he found his martyrdom, for defending the rights and legitimate freedom of the Church against the wishes of King Wenceslaus IV. The latter took part personally in his torture, then had him thrown from the bridge into the river Moldava.

"Some decades after the death of the man of God, the rumor spread that the King had had him killed because he had refused to violate the secrecy of confession. And thus the martyr of ecclesiastical freedom was venerated also as a witness to the sacramental seal.

"Since he was a priest, it seems natural that priests should be the first to drink at his fountain, to clothe themselves in his virtues, and be excellent shepherds. The good shepherd knows his sheep, their requirements, their needs. He helps them to extricate themselves from sin, to overcome the obstacles and difficulties with which they meet. Unlike the hireling, he goes in search of them, helps them to carry their weight, and always knows how to encourage them. He dresses their wounds and heals them with grace, especially through the sacrament of Reconciliation.

"In fact, the Pope, the bishop, and the priest do not live for themselves but for the faithful, just as parents live for their children and as Christ dedicated Himself to service of His Apostles: 'The Son of man came not to be served but to serve, and to give his life as a ransom for many' (Mt. 20:28)."

From the Word of the Gospel an Invitation to Courage

On May 18, 1979, just after his return from Monte Cassino, John Paul II delivered the following address to the Italian bishops gathered to take part in the final session of the Sixteenth General Assembly of the C.E.I.

Beloved and revered confrères of the Italian episcopate!

I deeply desired to meet you again at the end of this General Assembly, not only for the pleasure that renewed contact or—more exactly—communion certainly gives me and you, but also and above all to express to you my sincere appreciation for the commitment each of you has shown in these laborious days. I have just returned from the visit to Monte Cassino, and also this circumstance, recalling fundamental memories that concern both the history of Christianity and Italic civilization, makes me feel more deeply the spiritual tie that binds me to you. And also I want to thank you for having patiently waited for me, aware as I am that not a few of you should have returned to your respective sees for urgent requirements of your ministry.

1. On my side, I have been careful to follow your work—as far as was possible. I noted, with great satisfaction, its seriousness and clarity in the rightful and pre-eminent consideration you dedicated to the problem-theme of "Seminaries and Priestly Vocations." I have

already spoken of this subject during the concelebration in the Sistine Chapel, but its intrinsic importance and the special contributions made by the Rapporteurs prompt me to add some further considerations in this connection.

There is no doubt that the statistical data that have been presented should offer the necessary reference point for an exact evaluation of the problem; but, as pastors animated by living faith and prudent realism, we must always keep in mind that the most effective remedy, the adequate solution, lies in *an incessant, courageous and fervent vocational initiative.* It is not permissible to think of the problem in numerical and bureaucratic terms or in the key of mere recruiting: vocation is and remains an elect gift from God, which, far from dispensing from human collaboration, rather presupposes it and stimulates it. Nor is it permissible to think of its solution by eliminating or weakening those typical characteristics of the priesthood which represent inseparably its nobility and its difficulty: it is not a question of lowering the line so that the obstacle can be cleared! It is necessary to respond to the height of the ideal with generosity of dedication and capacity of sacrifice.

Brothers, you understand that a coordinated pastoral effort is necessary for that reawakening of vocations which is desired not only by us gathered here but by the whole People of God, to whose evangelization we are assigned with the indispensable help of the priests. It is to this effort that you have dedicated observations and resolutions in the course of this assembly. I make them my own, offering you my solidarity and most open collaboration.

2. I listened to the concluding *Communiqué*, drawn up at the end of your work. I am happy to express my convinced adherence to the indications contained in it. The intention that inspired you was to express collegially, in the riches of the contributions offered by you in these days, a unified, operational line. In this way too—I think—the community awareness of the whole episcopate is strengthened and increased, as likewise its capacity of

indicating with due deliberation a clear position which, while considering the different circumstances, is responsibly binding on each of the members of the conference. In such an important hour for the life of the nation, animated by a high sense of duty, you have opportunely pressed for the dignity and consistency of sound Christian conscience. And how could I fail to emphasize the importance and validity of such an approach, which—amid changing events or in the diversity of socio-cultural circumstances—assumes the value of a principle? Yours is an appeal which, objectively, deserves to be shared, and I hope it will be accepted and followed.

3. The fullness of the discussions, the seriousness of the subjects dealt with, and capacity in deciding, which you have also shown these days, are an eloquent sign of your affection for the people that is entrusted to you; for this Italian people, to whom I feel driven—almost by a natural impulse—to address a due word of gratitude and praise. Yes, I wish to express public and well-deserved praise to the good and generous people, tenacious and laborious, who add to the recognized virtues of ancient times the dynamism and brilliant achievements of the modern age. These were my thoughts this morning during the journey that took me to the venerated tomb of St. Benedict, patron saint and a luminous example for the whole of Europe. Also when visiting the nearby cemetery where lie—beside those of so many other victims—the remains of the sons of my Poland who shed their blood in this land, I was thinking of the history of Italy which, at critical moments, has always called upon its innermost and admirable energies, finding in them the secret and the courage for recovery. And I was thinking together with the Saint of Norcia, of Francis of Assisi and Catherine of Siena, a triad which draws the admiring eyes of the world, and not only the Christian world. And I was thinking of the multiform and symbolical relationship that throughout the centuries has marked the history of the Church and of Italy, so rich in admired testimonies of Christian faith. Beloved broth-

ers, this expression of praise bursts spontaneously from my heart, and I beg you to convey it to your priests and to your faithful when you return to your sees.

4. Allow me, finally, revered and dear brothers, to touch now upon another matter, which is of fundamental importance for the very activity of your conference.

a) Already some time ago, Cardinal Antonio Poma, who has filled the office of President of the Italian Episcopal Conference for ten years now, asked for his resignation from this post to be accepted. He had presented this request already to Pope Paul VI and then to Pope John Paul I; afterwards he turned to me, too, expressing the same desire. I asked him to remain in office for some time longer. We all know how important the presidency of the Cardinal Archbishop of Bologna was for the episcopal community of Italy during the years that witnessed the faithful and generous application of the norms issued by the Apostolic See in implementation of the provisions of the Second Vatican Ecumenical Council. I wish to say here before you all that Cardinal Poma has always been very close to me personally since the times of the Council, during which I was able to admire his high qualifications, his zeal, his prudence and his goodness. In this decade of his presidency there have also taken shape more and more clearly the structures, the sphere of competence, and the tasks of the Italian Episcopal Conference. It has assumed an increasingly organic, incisive and essential dimension, taking the opportune initiatives to increase the spiritual life of the country, in a view at once objective and hopeful, critical and stimulating, of the most serious problems on the plane of the overall apostolate. This is confirmed, among other things, by the interest that its decisions and its documents arouse in public opinion. Cardinal Poma's merits, though shrouded by his modesty, are certainly very great in the growing role taken by the C.E.I., and I am happy to acknowledge it today, publicly and with deep gratitude.

b) As a result of this resignation, I found myself up against a problem that we all consider very important.

The statute of the C.E.I. lays down in article 25: "In consideration of the particular ties of the Italian episcopate with the Pope, Bishop of Rome, the nomination of the President of the conference is reserved for the Sovereign Pontiff."

Realizing that the aforesaid principle set a very difficult task on the Pope, who does not come from the circle of the Italian episcopate, and, at the same time, wishing to act in a way that was not contrary to this norm, I considered it opportune—in view of the necessity of making provision for the nomination of the new President—to have recourse to the presidents of the regional conferences, asking them to express their opinions to ensure Cardinal Poma's succession.

At the conclusion of these contacts, I decided to call upon Archbishop Anastasio Alberto Ballestrero of Turin, proposing to him to accept the office of President of the C.E.I., since he had been indicated by the majority of the prelates consulted. Since Archbishop Ballestrero has accepted the nomination, I wish now to communicate to all of you present here that from today he is, for the period of three years—as laid down by the statute—the President of the C.E.I.

I would like to express to him, therefore, my hearty congratulations and my brotherly wishes, certain that I am interpreting the feelings of all.

In the spirit of the Gospel Word, which I wished to recall already during the recent concelebration, I renew to you a pressing invitation to trust and courage, in the certainty of the indefectible assistance of God, in whose name I willingly bless you, together with your faithful.

Keep Intact and Proclaim the Sacred Deposit of Christian Doctrine

On May 24, 1979, the Holy Father offered Mass which was attended by staff and students of the Venerable English College and of the Pontifical Beda College.
Pope John Paul II spoke as follows.

Dear sons and brothers and friends in Jesus Christ,

On this solemnity of the ascension of our Lord, the Pope is happy to offer the Eucharistic Sacrifice with you and for you. I am happy to be with the students and staff of the Venerable English College in this year in which you are celebrating your fourth centenary. And today, in a special way, I feel spiritually close to you, to your parents and families, and to all the faithful of England and Wales— to all who are united in the Faith of Peter and Paul, in the Faith of Jesus Christ. The traditions of generosity and fidelity that have been exemplified in the life of your college for four hundred years are present in my heart this morning. You have come to give thanks and praise to God for what has been accomplished by His grace in the past, and to find strength to go forward—under the protection of our Blessed Lady—in the fervor of your forefathers, many of whom laid down their lives for the Catholic Faith.

A cordial word of welcome goes also to the new priests from the Pontifical Beda College. For you, too, this is a moment of special challenge to keep alive the ideals manifested in your patron, St. Bede the Venerable, whom you will commemorate tomorrow.

With joy, then, and fresh resolves for the future, let us reflect briefly on the great mystery of today's liturgy. In the Scripture readings the whole significance of Christ's ascension is summarized for us. The richness of this mystery is spelled out in two statements: "Jesus gave instructions," and then "Jesus took his place."

In the Providence of God—in the eternal design of the Father—the hour had come for Christ to go away. He would leave His Apostles behind, with His Mother Mary, but only after He had given them His instructions. The Apostles now had a mission to perform according to the instructions that Jesus left, and these instructions were in turn the faithful expression of the Father's will.

The instructions indicated, above all, that the Apostles were to wait for the Holy Spirit, who was the gift of the Father. From the beginning, it had to be crystal clear that the source of the Apostles' strength was the Holy Spirit. It is the Holy Spirit who guides the Church in the way of truth; the Gospel is to spread through the power of God, and not by means of human wisdom or strength.

The Apostles, moreover, were instructed to teach—to proclaim the Good News to the whole world. And they were to baptize in the name of the Father, and of the Son, and of the Holy Spirit. Like Jesus, they were to speak explicitly about the kingdom of God and about salvation. The Apostles were to give witness to Christ "to the ends of the earth." The early Church clearly understood these instructions and the missionary era began. And everybody knew that this missionary era could never end until the same Jesus who went up to heaven would come back again.

The words of Jesus became a treasure for the Church to guard and to proclaim, to meditate on and to live. And at the same time, the Holy Spirit implanted in the Church an apostolic charism, in order to keep this revelation intact. Through His words Jesus was to live on in His Church: "I am with you always." And so the whole ecclesial community became conscious of the need for fidelity to the instructions of Jesus, to the Deposit of Faith. This solicitude was to pass from generation to generation—down to our own day. And it was because of this principle that I spoke recently to your own rectors, stating that "the first priority for seminaries today is the teaching of God's Word in all its purity and integrity, with all its exigencies and in all its power. The Word of God—and the Word of God alone—is the basis for all ministry, for all pastoral activity, for all priestly action. The power of God's Word constituted the dynamic basis of the Second Vatican Council, and John XXIII pointed out clearly on the day it opened: 'The greatest concern of the Ecumenical Council is this: that the sacred deposit of Christian doctrine should be more effectively guarded and taught' (Discourse of October 11, 1962). And if the seminarians of this generation are to be adequately prepared to take on the heritage and challenge of this Council they must be trained above all in God's Word: in 'the sacred deposit of Christian doctrine' " (Address of March 3, 1979). Yes, dear sons, our greatest challenge is to be faithful to the instructions of the Lord Jesus.

And the second reflection on the meaning of the ascension is found in this phrase: "Jesus took his place." After having undergone the humiliation of His passion and death, Jesus took His place at the right hand of God; He took His place with His eternal Father. But He also entered heaven as our Head. Whereupon, in the expression of Leo the Great, "the glory of the Head" became "the hope of the body" (cf. *Sermo 1 de Ascensione Domini*). For all eternity Christ takes His place as "the firstborn among many brethren" (Rom. 8:29): Our nature is with God in Christ. And as Man, the Lord Jesus lives forever to intercede for us with His Father (cf. Heb. 7:25). At the same time, from His throne of glory, Jesus sends out to the whole Church a message of hope and a call to holiness.

Because of Christ's merits, because of His intercession with the Father, we are able to attain justice and holiness of life in Him. The Church may indeed experience difficulties, the Gospel may suffer setbacks, but because Jesus is at the right hand of the Father the Church will never know defeat. Christ's victory is ours. The power of the glorified Christ, the beloved Son of the eternal Father, is superabundant, to sustain each of us and all of us in the fidelity of our dedication to God's kingdom and in the generosity of our celibacy. The efficacy of Christ's ascension touches all of us in the concrete reality of our daily lives. Because of this mystery it is the vocation of the whole Church to "wait in joyful hope for the coming of our Savior, Jesus Christ."

Dear sons, be imbued with the hope that is so much a part of the mystery of the ascension of Jesus. Be deeply conscious of Christ's victory and triumph over sin and death. Realize that the strength of Christ is greater than our weakness, greater than the weakness of the whole world. Try to understand and share the joy that Mary experienced in knowing that her Son had taken His place with His Father whom He loved infinitely. And renew your faith today in the promise of our Lord Jesus Christ, who has gone to prepare a place for us so that He can come back again and take us to Himself.

This is the mystery of the ascension of our Head. Let us always remember: "Jesus gave instructions," and then "Jesus took his place." Amen.

Pastoral Care for Religious Vocations

On May 26, 1979, the Holy Father received in audience a group of bishops from Uruguay on their visit ad limina Apostolorum.
John Paul II delivered the following address.

Venerable brothers,

Your presence reminds me of the message which, at the beginning of my pontificate, I addressed to you on the occasion of the first centenary of the foundation of the ecclesiastical hierarchy in your country. I felt immensely pleased that an event of such importance for the religious history of your land should have its final celebration on the solemnity of the Immaculate Conception, with a ceremony that culminated at the foot of the image of the Virgin of the Thirty-Three.

Today, seeing you here on your visit *ad limina Apostolorum*—and I feel present also the other brothers in the episcopate who will likewise come to *visit Peter*—I realize deeply that my union with you is becoming stronger: a strength that finds its perennial fruitfulness in the plan according to which Christ willed to construct His Church on Peter, with the mandate of strengthening his brothers, making his mission with them the unity of the Apostolic College. It is a question of the collegiality which the Second Vatican Council stressed insistently. The bishop is the visible source and foundation of unity of the particular Church of which he is pastor (LG 23); but as a member of the Episcopal College he is obliged to act in solidarity with his brothers when there arise problems common to other ecclesial communities, especially if these problems affect the whole territory of a nation. For this reason, I am filled with joy at the image the Church offers in your country, a manifest sign of salvation and sacrament of unity for all men (LG 1), and therefore a model for the brotherly coexistence of the nation.

I wish to dwell particularly on one point, when emphasizing the operating unanimity of your aspirations: adequate and intense pastoral care for religious vocations and, above all, priestly vocations. It is an indispensable necessity, for which I, too, feel anxious solicitude when I look at countries where, as in yours, there is still lacking an organic and adequate development of the body of the particular Churches, which are obliged, for their life and mission, to avail themselves of the precious and generous, but precarious, help that the clergy of other nations can offer.

For this reason I give fervent thanks to the Lord of the harvest who, for some time now, has been bringing forth a growing number of priestly vocations in your dioceses.

I consider it superfluous to call attention to the necessity of forming adequately the future workers in the vineyard. But allow me to stress that, in your mission as pastors, priority should go to care for the spirituality of those who will be your immediate collaborators, as well as of those whom the Lord has already put at your side. Let solicitude for your priests have all the vigor and all the delicate attentions that your fatherly office calls for, above all in order that supernatural inspiration, interpreting adequately the essence of the Gospel message, may play a decisive part in their attitudes and in their conduct.

Let this spiritual animation be your concern also in looking for, forming, and directing the other forces from whom the Church today asks a substantial organized contribution for the development of her mission.

In this way your five-year pastoral plan, prepared for the whole country, will be able to pass to a dynamic executive phase for the sanctification of the People of God. The moral and religious renewal of important sectors will also benefit, as is called for by serious necessities and fatal trends on which you have recently raised your voice.

I deeply appreciate your vigilant and efficacious zeal in the whole area of the specific mission of the Church. The latter, foreign to interventions that are outside her sphere of competence, renders a service—certainly not a contingent one—to the cause of humanity in general and of the people in the midst of whom she acts as mother and teacher. In this connection you have made an explicit and well-balanced pronouncement, and I myself dealt with this fundamental subject in the opening address of the Third General Conference of the Latin American episcopate. It is a way clearly marked out for evangelization in a continent which I love deeply and in which your country has had and keeps a place of great prestige. It remains for me only to tell you, in such a delicate field, that I rely greatly on your zeal and on that of all your collaborators. But I also wish to express the hope that the human and Christian wisdom of your fellow citizens will benefit trustfully from the Magisterium and the work of the Church.

I wish to return again to the starting point of this talk: in spirit I go on pilgrimage to the sanctuary of the Virgin of the Thirty-Three, commending to her motherly love your toil, your sorrows, your aspirations and those of all your priests, deacons, men and women religious, seminarians, all those engaged in pastoral work, and your whole people.

Receive the apostolic blessing which I willingly impart to you and which I wish to send to Antonio Cardinal Barbieri, this outstanding pastor who is completing in suffering and in prayer the long and precious service rendered to the Church in your country.

Abide in the Love of Christ

On May 27, 1979, twenty-six new bishops were ordained in the Vatican Basilica, in the course of a concelebrated Mass presided over by the Holy Father.
During the Mass, the Pope delivered the following homily.

1. *"Lord you know the hearts of all men; show which one of these two you have chosen"* (Acts 1:24).

Thus the Apostles prayed, gathered in the Upper Room at Jerusalem when, for the first time, they had to fill the place that had remained empty in their community. It was necessary, in fact, for the Twelve to continue to bear witness to the Lord and to His resurrection. Christ had duly constituted the Twelve. And now, after the loss of Judas, it was necessary to face for the first time the duty of deciding in the Lord's name who was to take the vacant place.

Then those gathered prayed precisely in this way: "Lord, you know the hearts of all men; show which one of these two you have chosen to take the place in this ministry and apostleship..." (Acts 1:24-25).

What took place so long ago in the early Church is repeated also today. Behold, those who are to take the different places "in the ministry and apostleship" have been chosen. They have been chosen after the fervent prayer of the whole Church and of every community that needs them and which they will serve.

So you have been chosen, dear brothers. Today you are here at St. Peter's tomb to receive episcopal consecration. Certainly today, too, as during the whole preceding period of preparation for episcopal ordination, each of you repeats in this Basilica: "Lord, You know the hearts of all men. You know my heart too. Lord, You Yourself have been pleased to choose me. You Yourself once said to the Apostles, after calling them: 'You did not choose me, but I chose you and appointed you that you should go and bear fruit and that your fruit should abide' (Jn. 15:16)."

2. "As far as the east is from the west..." (Ps. 103:12).

You have really come here today, revered and dear brothers, from the east and the west, from the south and the north. Your presence expresses the paschal joy of the Church, which can already testify in the various parts of the earth "that the Father has sent his Son as the Savior of the world" (1 Jn. 4:14).

At this point, I would like in beautiful and poetic and, at the same time, simple language, to describe and, as it were, gather the countries from which you ordinands come, beginning with the most distant East, the Philippines, India, and then, through Africa (Sudan and Ethiopia), to arrive at South America (Brazil, Nicaragua, Chile) and North America (United States, Canada), and then back again to Europe (Italy, Bulgaria, Spain and Norway).

Time, unfortunately, does not allow me to do so. The presence among the ordinands of a bishop from Bulgaria offers me, however, the welcome opportunity of addressing a special thought to that noble nation, which has been Christian for so many centuries. I take advantage of this happy occasion to send an affectionate greeting to all my Catholic brothers and sisters, of Latin and of Byzantine rite. Although their number is not large, they bear witness to the vitality of their faith in love for their country and in service of the communities to which they belong. A respectful greeting also to the venerable Bulgarian Orthodox Church and to all its children.

Among the ordinands there are also three archbishops, called to serve, particularly, the universal mission of the Apostolic See: the Secretary of the Council for the Public Affairs of the Church and two Pontifical Representatives. Their mandate springs, as a natural and necessary requirement, from the specific function entrusted to Peter within the Apostolic College and the whole ecclesial community. Their task is, therefore, to be ministers of "catholic" unity, as "servants of the servants of God," together with the one whom they represent.

3. And now, shortly, by means of episcopal consecration, you will receive special participation in Christ's priesthood, the fullest participation. In this way you will become pastors of the People of God in different places of the earth, each one with his own duty, in the service of the Church.

As the Second Vatican Council recalled, it was Christ Himself who willed that "the successors of the Apostles, that is, the bishops, should be pastors in His Church for all ages" (cf. LG 8). Obedient to this will of their Master, the Apostles "not only had various helpers in their ministry, but...in order that the mission entrusted to them might be continued after their death, they consigned...to their immediate collaborators the duty of completing and consolidating the work they had begun. ...Thus, according to the testimony of St. Irenaeus, the apostolic tradition is manifested and preserved in the whole world by those who were made bishops by the Apostles and by their successors down to our own time" *(ibid.*, no. 20). The Council illustrated amply the essential function that the bishops carry out in the life of the Church. Among the many texts which refer to this subject, let it suffice to recall the vigorous synthesis contained in that passage of *Lumen gentium* where, on the basis of the datum of faith according to which "in the person of the bishops...the Lord Jesus Christ is present...," it is deduced with logical consistency that Christ "above all through their signal service preaches the Word of God to all peoples and administers without ceasing to the faithful the sacraments of faith; that through their paternal care (cf. 1 Cor. 4:15) He incorporates, by a supernatural rebirth, new members into His Body; that finally, through their wisdom and prudence He directs and guides the people of the New Testament on their journey towards eternal beatitude" (no. 21).

In the light of these clear and rich conciliar affirmations, I express the deep joy it gives me to confer episcopal consecration on you today, dear brothers, and in this way bring you into the college of the bishops of Christ's Church: With this act, in fact, I can show particular esteem and love for your fellow-countrymen, your nations and the local Churches from which you have been chosen and for the good of which you are constituted pastors (cf. Heb. 5:1).

Together with you I meditate on the words of the Gospel today: "No longer do I call you servants, for the servant does not know what his master is doing; but I have called you friends, for all that I have heard from my Father I have made known to you" (Jn. 15:15). And I wish with my whole heart to congratulate you on this friendship. What could be greater? And, therefore, I wish you nothing else but this: Abide in the love of Christ! (cf. Jn. 15:10); abide in His friendship. Abide in it as He abides in the Father's love.

May this love and this friendship fill your life completely and become the inspiring source of your works in the service you assume today. I wish you abundant and happy fruits in this ministry of yours: "that you should go and bear fruit and that your fruit should abide" (Jn. 15:16), that the Father may give you everything you ask Him for in the name of Christ (cf. Jn. 15:16)—His eternal Son.

May your mission and your ministry lead to the strengthening of mutual love, common love, and of the union of the People of God in Christ's Church, since it is in love and union that there is revealed, in all its luminous simplicity, the face of God: Father and Son and Holy Spirit; God who is love (cf. 1 Jn. 4:16).

And what the world, that world to which we are sent, needs most is precisely love!

To Sustain and To Guide the Community of Faith

The Holy Father received in audience on May 31, 1979, eleven bishops of India who had come to Rome on their ad limina *visit. Pope John Paul spoke to them as follows.*

Dear brothers in our Lord Jesus Christ,

For the third time in a little over a month it is my joy to be with a group of Indian bishops making their *ad limina* visit. As I recall my meetings with your brother bishops, I offer to you also, for your encouragement and strength, the reflections I made previously with them. I spoke about the ministry of faith which is ours, which rests on the power of God, and which is eminently expressed in the Eucharistic Sacrifice and in the sacrament of Penance. I subsequently spoke about the holy name of Jesus, source of our strength and joyful inspiration for all our pastoral activities. And today I would like to continue to reflect with you on our common ministry of faith, exercised in the name of Jesus Christ, the Son of God and Savior of the world.

Day after day we are conscious of the challenge of Christ's words, spoken before the ascension: "Go out to the whole world. Proclaim the Good News to all creation" (Mk. 16:16). As bishops with this mandate we know what it means to experience limitations, to meet opposition, to face injustice, and to feel the effects of sin. And still we are filled with hope in our work, accepting as we do the words of God: *virtus in infirmitate perficitur* (2 Cor. 12:9). This, dear brothers, was likewise the conviction of all the bishops of the world as they began the Second Vatican Council. In their opening message they stated: "To be sure, we are lacking in human resources and earthly power. Yet we place our trust in the power of God's Spirit, who was promised to the Church by our Lord Jesus Christ" (October 20, 1962).

This then must be our attitude always, but especially today, as we wait, in the unity of apostolic fellowship, together with Mary, the Mother of Jesus, to receive anew at Pentecost the Father's gift of the Spirit, so that we can go forth to give witness to Jesus and to continue among our people His role as the Good Shepherd.

Only last Sunday I had the joy of ordaining twenty-six new bishops, including the Auxiliary of Calcutta. I could not help but reflect on the profound meaning of the ordination rite as I examined the candidates and asked: "Are you resolved as devoted fathers to sustain the People of God and to guide them in the way of salvation in cooperation with the priests and deacons who share your ministry?" These are indeed two key words: *to sustain* and *to guide*. Our pastoral ministry exercised in close union with our collaborators is above all directed to the good of God's people, of which our beloved laity are the great majority. For them we give our lives as devoted fathers to sustain them and to guide them in the way of salvation. And Paul VI completes our insight into the reality of this spiritual fatherhood of ours when he writes in *Ecclesiam suam:* "In the very act of trying to make ourselves pastors, fathers and teachers of men, we must make ourselves their brothers" *(AAS,* 1964, 56, p. 647). And so, in the brotherhood that we must also endeavor to exemplify, Jesus Christ is indeed our supreme exemplar—He who is the only begotten Son of God, but who became and is so rightly called "the first-born among many brethren" (Rom. 8:29).

In this time of Pentecost let us sustain our people, transmitting to them the encouragement of Jesus Himself: "Fear not, little flock, for it is your Father's good pleasure to give you the kingdom" (Lk. 12:32). In particular, let us do this by spelling out the exalted dignity of the laity within the community of the Church. Of primary importance in this regard is the fact that by Baptism and Confirmation the laity are commissioned by the Lord Himself to share in the saving mission of the Church (cf. LG 33). It is, therefore, no pragmatic reason that motivates us to sustain and guide them in their apostolate, but the very will of Christ for His people, for His Church. In so many circumstances the laity are the immediate heralds of faith giving authentic witness to God's kingdom, which is yet to be revealed in its fullness. It is up to the laity to order temporal affairs in justice and peace, in equity and freedom, in truth and love—in accordance with the divine plan of creation and redemption. After the fashion of leaven, they are called to work for the sanctification of the world from within, beginning with their own families. And all their efforts and struggles and sufferings on behalf of the kingdom of God are of immense value when united with the sacrifice of Christ. In the example of the laity the world must see the love of Christ manifested in His members. The nature of the Church as a community of prayer is readily perceived from the assemblies of the faithful gathered for the worship and praise of God.

In the community of the faithful—which must always maintain Catholic unity with the bishops and the apostolic See—there are great insights of faith. The Holy Spirit is active in enlightening the minds of the faithful with His truth, and in inflaming their hearts with His love. But these insights of faith and this *sensus fidelium* are not independent of the Magisterium of the Church, which is an instrument of the same Holy Spirit and is assisted by Him. It is only when the faithful have been nourished by the Word of God, faithfully transmitted in its purity and integrity, that their own charisms are fully operative and fruitful.

Once the Word of God is faithfully proclaimed to the community and is accepted, it brings forth fruits of justice and holiness of life in abundance. But the dynamism of the community in understanding and living the Word of God depends on its receiving intact the *depositum fidei;* and for this precise purpose a special apostolic and pastoral charism has been given to the Church. It is one and the same Spirit of truth who directs the hearts of the faithful and who guarantees the Magisterium of the pastors of the flock.

One of the greatest services then that we can give to our people is to proclaim to them, day in and day out, "the unsearchable riches of Christ" (Eph. 3:8), pointing out that Christianity is a unique and original message of salvation to be found in the name of Jesus Christ and in His name alone.

Brethren, each one of us must repeatedly confirm the *yes* of our episcopal ordination: We must indeed be resolved to sustain the People of God and to guide them in the way of salvation. And as we strive to fulfill this charge we must think of Jesus, who transmits to His disciples the great treasure of the Father's word: *Ego dedi eis sermonem tuum* (Jn. 17:14). We are called to continue His revelation of the Father, to transmit the Word of God.

As we exhort our people more and more to undiscriminating service of their brethren and to universal love, we wish them to realize the great dignity that is theirs as disciples of Christ, and the real consequences of this discipleship in their daily living. With humility, but with deep conviction, we must take our stand, clearly passing on the exhortation of St. Paul: "Do not be conformed to this world" (Rom. 12:2).

All of this, brethren, goes to describe the challenge that faces our laity, who must courageously take their place in loving union with their bishops in the *pusillus grex;* all of this clarifies the goals of the seminary training that we must uphold; all of this emphasizes the priestly task of true evangelization and gives us deeper insights into our own pastoral ministry as bishops of the Church of God.

Dear brothers, let us go forward—forward together, with each other and with our clergy—in the name of Jesus: strong in our communion of faith and love, serene in the face of obstacles, constant in prayer with Mary and to Mary—and, as fathers and brothers, sustaining our people in their distinctive vocation of Christianity, and guiding them in the way of salvation.

And together with the whole Church, let us await the Holy Spirit, who alone can supply for our weaknesses and bring to completion and perfection the ministry of faith that we exercise in the name of our Lord Jesus Christ, to whom be glory and honor, forever and ever. Amen.

Unity of Polish Bishops— a Recognized Source of Spiritual Strength

On June 5, 1979, Pope John Paul II took part in the Plenary Assembly of the Polish Episcopal Conference which was held in the Monastery of Jasna Gora. The Holy Father addressed the Polish bishops as follows.

1. First of all, I wish to express my joy and deep emotion at our meeting today. The Polish Bishops' Conference is the community and the setting from which Christ, by His inscrutable plan, called me on October 16, 1978, to the See of St. Peter in Rome, manifesting His will through the votes of the Sacred College, gathered in conclave in the Sistine Chapel. As today I have the good fortune to be taking part again in the plenary assembly of the Polish Bishops' Conference at Jasna Gora, I cannot fail to express especially my feelings of gratitude and fraternal solidarity, which go back to the very beginning of my nomination as

a bishop in 1958. I remember that the first Conference that I took part in as bishop-elect also took place at Jasna Gora, at the beginning of September.

During the twenty years of my membership and participation in the work of the Polish Bishops' Conference, I have learned a great deal, both from the individual members of this episcopal community, beginning with the eminent Primate of Poland, and also from the community as such. In fact, the quality that particularly characterizes the Polish Bishops' Conference is that unity which is the source of spiritual strength. The Polish episcopate, precisely through this unity, in a special way serves the Church in Poland and also the universal Church. Society is well aware of this, and has a justified and deserved confidence in the Polish episcopate. This confidence is shown to the whole of the episcopate, to all the archbishops and bishops in their dioceses, and especially to the Primate of Poland, of whom I wish to say here what I have already expressed several times, namely, that he is a providential man for the Church and for the motherland. This is the opinion not only of Poles but also of people belonging to the other nations of Europe and the world, who together with us thank the Lord for having given such power to man (cf. Jn. 1:12).

During the twenty years of my episcopal ministry, in the course of which I have been able to serve the Church in Krakow—first at the side of Archbishop Eugeniusz Baziak of blessed memory (Metropolitan of the orphaned Archdiocese of Lwow), then as the successor of the Metropolitan of Krakow, Cardinal Adam Stefan Sapieha, in the see of St. Stanislaus—there have accumulated in my heart great debts of gratitude, debts which I seek to repay, as best I can, with remembrance of and prayer for the Polish Cardinals, archbishops and bishops, living and dead. Those who have died do not fade from my memory, especially those with whom it has been granted to me to be closest by working with them, in the range of the influence of their personalities—as in the case of the Archbishops of

Krakow I have mentioned—the late Cardinal Boleslaw Kominek, Metropolitan of Wroclaw, Archbishop Anthony Baraniak, Metropolitan of Poznan, and so many magnificent and unforgettable bishops, both ordinaries and auxiliaries, men full of human originality and Christian authenticity, whom the Lord has called to Himself during these twenty years. I cannot fail to recall the late Cardinal Boleslaw Filipiak, who for many years of his life served the Holy See, and whom I met many times in Rome.

Taking part in the work of the Polish episcopate has enabled me to study at close quarters the problems of the modern Church in their universal dimension. This has occurred thanks in particular to the Council, in which I had the good fortune to take part from the first day to the last. In entering into all this vast combination of problems, which Vatican II pinpointed in all its documents, I have been able to realize what a special and responsible place Poland, and especially the Church in Poland, has on the great map of the modern world, that world to which we are all sent, as the Apostles were sent at the moment of Christ's ascension, with the words: "Go therefore and make disciples of all nations" (Mt. 28:19). This realization became even deeper during the year following the Council, thanks especially to work in the Synod of Bishops, in the Congregations of the Apostolic See, and thanks also to my meetings with representatives of the various episcopates, both from Europe and from the other continents. One of the opportunities consisted in the visits to emigré Poles which I made several times in the name of the Polish episcopate.

Today I remember all this with gratitude. My membership of the Polish Episcopal Conference and my many-sided participation in its work has been confirmed by Providence as the most appropriate means of preparation for that ministry which since October 16 I have had to exercise vis-á-vis the whole universal Church. I wish to say this at the beginning of my address, which is being given to this unusual plenary meeting of the Polish Episcopal Conference taking place here today.

2. In the Church in my motherland, the year 1979 is the year of St. Stanislaus. Nine hundred years have passed since his death at the hands of King Boleslaw the Bold at Skalka. The death of the Bishop who proclaimed to everyone—not excluding the King—the truth of the Faith and of Christian morality had a significance of special witness to the Gospel and to Christ Himself. Stanislaus of Szczepanow suffered death in such manner that, in the Church's tradition, he was included among the martyrs. At the beginning of our history, in the second century of Christianity in Poland, that martyr-bishop, blood of the blood and bone of the bone of the nation, was linked with another bishop, one who belonged to the first missionary generation and the time of the Baptism—St. Wojciech (Adalbert), who was of Czech origin. I mention him because, in the memory of the People of God on Polish soil, these two figures are linked together and surrounded by a special veneration and devotion.

Stanislaus of Szczepanow was bishop of Krakow and a member of the Polish episcopate at that time, and therefore the present Polish episcopate has particular reasons for surrounding his figure with special veneration, and especially the anniversary of his martyrdom. This has been taking place in the Archdiocese of Krakow since 1972, while in the Diocese of Tarnow, where Szczepanow, the saint's birthplace, is situated, they are celebrating the "Year of St. Stanislaus." As bishop and pastor of the see of Krakow, St. Stanislaus was one of the pillars of that hierarchical order which was established in the lands of the Piasts from the year 1000. We have special reasons for continually thanking God for the solid foundations of that order, instituted during the Congress of Gniezno upon the foundation of the apostolic mission of St. Wojciech and his martyrdom. It was precisely to that martyred body, which Boleslaw the Bold translated with veneration to Gniezno, that the legates of Pope Sylvester II and the Emperor Otto III came. The Poland of the Piasts, which from as early as 968 *cepit habere episcopum* at Poznan—relatively early, because it was scarcely thirty-four years after the baptism of Mieszko—gained its own ecclesiastical organization: the Metropolitan see at Gniezno with the episcopal sees at Krakow, Wroclaw and Kolobrzeg.

These facts are known by everyone. But it is impossible to fail to recall them and to refer to them on this extraordinary occasion that we are experiencing together.

The hierarchical order is a constitutive element of Christ's Church, as the Dogmatic Constitution on the Church, *Lumen gentium*, authoritatively reminded us. The Church, which as the People of God has been built up upon the mystery of the Incarnation and Redemption, and which is continually born from the descent of the Holy Spirit, is the visible reality of a clearly defined hierarchical order. This order determines the Church as a well defined community and society, which through its own hierarchical order forms part of the history of humanity, in the history of the individual peoples and nations. Therefore we rightly venerate St. Wojciech as the patron of the hierarchical order in our motherland. We rightly recall and appreciate the great leaders of the Assembly of Gniezno. Through the formal hierarchical structure that she gained in Poland at that time, the Church firmly became part of the nation's history. The year 1000 is a date that with good reason we link to the date of the Baptism that took place in 966.

Knowledge of the history of Poland will tell us still more: not only was the hierarchical order of the Church decisively inserted into the history of the nation in 1000, but also the history of the nation was in a providential manner rooted in the structure of the Church in Poland, a structure that we owe to the Assembly of Gniezno. This affirmation finds its confirmation in the various periods of the history of Poland, and particularly in the most difficult periods. When national and state structures were lacking, society, for the most part Catholic, found support in the hierarchical order of the Church. And this helped society to overcome the times of the partition of the country and the times of occupation; it helped society to maintain, and even to deepen its understanding of, the awareness of, its own identity. Perhaps certain people from other countries may consider this situation "untypical," but for Poles it has an unmistakable eloquence. It is simply a part of the truth of the history of our own motherland.

The episcopate of modern Poland is in a special way the heir and representative of this truth. There is a deep reason for the fact that for a thousand years of history the heritage of the holy martyr bishops Wojciech and Stanislaus has permeated the thoughts and the hearts of the Poles.

3. When in the year 1000 there arose in Poland the fundamental structure of the hierarchical order of the Church, it arose, right from the beginning, in the unity of the hierarchy with the order of the universal Church—that is to say with the Apostolic See. In this relationship the structure of the Church has lasted uninterruptedly in our motherland up till today. Thanks to this, Poland is Catholic and "ever faithful." The unity of the hierarchical structure, the bond between the Polish episcopate and the See of Peter, constitutes the basis of this unity in its universal dimension. The Church in Poland, throughout the centuries, has been firmly and unshakeably rooted in that universality which is one of the marks of Christ's Church. The Constitution *Lumen gentium* exhaustively studied this fact under various aspects, at the same time showing how the universal dimension of the Church is linked to the mission and ministry of Peter.

We are well aware that this fact that the Church in Poland is rooted in its catholicity—from the moment of the Baptism and of the Assembly of Gniezno and throughout history—has a particular meaning for the spiritual life of the nation. And it also has a meaning for the nation's culture, which is marked not only by the tradition of visible links with Rome but also possesses the characteristic of universality proper to Catholicism and the characteristic of openness to everything which in the universal exchange of good things becomes the portion of each of those who take part in it. This affirmation could be confirmed by innumerable instances taken from our history. One of these instances could also be the fact that we are together today, namely, that the Polish episcopate is meeting a Polish Pope.

It is generally stated that the Polish people's sharing in the Church's spiritual heritage, which results from its universal unity, has become an element of unity and security of the nation's identity and unity in the particularly difficult periods. Those periods were also particularly marked by the spreading of the Christian spirit. This is confirmed by the nineteenth century, and for us it is confirmed by the recent decades of the present century. After the period of occupation, which as everyone knows was a terrible and mortal threat for Poland's survival, there began a period of great transformations which found outward expression, for example, in the completely new definition of the boundaries of the State.

In this context, the bond between the life of the nation and the activity of the Church, a bond experienced for centuries, has been once more activated before our eyes. The normalization of ecclesiastical relationships in the sphere of the new boundaries of the Polish State, and in particular in the territories of the West and North, has clearly confirmed the meaning of the year 1000 or the times of Saints Wojciech and Stanislaus. The hierarchical order of the State has become not only the center of her pastoral mission, but also a clear support for the whole life of society, for the nation conscious of its right to exist, which, as a nation that is in the vast majority Catholic, seeks this support also in the hierarchical structures of the Church. Such is the eloquence of the events that began in the pontificate of Pope Pius XII in 1945, shortly after the end of the War and the Occupation, with the memorable mission of Cardinal Augustyn Hlond, Primate of Poland, and concluded with the final decisions of Pope Paul VI in June of 1972, when in the Archdiocese of Krakow there began the seven-year jubilee of the pastoral service of St. Stanislaus. It is significant that it was precisely during the Plenary Conference in Krakow, on June 28, that these important decisions of Paul VI were made public.

The Church's hierarchical order finds its keystone in the mission and ministry of Peter. The Apostolic See draws from this mission and ministry the character that is proper to it. This character is not one of secular and political structure, even though, for reasons that are still valid, there is still linked to the See of Rome a remnant of the old Papal States.

However, as in the case of that State, which in its historical aspect ceased to exist in 1870, so likewise the one which actually remains of it and which is only symbolical, is a guarantee of the sovereignty of the Apostolic See in regard to the world and constitutes a basis to support what is essential for the Apostolic See. This stems solely and exclusively from the nature of the Church, from her apostolic mission, from the evangelical service to truth and love, from the pastoral mission which, above all, the hierarchical order of the Church serves. The chapters devoted to this hierarchical order and its motivation are found in the Constitution *Lumen gentium*, after the chapters dealing with the mystery of the Church and the universal mission of the People of God.

It is only if we keep before our eyes this proper and correct image of the Church, and, in its organic whole, the proper image of the Apostolic See, that we can lay down exactly the meaning of the question that for many years has been of great relevance in Poland—the question of the normalization of relations between the Church and the State. It is necessary to speak here about this relevance which has new aspects because the already-mentioned question has behind it, for understandable reasons, a long and complex history which cannot be ignored. The Polish episcopate, in close collaboration with the Apostolic See, especially during the pontificate of John XXIII and of Paul VI, did a great deal for the cause of this normalization. In the first place, it laid down a series of concrete elements on which to base it. Of fundamental assistance in this pioneering work was the teaching contained in the documents of the Second Vatican Council; and especially the possibility of using the *Declaration on Religious Freedom*, a document that directly tallies with the principles promulgated in fundamental state and international documents, including the Constitution of the Polish People's Republic. It is clear that the concrete application of these principles can only respond to the idea of "religious freedom" when it takes into consideration the real needs of the Church linked with her many-sided activity.

I spoke about this subject, and also of the Church's readiness to collaborate with all countries and with all people of good will, on last January 12 to the Diplomatic Corps accredited to the Holy See. Here is a relevant passage:

"Maintaining contacts—among others by means of diplomatic representations—with so many and such different States, the Apostolic See wishes above all to express its deep esteem for each nation and each people, for its tradition, its culture, its progress in every field, as I said already in the letters addressed to Heads of State on the occasion of my election to the See of Peter. The State, as the expression of the sovereign self-determination of peoples and nations, is a normal realization of social order. Its moral authority consists in that. The son of a people with a millenary culture which was deprived for a considerable time of its independence as a State, I know, from experience, the deep significance of this principle.

"The Apostolic See welcomes joyfully all diplomatic representatives, not only as spokesmen of their own governments, regimes and political structures, but also and above all as representatives of peoples and nations which, through these political structures, manifest their sovereignty, their political independence, and the possibility of deciding their destiny autonomously. And it does so without any prejudice as regards the numerical importance of the population: Here, it is not the numerical factor that is decisive.

"The Apostolic See rejoices at the presence of so many representatives; it would likewise be happy to see many others, especially of nations and peoples which at times had a centuries-old tradition in this connection. I am thinking here particularly of the nations that can be considered Catholic, but also of others. For, at present, just as ecumenism between the Catholic Church and other Christian Churches is developing, just as there is a tendency to establish contacts with all men by appealing to good will, so this circle is widening.... The Apostolic See, in conformity with the mission of the Church, wishes to be at the center of this brotherly rapprochement. It wishes to serve the cause of peace, not through political activity but by serving the values and principles which condition peace and rapprochement, and which are at the basis of the international common good....

"We see clearly that humanity is divided in a great many ways. It is a question also, and perhaps above all, of ideological divisions bound up with the different state systems. The search for solutions that will permit human societies to carry out their own tasks and to live in justice is perhaps the main sign of our time.... Advantage must be taken of mutual experiences....

"The Apostolic See, which has already given proof of this, is always ready to manifest its openness with regard to all countries or regimes, seeking the essential good which is man's real good. A good number of exigencies connected with this good have been expressed in the 'Declaration of Human Rights' and in the international pacts which permit its concrete application" (*AAS* 70, 1978, pp. 170-179).

The Polish episcopate has its own experiences in this important field. Basing itself on the teaching of Vatican II, it has worked out a series of documents of theory, which are known to the Apostolic See, and at the same time it has worked out a series of pastoral attitudes that confirm readiness for dialogue. They clearly show that authentic dialogue must respect the convictions of believers, ensure all the rights of citizens and also the normal conditions for the activity of the Church as a religious community to which the vast majority of Poles belong. We are aware that this dialogue cannot be easy, because it takes place between two concepts of the world which are diametrically opposed; but it must be possible and effective if the good of individuals and the nation demands it. The Polish episcopate must not cease to undertake with solicitude initiatives which are important for the present-day Church. In addition, in the future there must be clarity in the principles of procedure which in the present situation have been worked out within the ecclesial community, regarding both the attitude of clergy and lay people and the status of individual institutions. Clarity of principles, as also their practical putting into effect, is a source of moral strength and also serves the process of a true normalization.

In favor of the normalization of Church-State relations in our time, the cause of fundamental human rights, including the right to religious liberty, has an undoubted significance, which under a certain aspect is fundamental and central. The normalization of Church-State relations constitutes a practical proof of respect for this right and for all its consequences in the life of the political community. Thought of in this way, normalization is also a practical manifestation of the fact that the State understands its mission to society according to the principle of subsidiarity *(principium subsidiarietatis)*, namely, that it wishes to express the full sovereignty of the nation. In relation to the nation, with regard to its special millenary and the present connection with the Catholic Church, this last aspect takes on a particular significance.

4. Throughout this consideration, especially, in its last part, we have penetrated deeply into the sphere of the ethical reasons that make up the fundamental dimension of

human life, also in the field of that activity that is called political. In conformity with the tradition of European thought, which goes back to the works of the greatest philosophers of antiquity and which found its full confirmation and deeper development in the Gospel and in Christianity, political activity also—indeed especially—finds its proper meaning in solicitude for people's good, which is a good of an ethnical nature. From here that whole so-called social teaching of the Church derives its deepest premises, a teaching that, especially in our time, beginning from the end of the nineteenth century, has been enormously enriched by all the problems of the present day. This does not mean that the Church's social teaching appeared only at the turn of the century; in fact it existed from the beginning, as a consequence of the Gospel and of the vision of the man that the Gospel brought into relationships with other people, and especially in community and social life.

St. Stanislaus is called the patron of the moral order in Poland. Perhaps it is precisely in him that we see most clearly how deeply the moral order penetrates—the moral order which is so fundamental for man, the *humanum*—in the structures and levels of the life of the nation as a State, in the structures and levels of political life. We can never meditate too deeply about the way in which that holy Bishop of Krakow, who suffered death at the hand of an eminent representative of the Piast dynasty, was later well received, especially in the thirteenth century, by the successors of that same dynasty, and later, after his canonization in 1253, venerated as patron of the unity of the motherland, which by reason of dynastic divisions found itself split up. Certainly, this unusual tradition of the cult of St. Stanislaus throws a special light on the events of 1079, during which the Bishop of Krakow suffered death, while King Boleslaw the Bold lost his crown and was forced to leave Poland. And even though Gall the Anonymous, writing his chronicle some decades later, used with regard to Bishop Stanislaus the expression *traditor*, this or similar expressions are found at that time applied to various other bishops (as, for example, St. Thomas Becket in England) and even to Popes (for example, St. Gregory VII) who earned the halo of sainthood. Obviously, the episcopal ministry has sometimes exposed bishops to the peril of losing their lives and thus of paying the price of proclaiming the truth and the divine law.

The fact that St. Stanislaus, whom history calls "the Patron of the Poles," has been recognized by the Polish episcopate especially as patron of the moral order finds its motivation in the eloquent ethical value of his life and death, and also in the whole tradition that has expressed itself throughout the generations of the Poland of the Piasts, of the Jagellonians, and of the elected kings, down to our own times. The patronage of the moral order that we attribute to St. Stanislaus is principally linked with the universal recognition of authority, of the moral law, that is to say, of the law of God. This law places an obligation upon everyone, both subjects and rulers. It constitutes the moral norm, and is an essential criterion of man's value. Only when we begin from this law, namely the moral law, can the dignity of the human person be respected and universally recognized. Therefore, morality and law are the fundamental conditions for social order. Upon the law are built states and nations, and without it they perish.

The Polish episcopate, with a deep sense of responsibility for the nation's destiny, always points out, in its pastoral programs, the sum of threats of a moral nature which the man of our time, the man of modern civilization, fights against. These threats relate both to personal life and to life in society, and they weigh especially heavily upon the family and upon the education of the young. Married people, the family nuclei, must be defended from sin, from grave sin against nascent life. In fact it is well known that the circumstances of that sin weigh upon the morality of society, and its consequences menace the future of the nation. And then one must defend people from the sins of immorality and alcoholic abuse, because these sins bear within them the lowering of human dignity, and have incalculable consequences in the life of society. Watchfulness is always needed, human consciences must always be kept alert, warnings must always be given in the face of violation of moral principles, people must be urged to carry out the commandment of charity, for inner insensitivity easily takes root in human hearts.

This is the eternal problem that has not only not lost its relevance in our times but has become even more clear and obvious. The Church needs a hierarchical order if she is to serve people and society effectively in the field of the moral order. St. Stanislaus is the expression, symbol and patron of this order. Given that the moral order is at the basis of all human culture, the national tradition rightly sees St. Stanislaus' place at the basis of Polish culture. The Polish episcopate must add to its present mission and ministry a particular solicitude for the whole Polish cultural heritage, of which we know to what degree it is permeated by the light of Christianity. It is also well known that it is precisely culture that is the first and fundamental proof of the nation's identity. The mission of the Polish episcopate, inasmuch as it is the continuation of the mission of St. Stanislaus, is in a certain manner marked by his historical charism—and therefore remains in this field clear and irreplaceable.

5. It is hard to think of our great jubilee of the nine hundredth anniversary of the death of St. Stanislaus and to prescind from the European context. Just as it is hard to think of and live the millennium of the Baptism of Poland without referring to that context. Today, that context has widened beyond Europe, especially because the sons and daughters of so many European nations—including the Poles—have populated and formed the life of society in other continents. Yet there the European context is undoubtedly at the very basis. The already mentioned analogies of the cause of St. Stanislaus with those of other nations and states, of the same historical period, clearly show how the Poland of the eleventh century formed part

of Europe and shared in its problems, both in the life of the Church and in the life of the political communities of that time. And so it is that we are rightly living the Jubilee of St. Stanislaus, a jubilee that has above all a Polish and native dimension, in the European context. We cannot do otherwise. Therefore, the presence of the representatives of the many European Episcopal Conferences who have come here for the occasion is highly valued and eloquent.

It providentially happened that on May 18 of this year I took part in the celebration of the thirty-fifth anniversary of the battle of *Monte Cassino* and the victory won there, a victory to which my fellow-countrymen contributed in great measure. On the same Monte Cassino we paid tribute to St. Benedict, with reference to the coming 1500th anniversary of his birth—that St. Benedict who was proclaimed Patron of Europe by Paul VI.

If I may allow myself to make this reference on today's occasion, I do so in relation to the European context of St. Stanislaus and also of his jubilee that we are celebrating. Europe, which during its history has been several times divided; Europe, which towards the end of the first half of the present century was tragically divided by the horrible World War; Europe, which despite its present and long-lasting divisions of regimes, ideologies and economical and political systems, cannot cease to seek its fundamental unity, must turn to Christianity. Despite the different traditions that exist in the territory of Europe between its Eastern part and its Western part, there lives in each of them the same Christianity, which takes its origins from the same Christ, which accepts the same Word of God, which is linked with the same twelve Apostles. Precisely this lies at the roots of the history of Europe. This forms its spiritual genealogy.

This is confirmed by the eloquence of the present Jubilee of St. Stanislaus, Patron of Poland, in which the first Polish Pope, the first Slav Pope in the history of the Church and of Europe, has the good fortune to be taking part. Christianity must commit itself anew to the formation of the spiritual unity of Europe. Economic and political reasons alone cannot do it. We must go deeper: to ethical reasons. The Polish episcopate, all the episcopates and Churches in Europe, have here a great task to perform. In the face of these many-sided tasks, the Apostolic See is aware of its own tasks in conformity with the character and ministry of Peter. When Christ said: "Strengthen your brethren" (Lk. 22:32), He meant by this: "Serve their unity."

Gospel Witness in the Priestly Ministry

On June 6, 1979, John Paul II met the diocesan and religious clergy in the Cathedral of Czestochowa and addressed them as follows.

1. My dear brothers in the priesthood, and at the same time, in the same priesthood of Christ, beloved sons.

We meet here at the feet of the Mother of God, before the face of our Mother: the Mother of priests. We meet in unusual circumstances, by which you certainly, like me, are deeply moved. And yet this first Polish Pope, who today stands before you, received the grace of a priestly vocation on Polish soil; he passed through the Polish Major Seminary (for the most part when it was underground, because it was during the Occupation); he studied at the Theology Faculty of the Jagellonian University; he received priestly ordination from the Polish bishop and inflexible prince of unforgettable memory, Cardinal Adam Stefan Sapieha; and, with you, he shared in the same experiences of the Church and the nation.

This in particular I want to say to you at today's meeting. Everything that was formed in me here, everything I have taken away from here, echoes in all the meetings I have had with priests since October 16, 1978. And so today, in this meeting with you, I wish especially to refer to the words that I have said on those various occasions. In fact, I believe that you all have some share in their formation, and in part you have authorship rights. I also hold that, though these words have been already said in Rome or elsewhere, they refer to you in Poland.

2. Here is a part of the talk I gave to the diocesan and religious priests of the diocese of Rome last November 9:

I said: "I remember the admirable, zealous and often heroic priests with whom I was able to share the concern and the struggles.... In my previous episcopal work the Priests' Council rendered me great service, both as a community and as a meeting-place for sharing, together with the bishop, common solicitude for the whole life of the presbyterium and for the effectiveness of its pastoral activity.... As I meet you here for the first time and greet you with sincere affection." I also said to the priests and religious of Rome, "I still have before my eyes and in my heart the presbyterium of the Church in Krakow: all our meetings on various occasions, the many talks that began right from the years in the seminary; the meetings of priests; ordination groups of the individual seminary courses, to which I always went and in which I took part with joy and benefit!" (*L'Osservatore Romano*, November 10, 1978, p. 1, nos. 2-3)

3. And now let us return together to the great meeting with the Mexican priests at the Shrine of Our Lady of Guadalupe. I said this to them:

"Servants of a great cause, on you largely depends the destiny of the Church in the spheres entrusted to your pastoral care. This imposes upon you the duty to have a deep awareness of the greatness of the mission that you have received, and an awareness of the need to make yourselves ever more fit for it. In fact, it is a question...of Christ's Church—with what respect and love this ought to fill us!—which you must serve with joy in holiness of life (cf. Eph. 4:13). This lofty and demanding service cannot be rendered unless you have a clear and firmly-rooted conviction of your identity as priests of Christ, stewards and ministers of God's mysteries, instruments of salvation for people, witnesses to a kingdom that begins in this world but reaches fulfillment in the world to come" (nos. 2-3; *AAS* 71 [1979], p. 180).

4. Finally, the fourth statement, and perhaps the best known one: the Letter to all the priests of the Church on the occasion of Holy Thursday, 1979. I felt the particularly strong need to address the priests of the whole Church precisely at the beginning of my pontificate. I wanted this to happen on the occasion of Holy Thursday, on the occasion of the "feast of priests." I had before my eyes that day in the Cathedral of Wawel, when we renewed together our faith in the priesthood of Jesus Christ and dedicated to Him anew, at His complete disposal, our whole being, soul and body, so that He might be able to work through us and carry out His salvific work.

"Our pastoral activity demands," I wrote, "that we should be close to people and all their problems, whether these problems be personal, family or social ones, but it also demands that we should be close to all these problems 'in a priestly way.' Only then, in the sphere of all these problems, do we remain ourselves. Therefore, if we are really of assistance in those human problems, and they are sometimes very difficult ones, then we keep our identity and are really faithful to our vocation. With great perspicacity we must seek, together with all men, truth and justice, the true and definitive dimensions of which we can only find in the Gospel, or rather in Christ Himself" (no. 17, *AAS* 71 [1979], p. 404).

5. Dear Polish priests gathered today at Jasna Gora, those are the thoughts that I wanted to share with you. The priests of Poland have their own history, a history that has been written, in close connection with the history of the motherland, by the entire generations of the "servants of Christ and stewards of the mysteries of God" (1 Cor. 4:1) whom our land has given.

We have always felt a profound bond with the People of God, with this people from the midst of which we have been "chosen," and for which we have been "appointed" (cf. Heb. 5:1). The witness of living faith that we draw from the Upper Room, from Gethsemane, from Calvary, from the faith that we absorbed with our mother's milk; from the faith that we strengthened amid the hard trials suffered by our fellow countrymen—this is our spiritual hallmark; the foundation of our priestly identity.

In today's meeting, could I fail to recall the thousands of Polish priests who lost their lives in the last war, especially in the concentration camps?

But allow me to limit the memories that crowd into my mind and heart.

I shall say only that this heritage of priestly faith, service and solidarity with the nation in her most difficult periods, which constitutes in a sense the foundation of the historical trust of society in the Polish priests, must always be developed by each of you and must, I would say, always be won again. Christ the Lord taught the Apostles what idea they were to have of themselves and what they were to demand of themselves: "We are unworthy servants; we have only done what was our duty" (Lk. 17:10). Dear brothers, Polish priests, as you recall these words and the experiences of history, you must always keep before your eyes the demands arising from the Gospel that are the measure of your vocation. It is a great blessing this trust that the Polish priest has to his credit with society when he is faithful to his mission and his attitude is clear and in keeping with the style developed by the Church in Poland in the last decades: namely, the style of the evangelical witness of social service. May God assist us in order that this style may not be exposed to any "hesitation."

Christ asks of His disciples that their light "shine before men" (cf. Mt. 5:16). We are well aware of the human weaknesses in each one of us. We think with humility of the trust that our Teacher and Redeemer had in us when He entrusted to our priestly hands the power over His body and His blood. I hope that, with the aid of His Mother, you will in these difficult and often unclear times be capable of behaving in such a way that "your light may shine before men." Let us pray for this without ceasing. Let us pray with great humility.

I also wish to express the earnest wish that Poland may not cease to be the motherland of priestly vocations and the land of the great witness given to Christ through the service of your lives: through the ministry of the word and of the Eucharist.

Love Mary, dear brothers! From that love do not cease to draw strength for your hearts. May she show herself for you and through you the Mother of all who have such a great thirst for this motherhood.

Monstra te esse Matrem
Sumat per te preces
qui pro nobis natus
tulit esse tuus.
Amen.

Seven Years of Community Work To Update the Church of Krakow

On June 8, 1979, John Paul II took part in the solemn closing of the Archdiocesan Synod of Krakow which he himself had initiated seven years earlier. His Holiness presided at the Mass in Wawel Cathedral, during which he preached the following homily.

Beloved Metropolitan of Krakow,
Reverend bishops,
Dearest brothers and sisters,

1. Today the ardent desire of my heart is fulfilled. The Lord Jesus, who called me from this see of Saint Stanislaus, on the vigil of his ninth centenary, permits me to participate at the closing of the Synod of the Archdiocese of Krakow, a Synod that has always been bound, in my mind, to this great jubilee of our Church. All of you know this very well, because I have dealt with this theme many times, and so I have no need to repeat it today. Perhaps I would not even be capable of saying everything

which, in relation to this Synod, has passed in my mind and in my heart—just what hopes and plans I have tied to it in this decisive period of the history of the Church and of the motherland.

The Synod has been linked, for me and for all of you, to the anniversary of the ninth centenary of the ministry of St. Stanislaus, who for seven years was Bishop of Krakow. The work program thus foresaw a period from May 8, 1972, to May 8, 1979. During this whole time, we wanted to honor the bishop and pastor (of nine centuries ago) of the Church in Krakow, and to try to express—according to our times and our needs—our concern for the salvific work of Christ in the souls of our contemporaries. Just as Saint Stanislaus of Szczepanow did it nine centuries ago, so too we want to do it nine centuries later. I am convinced that this way of honoring the memory of the great patron of Poland is the most suitable. It corresponds both to the historical mission of St. Stanislaus and to those great tasks facing today's Church and modern Christianity after the Second Vatican Council. The initiator of the Council, the Servant of God John XXIII, specified this task with the word *aggiornamento.* The aim of the work of seven years in the Synod of Krakow—in response to the essential goals of Vatican II—was to be the *aggiornamento* of the Church of Krakow, the renewal of the understanding of its salvific mission, as well as the exact program for its accomplishment.

2. The path that has led to this end has been marked out by the tradition of particular synods of the Church; suffice it to recall the two preceding synods during the ministry of Cardinal Adam Stefan Sapieha. The rules for conducting the synodal activity were laid out by the Code of Canon Law. However, we have taken into consideration the fact that the teaching of the Second Vatican Council opens new perspectives here and, I would say, creates new tasks. If the Synod was to serve the realization of the teaching of Vatican II, it was to do so above all with the same idea and with the same system of work. This explains

the whole plan of the pastoral Synod and its subsequent realization. One can say that for the formulation of the resolutions and of the documents, we have travelled over a longer, but a more complete path. This path has passed through the activity of hundreds of synodal study groups, in which large numbers of the faithful of the Church of Krakow have been able to express themselves. These groups, as is well known, were in the greater part made up of Catholic lay people, who have had on the one hand the opportunity to penetrate deeply into the teaching of the Council, and on the other hand to express in this regard their own experiences, their own proposals that manifested their love for the Church, their sense of responsibility for the whole of the Church's life in the Archdiocese of Krakow.

During the preparatory stage of the final documents of the Synod, the study groups became centers where extensive consultations took place; in fact, the General Commission that coordinated the activity of all the working commissions turned to them, as did the commissions of experts that had been summoned right from the beginning of the Synod. In this way, those matters matured, which the Synod, linking itself again to the teaching of the Council, wished to transfer into the life of the Church of Krakow. It wished to form, in accordance with those matters, the future of the Church.

3. Today, all that work, this journey of seven years, is already behind you. I never thought that at the close of the work of the Synod of Krakow I would take part as a guest coming from Rome. But if such is the will of God, permit me, at this time, to assume once again the role of that Metropolitan of Krakow who through the Synod had wished to pay back the great debt which he had contracted towards the Council, towards the universal Church, towards the Holy Spirit. Permit me also in this role—as I have said—to thank all the people who have built up this Synod, year after year, month after month, by their work, by their advice, by their creative contributions, by their

zeal. In a way, my gratitude goes to the whole community of the People of God of the Archdiocese of Krakow, both ecclesiastics and laity: to the priests, to the men and women religious. Especially to all here present: to the bishops, headed by my revered successor as the Metropolitan of Krakow; in a particular way to Bishop Stanislaw Smolenski, who as chairman of the General Commission has directed the work of the Synod. To all the members of the Commission, and once again to the Preparatory Commission, which in 1971 and 1972, under the direction of Monsignor Prof. E. Florkowski, prepared the constitution, the regulations and the program of the Synod. To the Working Commissions, the Commissions of Experts, to the tireless Secretariat, to the Editorial Groups, and finally to all the Study Groups.

In this circumstance, perhaps I ought to have spoken differently, but it is not possible for me. I have been too personally connected with this work.

I wish, then, in the name of all of you, to lay this finished work before the sarcophagus of St. Stanislaus in the center of the Cathedral of Wawel; the work had in fact been undertaken in view of his jubilee.

And together with all of you I ask the most Holy Trinity that this work may bear fruit a hundredfold. Amen.

The Work of the Local Churches for the Strengthening of Unity

On June 19, 1979, Pope John Paul II received in audience a group of bishops from Pakistan led by His Eminence, Cardinal Joseph Cordeiro, Archbishop of Karachi. His Holiness addressed the bishops as follows.

Dear brothers in our Lord Jesus,

In welcoming you this morning, I wish to greet the entire Church in Pakistan. With the Apostle Peter I say: "Peace to all of you who are in Christ" (1 Pt. 5:12).

The thoughts of my heart go to the communities of the faithful throughout the dioceses of your country: to the priests, who in union with yourselves build up the local Churches through the Eucharistic Sacrifice and the Word of God; to the religious, who through their ecclesial consecration to Jesus Christ give a special witness of hope to the destiny of all the children of God; to the seminarians, being trained to transmit the Word of God to the future generations; and to all the laity, who are called to share intimately in the Church's mission of evangelization, and who through their daily lives build up the kingdom of God. I am close to all of you in the love of the Savior—close to you in all your efforts to proclaim "the unsearchable riches of Christ" (Eph. 3:8).

At the same time, as Pastor of the universal Church, I can—and do—assure you and your people of the solidarity of all your brethren throughout the world. And I believe that in this solidarity you will find fresh vigor and strength to continue your joyful commitment to the cause of the Gospel. The communion of faith and love that we enjoy—this Holy Spirit—this is indeed a great unity that is effected in us by the gift of God.

Today at the tomb of Peter and together with his Successor, may you rededicate yourselves and your local Churches to all the exigencies of this Catholic unity. From this center may you take back to your people a message of hope and encouragement, so that they may continue to hold fast to the very core of Catholic life, so that like the faithful of the early Church they may persevere in devoting themselves "to the apostles' teaching, and fellowship, to the breaking of bread and the prayers" (Acts 2:42).

I am sure that at times, as bishops, you feel acutely the weight of the charge laid on you by the Lord. Especially because of your zeal, you experience deeply within your hearts the limitations and obstacles that hinder you in the exercise of your pastoral mission. But the success of our ministry is not measured by human standards; it is measured rather by our love and by our fidelity to the Word of

God. Christ has told us to go forth in the strength of His Spirit—and He assures us that He is with us until the end of time (cf. Mt. 28:20). It is with "the word of truth and the power of God" (2 Cor. 6:7) that we humbly but confidently present ourselves before the world, to fulfill the task entrusted to us by the Lord.

I wish to express my admiration for the faith of your people and for the sustained effort and joyful constancy with which your local Churches pledge their fidelity to Christ. At the same time I wish to add a word about one particular aspect of your witness to Christ. In the Acts of the Apostles, Jesus is presented to us in His activity: "He went about doing good..." (Acts 10:38). And this same activity is carried on in Pakistan, in Christ's members, in your people. The motivation is the love of Christ, the love of His Father, the love of His brethren. Through a whole network of generous endeavors—especially in the areas of charitable assistance, health and schools—the Lord Jesus continues to do good; He continues to show His love. The mystery of the Church as the extension of Christ goes on. The charism of the Good Shepherd is thus exercised among your people. God's love is from generation to generation, and it is ever newly manifested.

I believe that a consideration of this important aspect of the Church as a divine mystery is extremely beneficial in sustaining you and renewing you in your pastoral zeal. Your people too will find joy in reflecting on the fact that as an ecclesial community they continue among their own flesh and blood the loving activity of Jesus Christ the Son of God. In reflecting on the greatness of this mission, all obstacles seem secondary. There may be fleeting moments of discouragement, but the power of the Paschal Mystery does not admit defeat.

Our role then, dear brother bishops, is to continue to demonstrate the love of Christ and to proclaim His saving Gospel of redemption with all our energy. The rest is in the hands of God.

In pursuing our apostolate, the Word of God is the joy of our ministry. It is a lamp to our feet and a light to our path (cf. Ps. 119:105). It is by guarding and meditating on the Word of God that we are enabled to fulfill our mission of charity. By proclaiming to our people the unadulterated Word of God in all its richness, we equip them for the vocation of Christian living, Christian service and Christian witness that is theirs.

Dear brothers in the episcopate, in our special unity today do we not feel supported by the power of the Lord Jesus? Do we not sense His presence? Do we not hear Him telling us to continue, courageously and joyfully, in communion with the Catholic Church throughout the world, to proclaim His love and to spread His truth?

I ask our Blessed Mother Mary to assist you all in the service of her Son, to form you ever more perfectly in His likeness, so that your witness to Him may render great honor and glory to the most Holy Trinity.

And with my greetings and my prayers, I send my apostolic blessing to all who make up the community of the faithful in your land. My special encouragement goes also to the catechists and to the Christian families, to the youth and to those who suffer and work and pray—so that the world may see the face of Jesus in our midst.

Evangelization in Terms of the Future

On June 20, 1979, during a concelebrated Mass with members of the Council of Bishops of Europe, the Holy Father John Paul II spoke as follows.

Dear brothers!

1. I express cordial and sincere joy at our meeting. Joy in particular because the meeting takes place in the framework of the Symposium on the subject: "The young and faith."

I remember the preceding Symposium, in 1975, in which I had the fortune to participate actively as one of the speakers. At the same time I wish to express my happiness at meeting you today, concelebrating the Holy Eucharist. I hope that in this communion, in which our priestly and episcopal unity is expressed in the fullest and deepest way, we will receive greater light and strength of the Holy Spirit from Christ—the Prince of pastors, who as the one eternal Priest is also the one source and foundation of this unity, which we manifest and live in the Eucharistic concelebration.

We need so much this light and strength of the Spirit of Christ for all the tasks that derive from our mission—for example, in the sphere of the subject of your Symposium: Youth—but not exclusively. Those tasks as a whole, our whole mission, call for some particular grace in order that we may be able to meet with exact and full correspondence the signs of the times, which are the salvific *kairos* of Europeans and of the continent we represent, and to which "we are sent" as successors of those Apostles, those messengers of the Gospel from whom the history of Europe in the Christian era begins.

A NEW VITALITY

2. Your meeting—and, therefore, also our Eucharistic concelebration today—has its roots in that happy thought of Vatican II which reminds the bishops of the whole Church of the collegial character of the ministry they exercise. Precisely from this thought, expressed with the greatest doctrinal precision in the Dogmatic Constitution *Lumen gentium*, there have sprung a series of pastoral institutions and initiatives which already bear witness today to the new vitality of the Church, and will certainly constitute in the future the foundation of the further renewal of her salvific mission in a variety of dimensions and spheres of action.

Saying so, I have still before my eyes the marvelous assembly of bishops of the Church of Latin America, which I had the fortune to inaugurate at Puebla in Mexico on January 28 of the current year. The assembly itself was the fruit of a systematic collaboration of all the episcopal conferences of that immense continent, in which nearly half of the Catholics of the whole world now live. They are episcopates of varying numerical importance, some very numerous, particularly such as that of Brazil which alone has over 300 bishops. The methodical collaboration of all the episcopal conferences of Latin America has its support in the council commonly known as "CELAM," which makes it possible for these conferences to re-read together the tasks that await pastors of the Church in that great continent, so important for the future of the world.

The very title of the conference held at Puebla from January 27 to February 13, 1979, already very clearly bears witness to this. It was: Evangelization in the present and the future of Latin America. It is, therefore, already easy to understand from the title how useful at Puebla was the providential subject of the ordinary session of the 1974 Synod of Bishops, namely: evangelization.

CONTEMPORARY POINT OF VIEW

3. In connection with this fundamental subject every bishop in the world, as the pastor of his particular Church, of his diocese, could and should consider his Church from the contemporary point of view. And as evangelization expresses the mission of the Church, this look must be connected with the past and open up the perspective of the future: yesterday, today and tomorrow. And not only every single bishop in his diocese, but also the different communities of bishops and above all the national episcopal conferences can and must make that "key subject" of the 1974 Synod an object of reflection about society, with regard to which they have pastoral responsibility for the work of evangelization. The subject proposed by Paul VI for the Synod, five years ago, has multiform possibilities of application in various spheres.

At the same time, this subject induces us to reflect, in a fundamental way, if it is a question of realizing the Council itself and of carrying out its doctrine. The basic realization of Vatican II is nothing but a new awareness of the divine mission transmitted to the Church "among all nations" and "to the end of the world." The basic realization of Vatican II is nothing but a new sense of responsibility for the Gospel, for the Word, for the sacrament, for the work of salvation, which the whole People of God must assume in the way suited to it. The task of the bishops is to direct this great process. Their dignity and pastoral responsibility lie in this.

EVANGELIZING THE CONTINENT OF EUROPE

4. It is of great weight and fundamental importance to reflect on the problem of evangelization with regard to the European continent. I consider it a complex, extremely complex, subject. Moreover, as also for any other contest, it is necessary to bring out from an analysis of the present situation a vision of the future, since this situation is a consequence of the past, ancient as the Church herself is, and the whole of Christianity. In the analysis, we should reach every single country, every single nation of our continent, but also understand every situation of theirs, having before our eyes the great movements of history which—especially in the second millennium—divided the Church and Christianity on the European continent.

I think that, at present, in time of ecumenism, the moment has come to look at these questions in the light of the criteria drawn up by the Council; to look at them in a spirit of brotherly collaboration with the representatives of the Churches and communities with which we do not have full unity; and, at the same time, it is necessary to look in a spirit of responsibility for the Gospel. And this not only in our continent, but also outside it. Europe is still the cradle of creative thought, of pastoral initiatives, of organizational structures, the influence of which goes beyond its frontiers. At the same time, Europe, with its grand missionary past, is questioning itself at the various points of its present "ecclesial geography" and wondering if it is not about to become a missionary continent.

SELF-EVANGELIZATION

There exists, therefore, for Europe the problem that was defined in *Evangelii nuntiandi* as "self-evangelization." The Church must always evangelize herself. Catholic and Christian Europe needs this evangelization. It must evangelize itself. Nowhere, perhaps, so much as in our continent do the movements of the negation of religion, the movements of the "death of God," of programmed secularization, of organized militant atheism, take shape so clearly. The 1974 Synod provided a great deal of material in this connection.

It is possible to examine all this according to historico-social criteria. The Council, however, indicated to us another criterion: that of the "signs of the times," that is, of a special challenge of Providence, of Him who is "the Lord of the harvest" (Lk. 10:2).

Next year we will celebrate the fifteenth centenary of the birth of St. Benedict, whom Paul VI proclaimed patron saint of Europe. This might be, perhaps, the right moment for such a deep reflection on the problem of the "yesterday and today" of the evangelization of our continent—or rather, for reflection on this challenge of Providence, which, in its rich and varied historical complex, constitutes the Christian "today" of Europe as regards its responsibility for the Gospel—and also in the perspective of the future.

Our mission is always and everywhere turned towards the future. Either towards the future of which we are certain in faith: the eschatological future; or towards the future about which we can humanly be uncertain. Let us think of those who were the first to come to the European continent as messengers of the Good News, such as Peter and Paul. Let us think of those who, throughout the history of Europe, have opened the ways towards new peoples, such as Augustine or Boniface, or the brothers of Thessalonica, Cyril and Methodius. Not even they were certain of the human future of their mission or even of their own fate. Faith and hope were more powerful than this human uncertainty. The love of Christ that "drove" them (cf. 2 Cor. 5:14) was more powerful. In this faith, hope, and charity was manifested the operating Spirit. We, too, must become docile and effective instruments of His action in our age.

YOUTH AND FAITH

6. The subject of your Symposium is: "The young and faith."

It is well that it is. I think it is deeply and organically integrated in the great subject of reflection of the whole post-conciliar Church, which can never be far from our attention—the subject of evangelization. If we think of evangelization in terms of the future, it is necessary to turn our minds to the young: we must meet the intellects, the hearts, the characters of the young. This is the problem chosen, through which we arrive at the global problem.

The exchange of your experiences and suggestions must be a wide one, it cannot remain "particular." All practice of collegiality serves the cause of the universality of the Church. You, too, dear brothers, through this practice of collegial collaboration, which forms your Symposium, must, so to speak, "expand the spaces of love" (S. Aug. *de ep. Ioan. ad Parthos*, X, 5: *P.L.* XXXV, 2060). This expansion never takes you away from the responsibility entrusted directly to each of you; on the contrary, it makes it keener. The bishops and episcopal conferences of every country and nation in Europe must live the interests of all the countries and nations of our continent. And let those of you who are absent be present—I would say—even more intensely. It is necessary to work out special, effective methods to make those who are "absent" "intensely present." Their absence cannot be ignored or be justified with commonplaces.

Remember that just as all the episcopal conferences of Europe take part in this Symposium through their representatives, so, too, all the episcopates, all the bishops stand around this altar in the Eucharistic communion of love, sacrifice, and prayer. And in a certain way those who are missing, those who have not been able to attend, are present even more vividly.

Through everyone, the Church, as the People of God of our whole continent, "works out" her Christian future in union with Christ the Prince of pastors, with Christ the eternal Priest.

Amen.

Task of the Whole Community: To Transmit the Word of God

On June 23, 1979, Pope John Paul II received in audience thirteen bishops from the Tamil Nadu region of India. In reply to an address by H.E. Most Rev. Justin Diravian, Archbishop of Madurai, His Holiness spoke as follows.

Dear brothers in our Lord Jesus Christ,

It is difficult to express adequately the joy that I experience in being together with my brother bishops during their *ad limina* visits. Each meeting is an encounter with the pastor of a local Church, with the spiritual leader of an individual ecclesial community that has its own identity within the context of Catholic unity. The one, holy, Catholic and apostolic Church subsists in each of your dioceses, and in all of them together. An *ad limina* visit is indeed, therefore, a celebration of Catholic unity, and a manifestation of fidelity to Jesus Christ, "the chief Shepherd" (1 Pt. 5:4) of the universal Church.

As Successor of Peter and Vicar of Christ, I wish today to greet in your persons all the Catholics of the region of Tamil Nadu, as well as those represented by the other bishops who have joined this regional group. I wish, moreover, to render respectful homage to the ancient culture of your land—a culture that is steeped in wisdom, rich in human experience, and filled with spiritual values that point to God and His Providence in human history.

At a given moment in the life of your people, a unique and original message of revelation was offered and freely accepted by those who were to base their lives on "all that Jesus did and taught until he was taken up to heaven" (Acts 1:1). The name of Jesus Christ was preached and His Gospel was proclaimed in your midst. His divine Person became for many the center of their lives, and His message of gentleness and humility became the inspiration for their activities.

Through the action of the Holy Spirit, the seed of God's Word, sown in good ground, brought forth fruits of holiness, justice and love. And God continues to be praised in the marvelous works that His grace has accomplished in India.

The Word of God, containing the Good News of salvation in Jesus Christ, became forever a great heritage to be preserved and transmitted. It was accepted as a treasure to be passed on from generation to generation. On His part, Jesus spoke as the Father had instructed Him; He did nothing on His own (cf. Jn. 8:28). Indeed, Jesus insists on the fact that He speaks on the authority of His Father: "My teaching is not mine, but his who sent me" (Jn. 7:16). The transmission of this teaching, entrusted to the action of the Holy Spirit, whom the Father sends in the name of Jesus, awakens in the Church a realization of its vocation as a community that is called to hear and guard and do the Word of God. The transmission of the Gospel becomes the common responsibility of the entire community, living and acting under the guidance of the Holy Spirit.

CHARISM OF SERVICE

The same Holy Spirit who pervades the entire Body of Christ and consolidates it in unity implants in the community a charism of special service—the office of bishop—which becomes the specific instrument for safeguarding and proclaiming the Word of God. And this distinctive role is yours today, dear brothers, called as you are to govern the Church together with the Successor of Peter and in the unity of the episcopal college. Each of you experiences the importance and urgency of Paul's words to Timothy: "Guard the rich deposit of faith with the help of the Holy Spirit who dwells within us" (2 Tm. 1:14). This charge constitutes a vital aspect of your own ministry within, and for the benefit of the Church, which in her entirety is directed to the service of the living Word of God.

In fulfilling your role, you are assisted in the first place by your priests, who are indeed worthy of all your fraternal love and pastoral attention. As your co-workers they, too, have "as their primary duty the proclamation of the Gospel of God to all" (PO 4). I ask you to assure them, over and over again, how important a role they play in the fulfillment of the work of redemption.

In your local Churches I know that the catechists have a very particular role in the great task incumbent on the whole community—the task of transmitting the Word of God. Your leadership in this field is vital: to provide for the doctrinal and spiritual preparation of the catechists, to see that they are themselves trained in the Word of Christ, that they are imbued with the mystery of Christ's love, and that they share His zeal for service. Through your guidance, the catechists will understand that at the core of their mission is the urgency of communicating Christ: passing on His Word to their brethren, and eliciting a supernatural response of faith, hope and charity. Only by receiving the Word of God can the community of the faithful grow to full maturity in Christ the Head. Success in the catechetical field presupposes a consciousness of the common responsibility of the Church—a realization that all the faithful through their Baptism and Confirmation are commissioned by the Lord Jesus Himself to share in the apostolate of His Church (cf. LG 33). Be assured that the Pope supports you and encourages you in your efforts to prepare, sustain and perfect your catechists. And I pray that the Holy Spirit will lead you to find new opportunities to promote this great apostolic activity in your local Churches.

TRANSMITTING THE FAITH

In a very special way the transmission of the Faith is linked to the training given to students for the priesthood. The fidelity of the Church to her vocation of hearing, guarding and doing the Word of God depends on the effectiveness of seminaries. This is why the Second Vatican Council could well speak of the seminary as "the heart of the diocese" (OT 5). Every ecclesial community is affected by the condition of the seminaries that prepare its priests. The effects of seminary training last for generations. For this reason I recently spoke in Rome to a group of seminary rectors, expressing clearly my prayerful hopes for this important aspect of the Church's life. On that occasion I stated: "In a word, the first priority for seminaries today is the teaching of God's Word in all its purity and integrity, with all its exigencies and in all its power.... A second issue of great importance...is that of ecclesiastical discipline" (Address of March 3, 1979). And these two aspects—doctrine and discipline—I commend today to your pastoral zeal for vigilant promotion. Vocations to the priesthood are a great gift of God to the community of His Church. As bishops we must vocalize Christ's call to the young; we must encourage our young people to accept a vocation courageously and generously; and we must pray "the Lord of the harvest to send laborers into his harvest" (Mt. 9:38). And with keen responsibility we must promote the vocations that we have already received, by fostering the doctrine and discipline of our seminaries. This solicitude, dear brothers, I manifested last Holy Thursday, saying: "The full reconstitution of the life of the seminaries throughout the Church will be the best proof of the achievement of the renewal to which the Council directed the Church" (Letter to All the Bishops of the Church).

Catechetical activity and seminaries—these are indeed two privileged instruments for the Church to fulfill her vocation of transmitting the Word of God. Today I associate myself with your zealous efforts in these fields, and with all your other initiatives on behalf of the Gospel.

QUESTION OF FREEDOM

I am also confident that you will enjoy the benevolence and esteem of all men and women of good will in the question of religious freedom. The Vatican Council committed the Church anew to promoting the dignity of the human person, spelling out the exigencies of this natural dignity. And so it declared that the human person "has a right to religious freedom" (DH 2). In this document the Council feels itself allied with millions of people throughout the world who so sincerely embrace in all its practical applications article eighteen of the United Nations' Universal Declaration of Human Rights: "Everyone has the right to freedom of thought, conscience and religion...."

With these hopes and prayers, dear brothers in the episcopate, I renew the expression of my profound solidarity with you, in Christ and in the Church. I ask Mary, Mother of God and Mother of the Church, to sustain you in joy and strength, for the glory of her Son and for the generous service of your people. For the rest, brethren: "Let us keep our eyes fixed on Jesus, who inspires and perfects our faith" (Heb. 12:2).

Build the Church with Your Priesthood

Eighty-eight new priests were ordained by the Holy Father in the Vatican Basilica on June 24, 1979, the solemnity of the birth of St. John the Baptist.
John Paul II delivered the following homily.

1. *"Et tu puer propheta Altissimi vocaberis."*

"And you, child, will be called the prophet of the Most High" (Lk. 1:76).

These words speak of today's saint. With these words the priest Zechariah greeted his own son, after having regained the power of speech. With these words he greeted his son, to whom, by his will and to the surprise of the whole family, he gave the name John. Today the Church recalls these events, celebrating the solemnity of the birth of *St. John the Baptist.*

It could also be called *the day of the call* of John, son of Zechariah and Elizabeth of Ain-Karim, to be the last prophet of the Old Covenant; to be the messenger and immediate forerunner of the Messiah: Jesus Christ.

For he, who comes into the world in such unusual circumstances, already brings the divine call with him. This call comes from the plan of God Himself, from His salvific love, and it is written in the man's history right from the first moment of conception in his mother's womb. All the circumstances of this conception, as well as the circumstances of John's birth at Ain-Karim, indicate an unusual call.

"Praeibis ante faciem Domini parare vias eius."

"You will go before the Lord to prepare his ways" (Lk. 1:76).

We know that John the Baptist answered this call with his whole life. We know that he *remained faithful* to it until his last breath. And he breathed his last in prison by order of Herod, as a result of the wish of Salome who acted on the instigation of her revengeful mother, Herodias.

But the liturgy today does not mention all that, reserving it for another day. Today the liturgy bids us *rejoice just at the birth* of the forerunner of the Lord. It bids us thank God for the call of John the Baptist.

THIS DIVINE CALL

2. When on this day, my dear deacons and candidates for the priesthood, you present yourselves in St. Peter's Basilica in Rome, all of us wish to rejoice, too, at your call to further participation in Christ's priesthood.

God has written the mystery of this call in the heart of each of you. We can repeat with the prophet: "I have loved you with an everlasting love; therefore I have continued my faithfulness to you" (Jer. 31:3).

At a certain moment in life you became aware of this *divine call.* And you began to start on your way, you began to walk towards its fulfillment. The way to the sacrament of Holy Orders, which you receive from my hands today, passes through a series of stages and environments; to this belong your home, the years of elementary and secondary school as well as higher studies, the circle of friends, parish life. First and foremost, however, along this way is the *ecclesiastical seminary,* to which each of us goes to find a definitive answer to the question regarding his call to the priesthood. Each of us goes there in order that, finding this answer in a more and more mature way, he can prepare, at the same time, thoroughly and systematically, for the sacrament of Holy Orders.

Today all these experiences are already behind you. You no longer ask, like that young man in the Gospel, "Good Teacher, what must I do to inherit eternal life?" (Mk. 10:17) The Master has already helped you to *find the answer.* You present yourselves in order that the Church may stamp her sacramental seal on this answer.

POWER OF THE SPIRIT

3. This seal is stamped by means of the whole liturgy of the sacrament of Holy Orders. It is stamped by the

bishop, who acts with the power of the *Holy Spirit* and in communion with his presbyterium.

The power of the Holy Spirit is indicated and transmitted by the laying-on of hands, accompanied first by silence and then by prayer. As a sign of the transfer of this power to *your young hands*, they will be *anointed* with the *holy Chrism* to be worthy of celebrating the Eucharist. Human hands cannot celebrate in any other way than in the power of the Holy Spirit.

To celebrate the Eucharist means gathering the People of God and constructing the Church in her fullest identity.

The moment we are living here together is of great importance both for each of you and for the whole Church.

The Church has prayed for each of these persons called who receive the sacramental seal of the priesthood today. *The Church wishes* each of you to build her up with your own priesthood, with your own service, which—through the power obtained from Christ—"gathers and does not scatter" (cf. Mt. 12:30).

PRAY TO PERSEVERE

4. Today, too, the Church prays. Your parents pray, your families and the circles with which your lives have been bound up so far, your seminaries, your dioceses, your religious congregations.

Let us pray to the Lord of the harvest who has called each of you as workers for His harvest, *that you may persevere in this harvest until the end.*

Like John, son of Zechariah and of Elizabeth of Ain-Karim, whose father said on the day of his birth, *"Et tu puer propheta Altissimi vocaberis"* (Lk. 1:76).

May your perseverance be the fruit of the prayers we raise today. Persevere as prophets of the Almighty! Persevere as priests of Jesus Christ!

Yield abundant fruit. Amen.

Value of the Evangelizing Mission

On June 28, 1979, John Paul II received in audience participants in the national Study Meeting promoted by the Pontifical Mission Aid Societies. The meeting dealt with the subject, "The mission in the heart of the Church," in the light of the encyclical "Maximum Illud," the sixtieth anniversary of the promulgation of which falls now, and of the other pontifical teachings.

The Holy Father delivered the following address.

Beloved brothers in the episcopate, beloved daughters and sons,

It is with particularly warm feelings that I receive you today, thanking you also for having expressed the desire for this meeting. I extend my most cordial greeting to everyone, seeing in you, and in the many members of the Pontifical Mission Aid Societies which you represent here, particularly active members of the Italian Church who have a mature sense of responsibility as regards the missionary requirements of the People of God.

On the sixtieth anniversary of the encyclical *Maximum Illud*, issued by my Predecessor, Benedict XV of revered memory, your meeting opportunely chose as its subject of study "The mission in the heart of the Church."

The Church, in fact, was born missionary. On the very day of the first Pentecost, according to the narrative of the Acts of the Apostles (chapter 2), peoples of various origin were the spectators and at the same time the addressees and first beneficiaries of what the Spirit of God operated powerfully in the disciples gathered in the Upper Room in Jerusalem. Irresistibly invested by that Spirit, they could not but proclaim in different languages "the mighty works of God" (*ibid.*, 2:11). The Apostle of the Gentiles echoes these first heralds when he affirms: "Necessity is laid upon me. Woe to me if I do not preach the gospel!" (1 Cor. 9:16) All this applies in the first place and personally to individual missionaries, on the basis of their specific vocation. But it also applies, by extension to the whole Christian community, whose members, already because of the baptismal call alone, must "shine as lights in the world, holding fast the word of life" (Phil. 2:15-16), that is, must spread and communicate that treasure of faith and communion that every Christian possesses.

The Second Vatican Council, therefore, expressed itself rightly: "Missionary activity flows immediately from the very nature of the Church. Missionary activity extends the saving faith of the Church, it expands and perfects its catholic unity, it is sustained by its apostolicity, it activates the collegiate sense of its hierarchy, and bears witness to its sanctity which it both extends and promotes" (AG 6). And it is in this sense of common participation that the aforesaid encyclical of Pope Benedict XV must be read when, in advance of his times, he called upon the bishops to give some diocesan priestly vocations for the vaster and more urgent needs of the universal Church (cf. *AAS* 11 [1919], p. 452).

The mission, therefore, is not a marginal commitment, far less a superfluous one. To say that it is in the heart of the Church means stressing that it is a vital question for the Christian community. Not for nothing does St. Paul compare the proclamation of the Gospel to the action of planting (cf. 1 Cor. 3:6), laying the foundations (*ibid.*, 3:10) and begetting (*ibid.*, 4:15). They are all images which describe so many activities of primary importance, and which all converge in highlighting the fundamental value of the evangelizing mission. And they are not activities which are carried out once and for all, since it is necessary to cultivate the seed sown, to build the construction, to bring up what was born, "until Christ be formed in you" (Gal. 4:19). That calls for constant and careful attention; in fact, according to the parable of Jesus, it is not impossible, unfortunately, to fall asleep and thus encourage the intervention of the enemy who sows weeds (cf. Mt. 13:24ff.).

You, members of the Pontifical Mission Aid Societies, are certainly among those who watch out diligently and solicitously so that missionary action may really be fruitful and continuous, and that living consciousness of her responsibility in this connection may never fail in the Church. To you, therefore, go my most cordial applause and encouragement, with the sincere wish, entrusted to the hands of the Lord, for an ever greater impact of your useful action.

As a token of these wishes, I am happy to impart the most ample apostolic blessing to you all, extending it particularly to the well-deserving missionaries operating all over the world.

Consistory for the Creation of Fourteen New Cardinals

On June 30, 1979, in the Apostolic Palace in the Vatican and in the Paul VI Hall, John Paul II held the Consistory for the creation of Cardinals, for the provision of Churches and for the postulation of the sacred Pallia.

Revered brothers,

We rejoice deeply that it has been granted to us to celebrate with you this consistory, the first one since, by mysterious divine disposition, we were raised to Peter's See. It is a great event in the life of the Church. It is a question, indeed, of creating new Cardinals, who will then be part of the Sacred College, of those whom the Sovereign Pontiffs have as their main advisors and helpers in the government of the universal Church. Above all, according to the established norms, upon them falls the right and the duty to elect the Roman Pontiff, the Successor of him whom Christ constituted the "lasting and visible source and foundation of the unity both of faith and of communion" (LG 18).

Although the number of those who are added to this College today is relatively small—as you know, there exist some limits with regard to the number of Cardinals—nevertheless also these revered brothers of ours, who are about to be enrolled in the Senate of the Roman Pontiff, if this term can be used, represent the universal Church in a certain way.

1. It is not without reason and significance that we have convened this chosen gathering today, at the end of the month of June. It is well known that our Predecessor of unforgotten memory, Pope Paul VI, often gathered the Cardinals in his presence about this time and addressed very serious words to them, sometimes also for the nomination of new members of the Sacred College. He would take advantage of the occasion of the anniversary of his election—which was June 21—or of that of the solemn beginning of his pontificate, which was June 30, or of his name day, which was June 24. He was accustomed then to review briefly the internal problems of the Church. It is true that this same Predecessor of ours, following the custom of recent Roman Pontiffs, used to speak to the College of Cardinals also on Christmas Eve to deal with affairs and questions concerning the Church and the world; but generally moved by different reasons than in the month of June, and often treating wider subjects. Complying, therefore, with what has become a kind of tradition, we link up with the pontificate of that Predecessor of ours, to whom we are bound also by many other ties, as we set forth at greater length in the Encyclical *Redemptor hominis*. So today we think again with special intensity of Paul VI's pontificate, from which we are separated only by the very short interval of the apostolic ministry of John Paul I, as Successor of St. Peter.

2. The time that followed the Second Vatican Council is distinguished—as everyone knows—by the fact that the whole Church must commit herself to carrying out the decisions of the same universal Synod. They aim at nothing else than the *renewal* of the Church: It is necessary—to use the words of our Predecessor—"for her to restore herself to that conformity with her divine model, which is her fundamental duty" *(AAS,* 55 [1963], p. 850).

This renewal, according to the same Council, concerns many aspects: The most important one regards the constant effort that the Church must make to become increasingly more aware of her mission of salvation, which is also perpetual service of the fundamental cause of man, nations and the whole human family. This awareness must entail that certainty about the task of salvation, which is derived from confident faith and sincere humility, and makes us capable of carrying out courageously the work of renewal. This work must constantly be measured—so to speak—with the "universal yardstick" of the People of God, which, while it participates in the salvific mission of Christ Himself, at the same time completes it in various ways, according to the "gift" that each one receives, for the purpose of leading himself and others to salvation.

Certainly, it is difficult to measure correctly, with only human criteria of judgment, the process of this renewal, understood in such a wide sense. It may sometimes even happen that we are mistaken in judging what is happening, because divine Providence has its own ways to lead men, their society, nations and the Church. It follows necessarily that every criterion of ours to draw up a balance sheet of the situation of the Church is insufficient; yet we absolutely need such a balance sheet, especially in certain times, such as today. So when we speak and judge certain facts, we must always refer in the first place to God's loving plans, and to His holy judgments on human conduct.

3. One of the main instruments to make this renewal and unity characteristic of the Church, both local and universal, that is, of the People of God, is certainly the collegiality of the bishops. In this connection it is right to highlight the meeting of the bishops of Latin America celebrated in Puebla. Its fruits of keener awareness of the mission of the Church and of her task of evangelization in Latin America, in the wake of the Council and of the Apostolic Exhortation *Evangelii nuntiandi*, are already

beginning to be gathered, and open up hope for the future. Certainly, the subjects that were dealt with there were of supreme interest for the present and the future.

Perhaps we were granted the privilege of bringing something to this meeting, having presided over its beginnings. It is useful here to repeat the words that our Predecessor Paul VI spoke at the close of the third session of the Vatican Council, expressing himself on collegiality as follows: "It is this deep and essential relationship that makes the episcopate a unified assembly which finds in the bishop who is Peter's successor not a different and extraneous authority, but its center and its leader" *(AAS,* 56 [1964], p. 1011).

It should be added that in the last few months the life of the Church has had other events of this kind, such as the "Symposium" of the Council of the Episcopal Conferences of Europe, held in Rome, to deal with "the young and faith." These events were a significant manifestation of collegial conscience and of the duty regarding the pastoral ministry of bishops and of the episcopal conferences. But none of them can be compared for importance with that of Puebla. We also noted with pleasure the excellent work done by the Latin American Episcopal Council, or CELAM, for the preparation of that meeting, and the intense participation of many prelates.

4. It was also owing to the Puebla meeting that our first journey, at the beginning of the pontificate, was to Mexico, passing first through the Republic of Santo Domingo. In this way we were able to visit for nearly a week the Church established in that region. We still remember with deep gratitude how many people we met on that visit. Above all we thank God and His Mother, who, especially through the Guadalupe Shrine dedicated to her, has become the merciful Mother and Lady, not only of Mexico, but of the whole of America, particularly Latin America. In particular we recall the President of the

Republic of Santo Domingo and the President of Mexico, as well as the bishops, priests, and religious men and women of both nations.

But that visit to the Mexican Church gave us the opportunity to be in contact almost continually with the Catholic people of that State, who, moved by the spirit of faith, thronged around us enthusiastically wherever we traveled, wherever we stopped. So let our deep gratitude go to divine Providence, who granted us the possibility, by means of this visit at the beginning of our pontificate, to be able to bear witness to the love and reverence of the Apostolic See for that people which has experienced so many difficulties because of faithfulness to Christ and His Church. In the journey to Mexico, we also stopped and celebrated the Holy Eucharist in the place from which the evangelization of America started; just as on the way back we were able to meet the Christian community of the Bahamas.

5. We feel equally grateful for the recent journey to Poland, which gave us the opportunity to see again our native country from June 2 to 9; that is, to visit again the land from where the Lord in His inscrutable designs called us to the Roman See of St. Peter. The main reason for the journey was the jubilee of St. Stanislaus: It was the ninth centenary of the martyrdom, at the hands of the king, of that bishop of the see of Krakow (which we ourself, his heir, as it were, governed until a short time ago).

Invited by the Polish bishops headed by Cardinal Wyszynski, we celebrated the jubilee together with the citizens of our nation, almost following the historical course of the country: It begins at Gniezno and leads to Krakow passing through "Jasna Gora," the Bright Mountain. We stopped first at Warsaw, the present capital of Poland, and when we were staying at Krakow, we celebrated the Holy Eucharist at Oswiecim (Auschwitz), which has become a kind of Golgotha of our times, where, in the so-called starvation bunker, Blessed Maximilian Kolbe died, after having offered his life for a companion.

While making this journey, led by history, we renewed thanks to God One and Three for the gift of holy Baptism which our fellow-citizens received a thousand years ago. There was also the opportunity to greet the neighboring Slav peoples, who entered the Church in that same period. Finally we asked for the gifts of the Holy Spirit for their perseverance in faith and hope.

While this pontifical service in our native country is still present in our memory, we wish to emphasize again the significance of the invitation that the public authorities addressed to us. With it they not only recognized that they were aware that we—on whom it has fallen to hold the highest office in the Catholic Church—came from their nation, but they also manifested the dignity and importance due to the international character of this visit of ours. Therefore we are very grateful to the authorities both of the Republic and of the Church, which facilitated it, and then particularly to the immense multitude of those who, having been born in the same country in which we were born, came to meet us in the spirit of religious unity.

6. Paul VI, whom we cannot forget, introduced into his many journeys this way of carrying out the pontifical ministry. May such journeys be of use in the future to manifest the unity of the People of God in the various places of the earth, in the different regions and nations.

Parallel with these events which we have recalled with great joy, there has proceeded and proceeds the constant and orderly work of the Church, which is concentrated in the first place on the tasks that the episcopal college proposes to carry out under the guidance of Saint Peter's Successor.

The Synod of Bishops has become a very special instrument of this collegial cooperation, since it is extended to the universal Church. An apostolic exhortation will be published shortly in which there will be gathered the fruits of the work of the Ordinary Session of the Synod of Bishops celebrated in 1977, which had as its object catechesis. Likewise the following session in 1980 is already being prepared. It will examine the subject, already duly approved: "The role of the Christian family in the modern world." The General Secretariat of the Synod of Bishops, after its Council elected in the preceding session had examined points at a general meeting, has sent the *Lineamenta* (Outline Document) everywhere, so that they may be widely discussed in the episcopal conferences.

7. As regard the Catholic centers of study at the university level, an important thing has occurred, the promulgation of the Apostolic Constitution *Sapientia Christiana*, which at the time fixed therein, will replace the Constitution now in force, *Deus Scientiarum Dominus*. From that moment the *Normae quaedam*, issued in 1968, obligatory for the time necessary to prepare the new constitution according to the will and the mind of the Second Vatican Council, will no longer remain in force.

To prepare this constitution, several years were necessary. Without speaking of all the work carried out, let it suffice to recall that all the episcopal conferences and all Catholic centers of study at the university level were consulted.

We hope, therefore, that the sacred disciplines will receive a new impulse and be able to consolidate faith, guide morality, and drive out errors, in obedience to the Magisterium of the Church.

8. Finally, we cannot forget, but must recall at least briefly, ecumenism, which was one of the principal intentions of the universal Synod (cf. UR 1). It can be said, in short, that in these months various meetings have been held with representatives of the Christian religions not yet united with us in full unity. While we warmly rejoice at this, we urgently exhort everyone—because "the concern for unity belongs to the Church as a whole" *(ibid,* no. 5) —to persevere more and more eagerly in the noble effort to reconstitute this unity, willed by Christ.

It can also be added that there have been various contacts with non-Christians, and thus we have striven to obey the Second Vatican Council, which ordained that in this way "we work together to build up the world in a spirit of genuine peace" (cf. GS 92).

This, revered brothers, is what our heart urged us to say. May the holy Apostles Peter and Paul, whose feast we celebrated yesterday, and who bore witness to their love for Christ with their blood, protect this Roman Church and this Apostolic See, with which you have a special bond. Above all, however, let us ask for the help of the noble Mother of God, to whom we confidently entrust you and all our brothers and sons. To strengthen you in the high rank you occupy in the holy Church, we willingly impart to you the apostolic blessing.

ADDRESS ON CONFERRING OF BIRETTA

1. The Word of God has now spoken to us with its power, which is suitable for the moment we are living. While these our venerable and dear brothers in the episcopate, whose names are already known to the Church and to the world, are about to receive the sign of cardinalatial dignity, it is necessary that the meaning of this dignity should become crystal-clear for them and for us in the light of the words of God Himself. And thus, listening with gratitude to these words taken from the first letter of Saint Peter and from the Gospel of St. Matthew, we meditate for an instant on what the Lord wishes to express through them in this important and unusual moment.

2. Above all, through the words of the Apostle, the Lord manifests pastoral care for the Church, that is, for the flock. These words are truly marvelous! In them is fully opened up the soul of him to whom was given, "as a witness of the sufferings of Christ," the task of becoming the first shepherd of the flock. In his pastoral care for the Church, Peter has Christ continually before his eyes—Christ, who was revealed as the Good Shepherd giving His own life for His sheep, and who, as the chief Shepherd, will be revealed in that "glory of the Father" (cf. Jn. 17:24)

to which He leads us all. Fixing his gaze on Him, on Christ, the Apostle Peter—an "Elder," the Bishop of Rome—shares in turn his pastoral care with others, teaching them and, at the same time, asking how they must, together with him, conduct themselves as "elders and superiors." A particular reference to their personal example, to their selfless dedication and to their creative zeal. To be a shepherd of the flock means to be vigilant, so that a wild animal will not enter the flock. To be a shepherd of people's souls means to be vigilant, so that they will not be deceived and entrapped, and so that they will not be misled, losing their vital contact with the source of love itself and of truth. To be a shepherd of souls means, finally, to trust: to trust above all in Him who by His own blood acquired over these souls a divine right.

Venerable and dear brothers, accept today this message of the first Bishop of Rome—you who in a particular way must become sharers in the pastoral care of his unworthy Successor. The more deeply we draw from the very Gospel sources of this care, the more it will become effective and blessed. The present "time" *(kairos)* of the Church and of the world requires us to draw with particular diligence precisely from these sources.

3. The Word of God to which we have just listened contains in itself an appeal for courage and fortitude. In a significant way Christ invites us to courage and fortitude. We have heard Him say repeatedly: "Do not be afraid"; "Do not fear those who kill the body but cannot kill the soul" (Mt. 10:28); "Have no fear of men" (cf. Mt. 10:26): And at the same time, side by side with these decisive appeals for courage and fortitude, there is the exhortation: "Have fear"; "Rather fear him who can destroy both soul and body in hell" (Mt. 10:28). These two appeals, seemingly opposed, are reciprocally so closely connected that one results from the other, one conditions the other. We are called to fortitude and at the same time to fear. We are called to fortitude before men and, at the same time, to fear before God Himself; and this fear must be the fear of

love, filial fear. And only when this fear penetrates into our hearts can we be truly strong with the fortitude of the apostles, martyrs, and confessors. Strong with the fortitude of pastors. The invitation to fortitude is linked in an especially deep way with the tradition of the cardinalate, which even through the color of the cassock recalls the blood of martyrs.

4. Christ asks us above all to have this fortitude to confess before men His truth and His cause, without counting whether these people will be favorable or not to this cause, whether they will open their ears and hearts to this truth, or whether they will close them so as not to be able to hear. We cannot be discouraged before any program in which the ears and the intellect are closed. We must make our confession and proclamation in deepest obedience to the Spirit of Truth. He Himself will find the ways to reach the depths of consciences and of hearts. We must rather make our confession and render witness with such strength and ability that responsibility does not fall on us for the fact that our generation has denied Christ before men. We must also be "wary as serpents, innocent as doves" (Mt. 10:16).

And finally we must be *humble*, with that humility of interior truth that permits man to live with magnanimity because "God resists the proud, but gives grace to the humble" (Jas 4:6). This *magnanimity*, evolving from humility, evolving from cooperation with the grace of God, is a particular sign of our service in the Church.

5. Venerable and dear brothers, here is a program! The ample and demanding program which the Church links to your great dignity.

Accept this program with the same great confidence with which your predecessors in the same episcopal sees and in the same posts of the Roman Curia have accepted it! Accept it!

Look at the great, the magnificent examples they have left us.

On this new way may you be accompanied by the beloved *Mother of the Church* and also the holy Apostles Peter and Paul, in whose solemnity we rejoiced yesterday. In everything may God be specially adored: the Father, and the Son, and the Holy Spirit.

I wish to renew publicly, venerable and dear brothers in the episcopate who have been elevated to the cardinalatial dignity, my affectionate esteem and my sincere appreciation for the witness that you have given to the Church and to the world by your lives as priests and bishops completely dedicated to God and expended for souls in all the tasks entrusted to you in the course of your lives.

I likewise express my cordial and respectful greeting to the delegations from different countries, to the representatives of numerous dioceses and to the delegation sent to Rome by my beloved brother, Patriarch Dimitrios I, and to all who have come here to form a joyful circle around the new members of the Sacred College.

The Holy Father then greeted various groups who had come for the ceremony. To the English-speaking group he said:

With great affection in our Lord Jesus Christ, I extend a word of welcome to the English-speaking individuals and delegations that have come to Rome for this consistory. Today, in a special way, we are all experiencing together the universality of the Church. We are experiencing the strength and joy of being united in Christ, and in His one, holy, catholic and apostolic Church.

The Church as a Sign of God's Salvific Will

On July 1, 1979, John Paul II presided over a solemn concelebration in the Vatican Basilica with the fourteen new Cardinals created in the Consistory on June 30.
The Holy Father delivered the following homily.

Beloved brothers and sisters!

1. Today I wish, together with you, to contemplate the Church fully "subject to Christ" (cf. Eph. 5:24) as a faithful bride. The last few days, which we have lived meditating together on the sacrifice of the holy Apostles Peter and Paul, commit us to seek the manifestation of the mystery realized in their vocation, through the witness of faith and love, borne to the point of death. A manifestation, which we find throughout the history of the Church, throughout the centuries and the generations of her faithful sons and daughters, servants and pastors, going back in this way to that sublime love, with which our Redeemer and Lord "loved the church and gave himself up for her, that he might sanctify her, having cleansed her by the washing of water...that he might present the church to himself in splendor, without spot or wrinkle or any such thing, that she might be holy and without blemish" (Eph. 5:25-27).

To that sublime love, to that heart pierced on the cross and open to the Church, His bride, I wish today, together with you, to go on a spiritual pilgrimage, from which we ourselves must return "purified, strengthened and sanctified" in accordance with these days.

Here is the Church! The fruit of the inscrutable love of God in the heart of His Son!

Here is the Church! Bringing the fruits of the love of the holy Apostles, of the martyrs, of the confessors and virgins! Of the love of whole generations!

Here is the Church: our mother and bride at the same time! The goal of our love, our testimony and our sacrifice. The goal of our service and indefatigable work. The Church, for which we live in order to unite ourselves with Christ in a unique love. The Church, for which you, revered and dear brothers, created Cardinals in the Consistory yesterday, must live even more intensely from now on, uniting yourselves with Christ in a unique love for her.

2. The Church is in the world. You all constitute her living testimony in the world, arriving here from so many places distant in space, but, at the same time, close spiritually.

The Church is in the world as a sign of the salvific will of God Himself. Is she not the Body of Him whom the Father anointed and sent into the world "to bring good tidings to the afflicted, to bind up the brokenhearted, to proclaim liberty to the captives, and the opening of the prison to those who are bound...to comfort all who mourn...to give them a garland instead of ashes...the mantle of praise instead of a faint spirit"? (Is. 61:1-3)

Should not the Church be all this? Should she not live by all this, if she is to respond to the salvific mission of Him who is her Bridegroom and Head?

You know very well, revered and dear brothers—and all the Churches from which you come know it too—into what language of facts, experiences, aspirations, sadness, suffering, persecution and hopes it would be necessary to translate that ancient prophetic text of Isaiah, in order that it might express, in the language of our time, how the Church is rooted in the world; how much she desires to be, in the world, a living sign of the salvific will of the eternal Father with regard to every man and all humanity! The Church of our difficult age—of the second millennium that is drawing to a close—a period of extreme tensions and threats or of great fears and great expectations!

3. At all times this Church is simple with the same simplicity that our Lord and Master inspired in her with the word of the Gospel. How little is necessary for the Church "to begin to exist" among men! "Where two or

three are gathered in my name, there am I in the midst of them" (Mt. 18:20); and "If two of you agree on earth about anything they ask, it will be done for them by my Father in heaven" (Mt. 18:19).

How little is necessary for this Church to exist, multiply and spread! That is decided by those two or three gathered in Christ's name and united through Him, in prayer, with the Father. How little is necessary for this Church to exist everywhere, even in those places where, according to human "laws" she does not exist and cannot exist and where she is condemned to death! How little is necessary for her to exist, and realize her deepest substance!

For her to live her perennial youth! The same youth that the first Christians lived, who "devoted themselves to the Apostles' teaching and fellowship, to the breaking of bread and the prayers. Breaking bread in their homes, they partook of food with glad and generous hearts, praising God and having favor with all the people" (Acts 2:42, 46-47), as we read today in the second reading from the Acts of the Apostles. On reading this there reawaken not only the memories, but also the desires of simplicity on the part of the bride, who has just experienced the sacrifice of love of her crucified Bridegroom and rejoices in her generating fertility in the Holy Spirit when—as we read—"the Lord added to their number day by day those who were being saved" (Acts 2:48).

This Church is simple with the simplicity that is characteristic of her.

And she is strong with that unique strength which she received from the Lord: that unique strength! No other! "Whatever you bind on earth shall be bound in heaven, and whatever you loose on earth shall be loosed in heaven" (Mt. 18:18).

Here is the specific quality of this strength of the Church. Neither man nor humanity knows such a strength, in any other dimension of his individual or social existence. She does not draw this strength from any field of

her own temporariness or from any reserve of nature....
This strength comes only from God. Directly from God.
This strength is redeemed by the blood of her Redeemer
and Bridegroom. It is the strength of the Holy Spirit.

It forms an alliance with what is deepest in man: by
means of faith, hope and charity it seeks—immutably
seeks—the solutions in heaven of what cannot be fully
solved on earth.

4. Revered and dear brothers! How much we rejoice
at the fact that you, newly created Cardinals, wed this
Church today following the example of Christ! The sign of
this wedding is the ring, which I will shortly put on your
finger.

How we rejoice at these nuptials of yours, which bring
into the life of the People of God, all over the earth, a new
inflow of love and a new certainty of love! A new—we
hope—efficacy of love. Of that love with which we have
been loved and with which we must love one another.
Love which comes from the Bridegroom and is for the
Bridegroom.

Love, by means of which the Church must be loved
with renewed fervor by each of you.

Love, by means of which she must express herself
again in all the simplicity and the strength that she received
from the Lord.

Love, by means of which the Church must become
again *sine ruga et macula* for the Bridegroom.

I wish you this love, together with the whole People
of God in Rome and in the world. I lay my wish in the
hands of the mother of the Church, the bride of the Holy
Spirit.

Amen!

The Baptism of Blood of the Church of Rome

During the general audience in St. Peter's Square on July 4, 1979, the Holy Father gave the following address.

1. Last week, the Roman Church experienced holy and elevated moments, which deserve special mention before God and men.

Before God—to be able to express gratitude to Him and to renew trust. Before men—to satisfy the need of hearts, which at such moments unite and open to one another.

For the first time it happened to me, who am not a native of this city or of this land, to venerate the holy Apostles Peter and Paul in this very place, from which the Lord called them to Himself, on the day dedicated to the annual memory of their glorious martyrdom. I had already done so for many years in my native land, thus manifesting unity with Peter who unites the People of God in the Catholic Church. But here, at the very center of the Church, the mystery of that unusual vocation, which led Peter from the lake of Gennesaret to Rome, and then brought also Paul of Tarsus here in his footsteps, speaks to us with all the force of historical reality. With what deep emotion in the late evening of June 28 we recited the first vespers of the feast of the two patron saints. And then after the blessing of the Pallia, which are a symbol of the unity of the universal Church with St. Peter's See, we went down to the place where there are the sacred relics of the Apostle, once buried here, and in our times examined again by scientists.... How great is the eloquence of the altar in the center of the Basilica, on which the Successor of St. Peter celebrates the Eucharist with the thought that, in a place close to this altar, he himself, the crucified Peter, made the sacrifice of his life in union with the sacrifice of Christ crucified on Calvary—and risen again....

On the same day, according to a tradition, the Lord received also St. Paul's sacrifice.

And not only those two. The liturgy of June 30 commemorates all the martyrs of the Church who then, in Nero's time, suffered bloody persecution here in Rome. This is testified to by ancient historians such as Tacitus *(Annales* XV, 45) and Apostolic Fathers such as Clement of Rome *(Ad Cor.* 5-6). This, however, far from being the last persecution, was rather the first one. After it came others until the times of Diocletian, at the beginning of the fourth century, and then until the time of Julian the Apostate, after the middle of the same century. The Church of Rome was deeply implanted in this multiple testimony. This See of the ancient world was baptized not only with the baptism of water, but also with the baptism of the blood of the martyrs, "that speaks more graciously than the blood of Abel" (Heb. 12:24).

All of us, who live in the haste of modern civilization, in the restlessness of present-day life, must stop here and reflect how this Church was born, the Church to which it was granted by the will of the Lord to become the center and the capital of such a great mission: the Church to which there come on pilgrimage so many Churches, which find in it the foundation of their unity.

2. The memory of these events at the beginning of the Church of Rome, which God founded here on Peter (whose name means "rock") was united with other important events in the experience of the other days of last week. These events reflect the further historical development of that Holy See, which must always serve the unity of Christians in a Church that is catholic and at the same time apostolic.

We have had the fortune to introduce solemnly into the College of Cardinals of the Roman Church fifteen men. Of these, one remains "in pectore," while waiting for the decisions of divine Providence if one day it will allow us to reveal his name; the others are already commonly known to everyone.

In this sublime rite there was renewed the millenary tradition of the Roman Church, which has a great significance not only for the further stability of the Church, but also for adequate understanding of her character which is a double one: local and universal at the same time.

Our "local" Roman Church is linked with this city just as once, over nineteen centuries ago, the Apostle Peter linked it with this city. After Peter, this Roman Church elected its bishops successively, so that they might exercise pastoral service in it, and it did so in a way adapted to the possibilities and needs of the various eras.

The institution of the College of Cardinals in its origins goes back to this tradition, according to which the Bishop of Rome was elected by representatives of the Roman clergy. It was precisely these Roman electors, constituting already at that time an important College in the life of the Church, who began the institution which for nearly a thousand years has ensured succession to Saint Peter's See.

Succession to this episcopal See has a significance not only for the "local" Church, which is here in Rome. It has a significance for the universal Church, that is, for each of the local Churches, which in this way become part of a universal community. This is really a "key" significance, since Christ gave precisely to Peter "the power of the keys."

In recent times and especially during Paul VI's pontificate, the College of Cardinals has been increased and internationalized.

At present the Sacred College has 70 European Cardinals, 40 Cardinals from America (North, Central and South), 12 Cardinals from Africa, 10 Cardinals from Asia and 3 Cardinals from Australia and Oceania. They all fill particularly responsible offices such as pastors of important local Churches (or dioceses) or as superiors of the principal Departments of the Roman Curia, and they are at the same time the heirs of those ancient "electors" who came from the Roman clergy and chose the Bishop of

Rome. Therefore, together with the call to the College of Cardinals, they are given the title of one of the suburban dioceses or of one of the Roman churches. In this way the College of Cardinals unites in itself—and manifests in itself—both the constituent dimensions of the Church: the "local" dimension and the "universal" one. The Church built on Peter is "Roman" in these two dimensions.

3. In this way, therefore, the days of the past week enabled us to enter into a particularly deep familiarity with the reality of the Church, with her mystery and at the same time with her history, which, before our eyes, has been prolonged, in a certain sense, with a new stage.

If we return today to these important events, we do so to manifest how deeply we experienced these facts. Following the example of the Mother of Christ, it is necessary to "keep in our hearts" (cf. Lk. 2:51) such eloquent events, and at the right moment "manifest them outside," so that their interior importance will be consolidated in these manifestations.

My thought goes once more to the members of the College of Cardinals, and their new reinforcements. I commend each of them to the prayers of all of you gathered here, to the prayers of the whole Church.

To Jesus Christ, the "King of ages" (1 Tm. 1:17), I commend the Church built "upon the foundations of the apostles and prophets" (Eph. 2:20), the Roman Church founded on Peter and linked since the beginning with the memory of the Apostle of the Gentiles.

Irreplaceable Presence of the Priest in the Evangelizing Work of the Church

On July 6, 1979, John Paul II received in audience a group of bishops of Colombia on their visit ad limina Apostolorum. *The Holy Father, after listening to an address of homage delivered by the President of the Episcopal Conference of Colombia, Most Rev. Mario Revollo, made the following speech.*

Beloved brothers in the episcopate,

I receive you today with deep joy, pastors of the four ecclesiastical provinces of Nueva Pamplona, Barranquilla, Cartagena and Bucaramanga, who have come to Rome for your visit *ad limina Apostolorum.* Welcome, in Christ's name.

You form the first group of bishops of Colombia who will come to the eternal city this year to meet Peter and inform him of the achievements, hopes and difficulties of each one of your respective particular Churches.

Allow me in the first place to express my sincere appreciation and gratitude for the eloquent words uttered, on behalf of you all, by Archbishop Mario Revollo of Nueva Pamplona, President of the Colombian Episcopal Conference. They show clearly the central aim of the visit *ad limina:* to bear witness to and consolidate this close union of sentiments and intentions of the bishops with the Successor of Peter and Pastor of the whole Church: the guarantee of the necessary ecclesial union.

But this movement of ecclesial faith and love is not confined to us gathered here. Through that admirable and mysterious bond in the Mystical Body of Christ, we feel the presence of your priests, men and women religious, and faithful. They are the object of our common care; and this has been revealed both in the individual talks with each one of you and at this collective meeting.

Take to each one of the members of your flock my most cordial greeting in love of Christ, my encouragement to persevere in the firmness of faith, my exhortation not to fail in hope, and my prayer to grow strong in the bond of brotherly love. May the grace of the Spirit and the constant prayer of the Pope sustain them in their work and in their daily pilgrimage, so that they may be living witnesses to the resurrection of Christ and generous builders of the kingdom of God in their respective fields of activity.

PROBLEM OF VOCATIONS

Among the multiple cares that concern your souls as pastors, I know there is one that has a preeminent place: the problem of priestly and religious vocations. This is, in fact, a very important subject for the whole Church, for Colombia, and in particular for your four ecclesiastical provinces. I wish to confide in you that this is one of the points to which the Pope devotes special attention, in view of the enormous repercussion it has on the general progress of the Church, for the present and for the future.

Convinced of that, I wish to give you as your personal charge what I indicated in my opening address at the Puebla Conference: that you put care for vocations among your priority pastoral tasks. It is something vital, indispensable, since a Church that lacked qualified, stable agents, completely dedicated to this ministry, could not effectively carry out the work of evangelization.

It is certain that all the members of the ecclesial community, including laity—whose help must be appreciated and expanded in every possible way—must take part, by virtue of their Christian vocation, in the evangelizing task of the Church. But they cannot replace the indispensable presence of the consecrated minister or of the soul called to specific ecclesial dedication. What is more, the real maturity of the Catholic laity cannot help being reflected also in a practical opening to fully consecrated life.

THREE DIRECTIONS

In your concern for vocations you must aim in three directions: diligent search for these vocations, adequate preparation of them, and care for their perseverance. It will be opportune for this purpose to set up a well-prepared vocational apostolate which will pay careful attention to the family, the school, youth, apostolic movements; vital centers in which, if they are saturated with faith and good morals, there germinate so many decisions of commitment to the service of God and one's neighbor.

Do not, therefore, consider it superfluous or less productive on the apostolic plane to dedicate to this work well-qualified priests of great spirit, who attend preferably to this sector, in the framework of some good diocesan and even national plans to which I know you give careful attention. And, in that, interest all priests, men and women religious, and committed laity.

HOUSES OF FORMATION

You should give no less care to seminaries and houses of religious formation which—as indicated on various occasions, also recently, by the Holy See—must always be a center for the preparation of well-balanced human personalities, with all the healthy opening that the present moment requires, with a solid spiritual, moral, and intellectual basis, capable of disciplined life and the spirit of sacrifice. Without that, the interior structure of a vocation for the Church and the world of today cannot be constructed. A fundamental premise must never be forgotten: If we present debased values, the young people themselves are the first to reject them, since they do not discover in them a framework in which to pour all their generosity and longing for dedication.

Do not fail either to give due care to the apostolate of adult vocations, which in certain environments and also in Colombia are a more and more frequent and promising phenomenon.

BROTHERLY SERVICE

Finally, take to heart diligently the perseverance of those who are already living complete consecration. Do not fear to spend your time and best energies in this task. In the line indicated in my recent Letter to the Bishops, on the occasion of Holy Thursday, above all, be real friends and supporters, with your word and your luminous example, of priests and consecrated souls. May your life and effort be a precious help, in the spirit of brotherly service, to maintain in them clear awareness of their own identity as the chosen.

Beloved brothers: Here are some guidelines for you, to be completed with your zeal and creativity as pastors.

Let my last word be a brotherly call to hope and to prayer to the Lord of the harvest not to abandon us. May He make your efforts fruitful. May Mary, our Mother, accompany you always. As my prayer for you and for each member of your ecclesial communities accompanies you, I bless you all with special affection.

Apostolic Work of the Roman Curia

The Holy Father gave the following address to the large crowd assembled in St. Peter's Square on July 11, 1979.

1. Today, too, I wish to refer to the great solemnity that the Roman Church celebrates on June 29, recalling in this way every year the martyrdom of her patron saints, the holy Apostles Peter and Paul. The commemoration of these Apostles sets before our soul's eyes not only the moment of their death for Christ, but also their whole apostolic life. Although so remote in time, their lives, rich in the labor of evangelical witness, spent entirely in laying the foundations of the kingdom of God on earth, are always concrete and of topical interest for us. Both Apostles take shape before the eyes of our mind as real

figures; they express themselves with the words of their letters and with their works, recorded both in their writings and in the Acts of the Apostles. We can follow the events in which they took part and of which their lives were composed, in a certain sense, from outside and, at the same time, we can follow also their interior lives, always finding in them a living model of that *sequela Christi*, to which we are all called.

I would like to draw your attention today to one particular: The Apostles had numerous helpers and collaborators, who made possible and facilitated for them the accomplishment of the tasks connected with the proclamation of the Gospel. Many names of these disciples and apostolic helpers are known to us, especially from the letters of St. Paul. The commemoration of some of them is preserved in the martyrology or in the liturgical calendar of the saints of the Church.

2. This fact, which concerns the origins of the Church, enables us to cover nearly two thousand years of history, arriving at our own times. The fulfillment of the apostolic mission, and of Peter's ministry especially, has required numerous collaborators in every age. Our age, too, requires them, to an extent adequate to the needs of our times, in which it is incumbent on the Church to carry out the evangelical mission of salvation. I wish to speak today, on the occasion of the meeting with you participants in the Wednesday audience, precisely about all those who collaborate with Peter's Successor in Rome in the accomplishment of his service for the Roman and universal Church. I do so for theological reasons: The recent solemnity of the holy Apostles, in fact, prepares us for such reflection. I do so also for personal reasons: It is only right that I should express remembrance and gratitude to my collaborators, as we read in the letters of the Apostles and especially in St. Paul's letters. "We give thanks to God always for you all, constantly mentioning you in our prayers, remembering before our God and

Father your work of faith and labor of love and steadfastness of hope in our Lord Jesus Christ" (1 Thes. 1:2-3).

3. The circle of the closest collaborators of the Pope, Bishop of Rome and Successor of Peter, is constituted by the Roman Curia. As is known, it is at present a large and differentiated organism, on the updating of which, according to the tasks of Peter's ministry and according to the needs of the modern Church, the Second Vatican Council reflected deeply. Among its main suggestions in this field we read: "It is the earnest desire of the Fathers of the sacred Council that these departments, which have indeed rendered excellent service to the Roman Pontiff and to the pastors of the Church, should be reorganized and modernized, should be more in keeping with different regions and rites, especially in regard to their number, their names, their competence, their procedures and methods of coordination.... Furthermore, as these departments have been instituted for the good of the universal Church, it is hoped that their members, officials and consultors, as well as the legates of the Roman Pontiff, may be chosen, as far as it is possible, on a more representative basis, so that the offices or central agencies of the Church may have a truly universal spirit. It is urged also that more bishops, especially diocesan bishops, be co-opted to membership of these departments, who will be better able to inform the Supreme Pontiff on the thinking, the hopes and the needs of all the churches. Finally, the Fathers of the Council judge that it would be most advantageous if these departments were to have more frequent recourse to the advice of lay people of virtue, knowledge and experience, so that they also may have an appropriate role in the affairs of the Church" (CD 9 and 10).

Following the thought of the Council and in obedience to its indications, Paul VI gave concrete form to the updating of the Roman Curia, by means of the Constitution *Regimini ecclesiae universae*. This large and differentiated organism gathers within it offices and institutions with a long and sometimes centuries-old history, and alongside them, new organisms, which emerged directly from the ecclesiology of Vatican II, and which manifest that awareness of the Church's mission in the modern world that we owe precisely to the Council.

It would be impossible to make a detailed analysis of the whole complex of the Curia here. It would certainly be laborious to list in order the spheres of competence of the individual departments and the various offices, as well as their structure and internal organization; but this is perhaps not necessary. It is opportune, rather, to refer briefly to each of the departments in order to realize how each one corresponds to a definite field of the life and activity of the universal Church, and how it facilitates, in this sector, the carrying out of Peter's ministry before the Church, sharing in a deep and competent way the magisterial and pastoral concern of each Successor of St. Peter, Bishop of Rome.

The names themselves of the single departments express their spheres of competence. The task of the Bishop of Rome is, in the first place, concern for the integrity of the doctrine of the Faith: and here we have the congregation bearing precisely this name, which helps him in all that. Questions regarding the apostolic succession of the bishops in the dimension of the whole College are incumbent on the Bishop of Rome: hence the Congregation for Bishops. Then there follow all the other departments, which deal with the single tasks of Peter's ministry in the Church: the Congregation for the Eastern Churches which, though with different rites, are in communion with Peter's See; the Congregation for the Sacraments and Divine Worship, in charge of the sacramental and liturgical life of the Church; the Congregation for the Clergy, responsible for things regarding the ministry and life of priests; the Congregation for Religious and for Secular Institutes, which have such an important part in the living tissue of the Christian community; the Congregation for the Evangelization of Peoples, in charge of everything concerning missionary action; the Congregation for the Causes of Saints; and finally, the Congregation for Catholic Education, the activity of which regards Catholic schools, seminaries and universities scattered all over the world. Then there are the organisms for the administration of justice, that is, the Sacred Roman Rota and the Supreme Court of the Apostolic Signatura—as well as, for internal questions of conscience, the Sacred Apostolic Penitentiary—which endeavor to find a just solution to questions that may arise in the life of the Church and that concern the rights of the faithful or of communities.

There is, furthermore, as you well know, the Secretariat of State which assists the Pope from close at hand both in matters that regard the universal Church and for the coordination of the activity of curial organisms. There is, moreover, the Council for the Public Affairs of the Church, which deals above all with questions concerning relations with states and with governments.

The Church is like that man "who brings out of his treasure what is new and what is old" (Mt. 13:52).

Those organisms that arose as a result of the Council tell us a great deal about the Church of today and tomorrow: the Pontifical Council for the Laity; the Commission *Iustitia et Pax*; the three secretariats, for the Union of Christians, for Non-Christian Religions, for Non-Believers; various pontifical commissions and the Prefecture for Economic Affairs. Without mentioning, furthermore, the Synod of Bishops, which also came into being as a result of the Council, and which has its general secretariat at this Apostolic See.

4. The Apostolic See can, and should, be regarded as a complex of specialized offices, which by means of their tireless work facilitate knowledge of the essential affairs of the Church and the opportune decisions. It can and must be said that all these offices support the "ministry" of Peter's Successor and facilitate its accomplishment.

However, speaking of "ministry," it is always necessary to perceive that undercurrent which gives each of them a rightful meaning and causes the life of the whole

Church to throb in each one, by means of all the impulses which arrive from all sides and then branch out in all directions.

Perhaps, precisely for this purpose, the best thing is to go back to the times of the first Apostles, to their letters. With the same words that they wrote about their closest collaborators, allow me to express my gratitude to my present collaborators, uniting with them in solicitude for the Church which has her source in the heart of Christ the Good Shepherd.

Exemplary Fidelity in Ecclesial Service

On August 6, 1979, John Paul II concelebrated the solemn funeral rite for Cardinal Alfredo Ottaviani in the Vatican Basilica together with thirteen Cardinals, including the Dean of the Sacred College, Cardinal Confalonieri, and Cardinal Seper, Cardinal Ottaviani's successor at the head of the Sacred Congregation for the Doctrine of the Faith.
The Holy Father delivered the following homily.

Ecce Sacerdos magnus, qui in diebus suis placuit Deo et inventus est iustus (cf. Sir. 44:16-17): These are the first words that rise spontaneously to my lips at the moment in which we offer the Eucharistic Sacrifice to God and prepare to take leave of our revered brother, Cardinal Alfredo Ottaviani. He was really a great priest, distinguished for his religious piety, exemplary fidelity in the service of the Holy Church and of the Apostolic See, solicitous in his ministry and in the practice of Christian charity. And he was at the same time a Roman priest, in possession, that is, of that typical spirit, perhaps not easy to define, that those born here in Rome—as he was born, ten years before the end of the nineteenth century—have by inheritance, as it were; that spirit which is expressed in special attachment to Peter and to the faith of Peter and, again, in keen sensitivity to what the Church of Peter is and does and must do.

For this reason, I spoke of "exemplary fidelity," and now that he is dead after a long and laborious earthly day, it is easier to perceive this fidelity as the constant characteristic of his whole life. His was really *a tried and unflagging fidelity*. Without wishing to go through the phases of his activity in the different ministries, to which his brilliant intellect and the confidence of the Sovereign Pontiffs called him, he always distinguished himself for this moral quality, an extraordinary quality, a quality that means consistency, dedication, obedience. As Sostituto to the Secretariat of State, and then Assessor, Pro-Secretary, Pro-Prefect and Prefect of what was then the Sacred Congregation of the Holy Office, as Prelate Bishop and Cardinal, he gave proof of possessing this quality; a uniform, as it were, which characterized him and identified him in the eyes of those—and there were many of them both in Rome and outside—who knew him and esteemed him. Being responsible for the Congregation which is institutionally entrusted with the safeguarding of the sacred patrimony of faith and of Catholic morality, he expressed this same virtue in a behavior of perspicacious attention in the conviction—objectively founded and gradually more and more matured in experience of things and of men—that *rectitudo fidei*, that is, orthodoxy, is the indispensable patrimony and the first condition for *rectitudo morum*, or orthopraxis. His high juridical sense, which had made him, when still young, a teacher praised and listened to by many hosts of priests, sustained him in the tenacious work he carried out in defense of the Faith.

Always available, always ready to serve the Church, he also saw in reforms the providential sign of the times, so that he was able and wished to collaborate with my Predecessors John XXIII and Paul VI, as he had already done with Pius XII and even earlier with Pius XI. His existence was literally spent for the good of the holy Church of God. Our brother in everything, he was always *homo Dei, ad omne opus bonum instructus* (2 Tm. 3:17); and this is indeed an essential reference, a characteristic element, which highlights his spiritual and moral nature.

He was also a man with a great priestly heart: There are still many people who remember him in his daily ministry in the midst of the boys and youths of St. Peter's Oratory, who had him—alongside other unforgotten Roman priests and prelates—as a friend and brother, and I will say better: as a solicitous and affectionate father. This presence of his was not a distraction from the tedious weariness of official papers and bureaucratic commitments, but a necessity that arose spontaneously, intentionally and generously from a priestly program, a service offered at the bidding of his vocation.

He was born poor in the working class district of Trastevere, and this origin explains his tender love and preferential solicitude for the poor, for children and for orphans. And now it is just these innocent souls who—beside so many priests and laity who received from Cardinal Ottaviani the light of wisdom, the lesson of simplicity, the medicine of mercy—intercede for him before the altar of the Lord, in order that the reward destined for the "good and faithful servant" (cf. Mt. 25:21) may quickly be bestowed on him.

By a strange coincidence this sad rite takes place at the same time at which, exactly a year ago, my beloved Predecessor Paul VI was about to leave this world. And I am happy to recall with you the strong and moved voice of the Cardinal when he announced publicly on June 21, 1963, the elevation of Cardinal Giovanni Battista Montini to the pontificate. From the very tone of his words, though they repeated the usual Latin formula *Habemus Papam*, there could be felt the satisfaction of the old teacher who saw exalted a colleague and friend, so worthy of esteem, who would open an intense and promising season in the Church and for the Church. Both of them, in their respective positions of responsibility, in the obvious distinction of their individual personalities, have now concluded the cycle of earthly existence, to enter definitively—as we all hope and pray—that kingdom into which their ardent and intrepid faith had brought them in hope.

May the Lord now grant both of them rest in His light, in His peace. Amen!

A Long Life at the Service of the Lord and His Church

On September 6, 1979, in the Vatican Basilica, the Holy Father concelebrated the solemn funeral Mass for Cardinal Alberto di Jorio. It was the final homage which the Pope and the People of God made to a faithful servant of the Lord's Word, to a long life lived in the service of the Church.

Eighteen Cardinals concelebrated with the Pope at the Altar of the Chair, among whom were the Cardinal Secretary of State, Agostino Casaroli, and the Dean of the Sacred College, Carlo Confalonieri.

After the proclamation of the Gospel, John Paul II pronounced the following homily.

Your Eminences,
Revered brothers,
Beloved sons and daughters,

We are gathered today for the liturgical celebration of the funeral of the late Cardinal Alberto di Jorio, called to be a member of the Sacred College by John XXIII of happy memory, in 1958. The entire span of his long life was at the service of the Lord and of the Church. In particular, he gave much of himself to this Apostolic See, on whose behalf he exerted his greatest energies.

Consequently we have the duty of recognition towards him, which we discharge once more today, here, publicly before the Lord.

His whole earthly existence may be summed up in these three characteristics; he was a good priest, careful administrator, generous benefactor. The varied activity of the sacred ministry, exercised from the first years of the priesthood, is proof of the first. The second is proved by several decades of service both at the Roman Vicariate and at the Holy See. Various initiatives for social, cultural and ecclesiastical improvement are eloquent testimony of the third. Here we have a case of good qualities and good works which the Lord undoubtedly appreciates, in the same way as he praised, even though in terms of a parable, that good and faithful servant, who had fully exploited the talents received, not keeping them for himself but returning them multiplied to his master (cf. Mt. 25:14-21). Well, the reward for such lasting service, faithful and productive, cannot come to him but from the Lord Himself, and we are here precisely to implore it for him, in abundance and for his happiness.

It is the liturgy itself which directs us to this end, and enriches our meditation even more through the biblical readings we have just heard. All three are centered on the theme of communion with God, which already begins in this life by means of the redemption secured for us by Christ, and flowers in the future, never-ending life, beyond history.

In the Gospel according to St. John, Jesus solemnly asserts that it is the explicit will of the heavenly Father "that whoever sees the son and believes in him has eternal life" (6:40). But in the sense of St. John's Gospel, "eternal life" is not only reserved for the future of the after life, but it is also that which is already being realized in the adhesion of faith to the divine Logos, incarnate in this world, so that, from within our historical existence, so full of obligations, of activities, of preoccupations, it becomes a secret but dynamic principle of ferment and transformation of our whole being and action. This is the Christian and priestly principle, which surely sustained and inspired the existence of the eminent deceased and which must be the foundation of the life of every baptized man.

The very possibility of this marvelous reality is provided by the fact that, as St. Paul announces in the second reading, "while we were still sinners, Christ died for us" (Rom. 5:8), even overturning the human rules of heroism, which can, at the most, lead "to dying for a righteous man" (*Ibid.*, 5:7). That which Christ did on the cross is, on the one hand, an effective reason for our salvation or reconciliation with God (cf. *ibid.*, 5:10), but on the other hand, it must yet become a stimulus and parameter of our daily conduct: to offer life for men who are our brothers, and in particular for the poorest, for those of least account, for those who, by an excessively human reckoning, are regarded as being on the fringe of society. It is precisely here, in fact, that the beauty of Christianity shines forth, that is, in a totally gratuitous love, free of ostentatious motivations, disinterested, and therefore most pure. Such is the way of God Himself.

It is on these premises that the words of the first reading taken from the Book of Wisdom have a great significance: "The souls of the righteous are in the hands of God; those who are faithful to him will live close to him in love" (3:1, 9). The Christian is "right" not by his own power from within, but by a free and adorable divine gift, which, however, becomes the inspiration and source of activity, a principle of charity, in everyday life.

It is, in fact, at this point, that being "faithful" to God is measured, since fidelity to His love, in the concrete, is possible only by means of our love. And what is life after death if not precisely the definitive triumph of an indestructible and mutual communion? Therefore, "they will live close to Him in love"—those who already in this historical existence live or have lived in conformity with this supreme objective, which is not only chronologically at the end of the earthly road, but already dominates it ideally, or rather informs from within the sum total of our days.

Therefore, we pray to the Lord, that the soul of Cardinal Alberto di Jorio, redeemed by Christ and spent in the service of the holy Church in the name of charity, may actually and totally participate in the light, the peace and the love without end.

Let Us Go to Christ: He Will Cure Us

September 9, 1979, was a day of celebration for the numerous inhabitants of the Alban Hills. The Holy Father, visiting the Monastery of Grottaferrata, went in procession through the streets packed with cheering crowds. During the Mass, celebrated at an altar erected in front of the Abbey church of St. Mary at Grottaferrata, the Pope delivered the following homily.

Beloved monks of the Abbey of Grottaferrata, and you, priests and faithful who hear me!

1. It is not simply the nearness of place but above all of the spirit which has brought me here among you this evening, to celebrate the Sunday liturgy and give you a word of exhortation and encouragement. Our meeting takes place in the XVIth centenary of the death of St. Basil the Great, Bishop of Caesarea of Cappadocia. First of all, I would like to thank and greet the good religious who take their name from this illustrious Doctor of the Eastern Church, and who welcome us in the shade of their historic Abbey. I also cordially greet all those of you who have come in such great numbers and have given me proof of your respectful affection.

CHRIST'S HEALING

2. We have just heard the readings of the Holy Scriptures, rich in teaching and worthy of careful consideration. But I prefer to dwell on the *Gospel episode* which refers to the miraculous healing of a deaf and dumb man, by our Lord Jesus Christ. How wonderful, dear brothers, is that unanimous cry which rises from the crowd: "He has done all things well"! This exclamation provoked by keen surprise—as the evangelist observes—is more than a simple recognition of the Lord's power, or a tribute of admiration for the miracle. In reality, it implies the "violation" of an

order given by Jesus, who had asked for silence with regard to the event; furthermore—far more importantly—it is followed and, I would say, integrated by other words which make of it a clear messianic testimony. "He has done all things well"—said the bystanders—"he makes the deaf hear and the dumb talk."

Did they not recognize in these very actions some of those "signs" foretold by the prophets, which would occur on the advent of the Messiah? And have we not perhaps read in Isaiah's text, which preceded this Gospel, the inspiring words: "Then the eyes of the blind shall be opened, and the ears of the deaf unstopped. Then...shall the tongue of the dumb sing for joy" (Is. 35:6)?

Yes, brothers, basing ourselves on the probative value of such correspondence between prophecies and their fulfillment, and echoing the enthusiasm of the multitudes, we believe and confess that Jesus is truly the Messiah, that is, the Anointed of God, the Christ. *He was consecrated by God and sent into the world.* We can never meditate enough on this fact of our Credo, since it is so important and so rich in content: Jesus, the only-begotten Son of God, in fulfillment of the ancient promises, has come among us in the fullness of time; having become son of man, He is placed at the center of history to carry out in an authentic and definitive manner the plan of salvation conceived by the Father from eternity. Enlightened by faith, we must not only look to the figure of the Messiah but also to this function of His which concerns humanity in general and each of us in particular.

LIKE A CATALYST

Already in the Old Testament the Messiah is like a catalyst of the yearnings and expectations of the people of Israel, throughout the whole span of its history. Every hope of liberation and sanctification is focused on Him. But it is in the New Testament that this function of the Messiah is clarified as a mission of spiritual and universal salvation.

One day on finding Himself in the synagogue of Nazareth, Jesus read from a page of Isaiah: "The spirit of the Lord is upon me; because of this he has anointed me to preach the good news to the poor,...to give sight to the blind...," and He began the explanation with a significant remark: "Today this scripture has been fulfilled in your hearing" (cf. Lk. 4:16-21). To the disciples of John the Baptist who had come to ask Him: "Are you he who is to come, or shall we look for another?" Jesus answered, appealing to facts foreseen and foretold for the Messiah: "Go and tell John what you hear and see: The blind receive their sight...the deaf hear, and the poor have good news preached to them" (cf. Mt. 11:2-6).

Let us now take up again, in the light of these texts, the account in today's Gospel.

NEED FOR FAITH

3. The miracle also tells us something else with regard to the *modus operandi* followed by Jesus-Messiah. They had presented Him with a deaf and dumb man, begging Him to put His hand on him. Instead Jesus carries out various gestures in his regard: He takes him aside; He puts His fingers in his ears; He touches his tongue. Why all this? Because the condition which Jesus always demands from the suffering and the sick is faith, questioning them about it or urging them to it depending on the situation. Now, in the case of the deaf and dumb man, touching his impeded senses meets the situation perfectly: to communicate with one who can neither hear nor speak, and to arouse in him a movement of faith.

But there is more: Jesus raises His eyes to heaven, then sighs and pronounces the decisive word: *Ephphatha*, one of the few words preserved for us exactly as Jesus uttered it. Notice *the power of this word*, which has a dynamic charge, because it produces the effect it expresses. As in the case of other words of Christ, related in the Gospels, like *Talitha, koum*, which made Jairus' dead daughter rise from her bed (cf. Mk. 5:22-24; 35-43), or like the expression *Lazare, veni foras*, which made the friend whose body was already decomposing spring from the sepulcher alive (cf. Jn. 11:38-44), we are here in the presence of the mystery of miraculous power which is the connatural attribute of the Messiah Son of God. As the Word of the Father, the living Word of the Father, had already by the creative "Fiat" drawn forth all things from nothing, so likewise by the word uttered by His human mouth He has the capacity, that is to say, the absolute power of bending all things to His will.

Why, then, do we not try to experience in ourselves this permanent power of Christ? Together with His words producing physical miracles, how many other words are contained in the Gospel, which "probe" at an interior level and act on a supernatural plane? I recall briefly the words "Courage, my son: Your sins are forgiven," addressed to the cripple (Mt. 9:3); "Go, and do not sin again," to the adulteress (Jn. 8:11).

I also remember the miracle which Jesus' presence alone produced in Zacchaeus: "Today salvation has come to this house" (Lk. 19:9). And I could add the "Follow me" which is decisive for the vocation of the Apostles (cf. Mt. 4:19); or the "You are Peter, and on this rock I will build my Church" (Mt. 16:18), or the more mysterious and sublime words of the Last Supper: "This is my body; this is my blood" (Mt. 26:26, 28).

Deeply convinced of the miraculous force, of the *dynamis* of Christ, who on the verge of leaving this world claimed for Himself "all authority in heaven and on earth" (Mt. 28:18), we must go to Him to cure our weaknesses and our sins; by reason and in measure of our faith, we shall obtain hope, strength and salvation.

BASILIAN COMMUNITY

4. But what shall I say in particular to the Basilian religious and to all the monastic community of Grotta-

ferrata? The word of God, which I have wished to explain, certainly applies to them as well. But I know that they expect at least a thought, to strengthen their life of special consecration to the Lord in the spirit of the ascetic teachings of St. Basil.

Here, a few kilometers away from Rome, you, my dear brothers, are an expression of the fecundity of the monastic ideal of the Byzantine rite, and your Abbey—as my Predecessor Pius XI of venerated memory has already written in the act erecting it canonically—is "like a most brilliant eastern jewel" set in the diadem of the Roman Church (cf. Apost. Const. *Pervetustum Cryptaeferratae Coenobium*, in *A.A.S.* XXX, 1938, p. 183-186).

Moreover, I am aware of the singular bond of fidelity which this monastery has constantly maintained with the Apostolic See, since its foundation at the beginning of the 11th century; and this is not the least reason for the benevolence shown to it by the Supreme Pontiffs. I also know that such a relationship will always be stable.... Well, in the exemplary nature of your attachment to the See of Peter, take care to offer a valid witness to those who have occasion to meet you and to know you. Seek to radiate the pure evangelical light before men "that they may see your good works and give glory to your Father who is in heaven" (Mt. 5:6).

The practice of the virtues, beginning with brotherly charity, balance in the religious life, hard work, the loving study of Sacred Scriptures, the continual striving towards the "other life," as they are among the salient principles of the Rule of the great Basil, so must they be the qualities which distinguish you, confirming the authentic and unbroken tradition of spirituality which so honors your institute.

Precisely because you represent this Greek monastic tradition, another quality must distinguish you, namely, a special ecumenical sensitivity. On account of your position, of your formation, you can do much in this respect, involving yourself in dialogue and especially in prayer in order to promote the desired unity between Catholics and Orthodox.

In returning now to the celebration of the holy Mass, I invite you religious, and with you all the faithful who surround you, to unite with me in the common invocation that the Lord Jesus, renewing as it were the miracle of the deaf and dumb man, may open our ears to the ever faithful hearing of His word, and make fluent our tongues in praising and thanking His and our heavenly Father. Amen.

Dialogue with Christ in His Church

In the Sistine Chapel on September 15, 1979, the Holy Father conferred episcopal ordination on His Excellency, Most Rev. Jozef Tomko, who had been appointed Secretary General of the Synod of Bishops. Pope John Paul II delivered the following homily.

Dear brothers and sisters!

1. Here is our brother Joseph, whom today the "gift" of the Holy Spirit (cf. Eph. 4:11) makes a bishop of the Church. It includes him by means of my service in the circle of this college which receives, in inheritance from the Apostles, not only the living signs of the whole People of God, but also a particular priestly, magisterial and pastoral power with regard to the others.

This is a solemn and important moment not only for the bishop who is consecrated, but for the whole Church. Our brother Joseph must assume the important office of Secretary General of the Synod of Bishops, the organ which, in accordance with the decision of the last Council, has become a particularly fruitful expression and the instrument of episcopal collegiality.

2. Behold, at this moment an extraordinary *dialogue* takes place between the new ordinand and Christ living in the Church. The three stages of this dialogue are traced in the readings of the Liturgy of the Word today.

In the *first stage* we are witnesses of what is said by Him who knows us eternally, by Him who knows what is in every man (cf. Jn. 2:25): "Before I formed you in the womb I knew you" (Jer. 1:5). The man called by Him seems to answer: "Ah, Lord God! Behold, I do not know how to speak" (Jer. 1:6). In His turn, the Lord of the human heart says: "To all to whom I send you you shall go, and whatever I command you you shall speak.... Be not afraid of them, for I am with you to deliver you" (1:7-8). This is the *first stage.*

3. In the *second stage,* only the Lord speaks and he who is called listens. The *Lord*, in His speech, *expresses the requirements* with the words of the Apostle Paul in the letter to Timothy: "I remind you to rekindle the gift of God that is within you through the laying on of my hands.... Take your share of suffering for the gospel in the power of God.... (Christ) abolished death and brought life and immortality to light through the gospel.... Follow the pattern of the sound words which you have heard from me, in the faith and love which are in Christ Jesus; guard the truth that has been entrusted to you by the Holy Spirit who dwells within us" (2 Tm. 1:6-8, 10, 13).

These words come from Paul who addressed them to Timothy.

They contain a splendid expression of the apostolic succession. The episcopal consecration, which our brother Joseph receives today from the hands of John Paul, Bishop of Rome, is part of it and is a new link in it.

4. And finally the *third stage.* In the Gospel Christ Himself speaks. To the requirements just expressed He *adds His own example and model.* "I am the good shepherd. The good shepherd lays down his life for the sheep.... I am the good shepherd; I know my own and my own know me, as the Father knows me and I know the Father" (Jn. 10:11, 14-15).

Christ's words ring out with a special echo in the soul of each one who, together with the laying on of hands, receives the pastoral office, solicitude and responsibility.

Precisely with this allegory of His, with this example, Christ lays the deepest obligation on each of us. He wants us to be like Him: *the good Shepherd.*

These are the three stages of the dialogue which, during today's liturgy, takes place between Christ, living in the Church, and our brother Joseph, who receives episcopal ordination. It would be difficult to add anything else to these words of the Lord. They are full of wisdom and supreme love. Let all of us who are listening try to sustain our brother with prayer in order that these words may become the program of his life and the content of his new ministry in the Church.

The Holy Father then continued his homily in Slovak.

5. Today the persons closest to him sustain him with their prayer in a particular way, especially his parents, his sister and brother-in-law, and other relatives, who have been able to come here from their native country, Slovakia; then his confreres in the priesthood, the pilgrims from Kosice, Presov, Trnava and Bratislava, other pilgrims from all over Europe, and also from Canada, the United States of America and Australia, as well as those who join with us spiritually at this important moment.

My thoughts together with those of the new bishop, go, at this moment, towards those parts from which he comes. Towards the southern slope of the Tatra, not far from which is Udavské, his *native place:* the church from which he comes and which he entered by means of Baptism and Confirmation, by means of the Christian morals of his family, the example of his parents, the friendship of those of his own age. Our thoughts also go to that parish where, in the midst of the Christian community, he took his first steps and where, certainly, he heard the first words of Christ's call to the priesthood.

Today *we embrace particularly, in memory and with love,* all that country and the whole nation because today is the day of Mary, Our Lady of Sorrows, who is venerated on this very day, in Slovakia, as the principal heavenly Patron. Being present at the foot of the cross, she was fully united with her Son, our Redeemer. *Being present at the foot of the cross*, she remains for us the most splendid model of motherly fortitude when, with intrepid strength of spirit, she seems to repeat: "Behold, I am the handmaid of the Lord; let it be done to me according to your word" (Lk. 1:38). Being present at the foot of the cross, she accepts each of us as her children, as she accepted John.

So today she accepts also this son of the Slovak land who receives episcopal consecration from the hands of the Pope in the Sistine Chapel in Rome. And she seems to say to *all sons and daughters* of distant Slovakia: Stay with me! Stay with Christ! You are children of the supreme love with which God Himself "so loved the world that he gave his only Son, that whoever believes in him should not perish but have eternal life" (Jn. 3:16).

The Holy Father then concluded his homily in Czech.

There are also Czech confreres of the new archbishop, his fellow students at the Pontifical Nepomucene College, who also accompany him with their prayers. In this moment the memory of all of us and the assurance of being ever close to the Pope's heart go also to the dear Czech sister nation.

The Lovable Figure of Cardinal Wright

On September 22, 1979, the Holy Father presided over a solemn Eucharistic Liturgy—at the altar of the Chair, in the Vatican Basilica—for the soul of Cardinal John Joseph Wright, Prefect of the Sacred Congregation for the Clergy, just over a month after his death, which took place in the United States of America on August 10, 1979.

The special concelebration, with twenty-one Cardinals, was desired by the Pope not just to commemorate one of the most illustrious members of the Sacred College and of the Roman Curia, but above all to point out the characteristic features of his outstanding personality as a pastor who had, for ten years, the heavy task of guiding the Catholic clergy, on the pastoral plane.

The figure of Cardinal Wright was conjured up in moving words by John Paul II, who delivered the following homily, after the Gospel.

Lord Cardinals, Brothers and beloved sons:

I desired this special concelebration to commemorate, just over a month after his sad decease, the lovable figure of Cardinal John Joseph Wright. He left us silently, and his death, depriving the Sacred College and the Roman Curia of an authoritative member, was and still is a cause of sincere regret for us.

In actual fact who was Cardinal Wright? What are the characteristic features of his personality? We know very well the exterior elements of his biography: born in the United States of America of a family of Irish origin, after a youth marked by exemplary dedication to souls, he was nominated Auxiliary of Boston; then he was the appreciated Bishop of Worcester and of Pittsburgh, until, by the confidence reposed in him by my Predecessor, Paul VI, of venerated memory, he was called to Rome as Prefect of the Sacred Congregation for the Clergy.

But, beyond these external data, there emerged in him—and it presents itself to us now as the first and fundamental one—an outstanding pastoral quality. Endowed by nature with a rich and warm humanity, he always showed himself to be a pastor, with all the characteristics that must define the latter according to evangelical teaching, that is, solicitude, sensitiveness, understanding, the spirit of sacrifice for the sheep of his flock (cf. Jn. 10:2-18). It was precisely this attitude, matured in his long experience of diocesan life, that caused him to be given, in the post-conciliar period, the task of directing the important Congregation, which is the institution responsible for the guidance and inspiration of the clergy and the Christian people on the pastoral plane.

Wishing, however, to penetrate more deeply into the psychology of the Cardinal, we will find that the secret source that nourished this typical commitment of his was a constant and personal relationship of intimacy with Christ the Lord. He who had chosen as his motto the significant expression *"Resonare Christum,"* made it his concern to keep this contact with Him always fresh and alive. He was so convinced of this necessity that he never failed to instill it in priests both by writing and in words.

I am happy to quote, for example, the penetrating preface he wrote for the reprinting of the golden booklet *Manete in dilectione mea,* where we read the following sentences: "If you wish, beloved brothers, to *conservare in aeternum* your priestly identity in this age in which the world is too important for men, try to imitate the heart of Jesus today more than yesterday." And again: "If you want the Church to be really a sacrament of salvation for modern man, not to lose her own identity and suffer the sharp anguish of spiritual emptiness, direct your whole spiritual life to imitation of the heart of Jesus."

Here is the focal center, which explains our Cardinal's dynamism and zeal. Here is the permanently valid indication that he transmits to us, if we do not want—we bishops and priests—our ministry to be weakened or nullified. It is, in fact, an indication on which we shall never reflect enough, because it is a natural part of our state, because it calls us urgently to live an intense interior life, centered on Christ "gentle and lowly in heart" (Mt. 11:29), nourished by that charity of His, without which, even in the midst of resounding external success—as St. Paul warns us—one is nothing (cf. 1 Cor. 13:1-3).

A second lesson comes to us from this outstanding Cardinal: In the multiform ministry he carried out for brothers, priests and faithful, he kept and showed exemplary attachment to the Magisterium of the Church. He conceived this Magisterium as a living reality, a sacred function, a qualified service for the integrity of faith and in general for the cause of truth, set up within the Church by the Lord's will (cf. Mt. 28:19-20; 1 Tm. 3:15). One may well think that this fervent adherence and, I would say, devotion to the Church-Teacher, was not unrelated to the uninterrupted tradition of faithfulness of Catholic Ireland.

No text could be better indicated, for this liturgical assembly of ours, than the one of Matthew just proclaimed: After the sublime elevation to the Father *(Confiteor tibi, Pater...)*, Jesus addresses a persuasive invitation to His disciples to go to Him and accept the easy yoke of His teaching: *Venite ad me omnes....* Throughout his whole life, Cardinal Wright endeavored, precisely in that daily contact that I mentioned above, to study Jesus from close at hand, to learn directly from Him the eternal and salutary lessons of meekness and humility of heart. Prior to the *munus docendi*, which was incumbent on him as bishop and pastor, he held very dear the *Officium discendi*. We believe, therefore, because of the Lord's formal promise *(et invenietis requiem)*, that already on this earth he found relief and peace for his soul; but we also believe owing to the boundless charity of the same Lord, that he now enjoys these goods, in a full and unchanging form, in the glory of heaven. Amen.

The Family and the Young in the Church's Future

On September 25, 1979, John Paul II received in audience a group of bishops from Paraguay on their visit ad limina Apostolorum. *The group was led by Bishop Felipe Santiago Benitez Avalos of Villarrica, President of the episcopal conference of Paraguay. The Holy Father delivered the following address.*

Revered brothers in the episcopate,

Blessed be the Lord, for permitting me to have this brotherly meeting with you, the pastors of the Church in Paraguay. You have come to Rome "to see Peter," to share with him your joys and your solicitude in evangelization of the People of God entrusted to you, and to strengthen the bonds of charity between your respective sees and the See of Peter's Successor.

These moments of renewed communion that we spend together, after the individual meeting with each of you, offer me the opportunity to thank God for the harmony which reigns among you and which spreads beneficially in contact with your priests, with other pastoral workers, especially the religious, and with the faithful. I express to you, therefore, my satisfaction and ask the Lord that, as the fruit of this meeting with the one who has been set as the center and guarantee of communion with Christ, your unity of sentiments and wills may be perfected and strengthened, for the good of the Church in your country.

If you and your Christian communities maintain this brotherly communion, you will be able to face with greater ease and profit the challenges you have to meet at the present time and which can be seen from the reports you presented for this visit *ad limina.*

I know that one of the points that concerns you most in your pastoral task is the moralization of public, family and individual life. You are dedicating to this your efforts both personally and also as members of the episcopal conference. Rest assured that I am with you and encourage this work of yours, aimed at preserving, re-establishing and strengthening the moral sense in consciences, in order that the law of God and rectitude may govern social and family relations, as well as the private behavior of persons.

This is a chapter of great importance, for if the values of true moral integrity are not put into practice, the solid foundations of society will crumble and the level of life of the citizens will fall.

You should continue to dedicate particular attention to adequate pastoral care for the family, a guarantee of efficacy to obtain upright conduct in your faithful. It is well known, in fact, that where the family is sound, the whole of society feels its beneficial influence. It is precisely from a recognized lack of genuinely human and Christian values that so many of the evils that afflict the youth of today are derived. That of youth is another of the chapters to which I know you wish to dedicate further special care, because the future of the Church and of society depends on it.

In conclusion, some words on another point which has a front-ranking place in your concerns: the problem of vocations to consecrated life. I know of the shortage of priests, especially native ones, from which your Churches suffer. But together with that I am happy to note the promising increase in vocations which is now being perceived. If you and your Christian communities must commit yourselves generously to all aspects of evangelization, it is in the search, careful preparation and effort for perseverance of vocations that I ask you to use your best energies. It is worthwhile to dedicate to that all care and watchfulness. Do so yourselves and ask consecrated souls—especially those of contemplative life—as well as lay people of greater spiritual sensitivity, to ask the Lord of the harvest to send workers for it.

Beloved brothers: these reflections on subjects so important for your communities spring from the love that binds us to each member of them. On your return to your sees, tell priests and consecrated souls in particular that the

Pope encourages them in their faithfulness to Christ and His Church, and keeps them in mind in daily prayer. May Our Lady of Caacupé assist you in your efforts, console you and lead you to her Son, the Savior.

With great affection, I give you my blessing, which I ask you to transmit to all your dioceses.

Gather All Men in Christ

On September 25, 1979, the Holy Father received in audience a group of bishops from Colombia on their visit ad limina Apostolorum. *The group was led by Cardinal Anibal Muñoz Duque, Archbishop of Bogota, who delivered an address of homage. John Paul II spoke as follows.*

Beloved brothers in the episcopate,

I am happy to be with you today at this collegial meeting which culminates with your visit *ad limina,* after having listened and spoken personally to each of you in successive audiences. And just as I feel it, I wish to tell you, in the words of the Apostle St. Paul, something that wells up from my heart: "I give thanks to God always for you because of the grace of God which was given you in Christ Jesus, that in every way you were enriched in him..." (1 Cor. 1:4ff.).

I say this not out of empty flattery of your sentiments as pastors of the Church, zealous and diligent as you are in careful guidance of your respective flocks. I say so simply to dwell upon my sincere confidence in your apostolic activity, especially yours, Lord Cardinal, and also that of all the brothers present here, and to sustain you spiritually, according to Christ's mandate: "strengthen your brethren" (Lk. 22:32); all that, to stimulate that unshakeable charity which, humbly confessed by Peter, confers a characteristic profile on the one who, by the will of the risen Lord, has to "feed his lambs" (cf. Jn. 21:15ff.).

In this same charity, which is a bond of unity in the Church, I also wish to embrace and pay tribute to your diocesan communities. During these days they have been particularly present in my pastoral "anxiety for all the churches" (2 Cor. 11:28). It is an anxiety shared with you, with whom I wish to share likewise my deep satisfaction, since I am happy to "see your good order and the firmness of your faith in Christ...; live in him, rooted and built up in him and established in the faith, just as you were taught..." (Col. 2:5ff.).

Union in charity, firm and hopeful faith in Christ: there is here a complete expression of ecclesial vitality for those who have really taken root in Christ and feel built on Him. To all this must likewise be directed your prime mission as teachers and evangelizers of the People of God, according to the doctrine received in deposit.

1. There will be people who, with an attitude of facile criticism, think that this community of faith in Christ lives quite bewildered, in the midst of a society actuated by purely earthly motives and geared to profit and enjoyment, including what is just and honest, of material goods. They claim to reduce the Gospel to one doctrine among so many others of a humanitarian nature, which can serve very well as an alibi to escape from the burning human and social problems of our time. The pastors themselves— like consecrated persons and lay people engaged in the apostolate—are considered foolish people for preaching a hope (cf. 1 Cor. 1:18ff.) which is not easily reconciled with worldly gain.

Consequently, it would be viewed with pleasure if Christian communities would undertake other ways of salvation and give priority to alignment in favor of politico-social commitment, in the name of an alleged authentic interpretation of the evangelical doctrine which, in addition to "passing over in silence the divinity of Christ, claims to show him as politically committed, as one who fought against Roman oppression and the authorities, and also as one involved in the class struggle" (Opening address of the work of the Third General Assembly of the Latin American Episcopate, I, 4).

2. Beloved brothers: I wish to repeat here something that I already had the opportunity to say in Puebla before the Assembly of the Latin American episcopate. As pastors of the Church, let us be aware of being teachers of truth: This is what the faithful look for in us, when we proclaim the Good News to them (cf. *ibid.* 1, 1). Faith in Christ, which sustains ecclesial life, as you well know, is not a fruit of human invention nor is it the result of group enthusiasm or experiences. We preach the Son of God made Man, on His cross "a stumbling-block to Jews and folly to Gentiles, but to those who are called...the power of God and the wisdom of God" (cf. 1 Cor. 1:23).

The Christian mystery of creation and history converges on this divine wisdom, which in the Person of Christ assumes human weakness and grief, and in it the ultimate mystery of man and of his destiny is revealed. It then becomes necessary to be open to revealed truth, in order to understand the meaning of creation, which is not the result of natural forces or of human programs, but the work of God's plan, in which His designs of love for man stand out. It may happen, unfortunately, that the world does not recognize this meaning, that men do not accept this light of hope; but it is certain that Christ is this Light and that those who receive Him will become sons of God (cf. Jn. 1:9ff.).

You see already the pressing need for a more intense work of evangelization, which opens a way to the light of truth to show the world the specific mission of the Church: to root all men in Christ. As a community of faithful, the Church must always be in solidarity before God with everything human; as the *sacramentum salutis*, she must be responsible for the Good News of salvation in order to communicate it and put it into practice in all men (cf. GS 1). To be able to carry out this task adequately, priests, religious and faithful must live in communion with the Magisterium and with the guidelines issued by the ecclesiastical hierarchy.

3. With this, beloved brothers, I intended to emphasize what is the essence of our ministry: to build up the Church "speaking the word of God without fear" (cf. Phil. 1:14), proclaiming Christ, free of human fetters of a sociological, political or psychological slant (cf. Homily in the Cathedral of Santo Domingo), aware of being—and here my thought goes trustfully also to priests and consecrated souls—"companions and helpers," who serve God in the work of sanctifying mankind, by means of solicitous administration of the sacraments and guidelines of the People of God (cf. PO). We must then fill ourselves more and more with Christ in order to be able to present Him clearly to the world, to give credibility to our proclamation before those who seek Him with a sincere heart; in order that our actions for justice on behalf of the poor and oppressed may have the endorsement of a personal offering, following the example of Him who loved us even unto death and gave us new life (cf. Eucharistic Prayer IV).

I conclude with some words of St. Paul—I would be happy if they were really the motive summing up our lives and our ministerial tasks—"Only let your manner of life be worthy of the gospel of Christ, so that whether I come and see you or am absent, I may hear of you that you stand firm in one spirit, with one mind striving side by side for the faith of the gospel..." (Phil. 1:27ff.).

Assuring you of my abiding affection, I charge you, in deep love of Christ, to greet your priests, seminarians, religious and laity, on behalf of the Pope, who loves you all, prays for you all and blesses you all.

Unfading Crown of Glory

General audience of September 26, 1979, to priests, seminarians and students from Scotland.

I give a special welcome to the priests from the dioceses of Glasgow and Motherwell in Scotland, who are completing a month-long renewal course in theology. Tend the flock of God that is your charge willingly, eagerly, being examples to the flock. And when the chief Shepherd is manifested, you will obtain the unfading crown of glory.

The Unfathomable Mystery of Life and Death

On September 28, 1979, the Holy Father, John Paul II, presided over the solemn Mass for the soul of his Predecessor, John Paul I, on the first anniversary of his sudden death. Thirty-one Cardinals concelebrated with the Pope. During the Mass the Holy Father delivered the following homily.

Lord Cardinals, beloved brothers and sons!

1. With the help of the readings of today's liturgy we wish to relive that day one year ago, when Pope John Paul I was so suddenly called to God. Not so much today itself, as the night between September 28th and 29th marks the first anniversary of the death of this Successor to Saint Peter's See, who was able to remain there for just thirty-three days after his election. *Magis ostensus quam datus:* He departed almost before he had time to begin his pontificate. We have already dwelt on his unexpected departure, when visiting his birthplace, Canale d'Agordo, on August 26, that is, on the day when, through the votes

of the Cardinals in conclave, he had been called to be Bishop of Rome. Today it is fitting for us to celebrate the Eucharist for the first time on the anniversary of his death.

2. Listening to the readings of the liturgy, we find ourselves twice in the presence of the alternative of life, which the human heart often seems to oppose to death.

Martha addresses Christ with the words: "Lord, if you had been here, my brother would not have died" (Jn. 11:21).

Men often say near the corpses of persons dear to them: "Yet he might not have died; he might have lived longer...." Certainly also after John Paul I's unexpected death many people said, thought and felt like that: "Yet he might have lived longer...; why did he depart so soon?" Martha, the sister of Lazarus, passes from her human "yet he might..., if you, Christ, had been here" to the act of the greatest faith and hope: "And even now I know that whatever you ask from God, God will give you" (Jn. 11:12). Only Christ can be addressed with such words; only He has confirmed that He has power over human death. However, the human heart often opposes to death—this death which has already become a fact, this death of which everyone knows that, after all, it is inevitable—an alternative, the possibility of life: Yet he might have lived longer....

3. So let us allow St. Paul's apostolic voice to ring out again in our meditations. He, too, opposes the necessity of death to the possibility of life; he does so, however, in a way that corresponds fully to the light of faith, hope and charity that burned in his heart: "I am hard pressed between the two. My desire is to depart and be with Christ, for that is far better. But to remain in the flesh is more necessary on your account" (Phil. 1:23-24). The man who lives the faith like Paul, who loves like him, becomes, in a certain sense, master of his own death. The latter never surprises him.

At whatever moment it may come, it will always be accepted as an alternative to life, as a dimension which completes its whole meaning. "For me to live is Christ, and to die is gain" (Phil. 1:20). If Christ gives life all its meaning, then man can think of death in this way. He can await it in this way! And he can accept it in this way!

4. Let us penetrate with our thought the words of today's liturgical readings and try to follow their meaning. We perceive that they wish to bring us nearer to the answer regarding that death which took place, so unexpectedly, a year ago, and which today we not only remember, but, in a certain sense, relive. These readings wish to give us the answer to the question: *How did John Paul I die?*

Let us then ask a second question: What would this life have been if it had not been interrupted during the night between September 28th and 29th of last year? And we find the answer to this question, too, in Paul's text: "...life in the flesh, that means fruitful labor for me" (Phil. 1:22). So, therefore, not only does life bear witness to death, but also death to life.

5. This witness which John Paul I's death bore to his life becomes at the same time the testament of his pontificate: "I shall remain and continue with you all, for your progress and joy in the faith" (Phil. 1:25).

What is the main word in that testament? Perhaps the one that speaks of "joy in the faith." The Lord gave John Paul I thirty-three days in St. Peter's See in order that he might express this joy, this almost childlike joy.

This joy in faith is necessary in order that the further words of this testament may come true: that we may strive with one mind for the faith of the Gospel (cf. Phil. 1:27). We receive, in fact, the two indelible signs: the sign of son of God in Baptism, and the sign of confessor, ready to fight for the Faith of the Gospel, in Confirmation. John Paul I, Peter's Successor, manifested both these signs in his life and bore them strongly impressed on his soul, before God's majesty, like every true Christian.

6. We are celebrating the Eucharist: the liturgy of the death and resurrection of Christ. It becomes particularly eloquent when we celebrate it on the occasion of man's

death, during the funeral or anniversary of his death. In this connection I cannot but recall what the revered Cardinal Dean, the interpreter of the universal emotion, said during the sad funeral ceremony in St. Peter's Square, last year: "We are asking ourselves: Why so soon? The Apostle informs us with the well-known exclamation, full of admiration and worship: 'How unsearchable are his (God's) judgments and how inscrutable his ways! ...Who has known the mind of the Lord?' (Rom. 11:33) Thus the unfathomable mystery of life and death is brought up again in all its immense and almost oppressive grandeur" (cf. *L'Osservatore Romano*, English edition, October 12, 1978, p. 1).

Before this mystery, which is really impenetrable and insoluble for reason, no answering voice reaches man from man. With regard to it, what else can we hear but what Martha heard from Christ's lips? "Your brother will rise again.... I am the resurrection and the life; he who believes in me, though he die, yet shall he live, and whoever lives and believes in me shall never die. Do you believe this?" (Jn. 11:23-25)

The late Pope answered this question with the faith of the whole Church: I believe in the resurrection of the dead; I believe in the life of the world to come! And at the same time he confessed with the personal faith of his life: "Christ will be honored in my body, whether by life or by death" (Phil. 1:20).

"For I know that my Redeemer lives.../ And after my skin has been thus destroyed...,/ I shall see God" (Job 19:25-26).

The Church of Europe Owes a Debt of Gratitude to the Church in Ireland

The last meeting of the Pope's first day in Ireland took place on September 29, 1979, in the Dominican Convent in Dublin where the Holy Father met the Catholic bishops who had come to Ireland for his visit. The Pope spoke to them as follows.

Dear brothers in our Lord Jesus Christ,

That so many of you have come from different countries, to share with me the various moments of my visit, is a tribute both to Ireland and to yourselves, for it proves that you feel united with the Bishop of Rome in his "solicitude for all the churches" (2 Cor. 11:28), and at the same time it shows that you want to honor the faith of the Church in Ireland.

For is it not true that the Christian communities you represent have to discharge a duty of gratitude to the Church in Ireland? You who come from other European nations feel a particular relationship with the people that brought forth so many and so great missionaries, who in centuries past travelled untiringly across the mountains and rivers and through the plains of Europe to support the Faith when it was flagging, to revive the Christian communities, and preach the Word of the Lord. The vitality of the Church in Ireland made the establishing of many of your own communities possible. *Peregrinari pro Christo:* to be a voyager, a pilgrim for Christ was their reason for leaving their dear native land; and the Church in Europe was given new life by their journeyings.

Outside the continent, Irish immigrants, priests and missionaries were again the founders of new dioceses and parishes, the builders of churches and schools, and their faith succeeded, sometimes against overwhelming odds, to bring Christ to new regions, and to imbue new communities with the same undivided love for Jesus and His Mother, and with the same loyalty and affection for the Apostolic See in Rome as they had known in their homeland.

As we reflect on these historical realities, and as we witness together, during this visit, the piety, the faith and the vitality of the Irish Church, we cannot but feel blessed for these moments. Your presence here will in turn be an encouragement for the Irish episcopate and for the Irish Christians, since in seeing you gathered around the Bishop of Rome, they will see that it is the whole *Collegium Episcopale* that offers support to the local pastors and assumes its share of responsibility for the Church that is in Ireland. Let your love for Ireland and your appreciation of Ireland's place in the Church be expressed in prayer for a speedy return to peace in this beautiful island. Lead your faithful people in this earnest and untiring prayer to the Prince of Peace, through the intercession of Mary, Queen of Peace.

When the people of this beloved country see you, gathered together with the Irish bishops around the Bishop of Rome, they witness that special union that constitutes a core of the episcopal collegiality, a union of mind and heart, a union of commitment and dedication in the building up of the Body of Christ, that is, the Church. It is this profound union, this sincere "communion" that confers depth and meaning to the concept of collegiality and that carries it beyond a mere practical collaboration or a sharing of insights. It then becomes a bond that truly unites the bishops of the whole world with the Successor of Peter and among themselves, in order to carry out *cum Petro et sub Petro* the apostolic ministry which the Lord entrusted to the Twelve. Knowing that such are the sentiments that animate your presence here with me not only gives me satisfaction but also supports me in my own unique and universal pastoral ministry.

From this union among all the bishops will flow forth for each ecclesial community, and for the Church as a whole, abundant fruits of unity and communion among all the faithful and with their bishops, as well as with the visible head of the universal Church.

Thank you for sharing with me the privilege and the supernatural grace of this visit. May the Lord Jesus bless you and your dioceses with ever more abundant fruits of union in mind and heart. And may every Christian everywhere, and the whole Church of God as one, increasingly become a sign and a presence of hope for all of humanity.

Support of the Pope and Church in the Ministry of Bishops

On September 30, 1979, the Holy Father met the Irish Bishops led by the President of the Irish episcopal conference, Cardinal Tomás O'Fiaich, Archbishop of Armagh and Primate of all Ireland. The Holy Father spoke to them as follows.

My dear brothers,

1. Once again I want you to know how profoundly grateful I am to you for your invitation to come to Ireland. For me this visit is the fulfillment of a deep desire of my heart: to come as a servant of the Gospel and as a pilgrim to the Shrine of Our Lady at Knock, on the occasion of its centenary.

I come also as your brother Bishop from Rome, and I have greatly looked forward to this day so that we may celebrate together the unity of the episcopate of our Lord Jesus Christ, so that we may give public expression to a dimension of our episcopal collegiality, and so that we may reflect together on the role of pastoral leadership in the Church, particularly in regard to our own common responsibility for the well-being of the People of God in Ireland.

We are deeply conscious of the special charge that has been laid upon us as bishops. For "by virtue of sacramental consecration and by hierarchical communion" (LG 22) we are constituted members of the college charged with the pastoral mission of our Lord Jesus Christ.

2. The episcopal collegiality in which we share is manifested in different ways. Today it is expressed in a very important way: The Successor of Peter is present with you, in order personally to confirm you in your faith and apostolic ministry, and, together with you, to exercise the pastoral care of the faithful in Ireland. Thus, my pilgrimage as Pastor of the universal Church is seen in its deep dimension of ecclesial and hierarchical communion. And through the action of the Holy Spirit, the teaching on collegiality finds expression and actuation here and now.

In my first discourse to the College of Cardinals and to the world after my election to the See of Peter, I urged "a deeper reflection on the implications of the collegial bond" (October 17, 1978). I am also convinced that my meeting with the episcopal conference today leads to a better understanding of the nature of the Church, viewed as *People of God*, "which takes its citizens from every race, making them citizens of a kingdom which is of a heavenly and not an earthly nature" (LG 13).

3. In our present meeting, we are living the experience of the People of God in Ireland, first in the "vertical" dimension, climbing up, as it were, through all the generations to the very beginnings of Christianity here. At the same time we are mindful of the "horizontal" dimension, realizing how the People of God in Ireland are joined in the unity and the universality of the Church with all peoples on the earth, how they share in the mystery of the universal Church and in her great mission of salvation. The bishops of Ireland have, moreover, their own sharing in this dimension of the life of the whole Church because they share in the tasks of the College of Bishops: *cum Petro et sub Petro*. Hence this meeting of the Pope and the bishops

of Ireland is highly important and marvelously eloquent for Ireland and for the universal Church.

4. The basis of our personal identity, of our common bond and of our ministry is found in Jesus Christ, the Son of God and High Priest of the New Testament. For this reason, brethren, my first exhortation as I come among you today is this: "Let us keep our eyes fixed on Jesus, who inspires and perfects our faith" (Heb. 12:2). Since we are pastors of this flock, we must indeed look to Him who is the chief Shepherd—*Princeps Pastorum* (1 Pt. 5:4)—to enlighten us, to sustain us, and to give us joy as we serve the flock, leading it "in paths of righteousness for his name's sake" (Ps. 23:3).

But the effectiveness of our service to Ireland and to the whole Church is linked with our personal relationship to Him whom St. Peter also called "the Shepherd and Bishop of your souls" (1 Pt. 2:25). The secure basis for our pastoral leadership is then a deep personal relationship of faith and love with Jesus Christ our Lord. Like the Twelve, we too were appointed to be with Him, to be His companions (cf. Mk. 3:14). We can present ourselves as religious leaders of our people in the situations that deeply affect their daily lives only after we have been in prayerful communion with the Teacher, only after we have discovered in faith that God has made Christ to be "our wisdom, our righteousness and sanctification and redemption" (1 Cor. 1:30). In our own lives we are called to hear and guard and do the Word of God. In the Sacred Scriptures, and especially in the Gospels, we meet Christ constantly; and through the power of the Holy Spirit His words become light and strength for us and for our people. His words themselves contain a power for conversion, and we learn by His example.

Through prayerful contact with the Jesus of the Gospels, we, His servants and apostles, increasingly absorb His serenity and we assume His attitudes. Above all we take on that fundamental attitude of love for His

Father, so much so that each one of us finds deep joy and fulfillment in the truth of our filial relationship: *Diligo Patrem* (Jn. 14:31)—*Pater diligit Filium* (Jn. 3:35). Our relationship with Christ and in Christ finds its supreme and unique expression in the Eucharistic Sacrifice, in which we act to the full: *in persona Christi*.

Our personal relationship with Jesus is then a guarantee of confidence for us and for our ministry. In our faith we find the victory that overcomes the world. Because we are united with Jesus and sustained by Him, there is no challenge we cannot meet, no difficulty we cannot sustain, no obstacle we cannot overcome for the Gospel. Indeed, Christ Himself guarantees that "he who believes in me will also do the works that I do; and greater works than these will he do..." (Jn. 14:12). Yes, brethren, the answer to so many problems is found only in faith—a faith manifested and sustained in prayer.

5. Our relationship with Jesus will be the fruitful basis of our relationship with our priests, as we strive to be their brother, father, friend and guide. In the charity of Christ we are called to listen to and to understand them; to exchange views regarding evangelization and the pastoral mission they share with us as co-workers with the Order of Bishops. For the entire Church—but especially for the priests—we must be a human sign of the love of Christ and the fidelity of the Church. Thus we sustain our priests with the Gospel message, supporting them by the certainty of the Magisterium, and fortifying them against the pressures that they must resist. By word and example we must constantly invite our priests to prayer.

We are called to show generously to our priests that human concern, personal interest and sincere esteem whereby they will readily perceive our love. Despite the multiplicity of our commitments, our priests must recognize in us the faithful reflection of the Shepherd and Bishop of their souls (cf. 1 Pt. 2:25).

Our priests have made many sacrifices, including the renunciation of marriage for the sake of the kingdom of heaven; and they must be firmly encouraged to persevere. Fidelity to Christ and the demands of human dignity and freedom require them to maintain constancy in their commitment.

The pastoral solicitude we have for priests must also be shown to our seminarians. Let us exercise personally also our responsibility for their training in the Word of God, and for all the formation they receive in Ireland, and abroad, including Rome. In my *Letter to the Bishops of the Church on Holy Thursday*, I wrote: "The full reconstitution of the life of the seminaries throughout the Church will be the best proof of the achievement of the renewal to which the Council directed the Church."

6. Like Christ, the bishop comes among the laity as one who serves. The laity are the vast majority of the flock of Jesus Christ. Through Baptism and Confirmation, Christ Himself gives them a sharing in His own mission of salvation. Together with the clergy and the religious, the laity make up the one communion of the Church: "a chosen race, a royal priesthood, a holy nation, God's own people" (1 Pt. 2:9).

The greatest expression of the bishop's service to the laity is his personal proclamation of the Word of God, which reaches its summit in the Eucharist (cf. PO 5). As a faithful steward of the Gospel message, each bishop is called to expound to his people "the whole mystery of Christ" (CD 12).

As the bishop proclaims the dignity of the laity, it is also his role to do everything possible to promote their contribution to evangelization, urging them to assume every responsibility that is theirs in temporal realities. In the words of Paul VI, "Their own field of evangelizing activity is the vast and complicated world of politics, society and economics; the world of culture, of the sciences and the arts, of international life, of mass media" (EN 70). And there are other spheres of activities in which they can effectively work for the transformation of society.

In accordance with the will of God, the Christian family is an evangelizing agent of immense importance. In all the moral issues of authentic Christian living, the laity look to the bishops as their leaders, their pastors and their fathers. The bishops must constantly reply to the great cry of humanity, usually not articulated in words, but very real: "We wish to see Jesus" (Jn. 12:21). And in this the bishops have a role of great importance: to show Jesus to the world; to present Him authentically and convincingly: Jesus Christ, true God and true man—Jesus Christ, the Way and the Truth and the Life—Jesus Christ, the Man of prayer.

7. Bishops are called to be true fathers of all their people, excelling in the spirit of love and solicitude for all (cf. CD 16). They should have a special care for those who live on the margin of society. Among those most needing pastoral care from bishops are prisoners. My dear brothers, do not neglect to provide for their spiritual needs and to concern yourselves also about their material conditions and their families.

Try to bring the prisoners such spiritual care and guidance as may help to turn them from the ways of violence and crime, and make their detention instead be an occasion of true conversion to Christ and personal experience of love. Have a special care for young offenders. So often their wayward lives are due to society's neglect more than to their own sinfulness. Detention should be especially for them a school of rehabilitation.

8. In the light of our commitment to Jesus, and to His Gospel, in the light also of our collegial responsibility, our meeting here today assumes a special importance because of the present difficult time for Ireland, on account of the whole situation relating to Northern Ireland. These circumstances impelled some people to advise me against making a pilgrimage to Ireland. These very difficulties, however, made it all the more important to be here, to share closely with all of you these uncommon trials, and to seek in union with you the aid of God and good human

counsel. These reasons for coming here gain in eloquence if they are placed in the framework of my visit to the United Nations, where it will be my privilege and duty to seek out ways of living in peace and reconciliation throughout the world.

I am sure that the pastors of the Church in Ireland have a better understanding and deeper feeling for the painful problems of the present moment. Their duty, as I pointed out already, is to guide and sustain the flock, the People of God, but they can perform this duty in no other way than by suffering with those who suffer, and by weeping with those who weep (cf. Rom. 12:15).

On this point, I draw my conviction both from the Gospel and from the personal and historical experience that I had in the Church and nation from which I come. During the last two centuries, the Church in Poland has struck root in a special way in the soul of the nation. Part of the reason for this is that its pastors—its bishops and priests—did not hesitate to share in the trials and sufferings of their fellow countrymen. They were found among those deported to Siberia in the time of the Czars. They were found in the concentration camps at the time of the unleashing of Nazi terrorism during the last war. This self-sacrifice and dedication confirmed more fully the truth about the priest, that he is "chosen from among men...to act on behalf of men" (Heb. 5:1).

9. Because of this faithfulness to their brothers and sisters, to their fellow-countrymen, the sons and daughters of the same homeland, pastors, and especially bishops, must reflect beforehand on how to prevent bloodshed, hatred and terror, on how to strengthen peace, and on how to spare the people from these terrible sufferings. This was the message that Paul VI repeated over thirty times, in appealing for peace and justice in relation to Northern Ireland. He never ceased to condemn violence and to appeal for justice. "We earnestly beg"—he wrote to Cardinal Conway on the solemnity of Pentecost, 1974—"that all violence should cease, from whatever side it may come,

for it is contrary to the law of God and to the Christian and civilized way of life; that, in response to the common Christian conscience and the voice of reason, a climate of mutual trust and dialogue be re-established in justice and charity; that the real deep-seated causes of social unrest—which are not to be reduced to differences of a religious nature—be identified and eliminated."

These efforts, venerable and dear brothers, must be continued. Faith and social ethics demand from us respect for the established state authorities. But this respect also finds its expression in individual acts of mediation, in persuasion, in moral influence, and indeed in firm requests. For while it is true, as St. Paul says, that he who is in authority bears the sword (cf. Rom. 13:4), which we renounce in accordance with the clear recommendation of Christ to Peter in the Garden of Gethsemane (cf. Mt. 26:52), nevertheless, precisely because we are defenseless, we have a special right and duty to influence those who wield the sword of authority. For it is well known that in the field of political action, as elsewhere, not everything can be obtained by means of the sword. There are deeper reasons and stronger laws to which men, nations and peoples are subject. It is for us to discern these reasons and in their light to become, before those in authority, spokesmen for the moral order. This order is superior to force and violence. In this superiority of the moral order is expressed all the dignity of men and nations.

10. I recall with deep satisfaction a significant feature in the series of events connected with my journey to Ireland. It is highly significant that the invitation from the episcopate, through its four archbishops, was followed by invitations from other churches, especially from Irish Anglicans. I take the opportunity to stress this once again and to express my renewed thanks and appreciation to them. I see in this circumstance a very promising sign of hope. In view of the reasons with which you are all familiar, I have been unable to accept this truly ecumenical invitation by visiting Armagh in Northern Ireland, and

have been able to go no further than Drogheda. Nonetheless, the eloquence of this ecumenical readiness fully corresponds to what was expressed in my first encyclical: "In the present historical situation of Christianity and the world, the only possibility we see of fulfilling the Church's universal mission, with regard to ecumenical questions, is that of seeking sincerely, perseveringly, humbly and also courageously the ways of drawing closer and of union.... We must seek unity without being discouraged at the difficulties that can appear or accumulate along that road; otherwise, we would be unfaithful to the word of Christ, we would fail to accomplish His testament. Have we the right to run this risk?" (RH 6)

The witness to faith in Christ which we share with our brethren must continue to find expression not only in prayer for full unity but also in prayer and sustained effort for reconciliation and peace in this beloved land. This union of endeavor must lead us to take into consideration the whole mechanism of strife, cruelty, and growing hatred, in order to "overcome evil with good" (Rom. 12:12).

What are we to do? I earnestly hope that, in a continued effort, you and our brothers in the faith will become spokesmen for the just reasons of peace and reconciliation before those who wield the sword and those who perish by the sword. How sad it is to think of all the lives that have been lost, especially the lives of young people. What a terrible loss for their country, for the Church, for the whole of humanity!

11. Venerable pastors of the Church in Ireland: This service to justice and social love that is yours to perform in this present moment is difficult. It is difficult, but it is your duty! Do not fear: Christ is with you! He will give you His Holy Spirit: the Spirit of counsel and fortitude. And although this Spirit of God is frequently resisted, in the heart of man and in the history of humanity, by "the spirit of this world" and by "the spirit of darkness," nevertheless,

the final victory can only be that of love and truth. Continue steadfast in the difficult service that is yours, doing everything "in the name of the Lord Jesus" (Col. 3:17). Be assured that in your ministry you have my support and that of the universal Church. And all men and women of good will will stand by you in the quest for peace, justice and human dignity.

Dear brothers: In the name of Jesus Christ and His Church I thank you—and through you, all Ireland. I thank you for your fidelity to the Gospel, for your everlasting contribution to the spread of the Catholic Faith, for your authentic and irreplaceable service to the world.

As far as the future goes, brethren, courage and trust!

Walk in the illumination of the Paschal Mystery—in that light which must never be extinguished in your land! Go forward in the power of the Holy Spirit, in the merits of Jesus Christ!

And rejoice with a great joy in the unfailing intercession and protection of Mary, great Mary, Mother of God, Queen of the Apostles, Queen of Ireland, Queen of Peace!

Brethren, let us go forward together, for the good of Ireland and for the glory of the most Holy Trinity. And therefore, "Let us keep our eyes fixed on Jesus, who inspires and perfects our faith."

Homage to the Tradition of Faith and of Christian Life in Ireland

En route to Galway on September 30, 1979, the Pope's helicopter stopped for a brief visit to Clonmacnois, the seat of an ancient Irish monastery. He spoke to those gathered there as follows.

Dear brothers and sisters,

This visit to Clonmacnois gives me the opportunity to render homage to the traditions of faith and Christian living in Ireland.

In particular, I wish to recall and honor the great monastic contribution to Ireland that was made here on this revered spot for one thousand years, and whose influence was carried all over Europe by missionary monks and by students of this monastic school of Clonmacnois.

When we look at the works of faith, we must give thanks to God. Thanks to God for the origins of this apostolic faith in Ireland. Thanks to God for the saints and apostles and all who were the instrument for implanting and keeping alive this faith, and who "have done God's will throughout the ages." Thanks to God for the generosity of faith that brought forth fruits of justice and holiness of life. Thanks to God for the preservation of the faith in integrity and purity of teaching. Thanks to God for the continuity of the message of the apostles handed down intact to this day.

Never forget the wonderful boast and commitment made by St. Columban to Boniface IV in Rome: "We Irish...are disciples of Sts. Peter and Paul...; we hold unbroken that Catholic faith which we first received from you."

And in Ireland today, this Catholic faith is unbroken, alive and active. By the merits of our Lord Jesus Christ and by the power of His grace, it can, and must, always be this way in Ireland.

Clonmacnois was long the center of a renowned school of sacred art. The Shrine of St. Manchan, standing on the altar today, is one outstanding example of its work. This is, therefore, a fitting place for me to express my gratitude for the works of Irish sacred art, several pieces of which have been presented to me on the occasion of my visit.

Irish art embodies in many instances the deep faith and devotion of the Irish people as expressed in the personal sensitivity of its artists. Every piece of art, be it religious or secular, be it a painting, a sculpture, a poem or any form of handicraft made by loving skill, is a sign, a symbol, of the inscrutable secret of human existence, of man's origin and destiny, of the meaning of his life and work. It speaks to us of the meaning of birth and death, of the greatness of man.

Praised be Jesus Christ!

What the People Expect of You Is Fidelity to the Priesthood

On October 1, 1979, the Holy Father delivered the following address to the vast gathering of priests, religious men and women, missionaries and seminarians in St. Patrick's College in Maynooth, near Dublin.

My dear brothers and sisters in Christ,

The name of Maynooth is respected all over the Catholic world. It recalls what is noblest in the Catholic priesthood in Ireland. Here come seminarians from every Irish diocese, sons of Catholic homes which were themselves true "seminaries," true seed-beds of priestly or religious vocations. From here have gone out priests to every Irish diocese and to the diocese of the far-flung Irish diaspora. Maynooth has, in this century, given birth to two new missionary societies, one initially directed towards China, the other towards Africa; and it has sent out hundreds of alumni as volunteers to the mission fields. Maynooth is a school of priestly holiness, an academy of theological learning, a university of Catholic inspiration. St. Patrick's College is a place of rich achievement, which promises a future just as great.

Therefore, Maynooth is a fitting place in which to meet and talk with priests, diocesan and religious, with religious brothers, religious sisters, missionaries and seminarians. Having, as a priest-student in Paris, lived for a time in the atmosphere of the Irish Seminary—the College Irlandais in Paris, now loaned by the Irish Bishops to the hierarchy of Poland—I have profound joy in meeting with you all here in Ireland's National Seminary.

My first words go to the priests, diocesan and religious. I say to you what St. Paul said to Timothy. I ask you "to fan into a flame the gift that God gave you when [the bishop] laid [his] hands on you" (2 Tm. 1:6). Jesus Christ Himself, the one High Priest, said: "I have come to bring fire to the earth, and how I wish it were blazing already!" (Lk. 12:49) You share in His priesthood; you carry on His work in the world. His work cannot be done by lukewarm or half-hearted priests. His fire of love for the Father and for men must burn in you. His longing to save mankind must consume you.

You are called by Christ as the Apostles were. You are appointed like them, to be with Christ. You are sent, as they were, to go out in His name, and by His authority, to "make disciples of all the nations" (cf. Mt. 10:1, 28:29; Mk. 3:13-16).

Your first duty is to be *with Christ*. You are each called to be "a witness to his resurrection" (Acts 1:22). A constant danger with priests, even zealous priests, is that they become so immersed in the work of the Lord that they neglect the Lord of the work.

We must find time, we must make time, to be with the Lord in prayer. Following the example of the Lord Jesus Himself, we must "always go off to some place where [we can] be alone and pray" (cf. Lk. 5:16). It is only if we spend time with the Lord that our sending out to others will be also a bringing of Him to others.

To be with the Lord is always also to be sent by Him to do His work. A priest is *called* by Christ; a priest is *with* Christ; a priest is *sent* by Christ. A priest is sent in the power of the same Holy Spirit which drove Jesus untiringly along the roads of life, the roads of history. Whatever the difficulties, the disappointments, the set-backs, we priests find in Christ and in the power of His Spirit the strength to "struggle wearily on, helped only by his power driving [us] irresistibly" (cf. Col. 1:29).

As priests, you are privileged to be pastors of a faithful people, who continue to respond generously to your ministry, and who are a strong support to your own priestly vocation through their faith and their prayer. If you keep striving to be the kind of priest your people expect and wish you to be, then you will be holy priests. The degree of religious practice in Ireland is high. For this we must be constantly thanking God. But will this high level of religious practice continue? Will the next generation of young Irishmen and Irishwomen still be as faithful as their fathers were? After my two days in Ireland, after my meeting with Ireland's youth in Galway, I am confident that they will. But this will require both unremitting work and untiring prayer on your part. You must work for the Lord with a sense of urgency. You must work with the conviction that this generation, this decade of the 1980's which we are about to enter, could be crucial and decisive for the future of the Faith in Ireland. Let there be no complacency. As St. Paul said: "Be aware to all the dangers; stay firm in the faith; be brave and be strong" (1 Cor. 16:13). Work with confidence, work with joy. We are witnesses to the resurrection of Christ.

What the people expect from you, more than anything else, is faithfulness to the priesthood. This is what speaks to them of the faithfulness of God. This is what strengthens them to be faithful to Christ through all the difficulties of their lives, of their marriages. In a world so marked by instability as our world today, we need more signs and witnesses to God's fidelity to us, and to the fidelity we owe to Him. This is what causes such great sadness to the Church, such great but often silent anguish among the People of God, when priests fail in their fidelity to their priestly commitment. That counter-sign, that counter-witness, has been one of the set-backs to the great hopes for renewal aroused throughout the Church by the Second Vatican Council. Yet this has also driven priests, and the whole Church, to more intense and fervent prayer; for it has taught us all that without Christ we can do nothing (cf. Jn. 15:5). And the fidelity of the immense majority of priests has shone with even greater clarity and is all the more manifest and glorious a witness to the faithful God, and to Christ, the faithful witness (cf. Rv. 1:5).

In a center of theological learning, which is also a seminary, like Maynooth, this witness of fidelity has the added importance and the special value of impressing on candidates for the priesthood the strength and the grandeur of priestly fidelity. Here in Maynooth, theological learning, being part of formation for the priesthood, is preserved from ever being an academic pursuit of the intellect only. Here theological scholarship is linked with liturgy, with prayer, with the building of a community of faith and love, and thus with the building up, the "edifying," of the priesthood of Ireland, and the edifying of the Church. My call today is a call to prayer. Only in prayer will we meet the challenges of our ministry and fulfill the hopes of tomorrow. All our appeals for peace and reconciliation can be effective only through prayer.

This theological learning, here as everywhere throughout the Church, is a reflection on faith, a reflection in faith. A theology which did not deepen faith and lead to prayer might be a discourse on words about God; it could not be a discourse about God, the living God, the God who *is* and whose being is *Love.* It follows that theology can only be authentic in the Church, the community of faith. Only when the teaching of theologians is in conformity with the teaching of the College of Bishops, united with the Pope, can the People of God know with certitude that that teaching is "the faith which has been once and for all entrusted to the saints" (Jude 3). This is not a limitation for theologians, but a liberation; for it preserves them from subservience to changing fashions and binds them securely to the unchanging truth of Christ, the truth which makes us free (Jn. 7:32).

In Maynooth, in Ireland, to speak of priesthood is to speak of mission. Ireland has never forgotten that "the pilgrim Church is missionary by her very nature; for it is from the mission of the Son and the mission of the Holy Spirit that she takes her origin, in accordance with the decree of God the Father" (AG 2). In the ninth and tenth centuries, Irish monks rekindled the light of faith in regions where it had burnt low or been extinguished by the collapse of the Roman Empire, and evangelized new nations not yet evangelized, including areas of my own native Poland. How can I forget that there was an Irish monastery as far east as Kiev, even up to the thirteenth century; and that there was even an Irish college for a short time in my own city of Krakow, during the persecution of Cromwell? In the eighteenth and nineteenth centuries, Irish priests followed their exiles all over the English-speaking world. In the twentieth century, new missionary institutes of men and women sprang up in Ireland, which, together with the Irish branches of international missionary institutes and with existing Irish religious congregations, gave a new missionary impetus to the Church.

May that missionary spirit never decline in the hearts of Irish priests, whether members of missionary institutes or of the diocesan clergy or of religious congregations devoted to other apostolates. May this spirit be actively fostered by all of you among the laity, already so devoted in their prayer, so generous in their support for the missions. May a spirit of partnership grow between the home dioceses and the home religious congregations in the total mission of the Church, until each local diocesan church and each religious congregation and community is fully seen to be "missionary of its very nature," entering into the eager missionary movement of the universal Church.

...To you and to priests, diocesan and religious, I say: Rejoice to be witnesses to Christ in the modern world. Do not hesitate to be recognizable, identifiable, in the streets as men and women who have consecrated their lives to God and who have given up everything worldly to follow Christ. Believe that contemporary men and women set value on the visible signs of the consecration of your lives. People need signs and reminders of God in the modern secular city, which has few reminders of God left. Do not help the trend towards "taking God off the streets" by adopting secular modes of dress and behavior yourselves!

...To all of you I say: This is a wonderful time in the history of the Church. This is a wonderful time to be a priest, to be a religious, to be a missionary for Christ. Rejoice in the Lord always. Rejoice in your vocation. I repeat to you the words of St. Paul: "I want you to be happy, always happy in the Lord; I repeat, what I want is your happiness. There is no need to worry; but if there is anything you need, pray for it, asking God for it with prayer and thanksgiving, and that peace of God which is so much greater than we can understand, will guard your hearts and your thoughts, in Christ Jesus" (Phil. 4:4-7).

Mary, Mother of Christ, the Eternal Priest, Mother of priests and of religious, will keep you from all anxiety, as you "wait in joyful hope for the coming of our Lord and Savior, Jesus Christ." Entrust yourselves to her, as I commend you to her, to Mary, Mother of Jesus and Mother of His Church.

"I Am Happy To Be in Your Midst"

A crowd estimated at two million lined the route along which passed the cortege of cars that accompanied the Holy Father from the airport into the city of Boston on October 1, 1979. Stopping at the Cathedral of Holy Cross, the Holy Father met the diocesan and religious clergy, and the religious women of the Archdiocese of Boston and other dioceses of New England. The assembly of more than two thousand persons was led by Cardinal Humberto Medeiros, who delivered an address of welcome. After a brief Liturgy of the Word, Pope John Paul spoke to the group. The following are excerpts from his talk.

Dear Cardinal Medeiros, dear brothers and sisters in Christ,

On the first day of my pastoral visit to the United States of America, it is a great joy for me to come to the city of Boston, and in this Cathedral, and later tonight on the Common, to be able to meet with the Catholic community. It is the first time in history that a Successor of Peter is received in your midst. On this wonderful occasion I wish to render homage to the most Holy Trinity, in whose name I have come. And I make my own the greeting of the Apostle Paul to the Corinthians: "To you who have been consecrated in Christ Jesus and called to be a holy people, and to all those who, wherever they may be, call on the name of our Lord Jesus Christ, their Lord and ours: Grace and peace from God our Father and the Lord Jesus Christ" (1 Cor. 1:2-3).

My cordial thanks go to you, Cardinal Medeiros, Archbishop of Boston, for your welcome today. In your Cathedral church, I am happy to renew to you the expression of my deep esteem and friendship. Warm greetings also to the auxiliary bishops and to all the clergy, both diocesan and religious: You who are my brother priests in virtue of the Sacrament of Holy Orders. Through your priesthood, you are also God's gift to the Christian community. Because you are servants of the Gospel, you will always be close to the people and their problems. Because you share in the priesthood of Christ, your presence in the world shall always be marked by Christ's zeal, for He set you apart so that you might build up His Body, the Church (cf. Eph. 4:12).

...To all I want to say how happy I am to be in your midst. I pray for each one of you, asking you to remain always united in Jesus Christ and His Church, so that together we may "display to the world our unity in proclaiming the mystery of Christ, in revealing the divine dimension and also the human dimension of the redemption, and in struggling with unwearying perseverance for the dignity that each human being has reached and can continually reach in Christ" (RH 11). May this Cathedral, dedicated to the Holy Cross of Jesus, always be a reminder of our calling to greatness, for through the mystery of the Incarnation and of the redeeming sacrifice of Jesus on the cross we share in "the unsearchable riches of Christ" (Eph. 3:8).

Who Will Separate Us from Christ?

In the course of morning prayer in St. Patrick's Cathedral, on October 3, 1979, in the presence of numerous bishops, priests, religious, seminarians, laity and guests of other Christian faiths, Pope John Paul II gave the following brief address.

Dear brothers and sisters,

St. Paul asks: "Who will separate us from the love of Christ?"

As long as we remain what we are this morning—a community of prayer united in Christ, an ecclesial community of praise and worship of the Father—we shall understand and experience the answer: that no one—nothing at all—will ever separate us from the love of Christ. For us today, the Church's morning prayer is a joyful, communal celebration of God's love in Christ.

The value of the Liturgy of the Hours is enormous. Through it, all the faithful, but especially the clergy and religious, fulfill a role of prime importance: Christ's prayer goes on in the world. The Holy Spirit Himself intercedes for God's people (cf. Rom. 8:27). The Christian community, with praise and thanksgiving, glorifies the wisdom, the power, the Providence and the salvation of our God.

In this prayer of praise we lift up our hearts to the Father of our Lord Jesus Christ, bringing with us the anguish and hopes, the joys and sorrows of all our brothers and sisters in the world.

And our prayer becomes likewise a school of sensitivity, making us aware of how much our destinies are linked together in the human family. Our prayer becomes a school of love—a special kind of Christian consecrated love, by which we love the world, but with the heart of Christ.

Through this prayer of Christ to which we give voice, our day is sanctified, our activities transformed, our actions are made holy. We pray the same psalms that Jesus prayed, and come into personal contact with Him—the Person to whom all Scripture points, the goal to which all history is directed.

In our celebration of the Word of God, the mystery of Christ opens up before us and envelops us. And through union with our Head, Jesus Christ, we become ever more increasingly one with all the members of His body. As never before, it becomes possible for us to reach out and embrace the world, but to embrace it with Christ: with authentic generosity, with pure and effective love, in service, in healing and in reconciliation.

The efficacy of our prayer renders special honor to the Father because it is made always through Christ, and for the glory of His name: "We ask this through our Lord Jesus Christ, your Son, who lives and reigns with you and the Holy Spirit, one God, for ever and ever."

As a community of prayer and praise, with the Liturgy of the Hours among the highest priorities of our day—each day—we can be sure that nothing will separate us from the love of God that is in Christ Jesus our Lord.

Sacramental Priesthood Is Truly a Gift from God

The last encounter of Pope John Paul in the city of Philadelphia was the solemn concelebration on October 4, 1979, with representatives of the councils of priests of all the dioceses in the United States. Held in the Civic Center of the metropolis, the meeting included hundreds of religious men and women, as well as seminarians.

After the Gospel the Holy Father delivered the following homily.

Dear brother priests:

1. As we celebrate this Mass, which brings together the presidents or chairmen of the priests' senates, or councils, of all the dioceses of the United States, the theme that suggests itself to our reflection is a vital one: the priesthood itself and its central importance to the task of the Church. In the Encyclical Letter *Redemptor hominis*, I described this task in these words: "The Church's fundamental function in every age and particularly in ours is to direct man's gaze, to point the awareness and experience of the whole of humanity towards the mystery of God, to help men to be familiar with the profundity of the redemption taking place in Christ Jesus" (RH 10).

SIGN OF UNITY

Priests' senates are a new structure in the Church, called for by the Second Vatican Council and recent Church legislation. This new structure gives a concrete expression to the unity of bishop and priests in the service of shepherding the flock of Christ, and it assists the bishop in his distinctive role of governing the diocese, by guaranteeing for him the counsel of representative advisors from among the presbyterium. Our concelebration of today's Eucharist is intended to be a mark of affirmation for the good that has been achieved by your priests' senates during these past years, as well as an encouragement to pursue with enthusiasm and determination this important aim, which is "to bring the life and activity of the People of God into greater conformity with the Gospel" (cf. ES 16:1). Most of all, however, I want this Mass to be the special occasion on which I can speak through you to all my brother priests throughout this nation about our priesthood. With great love I repeat the words that I wrote to you on Holy Thursday: "For you I am a bishop, with you I am a priest."

GOD GIVES VOCATIONS

Our priestly vocation is given by the Lord Jesus Himself. It is a call which is personal and individual: We are called by name as was Jeremiah. It is a call to service: We are sent out to preach the Good News, to "give God's flock a shepherd's care." It is a call to communion of purpose and of action: to be one priesthood with Jesus and with one another, just as Jesus and His Father are one—a unity so beautifully symbolized in this concelebrated Mass.

Priesthood is not merely a task which has been assigned; it is a vocation, a call to be heard again and again. To hear this call and to respond generously to what this call entails is a task for each priest, but it is also a responsibility for the senates of priests. This responsibility means deepening our understanding of the priesthood as Christ instituted it, as He wanted it to be and to remain, and as the Church faithfully explains it and transmits it. Fidelity to the call to the priesthood means building up this priesthood with God's people by a life of service according to apostolic priorities: concentration "on prayer and the ministry of the word" (Acts 6:4).

In the Gospel of St. Mark the priestly call of the twelve Apostles is like a bud whose flowering displays a whole theology of priesthood. In the midst of Jesus' ministry, we read that "he went up the mountain and summoned the men he himself had decided on, who came and joined Him. He named twelve as His companions whom he would send to preach the good news...." The passage then lists the names of the twelve (Mk. 3:13-14). Here we see three significant aspects of the call given by Jesus: He called His first priests individually and by *name*; He called them for the service of His Word, *to preach the Gospel*; and He made them His own *companions*, drawing them into that unity of life and action which He shares with His Father in the very life of the Trinity.

PROPHETIC CALL

2. Let us explore these three dimensions of our priesthood by reflecting on today's Scripture readings. For it is in the tradition of the prophetic call that the Gospel places the priestly vocation of the twelve Apostles by Jesus. When the priest reflects on Jeremiah's call to be a prophet, he is both reassured and disturbed. "Have no fear...because I am with you to deliver you," says the Lord to the one whom He calls.... "For look, I place *my* words in your mouth." Who would not take heart at hearing such divine assurance? Yet when we consider *why* such reassurance is needed, do we not see in ourselves that same reluctance we find in Jeremiah's reply? Like him, at times, our concept of this ministry is too earth-bound; we lack confidence in Him who calls us. We can also become too attached to our own vision of ministry, thinking that it depends too much on our own talents and abilities, and at times forgetting that it is God who calls us, as He called Jeremiah from the womb. Nor is it our work or our ability that is primary: We are called to speak the words of God and not our own; to minister the sacraments He has given to His Church; and to call people to a love which He has first made possible.

Hence the surrender to God's call can be made with utmost confidence and without reservation. Our surrender to God's will must be total—the "yes" given once for all which has as its pattern the "yes" spoken by Jesus Himself. As St. Paul tells us, "As God keeps his word, I declare that my word to you is not 'yes' one minute and 'no' the next. Jesus Christ...was not alternately 'yes' and 'no'; he was never anything but 'yes' " (1 Cor. 1:18-19).

GOD'S GIFT FOR THE CHURCH

This call of God is grace: It is a gift, a treasure "possessed in earthen vessels to make it clear that its surpassing power comes from God and not from us" (2 Cor. 4:7). But this gift is not primarily for the priest himself; it is rather a gift of God for the whole Church and for her mission to the world. Priesthood is an abiding sacramental sign which shows that the love of the Good Shepherd for His flock will never be absent. In my letter to you priests last Holy Thursday, I developed this aspect of the priesthood as God's gift: Our priesthood, I said, "constitutes a special *ministerium*, that is to say, 'service,' in relation to the community of believers. It does not, however, take its origin from that community, as though it were the community that 'called' or 'delegated.' The sacramental priesthood is truly a gift for this community and comes from Christ Himself, from the fullness of His priesthood" (Letter, no. 5). In this gift-giving to His people, it is the divine Giver who takes the initiative; it is He who calls the ones "He Himself had decided on."

WHY ONLY MALE PRIESTS

Hence when we reflect on the intimacy between the Lord and His prophet, His priest—an intimacy arising as a result of the call which He has initiated—we can better understand certain characteristics of the priesthood and realize their appropriateness for the Church's mission today as well as in times past:

a) Priesthood is forever—*Tu es sacerdos in aeternum*—we do not return the gift once given. It cannot be that God who gave the impulse to say "yes" now wishes to hear "no."

b) Nor should it surprise the world that the call of God through the Church continues to offer us a celibate ministry of love and service after the example of our Lord Jesus Christ. God's call has indeed stirred us to the depths of our being. And after centuries of experience, the Church knows how deeply fitting it is that priests should give this concrete response in their lives to express the totality of the "yes" they have spoken to the Lord who calls them by name to His service.

c) The fact that there is a personal individual call to the priesthood given by the Lord to "the men he himself had decided on" is in accord with the prophetic tradition. It should help us, too, to understand that the Church's traditional decision to call men to the priesthood, and not to call women, is not a statement about human rights, nor an exclusion of women from holiness and mission in the Church. Rather this decision expresses the conviction of the Church about this particular dimension of the gift of priesthood by which God has chosen to shepherd His flock.

MISSION AND SERVICE

3. Dear brothers: "God's flock is in your midst; give it a shepherd's care." How close to the essence of our understanding of priesthood is the role of shepherd; throughout the history of salvation it is a recurring image of God's care for His people. And only in the role of Jesus, the Good Shepherd, can our pastoral ministry as priests be understood. Recall how, in the call of the Twelve, Jesus summoned them to be His companions precisely in order to "send them out to preach the good news." Priesthood is mission and service; it is being "sent out" from Jesus to "give His flock a shepherd's care." This characteristic of

the priest—to apply an excellent phrase about Jesus as the "man-for-others"—shows us the true sense of what it means to "give a shepherd's care." It means pointing the awareness of humanity to the mystery of God, to the profundity of redemption taking place in Christ Jesus. Priestly ministry is missionary in its very core: it means being sent out for others, like Christ sent from His Father, for the sake of the Gospel, sent to evangelize. In the words of Paul VI, "Evangelizing means bringing the Good News into all the strata of humanity...and making it new" (EN 18). At the foundation and center of its dynamism, evangelization contains a clear proclamation that salvation is in Jesus Christ, the Son of God. It is His name, His teaching, His life, His promises, His kingdom and His mystery that we proclaim to the world. And the effectiveness of our proclamation, and hence the very success of our priesthood, depends on our fidelity to the Magisterium, through which the Church guards "the rich deposit of faith with the help of the Holy Spirit who dwells within us" (2 Tm. 1:14).

A MAN FOR OTHERS

As a pattern for every ministry and apostolate in the Church, priestly ministry is never to be conceived in terms of an acquisition; insofar as it is a gift, it is a gift to be proclaimed and shared with others. Do we not see this clearly in Jesus' teaching when the mother of James and John asked that her sons sit on His right hand and His left in His kingdom? "You know how those who exercise authority among the Gentiles lord it over them; their great ones make their importance felt. It cannot be like that with you. Anyone who aspires to greatness must serve the rest, and whoever wants to rank first among you must serve the needs of all. Such is the case with the Son of Man who has come, not to be served by others, but to serve, to give his own life as a ransom for the many" (Mt. 20:25-28).

Just as Jesus was most perfectly a "man-for-others" in giving Himself up totally on the cross, so the priest is most of all servant and "man-for-others" when he acts *in persona Christi* in the Eucharist, leading the Church in that celebration in which this sacrifice of the cross is renewed. For in the Church's daily Eucharistic worship, the "Good News" that the Apostles were sent out to proclaim is preached in its fullness; the work of our redemption is reenacted.

How perfectly the Fathers of the Second Vatican Council captured this fundamental truth in their "Decree on Priestly Life and Ministry": "The other sacraments, as every ministry of the Church and every work of the apostolate, are linked with the Holy Eucharist and are directed towards it.... Hence the Eucharist shows itself to be the source and the summit of all evangelization" (PO 5). In the celebration of the Eucharist, we priests are at the very heart of our ministry of service, of "giving God's flock a shepherd's care." All our pastoral endeavors are incomplete until our people are led to the full and active participation in the Eucharistic sacrifice.

UNITY FOR THE SAKE OF THE GOSPEL

4. Let us recall how Jesus named twelve as His companions. The call to priestly service includes an invitation to special intimacy with Christ. The lived experience of priests in every generation has led them to discover in their own lives and ministry the absolute centrality of their personal union with Jesus, of being His companions. No one can effectively bring the Good News of Jesus to others unless he himself has first been His constant companion through personal prayer, unless he has learned from Jesus the mystery to be proclaimed.

This union with Jesus, modeled on His oneness with His Father, has a further intrinsic dimension, as His own prayer at the Last Supper reveals: "That they may be one, Father, even as we are one" (Jn. 17:11). His priesthood is one, and this unity must be actual and effective among His chosen companions. Hence unity among priests, lived out in fraternity and friendship, becomes a demand and an integral part of the life of a priest.

Unity among priests is not a unity or fraternity that is directed towards itself. It is for the sake of the Gospel, to symbolize, in the living out of the priesthood, the essential direction to which the Gospel calls all people: to the union of love with Him and one another. And this union alone can guarantee peace and justice and dignity to every human being. Surely this is the underlying sense of the prayer of Jesus when He continues: "I pray also for those who believe in me through their word, that all may be one as you, Father, are in me, and I in you" (Jn. 17:20-21). Indeed, how will the world come to believe that the Father has sent Jesus unless people can see in visible ways that those who believe in Jesus have heard His commandment to "love one another"? And how will believers receive a witness that such love is a concrete possibility unless they find it in the example of the unity of their priestly ministers, of those whom Jesus Himself forms into one priesthood as His own companions?

TO GIVE WITNESS

My brother priests: Have we not here touched upon the heart of the matter—our zeal for the priesthood itself? It is inseparable from our zeal for the service of the people. This concelebrated Mass, which so beautifully symbolizes the unity of our priesthood, gives to the whole world the witness of the unity for which Jesus prayed to His Father on our behalf. But it must not become a merely transient manifestation, which would render fruitless the prayer of Jesus. Every Eucharist renews this prayer for our unity: "Lord, remember your Church throughout the world; make us grow in love, together with John Paul, our Pope, ...our Bishop, and all the clergy."

Your priests' senates, as new structures in the Church, provide a wonderful opportunity to give visible witness to the one priesthood you share with your bishops and with one another, and to demonstrate what must be at the heart of the renewal of every structure in the Church: the unity for which Jesus Himself prayed.

TOTAL SELF-GIVING

5. At the beginning of this homily, I charged you with the task of taking responsibility for your priesthood, a task for each one of you personally, a charge to be shared with all the priests, and especially to be a concern for your priests' councils. The faith of the whole Church needs to have clearly in focus the proper understanding of the priesthood and of its place in the mission of the Church. So the Church depends on you to deepen ever more this understanding, and to put it into practice in your lives and ministry: In other words, to share the gift of your priesthood with the Church by renewing the response you have already made to Christ's invitation—"Come, follow me"—by giving yourselves as totally as He did.

At times we hear the words, "Pray for priests." And today I address these words as an appeal, as a plea, to all the faithful of the Church in the United States. Pray for priests, so that each and every one of them will repeatedly say *yes* to the call he has received, remain constant in preaching the Gospel message, and be faithful forever as the companion of our Lord Jesus Christ.

Dear brother priests: As we renew the Paschal Mystery and stand as disciples at the foot of the cross with Mary, the Mother of Jesus, let us entrust ourselves to her. In her love we shall find strength for our weakness and joy for our hearts.

Fidelity to the Truth in Love

On October 5, 1979, Pope John Paul II met the bishops of the episcopal conference of the United States at Quigley South Seminary, in Chicago, and delivered the following address.

Dear brothers in our Lord Jesus Christ,

1. May I tell you very simply how grateful I am to you for your invitation to come to the United States. It is an immense joy for me to make this pastoral visit, and in particular, to be here with you today.

On this occasion I thank you, not only for your invitation, not only for everything you have done to prepare for my visit, but also for your partnership in the Gospel from the time of my election as Pope. I thank you for your service to God's holy people, for your fidelity to Christ our Lord, and for your unity with my Predecessors and with me in the Church and in the College of Bishops.

I wish at this time to render public homage to a long tradition of fidelity to the Apostolic See on the part of the American hierarchy. During the course of two centuries, this tradition has edified your people, authenticated your apostolate, and enriched the universal Church.

Moreover, in your presence today, I wish to acknowledge with deep appreciation the fidelity of your faithful and the renowned vitality that they have shown in Christian life. This vitality has been manifested not only in the sacramental practice of communities, but also in abundant fruits of the Holy Spirit. With great zeal your people have endeavored to build up the kingdom of God by means of the Catholic school and through all catechetical efforts. An evident concern for others has been a real part of American Catholicism, and today I thank the American Catholics for their generosity. Their support has benefited the dioceses of the United States and a widespread network of charitable works and self-help projects, including those sponsored by Catholic Relief Services and the Campaign for Human Development. Moreover, the help given to the missions by the Church in the United States remains a lasting contribution to the cause of Christ's Gospel. Because your faithful have been very generous to the Apostolic See, my Predecessors have been assisted in meeting the burdens of their office; and thus, in the exercise of their worldwide mission of charity, they have been able to extend help to those in need, thereby showing the concern of the universal Church for all humanity. For me then this is an hour of solemn gratitude.

AN HOUR OF ECCLESIAL COMMUNION

2. But even more, this is an hour of ecclesial communion and fraternal love. I come to you as a brother bishop: one who, like yourselves, has known the hopes and challenges of a local church; one who has worked within the structures of a diocese, who has collaborated within the framework of an episcopal conference; one who has known the exhilarating experience of collegiality in an ecumenical council as exercised by bishops together with him who both presided over this collegial assembly and was recognized by it as *totius ecclesiae pastor*—invested with "full, supreme and universal power over the Church" (LG 22). I come to you as one who has been personally edified and enriched by participation in the Synod of Bishops; one who was supported and assisted by the fraternal interest and self-giving of American bishops who traveled to Poland in order to express solidarity with the Church in my country. I come as one who found deep spiritual consolation for my pastoral activity in the encouragement of Roman Pontiffs with whom, and under whom, I served God's people, and in particular in the encouragement of Paul VI, whom I looked upon not only as head of the College of Bishops, but also as my own spiritual father. And today, under the sign of collegiality and because of a mysterious design of God's Providence, I,

your brother in Jesus, now come to you as Successor of Peter in the See of Rome, and therefore as Pastor of the whole Church.

Because of my personal pastoral responsibility, and because of our common pastoral responsibility for the People of God in the United States, I desire to strengthen you in your ministry of faith as local pastors, and to support you in your individual and joint pastoral activities by encouraging you to stand fast in the holiness and truth of our Lord Jesus Christ. And in you I desire to honor Jesus Christ, the Shepherd and Bishop of our souls (cf. 1 Pt. 2:25).

Because we have been called to be shepherds of the flock, we realize that we must present ourselves as humble servants of the Gospel. Our leadership will be effective only to the extent that our own discipleship is genuine—to the extent that the beatitudes have become the inspiration of our lives, to the extent that our people really find in us the kindness, simplicity of life and universal charity that they expect.

We who, by divine mandate, must proclaim the duties of the Christian law, and who must call our people to constant conversion and renewal, know that St. Paul's invitation applies above all to ourselves: "You must put on the new man created in God's image, whose justice and holiness are born of truth" (Eph. 4:24).

PERSONAL CONVERSION

3. The holiness of personal conversion is indeed the condition for our fruitful ministry as bishops of the Church. It is our union with Jesus Christ that determines the credibility of our witness to the Gospel and the supernatural effectiveness of our activity. We can convincingly proclaim "the unsearchable riches of Christ" (Eph. 3:8) only if we maintain fidelity to the love and friendship of Jesus, only if we continue to live in the faith of the Son of God.

God has given a great gift to the American hierarchy in recent years: the canonization of John Neumann. An American bishop is officially held up by the Catholic Church to be an exemplary servant of the Gospel and shepherd of God's people, above all because of his great love of Christ. On the occasion of the canonization, Paul VI asked: "What is the meaning of this extraordinary event, the meaning of this canonization?" And he answered, saying: "It is the celebration of holiness." And this holiness of St. John Neumann was expressed in brotherly love, in pastoral charity, and in zealous service by one who was the bishop of a diocese and an authentic disciple of Christ.

During the canonization, Paul VI went on to say: "Our ceremony today is indeed the celebration of holiness. At the same time, it is a prophetic anticipation—for the Church, for the United States, for the world—of a renewal of love: love for God, love for neighbor." As bishops, we are called to exercise in the Church this prophetic role of love and, therefore, of holiness.

Guided by the Holy Spirit, we must all be deeply convinced that holiness is the first priority in our lives and in our ministry. In this context, as bishops we see the immense value of prayer: the liturgical prayer of the Church, our prayer together, our prayer alone. In recent times many of you have found that the practice of making spiritual retreats together with your brother bishops is indeed a help to that holiness born of truth. May God sustain you in this initiative so that each of you, and all of you together, may fulfill your role as a sign of holiness offered to God's people on their pilgrimage to the Father. May you yourselves, like St. John Neumann, also be a prophetic anticipation of holiness. The people need to have bishops whom they can look upon as leaders in the quest for holiness—bishops who are trying to anticipate prophetically in their own lives the attainment of the goal to which they are leading the faithful.

CONSECRATED IN TRUTH

4. St. Paul points out the relationship of justice and holiness to truth (cf. Eph. 4:24). Jesus Himself, in His priestly prayer, asks His Father to consecrate His disciples by means of truth; and He adds: "Your word is truth"—*sermo tuus veritas est* (Jn. 17:17). And He goes on to say that He consecrates Himself for the sake of the disciples, so that they themselves may be consecrated in truth. Jesus consecrated Himself so that the disciples might be consecrated, set apart, by the communication of what He was: the Truth. Jesus tells His Father: "I give them your word"—"your word is truth" (Jn. 17:14, 17).

The holy Word of God, which is truth, is communicated by Jesus to His disciples. This Word is entrusted as a sacred deposit to His Church, but only after He had implanted in His Church, through the power of the Holy Spirit, a special charism to guard and transmit intact the Word of God.

With great wisdom, John XXIII convoked the Second Vatican Council. Reading the signs of the times, he knew that what was needed was a council of a pastoral nature, a council that would reflect the great pastoral love and care of Jesus Christ, the Good Shepherd, for His people. But he knew that a pastoral council—to be genuinely effective —would need a strong doctrinal basis. And precisely for this reason, precisely because the Word of God is the only basis for every pastoral initiative, John XXIII on the opening day of the Council—October 11, 1962—made the following statement: "The greatest concern of the Ecumenical Council is this: that the sacred deposit of Christian doctrine should be more effectively guarded and taught."

This explains Pope John's inspiration; this is what the new Pentecost was to be; this is why the bishops of the Church—in the greatest manifestation of collegiality in the history of the world—were called together: "so that the sacred deposit of Christian doctrine should be more effectively guarded and taught."

In our time, Jesus was consecrating anew His disciples by truth; and He was doing it by means of an ecumenical council; He was transmitting by the power of the Holy Spirit His Father's Word to new generations. And, what John XXIII considered to be the aim of the Council, I consider as the aim of this postconciliar period.

SAFEGUARD DOCTRINE

For this reason, in my first meeting last November with American bishops on their *ad limina* visit I stated: "This then is my own deepest hope today for the pastors of the Church in America, as well as for all the pastors of the universal Church: that the sacred deposit of Christian doctrine should be more effectively guarded and taught." In the Word of God is the salvation of the world. By means of the proclamation of the Word of God, the Lord continues in His Church and through His Church to consecrate His disciples, communicating to them the Truth that He Himself is.

For this reason the Vatican Council emphasized the bishop's role of announcing the full truth of the Gospel and proclaiming "the whole mystery of Christ" (CD 12). This teaching was constantly repeated by Paul VI for the edification of the universal Church. It was explicitly proclaimed by John Paul I on the very day he died, and I too have frequently reaffirmed it in my own pontificate. And I am sure that my Successors and your successors will hold this teaching until Christ comes again in glory.

"I AM RESOLVED"

5. Among the papers that were left to me by Pope Paul VI, there is a letter written to him by a bishop, on the occasion of the latter's appointment to the episcopacy. It is a beautiful letter; and in the form of a resolution it includes a clear affirmation of the bishop's role of guarding and teaching the deposit of Christian doctrine, of proclaiming

the whole mystery of Christ. Because of the splendid insights that this letter offers, I would like to share part of it with you.

As he pledged himself to be loyal and obedient to Paul VI and to his Successors, the bishop wrote: "I am resolved:

—"To be faithful and constant in proclaiming the Gospel of Christ.

—"To maintain the content of faith, entire and uncorrupted, as handed down by the Apostles and professed by the Church at all times and places."

And then with equal insight, this bishop went on to tell Paul VI that, with the help of Almighty God, he was determined:

—"To build up the Church as the Body of Christ, and to remain united to it by your link, with the order of bishops, under the authority of the Successor of St. Peter the Apostle.

"To show kindness and compassion in the name of the Lord to the poor and to strangers and to all who are in need.

—"To seek out the sheep who stray and to gather them into the fold of the Lord.

—"To pray without ceasing for the People of God, to carry out the highest duties of the priesthood in such a way as to afford no grounds for reproof."

This then is the edifying witness of a bishop, an American bishop, to the episcopal ministry of holiness and truth. These words are a credit to him and a credit to all of you.

A challenge for our age—and for every age in the Church—is to bring the message of the Gospel to the very core of our people's lives: so that they may live the full truth of their humanity, their redemption and their adoption in Jesus Christ, that they may be enriched with "the justice and holiness of truth."

RELEVANCE OF GOD'S WORD

6. In the exercise of your ministry of truth, as bishops of the United States, you have, through statements and pastoral letters, collectively offered the Word of God to your people, showing its relevance to daily life, pointing to the power it has to uplift and heal, and at the same time upholding its inherent demands. Three years ago you did this in a very special way through your pastoral letter, so beautifully entitled, "To Live in Christ Jesus." This letter, in which you offered your people the service of truth, contains a number of points to which I wish to allude today. With compassion, understanding and love, you transmitted a message that is linked to revelation and to the mystery of faith. And so with great pastoral charity you spoke of God's love, of humanity and of sin—and of the meaning of redemption and of life in Christ. You spoke of the Word of Christ as it affects individuals, the family, the community and nations. You spoke of justice and peace, of charity, of truth and friendship. And you spoke of some special questions affecting the moral life of Christians: the moral life in both its individual and social aspects.

You spoke explicitly of the Church's duty to be faithful to the mission entrusted to her. And precisely for this reason you spoke of certain issues that needed a clear reaffirmation, because Catholic teaching in their regard had been challenged, denied, or in practice violated.

You repeatedly proclaimed human rights and human dignity and the incomparable worth of people of every racial and ethnic origin, declaring that "racial antagonism and discrimination are among the most persistent and destructive evils of our nation." You forcefully rejected the oppression of the weak, the manipulation of the vulnerable, the waste of goods and resources, the ceaseless preparations for war, unjust social structures and policies, and all crimes by and against individuals and against creation.

DIVORCE, CONTRACEPTION, HOMOSEXUALITY

With the candor of the Gospels, the compassion of pastors and the charity of Christ, you faced the question of the indissolubility of marriage, rightly stating: "The covenant between a man and a woman joined in Christian marriage is as indissoluble and irrevocable as God's love for His people and Christ's love for His Church."

In exalting the beauty of marriage you rightly spoke against both the ideology of contraception and contraceptive acts, as did the Encyclical *Humanae vitae*. And I myself today, with the same conviction of Paul VI, ratify the teaching of this encyclical, which was put forth by my Predecessor "by virtue of the mandate entrusted to us by Christ" *(AAS*, 60, 1968, p. 485).

In portraying the sexual union between husband and wife as a special expression of their covenanted love, you rightly stated: "Sexual intercourse is a moral and human good only within marriage; outside marriage it is wrong."

As "men with the message of truth and the power of God" (2 Cor. 6:7), as authentic teachers of God's law and as compassionate pastors, you also rightly stated: "Homosexual activity,...as distinguished from homosexual orientation, is morally wrong." In the clarity of this truth, you exemplified the real charity of Christ; you did not betray those people who, because of homosexuality, are confronted with difficult moral problems, as would have happened if, in the name of understanding and compassion, or for any other reason, you had held out false hope to any brother or sister. Rather, by your witness to the truth of humanity in God's plan, you effectively manifested fraternal love, upholding the true dignity, the true human dignity, of those who look to Christ's Church for the guidance which comes from the light of God's Word.

RIGHT TO LIFE OF THE UNBORN

You also gave witness to the truth, thereby serving all humanity, when, echoing the teaching of the Council—"From the moment of conception life must be guarded with the greatest care" (GS 51)—you reaffirmed the right to life and the inviolability of every human life, including the life of unborn children. You clearly said: "To destroy these innocent unborn children is an unspeakable crime.... Their right to life must be recognized and fully protected by the law."

And just as you defended the unborn in the truth of their being, so also you clearly spoke up for the aged, asserting, "Euthanasia or mercy killing...is a grave moral evil.... Such killing is incompatible with respect for human dignity and reverence for life."

And in your pastoral interest for your people in all their needs—including housing, education, health care, employment, and the administration of justice—you gave further witness to the fact that all aspects of human life are sacred. You were, in effect, proclaiming that the Church will never abandon man, nor his temporal needs, as she leads humanity to salvation and eternal life. And because the Church's greatest act of fidelity to humanity and her "fundamental function in every age and particularly in ours is to direct man's gaze, to point the awareness and experience of the whole of humanity toward the mystery of God" (RH 10)—because of this you rightly alluded to the dimension of eternal life. It is indeed in this proclamation of eternal life that we hold up a great motive of hope for our people against the onslaughts of materialism, against rampant secularism and against moral permissiveness.

RESPONSIBLE PASTORAL INITIATIVES

7. A sense of pastoral responsibility has also been genuinely expressed by individual bishops in their ministry as local pastors. To the great credit of their authors, I

would cite but two recent examples of pastoral letters issued in the United States. Both are examples of responsible pastoral initiatives. One of them deals with the issue of racism and vigorously denounces it. The other refers to homosexuality and deals with the issue, as should be done, with clarity and great pastoral charity, thus rendering a real service to truth and to those who are seeking this liberating truth.

Brothers in Christ: As we proclaim the truth in love, it is not possible for us to avoid all criticism; nor is it possible to please everyone. But it is possible to work for the real benefit of everyone. And so we are humbly convinced that God is with us in our ministry of truth, and that He "did not give us a spirit of timidity but a spirit of power and love and self-control" (2 Tm. 1:7).

One of the greatest rights of the faithful is to receive the Word of God in its purity and integrity as guaranteed by the Magisterium of the universal Church: the authentic Magisterium of the bishops of the Catholic Church teaching in union with the Pope. Dear brothers: We can be assured that the Holy Spirit is assisting us in our teaching if we remain absolutely faithful to the universal Magisterium.

In this regard I wish to add an extremely important point which I recently emphasized in speaking to a group of bishops making their *ad limina* visit: "In the community of the faithful—which must always maintain Catholic unity with the bishops and the Apostolic See—there are great insights of faith. The Holy Spirit is active in enlightening the minds of the faithful with His truth, and in inflaming their hearts with His love. But these insights of faith and this *sensus fidelium* are not independent of the Magisterium of the Church, which is an instrument of the same Holy Spirit and is assisted by Him. It is only when the faithful have been nourished by the Word of God, faithfully transmitted in its purity and integrity, that their own charisms are fully operative and fruitful. Once the Word of God is faithfully proclaimed to the community and is accepted, it brings forth fruits of justice and holiness of life in abundance. But the dynamism of the community in understanding and living the Word of God depends on its receiving intact the *depositum fidei;* and for this precise purpose a special apostolic and pastoral charism has been given to the Church. It is one and the same Spirit of truth who directs the hearts of the faithful and who guarantees the Magisterium of the pastors of the flock."

CUSTODIANS OF THE CHURCH'S UNITY

8. One of the greatest truths of which we are the humble custodians is the doctrine of the Church's unity —that unity which is tarnished on the human face of the Church by every form of sin, but which subsists indestructibly in the Catholic Church (cf. LG 8; UR 2, 3). A consciousness of sin calls us incessantly to conversion. The will of Christ impels us to work earnestly and perseveringly for unity with all our Christian brethren, being mindful that the unity we seek is one of perfect faith, a unity in truth and love. We must pray and study together, knowing, however, that intercommunion between divided Christians is not the answer to Christ's appeal for perfect unity. And with God's help we will continue to work humbly and resolutely to remove the real divisions that still exist, and thus to restore that full unity in faith which is the condition for sharing in the Eucharist (cf. Address of May 4, 1979). The commitment of the ecumenical council belongs to each of us; as does the testament of Paul VI who, writing on ecumenism, stated: "Let the work of drawing near to our separated brethren go on, with much understanding, with much patience, with great love; but without deviating from the true Catholic doctrine."

THE SACRAMENT OF PENANCE AND GENERAL ABSOLUTION

9. As bishops who are servants of truth, we are also called to be servants of unity, in the communion of the Church.

In the communion of holiness we ourselves are called, as I mentioned above, to conversion, so that we may preach with convincing power the message of Jesus: "Reform your lives and believe in the Gospel." We have a special role to play in safeguarding the Sacrament of Reconciliation, so that, in fidelity to a divine precept, we and our people may experience in our innermost being that "grace has far surpassed sin" (Rom. 5:20).

I, too, ratify the prophetic call of Paul VI, who urged the bishops to help their priests to "deeply understand how closely they collaborate through the Sacrament of Penance with the Savior in the work of conversion" (Address of April 20, 1978). In this regard I confirm again the norms of *Sacramentum paenitentiae* which so wisely emphasize the ecclesial dimension of the Sacrament of Penance and indicate the precise limits of general absolution, just as Paul VI did in his *ad limina* address to the American bishops.

Conversion by its very nature is the condition for that union with God which reaches its greatest expression in the Eucharist. Our union with Christ in the Eucharist presupposes, in turn, that our hearts are set on conversion, that they are pure. This is indeed an important part of our preaching to the people. In my encyclical I endeavored to express it in these words: "The Christ who calls to the Eucharistic banquet is always the same Christ who exhorts us to penance and repeats His 'repent.' Without this constant and ever-renewed endeavor for conversion, partaking of the Eucharist would lack its full redeeming effectiveness..." (RH 20). In the face of a widespread phenomenon of our time, namely, that many of our people who are among the great numbers who receive Communion make little use of confession, we must emphasize Christ's basic call to conversion. We must also stress that the personal encounter with the forgiving Jesus in the Sacrament of Reconciliation is a divine means which keeps alive, in our hearts and in our communities, a consciousness of sin in its perennial and tragic reality, and which actually brings forth, by the action of Jesus and the power of His Spirit, fruits of conversion in justice and holiness of life. By this sacrament we are renewed in fervor, strengthened in our resolves and buoyed up by divine encouragement.

CHRIST'S REAL PRESENCE IN THE EUCHARIST

10. As chosen leaders in a community of praise and prayer, it is our special joy to offer the Eucharist and to give our people a sense of their vocation as an Easter people, with the "Alleluia" as their song. And let us always recall that the validity of all liturgical development and the effectiveness of every liturgical sign presupposes the great principle that the Catholic liturgy is theocentric, and that it is above all "the worship of divine Majesty" (cf. SC 33), in union with Jesus Christ. Our people have a supernatural sense whereby they look for reverence in all liturgy, especially in what touches the mystery of the Eucharist. With deep faith our people understand that the Eucharist—in the Mass and outside the Mass—is the Body and Blood of Jesus Christ, and therefore deserves the worship that is given to the living God and to Him alone.

As ministers of a community of service, it is our privilege to proclaim the truth of Christ's union with His members in His Body, the Church. Hence we commend all service rendered in His name and to His brethren (cf. Mt. 25:45).

In a community of witness and evangelization may our testimony be clear and without reproach. In this regard the Catholic press and the other means of social communication are called to fulfill a special role of great dignity at the service of truth and charity. The Church's aim in employing and sponsoring these media is linked to her mission of evangelization and of service to humanity; through the media the Church hopes to promote ever more effectively the uplifting message of the Gospel.

11. And each individual Church over which you preside and which you serve is a community founded on

the Word of God and acting in the truth of this Word. It is in fidelity to the communion of the universal Church that our local unity is authenticated and made stable. In the communion of the universal Church local Churches find their own identity and enrichment ever more clearly. But all of this requires that the individual Churches should maintain complete openness toward the universal Church.

And this is the mystery that we celebrate today in proclaiming the holiness and truth and unity of the episcopal ministry.

Brothers: This ministry of ours makes us accountable to Christ and to His Church. Jesus Christ, the Chief Shepherd (1 Pt. 5:4), loves us and sustains us. It is He who transmits His Father's Word and consecrates us in truth, so that each of us may say in turn of our people: "I consecrate myself for their sake now, that they may be consecrated in truth" (Jn. 17:19).

Let us pray for and devote special energy to promoting and maintaining vocations to the sacred priesthood, so that the pastoral care of the priestly ministry may be ensured for future generations. I ask you to call upon parents and families, upon priests, religious and laity to unite in fulfilling this vital responsibility of the entire community. And to the young people themselves let us hold up the full challenge of following Christ and of embracing His invitation with full generosity.

As we ourselves pursue every day the justice and holiness born of truth, let us look to Mary, Mother of Jesus, Queen of Apostles, and Cause of our Joy. May St. Frances Xavier Cabrini, St. Elizabeth Ann Seton and St. John Neumann pray for you, and for all the people whom you are called to serve in holiness and truth and in the unity of Christ and His Church.

Dear brothers: "Grace be with all who love our Lord Jesus Christ with unfailing love" (Eph. 5:24).

Mary Is the Model of the Church

On October 6, 1979, the Holy Father went to St. Matthew's Cathedral, Washington, D.C., where some 1,400 priests, deacons and lay members of the archdiocesan council awaited him. During the Eucharistic celebration the Pope delivered the following homily.

Mary says to us today: "I am the servant of the Lord. Let it be done to me as you say" (Lk. 1:38).

And with these words, she expresses what was the fundamental attitude of her life: her faith! Mary believed! She trusted in God's promises and was faithful to His will. When the angel Gabriel announced that she was chosen to be the Mother of the Most High, she gave her "Fiat" humbly and with full freedom: "Let it be done to me as you say."

Perhaps the best description of Mary and, at the same time the greatest tribute to her, was the greeting of her cousin Elizabeth: "Blessed is she who trusted that God's words to her would be fulfilled" (Lk. 1:45). For it was that continual trust in the Providence of God which most characterized her faith.

All her earthly life was a "pilgrimage of faith" (cf. LG 58). For like us she walked in shadows and hoped for things unseen. She knew the contradictions of our earthly life. She was promised that her Son would be given David's throne, but at His birth, there was no room even at the inn. Mary still believed. The angel said her Child would be called the Son of God; but she would see Him slandered, betrayed and condemned, and left to die as a thief on the cross. Even yet, Mary "trusted that God's words to her would be fulfilled" (Lk. 1:45) and that "nothing was impossible with God" (Lk. 1:37).

This woman of faith, Mary of Nazareth, the Mother of God, has been given to us as a model in our pilgrimage of faith. From Mary we learn to surrender to God's will in all things. From Mary, we learn to trust even when all hope seems gone. From Mary, we learn to love Christ, her Son and the Son of God. For Mary is not only the Mother of God, she is Mother of the Church as well. In every stage of the march through history, the Church has benefited from the prayer and protection of the Virgin Mary. Holy Scripture and the experience of the faithful see the Mother of God as the one who in a very special way is united with the Church at the most difficult moments in her history, when attacks on the Church became most threatening. Precisely in periods when Christ, and, therefore, His Church, provokes deliberated contradiction, Mary appears particularly close to the Church, because for her the Church is always her beloved Christ.

I therefore exhort you in Christ Jesus to continue to look to Mary as the model of the Church, as the best example of the discipleship of Christ. Learn from her to be always faithful, to trust that God's Word to you will be fulfilled, and that nothing is impossible with God. Turn to Mary frequently in your prayer "for never was it known that anyone who fled to her protection, implored her help or sought her intercession was left unaided."

As a great sign that has appeared in the heavens, Mary guides and sustains us on our pilgrim way, urging us on to "the victory that overcomes the world, our faith" (1 Jn. 5:5).

Evangelization and Apostolate of Priestly Vocations

On October 13, 1979, the Holy Father received in audience at Castel Gandolfo the bishops of Chile on their visit ad limina Apostolorum. *The group was led by His Eminence Cardinal Raul Silva Henriquez, Archbishop of Santiago. John Paul II delivered the following address.*

Lord Cardinal,
Revered and beloved brothers in the episcopate,

I feel immense joy on receiving you today, bishops of the Church in Chile. I know that, at the cost of many sacrifices, you have undertaken this long journey *"Beatorum Apostolorum sepulchra veneraturi"* (CIC, c. 341, 1) and, as the President of your episcopal conference so aptly said, to confirm your filial adherence and close communion with the Sovereign Pontiff, Pastor of the Roman Church: *"ad hanc enim Ecclesiam, propter potiorem principalitatem, necesse est omnem convenire Ecclesiam"* (Iren. *Adv. Haer.* III, 3, 2).

This is not a sporadic meeting. The contact of the Pastor of the universal Church with the pastors of the local Churches is a permanent reality, through the interior bond of prayer and unity in faith, hope and charity, as also through representatives of the Roman Pontiff in each nation and of curial organisms, which work in his name and with his authority for the good of the Churches and in the service of their leaders (cf. CD 9).

But to meet here, gathered personally in the name of Christ, is a privileged moment. I am really very glad that your visit *ad limina* is a collective one, in a certain way as the manifestation of, and aspiration to, the unity of your souls; and it gives me great pleasure to be able to see you after your pilgrimage to the Holy Land, while I can well imagine the impressions you had as you traversed prayerfully the places sanctified by Jesus, the Founder of the Church.

I know very well your self-sacrificing and efficient labor, the tireless solicitude of your episcopal conference, and the pastoral plan on "Human Conduct," from which there spring, as from deep roots, precise guidelines for a deep and complete spiritual and religious renewal of the People of God entrusted to you.

As a modest contribution to your pastoral tasks, your aspirations and efforts, I would like to refer to two subjects which are of special importance in the exercise of your mission at the present moment: evangelization and vocations.

EVANGELIZATION AND VOCATIONS

Evangelization is the permanent and essential task of the episcopal ministry. "For the Church," our beloved Predecessor Paul VI said already, "evangelizing means bringing the Good News into all the strata of humanity, and through its influence transforming humanity from within and making it new: *'Now I am making the whole of creation new'* " (EN 18). "There is no true evangelization if the name, the teaching, the life, the promises, the kingdom and the mystery of Jesus of Nazareth, the Son of God, are not proclaimed" (*ibid.*, 22).

St. Matthew seems to interrupt his Gospel abruptly in order to conclude it by sending the Apostles to the world: "All authority in heaven and on earth has been given to me. Go, therefore, and make disciples of all nations, baptizing them in the name of the Father and of the Son and of the Holy Spirit, teaching them to observe all that I have commanded you; and lo, I am with you always, to the close of the age" (Mt. 28:18-20).

I strongly advise you to meditate on this text. What importance Christ attributes to the mission of the Apostles, since, in order to carry it out, He refers to the fullness of authority that He has received over the whole of creation! He transmits to you, the successors of the Apostles, the same mandate to proclaim Him as Savior, to bring about conversion and adhesion to Him and, finally, to incorporate everyone in the community in which the presence of God in the world is maintained and grows.

The Lord does not want the proclamation to be addressed exclusively to the intelligence, as a theoretical doctrine, since it must lead to deep unity of faith and life in everyday activities, on the personal and social, national and international planes. That cannot be achieved without sacrifice, without great care in applying the eternal Word to concrete circumstances, and showing yourselves to be living witnesses to the Gospel message.

Your mission is to follow in the footsteps of Christ, the Good Shepherd. You are not a symposium of experts, nor a parliament of politicians, nor a congress of scientists or technicians, but you are pastors of the Church, whom it behooves, as I recalled at the memorable gathering of the Latin American episcopate at Puebla, to be teachers of truth, signs constructing unity and defenders and promoters of man's dignity (cf. Opening Address, *passim).* In this way you will be able to contribute to the establishment of an order that is more and more Christian, and, for this reason, more and more just.

In your tasks you should address all men, without exception, both those who are already walking in the faith and those outside it, the poor and the rich, workers and professionals, the healthy and the sick, as the Master did. For the good of everyone, especially the neediest, it will be your careful concern to illuminate those who are active in the field of culture, science and technology, those who have a greater responsibility for the common good, in order that the light of the life-bringing Gospel may guide and promote this complete progress which, otherwise, ends up by turning against man.

As regards, in particular, the safeguarding of the dignity of man, his rights and his duties, as I already had the opportunity to say to you on another occasion, "let your resolutions be inspired by the principles of the Gospel, under the guidance of the Magisterium of the Church, aiming at Christ the Man, the Model, Teacher and Redeemer of His brothers." With renewed "confidence and hope I exhort you to an adequate effort of enlightenment, especially by stressing love, the indispensable foundation of the ecclesial community and of human society, in the perspective of the transcendent purpose of man, God's son. In this way, also in this important field, the Church will appear as the sign of salvation and sacrament of unity for everyone" (cf. LG 48).

SHORTAGE OF VOCATIONS

An essentially vital field for your Churches is that of the apostolate of vocations. Many of your dioceses, owing to the shortage of priests, have recourse to help from outside. This is a very valuable but precarious collaboration. The diocesan community must, for its organic maturation, bring forth from within itself the vital forces sufficient to ensure the spiritual progress of the faithful. For this reason I thank God and bless your precious efforts in this sector and observe with immense joy the promising increase of priestly vocations in Chile: the announcement of a new spring in your Churches.

Obviously the problem goes beyond a mere increase in the number of candidates; it also includes their thorough formation and follow-up during their priestly activities. It is necessary to make it clear that this is not an individual and isolated task of each one of you, since vocations are formed in the service of the Church. Therefore, you will keep in mind the national context, the requirements of the present and those of the future and act in everything in agreement with the other prelates, especially those of your own ecclesiastical province. You will also give due attention to the documents issued by the Sacred Congregation for Catholic Education referring to the formation of candidates for the priesthood: In them you will find reliable guidelines.

WORK OF THE PRIEST

The priest is also the "high priest chosen from among men...appointed to act on behalf of men in relation to God, to offer gifts and sacrifices for sins. He can deal gently with the ignorant and wayward, since he himself is beset with weakness. Because of this he is bound to offer sacrifice for his own sins as well as for those of the people" (Heb. 5:1-3).

Therefore, the priest is a man of prayer, the liturgist who leads the community to worship God with the services of the whole Church, a worthy and universal worship, of incomparable beauty. Seminarians must be formed theoretically and practically so that genuine liturgical renewal, in which is expressed one of the most insistent recommendations of the Council and of the Holy See, may be assured in the future.

Above all, right from the seminary, future priests must be formed in such a way that they are so clearly aware of their specific mission that they will not be tempted or induced later, for the sake of effectiveness, to adopt methods incompatible with the Gospel, based on purely human principles and geared to merely temporal aims.

PRIESTLY FORMATION

It is clear that the formation of the priest is based on a solid ecclesiology, starting from the Person of Christ as He is presented in the Gospel, excluding fallacious re-readings. I said so at Puebla, and because of its importance I wish to repeat it to you: Our duty is to proclaim liberation in the full and deep sense, as it was announced by Jesus Christ, liberation from everything that oppresses man, but especially from sin. "If the Church makes herself present in the defense of, or in the advancement of man, she does so in line with her mission, which, although it is religious and not social or political, cannot fail to consider man in the entirety of his being" (Opening Address, III, 2).

Many precious efforts made in the seminaries are sometimes lost as a result of lack of care afterwards. So follow your priests closely, with solicitude and trust, with fatherly love, so that, as they are integrated into the apostolate, they may be your precious and faithful collaborators.

This wide field that I have recalled to you, nay more, all pastoral action finds in you, as Vatican II teaches, the principal and visible foundation of the particular Church (cf. LG 23).

The unity of your Churches is constructed around each one of you and around you all in communion with Peter's Successor, in response to Christ's exhortation and prayer (Jn. 17:22), following the luminous line laid down by the Second Vatican Council (cf. LG 23).

RENEWED COMMITMENT

I warmly encourage you, therefore, to make this visit *ad limina* the occasion of a renewed commitment to continue your evangelizing task in full harmony not only of intentions, but also of methods and action.

The unity of the Church does not spring from external forms but from an interior force that is rooted in truth and in good. It cannot be obtained without interior struggle; it cannot be reached without self-denial; it cannot be attained except by questioning oneself daily and learning to accept others. *"Veritatem autem facientes in caritate crescite in Eo quod est caput Christus"* (Eph. 4:15): Christ must be the Inspirer and Center of unity, just as, in order to attain it, He gives us the grace to realize it in the full measure that He desires.

That ecclesial unity, the fruit of meeting in Christ, will be at the same time the great force that animates you and sustains you in generous dedication to the work of reconciling spirits, above any limits or barriers. In this connection I wish to express to you my satisfaction at the resolute support you have given to the cause of peace between your country and Argentina, a cause to which I have dedicated and am dedicating particular solicitude, as you well know. Continue with example, word and prayer, working in this noble task of brotherhood among men and peoples who recognize themselves as sons of the same Father.

To Mary, Mother of the Church, we commend the unity of pastors and of the faithful; to her, Mother and Queen of Chile.

The Lord will guide you and sustain you in your mission. In His name, with special affection and as a sign of communion, I bless you: you bishops and pastors of the Lord, your priests, deacons, men and women religious, your seminarians and ministers, and all your faithful: I pray for all, I live for all!

Consistent Testimony of Faith in a Brilliant Catechesis

On October 14, 1979, John Paul II presided over the solemn rite of beatification of the Spanish priest Henry de Ossó y Cervelló. The Holy Father delivered the following homily.

Praised be Jesus Christ!
Reverend brothers and beloved sons and daughters,

1. This morning, the Church strikes up a song of joy and praise to the Lord. It is the song of the Mother celebrating divine goodness and mercy, on proclaiming Blessed an outstanding son, who distinguished himself for the practice of Christian virtues to an eminent degree: the priest Henry de Ossó y Cervelló, the glory of beloved Spain, the land of saints.

To be present at the glorification of the new Blessed, you, his fellow-countrymen, have gathered in large numbers in this Basilica of St. Peter. Welcome to you all, bishops, priests, religious and faithful of Spain here present, as well as those of you who come from all those places to which there has spread the goodness sown by the Blessed Henry de Ossó and in which his person and his work have won just recognition and appreciation.

But above all, welcome to you, sisters of the Society of St. Teresa of Jesus, who have arrived with your present and former pupils, coming from various places and countries of Europe, Africa, and America, to offer a warm tribute of devotion and renewed faithfulness to your founder.

Allow me, however, to reserve a word of special greeting to representatives of the diocese of Tortosa, and more precisely to those of the village of Vinebre, the birthplace of this admirable figure of a man and a priest, whom the Church holds up to our imitation today.

IMAGE OF THE FAITHFUL PRIEST

2. Yes, the Blessed Henry de Ossó offers us a living image of the faithful priest, persevering, humble and courageous in the presence of contradictions, completely disinterested, full of apostolic zeal for the glory of God and the salvation of souls, active in the apostolate, and contemplative in his extraordinary life of prayer.

The period in which it fell to his lot to live was not an easy one, in a Spain divided by the civil wars of the 19th century and troubled by secularist and anticlerical movements in pursuit of political and social change, even giving rise to bloody revolutionary episodes. He, however, succeeded in remaining firm and intrepid in his faith, in which he found inspiration and strength to project the light of his priesthood upon the society of his time. He was clearly aware of what was his specific mission as a man of the Church, which he loved deeply, without ever seeking leading roles in fields that were alien to his condition, and being open to everyone without distinction, in order to improve them and bring them to Christ. He carried out his resolution: "I will always belong to Jesus, as His minister, His apostle, His missionary of peace and love."

His priestly life, which lasted barely thirty years, gave rise to a continual development of apostolic enterprises, well pondered and carried out with abnegation, with impressive trust in God.

His was an existence of continual prayer which nourished his interior life and informed all his works. In the school of the great saint of Avila, he learned that prayer, that "relationship of friendship" with God, is a necessary means to know oneself and live in truth, to grow in awareness of being sons of God, to grow in love. It is also an effective means to change the world. Therefore, he was also an apostle and teacher of prayer. How many souls he taught to pray with his work *Cuarto de hora de oracion (A quarter of an hour of prayer)!*

This was the secret of his great priestly life, which gave him joy, balance and fortitude; which made him—priest, servant and minister of all, suffering with all, loving and respecting all—feel happy to be what he was, aware that he had in his hands gifts received from the Lord for the redemption of the world, gifts which he, lowly and unworthy though he was, offered from the infinite superiority of the mystery of Christ and which filled his soul with ineffable joy. A witness and a lesson of ecclesial life that is fully valid for the priest of today, who can find, in the example of the saints and in the teachings or norms of the Church, not in extraneous suggestions or theories, secure guidance to preserve his identity and reach complete fulfillment.

Once more I wish to exhort my beloved brother priests, on this splendid occasion, to complete dedication to Christ, joyfully lived in celibacy for the kingdom of heaven and in generous service for brothers, especially the poorest, through a life centered on one's own pastoral ministry, that is, in the specific mission of the Church, and characterized by the evangelical style which I set forth in my letter on Holy Thursday and of which I spoke again in my welcome meetings with priests during my recent apostolic journey.

GREAT CATECHIST OF THE PAST CENTURY

3. If we wish to point out now one of the most characteristic features of the apostolic nature of the new Blessed, we can say that he was one of the greatest catechists in the 19th century. This makes him a very topical figure at this moment in which the whole Church is reflect-

ing—as she did at the last session of the Synod of Bishops also—on the duty of catechizing which is incumbent on all her sons.

As a brilliant catechist, he distinguished himself through his writings and through his practical work, taking care to make the *content of faith* known, adequately and in harmony with the Magisterium of the Church, and to help people to put it into practice in their lives. His active methods made him a forerunner of later pedagogical discoveries. But above all, the aim he set himself was to make known and awaken love of God, of Christ and of the Church, which is the center of the true catechist's mission.

In this mission he was familiar with all fields: that of childhood, with his unforgettable catechesis in Tortosa ("through children to the hearts of men"); that of youth, with the associations of young people, which spread far and wide; that of the family, with his religious propaganda writings, especially the Teresian review; that of the workers, endeavoring to make them acquainted with the social doctrine of the Church; that of education and culture, in which, in conformity with the mentality of the age, he struggled to ensure the presence of the Catholic ideal in schools, at all levels, including universities. He dedicated himself tirelessly to the ministry of the spoken word, through preaching, and of the written word, through the press as a means of apostolate.

THE·SOCIETY'S FOUNDER

4. But in his catechetical effort, his favorite work, the one that took up most of his energies, was the foundation of the Society of St. Teresa of Jesus.

To extend the range of his action in time and in space, to penetrate into the heart of the family, to serve society in an age in which cultural formation was beginning to be indispensable, he enlisted the aid of women who could help him in this mission, and dedicated himself to the task of forming them carefully. With them the new institute began. It was to be distinguished by the following features: as daughters of their time, esteem for the values of culture; as women consecrated to God, their complete commitment to the service of the Church; as their specific style of spirituality, assimilation of the doctrine and example of Saint Teresa of Jesus.

We could say that the Society of St. Teresa of Jesus was and is, as it were, the great catechesis organized by the Blessed Ossó in order to reach woman, and through her to instill new vitality in society and in the Church.

DAUGHTERS OF ST. TERESA

Daughters of the Society of St. Teresa: Allow me to say that I am happy to see that you remain faithful to your charism, within the renewal that the present time demands in the light of the guidelines of the Second Vatican Council and of my Predecessor Paul VI's Apostolic Exhortation, *Evangelii nuntiandi*. In accordance with the heritage of your founder and the spirit of the great saint of Avila, be generous in your complete donation to Christ, in order to yield a great deal of fruit in mission countries. Let your whole conduct reflect the richness of an interior life in which renunciation is love; sacrifice, apostolic efficacy; faithfulness, acceptance of the mystery that you are living; obedience, supernatural elevation; virginity, joyful donation to others for the kingdom of heaven.

Be before the world, with external signs also, a living testimony of great ideals that have become reality, catechizing and evangelizing always, with words and with apostolic action. Be a dazzling proof that, today as yesterday, it is worthwhile not to cut the wings of one's spirit, in order to give the modern world—which is in such great need of it and is looking for it, sometimes even without knowing it—serenity in faith, joy in hope, happiness in true love. It is, indeed, worth living for that; living one's vocation as a woman and as a sister in this way, in imitation of the Virgin Mary, to whom your founder professed such tender devotion.

EDUCATOR'S HERITAGE

5. For the Christian of today, plunged into an atmosphere of accelerated pursuit of a new ideal of man, the Blessed Henry de Ossó, the Christian educator, also leaves a heritage. This new man who is being sought cannot be truly such without Christ, the Redeemer of man. It will be necessary to improve him, educate him and ennoble him more and more in his multiple human aspects, but it is also necessary to catechize him, open him up to spiritual and religious horizons where he finds his dimension of eternity, as son of God and citizen of a world which goes beyond the present one.

What a vast field is opened to the generous dedication of fathers and mothers; to directors and teachers in schools and teaching establishments, particularly those belonging to the Church—which must continue to be, with due respect for everyone, centers of Christian education; to many of you, former pupils of schools of the Society of St. Teresa, who remain close to those who were once your teachers; to so many other souls, who, from different posts, private or public, can contribute to the cultural and human advancement of others and to their formation in faith! Be aware of your responsibility and possibilities of doing good.

SPAIN'S SPECIAL MISSION

6. I conclude these reflections with a cordial greeting to the members of the special mission sent to this ceremony by the Spanish government. I pray to God that the Catholic tradition of the Spanish nation, of which the new

Blessed spoke and wrote so much, may be a stimulus in the present phase of its history and that it may expand to include higher aims, looking decidedly to the future, but without forgetting, nay more, endeavoring to preserve and give new vitality to the essential Christian features of the past, in order that in this way the present may be an age of peace, material and spiritual prosperity, and hope in Christ the Savior.

Be Teachers of Religious and Social Truth

On October 20, 1979, John Paul II received in audience the bishops of Peru on their visit ad limina Apostolorum. *The group was led by His Eminence Cardinal Juan Landázuri Ricketts, Archbishop of Lima. The Holy Father delivered the following address.*

Lord Cardinal,
Beloved brothers in the episcopate,

With real brotherly affection I receive you at this collective meeting, pastors of the People of God in Peru, after having talked to each of you, during the past days, about the situation in each one of your respective ecclesiastical territorial divisions.

1. Through the reports you have presented, and in spite of the different concrete peculiarities that are revealed in them, I have been able to confirm that the Church in your country has accomplished and is accomplishing faithfully its mission of proclaiming the message of salvation and of bringing forth a community of new life in Christ.

I am well aware that this proclamation of the Gospel cannot be carried out without a considerable effort, owing to the difficult environmental circumstances in which it has to take place. Therefore, I wish to express right now, to you, and to your priests, men and women religious and all agents of pastoral work, my cordial appreciation and thanks in the name of Christ, because, despite the difficulties that this work frequently involves, you bear witness to self-sacrificing dedication to the Church. For this reason I wish to say to you with St. Peter: "May grace and peace be multiplied to you" (1 Pt. 1:2).

This evangelization of the People of God in which you are engaged is the great task offered to your zeal as pastors of the Church. You are dedicating your care to a portion of the Church which, centuries ago, received the first proclamation of the faith, thanks to a praiseworthy missionary effort. The seed sown has grown deep roots and produced precious fruits, which have left traces in the culture, the history and the whole life of your people.

However, your pastoral solicitude indicates to you that it is necessary to continue with this mission; that it is necessary to extend it and strengthen it, in order that faith may deepen more and more in your faithful and, raising them above what is imperfect, bring them to maturity of life in Christ.

A long task, which calls for good planning and persevering execution, in which it is necessary to use all ecclesial forces, both those already available and those that unlimited love for souls will succeed in bringing forth. Only with this evangelization in depth will it be possible to reach the aims that you desire for the true renewal and vitality of your Churches.

2. In the community of believers, guidance of the faithful has been entrusted to you. For this reason, allow me to stress to you, as instructions of this visit *ad limina*, the necessity of being "Teachers of Truth." Of the truth about Christ, the Son of God and Redeemer of mankind; about the Church and her true mission in the world; about

man, his dignity, his earthly and, at the same time, transcendent exigencies, as I set forth in the address delivered to the general conference of the Latin American episcopate, celebrated at Puebla. I know that you are aware of this duty, in harmony with the evangelizing mission of the Church and with the questions that our age raises. I encourage you, then, to continue along this way so that your priests and faithful may joyfully walk along safe and well-defined paths.

As part of your mission as teachers, pay attention also to the opportune diffusion of the social thought of the Church, in order that in society people may learn to respect those indispensable requirements of justice and fairness which protect persons, particularly those in greatest need, in the different spheres of their existence.

3. Thinking of the urgent needs of your dioceses and the shortage of priests that afflicts them, I give you, as a primary task, to work with might and main in favor of vocations for the priesthood and for religious life. This is an essential point for the Christian community. Precious, indeed, is the help given in pastoral work by deacons, religious who are not priests, sisters, catechists and other faithful aware of their responsibility in the evangelizing mission of the Church, a help that must be appreciated in all its value and promoted as a real ecclesial good. However, we cannot forget that Christ becomes present in each community through the priest above all.

In your effort to obtain true and sufficient ministers of Christ, preferably born in your own country, see to it that the priest has a clear awareness of his own identity, lives intensely the vertical dimension of his existence, and is the guide and educator in faith, the father of all, especially of the poor, the valiant servant of the Gospel cause, the true pastor interested in bringing everyone to Christ, in freeing man radically from what separates him from God in the first place.

Living very close to your priests and sharing, in sincere friendship, their joys and difficulties, help them to remain in joyful communion with their bishop and to avoid dangers and ideologies that may creep into the environment and that are not compatible with their mission and with the directives of the Magisterium.

4. As pastors of your faithful, also dedicate special care to the apostolate of the family. Let the family, "the domestic Church," be the object of your particular interest in the pastoral task.

Against the external attacks to which they are subjected today, propose and defend the genuine values of the family and of Christian marriage. Only by keeping firm these spiritual and human values is the family consolidated as an extremely important social cell and, at the same time, as "the first evangelizing environment."

You who live in contact with the family situation of your respective environments know very well their needs and the illusions that threaten so many homes. Never fail to take an interest in their fate and instill into your priests and evangelizing agents great esteem for this sector of the apostolate, which obtains so much fruit and with which so much good can be done.

5. Another subject of deep interest and great importance for the Church is that of youth.

In the Latin American world the young element prevails. Youth, consequently, must occupy a primary place in your pastoral work. The Church, and all those in it who feel a sense of responsibility, cannot let the young move away from Christ. It is necessary to be with the young, give them high and noble ideas, show them that Christ has a great deal to say to them. Jesus of Nazareth interests the man and youth of today when we know how to present him in the right way.

Among the many initiatives that your zeal as pastors will suggest to you in this field, I wish to call your attention to the importance of religious instruction in schools. There are, of course, also other environments in which this obligation can be carried out, but we cannot fail to use the opportunities offered to us and which, moreover, meet the desires expressed by so many fathers of families. It would be deplorable if, for trivial reasons, this sector of pastoral work were to be neglected.

It would be even more deplorable if, under the pretext of what are thought to be more profitable forms of apostolate, the possibilities of educating persons in their totality and youth in its integrality, which the educational establishments of the Church offer us, were to be abandoned. Certainly, they must be reformed—when necessary—to meet evangelical purposes and those of openness to all, but let us not easily abandon instruments that have produced so much human and social good, when we are able to use them adequately. It is an important service that we can render to society and to the Church today.

6. Beloved brothers, I would like to stay much longer with you, prolonging these moments of joy and communion. This visit *ad limina Apostolorum* is a sign of your cordial closeness to Peter's Successor. May this meeting strengthen and consolidate, at the same time, your mutual union as bishops and guides of the Church in Peru. All your activity will thereby gain in intensity and efficacy, which will redound to the good of your ecclesial communities.

We have thought of them also in these days and we have prayed for them, that they may grow in knowledge of, and faithfulness to, Christ. For one and all of their members, especially for priests, religious, deacons and sisters—whom I accompany with prayer in their difficult and meritorious labor—for seminarians and lay people committed to the apostolate, I leave you my affectionate greeting, my encouragement and my blessing.

I Follow Your Labor as a Father

To the heads of the Apostolic Union of the Clergy, during a General Audience.

Let a brotherly and cordial greeting go to those in charge of the Apostolic Union of the Clergy, international counsellors and national directors, coming from forty-four nations all over the world, who are holding the important International Assembly of the Association in Rome during these days.

Beloved priests! I thank you sincerely for your presence at the general audience, together with the People of God! Rest assured that I follow your labor with the anxiety of a father and friend, and appreciate your work, as my Predecessors did, because the diocesan clergy especially, in the various situations of the ministry, needs brotherly and concrete help.

The Apostolic Union, in fact, is intended precisely as a help for priests to live the spirituality typical of Christ's minister in a complete and authentic way. It is a service to ensure that the directives of the Pope and of the bishop may be accepted faithfully and put into practice with a spirit of generosity and conviction. Finally, it wishes also to be an ideal so that the priest, who feels the need of spiritual support and an elevating friendship in order to be steadfast in maintaining the commitments of his consecration, will know where to find it.

How necessary, therefore, is your work, especially today! Continue in your purpose in all the nations in which you operate. May the Sacred Heart of Jesus enlighten you and encourage you! May you be inspired by the Blessed Virgin, to whom, in particular, priests are entrusted in their joys and their tribulations! I hope that the Apostolic Union will be able to contribute effectively to realizing among the clergy the unity of doctrine, charity and discipline, which is absolutely necessary for evangelization.

I willingly bless you and all the members of the Union!

Theological Research Must Help the Church to Ever Deeper Knowledge of the Mystery of Jesus Christ

On October 26, 1979, John Paul II received in audience those taking part in the plenary session of the International Theological Commission. The theme for their discussions was certain actual problems of Christology. At the meeting with the Pope there were present among others, Cardinal Franjo Seper, President of the Commission, Cardinal Joseph Ratzinger, Archbishop of Munich, and Monsignor Delhaye, Secretary of the commission.

John Paul II gave the following address to his guests who this year are celebrating the tenth anniversary of the commission.

Esteemed brothers and beloved sons,

1. It is with great joy that we greet you, the members of the International Theological Commission, especially the President, Cardinal Franjo Seper, and Cardinal Joseph Ratzinger, as you come to visit us in the Vatican for the first time as Pastor of the universal Church.

We are pleased straightaway to make the following statement. We highly approve of your commission set up by our venerated Predecessor, Paul VI, in the year 1969. We value it greatly, and we expect a great deal from it. At the same time we thank you very much for the great work that has already been done especially during the last five years which have now come to an end.

DUTY OF ASSISTING

2. Not only are you expert investigators in the field of theology but the Supreme Authority of the Church has called upon you to help the Magisterium, especially the Roman Pontiff and the Sacred Congregation for the Doctrine of the Faith, by various forms of cooperation in theological matters. Your work also helps the local Churches which can be in touch with one another much more easily in our age than in the past.

There emerges from all this the grave duty or "responsibility" which you share in some way with the Magisterium. We say "in some way" for as our abovementioned Predecessor Paul VI advisedly said, the authentic Magisterium, which is divine in its origin, "is endowed with a certain charism of the truth, which cannot be communicated to others, nor can there be any substitute for it" *(Allocutio,* October 11, 1973: *AAS* 65, pp. 557ff.).

RELATION OF THE MAGISTERIUM

3. Moreover, in recent years you have already shown that this service of yours, which you make available to the Magisterium and to the whole Church, is well worthwhile, knowing that you must be involved in the life of the Church which today is assailed by so many difficulties, so many diverse and dangerous opinions. We want to mention a few things. With praiseworthy zeal and to no small advantage you have examined the question of the ministerial priesthood, one which has been the subject of much discussion in recent years. Then there was the very important topic of the unity of the faith and theological pluralism. You also discussed some questions on the methodology of moral theology and the criteria for judging the morality of an act. You carefully investigated the relationship between the Magisterium of the Church and theologians. You gave your attention to the consideration of a theme which has recently become particularly relevant—liberation theology. It has given rise to many studies, especially in certain regions of the Catholic Church, and it can open the way to conclusions which must rightly be called into question. Nor can we omit the fact that you have dealt with doctrinal questions concerning the sacrament of marriage. These really call for the work of theologians, so that the will of the Creator and Savior concerning them may be suitably and convincingly made known to the men of our time.

What you have so far done we cannot but appreciate and thank you for, and we invite, yes press, you with the same willingness to carry through to completion the work begun. In this way, in a world which, distressful that it is, still turn towards our sure Hope, you may for all the Lord's disciples clear a path to peace and joy in believing (cf. Paul VI, l.c., p. 557; cf. Rom. 15:13).

BINDING FORCE OF DOGMATIC FORMULAS

4. We know that in this plenary session you are discussing questions which you have selected on Christology and we hope that, as with your previous studies, your work will bear fruit. We have already seen a great number of references or works of historians and theologians on this subject and we will read attentively the conclusions which, in your wisdom, you will arrive at. New angles can be discovered in Christology which must be carefully examined, yet always in the clear light of the truths which are contained in the sources of Revelation and which have been proclaimed infallibly down the centuries by the Magisterium.

"You are the Christ, the Son of the living God" (Mt. 16:16). This is the witness which the prince of the Apostles, enlightened by grace and drawing on his own experience, clearly gave. "For flesh and blood has not revealed this to you, but my Father who is in heaven" *(ibid.* 17). In these words a certain summary, as it were, of our faith is contained. Indeed faith in Christ, which the Church professes, guided and strengthened by grace, is based on the experience of Peter and the rest of the Apostles and disciples of the Lord, who went about with Christ, who concerning the word of life looked upon and touched Him with their hands (cf. 1 Jn. 1:1). Then moved by the Holy Spirit, they understood what they had experienced in this way in the light of the cross and resurrection.

From this arose that first "synthesis" which is expressed in the confessions and hymns of the letters of the Apostles. Then in the course of time the Church, making continual reference to these forms of witness and making them a part of her daily life, has always expressed her faith in ever more precise wording in the decrees of the great councils. You as theologians of this commission have been engaged in the study of these councils, in a particular way in the councils of Nicaea and Chalcedon. For the statements of these general councils have a binding force that is permanent.

But the historical circumstances and the questions which were being raised in the Church in those days and to which the Church replied in the definitions of the councils must not be overlooked. Modern questions, however, are connected with those of past centuries and the solutions which were arrived at then are being put into new replies, since the modern replies always presuppose the traditional pronouncements in some way, although they cannot be wholly reduced to them.

This permanent binding force of dogmatic formulas is more easily explained by the fact that they were expressed in terms that are customary in everyday life, although at times, the language is philosophical in form. From this it does not follow that the Magisterium has adopted a particular school of thought, since these statements signify only what is to be found in the whole of human experience. You have also tried to see how these formulas are related to the revelation of the New Testament, as the Church understands it.

TO DEEPEN THE KNOWLEDGE OF CHRIST

5. It is clear that the study of theologians is not limited, so to say, to the mere repetition of dogmatic formulas; it must help the Church always to deepen her knowledge of the mystery of Christ. The Savior also speaks to the people of our time, for the Second Vatican Council points out: "Only in the mystery of the Word incarnate does the mystery of man take on light." In fact,

"the final Adam, by the revelation of the mystery of the Father and His love, fully reveals man to man himself and makes his supreme calling clear. For by His Incarnation the Son of God has united Himself in some fashion with every man. He worked with human hands. He thought with a human mind, acted by human choice and loved with a human heart. Born of the Virgin Mary, He has truly been made one of us, like us in all things except sin" (GS 22).

Therefore, with justification we wrote in the Encyclical Letter *Redemptor hominis:* "The man who wishes to understand himself thoroughly...must with his unrest, uncertainty and even his weakness and sinfulness, with his life and death, draw near to Christ. He must, so to speak, enter into Him with all his own self; he must 'appropriate' and assimilate the whole of the reality of the Incarnation and redemption, in order to find himself" (no. 10).

This being so, it is clear how important are the studies of those who, in their concern for a deeper knowledge of it, investigate this mystery of Christ. Appreciate your task! Appreciate the importance of your presence in the Church! Almost from the beginning of the Church, theology developed side by side with the pastoral practice and because of this very fact it had and has at present a great influence on catechesis. But this research of yours can come about in a variety of ways. It is already well known that in ancient times several schools of theology existed and even in this age diverse schools of thought and opinions are recognized as legitimate, so that one can speak of a healthy pluralism. Nevertheless, care must always be taken to preserve intact "the deposit of faith" and theologians must reject those philosophical tenets which are incompatible with this faith.

ROOTED IN FAITH

6. In passing, one refers here to the relationship between the "human sciences" and Revelation with which you have dealt at length. Some people expand the field proper to these sciences to such an extent that they empty

the mystery of Christ of its content as St. Paul very much lamented, and in their exaggeration of the importance of human wisdom they despise the foolishness of the cross. Fortunately, earlier theologians of repute, following the example of St. Thomas Aquinas, were convinced that philosophy must be put at the service of the faith. But every science is rooted in its own principles. Hence it is that theology in the end judges all questions calling for a solution according to the principles of faith. It would contradict itself, if by adopting principles foreign to it, it were to arrive at conclusions which are imcompatible with its own principles.

THE WORD OF GOD BINDS

7. Meanwhile, difficulties also arise which concern the relationship between the Magisterium and the theologians themselves. You dealt with this subject in a special meeting a few years ago, as we have already noted, when you considered three aspects of the matter, namely, the elements common to the Magisterium and to theologians and the difference between the Magisterium and theology. We wish to emphasize the first of these aspects, since it is of very great importance. In putting themselves at the service of the truth, the Magisterium and the theologians are joined together by common ties, namely, by the Word of God, by the *sensus fidei,* which has been alive in the Church in the past and is alive today, by the documents of tradition in which the faith of the people in general is set forth, and finally by pastoral and missionary considerations.

If all these points are duly taken into account, the difficulties will easily be overcome. Moreover, theologians, who teach theology to their students in centers of higher education, should always remember that they are not teaching on their own authority, but by reason of the commission that they have received from the Church, as is pointed out in the Apostolic Constitution *Sapientia Christiana* (cf. art. 27, par. 1).

All these matters which we have only touched upon illustrate very well the importance of theology and, therefore, of your work. Strive also in the future to enrich the Church with the results of your investigations and with your service. Act in such a way, as teachers, that you so form the young men of great ability, your students, that there will always be at the service of the Church really expert theologians of which she always has need.

8. We must take this opportunity of mentioning two members, Edward Dhanis and Otto Semmelroth, whom death has taken from your midst and we earnestly commend their souls to God.

Finally, with sincere love for you, we earnestly beseech the Lord, through the intercession of the Blessed Virgin Mary, whom we invoke as the Seat of Wisdom, to be with you always, to strengthen you, to reward you for your important work. May the apostolic blessing, which we willingly impart to you, confirm these wishes.

The Apostolate of the Family, a Priority in the Task of Bishops

On October 28, 1979, the Holy Father received in audience a group of bishops from Argentina on their visit ad limina Apostolorum. *After listening to a sincere address of loyalty by Archbishop Jorge Manuel Lopez of Corrientes, John Paul II delivered the following discourse.*

Beloved brothers in the episcopate,

1. I thank the Lord for granting me this desired meeting with you, bishops of the Church in Argentina. It is a meeting the joy of which is dimmed by the recent death of Cardinal Antonio Caggiano, who, during his long life, left so many examples of virtue and such fruitful works.

Today is the culminating point of your visit *ad limina*, which is at the same time a complement, as it were, to that of the other Argentine prelates who preceded you.

In this way I have been able to meet each of you personally and, through you, your collaborators: priests, religious men and women, and laymen of each of the dioceses of a country that is far away geographically, but very close to my heart as Pastor of the universal Church.

I want to express right now my gratitude and appreciation for your apostolic commitment, and I want to tell you how pleased I am with the Christian spirit that is reflected in the ecclesial communities entrusted to your responsibility.

2. I am following with special interest the commendable solicitude with which you have been setting up an organic apostolate of the family, and I look hopefully to the full development of the "Program of pastoral action for *Marriage and the Family*," which your episcopal conference—as the Archbishop of Corrientes has just mentioned—set into action with a special emphasis some years ago for all the various Churches of Argentina.

I am happy that, in view of this aim, you have been able to arrive at a joint apostolate, capable of uniting and fully exploiting the apostolic forces, at all levels, making them converge harmoniously towards nationwide goals. In this way an effective contribution is made to that happy result that only the concentration of intentions, action and methods can yield in a work of such importance as that of forming and guiding families in the whole sphere of a really Christian life.

3. Your decision to offer to the Blessed Virgin Mary the results of your work at the National Marian Congress, which you will celebrate at Mendoza next year, is also a reason of joy for me. I am sure that it will be a fruit most pleasing to the Lord, because it will ripen under the assistance of His Mother, devotion to whom you are endeavoring to stimulate in your ecclesial communities and families, as a guarantee for the success of your intentions.

I encourage you to continue your action along this way, as widely and deeply as possible, since its beneficial effects will be felt not only in the Church but also in civil society.

In this way you will walk along the paths laid down by Vatican Council II, which stressed, in its documents, the importance of marriage and of the family (cf. LG 11, 41; GS 47-52; AA 11; GE 3). It is likewise a subject to which I have referred on so many occasions, in this first year of pontificate.

4. Speaking to Latin American bishops, I do not wish to fail to indicate that at the opening address of the Puebla Conference I pointed out the subject of the family as one of the priority tasks to be carried out (IV, a). I also dedicated my homily at Palafox Seminary to it. I commend to your reflection what I said there.

It is a necessary duty of pastors to teach and defend the doctrine of the Church with regard to marriage and the institution of the family, in order to safeguard their constituent elements, their requirements and perennial values.

In your people, thank God, the sense of the family remains very deep-rooted; but we cannot fail to recognize that the permissive trends of modern society have a growing impact on this important area, which the Church must protect with all her energies.

Marriage, on which the family is based, is a community of life and love, instituted by the Creator for the continuation of mankind, which has not only an earthly destiny, but also an eternal one (cf. GS 48). Strive, therefore, to defend its unity and indissolubility, applying to family life the central thought of the Puebla Conference: *communion* and *participation*.

Communion, that is, an interior disposition of understanding and love of the parents for each other and for their children. Participation, namely, mutual respect and giving, both in happy moments and in times of trial.

Within this unity, vivified by love, marriage shines forth as a source of human life, in harmony with the laws established by God Himself. This indicates to us the necessity of stressing the Christian sense of responsible parenthood, in the line of Paul VI's Encyclical *Humanae vitae*. Do not hesitate, either, to proclaim a fundamental right of the human being: that of being born (cf. Opening Address at Puebla, II, 5).

An adequate family apostolate will have to take into great consideration the three dimensions which Latin American families must have: "education in the faith, formation of persons, promotion of development" (Homily at Puebla Seminary, 2).

In fact, the Christian home must be the first school of faith, where baptismal grace opens to knowledge and love of God, Jesus Christ and the Blessed Virgin, and where experience of Christian truths, that have become norms of behavior for parents and children, is gradually deepened. Family catechesis, at all ages and with various pedagogical approaches, is extremely important. It must become operative with Christian initiation from before First Communion, and it will have to have a special development by means of conscious and responsible reception of the other sacraments. In this way the family will really be a domestic Church (cf. LG 11, AA 11).

In the formation of persons, the family has a special role which gives it a certain sacred character, with its own rights founded in the last resort on the dignity of the human person, and consequently they must always be respected. I said so in my address to the Organization of American States: "When we speak of the right to life, to physical and moral integrity, to nourishment, to housing, to education, to health care, to employment, to shared responsibility in the life of the nation, we speak of the human person. It is this human person whom faith makes us recognize as created in the image of God and destined for an eternal goal" (*L'Osservatore Romano*, Oct. 8-9, 1979).

The family apostolate must, then, watch over the defense of these rights. In this way it contributes at the same time to making the family a real and effective agent of development.

On the other hand, it is evident that to be able to work efficaciously in this field, it is necessary to make a serious effort to eliminate the deep causes from which there spring so many factors that upset the balance of society and, consequently, of the family. Everyone can see, in this connection, the enormous repercussion, not only of a moral nature, that certain situations of clear social injustice have, or situations that affect likewise the area of labor relations.

Consequently, as part of your ministry, do not fail to preach and stimulate a sound public moral doctrine, in full harmony with the line marked by the social teaching of the Church. If the latter is put into practice faithfully and without tergiversations of any tendency, the exigencies of a human and evangelical nature that it intends to safeguard will become a fruitful reality.

5. If with rightful concern for the safeguarding of these human rights, you stress clearly the principles set forth above, you will find in lack of due respect for these principles the root of the unleashing of violence.

In order to contribute, to the best of your ability, to ending the fatal spiral of violence, proceed, venerable brothers, with all zeal in the accomplishment of your pastoral duties, endeavoring to bring it about that society and the first cell of this society, that is, the family, will take its place in that civilization of love, which my Predecessor Paul VI desired so much.

6. If in the light of the requirements of your vast and difficult program, the number of the collaborators at your disposal might seem inadequate—in spite of the recent increase in vocations—let the following promising assertion of the Council serve as an encouragement: "The greatest contribution is made by families which are animated by a spirit of faith, charity and piety and which provide, as it were, a first seminary" (cf. OT 2).

God wished to leave us a model very close to us in the Holy Family of Nazareth. May Jesus, Mary and Joseph inspire, accompany and encourage your family apostolate and the task of all your collaborators.

7. Before concluding this meeting, I wish to refer to the gratitude you expressed to me for the task of mediator that I have accepted, to contribute to peace and friendship between two brother peoples: Argentina and Chile. Rest assured that I really appreciate the fact that you are facilitating my work with your pastoral action, which, based on prayer and on the teachings of the Gospel, contributes effectively to creating the right atmosphere for the desired solution, for the good of everyone.

Finally, I charge you with a particular task: to take to your priests, deacons, religious men and women, seminarians, agents of the apostolate and all your diocesans, the greeting and blessing of the Pope, who thinks of everyone and prays for everyone with great affection and deep hope. With them I bless you all.

Let the Church Be Faithful to the Task of Evangelizing

On October 29, 1979, John Paul II received in audience a group of bishops of Colombia on their visit ad limina Apostolorum. After an address of homage by Archbishop Alfonso Lopez Trujillo of Medellin, the Holy Father delivered the following discourse.

Venerable brothers in the episcopate,

I receive you with deep joy at this collective meeting, which makes me extend my gaze, full of affection, to the beloved Church in Colombia, which you represent here, and which has become, and becomes, a spiritual pilgrim to see the Successor of Peter, with you and with your brother bishops who preceded you.

In these moments of communion, gathered in the Lord's name, we also feel the presence of your priests, men and women religious, seminarians, members of the movements of the apostolate and the whole faithful people, whom we are urged to serve with abnegation and joy by the commandment of love of the Divine Master.

In fact, love of man, the image of God, is a concrete expression of our faith in the Lord, a gift that unites us in the Church, the universal sacrament of salvation.

The vision of faith in the service of man, of all men, especially those in greatest need, implies that the exercise of the primary mission of evangelization, and with it, of catechesis, should "yield to no other care whatever in any way" (CT 63). Evangelization and catechesis, adequately conceived, are the very axis of your pastoral concern. As the Puebla Document opportunely puts it: "Service of the poor is the best measure, though not the only one, of our discipleship of Christ. The best service of our brother is evangelization, which prepares him to fulfill himself as a son of God, frees him from injustices and ensures his complete advancement" (no. 1145).

Evangelization has an indispensable place in the family, for which you must continue to work hard and hopefully. In homes the face of God is discovered in prayer, the values of true humanism are refined and the Church grows. On New Year's Eve, 1978, I pointed out: "The deepest human problems are connected with the family. The Church...wishes to recall that the fundamental values, which cannot be violated without incalculable harm of a moral nature, are bound up with the family.... It is necessary to defend these fundamental values tenaciously and firmly, because their violation does incalculable harm to society and, in the last analysis, to man.... The first is the value of the person which is expressed in absolute mutual faithfulness until death.... The consequence of this affirmation of the value of the person, which is expressed in the mutual relationship between husband and wife, must also be respect for the personal value of the new life, that is, of the child, from the first moment of his conception. The Church can never dispense herself from the obligation of guarding these two fundamental values, connected with the vocation of the family" (Homily on the last day of the year 1978, no. 2).

You know, likewise, the hope that the Church and the Pope have in youth. Repeat to your young people what I said in Ireland: "I believe in the young with my whole heart and with full conviction." Ensure by all means the most careful catechesis for children and the young: a complete catechesis, faithful to the whole content of the Gospel, in an adapted language, which does not empty the Creed of its content, which does not disturb spirits and which forms Christians firm on essential matters and humbly happy in their faith. These are some of the points to which I referred at length in the recent Apostolic Exhortation on Catechesis and which I offer as criteria to those engaged in this very noble task which the Church recommends to them.

Continue, then, to animate all sound efforts that are being made in the field of catechesis. You are well aware that, unfortunately, there have also been "articles and publications which are ambiguous and harmful to young people and to the life of the Church" (CT 49). It is deplorable to find that they are sometimes circulated, eluding the vigilance of pastors. The Spirit urges us to communicate the certainties of our Faith. Would that also Catholic publishing houses and bookshops, faithful to the mission and requirements that such a name entails, collaborate as far as they can in this important task.

Responsible as you are for the communities that the Lord entrusts to you, helped by all your provident collaborators, priests in the first place, bring the young to Christ—the only One capable of fully meeting their aspirations. As the bishops noted at the Third General Conference of the Latin American episcopate, "let the apostolate of the young be the apostolate of joy and hope which transmits the joyful message of salvation to a world that is often sad, oppressed and desperately in search of its liberation" (no. 1205).

I am well aware that you endeavor to exercise this evangelizing ministry in close contact with your faithful and following closely the concrete environmental circumstances in which their lives as Christians take place. That makes you witnesses of a good many painful situations, due to the lack of moral and religious formation, culture, work, and deplorable conditions of injustice, in which the gap between those who have too much and those who lack essentials continues to grow.

With a view to that, do not fail to do your utmost in favor of a complete formation of persons, giving all due attention to the social dimension that your ministry must also have, with the keen sensitiveness that distinguishes so many persons today, especially among the young, who are eager to see established a system of far more just social relations.

With great faithfulness to the Gospel and clear awareness of what the specific mission of the Church is, may you be—with your teaching, your work, and the encouragement given to your collaborators—efficient promoters of real justice in all fields, in harmony with the norms laid down by the Church in her documents on social doctrine.

Beloved brothers: strengthened by my words and encouragement, carry on your mission, and take to all members of your respective churches the Pope's affection and blessing. And with it, the desire for peace, joy and hope in faithfulness to Christ, the Savior.

The Religious Spirit of Your People Augurs Well for the Spread of the Gospel

On October 30, 1979, John Paul II received a group of bishops from Mexico on their visit ad limina Apostolorum, *led by Cardinal Jose Salazar Lopez, Archbishop of Guadalajara and President of the episcopal conference. The Holy Father delivered the following address.*

Lord Cardinal, beloved brothers in the episcopate,

1. Welcome to this meeting, the culminating point of your visit to the See of the Apostles Peter and Paul.

In the spirit of faith, you undertook this pilgrimage to Rome, with the keen desire to strengthen your communion with the Pastor of the whole Church, and let him participate in your successes, resolutions and hopes, as well as in the difficulties and obstacles that the apostolic service for your ecclesial communities meets with in its daily path.

Thank you for the special joy that your visit brings me. Yes, because through your faces, so familiar to me, the confidences received from your hearts as pastors and, more directly, through the expressive and touching words that the President of your episcopal conference, the Cardinal Archbishop of Guadalajara, has just uttered on behalf of you all, there are conjured up, beside you, the vast multitudes of your faithful—who represent almost half of the Church in your country—and of the whole beloved people of Mexico. With them I spent unforgettable days during my first apostolic journey, and they continue to occupy a very special place in my memory and in my heart.

I would like the harmony of sentiments created during those days of mine in Mexico and the abundant evangelical seed sown to bear their best fruit and complement in an increasing deepening of faith and Christian life in your country.

2. All that demands from you, aided by those who collaborate in the apostolic mission, a persevering and systematic work of evangelization at all levels, in order that each member of your communities may receive the Good News of salvation, develop in a more and more conscious and personal way the faith he has received and arrive at fullness of life in Christ. A long and urgent task, but a very noble and meritorious one, in which I am happy to see the spirit of mutual aid that reigns between your particular Churches, with adequate pastoral planning at the regional level and with reciprocal assistance between dioceses, enabling them to help those in greatest need with means and, above all, with qualified agents of evangelization.

You who come from lands the names of which are closely linked with such precious documents on evangelization do not need me to dwell at length on this point, on which I know you are committed with all your strength and conviction. Allow me, however, to encourage you once more in the fulfillment of this serious ecclesial responsibility, in order that the Church may carry out her mission faithfully. She always wishes to be "a good mother and to care for souls in all their needs, by proclaiming the Gospel, administering the sacraments, safeguarding family life with the Sacrament of Matrimony, gathering all into the eucharistic community by means of the holy Sacrament of the Altar, and by being lovingly with them from the cradle until they enter eternity" (Homily in the Basilica of Guadalupe, January 27, 1979).

3. As a starting point which will greatly facilitate your toil, you can rely on the deep religious spirit of your people, manifested in so many forms. In spite of the gaps it presents, it offers a field well-disposed to receive the Gospel. With opportune availability, you must be able to take advantage of it and make the best use of it.

In those cases in which Christian faith is mingled with less perfect forms of popular religion, a most prudent pastoral criterion is necessary, in order to not extinguish more or less genuine faith, but—starting from it—to purify it, strengthen it and gradually integrate it in conscious experience of the complete mystery of Christ.

4. A particularly important place is occupied, among your faithful, by devotion to the Virgin Mary, who from Guadalupe—a real "sanctuary of the people of Mexico"— and also from Zapopan or so many other places so dear to the soul of Marian Mexico, accompanies her sons in their pilgrimage of faith. Your history teaches you what a primary role the figure of Mary has had and has in the Christian life of your people.

Cultivate, therefore, lovingly this religious aspect of your faithful, who feel and live devotion to the Blessed Virgin as something that belongs to their own identity. Let it be Mary who leads your faithful, by means of perfect understanding of her place in the economy of grace, and following her example as a perfect Christian, along the path of true disciples of Jesus, the Savior. By means of a careful and well-guided apostolate, may her sanctuaries be "very special places for the meeting of an increasingly purified faith" (Homily at the Sanctuary of Zapopan, January 30, 1979).

5. One of the best-known characteristics of your ecclesial environment is the youth of the population, sixty percent of whom are under twenty years of age. This is a real challenge for you which the Church cannot ignore. These young people of today are the Church and the society of tomorrow, they are their future, their hope. It is necessary to be able to lead them to Christ, presenting Him to them as the one great Ideal that can meet their anxieties, their desires for freedom, justice, authenticity, and a change of hearts and, with it, a transformation of society that is so often unjust and sick. Only in this way, with noble ideas in their minds, and with generous experiences in their hearts, will they be able to overcome the existential emptiness that is at the root of the sad phenomena of vio-

lence, drugs and sex, or of deviations to ideologies which are, in the last resort, in contradiction with the worthy ideals for which people think they are fighting.

6. The cause of a deep moral education of consciences, particularly within the parish, the family, and formation centers, cannot ignore that opportune social-moral orientation which the Church has stressed so frequently in the documents dedicated to this subject, which form an important part of her teaching.

Throughout the history of your ecclesial community there has been no lack of examples and figures who, drawing upon the indications of the social doctrine of the Popes, especially since Leo XIII, have given proof—even in the midst of difficult external circumstances—of a fruitful integration in the social and associative field, by supporting the just claims of the needy working-class and peasant sectors, in a line of true humanism inspired by Christian principles. A work that continues, that must continue with renewed strength and commitment, under the impetus of the episcopate. Would that all those who work in this field—priests, religious, and Catholic laity—would abide by these principles, in order that their effort may be fruitful and ecclesial, without creating harmful discords, tensions or ruptures.

In this area I do not wish to fail to recommend to you special care for a particular sector of your flock: the communities of Indians. I remember with affection my meetings with some aboriginal groups at Cuilapan and I refer you to what I said there.

7. Beloved brothers, other points would deserve our attention, but I cannot prolóng this meeting any longer. I will refer to them on receiving the other members of the Mexican episcopate.

Continue your mission as teachers, pastors and fathers with renewed vigor and enthusiasm. Keep closely united with one another and also within the episcopal conference in developing your personal and collective responsibilities, for the building up of your Churches in the Faith.

To one and all the members of the latter, of the groups I met in the different stages of my pilgrimage in Mexico, and to all those who were unable to see me because of sickness or for other reasons, I extend my affectionate thoughts and my arms to bless them.

I conclude with a deep desire that becomes a prayer: May it be the sweet Lady of Tepeyac, the Mother of Guadalupe, to whose sanctuary the Pope continues to go on pilgrimage spiritually and whose image he keeps very close, who indicates to all: "go to Jesus," the Way, the Truth and the Life. Amen.

We Celebrate with Our Dead the Hope of an Eternal Life

On All Saints' Day, 1979, the Pope presided over a solemn Eucharistic concelebration at the cemetery of Verano in Rome, with the Cardinal Vicar, some auxiliary bishops of the diocese and about fifty parish priests of Rome. The Holy Father delivered the following homily during the Mass.

1. We are all gathered here today in the principal cemetery of Rome. All those for whom this cemetery has a particular value and eloquence have come here. It speaks to us of the dead who live in us: in our memory, our love, and our hearts. It speaks to us of our parents, those, that is, who gave us earthly life, thanks to whom we have all become participants in humanity. This cemetery also speaks to us of many others, whose love, example and influence have left lasting traces in our souls. We live still within the truth lived by them, in the problems which they served. We are, in a sense, their continuity. They live in us; and we cannot stop living in them.

Coming to this graveyard today, we wish to manifest all this. In this way the cemetery of Rome, like all cemeteries in Italy and in the world, becomes a marvelous assembly place: a place that bears witness that the dead do not cease to live in us, the living, because we, the living, do not cease to live by them and in them.

IT IS THE LORD'S

2. If this psychological truth, in a way a subjective one, cannot be false, we, following the words of today's liturgical feast, must confess the same thing as the responsorial psalm announces so simply and forcefully:

"The earth is the Lord's and the fullness thereof, the world and those who dwell therein" (Ps. 24:1).

It is the Lord's!...

If the world, this earth and all it contains, and if finally man himself, do not have that Lord, if they do not belong to Him, if they are not His creatures...then our sense of communion with the dead, our memory and our love break at the same point at which they come into being. Then we must abandon that in which each of us expresses himself so strongly; we must cancel what so strongly determines each of us.

For then there is revealed—with an almost implacable necessity—this second alternative: only the earth, which for a certain time accepts the dominion of man, turns out to be the master in the last analysis. Then the cemetery is the place of man's final defeat. It is the place where a final and irrevocable victory of the "earth" over the whole human being, rich as he is, is manifested; the place of the dominion of the earth over him who, in his own lifetime, claimed to be its master.

These are the inexorable logical consequences of the view of the world which rejects God and reduces the whole of reality exclusively to matter. At the moment in which man, in his mind and in his heart, makes God die, he must consider that he has condemned himself to an irreversible death, that he has accepted the program of man's death. This program, unfortunately, and often without reflection on our part, becomes the program of contemporary civilization.

CHILDREN OF GOD

3. We, gathered here, have come to this cemetery today to confess the presence of God and His lordship over the created world: to confess His salvific presence in the history of man. We are, as the psalm says, the generation of those who seek Him, who seek the face of the God of Jacob (cf. Ps. 24:6).

Yes, we have come here to confess the mystery of the Lamb of God, in whom we are endowed with salvation and eternal life. In fact, the Son of God, Himself divine, became a man and, as a man, accepted death in order to give us participation in the life of God Himself. The Apostle John speaks to us of this participation with the words of his first letter: "See what love the Father has given us, that we should be called children of God; and so we are" (1 Jn. 3:1).

This awareness accompanies us today, as we come to pray on the graves of our dear ones and to celebrate, amidst these graves, the Sacrifice of the body and blood of Christ. Offering it, let us think together with the author of Revelation of those who "have washed their robes and made them white in the blood of the Lamb" (Rv. 7:14).

We come here with faith. Faith raises the seals of these graves and allows us to think of those who are dead as of persons who, thanks to Christ, live in God. With this awareness, with this faith, we all, the Bishop of Rome and the parish priests of the individual Roman parishes, celebrate the Sacrifice of Christ here today. We celebrate it with the hope of eternal life, which Christ has given us. "Every one who thus hopes in him purifies himself as he is pure" (1 Jn. 3:3).

Christianity is a program full of life. Confronted with the daily experience of death, in which our humanity shares, it repeats tirelessly: "I believe in eternal life." In this dimension of life is found the final fulfillment of man in God Himself: "We know that...we shall be like him, for we shall see him as he is" (1 Jn. 3:2).

HOPE OF ETERNAL LIFE

4. Therefore, today also, we are called to gather round Christ, when He delivers His Sermon on the Mount. The Gospel of the eight beatitudes touches on these two dimensions of life, of which one belongs to this earth and is temporal, while the other bears within it the hope of eternal life.

Listening to these words, we can look towards eternal life from that which is temporal. But we can also, and must, look at the temporal, our life on earth, through the perspective of eternal life.

We must also ask ourselves what this life of ours must be like, in order that the hope of eternal life may develop and mature in it. Then we understand rightly what Jesus means when He proclaims "blessed" the poor in spirit, the meek, and those who mourn, and those who hunger and thirst for righteousness, and the merciful, and the pure in heart, and the peacemakers, and those who are persecuted for the sake of righteousness.

This is what Christ wants us to be. And this is what the Father expects us to be.

Let us not depart from this cemetery without a deep look at our lives. Let us look at them in the perspective of the living God, in the perspective of eternity. Then also our meeting with those who have left us will yield full fruit: "Their hope is full of immortality" (Wis. 3:4).

United in Truth and Charity

With the Holy Father there were present 120 Cardinals at the opening of the plenary meeting of the Sacred College in the Synod Hall on November 5, 1979. After an address of homage by the Cardinal Dean, Pope John Paul II delivered the following discourse.

Venerable brothers, members of the Sacred College:

The Cardinal Dean, with such kind words, has expressed to me, in his name and also on behalf of you all, good wishes for my name-day. For my part, I cannot fail to return those good wishes and express them publicly; and I must also thank him with affectionate sincerity not only for his remarks about this first year of my service as Pastor of the universal Church but also for the hopes that he has expressed, in your name, not only for me but also for the Church and for humanity itself: namely, that there should take place a general renewal, in practical acceptance of Christ's teaching.

In synthesis, is not this in fact the spiritual purpose of the Second Vatican Council, that great ecclesial event of our century, an event whose implementation is entrusted to the commitment of the whole People of God? The beloved Cardinal Confalonieri has rightly mentioned St. Charles Borromeo, my heavenly patron. How hard he worked; how much he suffered in order to render effective in the huge Archdiocese of Milan the wise directives of the Council of Trent in matters of doctrine, morals, pastoral activity and liturgy!

To him, my protector, at this moment of grace and blessing which finds us gathered together, I raise my fervent prayer that he may transmit to our hearts his zeal and devotion for the Church and for souls.

I

Venerable brothers,
members of the Sacred College:

1. At the beginning of this meeting of ours I especially wish to express my joy at seeing gathered here the whole of

the College of Cardinals, whose principal purpose is to elect the Bishop of Rome, as happened last year on two occasions. The sad duty of bidding farewell to the deceased Popes—first to Paul VI, after fifteen years of pontificate, then to John Paul I, after only thirty-three days of papal ministry—brought us together in Rome twice within a short space of time. In conformity with the directions of the Apostolic Constitution *Romano pontifici eligendo*, during the days preceding the conclave we held the Plenary Congregations, presided over by the venerable Dean of the Sacred College and by the Camerlengo, Cardinal Jean Villot, whom the Lord called to Himself at the beginning of March this year.

These frequent meetings of the whole College of Cardinals provided an opportunity to put forward the proposal that the College itself could meet, at least from time to time, also outside the times of conclave. In support of this proposal, I have thought of inviting the venerable Cardinals to this meeting, which I permit myself to open with the present address. In inviting you, I realized that your coming to Rome would involve giving up the many important tasks that occupy you in your countries and dioceses. And so today I wish to thank each one of you all the more cordially for being here.

2. Our meeting is fully justified by the character of the dignity that you possess and by the tasks that belong to the College of Cardinals which you constitute. In fact, venerable brothers, as well as having the task of electing the Bishop of Rome, you also have the task of sustaining him in a special way in his pastoral solicitude for the Church in her universal dimensions. Those among you who belong to the Roman Curia, filling the most responsible offices therein, share directly in this solicitude, in a continuous and permanent way. However, side by side with this group of worthy collaborators, all the other members of the Sacred College share with the Pope the common solicitude for the Church. Your link with this See of Rome is a special one, and the outward sign of union is,

for example, the churches of the Eternal City that enjoy the title, dignity and patronage of each of you. Precisely in this singular link with the Church in Rome is found the reason why the Bishop of Rome wishes to meet you more often, in order to profit from advice and your many-sided experience. In addition, the meeting of the members of the College of Cardinals is also one form in which episcopal and pastoral collegiality is exercised, a form that has been in existence for more than a thousand years; and it is fitting that we should avail ourselves of it in these modern times, too. This in no way weakens or diminishes the duties and function of the Synod of Bishops, the next ordinary meeting of which is fixed for the autumn of the coming year. The preparatory work for this meeting is going on now; the theme of the meeting, *De Muneribus Familiae Christianae*, in conformity with the suggestions of many episcopal conferences and various quarters, was laid down by Pope Paul VI of venerable memory.

3. It seems, therefore, that the meeting of the College of Cardinals this autumn can profitably occupy itself with an examination, at least a summary one, of certain questions rather different from those that the Synod of Bishops is working on. These questions, which as an introduction I wish at least to outline, are important ones, given the situation of the universal Church; and at the same time they seem to be more closely linked with the ministry of the Bishop of Rome than the questions that are to be the subject of the Synod of Bishops. It is obvious that here one cannot speak of any rigorous demarcation.

Right at the beginning, I also wish to make the point that, over and above the questions that I shall shortly put forward myself, I count upon proposals that the individual participants in this meeting of ours will put forward and elaborate. For this purpose we have provision for a due interval in the order of our sessions. This order, in contrast to what happens in the Synod of Bishops, is not based upon any particular statute. It has been prepared *ad hoc*, in accordance with the requirements foreseen for the present meeting (somewhat on the pattern of the Congregations held before the conclaves last year). I would like to add at once that, apart from the oral statements made during the meetings, all written observations and proposals will be very valuable. I am aware that this present work cannot be allowed to take too much time from the schedule of the venerable members of the Sacred College, and this too has been taken into account in the preparation of the program and order of our meeting.

II

4. By the grace of Almighty God and under the protection of the Mother of Christ and Mother of the Church, on October 16 last year I began the exercise of the universal pastoral service, to which I was called by your votes, venerable Cardinals, at the last conclave. As best I can, and according to my strength and with all possible goodwill—but especially with the help of the light and power of the Spirit, the Paraclete—I try to exercise this service and I do not cease to ask each and every person, and especially you, venerable and dear brothers, to pray for this intention. I do not intend to inform you here of the individual tasks that have filled the first year of the pontificate, also because they are already well known to you all. It is rather my wish to dwell once more on all the things that I was able to emphasize in my first talk on the day after the election. A consistent *putting into practice of the teaching and directives of the Second Vatican Council* is and continues to be the main task of the pontificate. This was, in substance, the content of that talk. In fact, the Council worked out and placed before the whole Church an "overall" vision of the tasks that have to be accomplished in the context of the mutual link and organic dependence, obviously with the use of many different methods and having available her own theological and historical perspective.

5. In the Constitution *Gaudium et spes* we read: "The Lord Jesus, when He prayed to the Father, 'that all may be

one...as we are one' (Jn. 17:21-22), opened up vistas closed to human reason. For He implied a certain likeness between the union of the divine Persons, and the union of God's children in truth and charity" (par. 24). The aspiration to the unity of men and women as children of God united in truth and charity does not cease to be something that the Church's whole life and mission looks forward to both within her own communion and outside it, in the radius of the individual "circles of dialogue," as Pope Paul VI called them in the first encyclical of his pontificate. We are all well aware that the aspiration to unity in truth and charity does not cease to be the aspiration to the truth in which we must meet one another, as also the aspiration to the charity through which we must be mutually united. It cannot be any different in the state of human existence on earth. In this sense especially I have allowed myself to stress, in the Encyclical *Redemptor hominis*, that Christ constantly shows to the Church, and in our own time in a special way through the voice of the Council, the road that man, every man, must take, and in this sense man in Christ becomes in a certain sense the road for the Church.

In this way we grasp in an ever new way the historical perspective of the Church's mission, that for us is linked with the theological perspective of faith, given that each individual and all people have been shown that "union in truth and charity," that is to say, the spiritual unity linked with the dignity of children of God. It is, therefore, a duty to ensure that this synthesizing formula, left to us by the Council in its pastoral constitution, should truly unite in itself all the individual efforts that make up the work of putting the Council into practice. This work, in its deepest reality, is symbolized by that tree of life by which man once broke the link through original sin (cf. Gn. 3:1-7), and which through Christ began anew to develop greatly in the history of humanity. The Council did not so much unveil before us the eternal mystery of this development as show in an unusually penetrating way its present stage. Therefore, obedience to the teaching of the Second

Vatican Council is obedience to the Holy Spirit, who is given to the Church in order to remind her at every stage of history of everything that Christ said, in order to teach the Church all things (cf. Jn. 14:26). Obedience to the Holy Spirit is expressed in the authentic carrying out of the tasks indicated by the Council, in full accordance with the teaching set forth therein.

6. These tasks cannot be treated as though they did not exist. It is not possible to claim to make the Church go back, so to speak, along the path of human history. But neither is it possible to rush presumptuously ahead, towards ways of living, thinking and preaching Christian truth, and finally to ways of being a Christian, a priest, a religious that are not envisioned in the integral teaching of the Council—"integral," that is to say, understood in the light of the whole of Sacred Tradition and on the basis of the constant Magisterium of the Church herself. The task that sets before us the command to carry out the Council is a great and many-sided one! It calls for constant vigilance regarding the authentic nature of all the undertakings whereby this putting into practice will become a reality. The Church, which is the living community of the children of God united in truth and love, must make a great effort, at this time, in order to step on to the direct road of putting Vatican II into practice, and in order to free herself from contrary proposals, each of which shows itself to be, of its own kind, a departure from this road. This road alone—that is to say, honest and sincere obedience to the Spirit of truth—can serve the unity and at the same time the spiritual power of the Church.

This road alone can, in addition, serve the work of ecumenism, that is to say, the renewed unity which, in its first meaning, we take to be union through charity, but which, in depth, we also look upon as a gradual meeting, in the fullness of truth, with all those who together with us believe in Christ. Only this road—the road of the internal union of the Church, the People of God—can serve the work of evangelization, that is to say, the effective manifestation to all people of that truth and life that is Christ Himself. This union in truth and charity is a particular requirement of our times, also because in these times of ours we are faced with the negation of this truth and with the radical questioning of the Gospel and of religion in general.

7. This glance at the situation as a whole also leads one to draw certain important conclusions, which can be defined as "practical" ones (insofar as the Second Vatican Council, basing itself on the Gospel and upon Tradition, only formed the skeleton of the whole of modern Christian *praxis*—the practice of the People of God).

The most important conclusion concerns the proper understanding and exercise of freedom in the Church. The Council, following the words of the Lord, desires to serve the development of this freedom—the freedom of the children of God, which in our own times especially has great significance, inasmuch as we are witnesses of many ways in which people are subjected to constraint, including constraint of their consciences and hearts. One must never forget that the Lord said: "You will know the truth, and the truth will make you free" (Jn. 8:32). For this reason the Church must preserve in the heart and conscience of each of her sons and daughters, and also, if possible, in the heart and conscience of every human being, the truth about freedom itself. Very often, freedom of will and the freedom of the person are understood as the right to do anything, as the right not to accept any norm or any duty that involves commitment also in the dimension of the whole of life, for example, the duties following from the marriage promises or from priestly ordination. But Christ does not teach us such an interpretation and exercise of freedom. The freedom of each individual creates duties, demands full respect for the hierarchy of values, and is potentially directed to the Good without limits, to God. In Christ's eyes, freedom is not first of all "freedom from" but "freedom for." The full enjoyment of freedom is love, in particular, the love through which individuals give themselves. Man, in fact, as we read in the same chapter of *Gaudium et spes*, "cannot fully find himself except through a sincere gift of himself" (no. 24).

It is this interpretation and this exercise of freedom that must be present at the basis of the whole work of renewal. Only the individual who understands and exercises his or her freedom in the manner indicated by Christ opens his or her spirit to the working of the Holy Spirit, who is the Spirit of truth and love. On the authentic affirmation of the freedom of the children of God depends the great work of vocations to the priesthood, the religious life, marriage. On it also depends effective ecumenical progress, and the whole of Christian witness, that is to say, the sharing of Christians in the cause of making the world more human. This is the first condition.

8. The second condition for the renewal of the Church in the spirit of the Gospel (that is to say, in the spirit of the Second Vatican Council) is constituted by a constant growth of solidarity, that is to say, of community (social) love, but within the Church and in relation to all people, without regard for their confession or convictions. Much has been done in this direction in recent times, as is shown by the activity of the Justice and Peace Commission and also by the Council *Cor Unum*. It is obvious that the Church's possibility of offering economic contributions in relation to the many different needs in the various parts of the world is limited. Here one should also stress that this solidarity of the Church *ad extra* demands solidarity *within*. I have tried to draw attention to this fact especially in the Wednesday talks last Lent.

The Church herself is a big community, within which there are different situations in the individual communities. There is no lack of people suffering material deprivation, but also there is no lack of people suffering oppression and persecution. In the whole Catholic community, in the individual local Churches, there must be an increase in the sense of particular solidarity with these brothers and sisters in the faith. In the modern world, in its own way dominated by the whole system of the exchange of information, it is necessary—both within the Church and outside her, in the face of world opinion—to have a permanent exchange of information about those suffering from poverty and also about those suffering for the faith. These latter must feel in a special way that they are not abandoned in their sufferings, that the whole Church remembers them, and that they are at the center of everyone's attention and not neglected.

In this field, the "rich and free" Church (if one may use such an expression) has enormous debts and commitments towards the "poor and constricted" Church (if one may use these expressions as well). Solidarity means above all a proper understanding and then proper action, not on the basis of what corresponds to the concept of the person offering help, but on the basis of what corresponds to the real needs of the person being helped, and what corresponds to his or her dignity.

Let us not forget that fundamental principle of the plan of salvation, according to which the person who offers to others saves himself or herself. Therefore, it is possible that the remedy for many interior difficulties from which some local Churches and some Christian communities are suffering is to be found precisely in this solidarity. Difficulties will be effectively overcome when (in a certain sense taking the gaze off themselves) they begin to serve others "in truth and charity." This principle interprets in a simpler way the missionary function of the Church—indeed this principle posits a stimulating postulate and, in a certain sense, a missionary imperative for our generation; for the generation to which Providence has entrusted a great work of renewal; the generation which sometimes is found to be hesitating and discouraged as it notes the collapse of certain fronts of the Church's traditional life, the crisis of fundamental institutions and still more the crisis taking place in people, in their attitudes and their consciences.

9. The renewal of the Church, in accordance with the splendid "program" set forth by the Second Vatican Council, cannot be, in its fundamental framework (and also in its concrete manifestation) anything other than an authentic conversion to God commensurate with the demands of our time. The call to conversion *(metanoeite)*, that is to say, to repentance, is not only the first word of the Gospel; it is also the Gospel's constant and irreplaceable word. From this word springs the Church's whole vitality. The Church finds herself all the more fully *in statu missionis*—that is to say, she fulfills her mission all the more fully—to the extent that she is converted to God. And only through this self-conversion does she become more powerful as the center of the conversion of individuals and of the world to the Creator and Redeemer Himself.

One must, therefore, view with a certain disquiet the widespread slowing down of these fundamental efforts, which always bear witness to the spirit of repentance and to the dynamic aspect of conversion among those who confess Christ. It is equally a duty, on the other hand, to thank God with joy for everything in which there is manifested the authentic "breath of the Spirit"; for the reawakening of the need for prayer, for the sacramental life and especially for sharing in the Eucharist; for the profound return to Sacred Scripture; for the increase, at least in some places, of vocations to the priesthood and religious life; for everything that can be termed a "spiritual reawakening." And this, venerable brothers, we must strive to foster with particular care, by creating the conditions necessary for a further development of these blessed currents, so needed by the Church and by humanity, which is becoming ever more clearly aware of where modern materialism in all its many manifestations is leading.

III

10. In the previous part of my talk I have tried not to deal directly with particular problems, but rather to indi-

cate the bases upon which depends the accomplishment of the task that faces the whole Church at the present stage of history. I hope that this will help the Cardinals assembled here to formulate the observations and proposals that we also await in the course of the present meeting.

After this general introductory talk, there will be three addresses of a more specific nature. They concern the practical questions about which the Apostolic See considers it useful to inform the Sacred College, in order to have its considered opinion.

In order that everyone should have an opportunity to express himself, provision has also been made for meetings in language groups.

The first address will be given by the Cardinal Secretary of State. Its subject will be the structures of the Roman Curia as a whole, as they have been reordered, following the suggestions of the Council, in the Apostolic Constitution *Regimini ecclesiae universae* of Pope Paul VI. These structures are organically linked with the many-sided activity of the Church today. The further putting into practice of the Second Vatican Council largely depends upon the efficient functioning of these structures, and upon their organized cooperation with the corresponding structures within the local Churches and episcopal conferences.

The subject of the second address, to be given by the Cardinal Prefect of the Sacred Congregation for Catholic Education, is a more specific but no less important question: the activity of the pontifical academies, and in particular the Pontifical Academy of Sciences.

This body, set up by Pope Pius XI, has a fundamental importance in the sphere of the relationship between faith and knowledge and between religion and science. Here, too, we have to give thought to a more collegial model in the formation of cooperation in this field, an important one for the Church in her universal dimension.

The Pastoral Constitution *Gaudium et spes* devoted a separate chapter to the question of the relationship between the Church and culture. Following the spirit of that document, it is necessary to seek a proper expression of the relationship between the Church and the wide field of modern anthropology and the human sciences, just as Pius XI sought the expression of the relationship between the Church and mathematics and the natural sciences when he set up the Pontifical Academy of Sciences.

And I am pleased that in a few days a solemn session of the Pontifical Academy to commemorate the centenary of the birth of Albert Einstein will be held, in the presence of all of you, dear and venerable brothers.

Finally, the third address, which will be given by the Cardinal President of the Administration of the Patrimony of the Apostolic See, will deal with the set of problems already touched upon in an introductory way during the Congregations of Cardinals that preceded the conclave in August of last year. Bearing in mind the different fields of the Apostolic See's activity, which had to be developed in relation with the putting of the Council into practice and in relation with the Church's present tasks in the spheres of evangelization and of service to people in the spirit of the Gospel, it is necessary to formulate the question of economic resources. In particular, the Sacred College has the right and duty to have an exact knowledge of the present state of the matter.

11. Venerable and dear brothers, this is a brief outline of the series of questions that are to constitute the subject matter of this meeting, which I have looked forward to very much. I hope that the Seat of Wisdom and Mother of the Church will obtain for us the light which we need in order to be able, in a relatively short space of time, to examine these questions and reach effective solutions to them in the future service of the Bishop of Rome.

An Important Stage on the Way to Collegiality

The plenary meeting of the Sacred College of Cardinals concluded its work on November 9, 1979, in the Synod Hall in the Vatican, in the presence of the Holy Father. In the course of the morning's work, John Paul II delivered the following address to the Cardinals.

Reverend brothers, members of the Sacred College!

1. *"Ecce quam bonum...habitare fratres in unum"* (Ps. 132:1). There are particular circumstances in the life of the Church in which we understand more thoroughly the beauty and truth of these words. We experienced them during the two conclaves, which we lived together last year, in a unique experience of our lives consecrated to Christ and to the People of God. We have experienced them also in these days, in all their interior richness and sweetness, when we met at this first historic meeting which I had so much desired, and which you favored with your presence and collaboration. *"Fratres in unum."* We have felt as *brothers, united in the same bond of vocation and mission:* gathered round the altar, near Peter's tomb, on November 5th, praying for the brothers of the Sacred College, most of whom were at our side in the past year, and who have been called to the Lord; united in this hall, where we felt that unique passion, which consecrates all of us "for the work of ministry, for building up the Body of Christ, until we all attain to the unity of the faith and of the knowledge of the Son of God" (Eph. 4:12f.).

2. And we feel, brothers, particularly today, in the bond of this Church of Rome of ours, to which we are very closely tied, I as Pastor, you as authoritative members of the Roman clergy, to which your *tituli* and *diaconiae* give you the native right to belong; today, I repeat, when the universal Church celebrates the dedication of the Lateran Basilica, *mater et caput omnium Ecclesiarum*, the See of the Bishop of Rome.

A reflection of that joy which is characteristic of the heavenly Jerusalem has spread out also and particularly on us, gathered here, at the conclusion of the meeting, precisely on the day sacred to the dedication of the See of Rome.

With these sentiments I thank you warmly: for having come to Rome from all continents, leaving for some days the pastoral concerns that unite you with your Churches, to which you are bound in Christ by a nuptial love; for having faced the discomforts of the journey regardless of the requirements of work. Thank you for the interventions, sound and well thought out, which you have let us hear, for the harmony with which the assembly and the single *Circuli* have worked, responding to the invitation to do so, and for the positive collaboration manifested.

But thank you above all for the atmosphere we have breathed here: an atmosphere of brotherhood, of the family, of co-responsibility, of love: *"caritas...Christi urget nos"* (2 Cor. 5:14).

3. I think that in this way our meeting has contributed:

—to covering in a short time an important stage on the way to collegiality, in the spirit of the Second Vatican Council;

—to the reanimation of this marvelous institution, which is the College of Cardinals, in conformity with its nature and its tradition.

Thanking you, I cannot but apologize at the same time:

—for the difficulties which you have had to face;

—for the tasks which, owing to their dimension, seemed to go beyond the possibilities of the time which you could dedicate to them.

It has been seen, however, that even in a relatively short time it has been possible to do quite a lot in this qualified assembly.

4. The principal elements will be reflected in the final communiqué.

In a sense, this meeting has been the introduction for a further exchange of ideas and pastoral concern.

There is no doubt that this meeting has had a highly pastoral character, animated by *"sollicitudo omnium ecclesiarum"* (cf. 2 Cor. 11:28).

5. It is not my intention to return to the subjects which have been submitted to your reflection, also for the months to come. Let it suffice for me to say that, as regards the organization of the Roman Curia, due account will be taken of the suggestions, advice and proposals which, animated by sincere love for the good of the universal Church, you have sent and will send here, to the very heart of the Church, in order that the organism of the Roman Curia, so articulated and complex, may be made fit to carry out a more and more qualified, precious and advantageous service for the bishops and episcopal conferences of the whole world.

6. You have seen the interest which, personally, and with the help of my direct collaborators, I intend to dedicate to the problems of culture, science and art, which were the object of special study by the Second Vatican Council, and which are awaiting a more willing contribution from all of us ecclesiastics. It was the Council that highlighted, in the Pastoral Constitution *Gaudium et spes,* the necessity of promoting the development of culture: "In their pilgrimage to the heavenly city"—it is said in the document—"Christians are to seek and relish the things that are above: this involves not a lesser, but rather a greater commitment to working with all men towards the establishment of a world that is more human. Indeed, the mystery of the Christian faith provides them with an outstanding incentive and encouragement to fulfill their role even more eagerly and to discover the full sense of the commitment by which human culture becomes important in man's total vocation" (GS 57).

This is the purpose of the concerns and perspectives which I took the liberty of pointing out to you, and which were subsequently illustrated by the Cardinal Rapporteur, qualified to do so. The interventions expressed clearly what your concerns are for the development of this vital field, in which the destiny of the Church and of the world is at stake, in this final close of our century.

I attach, therefore, very great importance also to the opinions you will send me on this central and inescapable question, for me and for everyone.

7. As regards the third subject, that is, the "economic" question, it seems opportune to point out:

—By continuing the exchange of information, started already in the month of August of last year, that is, before the conclave, you have been able, revered brothers, to obtain precise information about the state of the Holy See's financial problems.

—This is very important for the purpose of forming a correct public opinion in the Church and in the whole of Catholic society as regards this subject. That widespread fairytale about the finances of the Holy See has done it a great deal of harm. As in ancient times, in our days, too, myths come into being. The only thing to do in such a question is to consider the matter in itself objectively. In this connection, I must thank you heartily because in this field, too, you are generously ready to collaborate, according to the apostolic tradition confirmed by the experience of all the ages of the Church.

—In order to be able to serve the universal mission of the Church effectively, to be able to put into practice the pastoral program of the Council, and to work in favor of evangelization, the Apostolic See also needs financial means. These means, compared with those that the modern world spends, for example, on armaments, are, objectively, extremely modest.

In addition to this, the maintenance of that great monument of culture, such as is St. Peter's Basilica, and, connected with it, other institutions, for example, the Vatican Museums, is a duty of ours before history.

It seems to me, finally, that it can be said that the aims for which it was decided to convene this extraordinary meeting of the Cardinal Fathers have been achieved, *Deo adiuvante.*

And it is precisely to Him, to the "Father of lights," from whom there comes down "every good endowment and every perfect gift" (Jas. 1:17), that we express our common thanks. We entrust to Him our resolutions and our work. We ask Him for the grace to continue perseveringly along the way undertaken, for the elevation of man, for the true progress of peoples, for universal peace. *Aspirando praeveni, et adiuvando prosequere.*

And may Mary, Mother of the Church, Queen of Apostles, strengthen our common wishes and make them fruitful with her protection.

To her—and I say so gathering the unanimous wish expressed in this Hall—I entrust also myself and the whole of our assembly of pastors.

To all of you, beloved brothers, my special blessing.

To Lighten the Trials of Those Who Suffer for Their Fidelity

On November 12, 1979, in the Sistine Chapel, the Holy Father, in a solemn concelebration in the Byzantine-Ukrainian rite, conferred episcopal ordination on Archbishop Myroslav Lubachivsky, the new Metropolitan of Philadelphia of the Ukrainians. The co-consecrators were Cardinal Josyf Slipyj and Archbishop Maxim Hermaniuk of Winnipeg of the Ukrainians. Pope John Paul preached the following homily.

1. With deep emotion I come to the altar today in order to confer, together with you, venerable brothers, episcopal ordination on the new Metropolitan of Philadelphia of the Ukrainians.

A short time ago, during my journey to the United States, I had the joy of visiting his cathedral in Philadelphia. My meeting with the Archbishop-elect and the bishops of the ecclesiastical Province of Philadelphia, and with the priests, sisters and members of the faithful who had gathered in great numbers with their pastors, was for me a profoundly moving event. I am indeed well acquainted with the history of your people, the history of the Church that for centuries has been linked with this one, and this is the reason for my readiness today to lay hands, together with you, venerable brothers, upon the one whom the Holy Spirit calls to the episcopal ministry. At the same time, the Holy Spirit calls him to union with the Successor of Peter and with the whole hierarchy of this Church whose most eminent Hierarch is our venerable brother Cardinal Josyf Slipyj.

2. And so, Your Eminence, permit me to address myself in a special way to you. Not only the sons and daughters of your people but also the universal Church and the whole modern world know of the outstanding witness which by your difficult life and particularly by your many years of imprisonment you have given to Jesus Christ and the Church born from His cross and resurrection. That imprisonment tore you from the beloved See of Lviv, to which my esteemed Predecessor Pius XII had named you. It is consoling to find you with us today, after being freed many years ago through the concern of my esteemed Predecessor John XXIII and created Cardinal by Paul VI. You are therefore able to dedicate yourself to your people, on whose behalf in relation to God, to use the words of the letter to the Hebrews, you were appointed to act (Heb. 5:1).

You are still appointed to be the pastor who offers his life for the sheep (cf. Jn. 10:15), as an exile from that Church which, since 1596, has remained in union with the See of Peter, maintaining its fidelity to the alliance entered into almost four hundred years ago. This fidelity, particularly in the most recent centuries, has been paid for, and continues to be paid for, with great sacrifices. Your life as a pastor is a special example and proof of this.

3. I wish to avail myself of this occasion today in order to manifest the veneration that the Apostolic See and the whole Catholic Church have for your Church. The fidelity to Peter and his Successors, which has been attested, obliges us to special gratitude and also to mutual fidelity in relation to those who maintain it so firmly and so nobly. We wish to give them a tribute of truth and love. We wish with all our strength to lighten the trials they are undergoing precisely by reason of their fidelity. With all our heart we wish to ensure the internal unity of your Church and its unity with the See of Peter.

Your Eminence, allow me to address the same sentiments to the other co-consecrator, Metropolitan Maxim Hermaniuk of Winnipeg, Canada, and to the other representatives of the hierarchy of your Church here present. I also wish to manifest my esteem and affection for the entire Ukrainian Church.

4. We are celebrating the Eucharistic Liturgy of episcopal ordination on the day commemorating St. Josaphat, bishop and martyr, whom your Church venerates as its special patron. His remains, which since 1963 lie in Saint Peter's Basilica, constitute a further reason for today's ceremony, in which the new pastor is joined to the body of the bishops of your Church and is receiving episcopal ordination in Rome, close by the martyred relics of this saint. Today, together with you the whole Catholic Church is venerating St. Josaphat.

5. And you, Archbishop Lubachivsky, as a new pastor of the flock, are called to give witness to the fidelity that is so much a part of the tradition of your people. As a Catholic bishop you are called to be a sign of God's own fidelity to His covenant, a sign of Christ's undying love for His Church. And this is the ministry that is entrusted to you today: to offer unceasingly to the faithful the Bread of Life which, in the words of the Second Vatican Council, is taken from the table both of God's Word and of the body of Christ (cf. DV 21).

Yes, by word and sacrament you will sustain your people in their fidelity to the Gospel, and guide them in the way of salvation. The Word of God will be a lamp to their feet and a light to their path (cf. Ps. 119:105). And all your pastoral endeavors will be directed to this aim: that the Word of God may be the practical norm of Christian living, and bring forth fruits of justice and holiness of life in the community over which you preside and which you serve. And through the celebration of the Eucharistic Sacrifice you will continue to sustain your people in joy, confirming them in peace and unity and in the bond of charity. This, venerable brother, is a great mission, in which you find yourself the inheritor and guardian of a great tradition, which is both Catholic and Ukrainian. In the name of our Lord Jesus Christ, therefore, go forward in apostolic continuity and fidelity to proclaim to your people the Gospel of salvation.

On your return to your see, I would ask you to convey to your faithful my cordial greeting and my apostolic blessing.

6. May our special assembly here today, before the majesty of Almighty God in the Blessed Trinity, be a fresh confirmation of this path being followed by your Church and your people, in connection with the great thousandth anniversary of Baptism which you have this year begun to prepare for.

May the love of God the Father, the grace of our Lord Jesus Christ and the fellowship of the Holy Spirit, through the intercession of the blessed and Immaculate Mother of Christ and of St. Josaphat and of all the saints, be with you all. Amen.

Communion of Grace and Mission

On November 15, 1979, John Paul II received in audience a group of bishops from Venezuela on their visit ad limina Apostolorum. *The group was led by Archbishop Domingo Roa Pérez of Maracaibo, President of the episcopal conference.*

The Holy Father delivered the following address.

Beloved brothers in the episcopate,

It is a pleasure for me to receive you today at this audience, the culminating point, as it were, of the visit *ad limina* of all the Venezuelan bishops. At this moment I wish to express to you again my brotherly affection in apostolic communion.

Throughout the private audiences held up to now, I have been able to ascertain, on your side, identical correspondence in this same communion of grace and mission, in Christ, which must animate our pastoral service. So I make your concerns my own; I share, too, your afflictions and sacrifice for the sake of the Church; I likewise join in your joys and hopes for the spreading of the Gospel. I give thanks to the Lord for all that and rejoice that He "judged you faithful by appointing you to his service" (cf. 1 Tm. 1:12).

1. I will not describe now, since it is a thing we all know, what is the ecclesial function of the bishop in the midst of the Christian community. I would like, instead, considering that it is a fundamental aspect of every visit *ad limina*, to call you to a joint reflection, to intensify our collegial awareness, in order that our pastoral activity may be strengthened more and more in the exercise of the true mission, the aim of which "is love that issues from a pure heart and a good conscience and sincere faith" (1 Tm. 1:5).

Yes, beloved brothers: The realization of mutual love, the evident expression of a life grafted onto Christ the Savior is what gives credibility to our indispensable evangelizing task. Both of them, love and evangelization, take as their measure the inner man, that is, the human person who has to have "divine training" (1 Tm. 1:4), by means of the purification of hearts, the moral uprightness of consciences and orientation to God through living faith, expressed in works.

CAREFUL SERVICE OF TEACHERS AND GUIDES

2. Without losing sight of this urgency of credibility in the ecclesial mission, I feel the duty to propose to your reflection a field in which there is felt today more than ever in your country the need for a careful service on the part of those who are teachers and guides of the People of God.

I am referring to the institution of the family. I am well aware that it is a great concern of yours, too, and that you dedicate particular attention to it, because you are conscious of the invaluable and specific gift of the sacrament of marriage for Christian spouses: to "signify and share the mystery of the unity and faithful love between Christ and the Church. Christian married couples help one another to attain holiness in their married life and in the rearing of their children" (cf. LG 11). The sacrament of marriage and its historical perpetuation in the family are linked, therefore, with God's loving covenant with man, in creation and in redemption; a covenant which is perpetuated in the Church, the family of the People of God.

In our pastoral consideration on conjugal and family life, we must then go beyond strictly external perspectives, which sometimes ignore or dim, to some extent, its deepest and most genuine sense: the peculiar identity of love sanctified by the sacrament. We are sometimes content, perhaps a little superficially, to consult polls or statistics—carried out, maybe, on the basis of predetermined ideologies—which collect aspects that are changeable and can also be manipulated, the reflection, in turn, of changing situations of a cultural, sociological, political and economic character....

"DIVINE TRAINING" INSPIRES RESPECT

Let us not forget that, behind so many analyses and statistical data, there is a great vacuum which surrounds persons who, as a matter of fact, are confessing their own solitude, their own moral and spiritual emptiness, because they have not been sufficiently educated in the true meaning of the matrimonial union and of family life as a vocation to a fruitful, unique and unrepeatable experience of communication in harmony with God's initial and permanent plan.

A vocation from which there spring, of course, serious duties and responsibilities to which it is necessary to be faithful, for the sake of the children and in obedience to divine commands.

In view of this plain fact, we cannot but intensify our work with all the means within our reach. If we are really convinced that "it is man himself who must be saved: It is mankind that must be renewed" (LG 3), we must offer and cultivate this power and this truth in the family, within which the person is born and is regenerated thanks to grace. Where there is life, and it is appreciated and respected as a gift from God, the family and the community do not languish, moral conscience does not become lax, and daily existence does not fall a prey to boredom; on the contrary, with "divine training," it will feel its full meaning in its connection with divine Fatherhood.

HOME AS A SCHOOL

3. In the same way stress should be laid, because of its importance in the work of evangelization, on the task of the home as a school of formation. The Christian family, the "domestic Church," in the words of my venerated Predecessor Paul VI (EN 71), is the first suitable environment to sow the seed of the Gospel, and in it parents and children, as living cells, assimilate the Christian ideal of service of God and of brothers.

From this dynamic educative background there will certainly spring some vocations to the priesthood and to religious life—so necessary to be able to continue service of men, particularly on behalf of the poorest, those who are suffering in the flesh and in the spirit. So educate parents in the idea that to follow Christ is a reason which gives life its full meaning, because it is a generous response to the divine call.

AIM OF CATECHESIS

4. Another subject to which I wish to call your attention as pastors is that of catechesis. I know you are striving to bring your faithful to a progressive evangelization that will shape their entire Christian lives. I encourage you to continue and redouble your efforts in a field so vital for the Church, since it is only with systematic catechetical work, in depth, that your Christian communities will be able to arrive at complete experience of the message of salvation and at bearing witness personally and collectively to the deep reasons of their hope in Christ.

The accomplishment of this task will have to be centered on the mystery of Jesus, the Son of God and the Redeemer of man, who, in the revealed Word, continues to transmit His salvific teaching for the human being at each moment of history, and who, in the sacraments, continues to show today the efficacy of His divine power, which transforms those who approach Him.

This is the final aim of all catechesis: the vital, conscious and personal meeting with the Christ of faith, the Christ of history, the one Redeemer and hope of man. But a catechesis that is well planned and that starts from the true environmental reality, will not disdain all the aids and glimmers of true spirituality that are found in so many forms of popular religion. If well directed and made the object of a suitable catechesis, they can be valid paths towards the desired depth of a full life in Christ.

In this task and in order to give it the scope that the shortage of qualified agents of apostolate would otherwise prevent, use in every possible way the media of social communication, which can multiply your evangelizing voice. Also look, in this as in other fields, for the help of lay people and all persons who have had a good formation, who can offer you a precious collaboration. What wide perspectives could open up in this task for a good many of your best university graduates, for those who are aware of their Christian vocation and of their noble mission in the Church and in the present-day world!

SOCIAL SITUATIONS

5. There is another theme that you keep in mind and that recurs frequently in your five-yearly reports: concern about the social situations that you come up against in the ministry of your Churches.

You know very well that the priority and specific mission of the Church is evangelization. However, we cannot close our eyes to the repercussion that the message of the Gospel has also in the social order. The Church has shown throughout the centuries a deep sensitiveness for the human being, the victim of injustices, oppressions and violations of his dignity as a man and son of God. The sight of the worker who is not duly respected and remunerated, of the peasant without the possibility of access on suitable terms to a property in which he can fulfill himself with dignity, of the inhabitants of certain shantytowns without a house or means of culture or work, of the son of humble parents without opportunities for an adequate training for his life, of the emigrant, unwelcome or badly treated, these are realities—we could add others—that claim rightful attention on the part of those in the Church who can make a contribution in the tasks of a better humanization of structures and environments, so that they will be adapted to man and to his dignity.

It is an education of minds and hearts that is necessary, in the light of the great principles of the social and humanitarian teaching of the Church.

POPE'S BLESSING

6. In order not to lengthen this meeting further, I leave to your consideration and sensitiveness as pastors other chapters that we have touched upon in our conversations in the last few days.

I wish to tell you, finally, that the Pope feels deeply united with the aspirations and hope of the Church of God in your country. In my prayers to God the Father and to the Virgin of Coromoto, I keep one and all of the Venezuelans in mind, asking God One and Three to turn these wishes into Christian reality.

With great affection I give my special blessing to you and to the members of your Churches.

Intense Work for Native Vocations

On November 20, 1979, the Holy Father received in audience a group of bishops and of prelates of various Vicariates and Prefectures Apostolic of Colombia, on their visit ad limina Apostolorum. *Pope John Paul II delivered the following address.*

Beloved brothers in the episcopate,

1. Once more I feel the joy of seeing beside me a numerous group of bishops from Colombia, in this renewed communion of ecclesial sentiments and mutual affection, the aim and fruit of the visit *ad limina*.

Your presence, such a welcome one for me, makes me call to mind instinctively the members of the episcopate of your country who have preceded you. I feel that we are now prolonging the experiences and reflections which I had with them and which receive a complement with this meeting of ours.

ESTEEM AND THANKS

2. A special note characterizes our meeting today, since you, beloved brothers, as prelates of the various Vicariates Apostolic and Prefectures Apostolic of Colombia, bring to me the specific presence of the missionary Church in your country.

Consequently, my first word is one of esteem and thanks for your commitment in the work of building and consolidating the Church in each of the ecclesial districts entrusted to your pastoral care and responsibility.

In this task, such a vital and meritorious one, you receive precious help from the congregations and religious institutes to which your missionary districts are entrusted. I wish, consequently, to express here my sincere appreciation and gratitude, to which I add the testimony of my deep satisfaction and praise, to the members of these well-deserving religious families, who spend such generous energies in this task, in the midst of so many environmental difficulties and not a few privations. May the Lord reward them abundantly! These are sentiments which extend to all the others—sisters particularly—who work with abnegation in close collaboration with you.

THE WHOLE DIOCESE
SHOULD BE MISSIONARY

3. I know that you are engaged in the work of intense cultivation of native vocations. That makes me really very happy, and I encourage you to spare no effort in continuing along this way, which goes in the direction of the essential and prior needs of the Church.

However, looking at the overall panorama of the Church in your nation, we could ask ourselves if other more privileged dioceses were not able to offer you valuable help, by generously putting at your disposal personnel of evangelization, particularly priests and religious, which it seems they are in a position to give you.

This brotherly help between the various ecclesial communities, as well as being an evident sign of communion in Christ and maturity in the experience of the Catholic Faith, as well as contributing to correct quite considerable inequalities as regards evangelizing forces, would greatly aid the elevation of your missionary districts to dioceses of common law, an aim to which I myself look with favor and which I greatly desire, as soon as circumstances permit.

Active consciousness of the help that a particular Church can and must give to another one less privileged as regards pastoral agents and even material resources, far from reducing its own energies, will give it a new lease of life, by bringing forth new forces of ecclesial generosity and fruitfulness, as a reward for its own openness in the dynamic charity of the Gospel and a seed of certain divine blessings.

Then, too, if the missionary dimension is a necessary consequence of Christian vocation and if "the whole Church is missionary, and the work of evangelization the fundamental task of the People of God" (AG 35), every diocesan community—with its respective pastor, priests, men and women religious, seminarians and laity—must implement these vast ecclesial aims, which extend to other brother communities in the faith.

There is a fine evangelizing task here for everyone and more specifically for pastors, since, as the Second Vatican Council recalls, "by arousing, fostering and directing missionary work in his own diocese,...the bishop makes present and, as it were, visible the missionary spirit and zeal of the People of God, so that the whole diocese becomes missionary" (AG 38).

MAKE THE PRESENCE OF THE CHURCH A REALITY

4. At the conclusion of your visit to St. Peter's See, you are now preparing to return to your communities, to continue the work of evangelization, this work in which the two aspects of persevering preaching of Christ's saving message and help for those who are living in want and hardship are harmoniously united.

I would like the Pope's word, personal and full of affection, to reach each member of the Church working with you in the vineyard of the Lord, in order to encourage him in his toil for the kingdom of Christ, the spread of the faith, personal experience of the latter, and cheerful fortitude while waiting for the accomplishment of our hope. And also, at the same time, in order to manifest my approval for the praiseworthy dedication to the neediest, the poorest, and all those who are reached, perhaps, only by the support and aid inspired by charity carried out in Christ's name. Let them all know that in this way they are making the solicitous presence of the Church a reality, and that the Pope accompanies them, encourages them and is close to them.

I conclude, beloved brothers, by assuring you that I shall remember these intentions in prayer, in order that divine grace may be poured out abundantly on each member of your local Churches and on their initiatives.

May it be the Giver of all perfect good who brings to fullness the work begun. May it be the Mother of the Church, the Star of Evangelization, the perfect model of Christian life, who consoles and animates the courageous way, and causes it to leave in its wake fruitful evangelical and human achievements, in complete dedication to Christ and brothers. In order that it may be so, I give you my blessing, which is extended to all your collaborators and faithful.

Genuine Renewal

Excerpt from the general audience of December 9, 1979.

My special greeting goes also to the priests from the United States doing a course of continuing theological education at Casa Santa Maria. My brother priests: the genuine renewal of the Church in America depends to a great extent on the holiness of priests. Each one of you is called to a special intimacy with Jesus Christ, and it is only in union with Him that you will be able to make an effective and lasting contribution to the kingdom of God. And remember always the apostolic priorities that belong to the priesthood: concentration "on prayer and on the ministry of the word" (Acts 6:4).

Evangelization: Fundamental Mission of the Church

On December 11, 1979, the Holy Father received in audience the bishops of Ecuador on their visit ad limina Apostolorum. *The group, composed of over twenty prelates, was led by His Eminence Cardinal Pablo Muñoz Vega, Archbishop of Quito and President of the episcopal conference.*

The Holy Father delivered the following address.

Lord Cardinal, beloved brothers in the episcopate,

It is a great pleasure for me to have this collegial meeting with you, in the framework of the visit *ad limina* which you bishops of Ecuador are paying. These days of intense dialogue about your communities have been a great consolation for me, at a time when the real dynamism and the present promising perspectives of the Church in Ecuador have been unfolded before my eyes.

For that reason I give thanks to the Lord, "as is fitting, because your faith is growing abundantly, and the love of every one of you for one another is increasing. Therefore, we ourselves boast of you...for your steadfastness and faith in all your persecutions and in the afflictions which you are enduring" for love of the Church (cf. 2 Thes. 1:3ff.).

Your visit is a visible proof of communion and brotherly unity which, so desired by the Divine Master (cf. Jn. 17), is realized to the constant benefit of the one flock of Christ, gathered around its pastors.

This cause of deep communion within the Church, protecting it zealously and strengthening it by every possible means at every moment, is one of the essential aims of the meeting with the one who, as Successor of Peter and head of the apostolic college, is placed by divine will as the center and guarantee of unity in ecclesial faith and charity (cf. LG 23).

Therefore, while I express my deep joy at the union of minds and hearts that exists among you, I encourage you to preserve always this precious gift, so that, in all your initiatives and orientations as pastors, brotherly union may shine forth and that, as a reflection thereof, solidarity of intentions in the Christian communities entrusted to you may be strengthened.

2. The first field to which this experience of unity will be transferred very beneficially will be that of your priests, your most immediate collaborators in the care of souls. Here a truly ecclesial attitude is necessary, and the greater the needs of sufficient evangelizing forces, the more imperative it becomes. Precisely because these forces are insufficient today, it is increasingly necessary to avoid dispersion, which could be useless and even unproductive.

I am well aware that the concern to obtain an adequate number of Ecuadorian pastoral personnel is very much alive in your concern and programs as pastors. In fact, your sincere gratitude for the precious help you receive from other brother communities does not prevent you from being aware of the existing gap and of the necessity of a greater effort to obtain sufficient vocations for the priesthood and for consecrated life.

I encourage and bless with all my might these resolutions of yours, as well as your concern to obtain a suitable formation for all the apostolic personnel in the centers established by the Church at different levels. The careful dedication of the hierarchy to the promotion of these ecclesial centers, which can contribute so much to the good of your dioceses and the collective apostolate, cannot fail to yield outstanding fruits of evangelization, and is already doing so.

3. The aim that all engaged in the apostolate must set themselves is to bring about a really solid and deep evangelization, centered on Christ, the Son of God, the Redeemer and hope of man.

I know that you are studying carefully the Puebla Document, to which you wish to devote a national assembly, in order to apply its directives to the whole Church in Ecuador. It is a decision that merits my approval, since there are many concrete initiatives which it will help you to take in the important field of evangelization, which is the essential mission of the Church.

In the exercise of this mission, the concrete circumstances of the faithful must be kept in mind. Your people, in fact, have a good religious basis, which it has maintained admirably, in spite of the difficult experiences through which it has passed in the course of its history. The religious spirit of this people, the vast majority of which profess Catholicism, is frequently expressed in forms of popular piety, directed particularly to devotion to the Eucharist, to the Sacred Heart, to the Blessed Virgin and to the saints.

Keeping this in mind, it will be necessary to ensure an increasingly deep evangelization, taking advantage of this religious substratum, directing its manifestations, completing them and purifying them where necessary.

In this way you will enable the faithful to progress towards an adult faith, helping them to overcome the phenomena of secularization in its negative aspects of religious ignorance, indifferentism, practical or doctrinal materialism. In this way they will also be able to resist alien influences that may question their faithfulness to Christ and their convictions as Catholics; influences—as you well know—which are sometimes quite overt and against which the faithful must be immunized, so that they may always be aware of their faith and maintain the faithfulness promised.

Speaking of this evangelizing task, I wish to leave a word of special appreciation and encouragement for the missionary Church of your country, which is carrying out praiseworthy work. Let the most sincere thanks of the Pope and the Church, also in the form of a prayer, go to all those who generously dedicate themselves to it, even in the midst of serious environmental difficulties, and lack of personnel and means, and to all the religious families that devote such precious energies to this missionary effort, particularly the sisters, who sometimes write such admirable pages of ecclesial life.

4. Evangelizing work, which is the specific and primary task of the Church, must not, however, disregard what is its natural complement: concern for the social repercussion of the Gospel, which is geared to the human being, seen according to the divine plan. In fact, "the glory of God is living man" (cf. St. Irenaeus, *Adv. Haer.*, IV, 20, 7; P.G. 7:1037). And living according to the requirements of his dignity as a created being and son of God.

I know your sensitiveness as pastors in this field, attentive as you are to the process of transition from a prevalently agrarian civilization to an urban and industrial one; to the exodus of rural populations to the large centers of development, particularly Quito and Guayaquil; to the distribution of the national wealth, which sometimes remains palpably in the hands of the privileged. I know that you are hurt by the sight of excessive inequalities, which result in a few sectors of opulence alongside so many others of dire poverty, if not of want, which afflict whole strata of society, including most of the native population.

All that, in the framework of the new sources of wealth in your country, raises challenges for those who have to give guidance and an answer based on the Gospel, following the tradition of the great principles of the social teaching of the Church.

The document of the episcopate: "Social Justice in Ecuador" and the desired preferential option for the poor must become a vital reality, in the spirit of ecclesial communion of which I spoke before, and maintaining the irreplaceable balance between that action and pastoral solicitude which excludes no one, between evangelization and commitment for man. Only by keeping a clear vision of the Church and of the whole reality of man will it be possible to advance in the right way in this field, which is at once delicate and demanding.

5. Today, undoubtedly, youth is particularly sensitive in this field, to a greater extent than in past generations. It is necessary to be attentive to many just insights put forward by the young, for which they expect a due reply as well as a necessary answer to their anxieties and questions.

In the same way, the flourishing of youth movements, in which can be noted the pursuit of an intense spiritual life, are so many other factors that must serve the Church in Ecuador as a stimulus not to deceive newborn hopes.

That implies great attention to the work of human formation of the new generations, and their education in the Faith and in Christian witness. All this involves, in addition to the more directly pastoral sphere, also the school up to the highest level.

Since it is such an important field, the hierarchy and the whole Church in your country must commit themselves with all their energy to safeguard and renew their teaching centers, trying to give a truly human and Catholic education which, overcoming surrounding secular or materialistic trends, will form complete men, perfect Christians, with a great sense of service for the common good. There is here a fertile field of pastoral action and praiseworthy commitment also for lay people aware of their responsibility in the Church.

6. Looking to these great evangelizing and human aims in Ecuador, I have examined the projects that exist in the matter of social communications, in order to strengthen the voice of the Church and give it greater diffusion.

I warmly congratulate you on that and encourage you to continue in this direction, using all the means that technology offers us, to facilitate the spread of the saving truth, and the cultural and human education of the persons that lack means of formation most, in order to sustain and defend the family and the great values placed in it on behalf of society and the Church.

7. Beloved brothers: These are some reflections that spring from my intense love for the Church in Ecuador and for one and all of its members.

Tell them, on your return to your places of work, that the Pope appreciates their valor in the work of evangelization, their commitment to the Church in sacrifice, their testimony in hope, their faithfulness in practicing charity. My affection, remembrance in prayer, and my cordial blessing are extended to all.

Be Priests and Pastors of True Justice

On December 13, 1979, the Holy Father received in audience in the Sala Clementina about 70 participants in the seventh course for judges and officials of tribunals at the Pontifical Gregorian University.
After listening to the loyal address of homage given by the rector, Father Martini, the Pope delivered the following address.

Dear sons,

1. It gives us great joy to receive you all today, judges and officials of tribunals as well as the professors and

others who are giving the seventh renewal course. We extend a fatherly greeting to you. As we are about to speak freely with you, we are doing so willingly in response to your desire "to see Peter."

2. We have always regarded as important the work of justice in the Church. Its influence and importance are increasing from day to day. Because of this and following the example of our venerated Predecessor Paul VI, who on several occasions addressed those taking part in this renewal course, we wish to confirm this especially in his very own words. Together with him "we admit that we are very pleased that such men as yourselves, students of Canon Law, coming from various parts of the world, have followed this course so attentively and so diligently. Hence the confidence which we have in this institute of yours, providentially founded in our own Gregorian University, is clear to you. We see, not without fatherly consolation, that it is being even more effective."[1]

3. On this occasion we are very pleased to approve of and praise the new development of this faculty of Canon Law which has recently begun a special course in jurisprudence to encourage the practice of justice. It is right to support this venture with a word of praise and in a fatherly way to wish this special school and art of jurisprudence every success.

4. Finally, allow us to impress on your mind this sacred principle: Your office and your administration of justice is truly *priestly* and *pastoral* as the memorable Pope Paul VI also affirmed. You are "priests of justice" for in your noble ministry the light of God, who is absolute justice, shines forth, and your work as ecclesiastical judges serves and assists the members of the People of God who are experiencing difficulties.[2]

5. But this ministry is not really effective if Canon Law is not seen as hidden in the mystery of the Church,[3] if it is not cultivated as an element in the life of the Church, if it is not put at the service of redeemed man, if it is not proposed for the advancement of human dignity, and if it is

not understood in a manner that is in keeping with its proper character. For ecclesiastical law is not only a sign of human justice, it is also the expression of a deeper communion of life in Christ, in such a way that all canonical justice reflects charity just as canonical equity is itself the fruit of mercy and charity.

6. This divine charity, which regenerates redeemed man, reveals and throws light upon the true image of man. For man, created by God, is raised to the divine level so that he may recognize himself in God and portray his image in the love of the Trinity. It is necessary for all these things, which are illumined by a living faith, to shine forth in the life of the Church and also in your ministry. What would Church law be without charity? What would justice be without the defense of rights? What good would the defense of rights be if these rights were not applied sincerely and effectively? Apart from the solemn declaration of fundamental rights, what is more desirable today than the full recognition of these very rights? What more must one work for if not the true and genuine application of these rights?

7. Great importance must be given to the protection of rights especially in this age of ours in which the Church seems to be the sole guardian of redeemed man. "Christ the Redeemer...fully reveals man to himself. If we may use the expression, this is the human dimension of the mystery of the redemption."[4]

8. This truth concerning redeemed man must be preserved and protected especially in Christian marriage and in the Christian family. You especially are guardians of this holy Matrimony. You do not allow the indissoluble bond of love to be broken. You strive to keep intact the loving consent. You defend marriages that are valid. You respect marriages that are fruitful. You support spouses who are faithful so that you may not see their children scattered and abandoned.

9. Let this be your administration of justice which is a reflection of divine charity. For in Matrimony God has

placed these relationships of love which, in the very fruit of love, are reflected upon by mutual love and understood in their threefold purpose. For God created man, that is, man and woman, in His own image,[5] and He said to them, "Be fruitful and multiply."[6] Let no one destroy such a unity of love, for what God has joined together let no man put asunder,[7] and let no one abandon those whom mutual love has generated when they are deprived of their parents by death. This is a great sacrament which reveals the divine life by which man becomes an image of God.[8]

10. This dignity of marriage is entrusted to you as ministers of divine justice in a special way, so that it may be kept spotless, so that the Church may always see in this great sacrament a reflection of her own life in which Christ is the Spouse of the Church.

Beloved sons, we wanted to say this to you briefly and in all charity to give you courage, to strengthen your service to the Church and to make your ministry more fruitful. We confirm all these things with our apostolic blessing and we confidently commit them to almighty God.

Footnotes

1. Paul VI, Allocution to the participants in the Third Course of Canonical Renewal for judges and other members of tribunals, December 14, 1974, in *AAS*, 66 (1974), 10.

2. Allocution to the S.R. Rota on February 17, 1979, in *AAS*, 71 (1979) 422-427. See p. 423 text of Paul VI and *AAS*, 57 (1967) 234; Allocution to S.R. Rota, February 8, 1973, in *AAS*; 65 (1973), 101.

3. Cf. *Optatam totius*, no. 16a.

4. Encyclical letter *Redemptor hominis*, no. 10 in *AAS*, 71 (1979), 274.

5. Gn. 1:27.

6. Gn. 1:28.

7. Mt. 19:6.

8. Gn. 1:26.

Live Your Vocation with Authenticity, Intensity

On December 13, 1979, the Holy Father received in audience a group of Ecclesiastical Assistants of International Catholic Organizations, gathered at Villa Cavalletti, Grottaferrata, to discuss the subject "The role of Ecclesiastical Assistants in Associations of the Faithful." At the beginning of the audience, Cardinal Opilio Rossi, the President of the Pontifical Council for the Laity, the organizer of the gathering, delivered an address of homage to John Paul II, who replied as follows.

1. I welcome you, Lord Cardinal, your permanent collaborators, and the Consultants of the Pontifical Council for the Laity, and all of you, Ecclesiastical Assistants of numerous International Catholic Organizations and Associations, gathered in Rome for the first time on the initiative of the Council.

I hope that these few days of a meeting that has been most successful will produce good fruits for each of you and for the Organizations to which you give the best of your talents and priestly dedication.

AWARENESS OF VOCATION

2. I will recall to you in the first place a consideration of the letter I addressed to you on Holy Thursday of this year, 1979, a consideration which must constantly bring you joy, hope and spiritual comfort.

When a priest, in the course of his life, stops for a moment and casts a glance at his priesthood, he cannot help marveling at the abundance of grace that was given to him with the Sacrament of Holy Orders. Priests who exert themselves in the work that has been entrusted to them, whatever it may be: parish ministry, teaching, formation, if they remain aware of their vocation as priests and endeavor to act in everything and everywhere as priests, can see in the immense variety of their fields of action the supernatural fruitfulness of priestly grace that passes through them.

OPPORTUNITY FOR GROWTH

3. As for you, dear brothers, the Lord calls you for the moment to exercise your ministry as priests, full time or part time, in the very special field of ecclesiastical assistance to International Catholic Organizations and Associations.

There is no need for me to tell you the sincere esteem of the Church for the ICO. These Organizations, very varied, gathered in a conference for over fifty years, have a twofold aspect, which constitutes their value. On the one hand, thanks to their apostolic, spiritual or charitable aims, they make it possible for the Church to carry out her mission of salvation in the world; on the other hand, thanks to the status that some of them have, they ensure a special form of the Church's presence where the complex, delicate and important play of international life at its different levels is brought to bear decisively.

These Organizations and the other Associations which bear an identical witness are mostly made up of lay people, who must find in them the possibility of growing in their faith and in their apostolic commitment, and at the same time the means of taking part in the life and mission of the Church.

AUTHENTICITY MEANS NO TURNING BACK

4. Here, dear friends, is a field in which the grace of your priesthood can be exercised admirably if you prove capable of living your vocation as ministers of Jesus Christ with authenticity and intensity.

Authenticity means accepting your state as priests without turning back and unreservedly, this state of which you dreamed when you were young, for which you prepared lovingly, and which you accepted enthusiastically the day when the bishop and the presbyterium laid their hands on you. This state as priests gives you a clear and precise identity within the Church and in the midst of the

People of God. This identity must not be watered down, blurred or exchanged. It is necessary, on the contrary, to illuminate it and show it to the eyes of everyone.

In the organizations and associations which you serve—make no mistake about it!—the Church wishes you to be priests, and the lay people that you meet in them wish you to be priests and nothing but priests. Confusion of charisms impoverishes the Church; it does not enrich it in any way. Priests, be therefore within these groups architects of communion; educators in faith; witnesses to God's absoluteness; true apostles of Jesus Christ; ministers of sacramental life, especially of the Eucharist; the spiritual animators that the laity need both for their formation and to enlighten them in their commitment, which is often very difficult and even risky.

FERVOR OF SPIRIT DEFINES INTENSITY

5. *Intensity* is nothing but the fervor of spirit with which you must live your vocation with regard to the men and women whose pastors you are in your capacity as Ecclesiastical Assistants of important International Catholic Organizations and Associations. Is it necessary to remind you: the apostolic vitality and dynamism, the capacity of commitment, the effectiveness of the action of these communities or groups depend to a very large extent, when all is said and done, on the human and evangelical value to which your priestly life testifies.

6. You are not alone. Rest assured that the Pope follows your activities, which are very near to the concerns, the projects and the activities of the Holy See insofar as the latter is a major expression of the catholicity of the Church. Remain united with your bishops, your major superiors and, through them, with your spiritual families. Try to interest the other priests that you meet in your work; share with them your concerns and your achievements. Find among the lay people for whom you work a new lease of spiritual energy for your priesthood and for

your life. And I add: enrich all that by trying to meet one another as often as possible, to enlighten one another about your task, to help one another to grow in spirituality and missionary fervor, and to encourage one another. These meetings may be decisive for the authenticity and intensity of your priesthood. The Pontifical Council for the Laity will not refuse, I am certain, to help you to meet in this way.

May Christ the Priest, from whom there flows the immense grace of our priesthood, always be with you and assist you in your ministry. May He bless you. In His name, I give you the apostolic blessing, as a token of abundant divine graces.

Conform Always to the Image of Christ the Priest

On December 13, 1979, the Holy Father, John Paul II, paid a visit to the Pontifical Mexican College in Rome and delivered the following address.

Lord Cardinals; beloved brothers in the episcopate, superiors and students,

Allow me in the first place to express my most sincere appreciation and gratitude to Cardinals Miguel Dario Miranda and Ernesto Corripio Ahumada, as well as to my bishop confreres present here, for the special gesture of delicacy they have wished to make by coming from Mexico deliberately to be present at this meeting.

I feel particular joy at having the opportunity today of talking, even if only for a short time, with the numerous community of the Pontifical Mexican College of Rome, which I see as a kind of spiritual prolongation of those lands, distant geographically, but always so close to me, which I had the pleasure of visiting on my first apostolic journey outside Italy.

I wished to come to this college precisely to recall that visit which I paid to the beloved Mexican nation nearly a year ago. They were unforgettable days, during which the Mexican people, gathered in large multitudes, gave such an eloquent proof of warm and affectionate closeness to the Vicar of Christ, of joy at the first visit of a Pope, of communion around the religious and spiritual values which his presence signified.

All those manifestations of affection and so many others later, repeated throughout the year, have renewed in my heart feelings of deep appreciation and gratitude. They are feelings that I am very happy to manifest in this place, so significant of a distinguished presence of the Church of Mexico in Rome.

In this city, the See of the Pope and the center of the Catholic world, you are present, beloved priests and seminarians, to complete your ecclesial formation and then put yourselves at the service of your brothers, with richer experience and scientific preparation.

I wish to encourage you to take good advantage of the time that is now granted to you, in order to respond to the trust of your respective Ordinaries who have sent you here, to strengthen yourselves in that permanent docility to the teachings of the Magisterium which, in this environment, resound with particular intensity, and to adapt yourselves more and more to the figure of the priest who is able to integrate himself in the world of today, fully conscious of the needs of the present moment and with real interior strength which directs and determines all the activities of his own ecclesial service.

In this connection, I wish to repeat to you what I said to your confreres in the basilica of Guadalupe: "This high and exacting service cannot be carried out without a clear and deep-rooted conviction of your identity as priests of Christ, depositaries and administrators of God's mysteries, instruments of salvation for men, witnesses of a kingdom which begins in this world but is completed in the next" (Address to priests, no. 3).

With this clear perception of yourselves and your mission, nourish in prayer and the practice of the sacraments the vision of faith which must continually renew you in generous commitment to the Church and to man, your brother.

Nor can we forget that this meeting of ours takes place in the immediate proximity of the feast of Our Lady of Guadalupe, to whom every Mexican professes ardent devotion. Let it be she who guides you and teaches you the way to joyful and ready self-giving for the Church and for others.

I commend you in a repeated prayer to her, before whose image I had the happiness to pray in the new basilica, in that "sanctuary of the people of Mexico," in order that you may always succeed in conforming to the image of Christ the Priest.

With these wishes and hope, I impart with great affection a special blessing to you, to your superiors and to the sisters who exert themselves for you and to all the members of the Mexican community of Rome.

The Church Today in Defense of the Dignity of Every Person

On December 22, 1979, the Holy Father received the Sacred College of Cardinals, the Pontifical Household, the Curia and the Roman Prelature for the usual presentation of greetings on the eve of the Christmas festivities. At the beginning of the meeting, Cardinal Carlo Confalonieri, Dean of the Sacred College, delivered an address of homage to the Holy Father. John Paul II replied as follows.

Lord Cardinals,
Beloved brothers!

1. I am very grateful to the Cardinal Dean for his words of greeting, in which I felt the beat of his noble heart, and of yours, too, who have gathered here. May the

Lord reward his thoughtfulness. On this very special occasion, which is renewed every year, we feel more deeply the meaning and the riches of the approaching Christmas. Jesus is coming; He is now at the door. The heavenly Father makes us a gift of Him, the gift par excellence, in which we have all gifts, in the order of nature and of grace: He, who "in many and various ways spoke of old to our fathers,...in these last days has spoken to us by a Son, whom he appointed the heir of all things, through whom also he created the world" (cf. Heb. 1:1f.). And Mary, His Immaculate Mother, bears Him in her womb to offer Him to us who are represented by the shepherds of Bethlehem, and the Wise Men from the East; she offers Him for the salvation of all men. This hour, shared together, in a harmony of affection and prayer, with our hearts turned towards the holy cave, is full of joy and encouragement for me and for you, my beloved collaborators. And I thank you sincerely for this.

2. But I feel the whole Church present with you here: in her pastors, venerated brothers in the episcopate, in the priests, men and women religious, and all the faithful. The whole Church is preparing for Christmas and will live it again before long in the stupendous and mysterious bond of the holy Mysteries. And today my greeting goes to the whole Church, as well as my sincere "thank you" for the good wishes that have reached me from the five continents. Last year, on this same occasion—and it was my first Christmas with you in this See of Peter—I mentioned the commitment assumed, by divine mandate, in favor of the whole Church: "a commitment of dedication and love" (*AAS* 71, 1979, p. 50). And as the year is now fast approaching its end, I feel I can say that I have tried, humbly, simply, but with all my strength, using every opportunity offered to me, to remain faithful to that commitment, being well aware of my responsibilities before God.

My greeting and good wishes go, furthermore, to our brothers of the Christian communities, which are not yet in full communion with us. They go to members of non-Christian religions, particularly to those that worship the One, almighty God. My good wishes go to the heads of state of the whole world, to those responsible for the destinies of mankind, to politicians. They go to every person who lives, works, rejoices or suffers on the entire face of the earth.

3. The essential proclamation of Christmas is the Incarnation of the Son of God. The Word of the Father becomes flesh and dwells among us (cf. Jn. 1:14). He comes for man. For every man. "When the time had fully come, God sent forth his Son, born of woman...so that we might receive adoption as sons" (Gal. 4:4). As the Fathers and theologians of ancient times often pointed out, God becomes man in order that man may become God. The coming Christmas will be that "today" on which this "admirable exchange" takes place. A "today" that will never pass away, as long as a man is born on earth, bearing imprinted on his person, beyond his intrinsic frailty as an earthly creature, the royal image and likeness to God, the dignity of a son of the Father, redeemed by Christ. For this reason Jesus is born, in this "today" of Christmas, on which an Eastern writer comments so well: "On this day the Lord, the life and salvation of men, was born. Today the reconciliation of divinity with humanity, and of humanity with divinity, was carried out.... Today the death of darkness and the life of man took place. Today a way was opened for men towards God and a way for God towards the soul.... Beforehand, indeed, the whole of creation uttered a cry, swept along towards the corruption of the fall of Adam, who was master of created reality. But the Lord came to renew, as is fitting, the true image of God and to recreate it.... Today there is accomplished the union, communion and reconciliation between heavenly realities and earthly ones: God and man" (Ps. Macarius, Hom. 52, 1, *Macarii Anecdota*, ed. G.L. Marriott, Cambridge 1918, p. 24f.).

THE "REDEEMER OF MAN" IS BORN

The "Redeemer of man" is born. Humanity is born with Him. And the Church is born with Him, as Saint Ambrose stressed, commenting on the nativity of Christ: "Look at the beginnings of the Church that emerges: Christ is born, and the shepherds (that is, the bishops) begin to keep vigil in order to gather the flocks of the Gentiles in the Lord's hall" *(Exp. Ev. sec. Luc.* 2:50; *PL* 15, 1571). It is up to the Church, owing to her original mission, born at the birth of Christ, and received from Him with a solemn mandate, to defend the dignity of man: "of *each* man"—as I wrote in my first encyclical—"for each one is included in the mystery of the redemption, and with each one Christ has united Himself for ever through this mystery. Every man comes into the world through being conceived in his mother's womb and being born of his mother and, precisely on account of the mystery of the redemption, is entrusted to the care of the Church. Her care is for the whole man and is focused on him in an altogether special manner. The object of her care is man in his unique, unrepeatable human reality..." (RH 13).

4. This point of view, at once theological and existential, has been the leading motif, with God's help, of the first year of my pontificate. It is a line which, announced by the allocution at the solemn beginning of the pontificate, on October 22, 1978, assumed concrete shape in the encyclical mentioned above, in a trajectory that passes through the homily delivered at Drogheda, in Ireland, and arrives, as applied to life and to international problems, at the address to the Thirty-Fourth Assembly of the United Nations, in New York, on October 2, 1979. In fact, as I took the liberty of reminding the illustrious representatives of the whole world: "This relationship is what provides the reason for all political activity, whether national or international, for in the final analysis this activity comes from man, is exercised by man and is for man. And if political activity is cut off from this fundamental relationship and

finality, if it becomes in a way its own end, it loses much of its reason to exist. Even more, it can also give rise to a specific alienation; it can become extraneous to man; it can come to contradict humanity itself" (no. 6).

THE VOICE OF THE CHURCH AND MAN

I call to mind all this, in the vigilant expectation that characterizes this last period of Advent, to recall once more, together with Christ's mission of salvation entrusted to the Church, and perpetuated by her through the centuries, the intrinsic dignity of man, which must be served thoroughly. And if I have taken the liberty of quoting some sentences, both from the encyclical and from the address delivered in New York—at this meeting which deals mainly with the problems of the whole of mankind, leaving for another occasion, halfway through the new year, the treatment of the problems of the Church *ad intra*—it is because I see, and we all see, that the precious dignity of man, of every man, our brother, is not always respected as it should be.

5. At my meeting with the representatives of all the nations of the world, in New York, I recalled from that great forum the necessity of proclaiming and defending the "inalienable rights" of persons and of the communities of peoples. There are problems that challenge us in all their gravity; and the Church has the right and the duty to intervene, if she wishes to remain faithful to her mission which, in Christ (born for us), is geared to the salvation of the whole man and of every man. The Church asks nothing but the possibility of cooperating with all regimes and peoples, of any tendency and ideology whatsoever, for the constant improvement of mankind.

Actually, the various journeys that divine Providence has permitted me to carry out this year have also clearly indicated this dimension, this primary vocation of the Church in the modern world. It was not just a question, in fact, of contacts with the People of God, with this magnificent reality which constitutes and prolongs on earth the kingdom of heaven and prepares its definitive radiation; but those pilgrimages in nations and peoples so different in tradition, culture, intellectual and social formation, sociopolitical character, and form of government, afforded the opportunity to greet the illustrious representatives of those numerous states, at meetings rich in warmth and human and social significance. It was an absolutely positive expression which, better than any words, served to create a real and concrete rapprochement, nay more, a universal brotherhood among peoples, and to throw back further and further all kinds of barriers which divide the various systems from one another.

Thus, in this light there finds its *raison d'être* the network of relations that the Holy See maintains in the world, both through its own pontifical representations, in the service of the local Churches and of the nations in which they work, and in the Pope's contacts with heads of state and with the qualified representatives of governments and of the political life of the various peoples. And I am happy to mention the large number of ambassadors to the Holy See, a good many of whom I have received in the last few days for the presentation of the Letters of Credence.

6. In such a wide perspective of the actual possibility of the Church to establish a constructive dialogue with the forces that rule the world, she feels the duty to raise her voice for the defense of human rights. It is certainly not an interference in the internal affairs of states, nor an undue appropriation of tasks that are not hers, far less a mere rhetorical evocation of words, but not of facts.

The rights of man—as set forth in that fundamental "Universal Declaration of Human Rights," in 1948, which I desired to recall, from the platform of the United Nations—meet, unfortunately, with various obstacles in the world, which limit them and paralyze them, when they do not openly violate them and actually suppress them. Never has the dignity and the right of man to life fit for him been exalted so much, but never, too, have these declarations been belied so openly as today.

INTERNATIONAL TENSIONS

I am referring to international tensions which, unfortunately, still exist. To the wars and upheavals which, in addition to leading to very serious economic difficulties, have above all brought with them a tragic train of death and destruction. I am thinking of the internal struggles in which some nations are floundering, of the violation of unshakable principles of international law, causing very serious suffering to the persons concerned and to their families.

I am thinking of the dark and terrible plots of terrorism, which threaten the society of nations so dear to us, such as beloved Italy, and which, if they are not a real and veritable war, are a wicked and fierce substitute for it. I recall with horror the seizures, extortions, robberies; I think of the kidnapped, who suffer unspeakably, sometimes for long months.

In this context I cannot fail to recall the points of greatest danger in some parts of the world: the persistent crisis in the Middle East; the situation in South Africa; the strife in the Indo-Chinese peninsula: and here again one thinks of the miserable human caravans, wandering over the wide seas or in search of asylum, political refugees, exiles, prisoners, whose situation is and remains very painful owing to lack of food, clothes, housing, work, and above all, of any security for the future. The refugees are the real poor of today on the international plane, to whom is due the solidarity of all peoples, because the latter are all blessed with a better destiny, and cannot close their eyes to the tragedy of the refugees.

As I already said at the United Nations, the problem of armaments, too, is still one of very serious proportions, because "being ready (for war) means being able to start it" (Address to the United Nations, no. 10). It is an increasing outlay of means that are socially unproductive, which causes fatal psychological consequences in relations among states and in the internal life of the states themselves. In this context, the installation of more and more perfected arms, which, though conceived as an instrument of defense can become a source of destruction and ruin, cannot but arouse rightful concern.

HONEST PURSUIT OF GOOD AND TRUTH

In my recent message for the World Day of Peace, inspired by the principle that truth is the source of peace, I referred to various forms of "non-truth" which mortify man and make brotherly concord more and more difficult and problematical. What I mentioned above is also part of this framework of search for everything that can harm universal peace today precisely because it is opposed to the honest pursuit of good and truth, also in relations between peoples. In this Christmas message, therefore, I point out the need "to dig deep within ourselves, and going beyond the divisions we find within us and between us, to find the areas in which we can strengthen our conviction that man's basic driving forces and the recognition of his real nature carry him towards openness to others, mutual respect, brotherhood and peace. The course of this laborious search for the objective and universal truth about man and the result of the search will develop men and women of peace and dialogue, people who draw both strength and humility from a truth that they realize they must serve, and not make use of for partisan interests" (Message for World Day of Peace, no. 4).

THE CHURCH WITH SUFFERING MAN

7. The situations to which I have referred above are situations of hardship, are the source of sorrow. Today men are suffering. How much, how very much suffering there is in the world when it is forgotten that man is our brother! The Church, then, looking to the mystery of the Son of God made Man—and exposed as He was, owing to the injustice of men, to suffering and hunger, to poverty and exile—the Church cannot refuse to intervene, to commit herself, to become involved in order to help men, to

spare the suffering of men. Wherever a man suffers, Christ is there waiting in his place (cf. Mt. 25:31-46). Wherever a man suffers, the Church must be there at his side.

All that I mentioned above—threats and situations of war, terrorism, the problem of refugees—presents to our spirit a terrible weight of human pain.

I should mention, too, all that is a source of imbalance and hardship in the world, which offends the intrinsic dignity of man, because he is humiliated and wounded, and suffers for himself and for his dear ones. I am referring to blatant social inequalities, which still exist today. If, as the Second Vatican Council said, "man is the source, the focus and the end of all economic and social life" (GS 63), there remain in all their seriousness the "disturbing elements" that the Council denounced with absolute sincerity, speaking even of "a decline in the position of the underprivileged and contempt for the poor. In the midst of huge numbers deprived of the absolute necessities of life"—*Gaudium et spes* went on—"there are some who live in riches and squander their wealth" *(ibid.)*. Consequently, in some countries, people are dying of starvation today. These innocent victims can be counted in millions every year. How can we think of the imminent joy of Christmas before such atrocious, such inconceivable suffering? And this scourge, as we are well aware, brings with it a whole series of ills, which undermine the future development of whole populations: malnutrition, endemic diseases, inaction, want, despair. How could we fail to call for eager cooperation on the international scale? All peoples—who often destroy their products because of extraordinary market laws—must join together, even at the cost of sacrifice, to aid brothers who are suffering hunger. I recall here, with renewed intensity, what I had occasion to say at FAO, the organization of the United Nations which has as its prime purpose examination and solution of the problems of food and development in the world, both at the audience in July 1979, on the occasion of the Conference for Agrarian Reform, and in the visit I paid on last November 11. It is not possible to remain insensitive to a field of action of such great importance, which concerns whole vast areas of the earth.

Nor can I forget at this moment the unemployed, the underemployed, those who are finding it difficult to eke out a livelihood, with all the problems that grow in a delicate and economic moment such as the present one. The approach of Christmas makes the hearts of so many mothers and fathers sink, because their children will lack the joy, not of superfluous gifts, but of material tranquillity, perhaps of survival.

I think, too, of the suffering of the anonymous multitude of the humble, in every country, caused by sudden variations of the terms of trade, by the exorbitance of certain supplies, which lead to the increasing cost of the most elementary things of life, to the extent of producing very serious hardship in family and social life.

TRUE DIMENSIONS OF RELIGIOUS LIBERTY

8. But there are sources of more intimate suffering, which cannot be detected by statistical enquiries, and which deeply harm man's interior grandeur and nobility, because they prevent him from pursuing his highest and inalienable rights. I enumerated the most important of these rights in the address to the United Nations, mentioning among them "the right to life, liberty and security of person; the right to food, clothing, housing, sufficient health care, rest and leisure; the right to freedom of expression, education and culture; the right to freedom of thought, conscience and religion, and the right to manifest one's religion either individually or in community, in public or in private" (no. 13). In particular I would like to stress today precisely this right to religious liberty, sacred for all men, for which the Second Vatican Council made a solemn appeal: "Freedom of this kind"—the Declaration *Dignitatis humanae* said—"means that all men should be immune from coercion on the part of individuals, social

groups and every human power so that, within due limits, nobody is forced to act against his convictions in religious matters in private or in public, alone or in associations with others" (no. 2).

I must say that this is, unfortunately, a real problem, and a serious problem, for the life of different peoples in the world. In many countries the true dimensions of religious liberty do not exist. It is difficult to understand, for example, how the concept of scientific and social development can be considered bound up with the imposition of an atheistic program today. This continues to be the case in certain countries in the world, creating in actual fact, as I stressed further in the address to the United Nations, "structures of social life...in which the practical exercise of these freedoms condemns man, in fact if not formally, to become a second-class or third-class citizen" (no. 19). That causes deep suffering, incurable wounds, unrestrainable groans in the consciences of millions of persons, upright and just, who see the deepest aspirations of their spiritual being clipped away. The Pope is close to all these suffering brothers and sisters, with his sympathy, affection and prayer: he would like to reassure them that he neglects no opportunity to speak of their situation to those in charge whom he meets in his ministry. And today he lets everyone hear the just requirement that the Church and the Holy See should enjoy peacefully the right to help the faithful and priests all over the world: and this because she is animated only by the determination to help man, to facilitate his path in life, to raise his whole person to the horizons of the human and supernatural dignity to which he is called by God, in free and consistent exercise of his own convictions. The Church should be able to carry out her mission under every sky, in respect of mutual freedoms but also in the performance of her own indefeasible rights, as they are proclaimed in the Gospel. In this connection my thought returns with special affection to the great Chinese people, whom I already recalled on Sunday, August 19 of this year, at the recitation of the *Angelus*. As Christmas draws near, I send my greeting and my good wishes to the sons of the Catholic Church, as to all the members of that great nation, renewing "the hope that there may be positive developments, which will mark for our brothers and sisters of the Chinese continent the possibility of enjoying full religious freedom."

INTERNATIONAL YEAR OF THE CHILD

9. The International Year of the Child is drawing to a close, a year which brought to the center of universal interest the man of tomorrow, the man of the year 2000, who appears in life today with all his promises still in germ, and with all his expectations which cannot be disappointed. Very fine initiatives have flourished nearly everywhere, and that makes us hope that the problem will find space, at all levels, in the planning and concerns of politicians, sociologists, psychologists and pedagogues, doctors, teachers and men of culture, those responsible for the mass media; many have become promoters of worthwhile initiatives.

The Pope certainly cannot forget the tireless, loving and intelligent work of persons and charitable institutions, which is being carried out within the Church, often from inadequate means, but with an anxiety for the charity of Christ, which controls us (cf. 2 Cor. 5:14). Above all, my thought goes to the action of missionaries, whose evangelizing work is dedicated, in its educational and charitable aspects, precisely to the elevation and preparation of the growing generations. And I praise all that men and women, of every creed and religious conviction, are carrying out in the world, with a generous effort and an upright intention for the education and welfare of children.

But how could I fail to reaffirm solemnly that the life of the human being is sacred, from the time it springs into being below the mother's heart, at the moment of conception? How could I forget that, precisely in this year dedicated to the child, the number of lives suppressed in the mother's womb has reached frightful heights? It is a silent massacre, which cannot leave indifferent, not merely us ecclesiastics, but all Christian men and women of the whole world, and those in charge of the common good, persons concerned about the future of the nations. In the name of Jesus "living in Mary," borne by her in her womb in an indifferent and hostile world—in Bethlehem they refused to receive Him and in the kingdom of Herod His death was planned—in the name of that Child, God and Man, I beseech men, aware of the irrepressible dignity of those not yet born, to take up a position worthy of man, in order that this somber period that is threatening to shroud the human conscience in darkness may at last be overcome.

IN THE YOUNG IS THE HOPE OF TOMORROW

10. The International Year of the Child also comprises in its aims the human advancement of children and adolescents of both sexes, up to the threshold of youth. At this moment, therefore, my thought goes to the lively and joyful ranks of these dear boys and girls, who form the most joyful hope of the future all over the world. And further, following the growing generations, I also greet the immense host of young men and women of the whole world, the binding fabric of societies of every type, and a reserve of energies for the construction of a more just and serene future. This youth—in its various age-brackets which range from adolescence to the threshold of marriage—is upright, generous, and thirsty for truth and justice. It asks adults for acceptance with understanding and goodwill in operational sectors and vital managerial areas; it turns to the Church with renewed interest and with the deep desire for a clear answer to the fundamental "whys" of life. Today still, Christ looks in the eyes of these young people with sympathy, as He did with the young man in the Gospel (cf. Mk. 10:21).

In its search for certainties, youth cannot, must not be disappointed. I repeat to it the cry of the beginning of my pontificate: "Fling the doors wide open to Christ!" (October 22, 1978; *AAS* 70, 1978, p. 947) I know it will find a welcome! This is confirmed by my joyful and exalting contacts with so many young people to whom I have spoken, whose hands I have shaken, and with whom I have exchanged warm-hearted glances during this year, in Rome and in all parts of the world. I repeat to them: *the Church will never betray you, the Church will never disappoint you, the Church will always respect you* in your complete human personality. Do not be afraid.

But I am thinking also of the dark realities that threaten this very rich potential of life, adolescence and present-day youth, and which can change it into amorphous material, nay more, into a potential of destruction. How could I fail to recall that so many requests for work, cultural formation, professional employment, remain unheard, leaving in enforced inactivity so many young people, even though they have toiled and studied, and reached a preparation worthy of being utilized for the common good of society? And how could I fail to raise my voice vehemently against those who, in the background, ignobly, with perverse purposes, try to corrupt this stupendous youth with awful substitutes of betrayed values, with mortal enticements which, in an existence that is a prey to disappointment and sometimes empty of ideals, find an easy bait? How could I forget the innumerable victims of drugs, offered from the first years of adolescence, which then become an iron chain of shameful slavery? How could I forget the moral devastations, which an equally ignoble industry, or a permissive and hedonistic mentality —which permeates part of the publishing world and of the media of communication through the image—have produced in the spirit of so many young people, who take as their norm of life unbridled hedonism? How could I forget the manipulation of the personality of man in formation through the mass media, ideological indoctrination, the partial and distorted presentation of truth, pornography?

On all these alarming symptoms of moral regression there is grafted the factor of violence, in all its facets, which obeys solely a logic of destruction and death, and which might, God forbid, paralyze the common aspiration to orderly progress, constructive concord, industrious peace. To these young people, who today are not afraid to kill or wound other young people, other men, I address on my knees, like my Predecessor Paul VI, the cry of hope and the invitation that I let ring out at Drogheda: "I appeal to young people who may have become caught up in organizations engaged in violence. I say to you, with all the love I have for you, with all the trust I have in young people: do not listen to voices which speak the language of hatred, revenge, retaliation.... The true courage lies in working for peace. The true strength lies in joining with the young men and women of your generation everywhere in building up a just and human and Christian society by the ways of peace. Violence is the enemy of justice. Only peace can lead to true justice" (no. 12).

IMMENSE VALUE OF THE FAMILY

11. The formation of youth is inseparably bound up with a family life which works smoothly. The family, "the first and vital cell of society," as the Council defined it (AA 11), on which depends the fortunes or misfortunes of the society of the future, has, in fact, a continual and determining influence in the lives of the young, both in a negative and in a positive sense. So it cannot be absent from the order of reflection in this Christmas message, all the more so in that Christmas is *the* feast of Christian families, gathered round the crib in the simple joy that springs from true and deep union of hearts. The Holy Family, celebrated on the Sunday following Christmas, gives the key to understanding all the values that must be proclaimed to families of today: love, dedication, sacrifice,

chastity, respect for life, work, serenity and joy. The sources of imbalance, on the other hand, to which we have referred, make the family their first victim, and, with it, they sweep away youth. So much moral disorder, as so many acts of violence, spring precisely from the disengagement of the family, which is, unfortunately, the target of a coalition of disintegrating forces, which use all the means at their disposal.

In the journeys I carried out this year, if I got a good impression, it was certainly because the presence and work of Christian families are, as it were, the connecting tissue, the framework and the supporting structure of civil and ecclesial life all over the world. I thank the Lord for this, and with Him so many fathers and mothers throughout the world.

Also in defense of the values connected with the family, I lost no opportunity to raise the issues with the personalities whom I had occasion to meet during this year, including the leaders responsible for the life of nations, their diplomatic representatives and the civil and political authorities. And I spoke incessantly in favor of the family, on account of the various and complex problems it proposes to conscience and to society, in my addresses and appeals: in Mexico, in the homily at Puebla de los Angeles, in Poland at Jasna Gora, in the appeal and address to the workers, then at Nowy Targ, afterwards at Limerick in Ireland, and at Capitol Mall in the United States. Nor did I neglect reference to the catechetical action entrusted to the family, in the Exhortation *Catechesi tradendae* (no. 68). And I take the liberty of recalling the treatment I am carrying out at the general audiences, in preparation for the Session of the Synod of Bishops, which will take place next year, and will be dedicated to the family. It will be a very special opportunity, eagerly awaited by me, for the whole Church, through the representatives of her national episcopates, to pause and meditate and study the marvelous dignity of the family, the riches of its values, and the irreplaceable importance of its mission.

MEETING WITH CHRIST, WITH THE CHURCH, WITH MAN

12. Venerated brothers! This meeting while waiting for Christmas has permitted this general view of the most urgent and topical problems. I know that it is the indefeasible task of the Supreme Pastor of the Church to indicate the way to follow. And this way is Christ (cf. Jn. 14:6): He alone. Always Christ: *"Christus heri et hodie, ipse et in saecula"* (Heb. 13:8).

In this year of my pontificate, "the daily pressure upon me of my anxiety for all the churches" (2 Cor. 11:28) was solely that of meeting man, in order to let man meet Christ. The crowds that thronged to the Wednesday audiences week after week, the people I met on my pilgrimages, the weekly visits to the parishes of my Rome diocese, have given me the privilege of establishing this living contact, permitting a constant catechesis of the Magisterium, the lines of which I have laid down in the recent document *Catechesi tradendae*, which sums up the wishes expressed at the Synod of Bishops. It was a direct relationship with everyone: with living men, not with amorphous masses; with children and the young; with politicians; with workers in the various sectors, whom I visited also at their places of work; with people of the fields and of the mountains; with those in the scientific world—physicists, jurists, lecturers and university students; with the members of cultural and tourist institutions; with sailors; with those in aviation, and airline staffs that took me by air to the various continents; with the various sectors of the Armed Forces; etc. It was really a direct and personal meeting with the people of every country.

13. At the same time there was the meeting with the Church. She was instituted, in fact, by Christ for the salvation of man, every man, in the concrete situation of life. Today the Church is experiencing a really exalting moment of vitality, and is the center of orientation and interest for the whole world.

It was a very rewarding experience for me to meet this year the episcopates of most of the various continents: and if the charism of Peter and his Successors is *"confirmare fratres"* (cf. Lk. 22:32), no less great is the comfort I receive from the faith of these brothers, who come *"videre Petrum"* and to exchange the kiss of peace with him, in a brotherly embrace, in constant and strict exercise of episcopal collegiality, which is so dear to my heart. And above all the meeting with the members of the Sacred College—which aroused such joy, interest and participation in you first of all, venerated brothers who compose it—in consideration of the extraordinary nature of the event, was itself an expression of this collegiality.

Great joy fills my heart now, on recalling that a bishop of the Church of God, the esteemed Mons. Tchidimbo, has been restored to full freedom this year after a long period of suffering.

Nor can I forget the meetings and concelebrations with my beloved brothers in the priesthood, whom I love like the apple of my eye, and consider truly "my joy and crown" (Phil. 4:1) in their joyful, complete and irrevocable adherence to Christ, the sovereign and eternal Priest.

I have stamped on my heart the meetings with the religious of various congregations and institutes, and, among them, with the lay religious, and I rejoice in their special witness of love for Christ and for the Church.

In this way I recall the meetings with sisters, and I repeat to them all the confidence and expectation that the Church puts in them, in the exercise of a spiritual motherhood of offering and dedication, the source and inspiration of which is the Blessed Virgin, called to the noble dignity of Mother of God and of the Church, and provident Queen of the Apostles in the watchful silence of Nazareth, Calvary and the Upper Room.

There would not be time to recall the crowds of faithful met in the course of the year, in apostolic journeys and at audiences and visits, in Rome and throughout Italy.

ON THE WAY TO UNITY AMONG ALL CHRISTIANS

I wish to devote at least a brief reference to the effort to intensify the ties that unite the Catholic Church with the sister Churches of the Christian East, in pursuit of agreement and understanding, based on the charity of Christ and in common exaltation of divine glory. The instructions that the Second Vatican Council gave with regard to the delicate, difficult yet promising field of ecumenism, as one of its principal intentions for "the restoration of unity among all Christians" (UR 1), remain among the main commitments of the pontificate. In this spirit the embrace exchanged recently with the Patriarch of Constantinople, Dimitrios I, in whom I wished to embrace all the pastors and brothers of Christian Churches, took on special significance.

A SERVICE OF LOVE AND TRUTH

14. The office of the Supreme Magisterium in the Church, at this moment of great tensions but greater hopes, is that of offering man a service of love and truth. This was the spirit of the journeys I have carried out; and it will be that of the ones which, with God's help, I will undertake in the next year, for which invitations have reached me from the episcopal conferences and civil authorities of many countries. Expressing my thanks for such thoughtfulness, I give my assurance that I will satisfy as many as I can.

I ask the Lord to afford me the strength and assistance to continue along the way laid down by my unforgettable Predecessors: from the invincible and indomitable hope of John XXIII to the patience and heroic and far-sighted firmness of Paul VI, who will shine forth always for what he did for the Church in implementation of the Second Vatican Council; to the smile of John Paul I, who, in his swift passage, left a very deep furrow, reminding us once more that "the ways of God are not ours" (cf. Is. 55:8).

The Church continues on her way along this line, now, for the year that is about to begin, as for the future. Christ is with us, we do not fear, we do not hesitate: "Lo, I am with you always, to the close of the age" (Mt. 28:20).

I ENTRUST THE CHURCH TO MARY

15. All this, *per Mariam*. I entrusted the beginning of my pontificate to her, and I brought to her in the course of the year the expression of my filial piety, which I learned from my parents. Mary was the star of my way, in her most famous or most silent sanctuaries: Mentorella and St. Mary Major, Guadalupe and Jasna Gora, Knock and the national sanctuary of Mary Immaculate at Washington, Loreto, Pompei, Ephesus. I entrust myself to her. To her I entrust the whole Church, now ending a year and awaiting the dawn of the new one. With Mary, let us take the way to Bethlehem together.

Looking to the future, while reasons for anxiety are not lacking, reasons for confidence and hope are stronger and more outstanding. Supported by this hope, the Church continues her work. She remains faithful to Christ, to His Gospel, to His invitation to conversion, for "the kingdom of God is at hand" (Mk. 1:15). She will never tire of interceding with God for mankind, nor of intervening and paying the reckoning for the defense and ascent of man. Of the whole man, body and soul. Of every man (including the unborn child), because each man is the crown of creation (cf. Gn. 1:27ff.), each man is the living glory of God (cf. Eph. 1:12-14; St. Irenaeus, *Adv. Haer.* IV, 20, 7).

The Church continues to proclaim to the world this extraordinary reality: and tirelessly, without losing heart, she gathers her forces, advances in the world, proclaiming holiness, honor, the rights of God, and the grandeur of man. She walks in the light of God, in the joy of God. We are all involved in this pilgrimage. Let us go forward, let us walk and sing, as St. Augustine tells us: "Not to satisfy tranquillity, but to comfort fatigue. Let us do as travelers are wont to: sing, sing but walk; console weariness with song, do not be content with idleness; sing and walk.... Advance in good, advance in sound faith, advance in the good life; *Canta et ambula*" (Serm. 256, 3; PL 38, 1193).

In this walking may we always be guided by the star of Christmas, which leads to Jesus, the Son of God and the Son of Mary; to Jesus, the Redeemer of man.

The Episcopate: the Sacrament of the Way

On January 6, 1980, Feast of the Epiphany, Pope John Paul II conferred episcopal ordination on three bishops in St. Peter's Basilica. They were: Most Reverend Giovanni Coppa, titular Archbishop of Serta, Delegate for the Pontifical Representations throughout the world; Most Reverend Carlo Maria Martini, Archbishop of Milan, formerly Rector of the Gregorian University; Most Reverend Christian Tumi, Bishop of Yagoua (Cameroun). During the Mass the Holy Father preached the following homily.

1. "They offered him gifts...."

With this act the three Wise Men from the East carry out the purpose of their journey. It has brought them along the ways of those lands to which our attention is often drawn also by contemporary events. The three Wise Men were guided along these ways by that mysterious star "which they had seen in the East" (Mt. 2:9), and which "went before them, till it came to rest over the place where the child was" (Mt. 2:9). It was precisely to this Child that those unusual men went, called from outside the circle of the elect people to the ways of the history of this People.

The history of Israel had given them the order to stop at Jerusalem and ask—before Herod—the question: "Where is he who has been born king of the Jews?" (Mt. 2:2) In fact the ways of the history of Israel had been marked out by God—and therefore it was necessary to look for them in the books of the prophets: those who, in the name of God, had spoken to the people of its special vocation. And the vocation of the people of the covenant was precisely the One to whom the way of the Wise Men from the East led. As soon as they had asked that question in the presence of Herod, he had no doubt who—and what king—was meant, because, as we read, "assembling all the chief priests and scribes of the people, he inquired of them where the Christ was to be born" (Mt. 2:4).

In this way, therefore, the way of the three Wise Men leads to the Messiah, to Him whom the Father "consecrated and sent into the world" (Jn. 10:36). Their way is also the way of the Spirit. It is above all the Way of the Holy Spirit. Traveling along this way—not so much along the roads of the Middle East regions, as rather through the mysterious ways of the soul—man is led by the spiritual light coming from God, represented by that star, which the three Wise Men followed.

The ways of the human soul, which lead to God, bring it about that man finds an inner treasure in himself. Thus we read also of the three Wise Men, who, when they arrived in Bethlehem, "opened their treasures" (Mt. 2:11). Man becomes aware of what enormous gifts of nature and grace God has lavished upon him, and then there is born in him the need to offer himself, to give back to God what he has received, to make Him an offering of it as a sign of the divine donation. This gift takes on a threefold form—as in the hands of the three Wise Men:

"Opening their treasures, they offered him gifts, gold and frankincense and myrrh" (Mt. 2:11).

2. The episcopate, which you will receive from my hands today, venerated and beloved brothers, is a sacrament in which the gift must be manifested particularly. The episcopate, in fact, is the fullness of the Sacrament of Holy Orders, by means of which the Church opens, always before God, her greatest treasure—and from this treasure offers to Him the gifts of the whole People of God. The greatest treasure of the Church is her Bridegroom: Christ. Both Christ laid on straw in a manger, and Christ who dies on the cross. He is an inexhaustible treasure. The

Church continually stretches out her hand to this treasure to draw on it. And drawing on it, she does not diminish it, but increases it.

These are the principles of the Divine Economy. The Church, therefore, stretches out her hand to the treasure of the nativity and the crucifixion, to the treasure of the Incarnation and the Redemption. And drawing upon it, she does not impoverish that treasure but multiplies it.

The bishop is the administrator, at the same time, of that drawing and that multiplication.

He is a "steward of the mysteries of God" (1 Cor. 4:1). He is not just a Wise Man who walks along the impassable roads of the world towards the threshold of the mystery. He is set at its very heart. His task is to open this mystery and draw upon it. The more generously he draws, the more it multiplies.

Remember, beloved in Christ, that the Holy Spirit constitutes you in the midst of the Church today in order that, drawing abundantly on the treasure of the nativity and Redemption, you will multiply it with your life and your ministry.

3. Gold, incense and myrrh are always drawn from this treasure. Your life must be clad in this triple gift, since you are called to offer to God, in Christ and in the Church, your love, your prayer and your suffering. However, since you are constituted in the midst of the People of God as pastors and at the same time as servants, your personal gift must grow in this People. *"Fecit eum Dominus crescere in plebem suam."* Your vocation is the gift of the whole People. Each of you must remain the pastor and the servant of this love, prayer and suffering, which are raised by all hearts to God in Christ. Such gifts must not be wasted or lost. On the contrary, they must find their way to Bethlehem like the gifts in the hands of the Wise Men, who followed the star from the East.

Every bishop is the steward of the Mystery and the servant of the gift that is prepared incessantly in human hearts. This gift comes from the experiences of the generation to which the bishop himself belongs. It comes from the lives of hundreds, thousands and millions of men, his brothers and sisters. He himself, the bishop, is the servant of the gift, he who guards and who multiplies. You must penetrate deeply into the whole complexity of the lives of modern men, in order that what constitutes it will not be broken up in their works, their hearts, social relations and movements of civilization, but constantly find again its meaning as a gift. Christ Himself is the Pastor and Bishop of our souls, of all that is human, that desires to make us a perennial sacrifice pleasing to God (cf. Third Eucharistic Prayer), a gift to the Father.

The bishop is he who guards the gift, he who awakens the gift in hearts, in consciences, in the difficult experiences of his age, in its aspirations and in its bewilderment, in its civilization, in economy and in culture.

4. Today the three Wise Men come to Bethlehem from the East. They arrive by the way of faith. Can it not be said of the episcopate that it is a sacrament of the way? You receive this sacrament to find yourselves on the way of so many men, to whom the Lord sends you; to undertake this way together with them, walking, like the Wise Men, following the star; and how often to make them see the star again, which in some places has ceased to shine, in some places has gotten lost...to show it to them again!

Enter, you, too, dear brothers, this great way of the Church, which is marked out by the apostolic succession to the individual episcopal sees.

What shall I say here of the marvelous, rich succession to the see of St. Ambrose and then of St. Charles in Milan? It goes back roughly to the first decades of Christianity and abounds in martyr bishops...and, in our own century, has given the Church two Popes: Pius XI and Paul VI. Cardinal Giovanni Colombo, present here, received this see of Milan precisely after Paul VI, the then-Cardinal Giovanni Battista Montini, to transmit it today, when his strength is weakening, to his successor. With joy the Church of Milan greets this successor, a worthy son of St. Ignatius, the esteemed Rector of the *Biblicum* and then of the Gregorian University in Rome. With joy and trust the Church of Milan greets him who is to be its new bishop and pastor, the new steward of the gift, of which I have spoken, and the new witness to the star, that star which leads infallibly to Bethlehem.

The Holy See, too, greets with satisfaction its well-deserving son, former Official of the Apostolic Chancellery and for long years dedicated to the service of the Secretariat of State, as well as a zealous minister of God in so many works of the apostolate, who today receives episcopal ordination as titular Archbishop of Serta, to carry out the duties of Delegate for the Pontifical Representations.

We then greet the son of Africa, the new pastor of the young and dear Church of Yagoua in Cameroun, who up to today has dedicated himself, in his diocese of origin, as rector of the regional Major Seminary of Bambui and as a generous collaborator in various pastoral activities; and with him we address our cordial thought to the whole African continent.

5. The episcopate is the sacrament of the way. It is the sacrament of the many ways that the Church traverses, following the star of Bethlehem, together with every man.

Enter these ways, venerated and dear brothers, carry along them gold. Carry them with humility and with confidence. Carry them with courage and with constancy. May the inexhaustible treasure be opened, by means of your service, to new people, new environments, new times, with the ineffable riches of the Mystery that was revealed to the eyes of the three Wise Men, who came from the East, on the threshold of the stable in Bethlehem.

May the Teaching of the Council Guide Our Thoughts and Actions

The Synod of the Dutch Bishops started on January 14, 1980, with a Eucharistic concelebration presided over by the Holy Father. John Paul II delivered the following homily.

1. Today our thoughts and hearts turn to the Lord, who is the Shepherd of the Church.

It is He who is announced in the psalm of today's liturgy with words of peace and joy.

"The Lord is my shepherd, I shall not want; / he makes me lie down in green pastures. / He leads me beside still waters, he restores my soul. / He leads me in paths of righteousness for his name's sake" (Ps. 22[23]:1-3).

It is to Him, therefore, to Jesus Christ, that our thoughts and hearts turn because He is, above all, our Shepherd.

He is the Shepherd of the whole Church and of all Churches. He is the Shepherd of shepherds. The Shepherd of those to whom He entrusts pastoral solicitude for everything concerning the Church. He entrusts to them..., He entrusts to us this pastoral ministry which is nothing but service.

We have inherited from the Apostles this consciousness of the pastoral ministry. Through it we try to direct our behavior in relation to God and in relation to men, fixing our eyes on Christ.

Is there anything more marvelous than this image of the Shepherd, the Good Shepherd, which He Himself showed us as the model to imitate? This image emerges already in the prophet Isaiah when he speaks of the *Servant of the Lord* on whom God has made His Spirit to repose (42:1).

"He will not cry or lift up his voice / or make it heard in the street; / a bruised reed he will not break, / and a dimly burning wick he will not quench." And he adds: "He will faithfully bring forth justice" (42:2-3).

KEEPING THE TRUTH

2. However, at the end of all of the images known by Holy Scripture, there is this reality which is Christ Himself. He expressed it in the parable of the Good Shepherd and He realized it at the same time through all His works. He accomplished it above all in His last work, through which He offered His life for His sheep (cf. Jn. 10:11).

To prepare His Apostles for this work which is the paschal summit of His mission, He talked to them at length, and the evangelist St. John has handed down to us, in particular, His last speech. The words that we read in the Gospel today are part of it.

"If a man loves me, he will keep my word, and my Father will love him, and we will come to him and make our home with him. He who does not love me does not keep my words; and the word which you hear is not mine but the Father's who sent me" (Jn. 14:23-24).

Could Christ have laid a greater obligation on us, as shepherds and teachers of the Church, than the one contained in these words?

To be a pastor and bishop of souls, that means keeping the word. Keeping the truth. In it, it is the Father and He who comes continually to us: He who is the Word Incarnate; He who is Christ the Redeemer; He who is the eternal Shepherd of souls.

And He is above all the Shepherd of shepherds.

HEARING THE COUNCIL

3. In the same farewell speech of which we have just read a short passage today, Christ promises the Apostles the Holy Spirit, who is the Spirit of love and truth:

"But the Counselor, the Holy Spirit, whom the Father will send in my name, he will teach you all things, and bring to your remembrance all that I have said to you" (Jn. 14:26).

Here is the Church living by the Holy Spirit. The mouthpiece of this certainty is Paul of Tarsus in his letter to the Corinthians where he shows how, through the power of this Spirit, there is constructed this community which, in Christ, gathers as in one Mystical Body all those who "were made to drink of one Spirit" (1 Cor. 12:13).

In our difficult age, in our twentieth century, this Church has given, in the teaching of the Second Vatican Council, a particularly full expression of the truth about herself.

This teaching must be the measure of thought and action for all those who make up Christ's Church.

It must be, in particular, the measure of our own action, we who are the teachers and shepherds of the Church.

It must be the measure of our thought and action, of us who are gathered for this particular synod. The reason for this synod is nothing but a true and complete incarnation, in life, of this apostolic truth about the Church, which was shown in the teaching of the Second Vatican Council. It must remain its content, its inspiration and its purpose, from beginning to end.

UNPRECEDENTED EVENT

4. The synodal assembly in the course of which the bishops of the ecclesiastical Dutch Province meet the Bishop of Rome is an unprecedented event. We all realize this. The Synods of Bishops have already their multi-annual rhythm; on the contrary, a synod of this kind, a particular synod, is taking place for the first time.

The principle of the mutual penetration of the universal Church and the local Church is expressed especially in this synod. The Church of Jesus Christ, thanks to the

Spirit who is the soul of the whole body and all the members, is realized in these two dimensions. She is universal and at the same time composed of different parts. She is universal and local. The purpose of our meeting is to show the coherence of these two entire dimensions and to consolidate them.

That is why our thoughts and our hearts turn particularly to Christ: "For just as the body is one and has many members, and all the members of the body, though many, are one body, so it is with Christ..." (1 Cor. 12:12). Our thoughts and our hearts turn, therefore, to Christ. To the Shepherd and the Bishop of our souls. To the Shepherd of shepherds. Aware of the truth that we must serve, aware of the responsibility that we must assume, we meet together at this altar to celebrate the Eucharist, the sacrament of the death and resurrection, through which Christ continually gives us His Spirit, the Spirit of truth and love.

ACTING WITH LOVE

5. In this Spirit, let us go, therefore, towards this people, towards this community, which constitutes all the dioceses in the Netherlands.

Let us go with great love.

Love is aware of the difficulties. But above all, it is aware of good; it is aware of gifts: the gifts of nature and the gifts of grace, which the Good Shepherd has spread in this community. Which He has placed in the heart of every redeemed man, giving him the freedom of the children of God.

The gifts that He awaits.

And that is why we wish above all, in this sign of bread and wine, to accept the spiritual gift of your people, the spiritual gift of this land of which you are at once the sons and shepherds.

Let us pray to Christ to accept this gift.

Let us pray finally that He will imbue it with the light and grace of His Spirit, this Spirit who Himself operates all good, by giving "to each one individually as he wills" (1 Cor. 12:11).

This Spirit who builds up the Church and makes her "one body" (1 Cor. 12:12).

Unity Is Conversion to Christ

On January 25, 1980, the Holy Father presided over a Eucharistic concelebration in the Pauline Chapel with the Fathers taking part in the Synod of Dutch Bishops, at the end of the Week of Prayer for the Unity of Christians. John Paul II delivered the following homily.

Dear brothers,

Today we reach the end of the week of prayer for the unity of Christians. The subject chosen for this year was *"Adveniat regnum tuum,"* "Thy kingdom come": A prayer repeated very often, but which must always be new, if we are aware of its meaning. It implies, in fact, in a particular way for every Christian, for each of us, an interior change, a change of heart, thanks to which the kingdom of God spreads in the world, becoming truly realized in us.

1. The Netherlands are part of those regions in which the problem of ecumenism is of great historical and contemporary importance. For centuries, the religious situation of your country has been marked by the breaking of unity, and that not without suffering and tension. Today it is significant that Cardinal Johannes Willebrands should unite in his person the offices of Archbishop of Utrecht and of President of the Secretariat for the Unity of Christians, and all of us here know the merits he has acquired by dedicating himself completely to these two ecclesial functions, which are so important and delicate.

In a more immediate way, the particular synod which gives us the opportunity to be gathered round this altar also deals with the subject of ecumenism and it takes place itself in an ecumenical climate, for, if the concern with unity is constantly present in all its members, the assembly knows that it is supported, not only by the prayer of Catholics, but also by that of other Christians, as the Protestant pastors of the Netherlands have assured.

2. The week of prayer for unity finds its completion and its summit on January 25, the day when the Church commemorates in its liturgy the conversion of St. Paul.

This fact is a specially eloquent one. In the first place, it makes us become aware of a requirement: Unity cannot but be the fruit of conversion to Christ, who is the Head of the Body which is the Church. This conversion must be a deep one and reach members as a whole in the multiple aspects of their lives, in order that unity may truly be realized. St. Paul met the Lord: he gave himself to Him completely. This fact explains the formidable place that the Apostle has in the Church. In our turn, we must all progress in the unity which depends, in short, on Christ, and, therefore, on our adherence to Him, since it is in Him that we constitute the Church. In this spirit, we must continually ask ourselves how human expressions and the various dimensions of our efforts of Christian life and of our ecumenical proceedings show the search for unity as conversion to Christ.

Unity in Christ corresponds to the Father's eternal plan, to revelation of the mystery of salvation as proclaimed by the Apostle of the Gentiles: "to unite all things in him (Christ)" (Eph. 1:10); yes, before the Father, it is in Christ that the whole human family, redeemed by Him, finds its unity. We cannot seek it elsewhere.

3. A second point also calls for our attention and our meditation: This celebration of January 25 makes us become aware in a quite particular way that conversion, and therefore unity, is possible "for God," even if it may seem impossible "for men."

To enlighten us on this subject, we have the example of Paul of Tarsus, who became St. Paul. A mortal enemy of Christ and Christians—he who, as he himself says, was convinced that he "ought to do many things in opposing the name of Jesus of Nazareth" (Acts 26:9). He met the Lord; he became "the Apostle of the Gentiles"; love of Christ became his whole life (cf. Phil. 1:21).

4. Such a deep, such a radical change is, therefore, possible, by the grace of the Lord. To reach it, pressing and incessant prayer is necessary: The personal prayer of each one, like that of all of us during this week, and at the same time, community prayer, for when we pray together in this way, we have already a certain unity. And we also know that, in prayer, we enable the Holy Spirit to pray in us and for us Himself, even when, in the words of St. Paul, we do not know what we should ask for (cf. Rom. 8:26).

In this synodal community that we form, it is a good thing that we can pray for unity. It is a grace that this moment coincides with the week of prayer for unity. And this prayer is in the first place opening to the Holy Spirit: We pray to Him to extend the desires of our heart and to lavish upon us more than our hearts desire, more than the supplications that may spring from our lips, even if we do not find, perhaps, the adequate words.

Yes, let us pray to be more and more the instruments of God's salvific will, of His plan for unity, of His kingdom: Thy kingdom come!

Let No One Feel Neglected by the Pope

On the occasion of the first anniversary of his pilgrimage to Mexico, John Paul II sent the following message to the bishops, priests and the whole people of that nation.

Beloved brothers and sons of Mexico,

On the first anniversary of my visit to your country, I wish to send you my word of greeting, remembrance, thanks, and encouragement along the way to good.

On my arrival I kissed Mexican soil, as a sincere tribute to the nation and a proof of affection and esteem—

the beginning of that intense exchange of sentiments which was manifested in joyful harmony of hearts, during my stay in Mexico City, in Puebla, Oaxaca, Guadalajara and Monterrey, and which spread from there to all Mexican homes.

Recalling now those unforgettable moments, I wish to repeat my gratitude for your magnificent welcome, in the framework of that evangelizing ecclesial event which found its best concrete expression in the Third General Conference of the Latin American Episcopate.

Recalling here what was precisely the central purpose of my visit, namely, to offer on my part the best contribution possible to the cause of evangelization, I would like once more to encourage you to strengthen your Christian awareness, your life of faith, your joy in the confident implementation of Christ's message, your decision to work for the spiritual and material good of everyone.

It is not possible for me, in these brief moments, to tell you everything I would like, to help you along the path of faithfulness to Christ.

To my brothers in the episcopate I renew my trust and cordial benevolence, assuring them that I accompany them in their constant concerns and cares, as well as in their generous commitment to the Church and to the good of each one of their faithful.

With deep affection I encourage priests, men and women religious and all who are preparing for specific consecration to God and to their brethren, in their courageous choice, and I urge them to remain faithful to their vocation, always walking in love of Christ (cf. Eph. 5:2), looking constantly with the eyes of faith on their own identity and the value of their ecclesial dedication....

Beloved brothers and sons, let no one feel forgotten by the Pope, who embraces everyone in this overall survey. Let us all together, with me in your midst, make a pilgrimage of faith to the hearth and sanctuary of Mexico. At the feet of our Blessed Mother, the Virgin of Guadalupe, I wish to lay with you a prayer: that with her aid, this

Church of God, whose vitality I wished to increase with my visit, may experience a powerful growth, a renewed spiritual flourishing, an increase of Christian life, a strengthening of evangelizing forces, a constant drawing closer of faithful Mexico to Christ, the goal and aim of our everyday work.

As brother and friend I ask our Father in heaven to fill you with His grace and peace, while I willingly bless every Mexican, in the name of the Father, the Son and the Holy Spirit. Amen.

Our Task—To Proclaim the Sacredness of Life

About 150 bishops of the United States and Canada met in Dallas, Texas, from January 28 to 31, 1980, to study the medical, legal and moral problems raised by technological progress in the sphere of birth and death.

The Holy Father sent them the following message.

Dear brothers in our Lord Jesus Christ,

It is with great hope, and with great enthusiasm, that I send my greetings to all of you assembled in Dallas. This important workshop, sponsored by the Pope John XXIII Medical-Moral Research and Education Center, and generously supported by the Knights of Columbus, is a splendid initiative at the service of truth and at the service of the human person. The gathering of such a large number of bishops from the United States and Canada manifests a consciousness of your pastoral responsibilities as authentic teachers of God's people, who are called to live their Christian lives in the modern world.

The theme of your deliberations, "The New Technologies of Birth and Death," touches upon complex and vexing questions of medical ethics which face the Church and all of society. I had the occasion in *Redemptor hominis* (no. 15) to make the following statement: "The development of technology and the development of contemporary civilization, which is marked by the ascendancy of technology, demand a proportional development of morals and ethics. For the present, this last development seems unfortunately to be always left behind."

In your joint efforts in Dallas, you are zealously echoing the sentiments of my heart expressed last October in Washington, D.C.: "I do not hesitate to proclaim before you and before the world that all human life—from the moment of conception and through all subsequent stages—is sacred, because human life is created in the image and likeness of God." Our task is to proclaim ever more effectively this sacredness of human life. But, in order to do so, we must understand the new opportunities and new threats that are posed to the human person by ever-developing technologies. At this important moment of history, you are called, as bishops, to furnish timely leadership by examining new questions in the light of God's eternal Word, and with the help offered by the Church's teaching. In this context, your reflections, aided by physicians, theologians and attorneys generously sharing their knowledge and experience at this workshop, will help to contribute to that "proportional development of morals and ethics" which the contemporary situation so earnestly demands. Dear brothers: This is a great and vital contribution of the servant Church of Jesus Christ to the men and women of our day.

May God bless the Pope John Center in its desire and commitment to be of service to the Magisterium of the Church and to the cause of humanity. And may the Holy Spirit direct your minds and hearts to enter more fully into the mysteries of His divine wisdom and to be ever more inflamed with His love.

To all who are attending this meeting, and to all who have helped to make it possible, I cordially impart my apostolic blessing: In the name of the Father, and of the Son, and of the Holy Spirit. Amen.

We All Sincerely Desire a Church Which Corresponds to Christ's Will

On January 31, 1980, the work of the particular Synod of the Dutch Bishops concluded with a solemn Eucharistic concelebration in the Sistine Chapel, presided over by the Holy Father. At the end of the Mass, John Paul II signed the final document of the Synod, offered to him by Archbishop Tomko.

After the Gospel, the Holy Father delivered the following homily.

Venerable and dear brothers,

1. At this moment, we all cherish the same desire. We wish to thank God, Father, Son and Holy Spirit, for this ministry in which we have taken part in the course of more than two weeks. These days, indeed, during which we worked together in the framework of the particular Synod of the Dutch bishops, cannot be seen by us otherwise than by letting ourselves be guided by the truth of these words of the Second Vatican Council in the first chapter of the Constitution *Lumen gentium:* "Hence the universal Church is seen to be 'a people brought into unity from the unity of the Father, the Son and the Holy Spirit' " (no. 4).

Starting from that, our gratitude is addressed to this Unity in three Persons in which the unity of the Church, of the People of God, finds its origin. We wish to give thanks because we have been able to confess this Unity, and at the same time to serve It on every day and at every hour of our common work. We give thanks at the same time because, while looking for our mutual unity, we have been able to serve the unity of the Church—of the People of God—on the plane of the province which constitutes the Church in your country, and on a far wider plane. Yes, venerable and dear brothers, I am deeply convinced that our work has also served the Church of Christ in all her universality.

For this work which we have carried out together tenaciously, I wish to thank one and all of you very heartily. In the first place, I wish to say to the two Presidents Delegate, His Eminence, Cardinal Johannes Willebrands and His

Excellency, Archbishop Godfried Daneels, how I have appreciated at its rightful value the way in which they conducted the work of this assembly. To the bishops of the Netherlands, I express my deep gratitude for their generous availability and their deep love for their faithful and for the universal Church, and to the two religious superiors I wish to say how grateful I am to them for their original contribution to the Synod. I warmly thank their Eminences the Cardinal Prefects of the Congregations, my close collaborators, for their contribution to this work, to which they brought the experience acquired in their office. To the Secretary General, His Excellency Archbishop Jozef Tomko, to his assistant, His Excellency Most Reverend Albert Descamps, to the special secretary, Reverend Father Joseph Lescrauwaet, I express my deep gratitude for the competent services they all contributed. I do not wish to pass over in silence the dedication of the personnel of the secretariat of the Synod, of the press service, as well as of the assistant personnel. Allow me also to address a word of thanks to all the representatives of the media of social communication who, while respecting the reserve that necessarily had to surround the deliberations, devoted themselves to keeping in touch with the Church as a whole.

During all these days, I was able to be with you and take part in most of the assemblies in the mornings and in the afternoons. I was able to be a witness to the honesty, the attention and the objectivity with which you dealt with every problem. Such attention and such care merely manifest how close to your hearts are the problems we tackled together and how much you desire to dedicate all your strength to their solution. For this I thank Christ, and you, too, venerable and dear brothers. This atmosphere, tranquil, concrete and sincere, of an exchange of ideas on each of the subjects studied, showed that the Spirit of our Lord and Master was with us, and that we also received the assistance of His holy Mother, to whom we addressed our prayer every day, particularly in the recitation of the Angelus.

2. The problem studied by the Synod and which occupied completely the weeks of these discussions in Rome is expressed in the title of its agenda: "The exercise of the pastoral work of the Church in the Netherlands in the present circumstances, so that the Church may be more and more manifested as communion."

To deal with this important subject, we had continually to confront the multiple experiences of the Church in the Netherlands with the answer given some years ago by the episcopate of the whole world, gathered for four years in the Second Vatican Council, to the question that it asked itself: *Ecclesia quid dicis de teipsa?* This answer, expressed in an elaborate way by the conciliar Magisterium, has become for you at present, venerable and dear brothers, the systematic framework of reference, and at the same time the foundation that makes it possible to solve each one of the problems with which your experience as pastors and your conscience as bishops have to cope every day.

In the course of our discussions and our reflections, one thing has always been clear: We can desire only—and we actually desire it with our whole heart—a Church that corresponds completely with the intentions of Christ the Lord, as they were expressed and confirmed by the Council. We believe, in fact, that the Second Vatican Council has become for our age the very special subject and place thanks to which the Holy Spirit, the Spirit of Jesus Christ, "has spoken" to the whole Church (cf. Rv. 2:7) and led her towards the whole truth (cf. Jn. 16:13), and therefore also towards this truth of existence, "in the modern world," such as it appears to us through the "signs of the times."

Speaking to the whole Church, the Spirit of our Lord and Redeemer "has spoken" at the same time to each of the Churches which remain in the communion of this Church, one and universal. That is why the fundamental concern of all of us gathered in this synod was also the care to ensure that the existence of the Church in the Netherlands, its concrete existence in all sectors of life, should be able to possess and fully manifest the marks of this identity that the Second Vatican Council expressed again, in agreement with the whole of Tradition.

3. That is why, also, this daily effort of the synod, through the analysis of the different sectors of the life of the Church in your country, sought in the first place to reach a clearer awareness of everything that constitutes, so to speak, the daily life of the Church in her different aspects. It then tried to establish guidelines to be followed in the future. In fact, the identity of the Church is manifested precisely through this concrete form of her existence; it is manifested through her way of living every day, and through the way in which she carries out her work in the different sectors of life and activity.

In our analysis conducted according to these premises, we tackled, venerable and dear brothers, all the essential aspects, important from the point of view of the identity of the Church in the Netherlands for the present moment and for the future. There is no doubt, in fact, that, in the present activities of the Church, the future form of her life and her apostolate is worked out at the same time.

Thus we took as the starting point of our deliberations the reality and the fundamental exigencies of the communion of the Church, a communion at the same time local and universal, referring to the spiritual element as well as to the institutional one, aware that community of faith, hope and charity unites all believers with Christ and His Father, and unites them with one another. In the unanimous desire and determination to manifest this communion, we reaffirmed our agreement on the content of the Catholic Faith according to the teaching of the Magisterium of the Church, and we drew the necessary conclusions as to the function of the bishop as teacher of the Faith and as pastor, of every bishop in his diocese and of all the bishops together within the episcopal conference.

The Synod thus adopted resolutions referring to the ministerial priesthood, to the life of men and women religious, and to the participation of the laity in the evangelizing mission of the Church. It examined how to promote the sacramental life, and above all, the celebration and veneration of the Eucharist, the source of life and growth, and the Sacrament of Reconciliation. Finally, the Synod stressed the value of the liturgy celebrated according to the rules of the Church, the importance of doctrinal content and pastoral methods in catechesis, and finally the promotion of an ecumenism faithful to the orientation of the Council.

4. This all too brief reference to the subject matter and the conclusions of the synod is enough to show the riches of its discussions and the broad examination dedicated to the pastoral work of the Church in the Netherlands. The importance of all the subjects tackled for the future development of the pastoral efforts of the whole People of God has escaped no one. Allow me, however, to stress here a special point which turned out to be at the center of all the other questions raised and which will have a very great impact on the future of the Church. I am referring here to the true ministerial priesthood of priests, in its nature as well as in its relations with the bishop and in its relationship to the commitment of lay people in the mission of the Church.

The building up of the ecclesial community and the implementation of its mission are entrusted to the whole community, but, as the Dogmatic Constitution *Lumen gentium* says (cf. nos. 30-38), this responsibility is exercised in harmony with the charism and the place of each one in the Body of Christ. All vocations, all services, all charisms are ordained to manifesting in their variety the riches of the Church and to serving her unity. The Church must be able to express the fullness of her life through the riches of vocations and charisms, in the ministerial priesthood as well as in the apostolate of the laity, and also in religious consecration according to the spirit and the specific purpose of every institute.

But each of these ministries and these services has its own specific character, and they all complete one another without merging.

You rightly laid stress, dear brothers, on the importance and the necessity of the participation of the laity in the pastoral task of the Church; you also praised the active collaboration which is offered lay people in all the Dutch dioceses, and which they are called to intensify even more. For, without the work of the laity, it would be difficult for the Church to be present and to act in the world of today (cf. AA 1). But it is important, as you emphasized, to safeguard, in the attribution of tasks and in the delimitation of responsibilities, the distinction between the contribution of the laity and the tasks entrusted to priests and deacons. This shows the all importance of the conclusions at which this synod has arrived in the field of the collaboration of lay people in pastoral tasks as well as in that of the formation of future priests.

Unanimous in professing the essential distinction between the sacramental priesthood and the common priesthood of the faithful, as well as the permanent character of the sacramental priesthood, the bishops of the Netherlands have also expressed their concern and their will to be supported by a celibate clergy and to do their utmost to promote vocations to the priesthood. They feel the same concern as regards the religious vocation, through which men and women answer God's appeal in consecrated life. You have envisaged, ensuring the formation of candidates to the priesthood in real seminaries, either in seminaries that provide completely for formation, or in other institutions that possess all the characteristics of a seminary although part of the teaching is given by faculties of theology recognized by the Holy See.

In the same way, you are resolved to stress the opportuneness of a commitment along the way of the diaconate, in view of the specific task and importance of this permanent ministry, as restored by the Second Vatican Council. You then reaffirmed the importance of the specific contribution of the laity in the Church and you are determined to appeal to the collaboration of the laity in the pastoral tasks which can be entrusted to them according to the indications of the Holy See.

Those are resolutions which bode particularly well for the future of the Church in the Netherlands. The Pope is convinced that everyone will respond to this appeal, thus giving this Church its full dimension as a Christian community, which is manifested likewise by its missionary work, so bound up with its whole tradition.

5. In all the work we have carried out at the Synod —and in the work that awaits you after its conclusion —what was, what is and what will remain our bulwark and our strength, is the constant reference of our faith, our hope and our love to Christ, our Lord and Master, Christ the Redeemer of man, Christ who became in His Paschal Mystery the Bridegroom of His Church.

It was to Him that we tried to remain faithful in the course of our meetings in Rome, in our daily reflection and in our exchanges of ideas. His truth and His love were the source of light for our considerations, our resolutions and our decisions. And doing all that, we were more and more clearly aware that we need, for our service of the Church, great courage and at the same time great prudence. This courage and this prudence must be derived from our absolute trust in this love He gives everywhere to His Church, this faithfulness He gives in return to all those who try to remain constantly faithful to Him. This conviction makes it a duty for us to look to the future with evangelical hope: "Be of good cheer, I have overcome the world" (Jn. 16:33). Thus, we will be capable of carrying out our mission as bishops and pastors with regard to the Church in Holland, and at the same time with regard to the universal Church; we will be capable of serving the People of God in the way that the Spirit of Jesus Christ demands of us.

It is on Him, too, that we build our will and at the same time our hope for mutual unity, for "communio" among yourselves, bishops and pastors of the Church in the Netherlands, which is indispensable to carry out this pastoral ministry. The Synod has been for you, dear brothers, a time of happy union and deep exchanges of your thoughts; it has been a time of real dialogue of salvation. This dialogue, as Paul VI taught, is and must remain an exchange of thoughts in which respect and love are manifested, and which is at the same time subordinated to truth, to the good of the Gospel and the unity of the Church. At the moment when this happy time is drawing to an end, there remains nothing more for us to do than ask the Spirit of truth and the Lord of the harvest that the same style of dialogue and the same salutary climate of union may always continue to exist among you for the good of the whole Church, and in particular for the good of the dioceses of which the Holy Spirit has made you bishops.

6. Now that the Dutch bishops are preparing to go back to their respective dioceses, I turn my thought and my affection towards the whole Church in the Netherlands and towards one and all of those who constitute it. Rest assured, dear brothers and sisters, that the Synod is grateful to you for everything you have undertaken to contribute to the success of its deliberations. On behalf of the Synod, I thank you particularly for your prayers which have accompanied us during this period of grace.

I have received multiple echoes of initiatives which bear witness to your fervent response to the appeal I had addressed to you on the eve of the Synod. It was a real comfort and inspiration for its participants to know that the Church in the Netherlands was united with them through prayer in the parishes and schools, in religious houses, in groups of young people and houses of retreat. I thank particularly also the brothers and sisters of the Christian Churches and communities that joined the Catholics to implore the light of the Spirit on our work. It is with emotion and gratitude that I wish to recall here that a group of Protestant pastors sent a telegram at the beginning of the Synod to assure us all of their prayers. The spiritual union thus shown is a token of God's blessing for growing union among all those who profess the same faith and the same hope in Jesus Christ. May our expectation, our desire and our commitment correspond to the Lord's will! In this way, we will be able to promote an ecumenism that is without timidity because it is authentic, a dynamic ecumenism which will be a growth in the faith, an ecumenism, in a word, that is fully faithful to the Holy Spirit.

Now that the implementation of the decisions of this Synod is beginning, I entrust again to your prayers, dear brothers and sisters of the Netherlands, the way that has to be traversed. For it is on prayer, more than on deliberations and consultations, that the life and apostolate of the Church in the Netherlands will depend in the future. Gather round your bishops in prayer as in action. They are relying on you more than ever. Union in prayer, awareness that "every perfect gift is from above, coming down from the Father of lights" (Jas. 1:17), will help you to carry out this renewal and this conversion which each of us must practice continually. Prayer helps to believe, to hope and to love, even if human weakness puts us in situations of tension or brings about lapses. The fervent prayer of the whole Christian community, in the Netherlands as also elsewhere, brings the hope that everyone, priests and laity, men and women religious, will accept the conclusions of the Synod, in a spirit of faith and with sincere conviction. Now there is approaching the time of Lent, which prepares us to celebrate the resurrection of the Lord Jesus. We do not hesitate to request your prayer and your sacrifices in order that the seed of the Synod may fall on favorable land and yield fruit in abundance (cf. Mk. 4:8).

With very special confidence, I wish to address the young people of the Church in the Netherlands. In preparation for the Synod, a group of young people from your capital met to pray around a candle, the symbol of the light which is Christ, and afterwards they sent me this candle as a sign of their commitment and their union with the Synod. Dear young people, may the light of Christ illuminate your path as Christians and your aspirations which certainly find their place in the Church! Rest assured that your generosity and your sense of authenticity will help the whole community to make the choices which are necessary and to assume the consequences that faith in Jesus Christ and membership of the Church involve.

Venerable and dear brothers, at the moment of parting I call upon you to place the fruits of this Synod and the future of the Church in the Netherlands in the hands of Mary, Mother of the Lord and Mother of the Church. The last chapter of the Dogmatic Constitution *Lumen gentium* sheds light on the spiritual consequences that are derived, for the Church and for each Christian, from our situation with regard to the Son of God incarnate and to His holy Mother. It was because he was "born of woman" (Gal. 4:4) that our Lord Jesus Christ makes us real "adopted sons" (cf. LG 52). It was because she received the Word of God both in her heart and in her body that the Blessed Virgin has a unique role in the mystery of the Word incarnate and in that of the Mystical Body. She is closely united with the Church, of which she is the model in the order of faith, charity and perfect union with Christ. In this way, in answer to our devotion and our prayer, Mary, who gathers and reflects in a way in herself the highest aspirations of faith, calls the faithful to her Son and to His sacrifice, as well as to love of the Father. "The Church, therefore," the Council teaches, "in her apostolic work, too, rightly looks to her who gave birth to Christ, who was thus conceived of the Holy Spirit and born of a virgin, in order that through the Church He could be born and increase in the hearts of the faithful" *(ibid.,* no. 65). With the Virgin, the Church started her way through the history of this world two thousand years ago, in the Upper Room at Pentecost. Since then, the Church has traversed every stage of this way with her, who is the luminous sign of hope and comfort for the People of God *(ibid.,* no. 68). We must travel with her, too, the stage that we are beginning today, on the basis of this Synod. In the Netherlands, there are so many places where the Mother of God is venerated with particular fervor by the faithful. Let it suffice to mention, among so many sanctuaries which bear witness to their Marian piety, the name of the sanctuary *Ster der Zee* at Maastricht, that of *Zoete Lieve Vrouw den Bosch* and that of *Onze Lieve Vrouw ter Nood* at Heiloo, so dear to your hearts and mine. May these places become more and more the meeting places from which Mary will guide the People of God towards renewed faith and hope in the communion of love!

The Pursuit of Truth Is the Supreme Norm of Justice

On February 4, 1980, the Holy Father received in audience the Court of the Sacred Roman Rota, which had begun its new judicial year. John Paul II delivered the following address.

To see you around me, beloved sons, gathered for the opening of the new judicial year, gives me joy and comfort, as it does, too, to have listened to the confirmation of your sentiments of common gratitude from your worthy Dean, Most Reverend Heinrich Ewers. I, too, thank you heartily and confirm the sentiments of benevolence which I already manifested to each of you in the visit which your Dean mentioned.

1. On last December 8, as you know, I made public my message for the celebration of the 13th World Day of Peace, the content of which is summed up in these words: "Truth, the power of peace." On this occasion, I would like to talk to you, developing a particular aspect of the same subject, which is closely related to your ministry.

Truth does not become the power of peace except through justice. Holy Scripture, speaking of messianic times, asserts on the one hand that justice is the source and companion of peace: "In his days may righteousness flourish, and peace abound" (Ps. 72:7), and on the other hand it repeatedly stresses the bond that associates *truth* with *justice:* "Faithfulness will look down from the sky" (Ps. 85:11), and again: "He will judge the world with righteousness, and the peoples with his truth" (Ps. 96:13). Drawing inspiration from these and other texts of the sacred books, theologians and canonists, both medieval and modern, go so far as to affirm that justice has a relationship of dependence on truth. "*Veritas*—a famous canonical axiom asserts—*est basis, fundamentum seu mater iustitiae*" (A Barbosa, *De Axiomatibus Iuris usufrequentioribus*, *Axioma* 224, *Veritas*, no. 5; in *Tractatus varii*, *Lugduni* 1678, p. 136); and theologians, headed by St. Thomas *(Summa Theologica*, p. I, q. 21, a. 2, c.), have expressed themselves in the same way. Pius XII summed up the thought of the latter, affirming forcefully that "truth is the law of justice," and then commenting: "The world needs the truth which is justice, and that justice which is truth" (Address to the Sacred Roman Rota, October 1, 1942, in *AAS* 34 [1942] 342, no. 5).

2. To refer to the field which is specifically yours, in all ecclesiastical trials *truth* must always be, from the beginning to the sentence, the foundation, mother and law of *justice*. And since the main object of your activity is "the nullity or not of the marriage bond" as Monsignor the Dean has just stated—it seemed to me opportune, at this meeting of ours, to devote some reflections to matrimonial trials of nullity.

The immediate purpose of these trials is to ascertain whether or not the facts exist which, by natural, divine or ecclesiastical law, invalidate marriage, in order to be able to arrive at the promulgation of a true and just sentence with regard to the alleged non-existence of the marriage bond.

The canonical judge must establish, therefore, whether the marriage celebrated was a *true* one. He is, therefore, bound by *truth*, which he tries to investigate with commitment, humility and charity.

And this truth "will make free" (cf. Jn. 8:32) those who turn to the Church, tormented by painful situations, and above all by doubt whether that dynamic reality, involving the whole personality of two beings—which is the marriage bond—exists or not.

To limit as much as possible the margins of error in a precious and delicate service as yours is, the Church has elaborated a procedure which, with the intention of ascertaining the objective truth, will, on the one hand, ensure the person the greatest guarantees in sustaining his own reasons, and, on the other, consistently respect the divine command: *Quod Deus coniunxit, homo no separet"* (Mk. 10:3).

IMPORTANCE OF THE DOCUMENTS RELATING TO PRELIMINARY INVESTIGATION

3. All documents of the ecclesiastical judgment, from summons to the documents of defense, can and must be a *source of truth;* but the "documents of the case," and, among the latter, the "documents relating to the preliminary investigation" must be so in a special way, since the preliminary investigation has as its specific purpose that of gathering proofs of the truth of the alleged fact, in order that the judge may, on this basis, pass a just sentence.

For this purpose and on being summoned by the judge there will appear, in order to be questioned, the parties, the witnesses, and if necessary the experts. The oath to tell the truth, which is required from all these persons, is perfectly consistent with the purpose of the preliminary investigation. It is not a question of creating an event that has never existed, but of making clear and emphasizing a fact that took place in the past and that still continues, perhaps, in the present. Certainly, each of these persons will tell "his truth," which will normally be the objective truth or a part of it, often considered from various points of view, colored with the hues of personal temperament, perhaps with some distortion or else mingled with error. But in any case they must all act loyally, without betraying either what they think is objective truth, or their own conscience.

FROM MORAL CERTAINTY TO THE SENTENCE

4. Alexander III pointed out in the twelfth century: *Saepe contingit quod testes, corrupti praetio, facile inducantur ad falsum testimonium proferendum.* (It frequently happens that witnesses, corrupted by money, are easily induced to give false testimony. C. 10, *De praesumptionibus*, II, 23; ed. Richter-Friedberg, II, 355) Unfortunately not even today are witnesses immune from the possibility of acting dishonestly. For this reason, Pius XII, in the address on unity of purpose and action in matrimonial suits, exhorted not only the witnesses, but all those who take part in the trial, not to depart from the truth: "May it never happen that in matrimonial suits before ecclesiastical courts there will take place deception, perjury, bribery or fraud of any kind!" (*Address to the S. R. Rota*, October 2, 1944, in *AAS* 36 [1944] 282)

If this should happen, however, the documents relating to preliminary investigation would certainly not be limpid sources of truth and they might lead the judges, in spite of their moral integrity and their sincere effort to discover the truth, to err in passing sentence.

5. When the preliminary investigation is over, there begins for the individual judges, who will have to decide the case, the most important and delicate phase of the trial. Each one must arrive, if possible, at moral certainty concerning the truth or existence of the fact, since this certainty is an indispensable requisite in order that the judge may pass sentence: first of all, so to speak, in his heart, and then voting in the gathering of the judicial college.

This judge must draw this certainty *ex actis et probatis*. First and foremost *ex actis* since it must be presumed that the documents are a source of truth. Therefore, the judge, following the norm of Innocent III, *debet universa rimari (Iudex...usque ad prolationem sententiae debet universa rimari*, in c. 10, *De fide instrumentorum*, II, 22; ed. Richter-Friedberg, II, 352), that is, he must examine the documents carefully, letting nothing escape his attention. Then *ex probatis*, because the judge cannot limit himself to giving credence to affirmations alone; on the contrary, he must keep in mind the possibility that, during the preliminary investigation, the objective truth may have been obscured by shadows brought about by different causes, such as the forgetting of some facts, their subjective interpretation, carelessness and sometimes false representation and fraud. The judge must act with a critical sense. A difficult task, because there may be many errors, while truth, on the contrary, is one only. It is necessary, therefore, to look in the documents for proofs of the alleged facts, and then proceed to a criticism of each of these proofs, comparing it with others, in such a way that the earnest advice of St. Gregory the Great may be put into practice seriously: *ne temere indiscussa iudicentur (Moralium* L. 19, c. 25, no. 46. PL, vol. 76, col. 126).

The *memoriae* of the lawyers, the *animadversiones* of the Defender of the Bond, the possible *votum* of the Promoter of Justice, exist for the purpose of helping this delicate and important work. They, too, in carrying out their task, the first in favor of the parties, the second in defense of the bond, the third *in iure inquirendo*, must serve the truth, in order that justice may triumph.

6. It is necessary, however, to keep in mind that the purpose of this investigation is not just any knowledge of the fact, but the teaching of "moral certainty," that is, of that certain knowledge which "is based on the constancy of the laws and customs that govern human life" (Pius XII, *Address to the S. R. Rota*, October 1, 1942, in *AAS* 34 [1942] 339, no. 1). This moral certainty is a guarantee for

the judge that he has found the truth about the fact to be judged, that is, the truth which is foundation, mother and law of justice, and so makes him sure that he is—from this aspect—able to pass a just sentence. And this is precisely the reason for which the law demands this certainty of the judge, to enable him to pass sentence (can. 1869, par. 1).

Taking advantage of the doctrine and jurisprudence that has developed particularly in more recent times, Pius XII declared in an authentic way the canonical concept of moral certainty in the allocution addressed to your court on October 1, 1942 *(AAS* 34 [1941], 339-343). Here are the words that suit our case: "Between absolute certainty and quasi-certainty or probability, there is, as between two extremes, that *moral certainty* which is treated of in the questions submitted to your court.... It is characterized, on the positive side, by the fact that it excludes any grounded or reasonable doubt and, thus considered, it is distinguished essentially from the above-mentioned quasi-certainty; on the negative side, it allows the absolute possibility of the contrary to remain, and thereby is differentiated from absolute certainty. The certainty of which we are speaking now, is necessary and sufficient to pass sentence" *(ibid.,* pp. 339-340, no. 1).

Consequently no judge may pass sentence in favor of the nullity of a marriage if he has not first acquired the moral certainty of the existence of this nullity. Probability alone is not enough to decide a case. To any compromise in this connection, there could be applied what has wisely been said of other laws concerning marriage: Any relaxation contains within it an impelling dynamic, *cui, si mos geratur, divortio, alio nomine tecto, in Ecclesia tolerando via sternitur* (to which, if the practice be entertained, the way is opened to the toleration of divorce, under another name, in the Church—Letter from the Cardinal Prefect of the Council for the Public Affairs of the Church to the President of the Episcopal Conference of the U.S.A., June 20, 1973).

THE DUTIES OF THE JUDGE

7. The administration of justice entrusted to the judge is a service to truth and at the same time it is the exercise of a duty belonging to the public order. For the law is entrusted to the judge "for its rational and normal application" (Paul VI, *Address to the S. R. Rota*, January 31, 1974, in *AAS* 66 [1974] 87).

The plaintiff, therefore, must be able to invoke in his favor a law, which recognizes in the fact adduced a sufficient reason, for natural or divine, positive or canonical law, to invalidate the marriage; through this law the step will be taken from the truth of the fact to *justice* or recognition of what is due.

The judge's duties towards the law are, therefore, serious and multiple. I will mention only the first and most important one, which, moreover, implies all the others: faithfulness! Faithfulness to the law, to divine, natural and positive law, and to canonical, substantial and procedural law.

8. The typical objectivity of justice and of the trial, in the *quaestio facti*, finds expression in adherence to the *truth*, and in the *quaestio iuris*, is expressed in *faithfulness*; these are concepts which, as is clear, have a great affinity. The faithfulness of the judge to the law must lead him to identify himself with it, so that it can rightly be said, as M. T. Cicero wrote, that the judge is the law itself speaking: "*Magistratum legem esse loquentem*" (*De legibus*, L. 3, n. 1, 2; ed. of Association G. Budé, Paris 1959, p. 82). It will then be this same faithfulness that impels the judge to acquire that set of qualities that he needs to carry out his other duties with regard to the law: wisdom to understand it; learning to illustrate it; zeal to defend it; prudence to interpret it, in its spirit, beyond the *nudus cortex verborum*; careful consideration and Christian equity to apply it.

It comforts me to see how great your faithfulness to the law of the Church has been in the midst of the difficult circumstances of the last few years, when the values of married life, rightly highlighted by the Second Vatican Council, and the progress of the human sciences, especially psychology and psychiatry, have brought to your court new cases and new approaches to matrimonial trials, which are not always correct. It has been your merit, after a serious and delicate study of the doctrine of the Council and of the above-mentioned sciences, to think out "questions of law" in which you carried out excellently your duties to the law, separating the true from the false or bringing light where there was confusion, as, for example, by reducing a good many cases, which were presented as new, to the fundamental heading of lack of consent. In this way you confirmed, in a counter argument, the splendid teaching of my Predecessor, Pope Paul VI of venerable memory, on consent as the essence of marriage (cf. *Address to the S. R. Rota*, February 9, 1976, in *AAS* 68 [1976] 204-208).

FAITHFULNESS OF THE JUDGES TO THE LAW

9. This faithfulness will also enable you judges to give a clear and respectful answer to the questions submitted to you—as your service of truth demands. If the marriage is null and is declared such, the two parties are free in the sense that it is recognized that actually they were never bound; if the marriage is valid and is declared such, it is ascertained that the spouses have celebrated a marriage which binds them for their whole life and has conferred on them the specific grace to fulfill their destiny in their union, established in full responsibility and freedom.

Marriage, one and indissoluble, as a human reality, is not something mechanical and static. Its success depends on the free cooperation of the spouses with the grace of God, on their response to His plan of love. If, owing to lack of cooperation with this divine grace, the union had remained deprived of its fruits, the spouses can and must bring back the grace of God, which the sacrament has ensured them, and renew their commitment to live a love which is one not only of affections and emotions, but also and above all, of dedication—mutual, free, voluntary, total and irrevocable.

This is the contribution that is asked of you judges in the service of that human and supernatural reality, so important, but also so menaced today—the family.

I pray for you that Jesus Christ, the Sun of truth and justice, may always be with you, so that the decisions of your court will always reflect that higher justice and truth which proceeds from you. This is the heartfelt wish that I make for you at the opening of the new judicial year, and I accompany it with my apostolic blessing.

A Great Common Commitment

The meeting between the Holy Father and the Roman clergy took place on February 21, 1980, in the Hall of the Lateran University. The Pope delivered the following address.

Dear brothers in the priesthood!

"To all God's beloved in Rome, who are called to be saints: Grace to you and peace from God our Father and the Lord Jesus Christ" (Rom. 1:7).

With these words of St. Paul I extend to you my affectionate and cordial greeting in the Lord at the beginning of this brotherly conversation.

1. I greatly desired this meeting with you today. In it we are related to the tradition of similar meetings at the beginning of Lent, both with the preachers of the spiritual exercises and with the Roman clergy; but, at the same time, we also seek a dimension and a context a little different from the preceding ones. Therefore, it takes place here in the Lateran, where there is the See of the Bishop of the diocese of Rome and the Roman episcopal residence. Here is the center of the diocese, that is, of the particular Church, which is in Rome.

I wish to stress this reality in a special way. The Church has her universal and, at the same time, local dimension. "A diocese"—the Second Vatican Council stated—"is a section of the People of God entrusted to a bishop to be guided by him with the assistance of his clergy so that, loyal to its pastor and formed by him into one community in the Holy Spirit through the Gospel and the Eucharist, it constitutes one particular Church in which the one, holy, catholic and apostolic Church of Christ is truly present and active" (CD 11).

If the Church of Rome, precisely because it is Saint Peter's See, is of such fundamental importance for the universality of the Church, it is, however, in the first place, the Church of a "place": the Church that is in Rome. Christ wished it to be such. Here Peter initiated it as such, and as such have all his Successors had it in inheritance.

BISHOP OF ROME'S DUTY

2. It is not, in fact, the first time that I have emphasized the fact that I feel I am above all the Bishop of Rome, and that I, therefore, consider it my first obligation and duty to serve this Church. I can carry out this duty—which is in itself a very great one—thanks to the lasting and indefatigable collaboration of the Cardinal Vicar, the Archbishop Vicegerent and the auxiliary bishops, who all collaborate with me in the episcopal service and systematically share with me the pastoral work. It is well known that most of this commitment rests on their shoulders, and for this reason I wish to express to them today my sincere satisfaction and my sincere thanks.

I try, however, as far as possible, to make my personal contribution to one part; that is, to visiting the parishes. For these too, however, a considerable part of the work is carried out by the bishops of the individual areas. It can be said that the whole preparation, long and methodical, of the visit is entrusted to their zeal and their commitment. There remains for me, in a way, the final act, the conclusion, which, at the same time, is always a "synthesis." Within the limits of my other commitments, I have tried and am trying to visit the parishes as often as possible. In that way, I have already found my bearings to a certain extent in this field, which previously was almost completely unknown to me.

EXPERIENCE OF PARISH VISITATIONS

I am learning to know Rome as the Pope's diocese, as my Church; and in these Sunday meetings with the People of God and of the society of Rome, I am experiencing very deeply its needs, anxieties and expectations. In the first year, that is, up to the end of the month of last December, I visited eighteen parishes. I recall the visits to Garbatella and Testaccio, to St. Basil and to St. Luke; to St. Clement ai Prati Fiscali and to Our Lady of Sorrows at Villa Gordiani; to Spiaceto, Rustica, Trullo, Our Lady of Divine Love, and to the Twelve Apostles. This year I have already visited the parish of Mary Immaculate at Tiburtino, Our Lady of Guadalupe, the Ascension at Quarticciolo, Saint Timothy at Casalpalocco, and finally St. Martin ai Monti.

During these visits I met the parish priests, the priests who assist them in the ministry, and the faithful: fathers and mothers, the young, children, the sick, the various committed groups, the catechists. Each of these visits always gives me, in particular, a new opportunity for direct collaboration with you, priests of this Church "which is in Rome." And it is on these experiences that I wish to base our meeting today, which is intended not as an audience but as a talk.

MISSION OF THE BISHOP

3. I intend, first and foremost, to assure you that, although these brief periods of time which, on the occasion of the visits to the Roman parishes, I can dedicate to immediate collaboration with you, are objectively and relatively modest in proportion to my other occupations, yet I con-

sider them absolutely essential and fundamental for my apostolic mission. The mission of the bishop is to preside over his Church, to be its pastor, with the help of the priests as direct collaborators of his ministry. "The bishops, as vicars and legates of Christ, govern the particular Churches assigned to them" (LG 27), the Council proclaimed.

Such is the theological view of the bishop's pastoral ministry in the Church. The priests are the fulfillment and the completion of that priesthood which he possesses in pastoral fullness—only Jesus Christ possesses it in ontological fullness—with regard to His Church. The priests are His sons in that, by means of the sacrament of Holy Orders, He begets them, in a way, to the life of the priesthood; they are, subsequently, His brothers in this priesthood. *"Vobis sum episcopus, vobiscum sum sacerdos,"* I recalled to you, adapting St. Augustine's words (cf. *Serm.* 340, 1: PL 38, 1483) in the letter that I addressed to all priests of the Church on the occasion of Holy Thursday last year. Every visit I pay to a parish of the diocese makes me aware again of this apostolic truth of the life of the Church, and unites me more and more closely with you in this unity of the hierarchical ministry, which we constitute in our Church, which is in Rome. Every visit makes me meditate more and more deeply on the words of the same St. Augustine: *"Neque enim episcopi propter nos sumus, sed propter eos quibus verbum et sacramentum domini cum ministramus"*; and again, *"non propter nos, sed propter alios sumus" (Contra Cresconium Donatistam,* II, 11: PL 43, 474).

CLERICAL STATISTICS

4. The clergy of Rome—as has been pointed out in the various reports—is greatly differentiated and connected with different fields of apostolic work. Only a part of them are engaged in the parish apostolate, and in a minor percentage. There are about 5,280 secular and

religious priests resident in Rome. But only 1,153 of them have the care of souls in the parishes. To the latter it would be necessary to add the student priests who, in addition to attending the Pontifical Universities, make a certain contribution to the parish apostolate. On the other hand, the diocese of Rome is structured in parishes which, in the terminology adopted by Prof. J. Majka in his volume entitled *Sociologia della parrocchia* (Sociology of the parish), are called "gigantic parishes": in Rome there are 47 which have from 15,000 to 20,000 faithful; 31, from 20,000 to 30,000 faithful; 14, from 30,000 to 40,000 faithful; 5, from 40,000 faithful upwards.

Nor can we forget, in this brief but necessary review of the diocesan situation, that there are 70 parishes in which the premises used for worship are unsuitable, and whose faithful take part in the celebration of Holy Mass and of the sacraments in rooms, warehouses, etc. Fifteen recently formed Roman districts are still without places of worship.

The seriousness of the religious and pastoral problems of the diocese can be gathered from these few rough statistical data. There exists, in fact, an objective disproportion between the number of the faithful and the number of priests who devote themselves to the ministry. Not only the fundamental apostolate but also the specialized one becomes precarious and inadequate, in spite of the occasional availability of other priests, the help offered by sisters and by committed lay people themselves. At this point I would like to address my dear brother religious priests resident in Rome. Today there are about 3,644 of them. The diocese expects a great deal of them, of their generosity, their ecclesial sense, and the apostolic ardor that animates them.

It has just been mentioned that the first meeting of men and women religious of Rome concerning their presence and their mission in Rome took place in the early days of the month of January. This meeting was fruitful in indications and resolutions. I hope that the men and women religious of Rome, while fully respecting the specific charism of their own institutes, will be able to take their place in the overall apostolate of the diocese, on which the eyes of the world are fixed.

WORKING TOGETHER

5. In this heart-to-heart talk today to you priests of Rome, I consider it my duty to express to you my most sincere gratitude and deepest admiration for the priestly testimony of generosity, commitment and poverty, which distinguishes you. You must proclaim, live and get others to live the Gospel message in a city which has behind it, in fact in its bloodstream, 2,700 years of history, a history that is among the most complex and prestigious; a city in which the clash and the meeting between the classical world and Christianity took place in an exemplary way; a city which today is a real megalopolis, which in 1881, a hundred years ago, had about 274,000 inhabitants, and today has over ten times as many, that is, 2,900,000; a city in which the tensions and contradictions of contemporary society, the problems of urbanization, immigration, the shortage of houses, employment and work, violence and armed terrorism, are manifested and explode in a more and more acute way.

The clergy of Rome, called to tackle on the pastoral and evangelical plane the enormous mass of human and social problems, is largely not homogeneous, since it comes from nearly all the regions of Italy. This phenomenon, which is manifested in Rome to a greater extent, perhaps, than in any other urban diocese in the world, certainly has its positive aspects: every priest bears within him the diversity of traditions, experiences, schools of spiritual life, and apostolate. All this cannot be denied; in fact, particularly in Rome, such a phenomenon is appropriate. But it involves, at the same time, greater requirements as regards the construction and safeguarding of unity, so indispensable in the apostolate of this city. It is necessary to undertake, courageously and constantly, adequate efforts which will lead to this unity of direction in the overall apostolate. In this field, which is becoming more and more delicate and problematical, it is necessary to study together, reflect together, examine together, work together.

This precise meeting of ours today is intended as one of these efforts.

This unity must be, in the first place, the concrete and personal response of each of us to the prayer of Jesus to His Father: *"Ut unum sint"* (cf. Jn. 17:11, 21, 22). It must be a response matured in mutual love, with regard to the different problems that concern the clergy of Rome: problems of a spiritual, cultural, pastoral, human and economic character. It must be a response which will make it possible to overcome certain individualistic temptations and make us fully available for the organic plans indicated or prepared by the center, and not put us in a continual position of criticism or polemics with regard to directives, which are certainly the result of meditation and long reflection.

Beloved brothers! Maintain, around the bishop, the unity of the presbyterium, which is all the more necessary in a diocese such as that of Rome, inclined, owing to its very sociological and cultural structures, to a type of pluralism, that is sometimes ambiguous.

"Qui autem deseruerit unitatem, violat caritatem: et quisquis violat caritatem, quodlibet magnum habeat, ipse nihil est"—St. Augustine warns us. Quoting St. Paul's hymn to charity (cf. 1 Cor. 13:13ff.), he continues: *"Universa inutiliter habet, qui unum illud, quo universis utatur, non habete" (Serm.* 88, 18, 21: PL 38, 550).

In the midst of the deep and continual changes in all fields, the clergy feels the need to keep up with the breathtaking pace of this time: they feel the need for continual updating in order to be ready and vigilant in interpreting events in the light of God's Word, that is, in a Christian perspective.

The urgency, the necessity of an "ongoing formation," spiritual and cultural, of the clergy, as well as of the laity who are committed on the apostolic plane, is felt more and more. We must recognize that Rome, with the cultural riches of its universities and Pontifical Athenaea, could draw up really adequate initiatives. In this field, too, cordial and mutual availability and collaboration will be necessary.

NEED OF AWAKENING VOCATIONS

6. Among the prior duties which are incumbent on the bishop, the presbyterium and the whole Church of Rome, there is that of priestly and religious vocations.

In the specific report, stress was laid on my constant concern for this problem, and for this I am grateful. At the first meeting with the Roman clergy, I opened my heart to you with great sincerity and frankness, and I urged you to participate in this solicitude of mine. I have often returned to this subject, even a few days ago, when speaking to members of the Council and the Regional Secretaries gathered in Rome to reflect together on problems concerning the promotion of vocations at a meeting organized by the Italian Conference of Major Superiors. On this occasion I addressed in general all priests and religious who "live serenely, day after day, for their vocation, faithful to the commitments assumed, humble and hidden constructors of the kingdom of God, from whose words, behavior and lives there radiates the luminous joy of the choice made. It is precisely such religious and priests who, by means of their example, will spur so many people to receive in their hearts the charism of vocation" (cf. *L'Osservatore Romano*, February 17, 1980, p. 2).

The diocese has two seminaries: the Roman Major Seminary, which at present has 85 students, of whom 22 are Romans; and the Roman Minor Seminary, which has 13 boarders, who constitute the stable community; furthermore, 70 boys of the junior and senior secondary schools form the vocational community: They frequently meet in the seminary. Around them there gravitate another 200 boys of the secondary schools, whom the members of the seminary meet in parishes or in the seminary itself, to help them to study their vocation thoroughly.

From these statistical data there emerges the urgent necessity of an "awakening of vocations," of a conscious, constant, pondered and organized effort in order that also—and especially—in this field the diocese of Rome may be fruitful and fertile; that the diocesan seminaries, rich in glorious traditions of cultural and spiritual formation, may become more and more the reflection of the vitality of our particular Church. The vitality and maturity of a diocese are in proportion to the number and quality of its priestly and religious vocations. In the last fifteen years the number of diocesan priests coming from the Roman seminaries amounted to 122.

Will the diocese of Rome be so generous as to continue to give numerous and holy priests for the construction of the kingdom of God?

LAY PEOPLE'S ROLE

7. The various visits to the parishes have given me, furthermore, the possibility of seeing how groups of the laity, committed to the apostolate, are operating in these communities.

Lay people are rediscovering the parish. This is a consoling reality, because it shows how the faithful feel the need for a stable point of reference. As many as seventy associations of a national character are present, in varying numbers, in the different parishes; while there are about a hundred local groups working in the apostolate. My encouragement goes to these groups which, in the sphere of Christian faith, intend to bear a special witness either with community prayer or by means of religious listening to the Word of God, or in the commitment of charity to needy brothers.

But I would like no parish to be without the "group of catechists," composed of adults—mothers and fathers of families—and young people, thoroughly prepared and generously available to transmit catechesis to children and youth. "The parish community must continue to be the prime mover and pre-eminent place for catechesis.... Whatever one may think, the parish is still a major point of reference for the Christian people, even for the non-practicing." I wrote this in my recent Apostolic Exhortation *On Catechesis in Our Time* (CT 67).

In our parishes there exist the fundamental elements of those structures which make the parish a missionary unit of evangelization and catechesis. Although statistics indicate that the degree of penetration of the "mass" of that vast complex of parishioners is less than could be desired, it is necessary, however, not to lose heart and to dedicate a great effort to the problem of catechesis.

8. I am thinking at this moment particularly of the young, to whom my apostolic solicitude as priest, bishop and pastor of the universal Church goes in a special way. As you have heard from the report, in Rome—out of 2,900,000—500,000 are young people between 15 and 30 years of age! And of them, as many of 200,000 are looking for employment! Their human problems are serious. Even more serious are the spiritual ones. It is a question of their education and maturation in the Christian faith, their preparation for marriage, their integration in the society of adults, which has sometimes deeply disappointed them. What will the Church of Rome do, what will the priests of Rome do, to meet, in an adequate and modern way, the ideals, the religious, cultural and social expectations of these young people, a good many of whom are disappointed by ideologies and tempted to change society at any cost and by any means, even with violence?

I appeal to the young priests of Rome to dedicate their best energies to the apostolate among the young with generosity, enthusiasm and constancy, without letting themselves be discouraged by inevitable human failures.

Love the young! Make an effort to listen to them, to understand them! They have inexhaustible, hidden treasures of generosity and enthusiasm. Present to them Christ, the Man-God, our brother! Proclaim to them the Gospel message with all the vigor and all the rigor of its requirements!

UNITED IN CHARITY

9. Dear brothers in the priesthood!

I have listened with great interest and attention to what your representatives told me, on your behalf, about the situation of the Roman clergy, the parishes, the organic diocesan program, priestly vocations in Rome, the presence of men and women religious in Rome, the condition of the young.

On my side, I have tried to make myself the mouthpiece of your own voice, your thoughts, your desires, your hopes, but in particular of your commitment to be true priests of Christ in this Church, which is in Rome.

Let us continue together along our way of faith and pastoral commitment, strong in the power of Christ, which was manifested in His human weakness.

Today the Church celebrates the memory of St. Peter Damian, the austere hermit of Forte Avellana, called by God to take his place in the dramatic ecclesial events of the year one thousand, in a difficult and dangerous historical period. Let us listen to, and make our own, his call to love the Church united by the bond of mutual charity: *"Ecclesia siquidem Christi tanta caritatis invicem inter se campage connectitur, ut et in pluribus una, et in singulis sit per mysterium tota.... In omnibus sit una, et in singulis tota: nimirum in pluribus per fidei unitatem simplex, et in singulis per caritatis glutinem, diversaque dona carismatum multiplex; quia enim ex uno omnes" (Liber qui appellatur Dominus vobiscum,* 5: PL 145, 235).

In the Church of God which is in Rome, may the diversity of charisms always be united by charity.

May the Virgin, *Salus Populi Romani* and Mother of Trust, protect us from heaven.

With my apostolic blessing.

Renewed Commitment and True Solidarity

On February 22, 1980, the Holy Father received in audience the directors of the National Federation of the Italian Clergy, on the occasion of the recent election of the directors which took place on November 27, 1979. John Paul II delivered the following greeting.

Beloved sons!

I am happy to address my cordial greeting to you, receiving you this morning at this special audience reserved for you as members of the Board of Directors of the National Federation of the Italian Clergy. Through your persons, my greeting also intends to reach all the priests in the beloved Italian nation, who are exerting themselves in the pastoral ministry with admirable dedication and under conditions that are often not easy.

Your well-deserving association arose precisely to make provision for the problems raised by the present conditions, in which the activity of the Italian clergy takes place, and I am happy to take advantage of this circumstance to pay a due tribute of gratitude to all that your federation has done, in these years, to ensure suitable assistance for confrères in their necessities, both of a spiritual and of an economic and social nature.

I wish to encourage you to persevere with renewed commitment in this brotherly work of charity, which the present historical moment makes particularly delicate and urgent. The efforts made to guarantee every priest what may be necessary for him to live soberly, securely, but also decorously, releasing him from minor, sometimes harassing cares, due to the unforeseeable vicissitudes of life, and instilling in him a sense of tranquil detachment in the exercise of his ministry, are to be considered worthy of all consideration.

But beyond these concerns on the plane of welfare, it must remain your principal solicitude to stimulate among the clergy the growth of the spiritual values of solidarity, mutual understanding, brotherly emulation in dedication to the requirements of their vocation. To nourish in priests awareness of the deep union that the sacrament of Holy Orders has established among them and to work in order that in every diocese there may be a real family spirit within the presbyterium, gathered round its own bishop, this is the mission by which all your work must be animated and guided.

I entrust to the Blessed Virgin, the Mother of Christ and, in a special way, the Mother of every priest, these wishes of mine, confident that she will obtain light, generosity and energy for you, to continue, albeit in the midst of the inevitable difficulties, with your work, which is so important and delicate.

The apostolic blessing, which I willingly impart to you and to all the priests to whom your association is addressed, is an auspice of these heavenly gifts and a token of my benevolence.

Permanent Significance of the Christian Family

On February 23, 1980, the Holy Father presided over the meeting of the Council of the General Secretariat of the Synod of Bishops. After Cardinal Felici's greeting and report, His Holiness first of all thanked those present, stressing that he had gone to the meeting not only to say some concluding words, but also to listen. He recalled that he had been elected a member of the Council at the last session of the Synod of Bishops in 1977, and he then dwelt on the extreme importance of the subject, chosen for the next synod by Pope Paul VI of venerable memory with boldness and fortitude.

"The ordinary session of the Synod of Bishops"—he added—"is of great, in fact extremely great, value in the life of the Church, as has been proved by the experience of the past years. In this post-conciliar period, the synod contributes a great deal to implementing the subjects, the decisions, the policies of the Second Vatican Council, especially from the pastoral point of view. If we consider the themes of the preceding sessions—evangelization, catechesis—we realize that they are clearly subjects of great pastoral significance. Equally important is also the subject of the next synod: "The role of the Christian family in the modern world." In this perspective, it is necessary, then, to expect not only the participation of members of the synod in the formal sense, that is, those who are to be elected by the episcopal conferences, as well as those chosen by the Pope, but also the intermediate, indirect participation of others, since it is a question of a matter of great importance for the Church, for all her pastors, and also for the whole People of God, in particular for our brothers and sisters, who must carry out these tasks of the Christian family in their lives, in the life of the Church.

"The importance of this Synod"—the Pope said further—"its greatness and also its difficulty, lies in this. If, speaking just now of the decision taken by the late Pontiff, I called it a 'bold' one, I also added that it was reached 'with fortitude.' The Church, in things that concern the good of souls, must be bold and strong. At the next session of the synod, the same boldness and the same fortitude are to be expected of the Church, and in particular of those who take part in it. But we must also expect a special grace. We who have taken part in the past in various sessions of the synod have had the experience of this grace, as for example in the 1974 Synod. We expect the same grace also for the next synod; we hope for it; we must implore it with prayer, all of us and also those who are concerned about the good of the Church, her true mission."

The Holy Father went on to say that "it will be necessary to make provision for the problems regarding the next synod with our experience and with that of others, especially of the episcopal conferences, and, moreover, with due prudence. It will be necessary, indeed, to eliminate useless publicity, as far as possible. One thing is discussion, and the difficulty of the themes; quite another is the publicity aspect, which claims to present problems that are in themselves difficult and profound in an oversimple and superficial way. It will be necessary to eliminate and avoid all that, both in the preparation of the synod and also in the course of the session.

"Preparation will have to be continuous, in every aspect, and in that not only the work of the General Secretariat itself, of the Council and all the experts, is of great importance, but also that of the Committee for the Family, which has recently been deprived of its Vice-President Secretary, Mons. Gagnon, who has resigned. He has been replaced by Bishop Majdanski of Szczecin-Kamien, in Poland, at least for this period; we all expect help from this committee and other groups collaborating with it.

> "It seems to me that this session of the Council of the General Secretariat of the Synod of Bishops"—the Holy Father continued—"has done a great work, with the help of the experts and of the above-mentioned Committee for the Family. I, too, wish to offer my contribution to this work, since it is a matter of the utmost importance, which is very close to my heart. It was so in my preceding pastoral activity, and so it remains now too."
>
> Concluding his intervention, the Sovereign Pontiff recalled how he had taken part, in that same hall, in the work of a particular Synod, that of the Bishops of the Ecclesiastical Province of the Netherlands. "It was an unprecedented experience, unique so far. This experience, the experience of the work of twenty days," the Pope said, "left an excellent impression on me, in my mind and in my heart. I was able to see how important are the doctrine, theory and practice of collegiality in the Church; how, with the help of this principle, even difficult matters in the life of the Church can be solved. After the experience of the Synod of Dutch Bishops, I am happy and hopeful for the forthcoming session of the Synod of Bishops; with the same careful consideration, the same wisdom and pastoral prudence, the same doctrinal knowledge, the same spirit of responsibility, we will be able to achieve a great deal. I want to pray with you for this now."
>
> The Holy Father then delivered the following address.

Dear brothers in the episcopate,
Dear friends,

I. It is with joy that I meet you this morning in this hall which witnesses the First General Synod, and where you have kindly arranged to hold the last session of your council, thus making it possible for me to join in your work for a moment.

The next synod has as its subject: "The role of the Christian family in the modern world." Our age makes it necessary, in fact, to throw full light, in a comprehensible and suitable way, on the permanent meaning of this institution, which has long been rightly defined as "the domestic Church." On all sides, the secretariat of the synod has gathered the observations of the episcopal conferences, the experience of pastors, the way in which the evangelical ferment is at work in very different situations. On this basis, you are drawing up the background document which will permit thorough and fruitful work on the part of members of the synod.

In the first place, therefore, I am anxious to thank you, members of the Council of the General Secretariat of the synod, experts and members of the secretariat, for the service you thus render to the organism which is a very special expression of episcopal collegiality, through which pastors of dioceses share with the Bishop of Rome solicitude for all the Churches.

THE SYNOD AND ITS WORK

II. I do not wish to take up again here all the riches of your discussions or to dwell on all the problems which you think it necessary to submit to the next synod.

This synod will involve, in the first place, a description of the situation of families and of the different problems it raises. It is necessary to begin by looking clearly at the way in which family life is lived today, analyzing, as far as possible, the causes and lines of evolution, in order that evangelization may really penetrate this world.

An important part will be dedicated to theology, to the Catholic doctrine on the family. The synod must, in fact, strengthen the convictions of Christians. It is without doubt less a matter of giving again a systematic exposition of facts that are already well known and well established —as if we were starting from scratch, whereas the Church has been living by them for two thousand years—as of finding the language and underlying motivations that illustrate the permanent doctrine of the Church in a way that will reach and, if possible, convince the men of today, in their concrete situations, which will enable them to reply, for example, to certain tendencies which are spreading, such as that of consensual union. The synod will not provide an answer to all problems, but it will have to show clearly what it means to follow Christ in this field; it will have to define the values without which society plunges blindly into a dead-end; it will have to help Christians and men of good will to form on these points an enlightened and firm conscience, according to Christian principles.

Finally and above all, the synod will seek realistically how to permit families to find again these values or, having them, to live by them, to spread them around them, step by step. This will be the directly pastoral part.

IMPORTANT ASPECTS

III. I will merely stress some aspects which seem to me particularly important.

1. Considerations on the Christian family cannot be separated from *marriage*, for the couple constitutes the first form of the family and maintains its value even in the absence of children. And there, it is necessary to reach the deep meaning of marriage, which is a union and love: a union and love between two subjects, a man and a woman, a sign of the covenant between Christ and His Church, love that is rooted in Trinitarian life. The characteristics of this union must then appear in all their clarity: unity of the couple, faithfulness of the union, permanence of the conjugal tie.

2. The family must be envisaged as an *institution*, not only in the sense that it has its place and its functions in society and in the Church, that it must have juridical guarantees for the accomplishment of its duties, and in order to have the stability and influence expected of it, but in the sense that in itself it transcends the will of the individuals, the spontaneous projects of the couples, the decisions of social and governmental organisms: marriage is "the wise institution of the Creator to realize in mankind His design of love" (HV 8). It will be opportune to study more deeply this institutional aspect, which, far from being an obstacle to love, is its consummation.

3. It will be necessary to pay particular attention to preparation for love and for marriage, which is necessarily also a preparation for family life and family responsibilities. How can this preparation be ensured today? It is an essential point of pastoral work.

4. Priests, on their part, must be prepared and formed for the family apostolate, for a fundamental part of their role consists in supporting lay people in their responsibilities, personal and social, certainly, but also family responsibilities. Do they appreciate this family apostolate sufficiently? Are they initiated into its complex problems? As pastors, we do not have to solve all the problems of married couples ourselves, but we must be close to them in their difficulties as in their joys, and be able to help them, as the Lord wishes.

FORMATION OF THE LAY PEOPLE

5. The laity, of course, must also be able to find the conditions of their doctrinal, spiritual and pedagogical formation for their life as a couple, as well as for their responsibilities as parents at grips with all the problems of bringing up their children at the different stages of their growth. It is a question further of enlightening them in their attitudes towards all the members of the family in the wide sense, among whom there must be real solidarity: particularly with the sick, the handicapped and the old. The latter expect to receive special affection and support from the family, while themselves making a fine contribution, through their experience and their love.

The formation of these lay people is doubly important, in order to initiate them to real Christian values, and to enable them to bear witness to them, for, under present-day conditions, the evangelization of families will be carried out mainly by other families.

PASTORAL SOLICITUDE

6. Finally, we shall not forget the pastoral solicitude required by difficult cases: separated couples; divorced persons who have contracted another civil marriage, and who, without being able to have full access to sacramental life, must be accompanied in their spiritual needs and the

apostolate which is possible for them; widowers and widows; persons who alone are in charge of children, etc.

These few words, esteemed brothers and dear friends, give you an idea of all the interest the Pope takes in this synod, and the great hopes he lays in it for the Church. I address my heartiest encouragements to those who now have the task of making the final preparations. I am also thinking of all the future participants who are preparing for it in reflection and with the help of their Christian people. We will all pray to God to enlighten minds and prepare hearts in order that the experience of the synod may bring about an increase of convictions, resolutions and encouragement for the holiness of families. We are entrusting this work to the intercession of the Mother of Christ who is the Mother of the Church.

On the Mystery and Worship of the Eucharist

DOMINICAE CENAE

February 24, 1980

My venerable and dear brothers,

1. Again this year, for Holy Thursday, I am writing a letter to all of you. This letter has an immediate connection with the one which you received last year on the same occasion, together with the letter to the priests. I wish *in the first place to thank you cordially* for having accepted my previous letters with that spirit of unity which the Lord established between us, and also for having transmitted to your priests the thoughts that I desired to express at the beginning of my pontificate.

During the Eucharistic Liturgy of Holy Thursday, you renewed, together with your priests, the promises and commitments undertaken at the moment of ordination. Many of you, venerable and dear brothers, told me about it later, also adding words of personal thanks, and indeed often sending those expressed by your priests. Furthermore, many priests expressed their joy, both because of the profound and solemn character of Holy Thursday as the annual "feast of priests" and also because of the importance of the subjects dealt with in the letter addressed to them.

Those replies form a rich collection which once more indicates how dear to the vast majority of priests of the Catholic Church is the path of the priestly life, the path along which this Church has been journeying for centuries: How much they love and esteem it, and how much they desire to follow it for the future.

At this point I must add that *only a certain number of matters were dealt with in the letter to priests,* as was in fact emphasized at the beginning of the document.[1] Furthermore, the main stress was laid upon the pastoral character of the priestly ministry; but this certainly does not mean that those groups of priests who are not engaged in direct pastoral activity were not also taken into consideration. In this regard I would refer once more to the teaching of the Second Vatican Council, and also to the declarations of the 1971 Synod of Bishops.

The pastoral character of the priestly ministry does not cease to mark the life of every priest, even if the daily tasks that he carries out are not explicitly directed to the pastoral administration of the sacraments. In this sense, the letter written to the priests on Holy Thursday was addressed to them all, without any exception, even though, as I said above, it did not deal with all the aspects of the life and activity of priests. I think this clarification is useful and opportune at the beginning of the present letter:

I. THE EUCHARISTIC MYSTERY IN THE LIFE OF THE CHURCH AND OF THE PRIEST

Eucharist and Priesthood

2. The present letter that I am addressing to you, my venerable and dear brothers in the episcopate—and which is, as I have said, in a certain way a continuation of the previous one—is also closely linked with the mystery of Holy Thursday, and is related to the priesthood. In fact I intend to devote it to the Eucharist, and in particular *to certain aspects of the Eucharistic mystery and its impact on the lives of those who are the ministers of It:* and so those to whom this letter is directly addressed are you, the bishops of the Church; together with you, all the priests; and, in their own rank, the deacons too.

In reality, the ministerial and hierarchical priesthood, the priesthood of the bishops and the priests, and, at their side, the ministry of the deacons—ministries which normally begin with the proclamation of the Gospel—are in the closest relationship with the Eucharist. The Eucharist is the principal and central *raison d'être* of the sacrament of the priesthood, which effectively came into being at the moment of the institution of the Eucharist, and together with it.[2] Not without reason the words "Do this in memory of me" are said immediately after the words of eucharistic consecration, and we repeat them every time we celebrate the holy sacrifice.[3]

Through our ordination—the celebration of which is linked to the holy Mass from the very first liturgical evidence[4]—we are united in a singular and exceptional way to the Eucharist. In a certain way we derive *from* it and exist *for* it. We are also, and in a special way, responsible for it—each priest in his own community and each bishop by virtue of the care of all the communities entrusted to him, on the basis of the *sollicitudo omnium ecclesiarum* that St. Paul speaks of.[5] Thus we bishops and priests are entrusted with the great "Mystery of Faith," and while it is also given to the whole People of God, to all believers in Christ, yet to us has been entrusted the Eucharist also "for" others, who expect from us a particular witness of veneration and love towards this sacrament, so that they too may be able to be built up and vivified "to offer spiritual sacrifices."[6]

In this way our eucharistic worship, both in the celebration of Mass and in our devotion to the blessed Sacrament, is like a life-giving current that links our ministerial or hierarchical priesthood to the common priesthood of the faithful, and presents it in its vertical dimension and with its central value. The priest fulfills his principal mission and is manifested in all his fullness when he celebrates the Eucharist,[7] and this manifestation is more complete when he himself allows the depth of that mystery to become visible, so that it alone shines forth in people's hearts and minds, through his ministry. This is the supreme exercise of the "kingly priesthood," "the source and summit of all Christian life."[8]

Worship of the Eucharistic Mystery

3. This worship is directed towards God the Father through Jesus Christ in the Holy Spirit. In the first place towards the Father, who, as St. John's Gospel says, "loved the world so much that he gave his only Son, so that everyone who believes in him may not be lost but may have eternal life."[9]

It is also directed, in the Holy Spirit, to the incarnate Son, in the economy of salvation, especially at that moment of supreme dedication and total abandonment of Himself to which the words uttered in the Upper Room refer: "This is my body given up for you.... This is the cup of my blood shed for you...."[10] The liturgical acclamation: "We proclaim your death, Lord Jesus" takes us back precisely to that moment; and with the proclamation of His resurrection we embrace in the same act of veneration Christ risen and glorified "at the right hand of the Father," as also the expectation of His "coming in glory." *Yet it is the voluntary emptying of Himself, accepted by the Father and glorified with the resurrection,* which, sacramentally celebrated together with the resurrection, brings us to adore the Redeemer who "became obedient unto death, even death on a cross."[11]

And this adoration of ours contains yet another special characteristic. It is compenetrated by the greatness of that human death, in which the world, that is to say, each one of us, has been loved "to the end."[12] Thus it is also a response that tries to repay that love immolated even to the death on the cross: it is our "Eucharist," that is to say, our giving Him thanks, our praise of Him for having redeemed us by His death and made us sharers in immortal life through His resurrection.

This worship, given therefore to the Trinity of the Father and of the Son and of the Holy Spirit, above all accompanies and permeates the celebration of the Eucharistic Liturgy. But it must fill our churches also outside the timetable of Masses. Indeed, since the Eucharistic Mystery was instituted out of love, and makes Christ sacramentally present, it is worthy of thanksgiving and worship. And this worship must be prominent in all our encounters with the Blessed Sacrament, both when we visit our churches and when the sacred Species are taken to the sick and administered to them.

Adoration of Christ in this sacrament of love must also find expression *in various forms of Eucharistic devotion:* personal prayer before the Blessed Sacrament, Hours of Adoration, periods of Exposition—short, prolonged and annual (Forty Hours)—Eucharistic benediction, Eucharistic processions, Eucharistic congresses.[13] A particular mention should be made at this point of the Solemnity of the Body and Blood of Christ as an act of public worship rendered to Christ present in the Eucharist, a feast instituted by my Predecessor Urban IV in memory of the institution of this great Mystery.[14] All this therefore corresponds to the general principles and particular norms already long in existence but newly formulated during or after the Second Vatican Council.[15]

The encouragement and the deepening of Eucharistic worship are *proofs of that authentic renewal* which the Council set itself as an aim and of which they are *the central point.* And this, venerable and dear brothers, deserves separate reflection. The Church and the world have a great need of Eucharistic worship. Jesus waits for us in this sacrament of love. Let us be generous with our time in going to meet Him in adoration and in contemplation that is full of faith and ready to make reparation for the great faults and crimes of the world. May our adoration never cease.

Eucharist and Church

4. Thanks to the Council we have realized with renewed force the following truth: Just as the Church "makes the Eucharist" so "the Eucharist builds up" the Church[16]; and this truth is closely bound up with the mystery of Holy Thursday. The Church was founded, as

the new community of the People of God, in the apostolic community of those Twelve who, at the Last Supper, became partakers of the body and blood of the Lord under the species of bread and wine. Christ had said to them: "Take and eat.... Take and drink." And carrying out this command of His, they entered for the first time into sacramental communion with the Son of God, a communion that is a pledge of eternal life. From that moment until the end of time, *the Church is being built up through that same communion with the Son of God, a communion which is a pledge of the eternal Passover.*

Dear and venerable brothers in the episcopate, as teachers and custodians of the salvific truth of the Eucharist, we must always and everywhere preserve this meaning and this dimension of the sacramental encounter and intimacy with Christ. It is precisely these elements which constitute the very substance of Eucharistic worship. The meaning of the truth expounded above in no way diminishes—in fact, it facilitates—the Eucharistic character of spiritual drawing together and union between the people who share in the sacrifice, which then in Communion becomes for them the banquet. This drawing together and this union, the prototype of which is the union of the Apostles about Christ at the Last Supper, express the Church and bring her into being.

But the Church is not brought into being only through the union of people, through the experience of brotherhood to which the Eucharistic Banquet gives rise. The Church is brought into being when, in that fraternal union and communion, we celebrate the sacrifice of the cross of Christ, when we proclaim "the Lord's death until he comes,"[17] and later, when, being deeply compenetrated with the mystery of our salvation, we approach as a community the table of the Lord, in order to be nourished there, in a sacramental manner, by the fruits of the holy sacrifice of propitiation. Therefore in Eucharistic Communion we receive Christ, Christ Himself; and our union with Him, which is a gift and grace for each individual, brings it about that in Him we are also associated in the unity of His Body which is the Church.

Only in this way, through that faith and that disposition of mind, is there brought about that building up of the Church, which in the Eucharist truly finds its "source and summit," according to the well-known expression of the Second Vatican Council.[18] This truth, which as a result of the same Council has received a new and vigorous emphasis,[19] must be a frequent theme of our reflection and teaching. Let all pastoral activity be nourished by it, and may it also be food for ourselves and for all the priests who collaborate with us, and likewise for the whole of the communities entrusted to us. In this practice there should thus be revealed, almost at every step, that *close relationship between the Church's spiritual and apostolic vitality* and *the Eucharist, understood in its profound significance* and from all points of view.[20]

Eucharist and Charity

5. Before proceeding to more detailed observations on the subject of the celebration of the holy Sacrifice, I wish briefly to reaffirm the fact that Eucharistic worship constitutes the soul of all Christian life. In fact, Christian life is expressed in the fulfilling of the greatest commandment, that is to say, in the love of God and neighbor, and this love finds its source in the Blessed Sacrament, which is commonly called the sacrament of love.

The Eucharist signifies this charity, and therefore recalls it, makes it present *and at the same time brings it about*. Every time that we consciously share in it, there opens in our souls a real dimension of that unfathomable love that includes everything that God has done and continues to do for us human beings, as Christ says: "My Father goes on working, and so do I."[21] Together with this unfathomable and free gift, which is *charity* revealed in its fullest degree in the saving sacrifice of the Son of God, the sacrifice of which the Eucharist is the indelible sign, there also springs up within us a lively response of love. We not only know love; we ourselves *begin to love*. We enter, so to speak, upon the path of love and along this path make progress. Thanks to the Eucharist, the love that springs up within us from the Eucharist develops in us, becomes deeper and grows stronger.

Eucharistic worship is, therefore, precisely the expression of that love which is the authentic and deepest characteristic of the Christian vocation. This worship springs from the love and serves the love to which we are all called in Jesus Christ.[22] A living fruit of this worship is the perfecting of the image of God that we bear within us, an image that corresponds to the one that Christ has revealed in us. As we thus become adorers of the Father "in spirit and truth,"[23] we mature in an ever fuller union with Christ, we are ever more united to Him, and—if one may use the expression—we are ever more in harmony with Him.

The doctrine of the Eucharist, sign of unity and bond of charity, taught by St. Paul,[24] has been in subsequent times deepened by the writings of very many saints who are a living examples for us of Eucharistic worship. We must always have this reality before our eyes, and at the same time we must continually try to bring it about that our own generation, too, may add new examples to those marvelous examples of the past, new examples no less living and eloquent, that will reflect the age to which we belong.

Eucharist and Neighbor

6. *The authentic sense of the Eucharist becomes of itself the school of active love for neighbor.* We know that this is the true and full order of love that the Lord has taught us: "By this love you have for one another, everyone will know that you are my disciples."[25] The Eucharist educates us to this love in a deeper way; it shows us, in fact, what value each person, our brother or sister, has in God's eyes, if Christ offers Himself equally to each

one, under the species of bread and wine. If our Eucharistic worship is authentic, it must make us grow in awareness of the dignity of each person. The awareness of that dignity becomes the *deepest motive of our relationship with our neighbor.*

We must also become particularly sensitive to all human suffering and misery, to all injustice and wrong, and seek the way to redress them effectively. Let us learn to discover with respect the truth about the inner self that becomes the dwelling place of God present in the Eucharist. Christ comes into the hearts of our brothers and sisters and visits their consciences. How the image of each and every one changes, when we become aware of this reality, when we make it the subject of our reflections! The sense of the Eucharistic Mystery leads us to a love for our neighbor, to a love for every human being.[26]

Eucharist and Life

7. Since, therefore, the Eucharist is the source of charity, it has always been at the center of the life of Christ's disciples. It has the appearance of bread and wine, that is to say of food and drink; it is, therefore, as familiar to people, as closely linked to their life, as food and drink. The veneration of God, who is love, springs, in Eucharistic worship, from that kind of intimacy in which *He Himself, by analogy with food and drink, fills our spiritual being,* ensuring its life, as food and drink do. This "Eucharistic" veneration of God, therefore, strictly corresponds to His saving plan. He Himself, the Father, wants the "true worshipers"[27] to worship Him precisely in this way, and it is Christ who expresses this desire, both with His words and likewise with this sacrament in which He makes possible worship of the Father in the way most in conformity with the Father's will.

From this concept of Eucharistic worship there then stems the whole *sacramental style of the Christian's life.* In fact, leading a life based on the sacraments and animated by the common priesthood means in the first place that Christians desire God to act in them in order to enable them to attain, in the Spirit, "the fullness of Christ himself."[28] God, on His part, does not touch them only through events and by this inner grace; He also acts in them with greater certainty and power through the sacraments. The sacraments give the lives of Christians a sacramental style.

Now, of all the sacraments it is the Holy Eucharist that brings to fullness their initiation as Christians and confers upon the exercise of the common priesthood that sacramental and ecclesial form that links it—as we mentioned before[29]—to the exercise of the ministerial priesthood. In this way Eucharistic worship is the *center and goal of all sacramental life*.[30] In the depths of Eucharistic worship we find a continual echo of the sacraments of Christian initiation: Baptism and Confirmation. Where better is there expressed the truth that we are not only "called God's children" but "that is what we are"[31] by virtue of the sacrament of Baptism, if not precisely in the fact that in the Eucharist we become partakers of the body and blood of God's only Son? And what predisposes us more to be "true witnesses of Christ"[32] before the world—as we are enabled to be by the sacrament of Confirmation—than Eucharistic Communion, in which Christ bears witness to us, and we to Him?

It is impossible to analyze here in greater detail the links between the Eucharist and the other sacraments, in particular with the sacrament of family life and the sacrament of the sick. In the encyclical *Redemptor hominis*[33] I have already drawn attention to the close link between the sacrament of Penance and the sacrament of the Eucharist. *It is not only that Penance leads to the Eucharist, but that the Eucharist also leads to Penance.* For when we realize who it is that we receive in Eucharistic Communion, there springs up in us almost spontaneously a sense of unworthiness, together with sorrow for our sins and an interior need for purification.

But we must always take care that this great meeting with Christ in the Eucharist does not become a mere habit, and that we do not receive Him unworthily, that is to say, in a state of mortal sin. The practice of the virtue of penance and the sacrament of Penance are essential for sustaining in us and continually deepening that spirit of veneration which man owes to God Himself and to His love so marvelously revealed. The purpose of these words is to put forward some general reflections on worship of the Eucharistic Mystery, and they could be developed at greater length and more fully. In particular, it would be possible to link what has been said about the effects of the Eucharist on love for others with what we have just noted about commitments undertaken towards humanity and the Church in Eucharistic Communion, and then outline the picture of that "new earth"[34] that springs from the Eucharist through every "new self."[35] *In this Sacrament of bread and wine, of food and drink, everything that is human really undergoes a singular transformation and elevation.* Eucharistic worship is not so much worship of the inaccessible transcendence as worship of the divine condescension, and it is also the merciful and redeeming transformation of the world in the human heart.

Recalling all this only very briefly, I wish, notwithstanding this brevity, to create a wider context for the questions that I shall subsequently have to deal with: These questions are closely linked with the celebration of the holy Sacrifice. In fact, in that celebration there is expressed in a more direct way the worship of the Eucharist. This worship comes from the heart, as a most precious homage inspired by the faith, hope and charity which were infused into us at Baptism. And it is precisely about this that I wish to write to you in this letter, venerable and dear brothers in the episcopate, and with you to the priests and deacons. It will be followed by detailed indications from the Sacred Congregation for the Sacraments and Divine Worship.

II. THE SACRED CHARACTER OF THE EUCHARIST AND SACRIFICE

Sacred Character

8. Beginning with the Upper Room and Holy Thursday, the celebration of the Eucharist has a long history, a history as long as that of the Church. In the course of this history the secondary elements have undergone certain changes, *but there has been no change in the essence of the "Mysterium"* instituted by the Redeemer of the world at the Last Supper. The Second Vatican Council, too, brought alterations, as a result of which the present liturgy of the Mass is different in some ways from the one known before the Council. We do not intend to speak of these differences: It is better that we should now concentrate on what is essential and immutable in the Eucharistic Liturgy.

There is a close link between this element of the Eucharist and its sacredness, that is to say, its being a holy and sacred action. Holy and sacred, because in it are the continual presence and action of Christ, "the Holy One" of God,[36] "anointed with the Holy Spirit,"[37] "consecrated by the Father"[38] to lay down His life of His own accord and to take it up again,[39] and the High Priest of the New Covenant.[40] For it is He who, represented by the celebrant, makes His entrance into the sanctuary and proclaims His Gospel. It is He who is "the offerer and the offered, the consecrator and the consecrated."[41] The Eucharist is a holy and sacred action, because it constitutes the sacred species, the *Sancta sanctis*, that is to say, the "holy things (Christ, the Holy One) given to the Holy," as all the Eastern liturgies sing at the moment when the Eucharistic Bread is raised in order to invite the faithful to the Lord's Supper.

The sacredness of the Mass, therefore, is not a "sacralization," that is to say, something that man adds to Christ's action in the Upper Room, for the Holy Thursday supper was a sacred rite, a primary and constitutive liturgy, through which Christ, by pledging to give His life for us, Himself celebrated sacramentally the mystery of His passion and resurrection, the heart of every Mass. Our Masses, being derived from this liturgy, possess of themselves a complete liturgical form, which, in spite of its variations in line with the families of rites, remains substantially the same. The sacred character of the Mass is a sacredness instituted by Christ. The words and actions of every priest, answered by the conscious active participation of the whole Eucharistic assembly, echo the words and actions of Holy Thursday.

The priest offers the Holy Sacrifice *in persona Christi:* this means more than offering "in the name of" or "in place of" Christ. *In persona* means in specific sacramental identification with "the eternal High Priest"[42] who is the author and principal subject of this sacrifice of His, a sacrifice in which, in truth, nobody can take His place. Only He—only Christ—was able and is always able to be the true and effective "expiation for our sins and...for the sins of the whole world."[43] Only His sacrifice—and no one else's—was able and is able to have a "propitiatory power" before God, the Trinity, and the transcendent holiness. Awareness of this reality throws a certain light on the character and significance of the priest celebrant who, *by confecting the Holy Sacrifice and acting "in persona Christi,"* is sacramentally (and ineffably) brought into that most profound *sacredness,* and made part of it, spiritually linking with it in turn all those participating in the Eucharistic assembly.

This sacred rite, which is actuated in different liturgical forms, may lack some secondary elements, but it can in no way lack its essential sacred character and sacramentality, since these are willed by Christ and transmitted and regulated by the Church. Neither can this sacred rite be utilized for other ends. If separated from its distinctive sacrificial and sacramental nature, the Eucharistic Mystery simply ceases to be. It admits of no "profane" imitation, an imitation that would very easily (indeed regularly) become a profanation. This must always be remembered, perhaps above all in our time, when we see a tendency to do away with the distinction between the "sacred" and "profane," given the widespread tendency, at least in some places, to desacralize everything.

In view of this fact, *the Church has a special duty to safeguard and strengthen the sacredness of the Eucharist.* In our pluralistic and often deliberately secularized society, *the living faith* of the Christian community—a faith always aware of its rights vis-a-vis those who do not share that faith—ensures respect for this sacredness. The duty to respect each person's faith is the complement of the natural and civil right to freedom of conscience and of religion.

The sacred character of the Eucharist has found and continues to find expression in the terminology of theology and the liturgy.[44] This sense of the objective sacred character of the Eucharistic Mystery is so much part of the faith of the People of God that their faith is enriched and strengthened by it.[45] Therefore, the ministers of the Eucharist must, especially today, be illumined by the fullness of this living faith, and in its light they must understand and perform all that is part, by Christ's will and the will of His Church, of their priestly ministry.

Sacrifice

9. The Eucharist is above all else a sacrifice. It is the sacrifice of the redemption and also the sacrifice of the New Covenant,[46] as we believe and as the Eastern Churches clearly profess: "Today's sacrifice," the Greek Church stated centuries ago, "is like that offered once by the only-begotten Incarnate Word; it is offered by Him (now as then), since it is one and the same sacrifice."[47] Accordingly, precisely by making this single sacrifice of our salvation present, man and the world are restored to God through the paschal newness of redemption. This restoration cannot cease to be: It is the foundation of the "new and eternal covenant" of God with man and of man with God. If it were missing, one would have to question both the excellence of the sacrifice of the redemption,

which in fact was perfect and definitive, and also the sacrificial value of the Mass. In fact, the Eucharist, being a true sacrifice, brings about this restoration to God.

Consequently, the celebrant, as minister of this sacrifice, is the authentic *priest*, performing—in virtue of the specific power of sacred ordination—a true sacrificial act that brings creation back to God. Although all those who participate in the Eucharist do not confect the sacrifice as He does, they offer with Him, by virtue of the common priesthood, their own *spiritual sacrifices* represented by the bread and wine from the moment of their presentation at the altar. For this liturgical action, which takes a solemn form in almost all liturgies, has a "spiritual value and meaning."[48] The bread and wine become in a sense a symbol of all that the Eucharistic assembly brings, on its own part, as an offering to God and offers spiritually.

It is important that this first moment of the Liturgy of the Eucharist in the strict sense should find expression in the attitude of the participants. There is a link between this and the offertory "procession" provided for in the recent liturgical reform[49] and accompanied, in keeping with ancient tradition, by a psalm or song. A certain length of time must be allowed, so that all can become aware of this act, which is given expression at the same time by the words of the celebrant.

Awareness of the act of presenting the offerings should be maintained throughout the Mass. Indeed, it should be brought to fullness at the moment of the consecration and of the anamnesis offering, as is demanded by the fundamental value of the moment of the sacrifice. This is shown by the words of the Eucharistic Prayer said aloud by the priest. It seems worthwhile repeating here some expressions in the Third Eucharistic Prayer that show in particular the sacrificial character of the Eucharist and link the offering of our persons with Christ's offering: "Look with favor on your Church's offering, and see the Victim whose death has reconciled us to yourself. Grant that we, who are nourished by his body and blood, may be filled with his Holy Spirit, and become one body, one spirit in Christ. May he make us an everlasting gift to you."

This sacrificial value is expressed earlier in every celebration by the words with which the priest concludes the presentation of the gifts, asking the faithful to pray "that my sacrifice and yours may be acceptable to God, the almighty Father." These words are binding, since they express the character of the entire Eucharistic Liturgy and the fullness of its divine and ecclesial content.

All who participate with faith in the Eucharist become aware that it is a "sacrifice," that is to say, a "consecrated Offering." For the bread and wine presented at the altar and accompanied by the devotion and the spiritual sacrifices of the participants are finally consecrated, so as to become *truly, really and substantially* Christ's own body that is given up and His blood that is shed. Thus, by virtue of the consecration, the species of bread and wine represent[50] in a sacramental, unbloody manner the bloody propitiatory sacrifice offered by Him on the cross to His Father for the salvation of the world. Indeed, He alone, giving Himself as a propitiatory Victim in an act of supreme surrender and immolation, has reconciled humanity with the Father, solely through His sacrifice, "having cancelled the bond which stood against us."[51]

To this sacrifice, which is renewed in a sacramental form on the altar, the offerings of bread and wine, united with the devotion of the faithful, nevertheless bring their unique contribution, since by means of the consecration by the priest they become sacred species. This is made clear by the way in which the priest acts during the Eucharistic Prayer, especially at the consecration, and when the celebration of the Holy Sacrifice and participation in it are accompanied by awareness that "the Teacher is here and is calling for you."[52] This call of the Lord to us through His Sacrifice opens our hearts, so that, purified in the mystery of our redemption, they may be united to Him in Eucharistic Communion, which confers upon participation at Mass a value that is mature, complete and binding on human life: "The Church's intention is that the faithful not only offer the spotless victim but also learn to offer themselves and daily to be drawn into ever more perfect union, through Christ the Mediator, with the Father and with each other, so that at last God may be all in all."[53]

It is therefore very opportune and necessary to continue to actuate a new and intense education, in order to discover all the richness contained in the new liturgy. Indeed, the liturgical renewal that has taken place since the Second Vatican Council has given, so to speak, greater visibility to *the Eucharistic Sacrifice*. One factor contributing to this is that the words of the Eucharistic Prayer are said aloud by the celebrant, particularly the words of consecration, with the acclamation by the assembly immediately after the elevation.

All this should fill us with joy, but we should also remember that *these changes demand new spiritual awareness and maturity*, both on the part of the celebrant—especially now that he celebrates "facing the people"—and by the faithful. Eucharistic worship matures and grows when the words of the Eucharistic Prayer, especially the words of consecration, are spoken with great humility and simplicity, in a worthy and fitting way, which is understandable and in keeping with their holiness; when this essential act of the Eucharistic Liturgy is performed unhurriedly; and when it brings about in us such recollection and devotion that the participants become aware of the greatness of the mystery being accomplished and show it by their attitude.

III. THE TWO TABLES OF THE LORD AND THE COMMON POSSESSION OF THE CHURCH

The Table of the Word of God

10. We are well aware that from the earliest times the celebration of the Eucharist has been linked not only with

prayer but also with the reading of Sacred Scripture and with singing by the whole assembly. As a result, it has long been possible to apply to the Mass the comparison, made by the Fathers, with the two tables, at which the Church prepares for her children the Word of God and the Eucharist, that is, the Bread of the Lord. We must, therefore, go back to the first part of the sacred mystery, the part that at present is most often called the *Liturgy of the Word*, and devote some attention to it.

The reading of the passages of Sacred Scripture chosen for each day *has been subjected by the Council* to new criteria and requirements.[54] As a result of these norms of the Council a new collection of readings has been made, in which there has been applied to some extent the principle of continuity of texts and the principle of making all the sacred books accessible. The insertion of the psalms with responses into the liturgy makes the participants familiar with the great wealth of Old Testament prayer and poetry. The fact that these texts are read and sung in the vernacular enables everyone to participate with fuller understanding.

Nevertheless, there are also those people who, having been educated on the basis of the old liturgy in Latin, experience the lack of this "one language," which in all the world was an expression of the unity of the Church and through its dignified character elicited a profound sense of the Eucharistic Mystery. It is therefore necessary to show not only understanding but also full respect towards these sentiments and desires. As far as possible these sentiments and desires are to be accommodated, as is moreover provided for in the new dispositions.[55] The Roman Church has special obligations towards Latin, the splendid language of ancient Rome, and she must manifest them whenever the occasion presents itself.

The possibilities that the post-conciliar renewal has introduced in this respect are indeed often utilized so as to make us *witnesses of and sharers in the authentic celebration of the Word of God*. There is also an increase in the number of people taking an active part in this celebration. Groups of readers and cantors, and still more often choirs of men and women, are being set up and are devoting themselves with great enthusiasm to this aspect. The Word of God, Sacred Scripture, is beginning to take on new life in many Christian communities. The faithful gathered for the liturgy prepare with song for listening to the Gospel, which is proclaimed with the devotion and love due to it.

All this is noted with great esteem and gratitude, but it must not be forgotten that complete renewal makes yet other demands. These demands consist in *a new sense of responsibility towards the Word of God* transmitted through the liturgy in various languages, something that is certainly in keeping with the universality of the Gospel and its purposes. The same sense of responsibility also involves the performance of the corresponding liturgical actions (reading or singing), which must accord with the principles of art. To preserve these actions from all artificiality, they should express such capacity, simplicity and dignity as to highlight the special character of the sacred text, even by the very manner of reading or singing.

Accordingly, these demands, which spring from a new responsibility for the Word of God in the liturgy,[56] go yet deeper and *concern the inner attitude* with which the ministers of the Word perform their function in the liturgical assembly.[57] This responsibility also concerns *the choice of texts. The choice has already been made by the competent ecclesiastical authority, which has also made provision for the cases in which readings more suited to a particular situation may be chosen.*[58] Furthermore, it must always be remembered that only the Word of God can be used for Mass readings. The reading of Scripture cannot be replaced by the reading of other texts, however much they may be endowed with undoubted religious and moral values. On the other hand, such texts can be used very profitably in the homily. Indeed the homily is supremely suitable for the use of such texts, provided that their content corresponds to the required conditions, since it is one of the tasks that belong to the nature of the homily to show the points of convergence between revealed divine wisdom and noble human thought seeking the truth by various paths.

The Table of the Bread of the Lord

11. The other table of the Eucharistic Mystery, that of the Bread of the Lord, also requires reflection from the viewpoint of the present-day liturgical renewal. This is a question of the greatest importance, since it concerns a special act of living faith, and indeed, as has been attested since the earliest centuries,[59] it is a manifestation of *worship of Christ, who in Eucharistic Communion entrusts Himself to each one of us*, to our hearts, our consciences, our lips and our mouths, in the form of food. Therefore, there is special need, with regard to this question, for the watchfulness spoken of by the Gospel, on the part of the pastors who have charge of Eucharistic worship and on the part of the People of God, whose "sense of faith"[60] must be very alert and acute particularly in this area.

I, therefore, wish to entrust this question to the heart of each one of you, venerable and dear brothers in the episcopate. You must above all make it part of your care for all the churches entrusted to you. I ask this of you in the name of the unity that we have received from the Apostles as our heritage, collegial unity. This unity came to birth, in a sense, at the table of the Bread of the Lord on Holy Thursday. With the help of your brothers in the priesthood, do all you can to *safeguard the sacred dignity of the Eucharistic ministry and that deep spirit of Eucharistic Communion* which belongs in a special way to the Church as the People of God, and which is also a particular heritage transmitted to us from the Apostles, by various liturgical traditions, and by unnumbered generations of the faithful, who were often heroic witnesses to Christ, educated in "the school of the cross" (redemption) and of the Eucharist.

It must be remembered that the Eucharist as the table of the Bread of the Lord is a continuous invitation. This is *shown in the liturgy when the celebrant says: "This is the Lamb of God. Happy are those who are called to his supper"*[61]; it is also shown by the familiar Gospel parable about the guests invited to the marriage banquet.[62] Let us remember that in this parable there are many who excuse themselves from accepting the invitation for various reasons.

Moreover, our Catholic communities certainly do not lack people who *could participate* in Eucharistic Communion *and do not*, even though they have no serious sin on their conscience as an obstacle. To tell the truth, this attitude, which in some people is linked with an exaggerated severity, has changed in the present century, though it is still to be found here and there. In fact, what one finds most often is not so much a feeling of unworthiness as a certain lack of interior willingness, if one may use this expression, a lack of Eucharistic "hunger" and "thirst," which is also a sign of lack of adequate sensitivity towards the great sacrament of love and a lack of understanding of its nature.

However, we also find in recent years another phenomenon. Sometimes, indeed quite frequently, everybody participating in the Eucharistic assembly goes to Communion; and on some such occasions, as experienced pastors confirm, there has not been due care to approach the sacrament of Penance so as to purify one's conscience. This can of course mean that those approaching the Lord's table find nothing on their conscience, according to the objective law of God, to keep them from this sublime and joyful act of being sacramentally united with Christ. But there can also be, at least at times, another idea behind this: the idea of the Mass as *only* a banquet[63] in which one shares by *receiving the body of Christ in order to manifest, above all else, fraternal communion*. It is not hard to add to these reasons a certain human respect and mere "conformity."

This phenomenon demands from us watchful attention and a theological and pastoral analysis guided by a sense of great responsibility. We cannot allow the life of our communities to lose the good quality of sensitiveness of Christian conscience, guided solely by respect for Christ, who, when He is received in the Eucharist, should find in the heart of each of us a worthy abode. This question is closely linked not only with the practice of the sacrament of Penance but also with a correct sense of responsibility for the whole deposit of moral teaching and for the precise distinction between good and evil, a distinction which then becomes for each person sharing in the Eucharist the basis for a correct judgment of self to be made in the depths of the personal conscience. St. Paul's words, "Let a man examine himself,"[64] are well known; this judgment is an indispensable condition for a personal decision whether to approach Eucharistic Communion or to abstain.

Celebration of the Eucharist places before us many other requirements regarding the ministry of the Eucharistic table. Some of these requirements concern only priests and deacons, others concern all who participate in the Eucharistic Liturgy. Priests and deacons must remember that the service of the table of the Bread of the Lord imposes on them special obligations which refer in the first place to Christ Himself *present in the Eucharist* and secondly to all who actually participate in the Eucharist or who might do so. With regard to the first, perhaps it will not be superfluous to recall the words of the *Pontificale* which on the day of ordination the bishop addresses to the new priest as he hands to him on the paten and in the chalice the bread and wine offered by the faithful and prepared by the deacon: *"Accipe oblationem plebis sanctae Deo offerendam. Agnosce quod agis, imitare quod tractabis, et vitam tuam mysterio dominicae crucis conforma."*[65] This last admonition made to him by the bishop should remain as one of the most precious norms of his Eucharistic ministry.

It is from this admonition that the priest's attitude in handling the bread and wine which have become the body and blood of the Redeemer should draw its inspiration. Thus it is necessary for all of us who are ministers of the Eucharist to examine carefully our actions at the altar, in particular the way in which we handle that food and drink which are the body and blood of the Lord our God in our hands; the way in which we distribute Holy Communion; the way in which we perform the purification.

All these actions have a meaning of their own. Naturally, scrupulosity must be avoided, but God preserve us from behaving in a way that lacks respect, from undue hurry, from an impatience that causes scandal. Over and above our commitment to the evangelical mission, our greatest commitment consists in exercising this mysterious power over the body of the Redeemer, and all that is within us should be decisively ordered to this. We should also always remember that to this ministerial power we have been sacramentally consecrated, that we have been chosen from among men "for the good of men."[66] We especially, the priests of the Latin Church, whose ordination rite added in the course of the centuries the custom of anointing the priest's hands, should think about this.

In some countries *the practice of receiving Communion in the hand* has been introduced. This practice has been requested by individual episcopal conferences and has received approval from the Apostolic See. However, cases of a deplorable lack of respect towards the Eucharistic Species have been reported, cases which are imputable not only to the individuals guilty of such behavior but also to the pastors of the church who have not been vigilant enough regarding the attitude of the faithful towards the Eucharist. It also happens, on occasion, that the free choice of those who prefer to continue the practice of receiving the Eucharist on the tongue is not taken into account in those places where the distribution of Communion in the hand has been authorized. It is therefore difficult in the context of this present letter not to mention the sad phenomena previously referred to. This is in no way meant to refer to those who, receiving the Lord Jesus in the hand, do so with profound reverence and devotion, in those countries where this practice has been authorized.

But one must not forget the primary office of priests, who have been consecrated by their ordination to represent Christ the Priest: For this reason their hands, like their words and their will, have become the direct instruments of Christ. Through this fact, that is, as ministers of the Holy Eucharist, they have a primary responsibility for the sacred species, because it is a total responsibility: They offer the bread and wine, they consecrate it, and then distribute the sacred species to the participants in the assembly who wish to receive them. Deacons can only bring to the altar the offerings of the faithful and, once they have been consecrated by the priest, distribute them. How eloquent therefore, even if not of ancient custom, is the rite of the anointing of the hands in our Latin ordination, as though precisely for these hands a special grace and power of the Holy Spirit is necessary!

To touch the sacred species and *to distribute them with their own hands* is a privilege of the ordained, one which indicates an active participation *in the ministry of the Eucharist.* It is obvious that the Church can grant this faculty to those who are neither priests nor deacons, as is the case with acolytes in the exercise of their ministry, especially if they are destined for future ordination, or with other lay people who are chosen for this to meet a just need, but always after an adequate preparation.

A Common Possession of the Church

12. We cannot, even for a moment, forget that the Eucharist is a special possession belonging to the whole Church. It is the *greatest gift* in the order of grace and of sacrament that the divine Spouse has offered and unceasingly offers to His spouse. And precisely because it is such a gift, all of us should, in a spirit of profound faith, let

ourselves be guided by a sense of truly Christian responsibility. A gift obliges us ever more profoundly because it speaks to us not so much with the force of a strict right as with the force of personal confidence, and thus—without legal obligations—it calls for *trust and gratitude.* The Eucharist is just such a gift and such a possession. We should remain faithful in every detail to what It expresses in Itself and to what It asks of us, namely, thanksgiving.

The Eucharist is a common possession of the whole Church as the sacrament of her unity. And thus the Church has the strict duty to specify everything which concerns participation in It and Its celebration. We should, therefore, act according to the principles laid down by the last Council, which, in the Constitution on the Sacred Liturgy, defined the authorizations and obligations of individual bishops in their dioceses and of the episcopal conferences, given the fact that both act in collegial unity with the Apostolic See.

Furthermore we should follow the directives issued by the various departments of the Holy See in this field: be it in liturgical matters, in the rules established by the liturgical books in what concerns the Eucharistic Mystery,[67] and in the Instructions devoted to this Mystery, be it with regard to *communicatio in sacris,* in the norms of the *Directorium de re oecumenica*[68] and in the *Instructio de peculiaribus casibus admittendi alios christianos ad communionem eucharisticam in Ecclesia catholica.*[69] And although at this stage of renewal the possibility of a certain "creative" freedom has been permitted, nevertheless this freedom must strictly respect the requirements of substantial unity. We can follow the path of this pluralism (which arises in part from the introduction itself of the various languages into the liturgy) only as long as the essential characteristics of the celebration of the Eucharist are preserved, and the norms prescribed by the recent liturgical reform are respected.

Indispensable effort is required everywhere to ensure that within the pluralism of Eucharistic worship envisioned by the Second Vatican Council the unity of which the Eucharist is the sign and cause is clearly manifested.

This task, over which in the nature of things the Apostolic See must keep careful watch, should be assumed not only by each *episcopal conference* but by every minister of the Eucharist, without exception. Each one should also remember that he is responsible for the common good of the whole Church. The *priest as minister*, as celebrant, as the one who presides over the Eucharistic assembly of the faithful, should have a special *sense of the common good of the Church*, which he represents through his ministry, but to which he must also be subordinate, according to a correct discipline of faith. He cannot consider himself a "proprietor" who can make free use of the liturgical text and of the sacred rite as if it were his own property, in such a way as to stamp it with his own arbitrary personal style. At times this latter might seem more effective, and it may better correspond to subjective piety; nevertheless, objectively it is always a betrayal of that union which should find its proper expression in the sacrament of unity.

Every priest who offers the holy Sacrifice should recall that during this sacrifice it is not *only* he with his community that is praying but the whole Church, which is thus expressing in this sacrament her spiritual unity, among other ways by the use of the approved liturgical text. To call this position "mere insistence on uniformity" would only show ignorance of the objective requirements of authentic unity, and would be a symptom of harmful individualism.

This subordination of the minister, of the celebrant, to the *Mysterium* which has been entrusted to him by the Church for the good of the whole People of God, should also find expression in the observance of the liturgical requirements concerning the celebration of the holy Sacrifice. These refer, for example, to dress, and in particular to the vestments worn by the celebrant. Circumstances have of course existed and continue to exist in which the prescriptions do not oblige. We have been greatly moved when reading books written by priests who had been prisoners in extermination camps, with descriptions of Eucharistic Celebrations without the above-mentioned rules, that is to say, without an altar and without vestments. But although in those conditions this was a proof of heroism and deserved profound admiration, nevertheless in *normal conditions* to ignore the liturgical directives can be interpreted as a lack of respect towards the Eucharist, dictated perhaps by individualism or by an absence of a critical sense concerning current opinions, or by a certain *lack of a spirit of faith.*

Upon all of us who, through the *grace* of God, are ministers of the Eucharist, there weighs a particular responsibility for the ideas and attitudes of our brothers and sisters who have been entrusted to our pastoral care. It is our vocation to nurture, above all by personal example, every healthy manifestation of worship towards Christ present and operative in that sacrament of love. May God preserve us from acting otherwise and weakening that worship by "becoming unaccustomed" to various manifestations and forms of Eucharistic worship which express a perhaps "traditional" but healthy piety, and which express above all that "sense of the faith" possessed by the whole People of God, as the Second Vatican Council recalled.[70]

As I bring these considerations to an end, I would like to ask forgiveness—in my own name and in the name of all of you, venerable and dear brothers in the episcopate—for everything which, for whatever reason, through whatever human weakness, impatience or negligence, and also through the at times partial, one-sided and erroneous application of the directives of the Second Vatican Council, may have caused scandal and disturbance concerning the interpretation of the doctrine and the veneration due to this great sacrament. And I pray the Lord Jesus that in the future we may avoid in our manner of dealing with this sacred Mystery anything which could weaken or disorient in any way the sense of reverence and love that exists in our faithful people.

May Christ Himself help us to follow the path of true renewal towards that fullness of life and of Eucharistic worship whereby the Church is built up in that unity that she already possesses, and which she desires to bring to ever greater perfection for the glory of·the living God and for the salvation of all humanity.

Conclusion

13. Permit me, venerable and dear brothers, to end these reflections of mine, which have been restricted to a detailed examination of only a few questions. In undertaking these reflections, I have had before my eyes all the work carried out by the Second Vatican Council, and have kept in mind Paul VI's encyclical *Mysterium fidei*, promulgated during that Council, and all the documents issued after the same Council for the purpose of implementing the post-conciliar liturgical renewal. A very close and organic *bond exists between the renewal of the liturgy and the renewal of the whole life of the Church.*

The Church not only acts but also expresses herself in the liturgy, lives by the liturgy and draws from the liturgy the strength for her life. For this reason liturgical renewal carried out correctly in the spirit of the Second Vatican Council is, in a certain sense, the measure and the condition for putting into effect the teaching of that Council which we wish to accept with profound faith, convinced as we are that by means of this Council the Holy Spirit "has spoken to the Church" the truths and given the indications for carrying out her mission among the people of today and tomorrow.

We shall continue in the future to take special care to promote and follow the renewal of the Church according to the teaching of the Second Vatican Council, *in the spirit of an ever-living Tradition.* In fact, to the substance of Tradition properly understood belongs also a correct re-

reading of the "signs of the times," which require us to draw from the rich treasure of Revelation "things both new and old."[71] Acting in this spirit, in accordance with this counsel of the Gospel, the Second Vatican Council carried out a providential effort to renew the face of the Church in the sacred liturgy, most often having recourse to what is "ancient," what comes from the heritage of the Fathers and is the expression of the faith and doctrine of a Church which has remained united for so many centuries.

In order to be able to continue in the future to put into practice the directives of the Council in the field of liturgy, and in particular in the field of Eucharistic worship, *close collaboration is necessary* between the competent department of the Holy See and each episcopal conference, a collaboration which must be *at the same time vigilant and creative.* We must keep our sights fixed on the greatness of the most holy Mystery and at the same time on spiritual movements and social changes, which are so significant for our times, since they not only sometimes create difficulties but also prepare us for a new way of participating in that great Mystery of Faith.

Above all I wish to emphasize that the problems of the liturgy, and in particular of the Eucharistic Liturgy, must not be *an occasion for dividing Catholics and for threatening the unity of the Church.* This is demanded by an elementary understanding of that sacrament which Christ has left us as the source of spiritual unity. And how could the Eucharist, which in the Church is the *sacramentum pietatis, signum unitatis, vinculum caritatis,*[72] form between us at this time a point of division and a source of distortion of thought and of behavior, instead of being the focal point and constitutive center, which it truly is in its essence, of the unity of the Church herself?

We are all equally indebted to our Redeemer. We should all listen together to that Spirit of truth and of love whom He has promised to the Church and who is operative in her. In the name of this truth and of this love, in the name of the crucified Christ and of His Mother, I ask you, and beg you: Let us abandon all opposition and division, and let us all unite in this great mission of salvation which is the price and at the same time the fruit of our redemption. The Apostolic See will continue to do all that is possible to provide the means of ensuring that unity of which we speak. Let everyone avoid anything in his own way of acting which could "grieve the Holy Spirit."[73]

In order that this unity and the constant and systematic collaboration which leads to it may be perseveringly continued, I beg on my knees that, through the intercession of Mary, holy spouse of the Holy Spirit and Mother of the Church, we may all receive the light of the Holy Spirit. And blessing everyone, with all my heart I once more address myself to you, my venerable and dear brothers in the episcopate, with a fraternal greeting and with full trust. In this collegial unity in which we share, let us do all we can to ensure that the Eucharist may become an ever greater source of life and light for the consciences of all our brothers and sisters of all the communities in the universal unity of Christ's Church on earth.

In a spirit of fraternal charity, to you and to all our confreres in the priesthood I cordially impart the apostolic blessing.

From the Vatican, February 24, First Sunday of Lent, in the year 1980, the second of the Pontificate.

FOOTNOTES

1. Cf. Chapter 2: *AAS* 71 (1979), pp. 395f.
2. Cf. Ecumenical Council of Trent, Session XXII, Can. 2: *Conciliorum Oecumenicorum Decreta*, ed. 3, Bologna 1973, p. 735.
3. Because of this precept of the Lord, an Ethiopian Eucharistic Liturgy recalls that the Apostles "established for us patriarchs, archbishops, priests and deacons to celebrate the ritual of your holy Church": *Anaphora Sancti Athanasii: Prex Eucharistica*, Haenggi-Pahl, Fribourg (Switzerland) 1968, p. 183.
4. Cf. *La Tradition apostolique de saint Hippolyte*, nos. 2-4, ed. Botte, Munster-Westfalen 1963, pp. 5-17.

5. 2 Cor. 11:28.
6. 1 Pt. 2:5.
7. Cf. Second Vatican Council, Dogmatic Constitution on the Church *Lumen gentium*, 28; *AAS* 57 (1965), pp. 33f.; Decree on the Ministry and Life of Priests *Presbyterorum ordinis*, 2, 5: *AAS* 58 (1966), pp. 993, 998; Decree on the Missionary Activity of the Church *Ad gentes*, 39: *AAS* 58 (1966), p. 986.
8. Second Vatican Ecumenical Council, Dogmatic Constitution on the Church *Lumen gentium*, 11: *AAS* 57 (1965), p. 15.
9. Jn. 3:16. It is interesting to note how these words are taken up by the liturgy of St. John Chrysostom immediately before the words of consecration and introduce the latter: cf. *La divina Liturgia del nostro Padre Giovanni Crisostomo*, Roma-Grottaferrata 1967, pp. 104f.
10. Cf. Mt. 26:26-28; Mk. 14:22-25; Lk. 22:18-20; 1 Cor. 11:23-25; cf. also the Eucharistic Prayers.
11. Phil. 2:8.
12. Jn. 13:1.
13. Cf. John Paul II, Homily in Phoenix Park, Dublin, 7: *AAS* 71 (1979), pp. 1074ff.; Sacred Congregation of Rites, Instruction *Eucharisticum mysterium*: *AAS* 59 (1967), pp. 539-573; *Rituale Romanum, De sacra communione et de cultu Mysterii eucharistici extra Missam, ed. typica*, 1973. It should be noted that the value of the worship and the sanctifying power of these forms of devotion to the Eucharist depend not so much upon the forms themselves as upon interior attitudes.
14. Cf. Bull *Trasiturus de hos mundo* (Aug. 11, 1264): *Aemilii Friedberg, Corpus Iuris Canonici*, Pars II. *Decretalium Collectiones*, Leipzig 1881, pp. 1174-1177; *Studi eucharistici*, VIII Centenario della Bolla 'Transiturus,' 1264-1964, Orvieto 1966, pp. 302-317.
15. Cf. Paul VI, encyclical letter *Mysterium Fidei*: *AAS* 57 (1965), pp. 753-774; Sacred Congregation of Rites, Instruction *Eucharisticum Mysterium*: *AAS* 59 (1967), pp. 539-573; *Rituale Romanum, De sacra communione et de cultu Mysterii eucharistici extra Missam, ed. typica*, 1973.
16. John Paul II, encyclical letter *Redemptor hominis*, 20: *AAS* 71 (1979), p. 311; cf. Second Vatican Ecumenical Council, Dogmatic Constitution on the Church *Lumen gentium*, 11: *AAS* 57 (1965), pp. 15f; also, note 57 to Schema II of the same dogmatic constitution, in *Acta Synodalia Sacrosancti Concilii Oecumenici Vaticani II*, vol. II, periodus 2a, pars I, public session II, pp. 251f.; Paul VI, Address at the general audience of September 15, 1965: *Insegnamenti di Paolo VI*, III (1965), p. 1036; H. de Lubac, *Meditation sur l'Eglise*, 2 ed., Paris 1963, pp. 129-137.
17. 1 Cor. 11:26.
18. Cf. Second Vatican Ecumenical Council, Dogmatic Constitution on the Church *Lumen gentium*, 11: *AAS* 57 (1965) pp. 15f.; Constitution on the Sacred Liturgy *Sacrosanctum concilium*, 10: *AAS* 56 (1964), p. 102; Decree on the Ministry and Life of Priests *Presbyterorum ordinis*, 5: *AAS* 58 (1966), pp. 997f.; Decree on the Bishops' Pastoral Office in the Church *Christus Dominus*, 30: *AAS* 58 (1966), pp. 688f.; Decree on the Church's Missionary Activity *Ad gentes*, 9: *AAS* 58 (1966), pp. 957f.
19. Cf. Second Vatican Ecumenical Council, Dogmatic Constitution on the Church *Lumen gentium*, 26: *AAS* 57 (1965), pp. 31f.; Decree on Ecumenism *Unitatis redintegratio*, 15: *AAS* 57 (1965), pp. 101f.
20. This is what the Opening Prayer of Holy Thursday asks for: "We pray that in this Eucharist we may find the fullness of love and life": *Missale Romanum ed. typica altera* 1975, p. 244; also the communion epiclesis of the Roman Missal: "May all of us who share in the body and blood of Christ be

brought together in unity by the Holy Spirit. Lord, remember your Church throughout the world; make us grow in love": Eucharistic Prayer II: *ibid.*, pp. 458f.; Eucharistic Prayer III, p. 463.

21. Jn. 5:17.

22. Cf. Prayer after communion of the Mass for the 22nd Sunday in Ordinary Time: "Lord, you renew us at your table with the bread of life. May this food strengthen us in love and help us to serve you in each other": *Missale Romanum* ed. cit., p. 361.

23. Jn. 4:23.

24. Cf. 1 Cor. 10:17; commented upon by St. Augustine: *In Evangelium Ioannis* tract. 31, 13; *PL* 35, 1613; also commented upon by the Ecumenical Council of Trent, Session XIII, can. 8; *Conciliorum Oecumenicorum Decreta*, ed. 3, Bologna 1973, p. 697, 7; cf. Second Vatican Ecumenical Council, Dogmatic Constitution on the Church *Lumen gentium*, 7: *AAS* 57 (1965), p. 9.

25. Jn. 13:35.

26. This is expressed by many prayers of the *Roman Missal:* the Prayer over the Gifts from the Common, "For those who work for the underprivileged"; "May we who celebrate the love of your Son also follow the example of your saints and grow in love for you and for one another": *Missale Romanum*, ed. cit., p. 721; also the Prayer after Communion of the Mass "For Teachers": "May this holy meal help us to follow the example of your saints by showing in our lives the light of trust and love for our brothers": *ibid.*, p. 723; cf. also the Prayer after Communion of the Mass for the 22nd Sunday in Ordinary Time, quoted in note 22.

27. Jn. 4:23.

28. Eph. 4:13.

29. Cf. above, no. 2.

30. Cf. Second Vatican Ecumenical Council, Decree on the Missionary Activity of the Church *Ad gentes*, 9, 12: *AAS* 58 (1966), pp. 958, 961f.; Decree on the Ministry and Life of Priests *Presbyterorum ordinis*, 5: *AAS* 58 (1996), p. 997.

31. 1 Jn. 3:1.

32. Second Vatican Ecumenical Council, Dogmatic Constitution on the Church *Lumen gentium*, 11: *AAS* 57 (1965), p. 15.

33. Cf. no. 20: *AAS* 71 (1979), pp. 313f.

34. 2 Pt. 3:13.

35. Col. 3:10.

36. Lk. 1:34; Jn. 6:69; Acts 3:14; Rv. 3:7.

37. Acts 10:38; Lk. 4:18.

38. Jn. 10:36.

39. Cf. Jn. 10:17.

40. Heb. 3:1; 4:15, etc.

41. As was stated in the ninth-century Byzantine liturgy, according to the most ancient codex, known formerly as Barberino di San Marco (Florence), and, now that it is kept in the Vatican Apostolic Library, as Barberini Greco 366f. 8 verso, lines 17-20. This part has been published by F.E. Brightman, *Liturgies Eastern and Western*, I. Eastern Liturgies, Oxford 1896, pp. 318, 34-35.

42. Opening Prayer of the Second Votive Mass of the Holy Eucharist: *Missale Romanum*, ed. cit., p. 858.

43. 1 Jn. 2:2; cf. *ibid.*, 4:10.

44. We speak of the *divinum Mysterium*, the *Sanctissimum*, the *Sacrosanctum*, meaning what is *sacred* and *holy* par excellence. For their part, the Eastern Churches call the Mass *raza* or *mysterion*, *hagiasmos*, *quddasa*, *qedasse*, that is to say "consecration" par excellence. Furthermore there are the liturgical rites,

which, in order to inspire a sense of the sacred, prescribe silence, and standing or kneeling, and likewise professions of faith, and the incensation of the Gospel book, the altar, the celebrant and the sacred species. They even recall the assistance of the angelic beings created to serve the Holy God, i.e., with the *Sanctus* of our Latin Churches and the *Trisagion* and *Sancta Sanctis* of the Eastern liturgies.

45. For instance, in the invitation to receive Communion, this faith has been so formed as to reveal complementary aspects of the presence of Christ the Holy One: the epiphanic aspect noted by the Byzantines ("Blessed is he who comes in the name of the Lord: The Lord is God and *has appeared to us*": *La divina Liturgia del santo nostro Padre Giovanni Crisostomo*, Roma-Grottaferrata 1967, pp. 136f.); the aspect of relation and union sung of by the Armenians (Liturgy of St. Ignatius of Antioch: *"Unus Pater sanctus nobiscum, unus Filius sanctus nobiscum, unus Spiritus sanctus nobiscum"*: *Die Anaphora des heiligen Ignatius von Antiochien*, ubersetzt von A. Rucker, *Oriens Christianus*, 3ª ser., 5 [1930], p. 76); and the hidden heavenly aspect celebrated by the Chaldeans and Malabars (cf. the antiphonal hymn sung by the priest and the assembly after Communion: F.E. Brightman, *op. cit.*, p. 299.

46. Cf. Second Vatican Ecumenical Council, Constitution on the Sacred Liturgy *Sacrosanctum concilium*, 2, 47: *AAS* 56 (1964), pp. 83f., 113; Dogmatic Constitution on the Church *Lumen gentium*, 3 and 28: *AAS* 57 (1965), pp. 6, 33f.; Decree on Ecumenism *Unitatis redintegratio*, 2: *AAS* 57 (1965), p. 91; Decree on the Ministry and Life of Priests *Presbyterorum ordinis*, 13: *AAS* 58 (1966), pp. 1011f., Ecumenical Council of Trent, Session XXII, chap. I and II: *Conciliorum Oecumenicorum Decreta*, ed. 3, Bologna 1973, pp. 732f. especially: *una eademque est hostia, idem nunc offerens sacerdotum ministerio, qui se ipsum tunc in cruce obtulit, sola offerendi ratione diversa* (*ibid.*, p. 733).

47. *Synodus Constantinopolita adversus Sotericum* (January 1156 and May 1157): Angelo Mai, *Spicilegium romanum*, t. X, Rome 1844, p. 77; *PG* 140, 190; cf. Martin Jugie, Dict. Theol. Cath., t. X, 1338; *Theologia dogmatica christianorum orientalium*, Paris, 1930, pp. 317-320.

48. *Instituto Generalis Missalis Romani*, 49c: *Missale Romanum, ed. cit.*, p. 39; cf. Second Vatican Ecumenical Council, Decree on the Ministry and Life of Priests *Presbyterorum ordinis*, 5: *AAS* 58 (1966), pp. 997f.

49. *Ordo Missae cum populo*, 18: *Missale Romanum, ed. cit.*, p. 390.

50. Cf. Ecumenical Council of Trent, Session 22, chap. I, *Conciliorum Oecumenicorum Decreta*, ed. 3, Bologna 1973, pp. 732f.

51. Col. 2:14.

52. Jn. 11:28.

53. *Instituto Generalis Missalis Romani*, 55f.: *Missale Romanum, ed. cit.*, p. 40.

54. Cf. Constitution on the Sacred Liturgy *Sacrosanctum concilium*, 35, 51: *AAS* 56 (1964), pp. 109, 114.

55. Cf. Sacred Congregation of Rites, Instruction *In edicendis normis*, VI, 17-18; VII, 19-20: *AAS* 57 (1965), pp. 1012f.; Instruction *Musicam Sacram*, IV, 48: *AAS* 59 (1967), p. 314; Decree *De Titulo Basilicae Minoris*, II, 8: *AAS* 60 (1968), p. 538; Sacred Congregation for Divine Worship, Notif. *De Missali Romano, Liturgia Horarum et Calendario*, I, 4: *AAS* 63 (1971), p. 714.

56. Cf. Paul VI, Apostolic Constitution *Missale Romanum:* "We are fully confident that both priests and faithful will prepare their minds and hearts more devoutly for the Lord's Supper, meditating on the Scriptures, nourished day by day with the words of the Lord": *AAS* 61 (1969), pp. 220f.; *Missale Romanum, ed. cit.* p. 15.

57. Cf. *Pontificale Romanum. De Institutione Lectorum et Acolythorum*, 4, ed. typica, 1972, pp. 19f.
58. Cf. *Instituto Generalis Missalis Romani*, 319-320: *Missale Romanum*, ed. cit., p. 87.
59. Cf. Fr. J. Dolger, *Das Segnen der Sinne mit der Eucharistie Eine altchristliche. Kommunionsitte: Antike und Christentum*, t. 3 (1932), pp. 231-244; *Das Kultvergehen der Donatistin Lucilla von Karthago. Reliquienkuss vor dem Kuss der Eucharistie, ibid.*, pp. 245-252.
60. Cf. Second Vatican Ecumenical Council, Dogmatic Constitution on the Church *Lumen gentium*, 12, 35: *AAS* 57 (1965), pp. 16, 40.
61. Cf. Jn. 1:29; Rv. 19:9.
62. Cf. Lk. 14:16ff.
63. Cf. *Instituto Generalis Missalis Romani*, 7-8: *Missale Romanum*, ed. cit., p. 29.
64. 1 Cor. 11:28.
65. *Pontificale Romanum. De Ordinatione Diaconi, Presbyteri et Episcopi*, ed. typica, 1968, p. 93.
66. Heb. 5:1.
67. Sacred Congregation of Rites, Instruction *Eucharisticum Mysterium*: *AAS* 59 (1967), pp. 539-573; *Rituale Romanum. De sacra communione et de cultu Mysterii eucharistici extra Missam*, ed. typica, 1973; Sacred Congregation for Divine Worship, *Litterae circulares ad Conferentiarum Episcopalium Praesides de precibus eucharisticis: AAS* 65 (1973), pp. 340-347.
68. Nos. 38-63: *AAS* 59 (1967), pp. 586-592.
69. *AAS* 64 (1972), pp. 518-525. Cf. also the *Communicatio* published the following year for the correct application of the above-mentioned Instruction: *AAS* 65 (1973), pp. 616-619.
70. Cf. Second Vatican Ecumenical Council, Dogmatic Constitution on the Church *Lumen Gentium*, 12: *AAS* 57 (1965), pp. 16f.
71. Mt. 13:52.
72. Cf. St. Augustine, *In Evangelium Ioannis tract.* 26, 13: *PL* 35, 1612f.
73. Eph. 4:30.

Be Open to the Gifts of the Holy Spirit

On March 1, 1980, the Holy Father delivered the following address, at the end of the spiritual exercises held in the Matilda Chapel during the past week.

All of us, beloved brothers, feel a need at this moment: that of thanking our Lord particularly, for having granted us the possibility of entering into silence, solitude, even if relative, of opening ourselves to the gifts of the Holy Spirit, and of thus entering into communion with

Himself, as well as with one another. For all this we must give heartfelt thanks and we wish to do so now with the words of prayer, but above all with the interior voice, more eloquent than words and songs, especially at a moment such as this, when the spirit is full. This is the need we feel: to thank God, the Lord, and also the Virgin Mary, since our spiritual exercises reach their end on a Saturday, which is always dedicated to her.

We wish to thank our brother "Don Lucas" for the ministry of the word which he carried out for us. We call him so in order to be faithful not only to his episcopal and curial vocation, but also to his religious vocation. We must return, as the Second Vatican Council teaches us, to the spirit of the founders. St. Dominic founded an "Ordo Predicatorum"; the choice, therefore, was certainly a providential one. We had a preacher of the exercises who is our brother and at the same time a religious preacher of the Order of Preachers. We wish to thank the Lord for this service of the word, which our Lenten preacher carried out for us. And, thanking the Lord, let us thank him too, because he has given us a great deal, with his preparation and his lectures, four times a day.

We wish to thank you, beloved Don Lucas, particularly for the choice of the main subject of our exercises. Such a simple and at the same time such a topical and precious choice for each of us, because all of us present here are priests of Christ and there could not be any subject more important, both in the essential and in the existential sense, than the word and the subject you chose: "The Priesthood." Then there is also another reason why the subject of the priesthood is so important for us all. In fact, we here represent the Roman Curia, that is, a community of very great responsibility for the universal Church. The future of the Church is closely linked with the priesthood, and the real debate that is going on throughout the Church today, especially in Western countries, is that of the priesthood and its real meaning.

Then, the future of the Church depends on vocations to the priesthood. Everywhere, all over the world, in every country, in every local Church, the sign of the test, certainly a providential test, which the Church is going through in these post-conciliar times, is perhaps the test of vocations. You ended by speaking of joy; well, all news that arrives about the increase of priestly and religious vocations, about the awakening of the Spirit among the young in some countries and continents, gives us great joy; and in this way the Church of the divine, providential test does not cease to be also the Church of hope. Therefore, we are grateful to you for the choice of the subject of these exercises.

Then, we are also grateful for the method adopted in studying the subject from the point of view of the exercises, for the spiritual needs of the participants. You showed us above all the dimensions of the priesthood: first, the divine one of the relationship between God and man; then, the Christological or Christocentric one, on the second day; then, the ecclesiological dimension, on the third day, with the unforgettable lecture on the priesthood of the Church; and then the ecclesiologico-human dimension—if we may use this expression—on the relationship between the priest, men, and the People of God; and then the interior dimension, with a very precious emphasis on the Marian spirituality of the priest.

Following these dimensions which are really essential and existential aspects of the priesthood of each of us, you tried to study more deeply the various themes, always following the criteria established at the beginning, from the very first introductory lecture. These are precisely the biblical and theological criteria always centered on the doctrine, on the texts of the Second Vatican Council, which you always enriched with knowledge of the sources, of the Bible, of the Church Fathers, of theology, of St. Thomas, but also of contemporary literature and not only theological literature, but I would say also of lay and religious literature together.

I must say that in this way your addresses and sermons as a whole have given us a very rich, very accurate view. We have found in these lectures of yours personal enrichment, so much light for each of us, so many approaches. The structure of your lectures was clear, very clear, very simple and very deep, and for this we must thank the Lord, we must thank His Spirit, His Mother and we must also thank you, who have been a well-prepared instrument, who carried out good spiritual work. You were able, in your search, to find our spirits, to work on our souls, and you revealed yourself, in every lecture, as a pastor and instilled in us that our vocation is that of being priests and pastors here in the Curia. So if it is possible to sum up in a few words your lectures as a whole, I would say that you gave us a real good. We are grateful.

We are grateful to you for the spirit with which you spoke. But our gratitude, which goes at this moment to the preacher, returns to ourselves, to each of us. During the exercises, during this week, we have been these silent preachers, this silent community; but it was a silence full of content. This fullness is known only to the Holy Spirit and to each of us; it was a fullness of experience: experience of Christ, experience of His and our priesthood, experience of the spiritual exercises. This experience must remain for each of us as a fountain for the days, the weeks, the months of our lives, of our ministries, of our service here in the Roman Curia.

We must thank one another for the fact that we have been, that we have lived, as a praying unity in this silence and we must thank one another for prayers. The time of spiritual exercises is always the time of the most intense prayer: We have prayed, certainly, we have prayed more abundantly, more intensely; we have prayed also for one another, because in this community we have become more brothers.

We must remain so because this is the Word of our Lord. We must remain brothers, more brothers, in that brotherhood which He taught us, which He taught His apostles, His disciples; which He taught all generations. So our generation of disciples, of successors of the Apostles, must remain united in brotherhood around Christ, His Mother, and His mystical bride, the Church, always united in waiting for that mission of the Holy Spirit which, formerly manifested on the day of Pentecost, is always manifested, is renewed in every age, in every generation. We, too, must be united, waiting for this breath of the Spirit in order to manifest His light and His power to the Church, to the world and to our difficult but also promising age of history. Accept these words, which I have now spoken on behalf of you all, of this silent community. We remember a sentence of a confrère of ours, Cardinal Ratzinger: "The silent Church must again find her voice." And so, at last, beloved preacher, Don Lucas, the silent Church of the Roman Curia has regained, refound its voice to thank you and to thank, together with you, Almighty God, our Lord Jesus Christ, the Holy Spirit, the Virgin Mary and the Church: a real heartfelt thanks. Amen.

In the Service of the Renewal and Pastoral Progress of Rome

On March 4, 1980, the Holy Father went to visit the offices of the Vicariate of Rome, at St. John Lateran. John Paul II delivered the following address.

Venerated and dear brothers!

Among the Pope's various commitments there could not be lacking a particularly affectionate visit, dedicated exclusively to all those who carry out their meritorious pastoral work in the Vicariate of Rome. After the meeting with the Pontifical Lateran University, with the Major Seminary of Rome, and the one, even more recent, with the clergy of Rome, I wished to come here, to the curia of my diocese, to say a word of encouragement and good wishes to you, too.

1. A cordial greeting in the first place to beloved Cardinal Ugo Poletti, Vicar General for Rome and District, and, therefore, my direct and immediate collaborator in pastoral solicitude as regards Rome. To him goes my esteem and gratitude for his generous and indefatigable dedication. Esteem and gratitude which I wish to express also to the Archbishop Vicegerent, and to the auxiliary bishops, for the daily contact they have been able to establish with parish priests, assistant priests and the faithful. Esteem and gratitude which should be extended to all those who, in various ways and at different levels, offer their time, their qualifications, their intelligence and their spirituality in the various offices which make up the Vicariate. I wish to greet the Secretary Prelate with all the members of the General Secretariat; the officials of the "Pastoral Center for Evangelization and Catechesis"; those of the "Pastoral Center for Worship and Sanctification"; those of the "Pastoral Center for the animation of the Christian community and socio-charitable services"; those of the "Office for natural and juridical persons"; those of the "Administrative Office," the "Legal Office," and the "Technical Office"; those of the "Ordinary Court" and of the "Regional Court of Latium"; and finally those of the other offices and commissions.

My fatherly greeting to everyone!

2. I have come here also to tell you all, very simply and sincerely, my satisfaction, gratitude and appreciation for your work, which has made and makes a concrete and definite contribution for the renewal and pastoral progress of the diocese of Rome. The articulated and varied structure of the Vicariate of Rome—as it was wisely desired and planned by my Predecessor, Paul VI, of venerated memory, with the Apostolic Constitution *Vicariae potestatis* of January 6, 1977, in order to put into practice the theological, pastoral and organizational guidelines that emerged from the Second Vatican Council—needs a personnel adequate for the new requirements, qualified as a result of its specific preparation, its spirit of sacrifice, and especially its

limpid *sensus Ecclesiae*. And you, venerated and dear brothers, have shown in so many circumstances that you possess this sense of the Church to an outstanding degree, filled as you are with holy pride at living and working in Rome, in the Church founded by the Apostles Peter and Paul, and therefore deeply aware of the requirements that this privilege entails, according to the words of Paul VI himself in the above-mentioned document: *"Sed eadem illa dignitas ac praestantia officium quoque necessarium secum fert salubriter praemonstrandi exemplum christiane vitae toti Ecclesiae Christi, quae vivit et agit in variis communitatibus christianis, Ecclesiis scilicet particularibus, per omnem terrarum orbem dispersis"* (Apost. Const. Vicariae potestatis, Introd.).

Always offer an exemplary display of true Christian and priestly life both to the faithful of Rome, who are in contact with you, and to all those who, pilgrims of the world, come to this fortunate city, the center of Catholicism, to venerate the places sacred to the memories of the Apostles, martyrs and saints. Always operate in communion of faith and charity, participating and making your contribution of ideas, but especially of generous and constant action, in the overall apostolate in its various forms, especially those concerning catechesis; the apostolate of the young; the apostolate of the laity; charity; sacramental life; the relations between faith and social reality, without indulgence towards tempting forms of convergence with forces of opposed ideal inspiration.

In a serene and loyal spirit of service, always try to maintain a direct contact with pastoral life, in this Rome, in which human and spiritual problems are more and more vast and complex.

I am and always will be close to you with my affection and my prayer, certain of finding in you all good and thoughtful collaborators, capable of helping me and lightening my concerns in ruling and governing "my" diocese.

May the apostolic blessing, which I willingly impart to you, accompany you in your commitment and in your daily work.

Priests for the Church and for the Men of Today

On March 23, 1980, immediately after the meeting with the sisters, the Holy Father went to the Cathedral of Santa Maria Argentea, where the clergy of the dioceses of Spoleto and Norcia, and priests from other parts of Umbria were waiting for him. The Pope delivered the following address.

Dear brothers in the priesthood!

I wish to tell you, with great sincerity, how happy I am to speak to you, priests of the dioceses of Norcia and Spoleto, at a personal meeting, precisely in this fortunate place, in which St. Benedict and St. Scholastica were born. There is a set of external circumstances and interior emotions, which invite me and you to a short and serene reflection on the meaning of your priestly presence in this city, in this region, in this nation, that is, in modern society.

1. The society of today is certainly not that of the fifth and sixth century A.D. But man's fundamental problems—such as those of God and religion, the overall and definitive meaning of life, ethical behavior, justice, the dignity of man—are still similar today to those that the young Benedict came up against. They are the problems that you, priests of the eighties, live, sometimes dramatically, both in the secrecy of your conscience or of the confessional, and when you must say a word of guidance or give a concrete example to your brothers.

You are and must be priests for the Church and for the men of today, who live in a socio-cultural context which wishes to question everything, which raises doubts, sows uncertainties, or claims immediate solutions in all fields in which man finds himself acting or developing his personality.

And just as between the fifth and the sixth centuries, the presence of St. Benedict and his monks was providential for the society of that time, so there is no doubt that modern society, which lives between the end of the second and the dawn of the third millennium of Christianity, needs priests, precisely because it needs God.

And you, dear brothers, are "servants of Christ and stewards of the mysteries of God" (cf. 1 Cor. 4:1); you have been "chosen from among men" and "appointed to act on behalf of men in relation to God" (cf. Heb. 5:1). All your greatness and dignity lies here.

With the sacrament of ordination to the priesthood you have been configured to Christ the Priest as ministers of the Head, in order to build up and establish His whole Body which is the Church, as co-workers of the episcopal order—as the Second Vatican Council reminded you. By means of consecration you have been raised to the condition of living instruments of Christ, the eternal Priest, to continue in time His wonderful work, which restored the whole of mankind with divine efficacy (cf. PO 12).

PRIMACY OF THE SPIRITUAL

2. In the structure of the People of God, you, dear brothers in the priesthood, *occupy a specific and qualified role and place*, which is exercised, following the example of Christ's life, in a varied range of services for the Mystical Body; services which are the expression of the wonderful blossoming of Christ's own priesthood in which you participate. "The ways along which you fulfill your priestly vocation, dear brothers," I wrote in the Letter to Priests for Holy Thursday 1979, "are different. Some in the ordinary pastoral work of parishes; others in mission lands; others, again, in the field of activities connected with the teaching, training and education of youth, working in the various spheres and organizations, whereby you assist in development of social and cultural life; others, finally, near the suffering, the sick, the neglected; sometimes, you yourselves bedridden and in pain. These ways differ from one another.... Nevertheless, within all these differences *you are always and everywhere the bearers of your particular vocation:* you are bearers of the grace of

Christ, the eternal Priest, and bearers of the charism of the Good Shepherd. And you can never forget this; you can never renounce this; you must put this into practice at all times and in every place and in every way" (no. 6).

The consequence that must be drawn from the deep theological reality of the ministerial priesthood is the following: for the priest, *the center and fundamental reference point of his whole life and activity must be God:* God worshiped constantly, in particular in the beatifying sacramental presence of the Eucharist, entrusted especially to the ministry of priests; God invoked and supplicated in liturgical prayer, community and personal, in an affectionate dialogue between son and Father; God loved and served in our brothers, especially the suffering and the poor. This sense of God's presence, this primacy of the spiritual, which must direct the whole life and pastoral ministry of the priest, is the great and always topical teaching of St. Benedict: *"Ubique credimus divinam esse praesentiam...maxime tamen hoc sine aliqua dubitatione credamus cum ad Opus divinum adsistimus...ergo consideremus qualiter oporteat in conspectu Divinitatis et angelorum eius esse"* (Rule, chap. I). And again: *"Nihil Operi Dei praeponatur"* (ibid., chap. XLIII).

In the light of this essential theocentric view, the various tasks of the priest, the requirements of his functions, which come from the Gospel and are the very measure of the priestly vocation, are illuminated.

The priest is an immense gift that God has bestowed on His Church; and the priest's joyful response to the call of Jesus is, as St. John Chrysostom says, the greatest proof of love for Christ: "The Master asks the disciple (Peter) if he loves Him, not in order to know it Himself..., but He does so to teach us how close to His heart is care of the flock.... His intention, then, was not to show how much Peter loved Him..., but He wanted to show how much He loved His Church, and taught Peter and all of us what care we must lavish on this work" (cf. *Dialogue on the Priesthood*, II, 1).

YOUR IDENTITY AS PRIESTS

3. Beloved brothers! Your high and exacting service cannot be carried out—as I said to the priests of Mexico in the Basilica of Our Lady of Guadalupe—"without a clear and deep-rooted conviction of your identity as priests of Christ, depositaries and administrators of God's mysteries, instruments of salvation for men, witnesses of a kingdom which begins in this world but is completed in the next. In the light of these certainties of faith, why have doubts about your own identity? Why hesitate about the value of your own life? Why waver on the path which you have chosen?" (January 27, 1979)

Follow joyfully Christ, who loved you and called you; even if, as time goes on, your body feels the weight of fatigue and the wear and tear of time, let your heart always be awake and vigilant, burning with zeal for the souls that God has placed on your way. Ministers of Christ, love and be faithful to the Church, His bride; not to a utopian and abstract Church, but to the concrete, historical Church. Be firmly united, in serene concord and loyal obedience, to the bishop, whose direct collaborators you are; be united in brotherhood with one another, so that the presbyterium may be a visible sign of communion. In these times of the crisis of values and certainties, be, for everyone, "educators in faith" (cf. PO 6). And how could you be so more—as I said to all priests in my recent Apostolic Exhortation about *Catechesis in Our Time*—than "by devoting your best efforts to the growth of your communities in the Faith. Whether you are in charge of a parish, or are chaplains to primary or secondary schools or universities, or have responsibility for pastoral activity at any level, or are leaders of large or small communities, especially youth groups, the Church expects you to neglect nothing with a view to a well-organized and well-oriented catechetical effort.... All believers have a right to catechesis; all pastors have the duty to provide it" (CT 64).

CLOSE TO THE PEOPLE

4. A last thought, beloved brothers, to which I attach such importance. The priest, I said a moment ago, quoting the Letter to the Hebrews, is chosen from the people and appointed to act on behalf of the people (cf. Heb. 5:1). So you must be close to the people, beside the people, living their daily problems intensely, especially when they are suffering and find themselves in difficult moments and situations. And the present moment, dear brothers in the priesthood, is really difficult for the good Italian people, owing to the spreading temptation of hatred and violence rife in the country. The Permanent Council of the Italian Episcopal Conference announced precisely for today, March 23, a day of prayer and reflection against the fury of violence and for the victory of love. "The obligation of Christians," the message says, "is particularly the education of conscience, one's own and that of others, in the family, at school, in environments of work and in ecclesial associations. It is in consciences that the first and most decisive challenge to violence and terrorism takes place, a challenge that must be staked on the values of democracy, peace and love. The obligation of Christians is commitment in solidarity, participation, the sharing of the problems and of the fate of those who suffer, in humility and courage, willing, like Christ, to meet one's responsibilities squarely, and incarnating a Gospel of peace in oneself and in the world." And you, priests, must be the first to educate consciences to reject hatred and violence; the first to participate in, and share, the problems of those who are suffering.

I have opened my heart to you, dear brothers, on some aspects of priestly life and ministry. I invoke the grace of God on your commitments and your resolutions, through the intercession of St. Benedict and Saint Scholastica.

May the Blessed Virgin always help you with her motherly protection. With my apostolic blessing.

To Strengthen the Experience of Unity and Cooperation

On March 24, 1980, John Paul II presided at a solemn concelebration, in the Sistine Chapel, in the Byzantine-Ukrainian rite, to mark the opening of the Synod of Ukrainian Bishops. Concelebrating with the Pope were Cardinal Josyf Slipyj, Major Archbishop of Lwow of the Ukrainians, together with 14 other Ukrainian bishops. After the Gospel, the Holy Father preached the following homily in Ukrainian.

It is with great joy that, in the supreme act of communion with Christ, who brings about unity in charity in the Eucharist, in the sacrament "by which the unity of the Church is both signified and brought about" (UR 2), I address the most affectionate greeting to our venerated brother, Cardinal Josyf Slipyj, Major Archbishop of Lwow, and to all of you who have come from various parts of the world, in which your faithful are dispersed, for the celebration of this Synod.

Your origin cannot but recall to my mind the particular proximity of your glorious people to my people of origin. And the fact that, with your faithful, you have been found worthy "to suffer dishonor for the name of Jesus" (Acts 5:41) precisely for your faithfulness to Jesus Christ, to the Church, to this See of Peter, cannot but urge me to congratulate you.

SEE OF PETER

1. It was precisely to this See of Peter that you turned your trusting minds and hearts, when you were convened for this Synod which I have wished to celebrate with you. You can be sure that, on every occasion, as at this broth-

erly meeting of joy, Peter's humble Successor has only one desire: to be, as Vatican II said, "the perpetual and visible source and foundation of the unity of the bishops and of the multitude of the faithful" (LG 23). My most sacred commitment corresponds to what *Lumen gentium* says is the function of the Chair of Peter: It "presides over the whole assembly of charity and protects legitimate differences, while at the same time it sees that such differences do not hinder unity but rather contribute toward it" (no. 13).

This unity, the testament of love and the supreme wish of Christ in His great priestly prayer (cf. Jn. 17:11, 21, 23), is certainly the deepest anxiety of our spirits when they pause to consider the mystery of the Church in the world. It is an anxiety which, though it constitutes deep suffering in contemplating the division of the seamless garment of the Body of Christ, becomes at the same time incessant prayer which unites with Christ's invocation for unity, and is turned into wise and courageous action so that, while fully respecting everyone's freedom of choice, there may be recomposed in the Church the "unity of spirit in the bond of peace," as becomes those who are called to the one great hope which is Christ Jesus.

It is unity that reflects the mystery of that life as a result of which we are all "one body and one Spirit" in Christ, in the reality of "one Lord, one faith, one baptism, one God and Father of us all, who is above all and through all and in all" (Eph. 4:3-6). The multiple diversity of ministries, expressed also by the plurality of gifts, is directed to "building up the body of Christ, until we all attain to the unity of the faith..." *(ibid.,* 13).

This *attain* is part of our humble service. As pastors of God's flock, we are all committed to doing everything that depends on us in order that charity may realize in Christ the unity of His Church. It is the great ideal that must make us indefatigable, attentive, industrious, courageous in order that what Jesus, the supreme Pastor, invoked: "that they may all be one," may come true. What does this Synod of ours aim at, fundamentally, but this?

ADMIRABLE UNITY

2. The "Mystery of the Faith" which we celebrate around the altar manifests and realizes in a very special way this unity which we invoke with Christ and for which we work.

Certainly, "in the sacrament of the Eucharistic Bread the unity of all believers who form one body in Christ is both expressed and brought about" (LG 3; cf. also 11). This admirable unity should be seen not merely in the material bond that binds the faithful to the one table, but also in deep communion with Christ, "our paschal lamb" (1 Cor. 5:7). Jesus Christ, the Redeemer of man, is the principle of the new unity of all men. "Now in Christ Jesus we who once were far off have been brought near in the blood of Christ" (Eph. 2:13). It is precisely the "memorial" of the Lord par excellence, the Eucharist, which actualizes the mystery of grace, sealed fundamentally when Christ offered on the cross the reconciliation already signed at the Last Supper.

He who is "our peace," when His body, offered to the disciples at the Supper, was given up to death, sanctioned the unity that all men are called to have in Him. Then the dividing wall created by sin was broken down, hostility disappeared, peace and reconciliation were established, the "one new man" was set up (cf. Eph. 2:14-16). The mystery of the immolated body and of the blood shed to build up unity lives here in the Eucharist. Here is consummated the "new and eternal alliance" which renews and welds our union with Him. Here this union becomes a perennial "transfusion" of life which realizes the greatest Christian ideal, that of living for God: "He who eats me will live because of me" (Jn. 6:57).

To live for Christ is to live for God; it is to strain towards the glory of the Father; it is to realize with the Father the perennial prayerful communion which sustains the deep motion of the Spirit who elevates to Him (cf. Rom. 8:15; Gal. 4:6). It is to make the will of the Father our food, in faithful accomplishment of the work He has entrusted to us (cf. Jn. 4:34); it is to be perfect as the Father is perfect in the gift of merciful and generous love to all brothers (cf. Mt. 5:43-48). Thus divine life, through the Eucharist and by means of the Eucharist, "the font and apex of the whole Christian life" (LG 11), reaches fullness in man. The fullness of communion with the Father in the Spirit by means of Christ the Priest and Victim, the Bread of Life; fullness which is poured out in donation of charity, communion of grace, reality of "communication" among brothers.

Real deep unity among men arises in a very special way from the Eucharist. In it our Savior offers to the Church, His bride, the memorial of His death and resurrection as *sacramentum pietatis, signum unitatis, vinculum caritatis*, according to the well-known words of St. Augustine, adopted by *Sacrosanctum concilium* (no. 47). In the Eucharist, in the deepest experience of Christ, who "loved us and gave himself up for us, a fragrant offering and sacrifice to God" (Eph. 5:2), we learn to "walk in love" *(ibid.)*, or, rather, we are made profoundly suitable for the life of Christ which becomes our life, to imitate God as "beloved children" *(ibid., 1)*. In participation in the Eucharist, "partaking of the same loaf and drinking from the same cup" (cf. 1 Cor. 10:17), we realize in Christ the communion which permits us to be "of one heart and soul" (cf. Acts 4:32) and to be available to love as Christ loved (cf. Jn. 13:34), to the point of being ready to suffer and give our life for the brethren (cf. Jn. 15:13).

If we listen to the history of your Church, a history which, for some of you, has been a reality that was really experienced, it can be said with certainty that the power of faith, which becomes love and donation for brothers to the point of martyrdom, is an experience which springs from the Eucharist. In it your Church has found the source of heroism; through it your love has been expressed in the *confessio* which has strengthened the unity of pastors and faithful.

SESSION OF GRACE

3. "Because there is one loaf, we who are many are one body, for we all partake of the same loaf" (1 Cor. 10:17). This stupendous unity is realized in a quite remarkable way in this celebration which opens the session of grace and love which is the Synod of your Church.

You are united here with Peter, "by the fellowship of fraternal charity and by zeal for the universal mission entrusted to the apostles" (CD 36). And it is from this Eucharist, which we are celebrating, that we draw the necessary spirit which, while it binds us in Christ to God in the one love of the Holy Spirit, at the same time expands our heart to deep and real sensitiveness to the interest, the solicitude, the donation of apostolic charity.

The deep desire that the Synod should be celebrated *ad Petre cathedram* has no other purpose but to highlight "the unity we have received from the Apostles: collegial unity." Now, as I stressed in the letter I addressed to all the bishops on the first Sunday of Lent of this year on the mystery and the cult of the Eucharist, "this unity came to birth, in a sense, at the table of the Bread of the Lord on Holy Thursday" (III).

For it was in the Upper Room that the Apostles, at the Lord's table, received the mandate which, with the celebration of the Eucharist, ensures the "consummation" of the life of communion with God and with brothers, fixing the unity by which the Church lives and by which she must be a sign and sacrament in the world. Just indeed as it was in the Upper Room, precisely at the banquet of the Eucharistic Supper, that Jesus prayed for the unity of "His," of those Apostles of whose grace and mandate we bear the weight and the honor for the salvation of the whole world.

These days of grace, which begin with the common celebration of the Eucharist, must, therefore, be transformed into a special experience of unity, concord and collaboration. Thanks to the Eucharist, "we who are many are one body," as I said a moment ago with the words of

St. Paul. We are the Body of Christ! United with the whole Church of the Lord Jesus, with our eyes turned to Him, our Head, Teacher and Redeemer, and together with the heart that palpitates with all our brothers, especially with the faithful of your Church, in our deep union we must bear the witness that impels the world to believe (cf. Jn. 17:21). But to believe what? To believe that we have faith in Christ; to believe that we are dominated by His love; to believe that our adherence to the Gospel is unshakable; to believe that, above all human reality, we are convinced of the primacy of God and His action; to believe that we really love God and, through this love, we love the world and all men, for whom we are ready to offer joyfully our ministry, which is prompt, attentive, up-to-date, complete, if necessary unto death and death on the cross.

This is what springs up in our spirit in contact with the Eucharistic Mystery and the experience of its grace at the beginning of this Synod of ours. Gathered in the Cenacle, we do not feel isolated from the brothers for whom we are gathered here. They are with us, especially in this Eucharistic Celebration. They pray with us and for us, they invoke with us and for us the fullness of the Holy Spirit, they implore with us and for us that unity of spirit, in the bond of peace, which will help us to see the needs of their Church, the most urgent requirements, and at the same time give us the strength and the courage to bring them opportune assistance. Only in this way will this Synod, a typical expression of the unity of the Church, be a springtime of the Holy Spirit for us and for the beloved Ukrainian Church, present here, through you. Centuries of history of struggles and martyrdoms, demonstrations of faith and evangelical ardor, zeal for the proclamation of the Gospel in communion with the universal Church and with Peter, are present here in an extraordinary way at this moment. May this presence, a spiritual one, but real, deep and living, sustain our work, renewing us all in the spirit of the Apostles for the good of our faithful.

MARIAN TRADITION

The experience of the Cenacle would not reflect the hour of grace of the outpouring of the Spirit, if it had not the grace and joy of Mary's presence. "Together with Mary the mother of Jesus" (Acts 1:14), we read of the great hour of Pentecost. And it is this hour that we want to experience and renew. For this reason, with the very rich Marian tradition of your Church, we unite with the Blessed Virgin. May she, the mother of love and unity, bind us deeply, in order that, like the first community, born from the Cenacle, we may be "one heart and soul." May she, *mater unitatis*, in whose womb the Son of God was united with humanity, inaugurating mystically the nuptial union of the Lord with all men, help us to be "one" and to become instruments of unity among our faithful and among all men.

It is the grace that I entrust as a wish from the depths of my heart to the Virgin of the Incarnation. May the humble handmaid of the Lord "intercede with her Son...until all the peoples of the human family...are happily gathered together in peace and harmony into the one People of God, for the glory of the most holy and undivided Trinity" (LG 69). It is to her, "an example of that maternal love by which all should be fittingly animated who cooperate in the apostolic mission of the Church on behalf of the rebirth of men" (LG 65) that I entrust you all, one by one, with your Churches and your faithful, in order that by contemplating her and with her help, thanks also to this Synod, we may really be the Apostles of the new times.

New Vigor of Religious Life in Ukrainian Catholic Church

On March 24, 1980, John Paul II presided at the meeting of the Extraordinary Synod of the Ukrainian Bishops. Present were Cardinal Josyf Slipyj, Major Archbishop of Lwow of the Ukrainians, and the other 14 Ukrainian bishops. Also present were Archbishop Achille Silvestrini, Secretary of the Council of the Public Affairs of the Church, and Archbishop Mario Brini, Secretary of the Sacred Congregation for the Eastern Churches.

After an address of homage by Cardinal Slipyj in Ukrainian, the Holy Father replied as follows in the same language.

Your Eminence,

With my letter *Probe nostis* of March 1, 1980, I convened you here for an Extraordinary Synod, and I am happy to address a brotherly greeting to Cardinal Josyf Slipyj, Major Archbishop of Lwow of the Ukrainians, and to you metropolitans, exarchs, eparchs, the auxiliary and the apostolic visitor; and I send my best wishes, together with my prayers, to the prelates—the Most Reverends Malancsuk, Martenetz and Gabro—who, for reasons of health, have not been able to come to Rome.

In the Sistine Chapel this morning—as Pastor of the universal Church—I addressed to you a word of exhortation and encouragement about the new commandment that has been entrusted to us in the first place, as successors of Peter and the Apostles: the commandment to love one another as our Lord Jesus loved us; a commandment that must be lived, around the Eucharist, in unity of heart and soul at all levels of our being: human, Christian and ecclesial.

Already at the beginning of this solemn session, I wish to express to you prelates, and to the whole Ukrainian Catholic Church, my deep esteem for it and to assure you that I follow with particular attention the news that reaches me with regard to the conditions of the faithful in the Ukraine and in the diaspora. With deep admiration I follow your path in faith, now a millenary one, and I had the opportunity to dwell on this subject in the letter I sent to the Major Archbishop of Lwow precisely a year ago. I also want to assure you that your concerns are mine and that your pastoral cares—and those of your collaborators, priests, men and women religious and laity—are deeply shared by me and by the various organisms of the Holy See.

SYNODAL UNITY

The reason for this Extraordinary Synod is known to you: to propose candidates who actually meet the requirements of the Sacred Canons for the nomination of the one who can give valuable assistance today to the Major Archbishop Josyf Slipyj, and then succeed him in a worthy way.

I have desired all this to be the subject of a Synod, both because of the importance of the event, and to let the Catholic Ukrainian Church enjoy, by means of my intervention, a moment of synodal unity as an expression of its communion round the Vicar of Christ.

I feel deeply with you, in fact, the necessity of ensuring the continuity of the high office of the Major Archbishop of Lwow.

This Synod, which takes place by my convocation and under my presidency, is an Extraordinary Synod because it is a question of considering the nomination of a Coadjutor with the right to succession of the Major Archbishop, an act that requires the exercise of the pontifical authority; as well as the convocation, in this case binding, of the Ukrainian bishops who are outside the territory of the major archbishopric of Lwow. It takes place here in Rome, in the Pope's See, where all the Catholic bishops and faithful are, as it were, "in their Father's house"; in the See of Rome, with which all the other Churches must agree, according to the expression of St. Irenaeus: *"Ad hanc enim Ecclesiam propter potiorem principalitatem necesse est omnem convenire Ecclesiam" (Adversus haereses* 3, 3, 2).

I am aware of acting as the humble Successor of the blessed apostle Peter, by virtue of the divine mandate: "strengthen your brethren" (Lk. 22:32), happy to be able to sustain you in your anxieties, protect you from so many difficulties both external and internal, and give you a sign of special predilection. Moreover, this Extraordinary Synod may be followed by others, as I have already had occasion to point out to the Major Archbishop; it is a question of synods that he will be able to convene, when necessary, after having obtained the consent of the Sovereign Pontiff.

"SO TRIED, SO FAITHFUL"

Communion with Rome has been for centuries, and today more than ever, a fundamental and distinctive element of the faith of the Ukrainian Catholic Church. The Bishop of Rome, in his office as "the principle and foundation of the unity of ecclesial communion" (LG 23), has a special duty of gratitude and solicitude to his brothers in the Ukrainian episcopate, and among them particularly the venerable Major Archbishop Cardinal Slipyj, and to the whole Ukrainian Catholic Church, so sorely tried, so faithful.

I wish to address a word of special regard to you, Your Eminence. I wish to pay tribute to you for so many years of service and sacrifice on behalf of the cause of Christ and of His Gospel. I wish to recall the esteem and consideration shown by my Predecessors to your venerated person: Pope Pius XII who nominated you Coadjutor with the right of succession to the archiepiscopal See of Lwow of the Ukrainians; Pope John XXIII who obtained freedom for you after a long imprisonment; Pope Paul VI, who wished to recognize your merits and your sufferings by promoting you Major Archbishop (1963) and raising you to the dignity of the Cardinalate (1964). I want to thank the Lord, together with Ukrainian confrères present and absent, and the whole Catholic Church, for what He has carried out in you. We pray fervently to Him to lavish every grace on you, so that you may continue to gather joyfully every blessing *ad multos annos.* I have convened this Synod, as Pastor of the universal Church, to give support to your strength, and renewed vigor to the religious life of the Ukrainian Catholic Church.

The Pope exhorts pastors and faithful not to lose hope: There is a Providence that guides people and takes care especially of communities of believers. "God is faithful," as St. Paul says (1 Cor. 10:13). Afflictions, privations, hostility are sore trials, but they are also a stimulus to greater faithfulness: faithfulness to one's own Catholic Faith, to attachment to one's own rite, to ancient traditions, in a word to one's spiritual identity, which has in communion with the Pope and with all the bishops of the Roman Catholic Church the distinctive element of its own heritage of faith and life.

ECUMENICAL SPIRIT

The Pope would like this identity not to appear in the eyes of brothers of the Orthodox Church as a sign of antagonism and almost as a refusal to recognize the life and glorious traditions of the Eastern Church; and he hopes so precisely in virtue of the ecumenical spirit of today which follows the way of dialogue, mutual understanding, considering one another—as we actually are—brothers in common faith in Christ the Savior, members of Churches which are aiming at re-establishing the full communion willed by Christ.

This is the hope by which the ecclesial life of our beloved Ukrainian sons must be nourished, confident that their constancy will bear fruit one day in "the praise of his (God's) glorious grace" (Eph. 1:6).

Venerable brothers, before proceeding let us pray to God the Almighty Father that this Extraordinary Synod may really yield abundant fruit in the millenary history of the Ukrainian Catholic Church, so rich in religious traditions and fruitful in so many well-deserving confessors and martyrs of the Faith, the most illustrious of whom is Saint Josaphat. Let us insistently ask our Lord Jesus Christ, the Head of the Mystical Body, who called us to loving service and entrusted me with the task of "strengthening the brethren," to bless this important and historic event in the Ukrainian Catholic Church. Let us open ourselves without reserve to the Holy Spirit, so that He may enlighten us and guide us in our deliberations and decisions. Finally let us invoke the patronage of the Blessed Virgin Mary, the Mother of God. Tomorrow we will commemorate the mystery of the annunciation, which initiates the plan of redemption. The Byzantine liturgy especially stresses its importance in the divine economy, to such an extent that Good Friday is no longer aliturgical when the two commemorations coincide, since the passion and death of Christ would not have taken place if the Word had not become flesh in Mary's virginal womb. Let us implore, therefore, the Mother of God and ever Virgin Mary, Mother of the Church, to intercede propitiously in our favor and obtain from the Holy Trinity abundant favors and graces for us and for the Ukrainian Catholic Church in the mother country and scattered all over the world.

Persevere in Love!

On March 24, 1980, the Holy Father received in audience fourteen newly-ordained priests from St. Peter's Philosophical and Theological Institute, Viterbo, of the Congregation of St. Joseph (Giuseppini). The Pope delivered the following address.

Beloved newly-ordained priests, sons of St. Leonardo Murialdo!

Just ordained "ministers of the Lord" and after celebrating your first holy Mass, you ardently wished to meet the Pope to manifest your faithfulness to the Church, to listen to his word and receive his blessing.

And I am glad to welcome you and extend to you my most affectionate greeting: I thank you for this act of filial regard and I take part fully in your great joy for having been configured more closely to Christ by means of the sacrament of Orders, called to serve Him in the Church with His own divine powers.

And with you I also intend to greet cordially your superiors and teachers, your parents and relatives.

At this moment, such an anxious one for you, I have only one exhortation: persevere in love! Persevere in the "sacramental grace" and in the austere but stupendous mission of the salvation of souls!

And to persevere you have only to seek inspiration in the figure of your founder, St. Leonardo Murialdo, whose zealous life and passionate writings you certainly know.

Let the first means of perseverance be for you apostolic concern. The priest must have an "eschatological" view of existence and history and live in this perspective. Souls must be evangelized, saved and sanctified: This is God's will! The priest is responsible for this proclamation and this salvation. Never forget the apostolic concern of Murialdo, who said: "Let us not give ourselves the remorse of having to fear that some soul, redeemed by the blood of Christ, has been lost, partly owing to our cowardice, sloth and selfishness."

CHRISTIAN REALISM

A second means of perseverance is the sense of Christian realism. Murialdo, an eminently well-balanced and concrete spirit, in sad and dark times, had great faith and confidence in man. You know his programmatic adages: "Not words, but acts." "Seek holiness and seek it quickly." After the 1870 events, he wrote: "Our age has its good sides and its bad sides like all ages; but you cannot change the bad ones by shaking your head and withdrawing into Achilles' tent.... The Church and Christians will always be in a state of struggle on this earth.... On our side, let us unite with prayers, good works, Catholic zeal, the union of forces, ardor for the salvation of souls; but at once, without waiting for heavenly interventions and imaginary triumphs" (letter of May, 1872).

It is really an excellent program and extremely relevant today: not unrealistic optimism, nor pessimism, which does not do justice to Providence; but a healthy Christian realism, which accepts the reality of man and history in order to love it and save it in the name of Christ, with toil and patience.

PURITY OF THOUGHT

And, finally, a third means of perseverance is purity of thought, by means of orderly study and good reading. Your founder, in the ferment of the new rationalistic and materialistic philosophies of the century, had felt a deep urge to educate, especially the young, by means particularly of "good books and printed material." A century later the concern for "purity of thought" has multiplied enormously. How important it is to remain in "divine intimacy" by means of meditation on serious and solid books, which warm the soul at the fire of love of God and keep it serene and enthusiastic, whatever be the situation or duty in which one finds oneself.

Beloved newly-ordained priests! Imitate St. Leonardo Murialdo also in devotion to the Blessed Virgin and always ask yourselves: "Is the Blessed Virgin pleased with this decision of mine? What does she suggest to me? How would she behave in my place?"

So go now, joyful and courageous, to the place where obedience sends you and persevere in love, with the help of your saint and the comfort of my apostolic blessing.

Continuation of Your Church Assured

On March 27, 1980, John Paul II received in audience Cardinal Josyf Slipyj, Major Archbishop of Lwow of the Ukrainians, together with the other 14 Ukrainian bishops who had taken part in the Extraordinary Synod. During the course of the audience, His Holiness announced that he had appointed Most Rev. Myroslav Ivan Lubachivsky, Metropolitan of Philadelphia of the Ukrainians, as Coadjutor, with the right of succession of His Eminence the Major Archbishop of Lwow of the Ukrainians. The following is the translation of the Pope's address which he delivered in Ukrainian.

Venerable brothers in the episcopate,

Here we are, happily arrived, with the Lord's help, at the goal that we had set ourselves with the convocation of this Extraordinary Synod, that is, the nomination of an Archbishop Coadjutor with the right of succession for our venerated brother, Cardinal Josyf Slipyj, Major Archbishop of Lwow of the Ukrainians.

I wish to express to you in the first place my deep satisfaction at having been able to see with what sense of responsibility you have carried out your task.

The Lord will certainly reward you.

Seeing your assembly, there came spontaneously to my mind the sentence of the psalmist: "Behold, how good and pleasant it is when brothers dwell in unity!" (Ps. 133:1)

After having reflected for a long time and invoked the help of the Lord in prayer, I have decided to nominate as Coadjutor, with right of succession of Cardinal Josyf Slipyj, His Excellency Most Reverend Myroslav Ivan Lubachivsky, Metropolitan of Philadelphia of the Ukrainians. He is the first of the three candidates presented.

His outstanding piety, his pastoral zeal, his academic qualifications and the fine gifts of meekness and humility that adorn his spirit, make him worthy, moreover, of this high office. My confidence and my most sincere and hearty good wishes go to him. Your Eminence will have in him a worthy and fitting Coadjutor.

Now all of you, venerable brothers, return to your pastoral cares, happy to have been able to contribute in such a tangible way to a measure which constitutes for your Church an effective protection and a singular honor.

This happy synodal moment should remain as a token of unity of action and communion of spirits *in vinculo pacis* and direct your apostolate in close union of sentiments and resolutions with all the faithful of this select portion of the universal Church.

In the common concern of my heart and yours for the good of the Ukrainian Church, I recommend to your pastoral zeal the "holy cause" of priestly vocations, with the wish and the prayer that candidates *in sorte Domini vocati* may grow and be formed *in spem Ecclesiae Ucrainae.*

Through the intercession of the Mother of God, we implore from the Lord on all of you, on the clergy, the men and women religious and all the faithful of the Ukrainian Church, the joy of paschal love, the fullness of every consolation.

We Are Priests of Christ's Priesthood

On April 3, 1980, the Holy Father presided over the solemn concelebrated Mass for the blessing of the chrism in the Vatican Basilica. Two thousand five hundred priests concelebrated with the Pope.
John Paul II delivered the following homily.

Dear brothers,

1. We come to St. Peter's Basilica today and meet round this altar in the totality of our priestly community: the *presbyterium* of the Church of Rome.

We come, aware of the importance of the day, which unites us with the priests of the whole world, of the whole earthly globe. On this same day—on Holy Thursday—the communities of priests, the presbyteria of all the Churches, gather, like us, round their bishops all over the world, to proclaim—celebrating the Eucharist together—what we, too, wish to proclaim today. We proclaim it not only with words, but also with our whole *being*—because by the grace of God we are priests of Christ with our whole being. We proclaim it with the *liturgy*—this unique and extraordinary liturgy of Holy Thursday—which gathers in itself our human and priestly being, in order to proclaim, through it, the unfathomable mysteries of God.

THE DAY OF JESUS CHRIST

2. Holy Thursday is first of all the day of Jesus Christ. It is the first of those three holy days of His: *Triduum Sacrum*.

All these days constitute, in a way, an indivisible whole—they are, so to speak, *the day of our Redemption*, the paschal day, that is, the day of the Passover.

The day of Jesus Christ, that is, of the Anointed—whom the Father anointed with the Holy Spirit and grace, and sent into the world.

"The Spirit of the Lord God is upon me, because the Lord has anointed me to bring good tidings to the afflicted; he has sent me to bind up the brokenhearted, to proclaim liberty to the captives, and the opening of the prison to those who are bound" (Is. 61:1-2a).

Here Christ comes again—the Anointed of the eternal God—to promulgate another "new" year of grace. Grace, in fact, is mainly He Himself in His Paschal Mystery, that is, in the mystery of the Passover.

His day—the first of those three which constitute the one paschal day—will begin at sunset on Holy Thursday, when He will sit down at table with the Apostles for the supper prescribed by the rite of the Old Covenant.

We gather now already, in the morning of Holy Thursday, to be together from the morning with Him, Christ the Anointed, on this extraordinary, unique day.

It is the day of Jesus Christ—"the faithful witness, the first-born of the dead, and the ruler of kings on earth" (Rv. 1:5).

At sunset of this day He will begin to bear the last witness to Him who has sent Him, the Father.

He will begin to bear witness to such a love and suffering as no other human heart is able to penetrate.

He will begin to bear witness to eternal holiness, which was manifested to the world on the day of creation.

He will begin to bear witness to the Covenant, which the most holy God made with man from the beginning, and which, even when it was broken in the heart of the first man and then innumerable other times by the sins of other men, has not ceased, in expectation of this day and this hour of Christ, "the faithful witness."

Christ, the faithful witness, will begin, then, to bear witness to the holiness of God in that Covenant with man, which will have to be instituted definitively at the cost of the sacrifice, which will begin on Holy Thursday—this evening—in a bloodless way, and which will be fulfilled by means of His blood and His death on Calvary.

We come today to confess our faithfulness and our love, our unworthiness and our abandonment "to him who loves us and has freed us from our sins by his blood and made us a kingdom, priests to his God and Father..." (Rv. 1:5-6).

Lo, He will humble Himself, becoming obedient unto death—to be able to imprint on the souls of men, and in a way in the heart of the whole of creation, the new likeness to God by means of His one priesthood: to make us all "a kingdom of priests"—and in this way bear witness to the dignity of man and to the dignity of the whole of creation, according to God's eternal plan.

"Behold, He comes." Here comes "the faithful witness"—to fill with His priesthood the hearts of men and, at the same time, the whole of creation from beginning to end:

"I am the Alpha and Omega."

THE FEAST OF PRIESTS

4. Today, the day of Jesus Christ—Holy Thursday—is *our special day*. It is the feast of priests.

On this day we come, with the whole of our community, to thank Christ *for the priesthood*

—which He inscribed in the heart of man, the master of creation

—which He inscribed in a particular way in our hearts.

In fact, He invited us to the Last Supper—and today He invites us again. He invited us *in the person of those Twelve,* who were together with Him that evening. Before them, He took the bread, broke it, distributed it and said:

"This is my body which is given for you."

And then He took the cup filled with wine, gave it to His disciples and said:

"This cup which is poured out for you is the new covenant in my blood."

And at the end he added:

"Do this in remembrance of me."

We are, therefore, *priests* of His priesthood. We are priests of this sacrifice, which He offered in His body and in His blood on the cross and under the species of bread and wine at the Last Supper.

We are also *priests "for men,"* in order that all, by means of the sacrifice we carry out by virtue of His power, may become "a kingdom of priests"—and offer spiritual sacrifices in union with His sacrifice, of the cross and of the Upper Room.

We are, finally, *priests forever.*

For our place today is beside Him: beside Christ—and our lips and hearts wish to *renew the vow of faithfulness* to Him who is "the faithful witness" of our priesthood before the Father.

You Are Called to a Ministry of Charity

The Holy Father celebrated Mass on April 11, 1980, in the Hall of the Swiss in the pontifical palace at Castel Gandolfo, at which numerous newly-ordained deacons were present.

To the group, which numbered about 150 persons and included the superiors of the various colleges as well as relatives of the new deacons, the Pope addressed the following words.

Dear sons and brothers in Christ,

1. In the presence of the community of the faithful, represented by a group of your own parents, relatives and friends, you have come here to ratify the oblation of your lives as deacons of God's Church. In doing so you are filled with confidence because you know that your vocation and your ministry find their effective support in the power of Christ's resurrection, which the Church is celebrating with joyful gratitude and love throughout this holy season.

The Church has indeed placed a great treasure in your hands, for she has called you to be associated in a special way with the Lord Jesus in His worship of the Father and in His service to humanity. You are called to a greater conformity with Christ the Servant, and from now on your discipleship will be expressed in a *ministry of the word, of the altar and of charity.*

2. Your whole lives have to be rooted in the Word of God, which you are called to accept and to communicate in all its fullness, just as it is proclaimed by the one, holy, catholic and apostolic Church. In the Eucharistic Sacrifice —in which you participate and which will be forever the center of your lives—Christ Himself will offer your whole ministry of charity to His Father. From now on, you will have a particular relationship with the poor, the suffering and the sick—with all those in need. And remember always that the greatest service you will render to God's people is to bring to them His life-giving and uplifting Gospel of salvation.

3. To equip you for this task of service, the Church has solemnly invoked upon you the Holy Spirit and His sevenfold gifts. He it is, the Holy Spirit, who is able to configure you ever more deeply to the Jesus whom you represent, and who wishes to prolong through you His salvific contact with humanity. The people must be able to see Christ in you; the Master must be recognized in the disciple. It is in the name of Jesus that you are sent out, and everything that you are able to accomplish will be done "by the name of Jesus Christ the Nazarene" (Acts 4:10).

4. In order to be conscious of your task of ministering in His holy name, and in order to remain effectively united with Him, *you must pray.* You must frequently lift up your hearts to the Lord who has called you by name and entrusted you with a great responsibility. In this regard, the Liturgy of the Hours will be the enrichment of your lives and the guarantee of the effectiveness of your ministry of service. Prayer must sustain your service, and your service in turn must, time and again, lead you back to prayer. Be assured that Mary, the Mother of the risen Lord, will support you in your efforts and remain close to you with her love.

5. And finally, dear sons and brothers, so that your joy may be complete, remember the words of Jesus, the assurance He has given us, the wonderful promise He has made to us: "...if any one serves me, the Father will honor him" (Jn. 12:26). Yes, as deacons, you are called to serve Christ in His members and to be honored by His eternal Father, to whom be all praise and thanksgiving in the unity of the Holy Spirit, forever and ever. Amen.

Joyful Awareness of Your Own Identity

Before the beginning of holy Mass outside Turin Cathedral on April 13, 1980, the Holy Father met, inside the church, the priests of the archdiocese, who were to concelebrate with him afterwards. John Paul II delivered the following address.

Beloved priests of the Archdiocese of Turin!

"Grace to you and peace from God our Father and the Lord Jesus Christ!" (1 Cor. 1:3) I warmly greet you all alike, and in particular I embrace your Archbishop Cardinal Anastasio Ballestrero, who with you and for you spends his best energies as pastor for the benefit of this illustrious archdiocese. Accepting his invitation, I am among you today! I assure you that my greeting expresses a particular sense of affection and emotion, as well as great joy. Affection springs both from the common, though diversified, pastoral responsibility that we exercise in the Church of God, and from that sense of fatherhood which is characteristic of the Successor of Peter and which makes me repeat with the same solicitude: "Tend the flock of God that is your charge, not by constraint but willingly (as God would have you)" (1 Pt. 5:2).

But my greeting is also imbued with a particular emotion. I know, indeed, that I have before me the heirs to an extraordinary pastoral tradition characteristic of the Turinese clergy, which has the privilege of including in its ranks the resplendent figures of St. Joseph Benedict Cottolengo and St. John Bosco, as well as St. Joseph Cafasso and Blessed Sebastian Valfré. To them should be added so many other outstanding names, both of Turin and of the whole of Piedmont, which were a happy and efficacious reflection of those great ones....

PASTORAL CARE OF THE PRIESTS

Generosity, self-sacrifice, indefatigable pastoral care have always been the characteristic of whole generations of priests, wisely stimulated and guided by their bishops, particularly after the disorders of the war-torn Middle Ages and the Renaissance. Today I wish to pay tribute publicly to this noble pastoral tradition which is of prime importance for the life of the Church not only in Turin but also in Italy, and in fact for the universal Church, thanking God for having brought forth these "men who have risked their lives for the sake of our Lord Jesus Christ" (Acts 15:26). It is a tradition that made the priest the man of an intelligent and fruitful apostolate in all fields of human life: among the sick, young people, workers, students, prisoners and the condemned to death.

Today, too, there is no lack of new possibilities for the use of one's apostolic energies: there are, unfortunately, families in crisis, drug addicts, the violent, the derelicts of the underworld. This is where the whole dynamism of one's own priestly mission can find complete expression, in full and joyful awareness of one's own "identity," manifesting Christ's loving concern for all brothers, wherever they live and suffer, particularly for the neediest, since "those who are well have no need of a physician, but those who are sick" (Lk. 5:31). Try, therefore, new ways of approach to men and to their living conditions, in complete faithfulness to everything that is essential to your priesthood and, at the same time, with great pastoral elasticity, which will make you sensitive and open to the most urgent needs of the times in which we are living....

Finally, I remind myself and you that there are some fundamental properties which unite all those who share the ministerial priesthood in the Church, though exercising different tasks.

The first one is participation with the one Priest, sovereign and eternal, who is Jesus Christ; all of us, in fact, "have been sanctified through the offering of the body of Jesus Christ once for all" (Heb. 10:10), even if we always bear within us a sense of unworthiness for this extraordinary call which makes us "unworthy servants" (Lk. 17:10).

The second one consists in the peculiar pastoral responsibility, which distinguishes priests from the faithful on whom the ordinary baptismal priesthood has been bestowed, and reserves for him a specific task in the preaching of the Word, celebration of the sacraments and safe guidance of the community (cf. 1 Tm. 4:14; 2 Tm. 1:6). I am happy to stress, here, the typical ministry of St. Joseph Cafasso: that of the sacrament of Penance, which he carried out assiduously also in regard to St. John Bosco, in his faithful ministry in the service of the people and above all in the prisons for the benefit of large numbers of convicts. This is a "diaconia" (charitable service) that is still relevant and fruitful today, since it dispenses abundantly the Lord's mercy, as it is revealed in the Paschal Mystery which we are celebrating just in these days: *misericordia Domini in aeternum cantabo"* (Ps. 88:2). The priest is the one who, having felt the mystery of that Mercy in himself in a particular way, distributes it as widely as possible to others.

The third characteristic, closely connected with the preceding ones, concerns our special conformation to Christ, so that His sacrifice and His love become also our norm of life. Each member of the faithful should be able to say of each of us what every Christian, with St. Paul, confesses with regard to Jesus: He "loved me and gave himself for me" (Gal. 2:20), as the Holy Shroud, preserved here, opportunely reminds us.

CHARITY—THE MEANS

Finally, an essential ecclesial aspect must be kept in mind, the fact that every priest knows that his own dedication must be geared not to lacerating but to constructing the whole body (of Christ), joined and knit together (Eph. 4:16), also by means of sincere mutual charity, fruitful in community growth in the Spirit (cf. *ibid.*, 2:22). In particular, I call upon you always to cultivate close communion with your bishops, according to the classical teaching of St. Ignatius of Antioch: "In fact, your venerable Presbyterium, worthy of God, is harmoniously united with the bishop like the strings of a lyre; and in this way a concert of praise rises to Jesus Christ from the perfect harmony of your feelings and from your charity" *(ad. Eph.* IV).

Be sure that the Pope shares with you the extraordinary labors of this time of ours, connected with mutual reconciliation, with the failure of some pastoral efforts which in the past used to bear fruit, and with the "missionary" situation which you are living.

CONTACT WITH CHRIST

On these bases, my exhortation to joy becomes natural and almost obvious: let it be like that of the seventy disciples on their return to Jesus after their mission (cf. Lk. 10:17-20); and if it is accompanied by sufferings for the sake of the Church (cf. Col. 1:24; 2 Cor. 12:10), then it will be all the more deeply rooted and fruitful. And "no one will take" this joy from you (Jn. 16:22), especially because it springs from continual contact with Christ, who makes us men consecrated to renew His redeeming Sacrifice, men of the Eucharist, which must find Its warm and radiating centrality in our lives.

May the apostolic blessing, which I willingly grant to you, descend upon you as a token of the necessary divine grace, while we prepare together to concelebrate this solemn Sunday liturgy.

The Church Wishes To Collaborate in the Progress of Nicaragua

On April 17, 1980, the Holy Father received in audience the seven bishops of Nicaragua and delivered to them the following address.

Beloved brothers in the episcopate,

With special joy I share with you these moments of intense ecclesial experience, in the framework of the visit that you pay me today, venerable brothers, pastors of the Church of God in Nicaragua which is moving towards the goal of the Father.

If, in my concern for all the Churches, my thought has dwelt so often on the past of the Church that you represent, I wish to confide in you that I have remembered it particularly often and vividly in recent times.

So I thank the Lord for this opportunity of fruitful personal exchange which He gives us and which, for a moment, cancels geographical distances, which, however, have never prevented constant communion in affection and prayer. In fact, "God is my witness...that without ceasing I mention you always in my prayers" (Rom. 1:9). This assiduous memory, also become a prayer, is the expression of my permanent closeness to you, my uninterrupted participation in your troubles and concerns, my nearness to the anxieties and hopes of your portion of the Church and of each of its members.

These sentiments have found lasting echoes in my heart, which sum up the deep benevolence that your country deserves, with its everyday activities and its dignity in exceptional moments. I cannot help mentioning here—after the tragic earthquake that sowed such desolation and ruin, and the civil tension through which Nicaragua has passed, which has cost a great many tears and suffering—the present effort to procure for each member of this same people a better situation with regard to the future.

The Catholic Church, which has its roots in the very reality of the people of Nicaragua, cannot but share in its vicissitudes. Therefore, as I indicated recently to the delegation of the Government Commission of Nicaragua, the Church wishes to be close to this people, especially to the neediest sectors.

We are well aware, as the leaders and guides of the Church, that the latter has a serious mission to carry out today in order to project the light of faith on consciences, so that they will follow the paths demanded by the law of God and respect for the rights and dignity of persons, a divine voice imprinted on human beings.

Guided by this view of man in the light of the divine plan, the Church looks with favor and does not hesitate to promote all that raises the moral and human level of peoples in general and of persons in particular. Thinking concretely of Nicaragua, today she wishes to confirm this desire for collaboration and service, in which she willingly associates Catholic organizations and every individual who feels the call of the human being and the Son of God.

Therefore, Catholics of Nicaragua wish to be involved in this task, in a line of complete faithfulness to their own Christian vocation, with a responsible view of the human and spiritual values that must be at the basis of personal and family life and the organization of the whole of society. It is a collaboration which the Church wishes to continue to offer, above all in the field of education, health, the media of social communication, and Christian associations, in order to contribute to the civil and moral progress of the nation. It is clear, moreover, that the Church considers it a duty, to which there corresponds the right of being able to keep her own institutions for the normal accomplishment of her specific mission.

This attitude of service on the part of the Church is in agreement with the centuries-old Christian tradition of the people of Nicaragua, which, in its commitment for growing human advancement, greater social justice and a worthy future—above all for those in greatest need—confirms its desire to be faithful to its human and Christian nature. I know very well that in this perspective you are very close to your faithful, you pastors of the Church of God of Nicaragua. The Pope and the Church, who really love your people, are with you too.

The Church wishes to offer this commitment in favor of this people, which she is carrying out with the spirit of a Mother, in an attitude of deep respect for the institutions and convictions of every citizen. She believes, however, that an atheistic ideology cannot be an instrument to direct the effort to promote social justice, since it deprives man of his freedom, of spiritual inspiration and of the power of love for his neighbor, which has its most solid and operative foundation in love of God.

I would now like to call your attention especially to the importance of a systematic and solid work of catechesis, an extensive work of religious instruction, which will make use of all the resources available, in order that the stupendous spiritual values of your people may be loved with ever-increasing depth and strength. Together with this, I recommend to you, with special urgency, careful attention to the national seminary, so that future priests may receive a solid human, cultural and spiritual preparation, which will prepare them adequately for the delicate tasks they will have to assume on behalf of the Church and her faithful.

Allow me, beloved brothers, to express to you my deep trust in your ecclesial community. You can rely on a noble people, which loves good, solidarity, peace, justice, and the humanitarian impetus, and which cultivates lovingly the religious values of its existence. Take to it, then, my word of remembrance and affection; tell it that the Pope trusts it and encourages it to be faithful to the deep values of the Christian faith which it professes. This is my message of hope and encouragement, which I direct in the first place to priests, men and women religious, seminarians and laity committed to the apostolate.

To obtain due efficiency in ecclesial service, the unity between bishops and priests, both diocesan and religious, must always be firmly maintained. This unity, which must apply to inspiration and to pastoral action, cannot but be based on the awareness that we are called to serve the cause of the Gospel, which is at the same time the cause of man to the extent that he lives in truth, justice and love.

Return then, beloved brothers, to your place of work, to your own task as pastors and leaders of the Church, with renewed awareness of your important and indispensable mission. Be persevering and clear-sighted teachers of the truth about God, the Church and man at the present time. The Pope and the whole Church are close to you. Your people need you, that beloved people that prays to God as the common Father and invokes the Blessed Virgin fervently.

To her protection I entrust your ecclesial task and that of every member of the faithful in Nicaragua, on whom I bestow my cordial blessing with great affection.

Need To Evangelize, Reflect and Pray

The following are excerpts from the message of John Paul II for the Seventeenth World Day of Prayer for Vocations on Sunday, April 27, 1980.

In establishing the World Day of Prayer for Vocations, my unforgettable predecessor, Paul VI, wanted it to be celebrated between two great liturgical solemnities: Easter and Pentecost. This was a particularly happy choice, for those glorious mysteries of the Christian faith throw a strong light on the priestly vocation and on all other vocations consecrated in a special way to the service of God and the Church.

The Second Vatican Council says: "Rising from the dead, (Christ) sent His life-giving Spirit upon His disciples and through this Spirit has established His Body, the Church, as the universal sacrament of salvation" (LG 48).

This is how it happened at the beginning: a mysterious and profound transformation took place in the first disciples, who believed in the risen Christ and received the gift of the Holy Spirit. They were the same humble men whom Jesus had chosen, one by one, from among the members of His people. We know about their doubts and fears (cf. Mt. 28:17; Jn. 20:19); but they believed in the risen One, and, at the same time, were fully aware of their vocation and mission, in which the Holy Spirit would confirm them, as the Lord Himself promised: "But you shall receive power when the Holy Spirit has come upon you; and you shall be my witnesses in Jerusalem and in all Judea and Samaria and to the end of the earth" (Acts 1:8).

With the power of the Holy Spirit they were the Apostles, the priests and the witnesses of the risen Christ. They modelled their lives and activities with their gaze fixed on the unforgettable image of Jesus the Good Shepherd of men. They proclaimed His message to the world and worked for the salvation of men with His own sacred powers. They knew that the mission of Jesus the

Priest, Teacher and Shepherd was continuing through their own persons: "As the Father has sent me, even so I send you" (Jn. 20:21). They knew, in fact, that they had been constituted, in the midst of the world, as the sign and visible instrument of the living and active presence of the risen Lord; and they also knew that they had been constituted to form, by means of an ineffable gift of the Spirit, a new body of men endowed with an original and unmistakable character: the character of priests, teachers and shepherds of the New Testament.

SPECIAL CONSECRATION

Just as it happened at the beginning, so it has happened always. Centuries and millennia have passed, but the holy Church continues to be the Church of the risen Christ and of Pentecost. The bishops, successors of the Apostles, and the priests, co-workers of the bishops, are the bishops and priests of the risen Christ and of Pentecost. Thus it will go on happening in the future as well, for the risen Lord has guaranteed to His Church His constant assistance: "And lo, I am with you always, to the close of the age" (Mt. 28:20; cf. LG 19 and 28).

Side by side with the bishops and diocesan priests, in brotherly and filial communion with them, there were, there are and there will be other people called by the Lord to a life of special consecration. There have flourished and there are flourishing again the deacons, the servants of the People of God. There have flourished the multitudes of missionaries, sent out to found and guide new Christian communities. There have flourished the numberless forms of consecrated life in the religious orders and congregations and in the secular institutes, which show "to all men...wonderfully at work within the Church the surpassing greatness of the force of Christ the King and the boundless power of the Holy Spirit" (LG 44). All these men and women continue to find the pure source of their vocation in faith in the risen Christ and in the inexhaustible gifts of the Spirit.

INTENSE EVANGELIZATION OF GOD'S PEOPLE

Dear brothers in the episcopate, and all of you, priests, deacons, men and women religious, consecrated persons: my purpose in putting these thoughts before you is in order to extend to you a warm invitation: evangelize in an ever more intense and more effective way the People of God, especially the families and the young people, concerning these holy truths about the priesthood, the missions, the consecrated life. The People of God, when it prays for vocations, must know well why it is praying and for whom. The mysteries of the resurrection and of Pentecost enable you to speak, in the proper and most convincing way, about sacred vocations. The faithful, the families, the young people must realize ever more clearly that the Church and her priests, missionaries and other consecrated persons do not take their origin solely from human causes or motives or interests but from the merciful design of God, who desires the salvation of everyone through the strength of the dead and risen Christ and through the power of the Holy Spirit. And so the testimony of your personal lives, completely dedicated to the service of humanity, will confirm your words and confer upon them, with God's help, renewed and persuasive effectiveness.

INDEX

abandonment
  Christ's 208
  in the Lord 160
abnegation 207
abortion 116
absolution
  general 59, 226, 424; see also *confession*
abuse
  alcoholic 297
action
  Church's 110
  for justice 110
  missionary 351
  pastoral 66, 433
  priestly 148
activity(ies)
  apostolic 59
  Church's 107
  for the common good 71
  judicial 129, 132
  pastoral 43f., 46, 93, 116, 126, 144, 148, 193, 202, 242, 414
  political 296
  priestly 145
  scientific 170
adolescence 526
adolescents 88
adultery 59
advancement 109f., 115
Africa 122f.
age 99
aggiornamento 173f.; see also *renewal*
aggression 110
Ambrose, St. 111
America 90
angel 99
Angelus 151
anthropocentrism 105
anthropology 105f., 110
Apostle(s) 68, 76, 87, 99, 135, 153, 159, 180f., 190, 272, 349, 395, 409
  call of 405
  faith handed down by 418
  mission of 430
  Roman heritage of 70
  successors of 156, 279, 430, 622, 637, 660
  teaching of 339
  times of 353
  vocation of 362
apostolate 92, 161
  among migrants 61ff.
  and the Eucharist 409
  diocesan 138
  of emigrants 62
  of the laity 74, 552
  of the young 460
  vocational 347
Apostolic See 58, 62, 80, 121, 292, 352

Apostolic Union of the Clergy 446
arbitration 130
Aristotle 129
art 86
asceticism 149
Assembly of Gniezno 289f.
atheism 314
Augustine, St. 35, 102, 122, 235, 257
authenticity 62, 144, 210, 509
authority(ies) 66, 82f., 297, 390, 408
  civil 125
  ecclesiastical 28, 130
  of bishop 76
  of episcopal conference 76
  public 129f.
  Roman 99
  supreme, of the Church 58
  to forgive sins 93
  to offer the Eucharistic Sacrifice 93
availability 145, 190

Baptism 102, 140, 249, 283, 594
  of blood 341f.
  of catechumens 140
Basil, St. 363
beatitudes 414, 469
Belgian College 163ff.
Benedict, St. 268, 625, 627
  patron saint of Europe 77
Biblicum 537
bishop(s) 35f., 45, 53f., 57ff., 63, 66ff., 73, 75, 84, 90f., 93, 95, 101, 107ff., 114, 118ff., 125, 138, 140, 143, 146, 148, 180, 227f., 266, 275, 279ff., 308, 336, 345, 350, 364, 414, 421, 488, 497, 535f., 539, 567, 660
  American 40f., 415
  and laity 387f.
  and priests 185, 386f., 443f., 510
  brotherly cooperation of 76
  Canadian 56
  care of prisoners by 388
  collaboration with 137
  collegiality of 147, 328f.
  Colombian 345
  European 76
  evangelizing task of 228
  harmony of 371
  in ecumenical council 413
  in union with the Pope 422
  leaders in holiness 415
  mission of 569
  of Honduras 64
  of Hungary 69
  of Italy 258

of Rome 33, 36, 42, 136, 145, 147, 334, 350f., 567, 639
of Uganda 123
pastoral solicitude of 252
Sacred Congregation for 62
service of the 387
Synod of 73f.
teacher of faith 551
unity among 107, 445
Blessed Sacrament see *Eucharist*
Blessed Virgin Mary see *Mary*
blind 361
blood
of Christ 208
body 87
destruction of the 155
members of Christ's 402
of Christ 26, 102, 126, 208
bookshops, Catholic 460
Borromeo, St. Charles 36f., 470
brotherhood 34, 50, 67, 94, 110, 125, 143, 147, 434
of Apostles 181

calendar
liturgical 349
call 87, 156, 180, 213, 321f.
responsibility for 404
canon law 126f., 129, 505
cardinals 34, 42, 79, 119, 326, 340, 343f.
care
for the family 372
pastoral 65, 91, 118
Catechesi tradendae 529
catechèsis 74, 99, 137f., 144, 146, 221f., 261, 426, 459f., 575, 628, 657
aim of 493
family 456
fields of 438
of Bl. Henry de Ossó 439
catechetical instructions 104
catechism(s) 261
catechist(s) 58, 135, 221f., 237, 575
Bl. Henry de Ossó as 437f.
preparation of 318
youthful groups of 135
Catherine of Siena, St. 43, 268
CELAM 84, 96, 162f., 312
celibacy 47, 92, 143, 182, 195ff., 437
cemetery 466f.
Central America 118
Chair of Peter 85
character 111
priestly 187, 190
charism(s) 94, 108, 552
confusion of 510
of the faithful 422
pastoral 190ff.
priestly 47
charity 64, 86, 126, 128, 137, 159, 207, 230, 298, 369, 373f., 576, 591

bond of 124f.
brotherly 153
commitment of 144
Eucharist as source of 593
of Christ 420
pastoral 419
precept of 71
union through 475
chastity
consecrated 91
child 459
unborn 532
children 88, 524
of God 50, 113
Chile 82
bishops of the Church in 428ff.
chrism 207
Christ see *Jesus Christ*
Christian(s) 29, 49, 52, 77, 90, 98, 100, 102, 105, 114, 125, 127, 254, 358, 423
attitude of the 100
presence of 115
unity of 51
way of being a 475
Christianity 77, 111
beauty of 358
influence of 257
truth of 122
Christmas 78, 84, 86, 106, 514f., 527, 533
Christology 98
Chrysostom, St. John 93, 122, 125
Church(es) 23ff., 26, 29f., 33ff., 37f., 40, 49ff., 57ff., 65, 67ff., 70ff., 74f., 77ff., 83ff., 88, 90ff., 95ff., 101ff., 109ff., 119f., 126f., 129ff., 138ff., 150, 157, 159ff., 163, 169, 171, 173f., 186, 228ff., 232ff., 252, 257, 260, 272f., 275, 278, 283, 287, 289, 337ff., 343ff., 350, 353, 355, 362, 372, 404f., 408, 429, 460, 516, 628
and Eucharist 409, 589
and freedom 523
and Holy Spirit 540
and mankind 532, 628
and regimes 517
and state 292
and the suffering 520f.
and worship of the Eucharist 589
and youth 526
apostolic character of 68
beginnings of 256
building up 143, 418
bulwark of 126
call of 63
catholic character of 68
charism of 416
Christ's union with 425
communion of 234, 477, 55
community of faith 398
dedication to 442
destiny of 301
discipline of 28

doctrine of 61
domestic 116, 444
faith of 100f., 411
Founder of the 429
future of 372
good of 354, 371
growth of 257
guidance from 420
harmony within 232
hierarchical order of the 292
history of 24
in Honduras 64
in Hungary 71, 178
in Italy 257f.
in Krakow 32
in Poland 70, 290f., 389
in Rome 138, 341ff., 567, 575f.
in South America 84, 120, 162
in Uganda 124
in United States of America 69, 412
institutional dimension of 104, 142
judicial function of 126
life of 58, 352
local 45, 58, 76, 93, 95f., 172, 182, 185, 242, 343, 413, 426, 541
marks of 336
martyrs of the 342
mission of 60, 62, 76, 101f., 104, 153, 167, 185f., 203, 234, 328, 406, 433, 437, 441, 443, 463
missionary 324f., 398f., 478
Mother and Teacher 176
mystery of 158
Mystical Body 28, 184, 253, 345
nature of 25, 102, 104, 292
offices of 350
one 550
origins of 349
particular 345
pastors of 375, 414, 431
progress of 346
purification of 149
renewal of 442, 479
responsibility for 263
rights of 176
sacrament of salvation 26, 369, 459
sacramental discipline of 61
service of 356, 432
social teaching of 115, 296, 503
spouse of Christ 180
suffering within the 477
task of the 127, 403
teaching role of 53, 370
unity of 191, 233ff., 423, 434
universal 32, 39, 45, 48, 50, 54, 56, 67, 76, 85, 93, 336, 352, 541, 550
visible head of the 33
vocations in 174, 246
work of justice in 505
youth of 339
civilization 101, 105
Clement of Rome, St. 342

clergy 59, 90, 123, 139, 145f., 149, 400, 410
diocesan 45, 108, 140
of Rome 63, 139
ongoing formation of 573
religious 45, 140
collaboration 81, 93, 105, 138, 143, 170
faithful 137
collaborators 66, 79, 86, 88, 91, 126
of the Apostles 349
of the bishops 108
ecclesiastical 147, 159
College
of Bishops 58, 71, 74, 398
of Cardinals 30, 34, 36, 72, 78, 121, 342ff., 471
collegiality 26, 72f., 75, 139, 147, 181, 185, 329, 364, 384, 413, 416
episcopal 530, 581
Colombia 345f.
commandment
primary 112
Commission
Pontifical, *Iustitia et Pax* 49f., 52, 352
commitment(s) 113, 115, 119, 121, 131, 135, 141, 143f., 159
ecclesial 66
evangelical 99, 110
fidelity to the priestly 397
married 199
of catechetical groups 146
of charity 138
of laity 117
of life 88
of personal holiness 141
of priests 139, 190
pastoral 113, 137
politico-social 374
to the most needy 110
common good 130
communication
means of social 425
communion 79, 86, 93, 114, 130, 135, 139, 147, 358, 590
between bishops 107
between bishops and priests 46. 66; see also *bishops,* and *priests*
ecclesial 64, 129f., 226, 236f., 241, 413
Eucharistic 58, 203, 213, 590, 600, 605, 607f.
of Pope with bishops 371
of saints 37
with Christ 371
with the Church and her pastors 103
with the Father 633
community(ies) 93, 114, 127, 134, 141, 144
building the 142
Catholic 50, 62, 125
Christian 50, 63, 88, 93, 97, 116, 134f., 156, 351, 371f., 402
diocesan 374
ecclesial 39, 58, 63, 65, 71, 108, 127, 346

fraternal spirit in 180
international 51, 126
living 88
of believers 189
of Jerusalem 138
of persons 135
of the faithful 65
priestly 185
seminary 149
Word of God and the 422f.
concelebration 152, 404
conception 127, 421
conclave(s) 76, 153
confession 145, 424
auricular 59
first 58
individual 58, 225f.
of faith 99
seal of 265
confessional 625
confessor(s) 59
confidence
in God 198
Confirmation
sacrament of 207, 283, 594
conscience(s) 77, 98, 111, 199, 298, 335, 372, 476, 606, 629, 656
forming a social 115
of culture 112
of priest 142
problems of 145
questions of 352
consecration 600f.
episcopal 219, 365, 367
fidelity to 545
visible signs of 399
contemplation 135, 142
continent
African 123
American 119
Latin American 107
contraception 420
conversion 131, 226, 232, 236, 414, 423f., 479, 543
call to 423f.
Council for the Public Affairs of the Church 352
Council of European Episcopal Conferences (CEEC) 75ff.
Council of Jerusalem 156
Council of Parish Priest Prefects 44
Council of the General Secretariat 75
Council of the Synod of Bishops 72
Council of Trent 37, 59, 470
council
priests' 44, 185, 411
Court of the Sacred Roman Rota 126
courts
ecclesiastical 128
covenant 598
creation 141, 155, 375
Creed 102, 460

criticism 96, 374, 422
cross 124, 191, 249, 357, 401, 409, 635
culture 62, 86, 99, 101, 167, 170f., 192, 439, 484
Polish 298
Curia 44, 343, 350f., 621f.
history of 350
reform of 129
Roman 46, 73, 86, 484
structure of 351
Cyprian, St. 102, 107

De Ossó y Cervelló, Blessed Henry 435-441
deacon(s) 58, 117, 155f., 185, 216ff., 586, 606, 608, 649, 651, 660; see also *diaconate*
dead, the 466ff.
deaf, the 360
death 154f., 378ff.
of Peter and Paul 337, 348
unexpected 378f.
Declaration of Human Rights 113, 126, 131
Declaration on Religious Freedom 293
Decree on the Ministry and Life of Priests 65, 140
dedication 91, 156
democracy 629
destiny 98, 105
development 51, 101, 110, 112, 118, 130
liturgical 425
of peoples 51
of public education and culture 112
Di Jorio, Cardinal Alberto 356ff.
diaconate 553f.; see also *deacon(s)*
dialogue 51, 146, 295
stages of 364ff.
with God 64
dignity 71, 81, 94, 109, 116, 126ff., 131, 190, 297f., 320, 420
of Christian worship 61
Dimitrios I 531
diocese(s) 48, 54, 56, 64, 73, 138f., 578
of Rome 137f., 140
discernment 96, 193
disciple
of Christ 124, 242
discipline
of the Church 28, 41, 56, 149
penal 130
sacramental 58
discouragement 213
discrimination 30, 110, 113, 419
disputes
doctrinal 105
dissenter(s)
political 113
divorce 116

doctrine 40f., 54f., 68, 97, 112, 149, 166, 168, 177, 234, 241, 273, 374, 416f., 423
  social 115
donation
  ecclesial 66
  to Christ and the Church 210
drugs 526
dumb, the 360
duty(ies) 97, 106, 123, 476
  of evangelizing 101
  secular 115

Eastern Churches 68
ecclesiology 103, 143, 433
ecumenism 236, 294, 313, 332, 423, 475, 531, 542, 556
education 174, 297, 657
  Catholic 54
  Christian 166
  for peace 82
  of conscience 465
Elizabeth, St. 427
Elizabeth of Hungary, St. 179
emigration 63
encyclical(s)
  social 111
episcopal conference(s) 73, 93, 123, 312, 371
episcopate(s) 62, 73, 77, 82, 90, 107, 118, 181, 185, 223, 534, 536f.
  of Latin America 95, 120
  of Poland 285ff.
equity 126, 128
eternity 469
Eucharist 56f., 124, 141, 225, 227, 236f., 256, 409, 425, 479, 585-614, 627
  and conversion 424
  and the priest 213, 409
  celebration of 156, 185, 323
  First 208
  ministers of 598
  offering of 207
  sign of unity with Christ 163
Eucharistic Congress 124f.
Eucharistic Sacrifice 47, 93, 124, 177, 188f., 224
Europe 70, 76f., 299f.
  Christianity in 299
  history of 299
euthanasia 421
Evangelii nuntiandi 74, 96f., 115
evangelization 44, 53, 56, 66, 74, 76, 84, 96, 98, 100, 103, 107ff., 116f., 119, 122, 135, 162, 185, 200, 229, 239, 241, 255, 267, 276, 285, 312ff., 346, 371f., 375, 408, 425, 429f., 442, 459, 463, 475f., 490f., 494, 497, 501, 503f.
  and problem of vocations 346
  content of 228
  future of 148
  in Europe 313
  in Honduras 65
  in Latin America 103, 108, 311f.
  in the home 492
evangelizers 103, 114, 254
evil 134

faith 27f., 35, 44, 46, 53ff., 60f., 67f., 77, 80, 86, 90ff., 97f., 100ff., 122, 124, 139, 162f., 168, 171f., 179, 193, 223f., 288, 309, 345, 361f., 386, 398, 414, 422f., 428, 438, 459, 468, 598
  act of 120
  and theology 397f.
  certainty of 190
  content of 418
  convictions of 161
  defense of 354
  deposit of 27, 57, 408
  firmness of 172, 346, 374
  in Ireland 396
  integrity of 351, 370
  lack of 611
  Mary's pilgrimage of 427
  patrimony of 354
  spirit of 66, 160
  truths of 101
faithful, the 29, 31, 34, 39, 41f., 46, 55, 58, 61, 67, 83, 85, 94, 98, 103f., 108, 114, 123, 125, 135, 139, 143, 177, 189, 371f., 375, 428
  life of 101
  prayers of 38
  rights of 130, 352
  universal priesthood of 47
faithfulness 153, 160, 162, 213, 373, 439
family(ies) 90, 116, 135, 146, 238ff., 262, 297, 372, 459, 491f., 581ff.
  and ecclesial community 239
  and vocational apostolate 347
  apostolate of the 238, 444, 453ff.
  Christian 40, 74, 224, 239, 388
  community of grace 240
  community of love 36, 239
  first seminary 457
  holiness of 584
  human 79, 103
  of God 37
  pastoral care of 116
  values connected with 528
  vocation of 460
Father 102, 113, 229, 234, 264, 280, 339, 402
  will of the 357
  Word of the 362
  worship of the 237
father
  of families 88, 117
Fathers of the Church 111
fatherhood
  God's 50
  spiritual 91

Fatima 231f.
fear 49, 262
Federation of the Asian Bishops' Conference (FABC) 76
fidelity 25, 27ff., 102, 110, 114, 117, 199, 226, 354, 358, 397, 414, 426
  married 199
  of priests 387
  of seminarians 148
  of the U.S. bishops to the Apostolic See 412
  to the priesthood 404
  witness of 397
finances
  of Holy See 485
Fisher, St. John 34
formation 456, 461
  cultural 438
  houses of 347
  intellectual 202
  moral 81
  priestly 145, 158, 170, 202, 432
  scientific 170
fortitude 334f.
Francis of Assisi, St. 43, 268
freedom(s) 30, 49, 52, 71, 88f., 109, 113, 476f.
  in the Church 476
  knowledge of true 93
  of conscience 30
  of religion 30, 320
friendship
  with Christ 181, 280

Gaudium et spes 30, 50, 52, 54, 105
God 28, 50, 60, 65, 72, 83, 85f., 88, 91, 94, 97f., 100, 102, 104, 106, 113, 116ff., 124, 133f., 137, 141, 231, 402, 424, 468; see also *Lord*
  being of 398
  call of 407
  children of 50
  communion with 357
  confidence in 405f.
  conversation with 135
  dialogue with 64
  faithfulness of 397
  fear of 334f.
  glory of 123
  kingdom of 346
  mystery of 403, 408, 421
  presence of 134
  reconciliation with 358
  signs and reminders of 399
  union with 92, 153
  words of 405
good
  common 130f., 431
  individual 130
Good News 98, 102, 228, 254, 281, 375, 404, 408f.
  in the strata of humanity 430

Good Shepherd 144, 251ff.
Gospel 26f., 30, 39, 47, 49f., 53ff., 60, 65, 71, 73, 77, 91, 93f., 97, 99ff., 103, 105, 107ff., 114, 122ff., 133f., 141, 178, 229, 235, 241f., 272, 276, 374, 410, 418, 431, 596, 603
  a profession of life 92
  adherence to 635
  and philosophers of antiquity 296
  belief in 424
  conformity with 404
  fidelity to 489
  in homes 135
  partnership in 412
  power of 218
  proclamation of 156, 257f., 325, 430, 441, 635
  promoted through the media 425
  responsibility for 263
  servants of 400, 414f.
  social dimension of 44
  suffering for 365
  witnesses to 174
grace(s) 73, 102, 124, 135, 137, 141, 156, 194, 249, 373, 406, 424
gratitude 164, 286
  to American Catholics 413
Gregorian University 168, 537
Gregory the Great, St. 63, 135f.
Guadalupe 120
guide(s) 117, 135

habit
  ecclesiastical 210
heart(s) 476
  of the faithful 94
  priestly 355
hedonism 526
Hedwig, St.
  relics of 70
herald(s) 56, 105
heritage 80, 115
  Canadian 60
  Christian 76
heaven 99
hierarchy 93
  of Uganda 123
Hilary of Poitiers, St. 101
history 99, 103
  goal of 402
  of Christianity 77
  of salvation 99
  of the Church 109
holiness 142, 191, 201, 273, 424
  elements of 140
  in married life 491
  of priests 140, 499
  prophetic role of 415
Holy Father 64, 72, 75, 87, 90f., 118f., 126, 136f., 140; see also *Pontiff(s);*

INDEX 669

Pope(s); successor, of St. Peter; *Vicar of Christ*
Holy Land 429
Holy Orders 193, 198f., 203, 322f., 508, 569, 578
 fullness of 534
 sacrament of 47, 184, 187f., 191
Holy See 70, 75f., 82f., 85, 132, 342
 departments of 35
 relations of, with the world 518
 representative of 69
Holy Spirit 29, 40, 55ff., 67, 88, 102, 130, 207, 228, 234, 242f., 245, 256, 272, 282ff., 317f., 324, 365, 396, 477, 539ff., 621, 659
 and bishops 555
 and ecumenism 556
 and the Church 241, 550
 assisting the Magisterium 422
 gifts of the 190
 guidance of the 68
 help of the 408
 impulse and guidance of the 141
 obedience to the 474f.
 power of the 323, 416f.
Holy Thursday 180, 183ff., 203, 646f.
home(s) 78, 135
homily 603f.
homosexuality 420, 422
honesty
 intellectual 171
hope(s) 104, 117, 143, 345, 421, 468
Humanae vitae 420
humanism 105f., 459
 atheistic 105
 authentic 112
humanity 54, 96, 98, 110, 117, 128, 141, 360, 403, 408, 421, 430
humility 198, 304, 335, 370
 of Jesus 317
Hungary 70, 72, 179

identity 92, 103, 105, 136
 priestly 143, 188f., 195, 201, 303, 432, 443
ideologies 114, 444
Ignatius of Antioch, St. 159
Ignatius of Loyola, St. 175
ignorance
 religious 501
image
 of God 113, 459
immorality 297
Incarnation 132, 426, 451
indifferentism 501
individualism 127, 610f.
injustice(s) 30, 51, 81, 115, 126, 128, 13
integrity 372
 of life and service 189
 physical and mental 109
International Year of the Child 126

Ireland 388ff.
Irenaeus, St. 106
Isaiah 136
Italy 137, 259

Jeremiah
 call of 405
Jesus Christ 25, 34, 39, 41f., 46f., 49f., 52, 54f., 57, 59, 61, 71, 77, 84, 86ff., 91f., 94, 98ff., 102, 104f., 108ff., 113f., 117, 123, 133f., 141, 163, 207, 226ff., 234, 256, 261ff., 265, 272f., 277, 280ff., 343, 361f., 376, 380, 385, 388, 402, 404, 406, 426, 443, 474; see also *Lord*
 and Mary 203f., 428
 and pastoral activity 242
 and youth 444
 as a political figure 99
 as shepherd 385, 538
 attitude of 100
 belonging to 140, 219, 439
 Bishop of our souls 414
 body and blood of 73, 303, 425
 center of family life 240
 center of our lives 317
 commands of 27
 commitment to 65, 437
 crucified 341
 disciple of 124
 Divine Master 222, 500
 divinity of 99
 example of 142, 190
 faith in 101, 375
 flock of 403
 Founder of the Church 261
 full life in 493
 Good Shepherd 144, 190f., 194, 210, 234, 247ff., 251ff., 264, 333, 353, 365f., 407, 416, 431, 539
 Head of the Church 243
 heart of 369, 402
 holiness of 414
 in St. John's Gospel 357
 in the Eucharist and in Penance 424
 Infant 78
 intimacy with 141, 369, 409
 invitation of 87
 love of 149, 346, 401
 message of 76, 424
 mission of 100, 187
 mystery of 32, 57, 101, 140, 142f., 150, 185, 417f., 451
 Mystical Body of 28
 name of 56, 339, 345
 passion of 206, 208
 Pastor 144
 Person of 433
 personification of 214
 presence of 107, 133, 159
 priesthood of 48, 180, 182, 187, 189ff., 204, 279, 395, 530, 597, 626f.

priestly prayer of 48, 416
priests' union with 409
"prophetic function" of 171
Redeemer of man 178, 232, 440
relationship with 385f.
resurrection of 346
salvation in 234, 242
saving action of 61, 101
Savior 31f., 43, 59, 79, 84, 134
Servant of Yahweh 100
servants of 160
Son of God 53, 98f., 117, 360, 362, 375, 427f.
Son of man 360, 408, 520
Teacher 106, 177
the Lord 59, 80, 124, 206
the way 529
will of 70, 423
witnesses of 105, 399
John, St. 87
John Nepomucene, St. 265
John the Baptist, St. 321f.
disciples of 361
John XXIII, Pope 25, 40, 112, 531
John Paul I, Pope 23f., 28, 40ff., 63, 70, 80, 82, 95, 104, 149, 531
Josaphat, St. 488
joy 88, 379
judge 128f., 559ff., 620
jurisprudence 505
jurists 132
justice 50, 53, 57, 81, 104, 110, 112, 118, 126, 128f., 131f., 194, 389, 558f., 562

kingdom
of God 104, 108, 201, 272, 283
knowledge 116, 129, 161, 194
Kolbe, Blessed Maximilian 48, 135, 151

laity 47, 62, 65f., 108, 115, 146, 283f., 308, 346, 553f., 574
and witness 224
evangelizing work of the 387
Last Supper 362
Latin 602
Latin America 83, 85, 95f., 100, 108f., 117ff.
evangelization in 103, 311f.
Latin American Episcopal Conference (CELAM) 76
law 129ff., 564
Christian 414
divine 122, 297, 372
ecclesiastical 506
international 519
moral 297
Lebanon 69

Lent 138ff., 144
Leo XIII, Pope 85
liberation 97, 104, 109, 113ff., 360, 398, 433
Christian 113f.
of man 110
political, social and economic 104
liberty
preservation of 176
religious 110, 295, 523
life 102f., 135, 141, 191, 358, 372
active 142
Christ, source of 60
Christian 98, 137, 139
community 159
consecrated 346, 372; see also *religious*
contemplative 142, 372
ecclesial 24, 79, 138, 375
eternal 143, 357f., 468f.
family 113, 463
gift from God 492
human 524
interior 142, 145, 439
level of 372
liturgical 124
meaning of 178, 625
measure of 154
moral 419
moralization of 371
of the Church 97
of the faithful 101
priestly 185f., 191, 585
respect for 116
revision of 144
right to 57, 421, 547
seminary 148
light 106, 135
of the Word of God 115
Lippay, George 175
liturgist 432
liturgy(ies) 68, 87, 136f., 152, 180, 357, 425, 597, 601, 612f.
Liturgy of the Hours 402f.
lonely, the 110
Lord 82, 87, 90ff., 95, 100, 102, 107ff., 113f., 117, 125, 129, 132; see also *God* and *Jesus Christ*
of the harvest 146, 372
service of the 356
love 27f., 32, 37ff., 57, 59, 80, 89ff., 100ff., 110, 112ff., 125, 196, 199, 229f., 308f., 345, 358, 372, 402, 415, 431, 476, 490, 541, 592, 642
and Eucharistic worship 592
bond of brotherly 346
communion of 235
consecrated 39
fire of 395
for Christ 94, 186
for the Church 102, 186, 340
fraternal 59, 470
growth in 410

INDEX 671

in marriage 566
of bishops for priests 182
of Christ for the Church 337
of God 56, 99, 375
of Jesus Christ 42, 216f., 309, 346
of man 94, 459
school of 402
supernatural 59
truth in 422
Lumen gentium 25, 30, 52, 102, 108, 204, 290, 292
Lwanga, St. Charles 122

Magisterium 28, 103, 108, 114, 171, 177, 228, 283f., 370, 422f., 427, 431, 475, 531
attachment to the 370, 408
authentic 115
catechesis of 529
docility to teachings of 512
of Peter 28
reverence for 103
tradition of 185
man 81, 87, 89, 91, 94, 98, 105ff., 113f., 131, 141, 230, 235, 275, 426, 440; see also *person*
advancement of 294, 433
dignity of 235, 431, 517
manipulation of 193
marriage 196f., 238, 455, 491, 506, 559, 582
dignity of 507
indissolubility of 59, 420, 565
invalidation of 559, 564
nullity of 563, 565
preparation for 582
sanctity of 241
unity of 565
values of Christian 444
martyr(s) 122f., 342
martyrdom 123
of Peter and Paul 341
martyrology 122, 349
Mary 88f., 125, 163, 264, 272, 304, 399, 411, 426, 454, 514, 532
and unity 636
devotion to 464, 643
discipleship of 428
faith of 427
in the mystery of redemption 232
Model of the Church 427f.
Mother of Christ 40, 84, 86, 89, 102, 117, 204, 344, 427, 557
Mother of priests and religious 94, 203, 300
Mother of the Church 35, 40, 125, 136, 231, 336, 340, 557
Our Lady of Caacupé 373
Our Lady of Guadalupe 91, 94, 96, 117, 121
Our Lady of High Grace 90

Our Lady of Sorrows 366f.
Virgin 32, 428
Mass 97, 213f., 237, 587f., 596f., 600
concelebrated 404
sacrificial value of 599
see also *Eucharist,* celebration of, and *Eucharistic Sacrifice*
materialism 112, 220, 479, 502
matrimony 199, 463, 506
maturity 171, 346
in faith 146
priestly 198
Medellín Conference 101
media 120, 425, 494, 526f., 657
meditation 92, 177, 643
mercy
of God 114
Messiah 87, 360ff.
Mexico 78, 83, 91, 97, 117ff.
migrants 63f.
migration 62
minister(s) 116, 124, 131, 346
of the Eucharist 604, 608, 610
ministry 31, 39, 56, 63, 66, 73, 80, 92, 128f., 141, 156, 177, 185f., 194, 202, 204, 226, 246, 346, 352, 376, 408f., 418, 586, 650
among migrants 63
celibate 407
challenges of the 397
episcopal 57, 67, 71, 318, 487
of Jesus 405
of justice 132
of Peter 80, 351
of the community 104
papal 53, 61
pastoral 31, 35, 46, 140, 407, 437, 586
universal pastoral 31
mission 27, 57, 84, 92, 100, 102ff., 107ff., 129, 132, 138, 143, 145, 147f., 223f., 349, 407, 419, 438, 442, 652
of Jesus 99, 360
of the Church 30, 102, 104, 463
pastoral 79, 108, 119, 132
missions
parish 144
support for the 399, 413
missionary(ies) 31, 63, 123f., 237, 324, 524
morality 194, 297, 354
social 111
mother(s) 88
mystery 26, 228, 375
of Christ 101, 105, 141
of God's love 56
of man 105
Mystical Body of Christ 28, 184, 253, 345; see also *Church*

nation(s) 83, 99, 112f., 117
needy, the 100, 145, 242
Nero 342

Neumann, St. John 415
New Zealand 53, 55
Nicaragua 118
norms
  for judgment 115
  liturgical 28
  pastoral 59

obedience 93, 439
  to Holy Spirit 474f.
  to teaching of Vatican II 474f.
opportunism 110
order
  hierarchical 289f.
  moral 296, 390
  social 297
Orders see Holy Orders
Ordinary 66
ordination 147, 181f., 203, 278, 366
Orthodox Church 640
orthodoxy 354
orthopraxis 354
Ottaviani, Cardinal Alfredo 353ff.

Palafoxiano Major Seminary 95
paradise 249
parents 583
  rights of 176
parish(es) 45, 87, 133, 135, 139, 144f., 574f., 626, 628
Paschal Mystery 58
Passover
  of Christ 183
Pastor(s) 26, 41, 60f., 63f., 71, 73, 80, 84, 97f., 103, 106ff., 117, 129, 135, 138, 144f., 147, 153, 334, 345f., 396, 414, 421
  bishops as 348
  characteristics of 368f.
  duty of 97
  universal 33
Pastoral Constitution on the Church in the Modern World 54
Paul, St. 27, 56f., 77, 87, 89, 97, 139, 141, 149, 172, 254, 258, 336ff., 341, 344, 348f., 378f., 543f.
  proclaims the Gospel 257
Paul VI, Pope 23, 26f., 35, 39, 41, 43, 48, 50, 55, 58, 61, 69, 73ff., 95ff., 101, 110ff., 120, 122f., 128ff., 212, 244, 327, 350, 355, 424
peace 50, 53, 81f. 98, 102, 110f., 113, 118, 132, 233, 294, 389, 397, 434, 558f.
Penance
  sacrament of 225f., 281, 424, 594, 605f., 653
penitence 232
Pentecost 256, 324
  the new 416
People of God 26, 31, 38, 42, 45f., 56, 60f., 63, 65, 73f., 86, 91, 93, 99, 103, 114, 120, 127, 130, 134, 141, 173, 180, 182, 189ff., 197, 227, 237, 263, 282, 284, 289, 340f., 384, 398, 404
  apostolic vocation of 91
  collaboration of 105
  evangelization of 442
  mission of 187
  prayer for 418
  renewal of 148, 429
  sanctification of 233
  "universal priesthood" of 47
perfection 191
perseverance 182, 348
  means of 642f.
  of vocations 372
person(s) 113, 120, 126ff., 135; see also *man*
  autonomy of 131
  dignity of 593
  human-Christian 127, 130
  rights of the 113, 128
  value of 459
personality 129, 347, 526
  development of 199f.
  fulfillment of the 127
  priestly 144, 171, 193, 210
Peter, St. 26f., 38, 43, 58, 60, 73, 77, 87, 99, 107, 172, 184, 232, 242, 258, 334, 336f., 341ff., 348f.
  ministry of 349
  sacrifice of 341
  tomb of 57
  visit to 486f.
philosopher(s)
  of antiquity 296
philosophy 427
  system of 105
piety 101, 136
  Eucharistic 149
  popular 100, 136, 501
Pius XII, Pope 59, 85, 124
pluralism 609
plurality 62
Poggi, Archbishop Luigi 69f.
Poland 78, 286f., 289ff.
  Church in 389
politicians 97
Pontiff(s) 34, 62, 79; see also Holy Father; Pope(s); *successor,* of St. Peter; *Vicar of Christ*
  representatives of the 429
Pontifical Mission Aid Societies 255, 324f.
pontificate 79f., 85f., 95, 99, 101f., 125
poor, the 100, 104, 114, 156, 242, 355, 361, 418
Pope(s) 34, 38, 40, 42f., 51, 58, 66, 70, 73f., 76, 78, 80, 87, 90f., 94, 96, 111, 118f., 133, 136, 150, 346, 352, 373, 398, 523; see also Holy Father; Pontiff(s); *successor,* of St. Peter; *Vicar of Christ*
  election of 152, 471

presence of 120
"the chief shepherd" 241
population 116
pornography 527
power(s)
  civil 113
  of bishops 364
  political 110f.
  priestly 191
"**praxis**" 97
prayer 97, 120, 135, 149, 194, 201ff., 207, 232, 245, 257, 283, 396f., 409, 415, 428, 513, 544, 556, 627, 650
  community of 401, 403
preacher(s) 124
  of the Gospel 98
preaching 56
Predecessor(s) 27, 31, 60, 73, 79, 85, 95, 120, 122ff., 128
prefect(s)
  function and mission of 138
presbyter(s) 185
presbyterate 44f.
"**presbyterium**" 138, 143f., 146, 182, 185, 628
  of Rome 646
press
  Catholic 425
priest(s) 41, 45ff., 57ff., 66, 85, 91ff., 108, 116f., 125, 129, 132, 135, 137ff., 158, 161, 177, 211, 250, 260, 266, 318, 346f., 395ff., 406, 411, 433, 443, 599, 627, 649
  and celibacy 195ff.
  and Mary 204
  and mercy 653
  and the family apostolate 583
  as confessors 226
  feast of 208, 648
  garb of 47, 210
  identity of 301, 509f., 628
  lack of 200, 202f.
  ministry of 301f., 351
  parish 88, 134, 140
priesthood 31, 46ff., 93, 140, 144, 148ff., 186ff., 193, 197ff., 203, 212, 214, 241, 398, 403ff., 410f., 418, 510f., 552, 569, 586, 619f., 628, 648f.
  faithfulness to the 397, 653
  of Jesus Christ; see *Jesus Christ, priesthood of*
  of the faithful 93, 198f., 207
  origin of 406
  permanent character of 553
  social dimension of 143
  theology of 405
  understanding of 404
  vocations to 65, 620
principle(s)
  Christian and evangelical 111
  Christian and priestly 357
  ethical 112
  for reflection 115
  of faith 92
  of system of philosophy 105
prisoners 113, 388
problems
  family 193
  social 193, 374
procreation 113
profanation
  of Eucharistic mystery 597
programs
  catechetical 241
  pastoral 246
  spiritual 335
progress 431
  spiritual 201
promises
  priestly 182
  renewal of 182, 185
prophets 117, 533
Proverbs, Book of 139
Providence 77, 328, 402
  Mary's trust in 427
  of God 39
Psalms 402
Puebla 120f., 328f.
Puebla de los Angeles 83, 95
purity 128

racism 422
reading 643
realism
  Christian 643
reality 79, 84, 96, 113, 119f.
recollection 149
reconciliation 113, 397, 402
  sacrament of 92, 201, 266, 424
rector(s) 147f., 155, 157, 159
redemption 107, 283, 357, 403, 409, 516
reflection 97, 120, 135
refugees 519, 521
religious 31, 58, 62f., 90f., 93f., 108, 116f., 123, 125, 345, 371, 399
  identifiable as 399
renewal 40, 327ff., 414, 477ff., 499, 612
  liturgical 433, 604
renunciation 98, 439
responsibility 80, 83, 262
  pastoral 414, 421
  personal 198
resurrection
  of Jesus 217f., 649
  of the flesh 143
retreats
  of the bishops 415
right(s) 52, 81, 88, 106, 109f., 112f., 116, 126f., 131, 295, 419, 456, 518, 522
  protection of 129f., 506
rite(s) 28, 68f., 351, 640
Rome 77f., 93, 97, 119, 125, 134, 138ff., 158f., 164, 345, 571

center of Catholicism 624
Church of 341ff.
diocese of 43, 48
rosary
recitation of 92

sacrament(s) 102, 177, 188, 208, 405, 409, 463, 593f.
of faith 207f.
of the sick 208
Sacramentum paenitentiae 226, 424
Sacred Apostolic Penitentiary 352
Sacred College 33ff.
Sacred Congregation for Bishops 351
Sacred Congregation for Catholic Education 165f., 172, 351, 432
Sacred Congregation for Religious and Secular Institutes 351
Sacred Congregation for the Causes of Saints 351
Sacred Congregation for the Clergy 351
Sacred Congregation for the Eastern Churches 351
Sacred Congregation for the Evangelization of Peoples 351
Sacred Congregation for the Sacraments and Divine Worship 351
Sacred Congregation of the Doctrine of the Faith 354
Sacred Roman Rota 132, 352
Sacred Scripture 171, 359, 479, 602f.
Sacred Tradition 26, 171, 475, 551, 612
sacrifice(s) 51, 430, 439, 598, 600
spiritual 189
Salus Populi Romani 48, 136
salvation 61, 100, 102, 104, 131, 141, 176f., 190f., 194, 228, 284, 358, 360, 408, 478
message of 284
sanctification 141, 161, 360
sanctity
fruits of 122
Santo Domingo 118, 120
Scholastica, St. 625
school(s) 176, 503
Catholic 54, 166, 352, 412
religious instruction in 444f.
science 166, 426
scientists 97
Scripture see *Sacred Scripture*
secularization 44, 210, 314, 501
of priestly life 192f.
See
Archiepiscopal 90
of Krakow 70
of Peter 56, 70, 104, 343, 351, 363, 630
of Rome 33
seminarians 41, 116, 148f., 157, 237, 308, 433

holiness of 158
training of 387
seminary(ies) 42, 148f., 166, 174, 182, 284, 319f., 322, 347, 352, 433, 553
diocesan 45
major 177
service 51, 87f., 93, 107, 110, 147, 154, 193, 236, 348, 425
episcopal 44
God's call to 87
priestly 93, 189, 409
shroud 654
sick, the 88, 110, 114, 242
silence 360
sin 229, 297, 632
and the Church's unity 423
consciousness of 424
evil of 134
liberation from 433
mortal 595
slavery 110, 114
Slipyj, Cardinal Josyf 486f.
Slovakia 366f.
society 81, 88, 113, 116, 127f., 131, 178, 372, 457
Society of Missionaries of Africa 123
Society of St. Teresa of Jesus 438ff.
solidarity 131, 143, 147, 477f.
souls 145, 336, 346
consecrated 91, 372
pastors and guides of 138
service of 214
spirit
Christian 94, 112
missionary 398
of Christ 112
of sacrifice 347
of the Church 112
priestly 129
Spirit; see also *Holy Spirit*
impulse of the 130
of truth 335, 423
spirituality 92, 363
of the priest 143, 147
Stanislaus, St. 252f., 288, 296
Stephen, St. (of Hungary) 71, 177ff.
stewards
of the mysteries of God 141, 160
students 91, 157f.
in seminaries 148
studies
ecclesiastical 169f.
successor
of St. Peter 31, 33, 70f., 74, 76, 147, 215, 341, 349ff., 371, 400, 414, 418, 487, 500, 567, 637, 639, 651; see also *Holy Father, Pontiff(s), Pope(s), Vicar of Christ*
of the Apostles 156, 279, 430, 622, 637, 660
suffering(s) 98, 155, 520, 522, 654
superior(s) 159, 334
Supreme Court of the Apostolic Signatura 129, 352

Synod
  of Bishops 26, 73f., 352, 413, 472
system(s)
  economic 112f.
  human 131
  ideological 110, 114
  political 111, 113
  social and cultural 111

teacher(s) 58, 71, 117
  bishops' mission as 443
  of faith 97
  of the truth 97, 101
teaching
  apostolic 242
  of the Church 111, 166, 419
  social 115, 457
technology 547
temptation 198
thanksgiving 207
theologians 426ff., 448, 450
theology 110, 426ff.
  and faith 397f.
Thomas Aquinas, St. 111, 129, 427, 559
tradition 43f., 67f., 140; see also *Sacred Tradition*
  Church's living 114
  Greek monastic 363
  of fidelity 412
  prophetic 407
transubstantiation 213
Trinity
  life of the 405
  unity of 235
trust 102, 263f.
truth 95, 97f., 101f., 105, 107, 111, 126, 149, 194, 228, 335, 365, 370, 414, 416f., 422, 476, 520, 550, 558ff., 564
  bishops' ministry of 418f.
  historical 85
  openness to 375
  witness to the 420f.
Twelve, the 405; see also *Apostles*
  call of the 407

unborn, the 421
unemployed, the 522
union 46, 138, 476
  ecclesial 345, 383, 414
  sexual 420
  with God 153
United Nations Organization 113
unity 46, 56, 60, 62, 67, 73, 76, 94, 97, 104, 107, 131, 236, 279, 286, 307f., 342, 371, 401, 404f., 411, 482, 572, 612f., 632ff., 637
  among Christians 55, 235f., 391
  between bishops and priests 658
  collegial 604, 614

  ecclesial 107f., 182, 402, 434, 548, 631
  of Christian worship 61
  of faith and life 430
  of pastors 107
  of the presbyterium 572
  priestly 146
  sacrament of 431, 609
  source of 102
  synodal 638
universality 34, 67, 172
university(ies) 352
  Lateran 45
  of St. Thomas Aquinas (Angelicum) 168
  of Theological Sciences 45
  pontifical 158
  Urbanian 168
Upper Room 153, 159, 180

values 131
  Christian 372
  evangelical 77, 109
  human 105, 372
  supernatural 92
vandals
  persecution by 122
Vatican Council I 26, 74, 103
Vatican Council II 24ff., 30, 35, 37, 40, 47f., 52ff., 56, 68, 72ff., 102, 104, 112, 140f., 181, 185f., 311, 350, 416f., 421, 474
  and marriage 455
  and task of bishops 313
  ecclesiology of 351
  implementation of 173, 313, 470
  obedience to teaching of 474f.
vestments 610
Vicar of Christ 33, 80, 258; see also *Holy Father; Pontiff(s); Pope(s); successor, of St. Peter*
Villot, Cardinal Giovanni 64, 78, 152ff.
violence 110, 126, 389f., 527f., 629
  and society 457
  collective 113
virginity 439
virtue(s) 71, 129, 363
vocation(s) 46, 65, 87, 103, 116f., 140, 183, 192, 194, 200, 209, 213ff., 259ff., 267, 275, 346f., 429, 477, 479, 493, 500, 552, 574, 661
  and Eucharist 225
  apostolate of 432
  apostolic 91
  Christian 116, 346
  fostering of 245f., 250, 319, 443
  gift of 163
  living one's 440
  missionary 255
  native 496
  of first apostles 87
  of man 176

pastoral 197, 252
perseverance of 347
prayer for 244ff., 250
priestly 28, 47f., 65, 116, 180, 194, 201, 204, 346, 404, 553, 627
problem of 139, 346, 372
religious 28, 116, 180, 346
search for 146, 347
vows
priestly 208f.

war(s) 519
will
of God 153, 406
wisdom 135, 375
wise men 534ff.
witness(es) 92, 107, 117, 126, 229, 236, 254, 335, 345, 410
community of 425
credibility of 414
evangelical 348
for the Faith 122
of a holy life 207
of Jesus Christ 105
of Peter and Paul 337
to faith in Christ 194, 202, 391
Wojciech, St. 289
woman(en) 126, 131, 407
Word
ministers of the 177
ministry of 177, 404, 438
of the Father 416, 426
of truth 97
Word of God 41, 54, 57, 60, 63, 87, 99f. 102f., 114f., 131, 134, 144, 148ff., 177, 228, 273, 280, 283f., 310, 334, 385, 402, 416, 488f., 601ff.
basis for seminary life 149
fidelity to 308f.
meditating on 310
power of 57

proclamation of 180
relevance of 419
safeguarded by bishops 318
servants of 194
to be transmitted 317
work 97, 137, 220f., 396
of salvation 141
pastoral 192
significance of 121
worker(s) 220f., 494
for the harvest 372
pastoral 371
world 79, 81, 98f., 103, 111, 113, 115, 126f., 139, 141, 169
of culture 85
presence of the Church in 338
sanctification of 283
World Day of Prayer for Vocations 244
worship 124, 604
Christian 61
Eucharistic 588f., 594f.
social 124
Wright, Cardinal John Joseph 368ff.

young, the 88, 145, 159, 426, 460, 576
and evangelization 315
and vocations 246
youth 116f., 260, 311, 372, 461, 464, 503, 525f., 528
and faith 76
and vocational apostolate 347
education of 192, 241, 297, 445
formation of 178f., 527
pastoral work among 444

Zacchaeus 362
zeal
apostolic 241
pastoral 125, 309

Daughters of St. Paul

IN MASSACHUSETTS
 50 St. Paul's Ave., Jamaica Plain, Boston, MA 02130;
  617-522-8911; 617-522-0875
 172 Tremont Street, Boston, MA 02111; **617-426-5464;
  617-426-4230**
IN NEW YORK
 78 Fort Place, Staten Island, NY 10301; **212-447-5071**
 59 East 43rd Street, New York, NY 10017; **212-986-7580**
 625 East 187th Street, Bronx, NY 10458; **212-584-0440**
 525 Main Street, Buffalo, NY 14203; **716-847-6044**
IN NEW JERSEY
 Hudson Mall — Route 440 and Communipaw Ave.,
  Jersey City, NJ 07304; **201-433-7740**
IN CONNECTICUT
 202 Fairfield Ave., Bridgeport, CT 06604; **203-335-9913**
IN OHIO
 2105 Ontario St. (at Prospect Ave.), Cleveland, OH 44115; **216-621-9427**
 25 E. Eighth Street, Cincinnati, OH 45202; **513-721-4838**
IN PENNSYLVANIA
 1719 Chestnut Street, Philadelphia, PA 19103; **215-568-2638**
IN VIRGINIA
 1025 King St., Alexandria, VA 22314 **703-683-1741**
IN FLORIDA
 2700 Biscayne Blvd., Miami, FL 33137; **305-573-1618**
IN LOUISIANA
 4403 Veterans Memorial Blvd., Metairie, LA 70002; **504-887-7631;
  504-887-0113**
 1800 South Acadian Thruway, P.O. Box 2028, Baton Rouge, LA 70821
  504-343-4057; 504-343-3814
IN MISSOURI
 1001 Pine Street (at North 10th), St. Louis, MO 63101; **314-621-0346;
  314-231-1034**
IN ILLINOIS
 172 North Michigan Ave., Chicago, IL 60601; **312-346-4228
  312-346-3240**
IN TEXAS
 114 Main Plaza, San Antonio, TX 78205; **512-224-8101**
IN CALIFORNIA
 1570 Fifth Avenue, San Diego, CA 92101; **714-232-1442**
 46 Geary Street, San Francisco, CA 94108; **415-781-5180**
IN HAWAII
 1143 Bishop Street, Honolulu, HI 96813; **808-521-2731**
IN ALASKA
 750 West 5th Avenue, Anchorage AK 99501; **907-272-8183**

IN CANADA
 3022 Dufferin Street, Toronto 395, Ontario, Canada
IN ENGLAND
 128, Notting Hill Gate, London W11 3QG, England
 133 Corporation Street, Birmingham B4 6PH, England
 5A-7 Royal Exchange Square, Glasgow G1 3AH, England
 82 Bold Street, Liverpool L1 4HR, England
IN AUSTRALIA
 58 Abbotsford Rd., Homebush, N.S.W., Sydney 2140, Australia